AMERICAN FOOD

The Gastronomic Story

BOOKS BY EVAN JONES

Hidden America
(with Roland Wells Robbins)
The Father: Letters to Sons and Daughters
Trappers and Mountain Men
The Minnesota: Forgotten River
Citadel in the Wilderness
The World of Cheese
A Food Lover's Companion
American Food: The Gastronomic Story
Knead it, Punch it, Bake it: The Book of Bread
(with Judith Jones)
The L.L. Bean Book of New *New England Cookery*
(with Judith Jones)
Epicurean Delight: The Life and Times of James Beard

AMERICAN FOOD

The Gastronomic Story

THIRD EDITION

EVAN JONES

THE OVERLOOK PRESS
WOODSTOCK, NEW YORK

For Robert Lescher

This edition first published in the United States in 2007 by
The Overlook Press, Peter Mayer Publishers, Inc.
Woodstock & New York

WOOD STOCK :
One Overlook Drive
Woodstock, NY 12498
www.overlookpress.com
[for individual orders, bulk and special sales, contact our Woodstock office]

NEW YORK:
141 Wooster Street
New York, NY 10012

Grateful acknowledgment is made to the following publishers for permission to cite passages: Atheneum Publishers, Inc.: *The Margaret Rudkin Pepperidge Farm Cookbook* by Margaret Rudkin, copyright © 1963 by Margaret Rudkin, reprinted by permission; The Bobbs-Merrill Company, Inc.: *Soul Food Cook Book*, copyright © 1969 by Bob Jeffers, reprinted by permission; Chilton Book Company, Radnor, Pa.: *The Gold Cook Book* by Louis P. De Gouy, copyright 1947 by Louis P. De Gouy, reprinted by permission; Fawcett Publications, Inc.: *The Farmer's Daughter Cookbook* by Kandy Norton Henely, copyright © 1971 by Fawcett Publications, Inc., reprinted by permission; Herder and Herder, Inc.: *A Festival of Jewish Cooking* by Carole Lowenstein, copyright © 1971 by Herder and Herder, Inc., reprinted by permission; Houghton Mifflin Company: *Sam Ward "King of the Lobby"* by Lately Thomas, copyright © 1965 by Houghton Mifflin Company, reprinted by permission; Little, Brown, and Company: *West Coast Cook Book* by Helen Evans Brown, copyright © 1952 by Helen Evans Brown; Random House, Inc.: *Invisible Man* by Ralph Ellison, copyright 1947, 1948, 1952 by Ralph Ellison, reprinted by permission; Alfred A. Knopf, Inc.: *All Manner of Food* by Michael Field, copyright © 1965, 1966, 1968, 1970 by Michael Field, reprinted by permission.

Library of Congress Cataloging-in-Publication Data

Jones, Evan 1915 –
American Food: the gastronomic story / by Evan Jones.
p. cm.
Reprint. Originally published: 2nd ed. New York : Random House, © 1981
1. Cookery, American. 2. Food I. Title.
[TX715.J76 1990] 641'.0973—dc20 89-38960

Printed in the United States of America
ISBN-13 978-1-58567-904-1
10 9 8 7 6 5 4 3 2 1

CONTENTS

INTRODUCTION TO THE 2007 EDITION

The first edition of *American Food* was published in 1975, and it was ahead of its time. It was before America was quite ready to look seriously at its own culinary history and to take pride in its unique story. During the sixties the awakening to the pleasures of good food in this country had gained tremendous momentum. The spearhead of this revolution was, of course, Julia Child, who won the heart of America by demonstrating that cooking was fun and that if she could master the necessary technique to produce a good meal, so could you. But it was *soigne* French cooking she was enamored of. America was best known for the kind of food that could be eaten—or prepared—on the run, and the food industry had done a nice job of promoting fast and easy recipes and readymade products so that the poor, beleaguered housewife wouldn't have to slave away over a hot stove. But Julia was demonstrating just the opposite, extolling fresh ingredients, teaching us how to cook carefully, taking pride in our creations. With her buoyant spirit she managed to release the American appetite that had for so long been subdued by a Puritan ethic that belittled cooking.

Also, during this yeasty period ordinary people, not just the privileged, were getting on planes and vacationing in Europe as well as the Middle East and Far East. There they experienced new tastes that they were eager to reproduce at home, and ethnic pockets all over America were ready to oblige them. Soon good old spaghetti and meatballs were augmented with interesting Italian regional dishes; Greek restaurant proprietors added moussaka and spanikopita to their steak-and-potatoes menus; chop suey and bland stir-frys gave way to hot and spicy Szechuan and Hunan dishes.

As a result of this gastronomic awakening it was inevitable that we finally take a look at our own heritage, and this seminal book led the way. It was the first attempt to tell the American food story, to show us who we are and how we got that way.

I remember MFK Fisher saying that what she particularly loved about Evan's book was that it was written as though he were having a lively conversation with the reader, telling one good story after another. And that is how the book evolved. Evan was drawn to the subject because he found that food was a way of telling the social history of a people, and in the case of America there were so many different strands to be traced. But the only way to get at the sources was by going to original documents such as Jefferson's garden notebooks, old plantation records, farm journals, local recipe collections and menus, and, above all, talking to people all around the country and getting their stories.

Sometimes when Evan was doing research for this project, I would join him at the Society Library and we would go through the stacks of books on American history. We would look in the indexes for entries on food lore, checking subjects like corn or cheesemaking or church suppers. There were none. Clearly food and cooking weren't subjects deemed worthy of scholarly pursuit.

James Beard, a huge champion of American cookery, particularly appreciated what Evan had accomplished, and when the book was published, he wrote in his weekly syndicated column that it was the kind of book that we should send to all our friends in other countries "to give them a new insight into our gastronomic traditions and reassure them that there are many of us who, like Evan Jones, deplore and resist convenience foods, TV dinners, and the let's-grab-a-bite theory of eating."

That, of course, was written more than thirty years ago and a lot has changed since then. Today American food is considered perhaps the most interesting and innovative in the world. We are unique in that what we call American food is no one style but a merging of many different influences, as this book makes clear. Now we are increasingly open to new taste experiences, borrowing them, adapting or fusing them, and making them our own. We are more conscious than ever about cultivating good ingredients, and the emphasis on organic and locally grown produce has done a lot to restore the authentic tastes that we took for granted in the past.

It is an exciting and challenging time in our food history, and I only wish that both Evan and Jim Beard were still around to enjoy it all.

—Judith Jones
October, 2006

INTRODUCTION

In 1975, when the first edition of this book was published, there was a good deal of talk about the food Americans eat but not much confidence in a singularly American style of cooking. Any restaurant laying claim to distinction had a kitchen guided by a French-born chef or one who had been trained in haute cuisine. Southern Italian restaurants scattered throughout the United States had long been considered place where one could count on good, inexpensive, well-seasoned meals, and in Scandinavian parts of the country, the smorgasbord style was embraced by the adventurous. So was he robust fare of the Pennsylvania Dutch. And the flavors of Cajun and Creole cooking in Louisiana were sought by tourists visiting the region. But those local accents had not yet traveled to become part of the mainstream of American cookery.

It took a "food revolution," as it has been called by some observers, to bring about the change that has made us proud enough of our rich heritage to celebrate it at restaurant tables. James Beard, the foremost exponent of America's gastronomic excellence, proclaimed the revolution "a grand new era of liberation touching professionals and nonprofessionals alike," and he traced its origin to the ears after World War II, "when Americans began to think of eating as pleasurable."

In my own effort to explore three centuries of American cooking and eating, I find the awakening of he American—engendered by the war and its aftermath of unprecedented travel for the average citizen—has resulted in almost two decades of exciting awareness of good eating and experimentation and finally in delight over our own varied and yeasty culinary tradition.

Julia Child, as a leading culinary figure of the television age, has instilled confidence among millions of wishful lovers of good food, and many of them have begun to cook with enthusiasm and good taste. Now, in the last decade of the century, television offers almost as many how-to-cook programs as soap operas. Also, since the first publication of *American Food: The Gastronomic Story*, almost every major newspaper in the country has established a substantial food section, filled not only with recipes but with news about sources of regional wild foods such as chanterelles, stuffed milkweed pods, and sea urchins. In those fifteen years, food magazines have doubled in number—and much of their readership believes that food itself is entertainment.

I'm convinced that the delights to be found in eating abroad (still among the rewards of travel) changed the complexion of the restaurant scene at home. Many dining rooms have become less formal and almost as casual as the current mode of dress. Today there are as many menus featuring the regional—and the bistro—fare of France as once there were others offering only the classic dishes of *haute Paris*. Our recognition of the distinctive style of Northern Italian food continues to increase, and with the more recent acceptance of Southeast Asian influences there has been a proliferation in this country of another kind of cooking that is "light" in its traditions and appealing in the same way as Chinese and Japanese cuisines.

In 1981, a revised edition of this history emphasized gastronomic changes that today are firmly established. For example, in supermarkets now, the availability of fresh garlic can be counted on by small-town shoppers who only a few years ago had to make do with garlic powder; fresh gingerroot, fresh watercress, parsley, and several kinds of lettuce are widely available as well. The demand for fruits and vegetables has made plastic-chocked produce no longer acceptable, and in most regions there are markets where good things from gardens and orchards, picked only hour before, are freely arranged and sold from portable stands or the backs of trucks. As a result, superior supermarkets in urban precincts have followed suit. The pervasive trend of mail-order shopping has made it easy to fill kitchens everywhere with such fundamental traditional foods as cured and smoked country hams and fish and varied cheeses made by young Americans at home.

The American search for better health—almost a national obsession—has led to the mushrooming of the natural food business to an even greater degree today than in other historic periods. Frightened by reports of possibly toxic ingredients in everything and armed with a new awareness of compromises with safety by the food manufacturing industry, consumers have returned to patronizing health food stores, where organic foods beckon. A new generation has been willing to pay premium prices for health foods—and rush to consume vast quantities of such foods as oat bran and breakfast mixtures of fruit, fiber, and yogurt.

Away from the table, there is a serious new regard for the subject of food in general. Both the American Institutes of Wine and Food and the International Association of Cooking Professionals have sponsored symposia to explore the subject of food in terms of the environment. The intense involvement in what is happening to the soil and air above it, to the nation's waters, both the fresh and salt, has become a cause for many dedicated and politically aware people. Out of the consciousness of the need to rejuvenate the elements in order to produce food, there will come, I trust, more and more recognition of the values of the past.

The story is ongoing. In this country there is no need to lay claim to something called *cuisine*—it is the country's great bounty and its many evolving cooking styles that make American food worth hailing.

—Evan Jones
New York 1990

AMERICAN FOOD

The Gastronomic Story

PURITANS AND PLANTATIONS

Almost anyone who ever has been host to a friend from another country has had to deal with the question, "What is American food?" A visitor from abroad—in whatever region his discovery of the United States may begin—encounters so many public eating places that specialize in dishes from Europe or the Orient that it would be surprising if he failed to ask when he might sample indigenous food. It's a question that seldom gets a satisfactory answer. Public food in America is apt to be pretentious and derivative, or vulgarized like hot dogs and hamburgers, oozing with spicy-sweet, not very interesting sauces. But there is a difference between restaurant talk of cuisines and the reality of good home cooking. The true style of American food is the sum of many parts, and most of it came over with immigrants. In addition, there developed after World War II a new generation of lovers of food, who, having traveled or lived abroad, returned with recipes and whetted palates as well as with enthusiasm for the art of creating good things to eat. They were repeating the pattern of bringing from abroad new ways of cooking that would be incorporated into an American style that has been evolving since the beginning of settlement.

Like the vegetables discovered in the New World, much of the best of indigenous food is simple but good. Foreign travelers are apt to consider wild rice a delicacy to be coveted as much as truffles from France or Italy. Pompano from American waters, filleted and sautéed in butter with lemon juice and parsley and served with tiny boiled potatoes, can be worth a special journey. As can Long Island duckling, roasted with sage and onions. Abundance and the quality and variety of raw ingredients are basic to the American way with food, and they have been from the earliest years. Basic, too, is the assimilation of ideas from many other cuisines.

Even a primitive American cooking style cannot be said to have simmered into being over the first white man's campfire beside Virginia's James River. No more so on that cold winter day at Plymouth when Myles Standish and friends shot and roasted over coals an eagle "which was excellent meat"—so they said, thinking of Merrie England—"hardly to be discerned from mutton." Not even the penchant among Indian tribal cooks for stewing corn and dried beans into palatable meals can be assessed as a distinguishable branch of epicurism.

Nevertheless, the first important influences evolved in the colonial period. Britishers had come to the New World in many cases to gain religious freedom, and they were intent also on emulating the daily life of their homeland; their feelings were well expressed when they used the term *New England*. For their part, those who were Puritans exercised "the plain style," as they called it, as a fundamental of life. The preparation of food, quite naturally, was affected by this philosophy.

To both Plymouth and Jamestown, colonial women brought the incontestably British cooking style they had learned at home. There was a forthrightness about their preparation of various raw ingredients, and nothing at all about the way they cooked (in contrast to the French, for instance) could be described as tricky. The kitchens they left behind were rudimentary—open-hearthed and usually equipped with a spit or two. The limited character of their utensils can be recognized in John Winthrop's admonition to his wife to be sure to bring to Massachusetts Bay "2 or 3 skillets of several sizes, a large frying pan, a small stewing pan, and a can to boil a pudding in." These were women who always had done a good deal of their own work, but many of them had come from urban rather than rural homes and some had to accustom themselves to the care of poultry and dairy animals and to such chores as butchering.

In New England the traditional Yankee way of cooking remains strongly influenced by two factors—weather and religion. Without central heating, a family needed fortifying food from earliest times to see themselves through the unrelenting winters, and cooking was kept simple in order to satisfy a strict New England conscience. The Puritan sabbath began at sundown on Saturday and lasted until sundown on Sunday. Only work that was absolutely necessary was permitted, and even cooking had to be reduced to an absolute minimum. The immigrant women from England devised dishes that could be baked on Saturday and simply warmed up for supper Saturday evening, for Sunday breakfast, even for dinner after church. Out of the observance of religious strictures a general Yankee frugality was born; no more excuse was made for profligacy in cooking than in anything else. Good, plain food evolved from the respect of New England cooks for the ingredients at hand, and choosing the best remains important in contemporary kitchens.

In Virginia, where life was generally easier, colonial housewives also continued to prepare meals as their forebears had, but their mood was a lot more relaxed. What difficulties they had to deal with were not uncommon on either side of the Atlantic. Except for fair-weather days, when they might cook outdoors, all their roasting, broiling, boiling, and baking were done in the blistering temperatures of the wide kitchen fireplace with its spits and its heat reflectors, its trivets, its drip pans, griddles, Dutch ovens, hanging pots and trammels and cranes, and its long-handled peels, which were used to recover food or containers buried in the coals. The challenge was to apply English methods to whatever food supplies there might be, whether sent from England or grown or caught in the colonies. The earliest inventory at Jamestown showed sixty-odd domestic pigs, offspring of three English sows, in addition to some five hundred similarly bred chickens; but great damage had been done to other food supplies by rats, which had arrived on the first ships and had persistently multiplied.

No problems attended the boiling or broiling of chickens or pork, but in order not to tax these resources, more than sixty colonists in 1610 were packed off down the James to live on oysters and other seafood at the river's mouth. There they found sturgeon in such great abundance that they dried the surplus, then pounded the hard flesh and mixed it with roe and sorrel to provide, as some said, both bread and meat.

"Baked sturgeon" was apt to be cooked by those early Virginians in a cast-iron oven-pot that sat with its heavy, deeply edged iron cover on three squat legs among the glowing fireplace coals. Sometimes more coals were packed in, red hot, on the rimmed top—when the objective was to brown the surface of a meat roast, for instance. This was pure, untainted English cooking of the period, as are these instructions: "To roast a piece of fresh sturgeon, fasten it on the spit, and baste it well with butter for a quarter of an hour, then with a little flour, then a grate of nutmeg all over it, and a few sweet herbs. . . ." Average English tastes called for the use of some spices, and those who could afford it bought pepper, cloves, mace, cinnamon, and ginger when an occasional ship brought new supplies. Even the Pilgrims, who had to eat ground nuts during the first hard winter, preferred such conventional seasonings when they were available. And some early Virginians insured the succulence of their spitted sturgeon with an artful sauce: an anchovy, an onion, a little lemon peel, a bundle of sweet herbs, and spices simmered in a mixture of white wine and walnut catsup, with "the inside of a crab bruised fine"—or with lobster, shrimps, prawns, and about a dozen oysters, all of it thickened with butter rolled in flour.

Untainted Yankee cooking has never been quite so extravagant with the sea's bounty. Yet fish was a staple of life for all who had come to colonize. Some of the Pilgrims, after they had managed to stay alive on the *Mayflower* on a diet of "salt horse" (as they called preserved beef), hardtack, beer, dried fish, and moldy cheese, sent enthusiastic messages about their food sources back to England. As Edward Winslow wrote a friend, "Fresh cod, in the summer, is but coarse meate with us." He reported the bay full of lobsters all summer and said that in September a hogshead of eels could be taken in a night. All winter Winslow and his neighbors had mussels and clams "at our doors. Oysters we have none near," he wrote cheerfully, "but

To Roast a Large Fish

Take a large [fish of any kind], gut it and clean it, and lard it with Eel and Bacon, as you lard a Fowl; then take Thyme and Savory, Salt, Mace, and Nutmeg, and some Crumbs of Bread, Beef-suet and Parsley; shred all very fine, and mix it up with raw Eggs; make it a long Pudding, and put it in the belly of your Pike, skewer up the Belly, and dissolve Anchovies in Butter, and baste it with it; put two Splints on each Side of the Pike, and tie it to the Spit; melt Butter thick for the Sauce, or, if you please, Oyster-sauce, and bruise the Pudding in it. Garnish with Lemon.

—Eliza Smith,
The Compleat Housewife, 1742

can have them brought by the Indians when we will." Also for the taking, they found wild fruits (including cranberries and beach plums, about which maritime Yankees feel possessive) as well as herbs in variety and a "great store of leeks and onions."

In the spring the white blossoms of a species of plums unknown in Europe distinguish the sandy coasts from Virginia to Nova Scotia and—like the cranberries cooked with maple syrup by Indians—beach plums were among the first foods that colonists learned to adapt. Mixed with equal parts of sugar, the fruit can be turned into tart, shimmering purple jellies much admired on Cape Cod and Martha's Vineyard. On Long Island a recipe for a sweetmeat, kept in one family for generations, combined oranges, raisins, and walnuts with beach plums. The piquant plums discovered by the first settlers may be at their best, however, when served as a jelly in concert with soft-shell crabs that also were an immediate source of sustenance at both Plymouth and Jamestown. "It was a kindly providence," said a later beachcomber, "that arranged for Soft-Shelled Crabs and Beach Plums to be found in the same localities, and even saw to it that they were in season at the same time of year."

Discovered in the same fall season, all those eels that Edward Winslow valued were cooked as simply as possible—not with dozens of shrimps and mushrooms and parsley roots sautéed in herbs (as in a Pennsylvania Dutch soup) but with nothing more than a morsel of fat and a little onion, as wild as the beach plums. The Pilgrims called so unadorned a dish an eel stifle; later accented with the salt pork and potatoes, it evolved into a classic Yankee supper.

Stifle is the kind of word for which old-time Yankees seem to have had a hankering. It is an archaic term, related to early forms of the word *stew*, for which it is an uneasy synonym. A Martha's Vineyard variation, called a chicken and oyster stifle, requires browning chicken pieces in butter, then making a white sauce in the pan; covered with the sauce, the chicken is baked in a casserole for about an hour with a liberal amount of cream and a pint of oysters added for a final quarter-hour in the oven. For such straightforward cooking, the language of the past seems fitting.

English cookery of the colonial period was described by contemporary observers as fare that required no imagination, a comment that may suggest prejudice. At home the affluent British then were dining on pork that had been fed apples, on juicy roast beef, stubble geese, and other earthily good British provender such as mutton or firm cheeses made by dairy maids. Kippered herrings were long established as breakfast musts. Colonists, not strangely, were inclined to feed themselves in just that simple way when they settled in America. In 1622, when he was en route to London after a short residence in Jamestown, John Pory spoke for the average English palate when he described Plymouth Bay's bluefish as "of a taste requiring no addition of sauce." There were more than two hundred different fish that could be caught for eating in those New England waters. In Chesapeake Bay Captain John Smith once saw so many sea bass "that it seemed to me that one might go over their backs drishod." The New World plenitude was such that it may have made the earliest colonial cooks less inventive than they might have been—had there been less from which to choose.

"What but plenty makes hospitality and good neighbourhood?" asked another seventeenth-century Englishman traveling through Virginia and Maryland. Everywhere he looked he had found "as sweet and savoury meat as the world affords," along with good butter and cheese, fish, fowl, and venison; he noted prosperous orchards and gardens. Many later travelers were as lyric as their predecessors about the abundant wild fruit, the strawberries and wild grapes that had been successfully transplanted into domestic plots, the variety of melons, the pumpkins and squash, the corn that was sometimes white, sometimes blue, sometimes yellow or red. Pilgrim women had brought seeds to grow cabbages, turnips, onions, parsnips, peas, herbs, and other vegetables that were common in England; they even had planted some string beans they called French beans. Virginians planted artichokes, asparagus, beets, broccoli, cauliflower, cress, cucumbers, and the mustard and other greens that were to help make the South famous for its "pot likker." Robert Beverley, who wrote Virginia's first history, emphasized the cultivation of "all the Culinary Plants that grow in England."

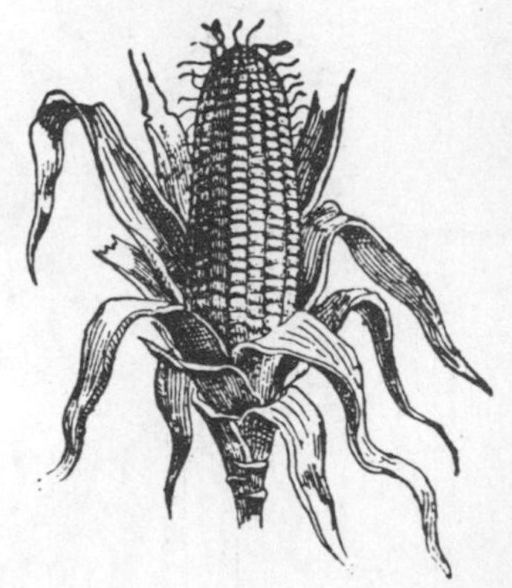

To incorporate such garden produce into the kind of meals they liked, affluent housewives of the southern colonies turned for culinary guidance to their memories of England. Considering themselves to be as British as any hostess in the home counties, they set the pattern of stylish entertainment for which plantations in Virginia and other southern states remain famous. Their European guests often noted that colonial housewives who wished to be fashionable had no problems in dealing with the choice of ingredients available in America. Following the prevailing mode in elegant dining rooms, the hostess herself ladled a fine soup as a first course when guests gathered for dinner in midafternoon; the table itself might be almost covered with large roasts of meat on platters, whole fowls, boiled or baked fish, as well as supplementary meat dishes, game birds, sometimes seafood casseroles, and the home-grown and distinctly Anglo-Saxon puddings, pastries, jellies, and the inescapable sweetmeats of the seventeenth and eighteenth centuries. ("In old Virginia life," commented Mary Stuart Smith in her *Virginia Cookery-Book*, "the carver was always the gentleman of the house, until the oldest son took his place, both for the sake of his own education in what was esteemed a gentlemanly accomplishment, and to relieve his parent of an onerous duty. In many families it was the invariable custom, when a roast turkey was served, to cut off the legs, or one leg, when the fowl was first carved, and send it to the kitchen with the gizzard and liver to be deviled, and brought in as an entremets later on in the meal. The deviling consisted in merely gashing the said parts of the fowl deeply, strewing them thickly with black pepper and butter, slightly with salt, and then broiling, sending in to table hot, when each person who wished it was helped to a small piece.")

Within a few years after the founding of Jamestown the kitchens of

plantations had become as creative in adapting Indian culinary methods as in pursuing the traditional English recipes. As it happened, in the first year of the Jamestown settlement a number of families—to minimize their dependence on food supplies that had to be imported from England—had been billeted with friendly tribesmen to learn to recognize strange varieties of edible roots and how to prepare them. Thus they were introduced to the potato, and they learned to master the imaginative ways that the local Indians had devised for making use of corn. All the colonists quickly accepted the need for cornmeal as well as flour in making bread, and gradually one good recipe followed another—from the most primitive ashcakes to hoecakes ("so called because baked on a Hoe before the fire," a colonial Williamsburg tutor wrote) to corn pones to corn sticks to johnnycake (then spelled "Jonny" and made with white cornmeal in Rhode Island) to hush puppies fried in deep fat, which were as necessary to fried fish, a southern cook once said, as woman is to man.

Among the young women who set out to adapt to the produce of New World harvests were Joane Pierce, Elizabeth Joones, and Temperance Flowerdieu. Those who were first to live side by side with Indian women in order to learn their cooking secrets are not named, but it isn't hard to imagine them as they experimented with the aboriginal way of pounding parched corn into meal. Or to share the wonder as the squaws built fires beside the corn fields, heated water to a boil into which to toss the freshly picked and husked ears of corn, then to watch the eating, the moving of cobs across hungry mouths like harmonicas. Never had they seen a vegetable eaten in such fashion, but the newcomers took to the idea immediately. They also quickly accepted the various Indian ways of mixing corn with beans and meat, both in summer and in winter (when the vegetables that were dried in the fall were soaked before cooking).

Hominy and the Pervasive Indian Influence

Virginia cooks did more than accept the hulled, dried corn called hominy; they made a sort of Southern fetish of it. Those young Jamestown women camping among the squaws observed the Indian use of ashes and water to remove the skin from dried corn kernels, and they recognized a difference in flavor when the hull-less kernels, puffed and white, were cooked in any of a number of ways. Whole hominy—it is sometimes called big hominy—is good when stewed with meat and wild greens, and Indians in the South sometimes crushed the parched grain, mixing it with dried eels and other fish to make thin but nourishing soup. When coarsely ground, hominy has been known, since colonial times, as grits, and it is one of the most characteristic foods of the South. "Hawg 'n' hominy," that special combination of salt pork and corn, is often given credit for keeping the pioneers alive in every phase of the westward migrations.

Many colonial women cooked grits as a stick-to-the-ribs gruel to which they added maple syrup, as the Indians sometimes did. From the natives they had also learned that the plump, unground kernels of whole hominy served as well as beans when prepared in the same fashion. Dried beans and dried corn, cooked together, continue to be a Yankee specialty. When it is cooked to a porridgelike consistency that is known as samp, whole hominy is the stuff of which undying New England legends are made. Aging Yankees tell tales of sailors lost in coastal fogs who found their way to port by listening to the sounds of dried corn being pounded in mortars as a preliminary to making samp. Other coastwise skippers used to swear they could tell when they were nearing East Hampton, on Long Island, by the smell of samp simmering in scores of pots. Like beans, samp was often cooked with salt pork or with pig's knuckles according to the method of some fishermen's wives.

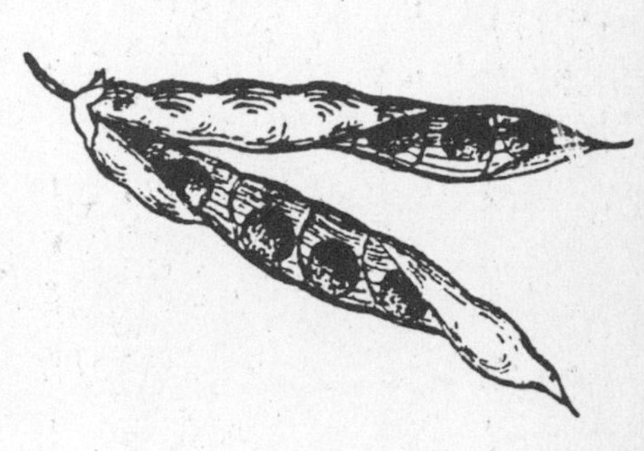

The combination of dried beans and whole corn is a variation of the Narragansett *msickquatash*, introduced to colonial cooks by the Indians and subsequently known as succotash. A similar corn-bean dish may have been served by Pilgrim housewives at the first Thanksgiving dinner in 1621 (along with venison, roast duck, roast goose—no turkey has been reported—clams, eels, wheat and corn breads, leeks, watercress, wild plums, homemade wine), and it became without question a staple in the colonial diet, especially in New England. The oldest succotash recipe on record requires the boiling of two fowls in a large kettle of water. Meanwhile, two quarts of dried white beans are simmered with a half-pound of lean salt pork "until like soup." Fat is skimmed off the broth from the fowls, and in goes a four-pound freshened piece of cornmeal brisket, a diced turnip, five or six sliced potatoes; the cooked chicken and pork are set aside to keep warm. The beans "like soup" are added to the broth along with salt, pepper, and four quarts of cooked dried corn. "Before serving, add the meat of one fowl," the original recipe says firmly. "The second fowl should be served separately, as also the corned beef and pork." Such a succotash, made according to these instructions, was the *pièce de résistance* in 1769, when a dozen or so Plymouth young men of *Mayflower* stock formed the Old Colony Club at a dinner to celebrate the landing of the Pilgrims.

There may be a dozen "authentic" ways to make succotash. Lima beans seem to be chosen most frequently to combine with corn, but New England cooks who cling to a sense of tradition say that the true succotash beans are known as horticulture or cranberry—or just plain shell beans—the kind with "cranberry-sauce colored splashes on the pods." Summer succotash as made by Yankees requires the shelled beans to be cooked a couple of hours with diced, thickly sliced bacon and a little onion, and—when the beans have become tender—corn freshly cut from the cob is added with salt, several grindings of black peppercorns, and thick cream. Indian women, who tutored those first English cooks long ago, would freeze their winter succotash (made with dried vegetables, of course) and use an idle tomahawk to chop off chunks to melt over a fire as needed. In summer they too made a similar stew with corn cut from the cob at the milky stage and stewed with fresh beans along with whatever meat was available.

Among the variations that have evolved in the last three hundred years, one popular with some Southern cooks consists of onions, okra, and tomatoes in addition to lima beans and corn, and a final generous sprinkling of grated nutmeg. Traditional Pennsylvania Dutch kitchens turn out a similar concoction in which green pepper is substituted for okra and which is further embellished by potatoes and dumplings. Succotash may mean all things to all men. I once found an unpublished diary of a pioneer Vermont farmer in which he was moved to mention food only once in an entire year. "This day," he noted in mid-August 1808, "I din'd upon Succotash." A noble dish, that succotash must have been, to warrant mention by so taciturn a frontiersman.

The English colonists not only had learned Indian ways of cooking corn and beans together but, as every schoolchild should know, they had learned from Squanto how to make use of the growing corn stalks to support the bean vines by planting the two together. They had also found that corn, unlike other grains, which require smooth and well-tilled fields, could be grown in patches where trees had been cut down, leaving stumps behind; they accepted the boon that corn could be raised easily on land that not long before had been heavily forested. This fact alone may have made America a corny country. The adjective when applied to sentimental things is said to derive from the supposedly unsophisticated humor of the early farmer; it might as well apply to a provincial American style of unpretentious cooking.

Corn in the American Kitchen

A contemporary American cookbook with encyclopedic intentions may include, perhaps, twenty to thirty recipes for preparing corn. Most of these, basically, are the dishes that English cooks devised in modifying Indian food to conform to the familiar tastes of the British Isles. In both early New England and the South of plantations those cooks made corn puddings, sometimes as one-dish meals, sometimes to accompany meat, sometimes to finish the meal as a dessert. The legendary Yankee hasty pudding is an adaptation of an English recipe for an ancient porridge that combined wheat flour, butter, spices, milk, and sometimes an egg. Because cornmeal was less expensive, as well as immediately at hand, colonial American cooks substituted it for flour and the mixture was thereafter called Indian pudding as often as by its old-country name. Records show that it was served as a vegetable to accompany the meat course—an eighteenth-century diarist noted "a very good Hasty Pudding" that he ate with "roste Alewive" in a Massachusetts tavern. By John Adams's time it was so accepted a Yankee institution that the Adams family served it habitually for Sunday night supper. Harvard University historians have written that the Hasty Pudding Club was founded in 1795 by students who sought relief from food the college provided by cooking their own hasty puddings in fireplace pots. Perhaps there are as many variations of hasty pudding (or Indian pudding)

as there are ways of making bread. As produced in many parts of the country, they are often sweet in flavor and baked in an oven, with accents of maple syrup, molasses, or grated orange.[1]

In the smoothest, most luscious corn pudding I know, much depends on the amount of liquid in the corn pulp. Some Kentuckians say this delicacy must be made with young field corn, and served as a vegetable. A razor-sharp knife cuts down the center of each row of kernels. No husk or skin is supposed to come close to the finished product. The blunt, non-cutting edge of a knife is used to depress the kernels when the ear is held upright over a bowl. Out spills the tender inside only, to be mixed with eggs, milk or cream, butter, salt, pepper, and a hint of sugar. This mixture is baked in a buttered casserole at about 350°F. for about forty or forty-five minutes. "When it doesn't shake," say some Southern cooks, "it is ready."

Corn oysters, which are sometimes called mock oysters and are considered by some to taste like marine oysters fried in deep fat, are usually made with whole kernels, but are incomparably better when the corn is minced. In this fashion they sometimes fool the unalert into thinking they are real oysters, and they are given a very precise title by M. F. K. Fisher in a recipe she received from by a Southern lady. "One-and-Only Unique Real Corn Oysters" calls for a dozen ears of shucked corn that have been scored with a sharp blade through the center of each row of kernels. The corn is then cut away from the cobs and put through a fine grinder. This pulp and all its milk is set aside for about three hours or until it reaches a custardlike consistency. If the mixture becomes very stiff, two beaten eggs are added (one if it is thinnish) along with salt and pepper to taste. Crisp, golden corn oysters form when this batter is dropped from a spoon into deep hot fat, and they earn their advance billing when served immediately on hot plates.

A recipe like this one provides a means of making something good of corn when it is impossible to cook within minutes after picking. For the fact is that freshly picked corn is never quite so edible as when cooked immediately. The lesson is one learned early from the Indians. "They delight much," Robert Beverley wrote of Virginia's tribesmen, "to feed on roasting ears; that is, the Indian corn, gathered green and milky, before it is grown to its full bigness, and roasted before the Fire, in the Ear." Even

[1] The loyalist Benjamin Thompson, who in 1776 went to live in Europe, later becoming Count Rumford, was as interested in the chemistry of food as he was in the physics of heat. He invented a cooking range, a pressure cooker, and his name was given to a baking powder mixture. In *An Essay on Food*, he wrote that "hasty pudding, when done, may be put, while hot, by spoonfuls into a bowl of milk, and eaten with the spoon in lieu of bread; and used this way it is remarkably palatable. It may likewise be eaten, while hot, with a sauce composed of butter and brown sugar, or butter and molasses, with or without a few drops of vinegar; and however people who have not been accustomed to this American cookery may be prejudiced against it, they will find upon trial that it makes a most excellent dish. . . . The universal fondness of Americans for it proves that it must have some merit; for, in a country which produces all the delicacies of the table in the greatest abundance, it is not to be supposed that a whole nation should have a taste so depraved as to give a decided preference to any particular species of food which has something to recommend it."

when he had a garden in Paris, Thomas Jefferson cultivated Indian corn "to eat green in our manner," meaning as quickly after it left the stalk as possible. Fresh picked vegetables, it has been said, should be "run from garden row to the kettle boiling for them, before the shock of being picked has had a chance to make them nervous or revengefully tough. Green-corn, of course, is the most immediate of all vegetables. It should be cooked before the flow of honey has stopped on the stem it has been pulled from."

When not so swiftly managed, about 90 percent of the sugar in sweet corn turns to starch within an hour of picking, and no store-bought corn remotely compares with that cooked in the field. The early American cooks learned this lesson well, but twentieth-century urbanization makes the practice almost impossible. To help a little, some modern cooks add sugar to the boiling water and refrain from any salt whatever, for salt water cooking toughens the kernels even more than prolonged exposure to air. An even better recipe for those who cannot toss their corn directly from the stalk into the pot is this one still used in Coahoma County, Mississippi (a good enough method, incidentally, to have been adapted by a Paris restaurant known for its *Maïs Frais Américaine*):

For a dozen ears, as fresh as availability permits, some Southern cooks bring to boil two quarts of milk mixed with an equal amount of water and a half-pound of butter. They say the corn may be cooked as much as eight to ten minutes, depending upon how fresh it is. And some say corn will keep in the milk-water mixture for at least an hour after the pot is taken from the fire, tasting as fresh as when cooking stopped.

Just as Jefferson planted corn in France in order to be able to pick ears right out of his Paris garden, Benjamin Franklin hungered for it in cooked form when in 1765 he was representing the colonies in London. He wrote to his wife asking her to send his favorite fruits—he was partial to York County apples—along with buckwheat flour and cornmeal; then he put his English cook through her paces until she mastered various corn breads and cakes. "The buckwheat and Indian corn meal are come safe and good," one letter said. "They will be of great refreshment to me this winter; for since I cannot be in America, everything that comes from thence comforts me a little, as being something like home." Earlier he had dealt with British ignorance of such things, responding to a letter in the London *Gazetteer* that had demeaned cornmeal as "not affording an agreeable or easy digestible breakfast." Franklin invited the letter writer to join him in America for proof that the colonies could offer dairy products and all the edible grains "as good as the world affords," and he listed the fruits of the forest and even of the islands off the Florida coasts:

> Pray let me, an American, inform the gentleman, who seems ignorant of the matter, that Indian corn, take it all in all, is one of the most agreeable and wholesome grains in the world; that its green leaves roasted are a delicacy beyond expression; that samp, hominy, succatash, and nokehock [nocake: corn parched in hot ashes and pounded into meal], made of it, are so many

pleasing varieties; and that johny or hoecake, hot from the fire, is better than a Yorkshire muffin.

Beans—and the Yankee Character

Other Americans have become convinced that Boston brown bread, also a product of Indian corn, is equally superior to muffins of any sort; and, along with Boston beans, the steamed bread from Benjamin Franklin's birthplace has remained a gastronomical standard wherever Yankees have settled in the United States. At least one Yankee cookbook, carried west in a covered wagon, rhymed a recipe in which it seems simple enough to produce a highly appetizing loaf as dark as chocolate and rather moist, not quite so dense as a Christmas steamed pudding:

BOSTON BROWN BREAD

One cup of sweet milk,
One cup of sour,
One cup of corn meal,
One cup of flour,
Teaspoon of soda,
Molasses one cup;
Steam for three hours,
Then eat it all up.

The traditional coupling of Boston brown bread with Saturday night suppers of baked beans, or Sunday morning breakfasts of fish cakes, was welcome wherever New Englanders migrated in the settlement of the rest of the country. I remember this from a childhood in Minnesota. It was more than a thousand miles from Boston but was nevertheless a place, like so many other not-so-long-ago frontiers, influenced by a kind of New England hauteur among families with origins in the East. Our home-steamed Boston brown bread was served by my mother—with her own all-night-long-baked Boston beans—sometimes even as a repository for what in our house was invariably a cheese (of domestic manufacture) called "Olde English," very orange-yellow and, as my parents would say between appreciative munches, "good and sharp."

BEAN POT

The beans were the genuine article. They related my part of America to one of its beginnings, to the dour climate of New England that helped to produce a style of cooking with no more subtle embellishments than the food of Britain, which so many had left behind. Early New Englanders very soon discovered—as should be proved by whatever case there may be for brown bread—that sweeteners added *something* to the quality if they did not necessarily improve the taste of food; the sugar content fortified their bodies against bitter and seemingly endless winters. They had learned this, perhaps, watching Narragansett and Penobscot squaws mixing maple sugar in with beans to bubble gently for a day or so in pots buried in pits lined with coals.

Few real Yankees admit to disliking baked beans, no matter what the recipe, and some colonists may have tasted one or another version in England. George III is said to have been fascinated when he first found beans and bacon being eaten by workmen constructing a military establishment at Woolwich, not far from London; the king ate baked beans alfresco with his subjects and so liked the taste (or the idea of so democratic a repast) that he instituted an annual bean feast. With no such kingly interests "baked bean days" are annual community celebrations in many parts of the United States. Recipes vary with the region, naturally. Throughout New England the various ways of cooking beans comprise a controversial subject, as energetically debated as the differences among Frenchmen who argue the fine points of the *cassoulets* of Castelnaudary and Toulouse. Yankee cooks have been equally opinionated since they traveled in oxcarts with frozen slabs of beans—to be heated at midwinter campfires—hanging from the wagon sides.

Salt pork is considered the heart and soul of Maine beans because, some say, it should constitute about a quarter of the pot's contents. My feeling is that the pork should have an instantly recognizable strip of red down its middle and that its rind should be slashed at about one-and-a-half-inch intervals so that meat lies flat instead of curling. Every bean in a real Maine bean pot "should be treated like a voter in an election. You must understand each bean to bake a collection of them," according to a Lewiston, Maine, newspaper that emphasized that meat is much less important than the beans. "Leaving aside our different families of beans, such as pea-beans, 'yaller-eyes,' 'marrer-fats,' kidney, lime and 'crambry,' we note a difference among themselves in each tribe. They never wholly assimilate or mash. That is, they never do in Maine. You do get in Boston a sort of brown paste with small nubbly particles in it, dejected in appearance. It should be called 'bean butter'."

Some New England cooks insist that the best beans for baking are the Jacob's Cattle, Yellow Eye, and Soldier varieties. Southwesterners are partial to the chili bean, pinto, Hopi, and Red Mexican, which developed deep tap roots that help them survive in the hard, dry soil of the region. Vigna beans, trained to poles, are common in the South, where dried beans are often cooked with butter to make them soft and flavorful. In the Midwest a regional favorite has been the so-called Swedish Brown bean, planted by Scandinavian immigrants in the nineteenth century. Of the almost one thousand varieties native to the Western Hemisphere, many kinds were taken to Europe after Columbus's discovery and later returned in immigrants' bags with new names. Pale green flat beans brought back from Lima, Peru, in 1824 by U.S. Navy captain John Harris were cultivated on that officer's farm near Chester, New York; they are the kind known as Lima, of course, and they are cooked in various ways all over America.

Among baked-bean connoisseurs, some Vermont purists still demand that yellow-eye beans be accented in the old Indian way, with maple syrup—four cups of beans to a pound of salt pork or smoked bacon and a quarter cup of syrup—while others in the same Green Mountains, where people are apt to be snowed in, speak for a quart of soldier beans to half a pound of salt pork and a half-cup of shaved maple sugar rather than syrup. Still others are happy, and produce marvelous results, using navy or pea beans instead of yellow-eyes, with no other deviations. Pea beans were also the stuff of which "Algonquin Maple Baked Beans" were made in Depression days, when literary New Yorkers used to dine regularly at the Algonquin Hotel on American fare; this recipe called for *two* pounds of salt pork and some molasses heightened by maple syrup.

True to British heritage, more Americans put gluttonous emphasis on meat, and at least one version of the recipe, in traveling from New England to Missouri, added an equal amount of country ham to the salt pork, tossing out maple, molasses, and sugar in favor of New England rum. In pioneer Michigan, in the rough country of that state's peninsula, apparently almost nobody used molasses—the style being to bake beans in a dripping pan with a layer of sliced salt pork covering the top; these beans were cut out of the dripping pan in slices and served with a colorful sauce of homemade tomato catsup.

A more prevalent method employing baked beans in a thoroughly American way is called New England baked bean soup. If you want to follow the traditional directions, simmer three cups of baked beans, four cups of water, one small onion and one stalk of celery for half an hour. Meanwhile, brown a half cup of diced salt pork and blend in two tablespoons of flour. Add two cups of chopped tomatoes, a teaspoon of salt, freshly ground pepper to taste, and stir while the mixture cooks and thickens. Put beans, onions, and celery through a sieve and combine with the tomato mixture, then cook for about an hour. In Washington, D.C., a flavorful version became famous as "Senate bean soup." It was officially introduced by Senator Henry Cabot Lodge after World War I, and is made with pea beans thickened by mashed potatoes, pungently fortified by a hambone with some meat on it.

The cooking of New England baked beans may have been varied in other regions, but ritual prevails where outdoorsmen still follow the "bean-hole" method; the cook digs a pit into which to sink an iron pot full of beans, seeing to it that hot coals are settled on both top and bottom surfaces, with a covering of earth to prevent the heat from escaping. Other carryovers from the past are also still around. People who own old New England houses on rare occasions make use of the brick ovens built into colonial fireplaces. About two hours before putting the bean pot in to bake they build a fire and let it burn until the black soot comes off the oven walls and the top surface has turned white. The coals are then swept out (a turkey wing was long ago recognized as just the right natural tool); the pot is put in to bake and the iron door of the oven latched tight for the nocturnal slow cooking.

Brick ovens were designed to turn out at the same time not only baked beans but bread, Indian puddings, meat pies, and rustic desserts known as pandowdies. Although lexicographers say that the origin of this last term is obscure, pandowdy has a fine Yankee ring to it and, according to some cooks, it also has synonyms that range from apple Jonathan and apple pot pie to Yankee apple John and brown Betty.

Whatever the name, there remains a pioneer quality in such apple desserts—as in these instructions of Connecticut's Mrs. Israel Putnam, whose husband was a Revolutionary general with descendants who have been proceeding as directed for five or more generations. The instructions call for four cups of apple slices arranged in a buttered baking dish with a half cup of cider, a dusting of cinnamon, cloves, nutmeg and brown sugar, and dots of butter. The seasoned apples are covered with a sturdy lid of baking powder biscuit dough, slashed for the escape of steam. When the apple Jonathan has been baked—in the same oven with beans—it is served warm.

In brick-oven bread cookery the dark loaves of rye flour and cornmeal, known as ryaninjun, have remained the standard bread. Two cups of meal made of white flint corn are scalded as the first step in producing one of these dome-shaped loaves, and after ten minutes enough cold water should be added to make a soft batter. Then a yeast cake dissolved in lukewarm water, a half cup of molasses, and two cups of rye flour are stirred in. When the dough seems well mixed, it should rise overnight in a warm place. Punched down in the morning, the dough should be shaped into round loaves, which are allowed to double in size. Baking takes about two hours, either in a brick oven or a modern range at a temperature of 325°F.

When the prosperity of Southern plantations was at its height, many households took pride in developing private bread recipes. In South Carolina's Low Country, where rice was the money crop, there were several kinds of loaves in which cooked rice was incorporated with wheat flour or, in the case of the splendid Beaufort plantation, mixed with rice flour and grits to make a thick batter—beautiful yeast-risen loaves resulting in each instance. "Take two and butter 'em while they're hot" is still a phrase to underscore the Southerner's fondness for hot breads. Housewives produce hot rolls and other famous regional specialties like spoon breads, beaten biscuits, batter breads, egg breads, popovers, ham biscuits, and sweet potato biscuits. Waffles have been made in both the North and the South since Dutch settlers founded New York—along with pancakes and other simple forms of skillet bread. The basic recipes had evolved in Europe, but American cooks added their own modifications. Indeed, the common European way of eating waffles with butter and sometimes sugar obtained until Americans discovered how much the cakes were enhanced by maple syrup.

Colonists found maple trees in abundance. The harvesting of "sugar trees" in seventeenth-century Virginia is a part of the record left by Robert Beverley. (An annual Maple Festival continues to be celebrated in Virginia's Shenandoah country, even though the syrup has become a factory product.) However, it is in the North, and particularly in New England, that Americans established maple sugar and maple syrup as one of the great indigenous culinary ingredients. Nowhere else in the world has "sugarin' off" been important in farm life, for it is a part of living off the land learned from Algonquin Indians by the founders of Massachusetts. From the Atlantic coast to Ontario and Minnesota, various tribes traditionally went into the woods in March to make cuts in the bark of hard maples and then to channel the tree sap into rustic vessels set to receive it. Indian women boiled it down to sugar, adding it to porridges made of ground corn; mixing it into cold water, they drank it as a tonic in hot weather. The Indians also used crystallized maple syrup as a seasoning for meat and fish dishes, a flavoring they much preferred to the European use of salt. And there is an echo of this when some Americans add maple syrup to the water in which country hams are boiled.

Pork—and the Anatomy of Boiled Beef

Pork in its various forms served frontier America well because pigs required almost no supervision and could be raised on edible discards of all kinds. Porkers did their bit for Southern cooks, but not quite so inclusively as they abetted the northern pattern of frugal life. Long, bitter, blustery winters kept menus anchored to the pork barrel in the cellar of the house, where red-streaked creamy slabs of side meat had been laid down in brine thick enough to let the pork pieces float when the heavy hewn-oak cover was lifted. This is an image of treasury—in this bursary of food one gets telling glimpses of the American past; the old political reference to dipping into the pork barrel still turns up in accounts of lawmakers' machinations.

And America moved west with pigs in droves, foraging on mast in virgin woods, rooting and snorting and running untended in the streets of burgeoning towns and cities. When venison and wild birds were in short supply, pork was the staple meat in every diet; and instead of wearing out its welcome, it incited sentimentality in hundreds of memoirs. One such remembrance of a Midwest childhood reports, "For breakfast we had bacon, ham, or sausage; for dinner smoked or pickled pork; for supper ham, sausage, headcheese or some other kind of pork delicacy." Note that nostalgia settles on the word *delicacy*. Salt pork, this choice of language makes it easy to believe, could be cooked with skill and undoubtedly love, could be served three times a day in such variety that it did not pall. No wonder it has been said, perhaps too often, that America's forests and prairies were turned into farms, and "her railways laid, her canals dug, her ships kept at sea on a porcine diet."

It is doubtful that anyone recently has had three consecutive meals based on no other meat than pork. But of course such redundant menus were the result of necessity, despite the cheerful memoirs. More often, the meat preserved in brine was an accent, to enrich flavor in a more substantive dish. Daniel Webster's mother, so her Yankee son told friends, was an artist at simmering together chicken and salt pork "in her own rare manner" to serve with pork gravy whenever Webster visited her in New Hampshire.

Yankees going south seem always to have been impressed by Southern amenities. A Massachusetts man who visited Virginia during the Madison administration applauded the Southern appetite for hominy, no matter how it might be prepared, because in his opinion it was a good substitute for potatoes—which he said "don't keep sound during the winter" in the South. While he noted that puddings and pastries were seldom served, there was always a great array of meats, "six or seven kinds . . . flesh, fowl and fish." And while neither cider nor home brew were as prevalent as in New England, preCivil War Virginia tables offered weak toddies for the ladies, and for the men whiskey, apple or peach brandy, "with decanters on the sideboard." People in those days said that one could get good beef and bad bacon north of the Potomac, and south of the river there were good bacon and bad beef.

It is true that pork was and remains a Dixie favorite. During the colonial period on one plantation alone twenty-seven thousand pounds of pork were annually consumed but only about one-third that amount of beef. Young pigs, stuffed and roasted whole, stuffed spare ribs, shoat's head simmered in herbs, chine stewed with sweet potatoes appeared regularly on Southern tables, and they still do, along with boned, breaded pig's feet that resemble fried chicken legs and sometimes nestle in a winy raisin sauce. Pork fat, of course, distinguishes the preparation of traditional Southern fried chicken as well as deep-fried fish and slabs of sizzling cornmeal mush. "Living high on the hog" is a Southern phrase still in use, and it takes in garlands of highly seasoned sausages as well as baked fresh ham—sometimes called a leg of pork—that has marinated in a peppery barbecue sauce. When Frederick Law Olmsted toured the South before the Civil War, he described a sumptuous meal at which were served "four preparations of swine's flesh"; and beside a variety of fowls there was oppossum, said to "somewhat resemble baked suckling pig."

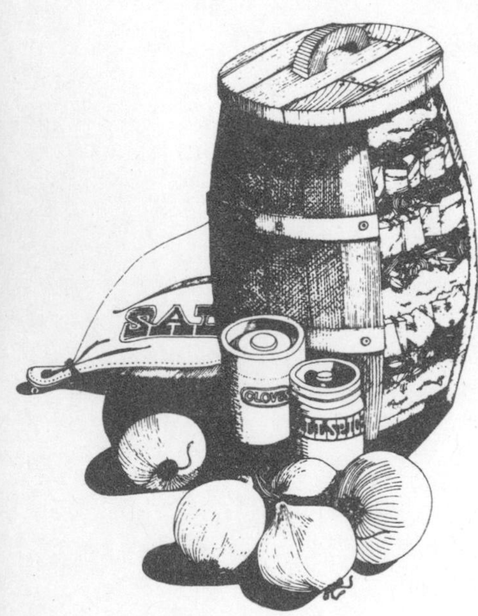

Whether in the form of ham, bacon, jowl, or tenderloin, pork—before the advent of twentieth-century beef—was the meat all Americans served most often. And most travelers were persuaded that Virginia ham was the best—good enough in very early colonial years to cause Sir William Gooch, royal governor of the Old Dominion, to send his home-cured hams regularly to his brother, the bishop of Norwich, and also to the bishops of Salisbury, London, and Bangor. William Byrd, who built up the great tidewater plantation called Westover, considered ham so serious a subject that his recipe was written in the flyleaf of his Bible:

> To eat ye Ham in Perfection steep it in half Milk and half Water for thirty-six Hours, and then having brought the Water to a boil put ye Ham therein and let it Simmer, not boil, for 4 or 5 Hours according to sise of ye Ham—for Simmering brings ye Salt out and boiling drives it in.

In the South hams have been a serious subject ever since the days of Gooch and Byrd. British methods of curing were employed from the first years along the James estuary, but it was the planting of peanuts, used for cheap food on slave ships, that helped to give Virginia hams their special flavor. Many of them were cured and smoked at a tidewater settlement called Smithfield after the London market area, and soon hams bearing that name were being favorably compared with the long-famous hams of York, Westmoreland, Suffolk, and Bradenham. By the nineteenth century in England, Gloucester and Buckingham hams were considered the best in the kingdom because the pigs in those counties were fed on beech mast. Yet the American peanut-fed hams appealed to Queen Victoria, and a standing order went out from the palace for six of those Virginia hams each week; Sarah Bernhardt, the superstar of the nineteenth century for whom the world's great chefs had created dishes, had Smithfield hams sent to her in Paris.

The best-known hams of France, *jambon de Bayonne*, are so called because they are cured with salt from the Basque port of Bayonne. The best-known hams of America have been cured in Smithfield, Virginia, for almost 350 years, and their flavor and texture set them apart from all others. They are lean and firm, with a strong salt taste, and are slightly oily, a quality that was first developed in colonial times when Virginia pigs grew to marketable size on a peanut diet almost exclusively. Economy now causes hogs in the South to be turned loose to root for acorns and nuts in the woods, and they enter the peanut fields in the wake of the harvest and eat what is left.

It is the curing process, rather than the feed, that gives a ham its Smithfield flavor. For thirty-five days it lies in salt and for twenty-one more days it is put aside to let the salt penetrate the meat. For five days then it is smoked over red oak or hickory coals, and afterward it is rubbed thoroughly with black pepper. Encased in porous cotton, it is hung up and air-cured for a minimum of six months—or from eighteen to twenty-four months for ham lovers convinced that aging is as essential to good ham as it is to good bourbon. The longer a ham hangs, the stronger the taste becomes, for moisture in the meat evaporates gradually, and it is moisture that keeps the flavor mild.

"To cure Virginia hams," according to a yellowing copy of Mrs. Smith's *Virginia Cookery-Book*, one must have "for each hundred pounds of hams, ten pounds of salt, two ounces of saltpetre, two pounds of brown sugar, and one ounce of red pepper, and from two to four and a half gallons of water, or just enough to cover the hams after being packed in a water-tight vessel (or enough to make a brine to float a fresh egg high enough—that is to say, out of the water). From five to six weeks in brine; then hang up, smoke, and put in papers before the fly appears in the spring—and bagged with the hock turned down, and hung until wanted. Boil till well done, for bad cookery can spoil the best ham." The process is, essentially, simple.

"A good Virginia Ham ought to be 'spicey as a woman's tongue, sweet as huh kiss, an' tender as huh love.' " So, they say, spoke one of the most talented country cooks as he demonstrated ways to prepare a perfectly aged ham. Most Virginia cooks, like Mrs. D. W. Sykes, whose colonial inn in Smithfield was widely known in the first half of the twentieth century, cook hams as simply and as carefully as suggested by William Byrd, already mentioned. Thomas Jefferson, at Monticello, had a boiled ham stuck with cloves, covered with brown sugar, baked for two hours while it was intermittently laced with a good white wine. A variation in nearby Charlottesville calls for cutting end-to-end gashes an inch apart and deep enough to touch the bone. These apertures are stuffed with brown sugar mixed with chopped sweet pickles and crumbs of corn bread. While the ham is baking, it is basted with a sauce made from the water in which it simmered, plus vinegar and brown sugar. In southern Maryland the most typical old-fashioned way of stuffing is with a combination of greens—seasoned spinach or mixtures of kale, watercress, cabbage, celery, plus red pepper, mustard seeds, Tabasco.

Country-cured hams demand more respectful attention than contemporary steam-injected pork products. Like fine Italian *prosciutto*, the country ham should be sliced with a hand as steady as that of a surgeon, "almost as thin as this page you hold in your hands." And the choice of other foods with which to serve such ham warrants much careful consideration, according to proud Southerners. "The making of a ham dinner," one of them wrote, "like the making of a gentleman, starts a long, long time before the event." The rich, nutty, pungent flavor of country ham made America famous (in ways different from other countries) for ham and eggs as a classic breakfast, lunch, or dinner; and it made the South famous for red-eye gravy, which goes better—they say in Blue Ridge and Blue Grass country—with hot biscuits and boiled hominy grits traditionally served with fried ham. (They also say in the South that the smell of frying ham is enough to make a person dissatisfied with anything else he might be served. To enhance ham with red-eye gravy, put the fried slices aside and add one-half cup of ice water to the drippings, letting it bubble until it turns red. Some cooks use strong black coffee; others stir in one teaspoon of brown sugar until it caramelizes, then add the ice water.) In the days of a cavalier style of life below the fortieth parallel, assertive ham was the characteristic *pièce de résistance* at meals that included baked yams, or homegrown sweet potatoes, baked with Virginia apples and chestnuts flamed in rum brought down the coast from New England.

There are more frugal cooks who maintain the art of preparing the traditional Yankee "salt pork dinner," which combines such winter vegetables as turnips, carrots, beets, and potatoes, sautéed sliced apples, with salt pork that has been boiled, then slowly fried until its dusting of cinnamon-scented flour is browned into the meat and all the excess fat is rendered. The meat slices are served on a platter surrounded by sliced apples, mounds of boiled vegetables, a separate dish of potatoes baked in their skins, and a gravy boat steaming with a delicate sauce made by stirring flour into a little of the pork fat and blending in thick sweet cream; sometimes an equal amount of sour cream gives extra piquancy. "Sounds awful," a good cook once said, "but it's heavenly." In Vermont this salt-pork dinner is ritual eating: Diners open and mash the potatoes, strewing them with bits of pork they have cut up; then they cut in the vegetables they like; the fried apples go alongside, and there is usually a New England relish such as piccalilli or small green tomatoes pickled in dill. Thrift is often the mother of inventive cookery. In Normandy beef tripe, ox feet, a few vegetables, cider, and brandy are turned into the rich and succulent *tripes à la mode de Caen* that used to be left off at a nearby baker's because of the need for so many hours in the oven. It became one of the region's famous dishes. In Yankee country the method used by the old Parker House to prepare honeycomb tripe may have been simpler, but its fame is so touching to thousands who once lived in New England, or dined on tripe at Boston's now vanished hotel, that it still evokes letters to the editors of food magazines. Broiled tripe Parker House makes up in nostalgia what it may lack in sophistication. "This tripe was excellent and as famous," a man in Texas wrote once, "as Parker House rolls and the apple pie at Thompson's Spa." Sometimes referred to as *tripe diable* by displaced Americans, its secret, according to those who have claimed to know, is to simmer the tripe in milk seasoned with thyme, clove, salt, and pepper for about twenty minutes. After the tripe has cooled in the fragrant milk, it is drained well and coated with a sauce made of butter, powdered mustard, cider vinegar, Worcestershire sauce, salt, cayenne, and an egg yolk, then broiled. Or a somewhat quicker method, with a finished product that those haunted by Parker House memories swear by, requires tripe cut into rectangles four by six inches to be salted and peppered, sprinkled with flour, dipped in olive oil, and coated with bread crumbs. Then it is broiled over charcoal and served with a basic mustard sauce made with cider vinegar.

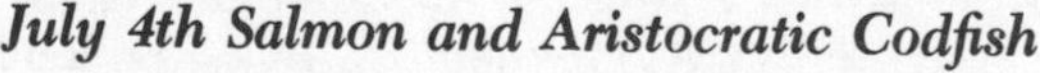

July 4th Salmon and Aristocratic Codfish

Even as early as 1630 a passing traveler said that the Maine coast "had the smell of a garden." That image still prevails, though much of the terrain is rugged and the soil stony. Produce of the sea and earth are brought together in special ways in this state, particularly in the traditional New England Fourth of July menu that calls for freshly picked green peas, gently simmered Maine salmon, and a creamy sauce containing hard-boiled eggs.

Like Independence Day salmon, salt cod seems synonymous with New England. In addition, shellfish were so abundant in the beginning that Pilgrim cooks at Plymouth, according to early cookbook writers, had nearly fifty ways of serving clams and lobsters. There may be fewer ways to prepare codfish for the table, but the Massachusetts affection for cod is such that a wooden replica of the fish is enshrined in the state legislature, and in the nineteenth century its economic importance was the source of status and fortunes for families who belonged to what was known as the

"codfish aristocracy." In those days in every home there was a box containing hard, whitish slabs in the back pantry, and in many cracker-barrel stores a long, dried fillet of salt cod hung next to the rum barrel as a kind of free lunch to whet the thirst. Cod was considered a must for Saturday dinner for generations of seagoing New Englanders and was known as "Cape Cod turkey" when it was cooked with pork scraps and served (like fresh salmon) with an egg sauce, boiled potatoes, and boiled beets decorating each side of the platter. Another garnish for salt fish consisted of sliced parsnips, a much-loved New England root, parboiled and sautéed in butter so slowly that all the butter is absorbed and the parsnips turn yellow, slightly flecked with brown.

Cooks in Gloucester, Massachusetts, became famous for their codfish balls (call them cakes if you will) as did others on Martha's Vineyard. In the homes of Boston Brahmins for many generations "eating fish balls on Sunday morning was like reading The Transcript or taking visitors to see the glass flowers." Knowing enough to appreciate codfish balls was essential to becoming a proper New Englander. As Senator Lodge was to do for bean soup, Senator George Hoar, concerned about pure food laws, saw fit to make Congress alert to Puritan Yankee palates by extolling "the exquisite flavor of the codfish, salted, made into balls, and eaten . . . by a person whose theology is sound, and who believes in the five points of Calvinism."

Some cooks in Rhode Island devised a boost for the flavor of cod by stuffing the whole fish with onions, celery, bread crumbs, and oysters before baking; others baked fresh cod in a custard and served it with the state's famous white-meal johnnycakes. (The epicure and music critic Henry T. Finck wrote in 1913: "It is for the cod that I wish to plead most earnestly. Some persons [usually persistent smokers, or individuals whose sense of smell is not well developed] maintain that cod is 'tasteless.' As a matter of fact it has a subtle but most delicious Flavor which, when the fish is fresh, reminds me of the flesh of crawfish.") And anywhere along the New England coast the choicest fresh cod is young, weighing between one and two pounds, and is the only fish entitled to be called scrod. According to the venerable *Century Dictionary and Encyclopedia*, scrod is strictly a New England dish and the term is defined as "a young codfish, especially one that is split and fried or boiled." Broiled scrod was one of the dishes that made Boston's Parker House famous for its dining rooms and its recipe is classic: Split the young fish and remove all the bones. Sprinkle with salt and pepper and dip in olive oil, then dip in bread crumbs seasoned with salt and pepper. Broil it over charcoal, put it on a hot platter, and cover it lightly with melted butter mixed with chopped parsley and a little lemon juice.

With scrod hard to come by, haddock is a common New England substitute, some cooks considering haddock more flavorful than its cousin the cod. In early Yankee kitchens the combination of fish and salt pork became common, and a method long used in Ogunquit, Maine, is simplicity itself—a dressed haddock is notched along the back at one-inch intervals and wedged with strips of salt pork that subtly flavor the fish when it is baked.

New England boiled haddock is simmered about half an hour, then garnished with crisply fried salt pork, parsley-sprinkled potatoes, and buttered beets; it is usually served with an egg sauce.

This is good food that squares with the characteristic Puritan conscience, and it doesn't threaten the budget—but then neither did lobster when New England was young; so plentiful was it then that it was used as bait for codfish. Indeed, among the earliest colonists in Maine there were some who considered lobster the bane of their tenuous existence. In 1608 members of Maine's ill-fated Popham colony went on strike because they were being fed lobster for breakfast, lunch, and dinner. In the Northeast one early traveler after another reported his surprise over these long-clawed crustaceans, grown to five or six feet in length and weighing twenty-five to thirty pounds. Somewhat wryly, perhaps, one writer said that these giants began to disappear from New York Harbor as the result of "incessant cannonading" during the Revolutionary War. Sixty years or so later, however, the visiting English captain Frederick Marryat, of the Royal Navy, noticed the prodigious size of lobsters off the Boston coast and said that each one "could stow a dozen common English lobsters under their coats of mail." By the end of the nineteenth century lobsters were no longer permitted to grow so large and the going price in Maine—per *dozen* whole lobsters—was reported to be twenty-five cents.[2]

European travelers were accustomed to lobsters known as *Homarus gammarus*, which are dark blue tinged with purple and are found in Norwegian waters and down the continental littoral to the Mediterranean. *Homarus americanus* is the creature of cold North Atlantic waters from Labrador to Cape Hatteras. The clawless crayfish of Florida and the West Coast are widely known either as spiny lobsters, rock lobsters, or as Key West crawfish and are slightly blander, lacking the true lobster's exotic flavor. Thus, in this instance at least, Puritan food had a recognizable advantage over that of the plantations, opulent though the Southern cuisine was soon to become.

New England's Seafood Ritual

The two regional cooking styles had many shellfish in common in their beginnings, but the Algonquin way of cooking seafood packed in seaweed, with ears of corn added—the so-called clambakes—has remained for 350 years a characteristic New England ritual. The Pilgrims learned the ingenious technique from the Indians; seaweed was laid over stones hot enough to cause it to steam, thus cooking corn and shellfish in perfect concordance. In southern New England clams have given their name to this outdoor banquet, but no such occasion would be complete without lobster, and in

[2] The lobster for which Maine has become famous is marketed (an $80 million Maine industry as recently as 1977) when about one pound in weight, rarely over five pounds. Bigger ones are used by commercial canners. However, along the Jersey shore, lobstermen who drag the bottom bring up lobsters weighing as much as twenty pounds, which are often grilled over open fires by summer residents.

Maine substantially the same kind of picnic is advertised by hundreds of resorts as a "lobster bake."

In either case some seaside chefs add a variety of fish, along with chicken or sausages, and potatoes usually join the ears of field-fresh corn. One white-haired clambake patriarch I know substitutes a domestic washboiler for the Indian's method of digging a pit. This man's fire is laid in a trench, and he covers the bottom of his boiler with about three inches of common rockweed, on which he spreads about a dozen hard sea clams, which he describes as too tough to eat but good for flavor. He layers these with more seaweed and spreads out a piece of cheesecloth to receive six small broiling chickens, split in half, and a pound of frankfurters. More rockweed is needed to bury a dozen each of white and sweet potatoes, then come ears of corn with the silk removed, followed by split lobsters wrapped in butcher's paper, more seaweed and cheesecloth, and three pecks of soft steamer clams. Rockweed has tiny sacs containing seawater, which jets, when heated, into the steaming meat and seafood. Thus when cooked, the chicken tastes like something between fish and fowl; the lobster gathers subtlety from the other meats; and the vegetables acquire an aromatic marine flavor from the steam.

Lobsters that escape immolation in clambakes have been easy for cooks of the Northeast to obtain, and some of the most chauvinistic are sticklers for detail. The Maine poet Robert P. Tristram Coffin may have spent as much time considering the bounty of Casco Bay as he did writing in iambic pentameter, and one of his many enthusiasms was lobster stew. Here is his method:

> Bring two cups of Maine sea water to a boil in a steamer and lay in twelve medium lobsters shell-side down to steam in their own juice; cover tightly, keep heat high ten to fifteen minutes. Remove and pick meat from shell while hot, discarding intestinal vein and lungs. Let picked meat cool overnight. Melt half a pound of butter in a large pot and in it heat lobster meat until it seethes. Turn heat low and slowly add one quart of milk, stirring clockwise to keep mixture from coagulating. Add a second quart of milk a little at a time. Bring the liquid to a froth and immediately pour in a third quart of milk, stirring constantly. Let the stew come to a boil and stir in one pint of cream; when this starts to bubble add another pint of cream. Let it simmer a few minutes without permitting it to boil, then remove from heat. Cool twelve to twenty-four hours while flavor develops. Reheat, season to taste, and serve to ten or twelve.

Early-nineteenth-century cookbooks made note that lobsters already boiled were sold in Boston markets "and are always fresh and good." A pie made of boiled lobster was a great Yankee favorite in colonial days and remained so for generations after the Revolution. Recorded sometime before 1763, the instructions of Mrs. Sylvester Gardiner lead to an interesting pie that contains pieces of lobster claws, lobster meatballs, and oysters:

> Take the meat out of the tail and claws of a boiled Lobster & cut them in Slices, & season them with grated Nutmeg, Pepper and Salt; then take the

> Meat out of the Body, and season with the Yolk of an Egg, a little Flour, Nutmeg, Pepper and Salt. Make these Ingredients into [small meatballs] and fry them brown with Butter; then [make a pie crust to line] your Dish and lay the pieces of Lobster in with some Oysters, an Anchovy slired, & Force-meat balls over them, to which add half a pound of good fresh Butter, laying it uppermost. Close your Pie and bake it half an Hour, and then put in a Layer of good rich Gravy [made with fish stock].

This lobster pie (and other versions popular in colonial New England) was in the tradition of British meat pies. So is the common clam pie, variations of which will be found from the saltwater farms of Maine—where a simple combination of minced clams, clam liquor, cracker crumbs, butter, eggs, and milk is encased in a shell—to a vegetable and salt pork mélange of Cape Cod or Long Island. Around Chatham on the Cape some good cooks think a delectable clam pie can be made only after a night of a full moon. They disdain quahogs, or common long-necked hard-shell clams, insisting on giant sea clams, so large that four are sometimes sufficient for a pie. When a round, white moon fills the sky over Monmoy Point and the tide is way out, diggers walk out as far as possible toeing the oozing sand with investigatory feet. When it is time to make the pie, they wash away the grit from the clams and strain the liquor, chopping off the heads and cutting away the stomachs. The body meat is chopped fine and combined with minced onion cooked with salt pork, some flour, milk, and cayenne. Sometimes diced potatoes take the place of the flour-and-milk white sauce. Mashed potatoes, carrots, and celery may be incorporated in the pies made from Chesapeake Bay clams in Virginia and Maryland. But in no other region is the clam so esteemed as in New England.

It is true, of course, that sentimental Yankees established their old place-names, such as Salem and Portland in the Pacific Northwest, and they also brought their appetite for clams—to the extent that a verse entitled *The Old Settler* includes this quatrain:

No longer the slave of ambition,
I laugh at the world and its shams
As I think of my pleasant condition,
Surrounded by acres of clams.

There were, as pioneers came to expect, some hard times for those New England settlers of Oregon and Washington, and a Judge Cushman of Tacoma has read into the record the fact that Puget Sound people had to rely so heavily on products of the sea, particularly the many Pacific varieties of clams, that "their stomachs rose and fell like the tides." These transplanted Yankees, according to a story sometimes told in Seattle, were so disheartened when they found themselves without corned beef that they replaced it with easily available local clams when they made hash. As they worked it out, clam hash has crumbled bacon and sautéed onion bits mixed with the clams, diced potatoes, and two beaten eggs, and the conglomerate is baked in a moderate oven for about a half hour.

Clam broth was said to have saved the lives of many Northwest pioneers, and clam chowder recipes traveled across the prairies, to be used sometimes just as they had originated in New England and sometimes with such regional flourishes as the substitution of cooked rice for potatoes, or the addition of tomatoes, chopped carrots, and cabbage, as well as potatoes, crackers, butter, and cream. The authenticity of the original Yankee clam chowder may be difficult to prove, but the following New England recipe appeared in 1833 in *The Cook's Own Book*, published in Boston:

> Take of salt pork cut in thin slices as much as will make half a pint of fat, when tried, which will do for a sufficient quantity of clams instead of two good sized cod, the heads or hard leathery part being first cut off. Be careful not to burn the fat. First, put your fat in the pot. Secondly, put a layer of clams on the fat; pepper, salt and a few cloves, then a layer of the slices of pork, strewed over with onions cut fine; then a layer of ship-bread or hard crackers dipped in water; then your thickening. Go on again with clams, &c. &c. as above, till your pot is nearly full, then put in water until you can just see it, and let it stew slowly. After coming to a boil, it will be done in twenty-five or thirty minutes. N.B.—Some like potatoes cut in slices, which may be introduced between each layer. Likewise wine or cider, as you fancy. This receipt is according to the most approved method, practised by fishing parties in Boston harbor.

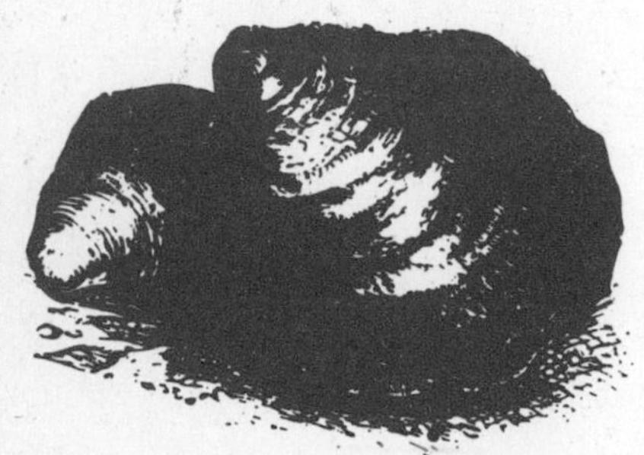

Whether brewed in a ship's galley or on the home stove, mention of clam chowder has spurred debates for generations. Real Yankees think of chowder as a whole meal by itself, and some feel so strongly about the ingredients that a Maine legislator named Seeder finally, in 1939, introduced a bill to make it illegal to add tomatoes to the pot. Long Islanders and other defenders of the so-called Manhattan clam chowder point out that their version should be served as a soup course, and for them fresh tomatoes have been the source of necessary flavor and color, since Long Island tomato growers and some neighborly old salts were mutually persuasive about merging fruits of the garden and the sea.

Marylanders, down on Chesapeake Bay, want no part of the tomatoes-or-not brouhaha. Early cooks of the region often combined chicken, vegetables, and seafood. One formula for Maryland clam chowder calls for chicken broth, chicken breast, celery, soft-shell clams, chives, minced onion, carrots, potatoes, corn, peas, pimiento, clam juice, parsley, and fresh thyme. It derives from an ancient recipe for "a sea dish" in which minced clams were combined with chicken broth, leeks, onions, celery, carrots, flaked rock fish, milk and cream, and a half-pound of crab meat. A colonial hostess in Anne Arundel County preserved her method in a longhand notebook labeled "Miss Fanny's Receipts."

So naturally blessed with good things from land and sea, the hospitality of Chesapeake Bay—indeed, wherever affluence encouraged southerners—often focused on informal alfresco entertainments. In the early days of the nineteenth century there was often a feeling of privileged informality when country people gathered to feast on oysters, or other seafood, as guests of the country gentleman who ran for political office—at least plantation aristocrats thought it was informality. Handymen carted big stoves onto the meadow and set them up in long lines facing each other. In between these lines serving girls set tables, also in long lines, impeccably decorating them with ancestral napery, fine china, and gleaming silver. When, at the appointed hour of one P.M., a hunting horn sounded from the portico of the great house, oysters by the barrelful were spread out to roast. A butler discharged his troops with whiskey punch for men and eggnogs for women. After the leisurely drinks, a guest once recorded, there came "battalions of pickaninnies bearing platters of sputtering oysters." And after an hour or so of feasting on oysters, there was an hour's rest while the linen was changed and order restored to the dining tables. Then crayfish in aspic, shrimp and watercress salad, red snapper baked whole with a wine sauce, terrapin stew and venison patty, pudding made of palmetto hearts, and yams "baked so tenderly they fell into the mold of any hand they touched." Not until sundown was there a hint of the real reason for the picnic; then the host announced to his sated guests that he was standing for office and would appreciate their votes.

There was a landed-gentry Englishness to scenes like this. Much of the colonial South had been founded by cavaliers, loyal to England's king. The average plantation owner was a man of the middle class who acquired land and devoted his energies to building a life of greater security and more evidence of affluence than he or his forebears had known before. Social status was of grave concern and was marked by emphasis on horse racing and fox hunting, six-in-hand coaches and ten-gallon punch bowls. Hospitality, above all, was *de rigueur*, not only because there were few taverns in the early days but because guests added interest to the isolation of plantation life. Entertaining was easy enough, with so many servants, easier because so many had an affinity for cooking well. The colonial South, said Sir William Berkeley, a Virginia governor in the seventeenth century, was "the land of good eating, good drinking, stout men and pretty women." With these planters' wives a good table was a point of honor. Meals on most plantations were prepared in detached kitchens and sped to the table under cover by waiters recruited from the slave population—"long trains of slaves," as an early traveler wrote, "passing to and fro, with the different viands."

Toward a Uniquely Southern Cuisine

Aside from the service, the Southern menu itself, of course, had little of the New England puritanism. Plantation breakfasts were generally so luxurious that one traveler after another described them in detail, and one reported that the ample breakfasts of England were, in comparison, "meager repasts." More often than not, a man's day started with a julep "made of rum, water and sugar," or sometimes the eye-opener was brandy. In antebellum days a Southern gentleman may well have rated drinking among the arts. Henry Clay, the distinguished Kentuckian and a presumed expert on bourbon, entered his julep recipe in his diary:

MINT

> The mint leaves, fresh and tender, should be pressed against the goblet with the back of a silver spoon. Only bruise the leaves gently and then remove them from the goblet. Half fill with cracked ice. Mellow bourbon, aged in oaken barrels, is poured from the jigger and allowed to slide slowly through the cracked ice. In another receptacle, granulated sugar is slowly mixed into chilled limestone water to make a silvery mixture as smooth as some rare Egyptian oil, then poured on top of the ice. While beads of moisture gather on the burnished exterior of the silver goblet, garnish the brim of the goblet with choicest sprigs of mint.

A visitor in 1774 observed that the average planter rose early, had his drink (because "a julep before breakfast was believed to give protection against malaria"), then inspected his stock and his crops before breakfasting at about ten o'clock on "cold turkey, cold meat, fried hominy, toast and cider, ham, bread and butter, tea, coffee and chocolate." It is clear that breakfast has been as worthy of attention in the minds of some as the art of drinking. Tables were often laden with grilled fowl, prawns, ham and eggs, "potted salmon from England," vegetables, cornmeal mush, and hominy cooked in a variety of ways. Southerners of the nineteenth century may not have indulged as often as did New Englanders in a slice of pie for breakfast, but they made up for such a lack in sweet breads of all kinds.[3]

It may be true that no other people on earth have been reared to expect habitually a breakfast like those that are common in the South. It is a Georgia habit in coastal areas to start the day with shrimp, either simply boiled or sprinkled with a little salt, rolled in bread crumbs mixed with eggs, and fried in deep fat. Boiled hominy grits with a small pool of butter in each serving is the accompaniment. Another dish with an inelegant name, shrimp gravy, is served with grits at breakfasts in Beaufort, South Carolina, and its preparation begins with a couple of strips of bacon frying in an iron skillet. You set the bacon aside and sauté a quarter-cup of chopped onion in the fat, then add two cups of peeled raw shrimp and stir about two minutes; sprinkle in two tablespoons of flour, coating the shrimp evenly, and add four tablespoon of Worcestershire sauce and enough water to give the shrimp a slightly liquid binding. The mixture should be salted to taste, given a turn or two of the pepper grinder, and brought to the breakfast table with a steaming dish of grits.

A lesser-known South Carolina breakfast dish is a sort of gargantuan pancake known as a plantation skillet cake. Well-beaten eggs are made into a batter with flour, salt, milk, and a little oil, then poured into a well-

[3] A nineteenth-century writer decided that in northern New England "all the hill and country towns were full of women who would be mortified if visitors caught them without pie in the house." As he saw things, the absence of pie at breakfast " was more noticeable than the scarcity of the Bible."

buttered iron skillet and baked in a hot oven (400°F.) for about twenty minutes. The cake puffs, turns light brown at the edges, and comes out looking a good deal like Yorkshire pudding; with hot applesauce and brown sugar it makes a comforting start to the day.

It is unlikely that many colonists had encountered sweet potatoes before they came to the Virginia settlement, but in Britain the pithy tuber, the color of terra cotta, had made such a hit at the royal court that Henry VIII indulged in liberally spiced sweet potato pies. At Jamestown, early cooks most often roasted sweet potatoes in ashes, the way their Indian neighbors did. As kitchen equipment improved, sweet potatoes were frequently sliced and broiled with butter; they were baked with molasses and mated with oranges when that fruit was available, and many sweet potato puddings and other desserts—there is, of course, sweet potato ice cream—were devised. But ham and sweet potatoes have been prepared companionably at least since the publication of Virginia's first purely local cookbook in 1824. To serve "Sweet Potatoes Stewed" according to Mrs. Randolph's method, you slice them in half, cover them with slices of Virginia ham, "and on that, one or two chickens cut up with pepper, salt, and a bundle of herbs." It is a meat-and-potatoes dish of long-established tradition.

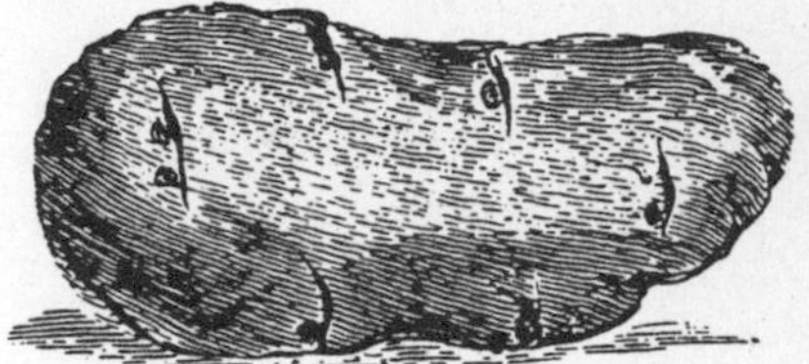

Southern colonists, following English culinary custom, added slices of ham to beefsteaks cooked in gravy, sealing in the meats with a crusty top to make a meat pie. They maintained the Tudor custom of spiced beef, marinated a fortnight at least, then roasted and served cold; slices as thin as parchment are still eaten with beaten biscuits made by pounding (for a half hour, until the dough blisters and is therefore full of air) a mixture of flour, lard, and water. In Baltimore and on the Eastern Shore, where these little hot breads are still made, sometimes with a machine designed to do the work of the tedious pounding, they are known as Maryland biscuits. (Beat, they say in Caroline County, at least thirty minutes and forty-five for company.) At a buffet supper in Annapolis, tiny Maryland biscuits might accompany deviled Maryland ham, crab-meat balls, hot chicken mousse, deviled crabs, a casserole of rice, oven creamed mushrooms, spiced beef, lobster salad, green salad, sweet rolls, strawberry ice, lemon sherbet, and a fluffy vanilla cake. Deviled ham may come in cans, but it is better, as are most things, when produced at home. The process is a variation of the old English method of making potted ham, and it is simple. Combine two cups of finely minced or ground country ham with a sauce composed of a cup of cream, four tablespoons of butter, one tablespoon of flour, a dash of red pepper, one-half tablespoon of dry mustard which has cooked about ten minutes and become thick. Pack the ham mixture in a mold and chill; it is served sometimes for Sunday evening suppers or used as a spread on crackers or cocktail canapes. An even easier version is a mixture of the same amount of ground ham with two teaspoons each of Dijon mustard and mayonnaise to serve as a binder.

Southern ham is a natural foil for birds and fish, and it is often served with shrimp or crab or duck in so-called "made dishes" typical of the cooking style that may be called Southern. One of the best of such collaborations between ham and seafood calls for crabmeat rolled in thin slices of ham, served straight from the fire, piping hot.

Early Virginians were likely to serve crab, shrimp, and lobster in traditional English fashion: very simply. They minced the meat of the crab, cooked it in some white wine and vinegar touched up with gratings of nutmeg; they made an anchovy sauce with plenty of butter and a couple of egg yolks, then combined sauce and crabmeat and served it hot in the shell. Along the Eastern Shore and in the Carolina Low Country soups and stews made with crabs and a milk-and-butter stock, or chicken broth, have been popular since the seventeenth century.

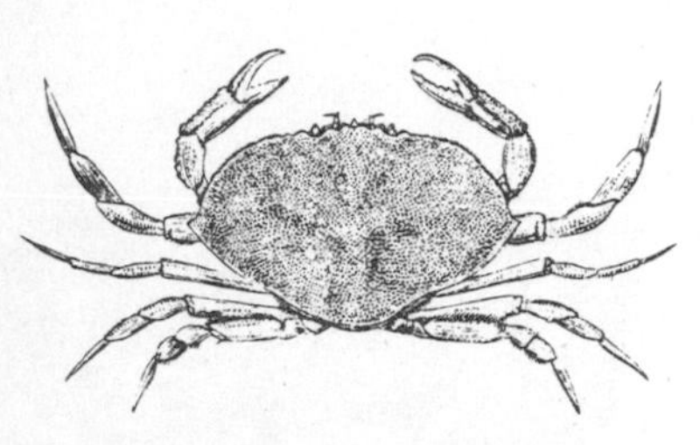

To Dress Crabs

Take out the meat and clean it from the Skin. Put it into a Stew-pan with half a pint of white wine, a little nutmeg, pepper and salt, over a slow fire,—throw in a few crumbs of bread, beat up one yolk of an egg with one spoonful of vinegar, then shake the Sauce pan round a minute, and serve it upon a plate.

—*Miss Ann Chase's Book*, 1811

Cookbooks before Miss Fannie

The crab loaf that is sometimes on the menu at organized roasts represents an old English custom that may first have been described in a cookbook in 1741, when Edward Kidder published his *Receipts of Pastry*. The Kidder method starts with bread rolls that have been hollowed out and fried in deep drippings, then stuffed with a mixture of chopped oysters and eels in a sauce of anchovies, mushrooms, and wine. There was then a similar treatment of crisp, golden rolls filled with lobster stuffing—essentially the same as the crab loaves that today begin with split French or Italian loaves hollowed out and filled with a crab and bread crumb mixture that is seasoned with dry mustard, celery seeds, salt, and pepper and bound with a little heavy cream and a good deal of butter. With the top replaced, the crab loaves are heated in a hot oven (or sometimes wrapped in foil and toasted over coals outdoors), then cut into sizzling slices.

The Kidder book was published in London, and it was there that a Virginia printer named William Parks in the same year found one of the ten editions of *The Compleat Housewife* by Eliza Smith and decided it was time for Old Dominion cooks to have a cookbook of their own. In the style of the times, Parks simply appropriated from Mrs. Smith's various editions recipes he considered useful (including one for oyster loaves) in colonial kitchens; he left out those containing ingredients not obtainable or which would, he said, merely "swell out the book and increase its Price." His pirated version went on sale in Williamsburg, and soon other English cookbooks were made available to the colonies. The first original American cookbook appeared a half century later, when George Washington was retiring as the new nation's first president. *American Cookery* was published in Connecticut in 1796, for the first time giving printed instructions for the cooking of corn and other colonial produce.

"An American Orphan," designated as the author of this book, turned out to be a Connecticut cook named Amelia Simmons, who gave the earliest professional directions for making Indian pudding, johnnycake, and spiced watermelon pickles. For those in such port cities as Boston, New York, Philadelphia, and Charleston, where it was possible to buy spices such as coriander that were cultivated in the West Indies, Miss Simmons described the making of cookies with a stiff dough of butter, sugar, thick sour cream, and flour, highly seasoned with coriander that the cook ground in her kitchen. The word *cookie* seems to have been borrowed from the Dutch settlers in New York and transformed into one of the most basic of American sweets.

Between 1796 and 1808, Amelia Simmons's *American Cookery* was published in four editions, and its repertoire widened to include Independence Cake, Federal Cake, and Election Cake (a rich, spicy, fruit-strewn loaf designed for town meeting occasions)—all three titles speaking of a new nationalist fervor. There was talk of an "American mode of cooking." The Simmons book was the first to tell how to deal with the knobby root of a type of sunflower plant cultivated by the Indians that had become known as Jerusalem artichokes.[4] It introduced the use of molasses as a synonym for the English word *treacle*, and gave instructions for making pumpkin "slapjacks" by combining cornmeal with boiling water, then adding milk and puréed pumpkin, a little flour, pearl ash or baking powder, salt, sugar, and a beaten egg. They were fried on a hot griddle like pancakes, then served with maple syrup.

In 1808 Lucy Emerson of Montpelier, Vermont, did to Miss Simmons what William Parks had done to Mrs. Smith—she reprinted most of the Simmons recipes in a volume she called *The New England Cookery*. But her version did not warrant such a specific title; it remained an essentially English text, concentrating on English ways in the kitchen. The first genuinely regional cookbook available to Americans was Mary Randolph's *The Virginia Housewife*. In Mrs. Randolph's pages there was a candid breaking away from the English past and an admission of other influences in the gastronomy of the United States. Hers was the first book to devote an entire section to vegetables and to feature some not commonly served in England, such as sweet potatoes, pumpkins, squashes, and tomatoes. "Peel the skin from very large, full, ripe tomatoes," she wrote in a recipe that seems to have an appetizingly modern stance. "Put a layer in the bottom of a deep dish, cover it well with bread grated fine; sprinkle on pepper and salt, and lay some bits of butter over them—put another layer of each, till the dish is full—let the top be covered with crumbs and butter—bake it a nice brown."

The white potato appears to have been given its first published recipes four or five years later in a book by Eliza Leslie, which called attention to its American emphasis. But cookbook users were also doing new things with old ingredients. Mrs. Randolph, stressing her Southernness, claimed to be the first writer to recommend various preparations of fresh, young turnip tops, which, she declared, "are still better boiled with bacon in the Virginia style."

[4] "Jerusalem" appears to be a mistaken pronunciation of the Italian word for sunflower, *girasole*.

BAKING AND COOKING RECEIPTS.

LOTTE RUSSE.—Take 1 pt. milk, dissolv
ss and 1 lb. sugar; add, after it is cool
lour, suit your taste and line out som
d put the cream in it and cool.
JELLY.—Take 1 pt. water and 3 c
of 2 lemons, and dissolve that
wine, brandy and spice to your ta
r flannel cloth and put it in mould.
KE APPLE MOLASSES.—Take new
ade from sweet apples, and boil it
molasses. It should be boiled in br
that would injure the flavor. It will keep
aid to be as good, and for many purposes
nolasses.

☞ Acid fruits should be cooked
metal, and poured out as soon as t
essels should never be used, as th
poison which very readily unites w
JELLIES.—*Lemon Jelly.*—Isinglas
gar, 1 lb.; clarify; and, when
nons, and the grated yellow rin
well, strain off the peel, and po
rtshorn Jelly.—Hartshorn, 1 lb.;
over a gentle fire till su

Most methods of cooking were, of course, passed on from generation to generation through practice and word of mouth, and housewives who could read and write kept their most valued "receipts" in handwritten notebooks. At Pennsbury, outside Philadelphia, the family of William Penn had a copybook headed "My Mother's Recaipts for Cookerys Presarving and Chyrurgery," which had been transcribed for William Penn, Jr. An eighteenth-century Maine household's recipes were written down by the same Mrs. Gardiner whose method for making lobster pie appears in this chapter and whose instructions for "A Savory Veal Pie" combine loin of veal with oysters, hard-boiled eggs, lemon peel, and judicious sprinklings of spices and fresh herbs. Mrs. Penn's partridge pie recipe calls for seasoning the wild birds with nutmeg, mace "and a Littell suger," and she was prepared to substitute venison round for a leg of mutton, making a sauce of sweet butter, vinegar, sugar, gooseberries, and barberries.

Housekeepers for the Penn and the Gardiner families were no strangers to wild food, of course, and they were among the average colonial women who adapted traditional culinary techniques whenever they encountered ingredients unknown in Europe. American gastronomy made the most of the bounty of the sea and the garden, of forest game and domestic livestock. As settlers with varying ethnic backgrounds arrived and began to live off the land, there was greater inventiveness in the kitchen. And, inevitably, perhaps, there were some changes made in that abstraction we tend to call American food.

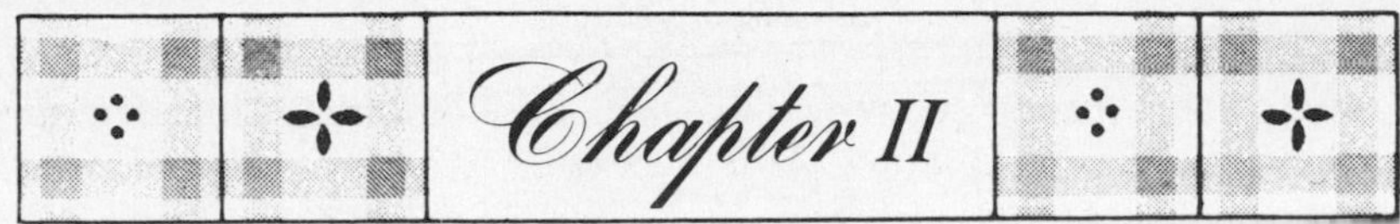

THE FRENCH TOUCH

Some travelers from abroad viewed this country in its earliest epochs not only with alarm but with alimentary disdain. The initial criticism was based not on notions of French *haute cuisine*—which Puritan England found sinful—but on the recognition that raw materials were too often treated without sufficient respect. Travelers were always, in those days, impressed by the abundance of fish, meat, and vegetables, but they deplored what happened in the kitchen to such good things. In 1796, on a visit to New York's city market, one observer counted sixty-three kinds of fish, fourteen kinds of mollusks and crustaceans, fifty-two of meat and fowl, along with twenty-seven garden vegetables for sale. (A whole pig, it was noted, could be bought for fifty cents.) Bounty, however, has rarely had very much to do with culinary excellence.

England's seagoing novelist Captain Frederick Marryat made it a matter of record that in the early nineteenth century there were "plenty of good things for the table in America; but . . ."

It was a big "but" that Marryat managed to soften by a frequently used quotation: " 'God sends meat, and the devil sends cooks,' " he wrote in his *Diary in America*, adding, "such is and unfortunately must be the case for a long while, in most of the houses of America, owing to the difficulty of obtaining or keeping servants." The situation was no different in public hostelries. Traveling through shingle-roofed hamlets and tree-stump-studded countryside, visitors generally agreed that taverns themselves were dreadful and the food served in them was occasionally close to inedible.

One of these Britons, for a half-dozen years a consul for Her Majesty in Transcendentalist Boston, had no doubt that the worst of the trouble was in the cooking. "The great evils," Thomas Colley Grattan said in a book he chose to call *Civilized America*, "are the odious attempts at *la cuisine française*, and the bad butter used in the sauces." It was the first of these evils that upset Mr. Grattan the most. "Every broken-down barber, or disappointed dancing master . . ." he declared, "sets up as a cook. . . . In a word, the science of the table is at the earliest stage of infancy in the United States. In all the doubts and fears expressed as to their future fate, nothing sounds so terribly ominous as that aphorism in [Brillat-Savarin's] 'Physiologie du Gout,' which solemnly says, '*La destinée de Nations dépend de la manière dont elles se nourissent.*' "

Ominous, no doubt—but it isn't too easy to find a direct connection between this nation's destiny and the way it nourishes itself, Brillat-Savarin to the contrary. Almost thirty years before he published *The Physiology of Taste* in 1825, this most celebrated of France's gastronomes did spend a couple of years in New York, for a time as a fiddler in a theater orchestra, but he wasn't enough impressed with the city's food to mention it in his classic volume. He was in fact a little like the more pretentious American cooks of the period. He went out one day in Connecticut and shot a turkey, then served it, of course, with the most subtle French touches he could devise. Naturally, this gallicized repast was a resounding success with the guests who gathered near Hartford.

Another Debt to Jefferson

Brillat-Savarin had no effect on American culinary ways, but by this time Thomas Jefferson's admiration for the food of France had begun to have limited influences, especially in his native South. In his five years in Paris, where he followed Benjamin Franklin as U.S. envoy, as much of Jefferson's attention as he could spare was devoted to recipes rather than treaties, to the intimate secrets of the kitchen rather than those of state. Jefferson, as Marshall Fishwick put it a little too neatly, "wed Virginian and French cooking in one of the happiest unions recorded in the history of cookery."

At any rate, he did his best to do so. It was Jefferson who ensconced the first French chef in the White House. And he carried his point further when, bringing eleven servants to staff the executive mansion, he assigned two black girls, Edy and Fanny, as apprentices to Chef Julien so that they might learn advanced culinary ways. He was convinced that the Paris influence in the kitchen was worth paying for. "I have understood that twenty dollars a month is what is given to the best French cook," he wrote a friend, going on to say that he was so determined to find a superlative chef that he authorized his agent "to go as high as twenty-eight dollars." Forty percent more than the prevailing wage was simply not too great a premium for the assurance of having the best food in Virginia.

Patrick Henry permitted himself to get so riled by Jefferson's Gallic admirations that he once told a political rally that the author of the Declaration of Independence "abjured his native victuals." This was missing the point. For at the same time Edy and Fanny arrived to develop their skills under Julien's tutelage, Annette, the Monticello children's governess, joined

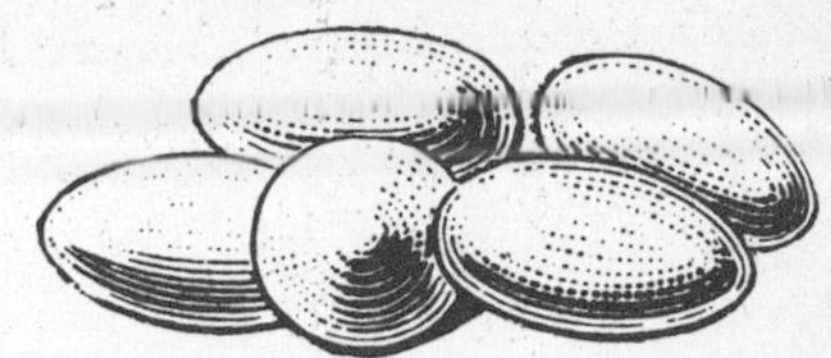

the White House crew to make sure that the president also got the kind of Southern food he had grown up with. Annette knew "just how he liked batter cakes, fried apples, and hot breads served with bacon and eggs at breakfast." Far from abjuring anything, Jefferson was determined to surround the best of Virginia food with the best from the European cuisine.[1]

In this spirit Annette left a record of her way of making chicken hash, under the title *Capitolade* and with the stipulation, "This dish is for breakfast." Rich in chopped cooked chicken, mushrooms that came from nearby woods, homegrown shallot onions, and garlic, *Capitolade* is the kind of dish that Southerners have often found at plantation breakfasts, and its sauce of dry white wine combined with chicken stock suggests the use of Jefferson's French vintages in the kitchen.

A waffle iron purchased in Holland had also been brought home by Jefferson, and waffles were made by cooks like Annette from the same mixture of ingredients as batter cakes, the Southern term that Yankees or Westerners might translate as pancakes or griddle cakes. In Jefferson's South the French urge for the thinnest of batters was more often than not suppressed. One New World pancake, for instance, blended unbolted wheat flour with yeast and cooked hominy grits, whose pearly contribution made the cakes that sizzled on the griddle seem slightly heavy though smoothly textured and unlike any European forerunner. As rice became important among Southern crops, Mrs. Randolph provided a method for producing "Rice Woffles" that was simple enough: "Boil two gills of rice quite soft, mix with it three gills of flour, a little salt, two ounces melted butter, two eggs beaten well, and as much milk as will make it a thick batter—beat it till very light, and bake it in woffle irons."

George Washington's mother was one of the plantation hostesses who served such breakfast fare, and records show that she made sure that cakes like these were even more American by serving them with a mixture of maple syrup and honey, heated together. There were, as well, efforts to emulate French chefs more closely by making very thin dessert crêpes, still known in Virginia vernacular as "Quire-of-Paper Pancakes." These are mixtures of egg yolks, flour, butter, sugar, and white wine, and when they come hot off the griddle, the paper-thin cakes are stacked, with sprinklings of maple sugar on each surface, then cut in wedges like pie. One recipe, from Mildred Lee of the colonial Virginia family, "which we used to use at Arlington," gives directions as follows:

> Beat 4 eggs light and frothy; beat in ½ cup sugar. Sift together ½ cup flour and nutmeg gratings and add to egg mixture alternately with 1 cup milk. Use

[1] Perhaps others in the fledgling U.S. government might have learned from Jefferson. A French traveler during Washington's administration pointed out the importance of food in some diplomatic situations. He said of his country's minister to the new nation that his "maladroitness was such that when he dined at the home of M. [Alexander] Hamilton . . . he took with him two or three dishes cooked in the French fashion on the pretext of being on a diet." Needless to say, had the French minister dined with Jefferson, such precautions would have been even more gratuitous.

a rotary beater if necessary to remove lumps, then stir in 1/2 cup melted butter and 1/4 cup Madeira or sherry. Heat 5-inch griddle or frying pan, painting with butter. Put about 2 Tbs batter on hot griddle, tilting immediately to spread thin layer over entire surface. Cook about 2 minutes till brown on bottom and well done on top. As each cake is finished stack on pie plate in 200° oven and dredge with powdered sugar; keep stack covered with another pie plate turned upside down. To serve, cut stack in wedge-shaped pieces like a pie.

Dating back to the same colonial period, "Pink-Colored Pancakes" also sometimes turned up as dessert on Virginia tables. There was nothing very French about these; they got their color from beets pulled fresh from the kitchen garden and their sweetness from coatings of preserved fruits. More generally speaking, dessert pancakes remain a French influence and one that continues to gain in popularity. A modern Virginia recipe combines flour, baking powder, sugar, and salt with beaten eggs, melted butter, and enough milk to make a thinnish batter into which cooked blueberries (which grow wild east of the Appalachians, from Canada to Florida) are folded; the cakes are served with a sauce prepared by boiling the juice of the berries with sugar. In Virginia also, lacy rice pancakes, made with a batter of flour, milk, egg yolks, and cooked rice—lightened by the addition of stiffly beaten egg whites—are served with crushed berries.

There is no doubt that Jefferson's garden served his cooks well, providing such uncommon fruits as carnation cherries. He had noted that of the fruit sold in Paris only pears and apricots were better than the produce of American orchards. Virginia melons, he said, were far superior to those of France, for "there is not enough sun enough to ripen them and give them flavor." At Monticello he grew every possible kind of fruit, in several varieties—cloudberries, dewberries, persimmons, mulberries, even "indigenous oranges of Florida." And he was making plans for a botanical garden at the University of Virginia (of which he was the spiritual as well as actual architect) until two months before his death in 1826. For his own kitchen, he had planted such continental delicacies as broccoli and endive, together with vegetables about which even Patrick Henry could find no reason to complain. He grew and ate tomatoes when the relatively few Americans who had heard of them still considered the red fruit to be poison apples. Jefferson loved tomatoes—especially one variety called Spanish, which were fine and large, very much the type that twentieth-century shoppers call beefsteak tomatoes. Jefferson's garden got his closest attention, and for years he joined his neighbors in vying for the earliest harvest of peas, the winner playing host to the losers and serving the victorious crop as a highlight of a celebratory meal.

Just how keen on "native victuals" Jefferson really was can be seen in these entries from his 1774 *Garden Book*, ending on August 3 in a crescendo of pride for home-grown things:

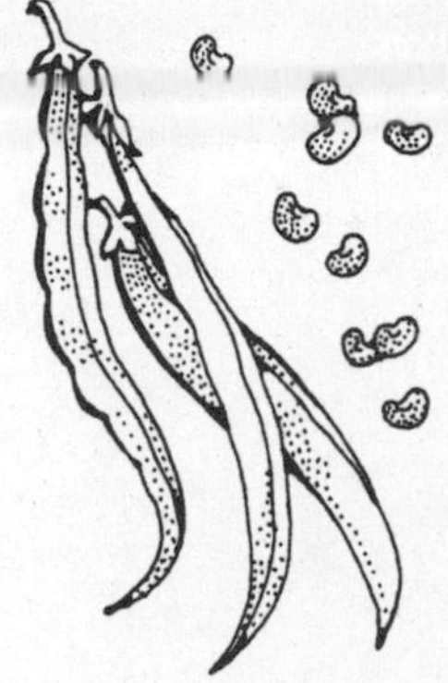

May 16.	First dish of peas from earliest patch.
May 26.	A second patch of peas comes to the table.
June 4.	Windsor beans come to table.
June 5	A third and fourth patch of peas come to table.
June 13.	A fifth patch of peas come in.
July 13.	Last dish of peas.
July 18.	Last lettuce from Gehee's.
July 23.	Cucumbers from our garden.
July 31.	Watermelons from our patch.
Aug. 3.	Indian corn comes to table.
	Black-eyed peas come to table.

Indian corn so ready on August 3, of course, would be corn on the cob, picked and husked and cooked in the swiftest progress from field to hungry mouths. The black-eyed peas Jefferson noted that day really belong in the bean family (botanically *Vigna sinensis*); they would have been picked and shelled early in the morning, when still a bit dewy, kept in spring water until an hour before dinnertime, then cooked in the French manner, with bacon or white meat (salt pork) just long enough to preserve their garden tenderness. Monticello cooks may also have picked black-eyed peas before they were ripe, snapping them from the vines when only two or three inches long and following a Paris recipe for cooking the pods as one would prepare so-called French beans.

During the winter, dried black-eyed peas—they've also been known as field peas, cowpeas, whippoorwills, Jerusalem peas, Tonkin peas, and marble peas—from earliest times have served the South in the same fashion as beans often staved off hunger for most of the rest of the country. Like all other beans, these marbled black and white legumes are enhanced by the flavor and fat of one or more kinds of meat. They would not have been found per se by Jefferson during his stay in France. But while U.S. minister he had toured much of France and had seen the bean fields of Languedoc; there is at least a chance that he tasted a leguminous *cassoulet* at either Castelnaudary, Carcassonne, or Toulouse, for he stopped at each of these hometowns of the classic French baked-bean dish. He investigated the provincial food with enthusiasm, and he wrote his friend Lafayette that the traveler who would learn about French food "must ferret people out of their hovels, as I have done, look into their kettles, eat their bread." Though he told Lafayette he had considered "the throwing of a morsel of meat" into some of the pots he saw, he didn't, so far as we know, include a recipe for *cassoulet* among all his notes on food; nevertheless there remains in some parts of Jefferson's South a casserole recipe that seems to demonstrate how a little of that kind of French influence is still recognizable in a forthright American dish of black-eyed peas.

This version of baked beans requires some cooked country ham and some leftover duck, wild or domestic. After soaking overnight, the black-eyed peas are simmered an hour or so, then accented with chopped and sautéed onion, green pepper, celery, some cooked tomatoes. The meats, including some pork sausages, are mixed with the vegetables, and the casserole bubbles in the oven under a layer of buttered baking-powder biscuit crumbs. Delicious as this can be, such elaborations are not considered necessary among many Southerners.[2] Throughout the region there are many recipes for serving salad dominated by black-eyed peas. A dish to serve as a first course, called Texas caviar, requires two cups of the drained cooked legumes, combined with thin slices of green pepper and green onions, marinated overnight in oil and vinegar accented by dried red pepper and garlic. Sometimes, when black-eyed peas are served as a vegetable with sliced meat, no more than a dash of cream and some black pepper are added. When fresh black-eyed peas accompany roast meat, they are sometimes embellished with sour cream, cucumber, dill, caraway seeds, oregano; this last may be the only one of the herbs listed that did not grow in Mr. Jefferson's garden.

In his years as president he took time when he could to oversee all phases of supply and preparation of White House food. "He would get out the wagon early in the morning," his overseer Edmund Bacon later wrote, "and [his steward] Lamar would go with him to Georgetown to market." Bacon emphasized that "it often took fifty dollars to pay the marketing they would use that day." At Monticello, according to Bacon, guests came "in gangs," with or without invitations, "and they almost ate him out of house and home. . . . I have killed a fine beef and it would be all eaten in a day or two. There was no tavern in all that country that had so much company." Jefferson himself, said Bacon, "was never a great eater, but what he did eat he wanted to be very choice. . . . He was especially fond of Guinea fowls, and for meat he preferred good beef, mutton, and lamb." With a sense of the history he played a part in, Bacon added that "Merriweather Lewis' mother made very nice hams. And every year I used to get a few from her for [the president's] special use."

Edmund Bacon is one of many who has left impressions of both Jefferson as host and of the French influences he brought to his table, which the overseer described as "chock-full [of] Congressmen, foreigners, and all sorts of people." He said they would sit down to a four P.M. dinner and talk on into the night. One of them, Congressman Manasseh Cutler of puritan Massachusetts, preserved a Jefferson menu for February 6, 1802, which had offered White House guests "rice soup, round of beef, turkey, mutton, ham, loin of veal, cutlets of mutton, fried eggs, fried beef, and a pie called macaroni." Desserts, said Cutler, included "ice cream very good, crust wholly dried, crumbled into thin flakes; a dish somewhat like a pudding—inside white as milk or curd, very porous and light, covered with cream

[2] A legendary Southern bean dish is known as Hoppin' John, most closely associated with the Carolinas. Variations of Hoppin' John are served also in Georgia and Florida—in fact in most states of the Old South. The dish is traditionally a high point of a New Year's Day meal, when a shiny dime is often buried among the beans before serving. He who gets the coin in his portion is assured good luck throughout the year.

sauce—very fine. Many other jimcracks, a great variety of fruit, plenty of wine (and good)." A list Jefferson had made of desserts fashionable at the French court when he lived in Paris included pastries, custards, cakes, sweet fritters, and a variety of fruit compotes. He had brought home a delicate recipe for blancmange made with almond paste and gelatin, and some of the French sauces he instructed his Virginia kitchen to duplicate were those known as *hachée, tournée, piquante,* and *Robert.*

Among the numerous recipes Jefferson collected in Europe was one for homemade noodles to be served "like macaroni," and it is unlikely that he was aware of Cutler's lack of enthusiasm for the so-called macaroni pie. In a somewhat caustic description of it, the Massachusetts congressman said it "appeared to be a rich crust filled with strillions of onions, or shallots, which I took them to be, tasted very strong, and not agreeable. Mr. Lewis [Jefferson's secretary, later to be sent with William Clark to explore the Louisiana Purchase] told me there were none in it; it was made of flour and butter, with a particularly strong liquor mixed with it."

The fact is that Jefferson's recipe for pasta dough calls for two eggs beaten with a wine glass of milk, a teaspoon of salt, and enough hard flour to make a smooth, firm dough, not unlike methods used today. His interest was keen enough for his papers to include a drawing and description of a machine for shaping this kind of dough into the tube shapes that distinguish macaroni from other forms of pasta. And as a result of a visit to a cheese dairy he had some Parmesan shipped to Virginia and made extensive notes of the process of manufacturing the cheese so complementary to pasta. Long before the great wave of Italian immigration to the United States, Jefferson introduced pasta to his countrymen, making macaroni and cheese a staple in the American diet.

At the risk of the death penalty, Jefferson also had brought home some rice in his own pockets, in addition to a sack of rough rice he had paid an Italian muleteer to smuggle out of Piedmont. Later he got some "dry rice" from Africa that could be grown without having to deal with the unhealthily swamped fields characteristic of the Carolinas. In his lifetime rice became an important grain in many American kitchens, and he would indeed be pleased today, as Jane Grigson has written in *Eating with the Famous,* "to see packets of Carolina rice on sale in every French supermarket."

Rice soup, as served at the White House dinner attended by Manasseh Cutler in 1802, went out of fashion some time in the nineteenth century, but for many years it had been one of the culinary reflections of a new influence in Southern agriculture. In the Carolina Low Country great fortunes had been made on rice plantations during the Jefferson era. Rice was a cash crop for Louisiana farmers. The pearly soup—worth noting by a Yankee visitor—was prepared by boiling rice until very tender, then mashing it and rubbing it through a sieve; egg yolks beaten with cream might be added with the rice purée to hot chicken stock before serving in a tureen, along with croutons. Soft boiled rice was the basis of a version of blancmange for which the mushy grain was strained, sweetened with sugar, and seasoned with spices, brandy, or wine. Then the rice mixture was combined with thin custard and served with quince marmalade.

Some historians perceive the ice cream dessert that was served in a crust to Manasseh Cutler and the other dinner guests to have been a forerunner of baked Alaska, and it has been recorded that Jefferson had an eighteen-step method for making frozen dessert in the "cream machine for ice" he purchased in the spring of 1784, before he went to France. A recipe from the Jefferson kitchen at Monticello tells the cook to beat six egg yolks until thick and lemon-colored, then to add a cup of sugar gradually, along with a pinch of salt. "Bring 1 quart heavy cream to a boil and pour it over the egg mixture. Put it into the top of a double boiler and cook it until it thickens. Remove and strain through a fine sieve. When it is cold, add teaspoon of vanilla. Freeze as usual."

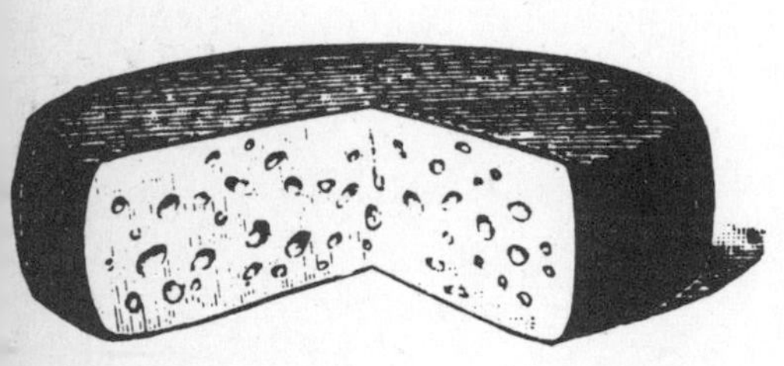

Not all American voters may have realized how serious Jefferson's interest in food was, but his popularity sometimes evoked gifts for his table. Among those present at the White House on New Year's Day 1802, Congressman Cutler observed hordes of visitors digging into a 1,235-pound "Cheshire" cheese, from the Massachusetts town of that name, which had been produced from the milk of 900 cows (reputedly at one milking), and presented to the president as a "peppercorn" of the esteem of Jeffersonians in New England. Philadelphia butchers, about the same time, sent Jefferson the hind quarter of an exemplary veal in admiration for his overcoming the European prejudice that New World meat was inferior. If some thought he had highfalutin ways at the table, there was ample recognition of his belief in American food production.

Jefferson had brought several kinds of figs from Europe to Virginia, and he had tried hard to establish olive orchards to augment the "natural bounty" of the South. "Of all the gifts of heaven to man, [the olive]," he said, "is next to the most precious, if it be not the most precious." Having observed the blessings the olive shed on the poor of southern France and Piedmont, he hoped to see successful crops of olives in South Carolina and Georgia—he was also interested in growing capers. But when he was nearly seventy, he was "disheartened by the nonchalance of our southern fellow citizens," and felt that none of the five hundred olive plants he imported from Aix survived except as curiosities in formal gardens. Still, he continued to hope that a suitable climate for growing olives would be found in America.

Margaret Bayard Smith, who played an active part in the first forty years of the capital's social life, recalled long after Jefferson's death that the president's dinners were beyond comparison with any others given in the White House. She said succinctly that "republican simplicity was united to Epicurean delicacy" in a style of hospitality not emulated often enough in the new nation. Seeing things differently, John Adams was nonetheless still impressed when he wrote: "I held levees once a week that all my time might not be wasted by idle visits. Jefferson's whole eight years was a levee.

I dined a large company once or twice a week. Jefferson dined a dozen every day." (Some clue to dinner à la Adams may be found in these lines by John Quincy Adams, second member of that family to be a White House host: "At home I find the table spread, / And dinner's fragrant steams invite. / But first the two fold stairs I tread, / My atmospheric tale to write. / Then seated round the social board, / We feast, 'til absent friends are toasted, / Though sometimes *my* delays afford / The beef or mutton *over-roasted*.")

The open-handed hospitality that distinguished Jeffersonian dinners invested all the meals at which he presided. "The French style" was duly noted by the New England educator, George Ticknor, who was a Monticello visitor as a young man; and Ticknor was impressed as well with the breakfasts that might on the same day include braised partridges, eggs, bacon, cold meats, fried apples, various hot breads, along with the ever-present batter cakes, and a tansy pudding that may have softened the bitter taste of that herb with sweeteners, brandy, eggs, milk, citron, and spices. Except for European gypsies, who still use tansy for culinary purposes, few cooks pay attention to the feathery-leafed plant with clustered yellow flowers that grows on roadsides. But when America was young, tansy gave an interesting accent to a dessert, sometimes boiled and sometimes baked, which required a pound of powdered almonds to be stewed with butter and bread crumbs and seasoned with rosewater, lemon rind, nutmeg, brandy, and two tablespoons of tansy juice; three cups of milk and eight beaten eggs turned the final effect toward custard. In her chronicle of capital life Margaret Bayard Smith noted breakfasts of similarly rich dishes, describing one as a "most excellent Virginian breakfast" when she visited James and Dolley Madison in the White House. And *pannequaiques*, a festive recipe Jefferson had picked up from his chef in Paris, also became a deluxe French addition to Monticello breakfasts.

Triumphs for La Haute Cuisine

Jefferson's luxurious menus were not unique by any means. Increasingly French influences were acknowledged. Even the Williamsburg edition of Eliza Smith's 1742 cookbook had a good share of recipes with French titles, albeit of bastardized spelling, as when *poupeton* came out as "pulpatoon." Much the same is true of America's oldest manuscript cookbooks, some belonging to early eighteenth-century households. One of these, kept by Frances Parke Custis, the mother of Martha Washington's first husband, includes French bread, and in it the terms *à la mode, à la braise, à la daube* are common. No matter that Eliza Smith had written in an introduction to one of the London editions of her manual: "To our disgrace, we have admired the French tongue and French messes. . . . [French chefs are] upstarts who do such preposterous recipes as stuffing a roast leg of mutton with pickled herring." No matter that the famous Mrs. Hannah Glasse warned, "If gentlemen will have French cooks, they must pay for French tricks." In her *The Art of Cookery, Made Plain and Easy*, one of the most popular cookbooks in colonial Virginia, Mrs. Glasse fairly exploded at "the blind folly of this age, that would rather be imposed upon by a French booby, than give encouragement to a good English cook!"

French cooking threatened that of the English because it was better, of course, and also because of the enforced exodus of many of the best exponents of the Parisian cuisine. The French Revolution caused such chefs as Louis Eustache Ude to seek refuge (Ude had been Louis XVI's cook) in Great Britain, where they began to tantalize the upper classes with the joys of *haute cuisine*. An English translation of LeSieur Menon's *La Cuisinière Bourgeoise* had been published in London as early as 1763 (for Christmas in 1791 Jefferson gave a copy to his daughter Martha), and Ude's *The French Cook* came out in English in 1813, when the author, working as *chef de cuisine* for the earl of Sefton, was introducing British high society to the subtleties of Paris dining. "French tricks" seemed bound to gain acceptance in spite of Mrs. Glasse.

Affluent Americans, Martin Van Buren among them, were influenced by the French style when they visited London. As United States minister to Great Britain, Van Buren dined with Talleyrand (who was vastly admired for his skill in combining dinner parties with diplomacy), and the American, perhaps hoping to emulate the man who had served Napoleon and his successors, hired a French chef to serve him on his return to Washington. Later, in the White House, the Van Buren hospitality was far more rigidly French than it had been in Jefferson's day. By this time the capital was full of cooks from Paris, according to Jessie Benton Fremont (whose father was a senator and who married a frontier hero who later ran for president). "The foreign ministers all brought them," Mrs. Fremont wrote; "when they returned [to their home countries]—if not sooner—the cooks deserted and set up in business for themselves [in Washington]. These not only went out to prepare fine diners, but took as pupils young slaves sent by families to be instructed. In that way a working knowledge of good cookery of the best French school became diffused among numbers of the colored people—"

One of the results was that reprints of cookery manuals including Ude's were widely used on this side of the Atlantic. Many Americans, who had become Francophiles as a result of the national hero-worship of men like the Marquis de Lafayette, were—much more than their English cousins—quick to show interest in recipes from French kitchens. As a consequence these "tricks" of chefs were pirated without shame or apology. One such collection of loot, called *Domestic French Cookery*, was compiled in 1832 by Eliza Leslie of Philadelphia, five years after she had published *Seventy-Five Receipts* which she described as "in every sense of the word, American."

Miss Leslie's American book did offer such New World ideas as Indian pound cake, made with equal amounts of cornmeal, sugar, butter, and eggs, and a boiled Boston pudding, for which she suggested a filling of cranberries. She also gave instructions for "New York Cup Cakes" and she balanced her recipe for "Common Gingerbread" with one entitled "LaFayette Gingerbread," which was richer for the use of lemon juice and a sweetening of brown sugar in addition to molasses. But French recipes dominated as Miss Leslie compiled other cookbooks in a career that kept her work in print for more than forty years. Even for her, French recipes in themselves were not enough. For Americans living in good-sized towns Miss Leslie defied Mrs. Glasse altogether. Her advice in 1837 stipulated that the "safest way to avoid a failure in an omelette soufflé . . . is to hire a French cook to come to your kitchen with his own utensils and ingredients and make and bake it himself."

In that same period the first real restaurants appeared in major American cities, and along with hotels, country inns, and local taverns they too began to persuade American housewives that keeping up with one's neighbors meant staying abreast of the French. Reactions, however, were sometimes mixed. In 1838 the distinguished Philip Hone, prominent Whig and long-time mayor of New York, protested the new style of serving one course at a time, instead of placing all dishes on the table at once. "One does not know how to choose," he wrote in his diary, "because you are ignorant of what is coming next, or whether anything is coming. Your conversation is interrupted every minute by greasy dishes thrust between your head and that of your next neighbor, and it is more expensive than the old mode of showing a handsome dinner to your guests and leaving them free to choose. It will not do. The French influence must be resisted. Give us the nice French dishes, *fricandeau de veau, perdix au chous*, and *cotelettes à la province*, but let us see what we are to have." The Astor House, the preeminent New York hotel when Miss Leslie's second book appeared, had begun to pursue this French trend as early as 1838 in somewhat haphazard fashion by presenting a menu with "Boiled Cod Fish" and "Oysters and Roast Turkey" listed alongside Paris dishes like *Ballon de Mouton au Tomato* and *Roulleau de Veau de la Jardinière*.[3]

"Delmonico" Enters the Language

The previous fall had seen the opening of a restaurant that was to do perhaps more than any other to set high standards for Americans interested in good food. The soon-to-be-famous Delmonico's established a cuisine that was exclusively continental; the French-speaking family from Switzerland wrote their menu in French, then paid a hundred dollars for a translation and henceforward had their bills of fare printed with matching columns of English and French. Their two-language menu was widely imitated, and for the rest of the nineteenth century the Delmonico restaurants set many styles that increased the French influence on American food. Twentieth-

[3] It may be that this custom is not unknown today. At any rate, as late as 1855 at one of the great hostelries of the period, the United States Hotel at Saratoga, New York's renowned resort, ineptly scattered its menu with compromise language: "Filet of veal à la Gardiniere," "Tenderloin of Mutton à la Maire d'Hote," "Currie of Veal en Bordured de Riz."

century cookbooks continue to give instructions for restaurant dishes that have become standards: Delmonico potatoes are creamed and baked with cheese; finnan haddie got its Delmonico touch in a similar treatment, with cream, hard-boiled eggs, and cheese; a delicate, custardy pudding also bears the name. And good old-fashioned butchers, wherever they may be, can still offer a Delmonico steak, which dictionaries define as a piece cut from the short loin.

Although "Delmonico" still carries with it a connotation of excellence, and although chefs who received training at those restaurants moved on to establish *la grande cuisine* in such far-flung hostelries as San Francisco's elegant old Palace Hotel and the Broadmoor Casino in the Rockies, the name is as apt as not to remain attached to unsophisticated dishes that have no clear lines of heritage. I know of one, to be found in a "Collection of Choice Recipes from a Golden Era of St. Louis Living," and it takes the cookbook browser back a hundred years or so to "cook's night off" and the chafing dish that became so necessary a part of American dining room paraphernalia.

Veal hash Delmonico may not have earned its credentials from any chef, but the preponderance of precooked ingredients make it an easy and savory meal to conjure up in a chafing dish, with little or no kitchen experience—and with egg yolks added at the end, there is a distinctive French touch hinting at the delicacy of *blanquette de veau.* Chopped onion is cooked gently in oil, diced veal and potatoes are scattered in and accented with chopped pimiento, chopped olives, and chopped eggs. Equal amounts of stock and good thick cream are then poured into the chafing dish, and as these cook down a bit, a little of the resulting sauce is stirred into lightly beaten egg yolks so there will be no curdling over the heat. When this mixture has blended well, it is turned into the hash and served hot, still quite liquid in consistency, over toast or English muffins.

Sometimes there seems no end to dishes of this sort, so clearly American in their amalgamation of various ingredients but with touches that betray a debt to Parisian cooks. While the Delmonico reputation was just beginning to affect some American householders, others more affluent were already going more directly to French sources by taking their cooks along when they traveled abroad. In the South generally, cooks who had been born as well as trained in France were common enough in the mid-nineteenth century to cause one lady of a great Charleston family to point out that cookbooks published especially for the use of those cooks—and in their own language—were "to be found in every book store." There was no ignoring the various degrees of interest in the cooking of Paris. In and around Charleston many plantation cooks in late antebellum days were guided by a volume entitled *The Carolina Housewife*, described modestly by its author as "a selection from the family receipt books of friends and acquaintances who have kindly placed their manuscripts at the disposal of the editor"; in fact, it also included general hints from the French along with several receipts culled from *Maison-Rustique*, a manual written by the accomplished Mme. Stephanie-Felicité de Genlis, an intimate of the French royal household. The appearance in Charleston of the Genlis recipe for lyonnaise potatoes seems to have been the first notice of that dish in these United States, setting off a chain reaction that has come close to making American restaurant menus seem incomplete unless they include potatoes fried with onions in the manner of France's second largest city.

Sarah Rutledge, the compiler of *The Carolina Housewife*, who belonged to one of the South's first families, hoped that her selected foreign recipes would, as she said, add value to her book. In addition to Mme. de Genlis's instructions for souffléed omelets and various fricandeaus, there was a dessert called "Nudel Pudding" and a pasta recipe *à la sauce blanche*, an apparent forerunner of the American standby, macaroni and cheese. On the other hand, Horace Mann's wife, one of the cultivated Peabody sisters of Boston, had a warning for her readers when she appended a section of French recipes to her no-nonsense book called *Christianity in the Kitchen*. It was all very well, she said, that citizens of France believe that health and happiness are connected to good cooking and that the French "have applied themselves to the task of improving the art"; nevertheless she thought they used too much butter, oil, and lard, and she exhorted Americans to eschew the Gallic penchant for "injurious ingredients."

As one who believed herself to be descended from Boadicea (early Britain's warrior queen who defied the Roman occupiers), Mary Peabody Mann may have had reason for her aversion to any sort of Latin touch in Anglo-Saxon kitchens. Boadicea has gone down in history as having excoriated the southern invaders who wanted to impose fancy ways on straightforward Britons. Eyes flashing and untamed red hair flowing down her back, she told her troops that from across the Channel had come men "who bathe in warm water, eat artificial dainties, drink unmixed wine." Centuries later, in the Victorian times in which Mrs. Mann wrote, Boadicea had become for some Anglophiles a symbol of romantic revolt. In her own time the warrior queen had brought her cheering followers to their feet by praising them for eating the poorest of vegetables instead of bread, rejecting wine in favor of water, and using the juices of plants instead of fats or oils.

Paeans for the Food of Early New Orleans

Both Boadicea and Mrs. Mann fought losing battles. In America the invasion, albeit more specifically gastronomical, was not limited to a single front. As the immigration of chefs continued through Eastern Seaboard ports, the French influence emanating from the Gulf of Mexico became more and more recognizable in the repertoires of good cooks in other parts of the country. New Orleans, founded as a French town and enriched by an interim of Spanish occupation, had developed its own cuisine early in American history. Some travelers who had tried Louisiana eating, and who damned the food of America generally, resorted to paeans when trying to do justice to the Crescent City of the South (so called because it is built on a curve of the Mississippi). And well-traveled William Makepeace Thackeray, whose appreciation of French gastronomy moved him to write the "Ballad of Bouillabaisse," was similarly affected by epicurean New Orleans. He described the city after his visit in the 1850s as the place where "of all the cities in the world, you can eat the most and suffer the least, where claret is as good as at Bordeaux, and where a 'ragout' and a 'bouillabaisse' can be had, the like of which was never eaten in Marseilles or Paris."

It is not possible to know what characteristics made the Creole bouillabaisse so memorable to Thackeray when in 1856 he sat at a table at Boudro's on Lake Pontchartrain. Even in Marseilles, where the term *bouillabaisse* is most at home, there is no inviolate formula; French authorities are very clear on this point. Every locality along the Côte d'Azur has some claim to a genuine bouillabaisse, and so, using the same logic, did every Provençal cook who came to make his home in Louisiana. In New Orleans French chefs began to improvise with ingredients abundantly available in hauls that fishermen brought in from waters of the Gulf of Mexico. The most important thing about any bouillabaisse is that the fish must be spanking fresh from the sea, and of diverse kinds. It is true that some Louisiana cookbooks maintain that redfish and red snapper alone give the local fish stew its authenticity. But the version that so impressed Thackeray must have been more closely related to the Marseilles recipes that call for at least one variety of shellfish as well.

An old Delta formula requires one each of redfish, red snapper, blackfish, crabs, shrimp, and crawfish. You remove the heads of the fish, cover them with water, and boil fifteen minutes a pound to make a quart of stock, seasoning it with thyme, bay leaves, chervil, and onions. Slice the fish and rub with salt, pepper, dill, thyme, and olive oil. Add two cups of white wine to the fish stock, and in it cook a dozen crabs, about four pounds of shrimp, and six pounds of crawfish. Fry the fish slices in olive oil, turning once, remove them, and to the oil add a garlic clove, a small bunch of minced green onions, six fresh tomatoes that have been cut up, and the stock. Simmer five minutes. Rub fish slices with saffron mixed with stock, then put them and the shellfish on a hot platter and serve the soup with chunks of French bread. The result is a dish that has given several New Orleans restaurants long-lasting reputations for excellence.

Lavish praise was often earned by the food served in private homes as well, for Louisianans dining in public demanded that restaurant cooks be at least as talented as those employed by private citizens.[4] Such rivalry could not go unnoticed. Guests in New Orleans compared the food with that of Delmonico's and the equally outstanding dining room of the Hotel Brunswick in New York. And dining out in the Crescent City also brought to

[4] "The Creole cookery in private houses is," British journalist George Augustus Sala wrote, "exquisite. The question whether Life be worth Living for can be immediately answered in the affirmative after you have partaken of white mulligatawny pepperpot and turkey with plantain sauce; and the New Orleans 'drip' coffee is the most aromatic and most excellent preparation of that beverage that I know."

mind some favorable comparisons with Paris's Café Anglais, La Maison Dorée, Durand's, and Bignon's, some of the best of nineteenth-century Continental hostelries.

Just east of New Orleans, along the Gulf of Mexico, nineteenth-century travelers could also find French food in Biloxi, Mississippi, and Mobile, Alabama, both of which predated the Crescent City as settlements with French and Spanish beginnings. In the twentieth century both towns (even though Mardi Gras is a carefree and Gallic event in Mobile) have become more typically Southern, with an emphasis on provender netted in the Gulf.

In Biloxi, founded in 1699, a crab soup may be made by boiling eight to ten hard-shell crabs until they are bright red. When the meat has been picked out, the shells are simmered in fresh water to make a broth. A cup of chopped onion and four cloves of garlic are sautéed, then a spoonful of flour is browned in the same pan and a cup of chopped tomatoes added to the onion mixture, along with a little thyme and bayleaf. When this has cooked about five minutes, you pour in the reserved broth and the crab meat, turn the heat low and simmer the soup for about an hour. Season with salt, pepper, and a dash of cayenne to taste, and stir in two beaten egg yolks mixed with some of the hot soup, just before serving.

Mobile is celebrated for the crab salad served in local seafood restaurants and, along with other Gulf towns, for pompano. The beautiful silvery fish with the deeply forked tail is a famous dish when served *en papillote*, and it is equally good broiled with butter and lime juice or poached and garnished with a sauce of minced mushrooms, shallots, shrimps, and herbs.

Cuisine Among the Lagoons

In the bayou country, west and south of New Orleans, a French patois is spoken, a language that is closer to the speech of Quebec than to that of Paris. And for similar reasons the cooking in this low-country region may be closer to the earliest years of colonial America than any other. These waterlogged parishes of Louisiana are, as the inhabitants say, Cajun country, to which French Canadians who refused to swear allegiance to the British crown were exiled after 1755. Leaving Acadia (the original name for Nova Scotia), French refugees who were fishermen and wetlands farmers moved south and for more than two centuries successfully preserved Gallic folkways along Gulf Coast lagoons and sluggish streams. At first isolated from the more sophisticated French of New Orleans, the transplanted Acadians became "Cajuns" in the same way that frontier language corrupted *Indians* into "injuns."

Cajun cooking has little to do with the cuisine of either New Orleans or Paris. The dishes are essentially country food bearing the influence of Louisiana Indians and slavery, as well as that of ancient France. Gumbo is as famous as any of them—its name is believed to derive from the African word *kingumbo*, meaning "okra,"the seeds of which captured Africans brought to the New World. Without okra, a Cajun gumbo, or stew, may be made with filé powder, which Choctaw women ground from dried sassafras, a seasoning and a thickener for their own mixtures of vegetables and meat or fish. Whatever additions, no authentic gumbo is to be made without preparing the flour-and-fat base known as roux, which it seems is seldom absent from either Cajun or other forms of Louisiana cooking.

Along with herbs, a good rich stock, and iron vessels to conduct gentle heat, the roux is a Louisiana culinary requisite. A gumbo begins with flour that is so carefully stirred into melted butter or shortening that it may take twenty minutes for the mixture to turn a deep brown; it must not burn. When it is as dark and as thick as chocolate syrup, chopped onions, garlic, minced parsley, and sometimes green pepper are added and cooked a little before stirring in fish, crustaceans, or a choice of meats, including sausage or game—then the required liquid. There are plain shrimp gumbos and plain crab gumbos. There is a green gumbo called *gumbo zhèbes* (*gumbo des herbes*), which combines, during Lent or in the absence of meat or fish, as many as seven vegetables, including mustard, beet, or turnip tops; spinach; collards; lettuce; and cabbage. (In 1803 a highlight of the social season in New Orleans was a banquet at which twenty-four different gumbos were served.) Appetizingly tacky with the gelatinous texture of okra or the aromatic thickening of filé powder, and with a sharp piquancy from hot pepper that marks many dishes as Louisianan, gumbo is served with rice, the principal starch of the regional diet.

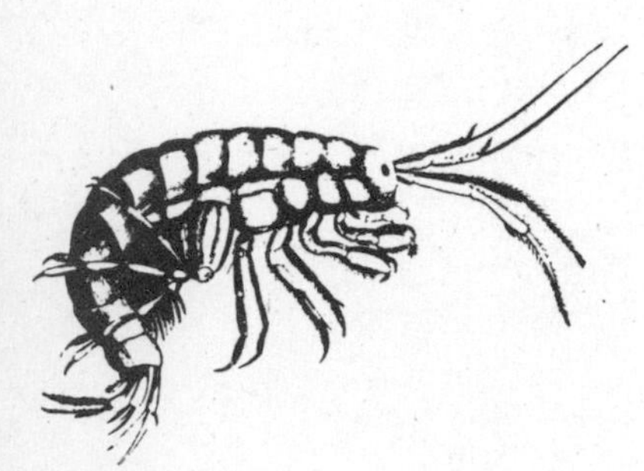

Rice grown by Cajuns is the foundation of jambalaya, a mélange of seafood and meat that surely evolved when Spaniards briefly occupied the Louisiana Territory—it is a kind of rich hybrid of gumbo and paella in which a roux, some kind of fowl, ham, sausage, crawfish, tomatoes, and some sautéed vegetables are simultaneously cooked in stock with raw rice. The rice puffs out as it absorbs the juices and contrasting flavors, and jambalaya, simmered slowly out of doors in iron pots, is the cause of festivals of eating at which Cajun cooks draw great crowds annually along the Mississippi.

Crawfish in Cajun country are simply the same crayfish to be found in various parts of the United States, but they have a way of seeming to dominate the local cooking. Crawfish étouffé is a classic stew that starts with the usual roux, onions, celery, green pepper, and garlic cooked in yellow crawfish fat, along with tomatoes and crawfish tails tossed in at the end. Whole green peppers are stuffed with minced crawfish meat, and crawfish pie is covered with golden pastry and served hot as a main dish. The miniature lobsterlike fish are eaten from November to early summer, and the demand is such that crawfish "farming" helps augment the natural supply.

If Cajun food remains close to that of France's littoral, the chefs of New Orleans and of Louisiana's River Road plantations have been responsible for the distinctive cuisine most often described as Creole. That word has French, Spanish, Portuguese, even Latin roots, and is applied to persons of

European descent who are born in the New World. In culinary precincts it is used frequently to identify spicy concoctions often dominated by tomatoes, green peppers, onions, and garlic. Creole is also used to describe the cooking of some of the Caribbean islands, and there are in fact some likenesses between the kitchen styles of both regions. But Louisianans generally have no doubt that it is *sui generis*, a label warranted only by the best of the state's indigenous cuisine.

The Louisiana Dowry

Sometimes cooks in other regions find that Louisiana's best seems to extend beyond reasonable limitations; the Creole repertoire is a formidable list, yet one that magnetizes those who like to cook. Distinguished not only by seafood and other fish dishes, Louisiana's cookery owes much to the fact that the state is one of the country's biggest producers of rice. It also grows a lot of corn, and since the end of the eighteenth century, before Thomas Jefferson made the Louisiana Purchase, sugar cane has been a money crop, one that was transplanted from the Creole economy of the West Indies. Other transplants include the ice-green squash that grows rampantly in New Orleans backyards as well as in cultivated fields and is called chayote after the Mayan word *chayotl.* Creoles train the vines to grow on fences, arbors, and trellises and call it mirliton, and it is also known as the vegetable pear. Stuffed with meat or fish, or cooked in other ways common to squash, it has been cultivated as a South Florida crop as well and welcomed by cooks in the North.

But Louisiana cookery also has developed character of its own because settlers made use of such native foods as the pecan, a variety of hickory nut that thrives in riverlands of Southern states. Louisianans may or may not have been the first to bake oozy, sticky pecan pies, but certainly pecan pralines are considered a New Orleans invention, so successfully commercialized that a visitor is expected to buy them as a souvenir. French cooks coated the nuts they found growing wild with sugar as a variation on an ancient old-country confection. Pecan meats are annually consumed by the hundreds of tons—in candy bars, ice cream sundaes, layer cakes, waffles, brownies, coffee cakes, cinnamon buns, and candied sweet potatoes. Louisiana cooks are sometimes considered less than loyal to their native state if they are not expert at such endeavors. There is a tradition, one of their historians wrote in the mid-twentieth century, that may help to explain: "When a girl marries she receives, as part of her dowry, the ancestral skillet. She is considered a social failure unless she develops a *haut ton* and applies it to her cookery. And in Louisiana today gastronomes may travel to the North, to the South, or to the City [of New Orleans] and find *un vrai regal* on the native tables."

This could mean a simple fish course of sea trout cooked with a sauce of green peppers, shallots, wine, and toast crumbs; or a dinner menu including shrimp in highly spiced oil and vinegar, turtle soup, Gulf trout filleted and served with sautéed shoft-shell crabs and a sprinkling of buttered almond slivers, along with new potatoes, broccoli from farms just up the river, a cabbage palm salad, and Louisiana pecan-molasses ice cream. It also could mean a preparation of shrimp that is one of the simplest yet most interesting ever devised. Sautéed in oil to which has been added several sticks of cinnamon, three or four cloves, and a generous grating of nutmeg, the shrimp are left to steep in the spices a half hour or so; then warm light rum is flamed and poured over them. Or a true Creole regalement might include thin pancakes stuffed with oysters in a hot Hollandaise-like sauce that Louisiana cooks used to make from homegrown peppers and whose flavor, they maintain, is unsurpassed.

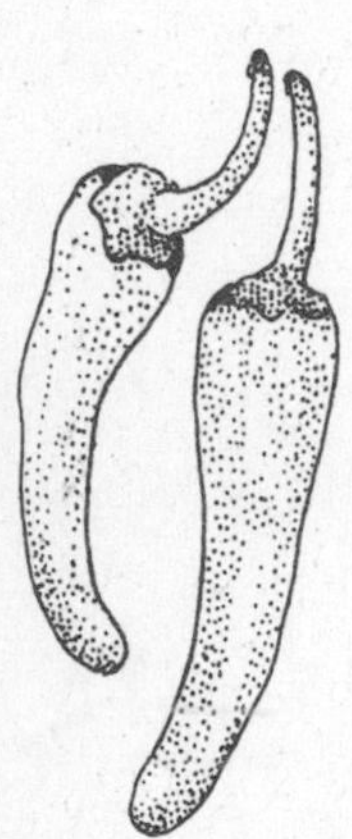

Just as few cooks anywhere continue to produce their own catsup, there are not many who take the trouble to compete with the manufacturer of commercial Tabasco sauce, even though the basics seem simple enough. A traditional method calls for the scalding of three dozen Tabasco peppers, finely chopped, along with minced garlic, then to press the pulp through a sieve and thin it to the consistency of rich cream by adding spiced vinegar. The name *Tabasco* however, is patented and derives from the impulse of a soldier in the Mexican War to bring home from the state of Tabasco some red-pepper seeds he thought would produce handsome blossoms to line a flower garden. On Avery Island, in the bayou country, where the seeds were planted, a plantation cook developed a hot sauce as a result, and when the Civil War ended and the Avery family faced the need for a new source of income, the sauce was bottled as a condiment with unique flavor. The family kept its recipe a secret. Yet the success of Tabasco sauce was such that it is used in many of the world's cuisines and, according to a story told about Lord Kitchener, was found deeper in the desert of Sudan than any other manufactured product. There are numerous New Orleans seafood recipes that cannot be duplicated without Tabasco sauce. The usual oyster cookery is not among them, however.

Not only do gifted Louisiana cooks prepare oysters in dozens of French-accented ways, the streets of the Vieux Carré of New Orleans are punctuated with oyster bars maintaining that nineteenth-century tradition that made ostreomaniacs of a majority of United States citizens. Oysters can be eaten freshly opened in these quick-service places, they can be popped steaming into one's mouth, or they may be carried home under a wondrous title, *La Médiatrice*—the famous "peacemaker" of New Orleans days when husbands sometimes stayed out long enough to want means to placate wives. "Right justly is the Oyster Loaf called the 'Peacemaker,' " a turn-of-the-century book says with a hint of Edwardian naughtiness, "for, well made, it is enough to bring smiles to the face of the most disheartened wife."

Women needn't wait for men to turn wayward to enjoy an oyster loaf. It is identical in concept to the crab sandwiches of the Eastern Shore. But it still carries with it the connotation of a man making amends for indiscretions. Buttery sautéed oysters confined in a hollowed out and toasted loaf of

French bread became famous in San Francisco's gayest days as "the squarer"; even in puritan Connecticut the idea—here called boxed oysters—may have helped to get a mild philanderer out of trouble. Doubtless no such problems lurked behind the fact that Mrs. James Monroe noted that her recipe for oyster loaves came to her from Martha Washington, or that she sometimes substituted clams or shrimp in the same formula.

Seafood in all its forms distinguishes New Orleans menus. Local oysters from Bayou Cook, Lac Barre, and Barataria Bay, once in almost unlimited supply, were as famous in the nineteenth century as Long Island's Lynnhavens, the Chincoteagues from Chesapeake Bay, or the tiny Olympias from Puget Sound. Louisiana's shellfish are now most apt to come from Houma or Morgan City, whence they are trucked by the ton across bayou country to French restaurants of New Orleans that have built worldwide reputations on their saltwater cuisines. Antoine's, where Jules Alciatore created oysters Rockefeller, may be the "Frenchest" of them all, and the secret "Rockefeller" recipe has become so much a part of American cooking lore that its original similarity to the Burgundy sauce that sometimes dresses snails may have been lost. For the record, a New York chef recorded the instructions he got at the source:

> "Take selected oysters, open them and leave them on the deep half shell. Place the shells containing the oysters on a bed of rock salt in a pie pan. The sauce for the oysters is compounded as follows:
>
> "Take the tail and tips of small green onions. Take celery, take chervil, take tarragon leaves and the crumbs of stale bread. Take Tabasco sauce and the best butter obtainable. Pound all these into a mixture in a mortar, so that all the fragrant flavorings are blended. Add a dash of absinthe.
>
> "Force the mixture through a fine-meshed sieve. Place one spoonful on each oyster as it rests in its own shell and in its own juice on the crushed rock salt, the purpose of which is to keep the oyster piping hot. Then place them in an oven with overhead heat and cook until brown. Serve immediately." Thus spoke Monsieur Alciatore to your humble servant.

The recipe cities no spinach, which is considered by most chefs to be the basic ingredient, after the oysters, nor does it mention watercress or fennel. Yet whether oysters are blanketed in combinations of spinach, shallots, herbs, and anchovy, or lettuce, spring onions, anise, lime juice, and Tabasco—to suggest only two of the secret's variations—oysters Rockefeller is one of the most-appreciated discoveries of diners-out who like exploring unfamiliar culinary paths.

One way or another the Frenchness of Louisiana cooking has branched out and made its mark. Oysters Bienville, named for one of the heroes of the city's history, is the creation of another French-born restaurateur. The Bienville sauce, as prescribed by the founder of Arnaud's restaurant, surrounds oysters with a sauce of Parisian elegance. When made in the Vieux Carré, the sauce is dominated by minced shrimp. In a Baltimore modification the shrimp are joined by clams and are puréed. There is a similar variation on a theme in another French Quarter recipe, one that calls for frogs' legs: *Grenouilles en fricassees à la Vieux Carré* embellishes a classic method by adding oysters. Up the Mississippi at St. Louis cooks went even farther afield with a dish of frogs' legs hidden behind the title of *pigeons de marais* because somebody at Tony Faust's oyster house thought a fastidious Victorian lady would be repelled at the image instilled by a more accurate description.[5] In this preparation of "marsh pigeons" the shellfish is crab—instead of the oysters that are used in the traditional New Orleans fricassee—and the meat of the frogs' legs is stripped from the bone before simmering in wine. As it is made today, the final result—and it is delicious—is a combination of boned crab and frog meat cooked with mushrooms; there is a cream sauce accented with sherry and applejack, plus a dash of cayenne pepper that marks so many colonial Louisiana specialties.

A Gallic Pervasiveness

Eighteenth-century settlers already had carried up the Mississippi and onto its tributaries much of traditional Gallic cooking. St. Louis was a thoroughly French community before Thomas Jefferson moved into the White House. So were smaller places, such as Terre Haute and Vincennes on Indiana's Wabash River. On the Ohio there is Louisville (named by an American admirer of Louis XVI), where French glimpses can be seen in recipes from downriver that are now acclaimed as Kentucky's own. One of these is called Louisville rolled oysters, little more than fist-size clusters of tiny bivalves from Mississippi Sound dipped in egg and seasoned cornmeal and deep fried; simplicity itself, this is an encrusted, seethingly hot bunch of oysters that can taste of the Vieux Carré when eaten at family gatherings in Blue Grass backyards.

Nothing about things of this sort seems remarkable enough to claim as a regional achievement. But good, simple cooks, loyal to their home turf, don't need to dazzle to establish their competence. They leave spellbinders, often enough, to those who cook for the public. In Louisville and Natchez and the plantations along the River Road, many of the best of the public cooks by 1850 were black and male and so well trained that those of them who took over the galleys of the luxury steamboats plying the Mississippi and the Ohio were masters of the intricacies of *haute cuisine*. Aboard the shining white, gold-trimmed sternwheelers and sidewheelers, these chefs created plantation meals for passengers from all over the country and many parts of the world. Among voyagers dining under chandeliers swaying to

[5] To utter the word *leg* in front of ladies was considered crude, vulgar, even insulting. The gallant Captain Marryat tells of such a blunder on his part, after which the lady involved instructed him always to use *limb* to placate tender female sensibilities. She is quoted by Marryat as saying, "Nay, I am not so particular as some people are, for I know those who always say limb of a table, or limb of a pianoforte." Sometime after this colloquy Marryat entered a room in which, he later wrote, there was a "pianoforte with four *limbs*. . . . [In order] to preserve in their utmost purity the ideas of the young ladies in her charge, [the mistress of the establishment] had dressed all these four limbs in modest little trousers, with frills at the bottom of them!"

the boat's motion they spread the enthusiasm for food of the Vieux Carré and Greek revival mansions.

Chickens, pigs, lambs were shepherded on board—because of lack of refrigeration—and fish were hooked or seined from the waters that turned to foam as the steamboats churned forward. In the galleys pompano were plucked from tanks and prepared *en papillote*, and the succulent Mississippi catfish were trimmed into *paupiettes*, rolled around a stuffing of pecans and capers, poached in white wine, and finished with a wine sauce encompassing mushrooms and oysters. Surely, the chef of a vessel such as the *Robert E. Lee* had his men regularly turn out a caldron of New Orleans court bouillon which, in some ways close to a bouillabaisse, is a soup of several chopped vegetables with fish fillets added at the end.

Far better known and considered so great an example of the burgeoning American style of cooking that Lafayette gave it as one of his reasons for returning to the nation he helped to liberate, turtle soup was termed a national dish from the bayou to the diamondback breeding grounds on Chesapeake Bay. Louisianans maintain that only a good Creole cook knows how to brew the aromatic mixture they still sometimes refer to as *soupe à la tortue*. The basic method is French. Sometimes ham is added to meld with the flavor of the green turtle, white wine or sherry is stirred in, or quenelles exuding the fragrance of laurel and nutmeg are floated on the surface. Louisiana ways with green turtle soup spread across the South, augmenting rather than nullifying the Gallic base from which this kind of good soup or stew is apt to evolve. And in Baltimore, where French-trained cooks, driven by Haiti's war of independence, arrived in small legions, the diamondback terrapin became the center of the gourmet rivalry that pitted Marylanders against Philadelphians.

The French influence was never overt in Baltimore, but Philadelphia, for many early decades the country's largest city as well as briefly the capital, was long a cosmopolitan center. It was the kind of place at which Puritans and perhaps some others looked askance. "A most sinful feast again," John Adams wrote in his diary while attending the Continental Congress, "everything that would delight the eye or allure the taste—meats, turtle and every other thing . . . Parmesan cheese, punch, wine, porter, beer, etc." That phrase "turtle and every other thing" gives one pause. Turtle soup and turtle steak appeared on most formal Philadelphia menus when, in the early nineteenth century, at least one Fairmont Park hostess emulated Mme. Récamier, priding herself not only on her "salons" of intellectuals but on her superior French dinners. (She had a dining room large enough to seat one hundred guests on gilded chairs imported from Paris.) The turtle served with dinners in Philadelphia got talked about a good deal—by intellectuals from abroad and by connoisseurs with upturned noses in Baltimore.

Finally, in 1893, some historians insist, members of Philadelphia's Rittenhouse Club and Baltimore's Maryland Club considered the matter serious enough to sit down at the same table. In Philadelphia old-time purists believed that cream sauce should be blended with the turtle broth just before pieces of the meat are dropped in; in Baltimore "Maryland Club terrapin" is a clear soup laced with butter and sherry and dominated by picked turtle meat untainted by herbs or cream. In the famous meeting of the two clubs, according to an account that comes to me from a Chesapeake Bay acquaintance, the latter, simpler version got the nod from the impartial jury.

In New York, Ward McAllister (the social arbiter whose roots were in Georgia) would have agreed essentially, substituting Madeira for sherry. But in Savannah, where this self-styled "Autocrat of the Drawing Rooms" had spent a good many youthful days, terrapin from a nearby terrapin farm on the Isle of Hope is turned into a stew incorporating steamed turtle that has been allowed to cool in its own aspic and is molded with chopped egg whites, yolks rubbed with butter and flour, cream, and a good wine accented by onion, nutmeg, red pepper, Worcestershire sauce, and lemon.

McAllister's numerous claims to notoriety include the coining of the phrase "the Four Hundred" to describe New York's most eligible members of the upper class. His cousin, Sam Ward, was both more respected and more influential, and Ward's knowledge of gastronomy was taken seriously among people beginning to care about improving the quality of American food. Sam Ward took the trouble to fully describe the proper culinary treatment of the fashionable terrapin:

How to Cook the Toothsome Terrapin as It Ought to Be

> Immerse the live terrapin in spring water, boiling hot, for five minutes, to loosen the skin. The skin is then removed with a knife, thoroughly polished to free it from any foreign substance, with a piece of chamois leather. Then replace the terrapin in boiling water. When the claws become so soft as to pinch into a pulp by a moderate pressure between the thumb and forefinger, take it out and remove the bottom shell first, as the convexity of the upper shell catches the rich and savory juices that distinguish the terrapin from the mud turtle and the slider. Cut off the head and claws, and carefully remove the gall and sandbag. A little gall does not impair the flavor of the terrapin, but the sandbag requires the skillful touch of a surgeon, the heart of a lion, the eye of an eagle, and the hand of a lady.
>
> Cut up the remainder into pieces about half an inch in length. Be careful to preserve all the juice. Put in a chafing dish, and add a dressing of fine flour, the yolks of eggs boiled so hard they are mushy, *quantum sufficit* of butter fresh from the dairy, salt to taste, red pepper, a large wine-glass of very old Madeira (to each terrapin) and a small quantity of rich cream. The dish like everything else fit to eat except Roman punch and Stilton cheese, should be served smoking hot. Some persons have been known to season with spices, but this, like the rank perfume which exhales from the handkerchiefs of underbred people, is apt to arouse suspicion.

Sam Ward's knowledge of gastronomy was said to be greater than that of any other American, and restaurant and hotel dining rooms frequently offered dishes *à la* Sam Ward. As with his way with terrapin, his recipe for grouse—his era's most popular game bird—followed classic precepts. To roast these birds, the cook was enjoined to "take two fine fat grouse . . . truss them nicely." After putting them in a roasting pan "a piece of broiled toast four inches long and two wide" is to be put inside each bird. "Drip in on on each toast, with a spoon," the instructions continue, "a small glassful of good Madeira wine or sherry . . . spread a little butter over." Simple enough; the grouse were pleasing to Ward when roasted in a hot oven and served with red-currant jelly. His favorite way with mushrooms, under glass, called for serving them over thinly sliced Virginia ham on toast, with a sherry-flavored cream sauce.

Lessons from Mrs. Habersham—and Others

Ward's manner with delicacies of this sort became relatively common. His instructions for the terrapin represents more than a classic recipe of the South. The formula was given coinage early in the twentieth century by a Savannah woman whose family background was the kind that didn't cause one to think of her in the kitchen, let alone teaching others of her social set how actually to prepare meals. The history-minded Harriet Ross Colquitt looked in on this episode of Southern gastronomical development:

> Long before it was fashionable for society women to have a career, or do anything in the least practical, Mrs. Fred Habersham, who was famous for her table, conducted a cooking school at her home in Savannah, and here all the young society matrons gathered once a week, pencil in hand, and wrote down the words of wisdom which fell from her lips, while she illustrated by cooking as she talked . . . teacher and pupils fell to and ate all the delicacies which she had wrought, so that the undertaking could not have been a very profitable one for the teacher.

Mrs. Habersham may have been the first Savannah "society woman" to share her ability to create exceptional American food, but by the last quarter of the nineteenth century there were scores of teachers available to any female American who wanted to cook. By the time Thomas W. Lawson sent each of his four daughters to a teacher ensconced in a cottage on his Cape Cod estate—and offered each of them $100,000 when she could cook a formal dinner, including the making of bread and butter—the study of the art of cooking had become to some degree fashionable.

Of the teachers who became fashionable, most were French. Probably the best known was Pierre Blot, who arrived about the time of the Civil War. Blot was a Paris-trained chef and, as he advertised himself, a "Professor of Gastronomy" who believed American women were interested in the finesse of the French approach to food; after his "tour of Lectures" in the East, the New York Cooking Academy that he established was successful enough to persuade many that his point was well taken. His book *What to Eat . . . And How to Cook It*, published in 1863, seems to reflect his classroom straightforwardness, and his school continued, under the aegis of

Juliet Corson, to give Americans opportunity to learn the fundamentals of classic cookery for years after the professor returned to France.[6]

A generation after Pierre Blot, a Philadelphia mother of three named Sarah Tyson Rorer opened a cooking school in her hometown—following a trip through Europe that made her exuberant about French food and disdainful of German cooking. (As a result of an evening meal in Germany that included a rye bread sandwich, cheese, and beer, she asked her students, "Why would not one think death a joy after a month of such fare?") In her school she was a champion of the chafing dish, and she preached that fresh green salads should be eaten every day of the year. She taught that bad cooking was responsible for "crowded conditions in our insane asylums, almshouses, prisons, and hospitals." Her students were reported to come "almost exclusively from families of wealth, refinement and fashion."

Mrs. Rorer's cooking classes and demonstrations made her nationally famous at the time the Boston Cooking-School was making its own reputation. It was a decade after the publication of Mrs. Rorer's cookbook, however, that Fannie Farmer, whose name was to become synonymous with the Boston school, published another American cookbook. Miss Farmer's book emphasized the value of precision in recording recipes, and the Boston Cooking-School became noted for teaching uniformity and accuracy to practical cooks, rather than enrolling ladies of leisure. Her students learned by doing. "They do the work themselves, prepare lunch, take turns serving it, and eat it," Miss Farmer told a French journalist. "From time to time, French chefs come and help—those from the best hotels in Boston, and sometimes from a transatlantic liner." But while some women studied French ways in classrooms, affluent American males of the nineteenth century prided themselves on mastering the art of French cooking by habitual dining out in the best hostelries. Others, like Thomas Jefferson, developed their epicurean sensibilities by dealing directly with their own French cooks.

General of Gastronomy

General Winfield Scott failed to make it to the White House in the election of 1852, but he was as devoted as his Virginia forerunner to the French cooking he learned first from an aged French colonist forced to take shelter near Petersburg after the Haitian revolution. While still a boy, Scott was taught to cook by this émigré, who was too poor to afford a servant but too

[6] A sixty-page pamphlet was published in 1866 after Blot's "immensely popular" lectures in Boston's Mercantile Hall. In it a series of the Frenchman's recipes is followed by questions and answers: "Is a cook a chemist?" Well, said the professor, "A cook is a person whose duty it is to keep in order the animal mechanism. A chemist is called when the mechanism is out of order." M.D.s please note. His successor, Miss Corson, conducted cooking classes in both the U.S. and Canada and was awarded a prize at the Columbian Exposition in 1893 for scientific cooking and sanitary dietetics. Her lectures and demonstrations at the University of Minnesota in 1884 drew 1,200 persons, who learned about such topics as "Cheap Dishes for Rewarmed Foods" and—foreshadowing the health-food enthusiasm of the twentieth century—the strength-sustaining values of lentils, fresh and dried peas, and beans.

respectful of the meals he prepared himself to fail to dress for dinner. These lessons Scott amplified by trips to Paris where he got to know the chefs of Les Trois Provençaux, Very's, and other great restaurants. Traveling to every out-of-the-way corner of the United States as a career officer, Scott knew all about the food available to Americans and—as few others did—what should be done to make it more palatable.

More than that, he talked food and touted French culinary tricks wherever he went. "I know of no flesh of beasts, or edible fishes, or fowl, or herb, or root, or grain, the preparation of which for food," his aide Erasmus Darwin Keyes wrote in a book largely about Scott, "was not many times the subject of his conversation." The general, who was chief of staff of the army, was known as "Old Fuss and Feathers," but in the memories of maîtres d'hôtel in New York, New Orleans, Washington, and throughout the country he was respected as the nation's best-known gourmet (when that word had a meaning worthy of real respect). Opponents of Scott's presidential aspirations accused him of gustatory xenophilism, yet his mind was usually on the bounty of his native land. During the Civil War, after he had had to reassign General Benjamin Franklin Butler to a command at Hampton Roads on Chesapeake Bay, Scott softened the blow by writing, "You are very fortunate . . . it is just the season for soft-shelled crabs, and hog fish have just come in, and they are the most delicious pan fish you ever ate." He needed no elaborate reasons to pass on his culinary enthusiasms. For a lady of his acquaintance he described a dish not then widely known, writing the directions in his own firmly masculine hand.

> Recipe for making the soup called, by French Creoles, "Gumbo filé," say for twelve plates:
>
> Take a grown chicken, cut it into many pieces, which fry, and then boil them to rags: 12 to 20 minutes before dishing, put in 30 to 40 oysters, with their liquid, and 6 to 10 minutes later add 23 spoonfuls of sassafras powder; stir the powder in, and if, on lifting the spoon, the composition drains out into a thin thread, you have a genuine "gumbo filé." If it does not rope sufficiently, stir in more of the powder. A small piece of bacon, or pork—say 2 or 4 ounces—may be put into the pot at the same time with the fried chicken. Rice, boiled dry, well cooked and each grain perfect, ought to be served separately, to be put into the plate with the gumbo soup.
>
> For Mrs. [George W.] Blunt—with the compliments and respects of
>
> General Scott

Old Fuss and Feathers might have instructed General Butler and other friends to prepare molting crabs for frying in deep fat, or he might have urged Mrs. Blunt that lump-back crab meat be dressed in mayonnaise, sending along another recipe, one published in Charleston in 1847. Far from being confined to Delmonico's for dishes turned out in the French manner, even epicures like Scott took for granted the increasing number of Gallic recipes that had come to be accepted as American. Mayonnaise, in fact, was being prepared in U.S. kitchens very early in the nineteenth century. As for Winfield Scott, he ended his days living in the same building as one of Delmonico's dining rooms; his enormous weight so curtailed his travel that he made sure of being close to the best of kitchens.

By the end of that century, when Fannie Farmer was well on her way to a lasting reputation as the arbiter of Yankee dining habits, her cookbook proved how easily thousands of Americans took to the influence of *haute cuisine*. *The Boston Cooking-School Cook Book*, by Fannie Merritt Farmer, published in 1896, did not bother to americanize such recipe titles as hollandaise sauce, chops en papillote, soufflé au rhum—or scores of others. Quoting John Ruskin in her foreword, the author of the cookbook that was to sell more than three million copies in the U.S. alone defined the meaning of cookery as, among other things, a capacity for "English thoroughness and French art." Thus Miss Farmer cited the two most important influences on what was to become—however tenuously—American food.

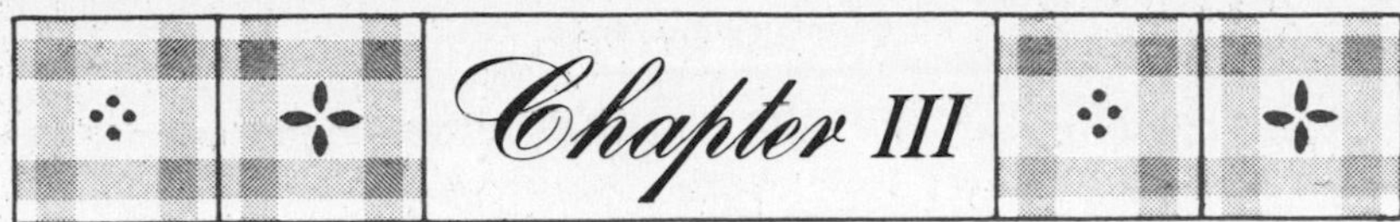

PADRES AND CONQUISTADORES

In *Death Comes for the Archbishop* Willa Cather tells of two French priests who helped to bring civilization to New Mexico. As Spaniards had done before them, these missionaries planted orchards and gardens and nurtured vineyards. But Father Vaillant and Bishop Latour[1] never succumbed to the peppery tastes in cooking that had evolved after the Spanish conquest. Once, visiting a parishioner near Santa Fe, Father Vaillant is told that his host's dinner of young lamb is to be stewed "with chili and some onion." The prospect causes the priest to ask leave to personally roast his portion quickly, as it would be done in France.

"Cook a roast in an hour! Mother of God, Padre," the *rancho* cook cries, "the blood will not be dried in it!"

"Not if I can help it!" says Miss Cather's priest, and she pictures him carving while watched by serving girls appalled at "the delicate stream of pink juice that followed the knife."

Priests so gastronomically inclined are far from unique, and this scene rings with the accuracy of many occasions never recorded in either fact or fiction. In the Southwest, nevertheless, there were few Frenchmen, in or out of cassocks. There the European influence on food established by clerics and settlers alike was Spanish, with some Aztec and other Indian overtones. In the Southeast, and in Florida particularly, the Continental Spanish influence has been modified by the produce of tropical islands. It

[1] Father Joseph Machebeuf, and Jean-Baptiste Lamy, who became archbishop of Santa Fe in 1875, were the Franciscans whose letters and papers Miss Cather used to document her novel.

developed the distinction that is described as Creole along the rim of the Gulf of Mexico.

In New Orleans, where that city's best restaurant food is still as French as it ever was, the most authentic Creole cooking is apt to be found in private homes. The cuisine indigenous to Louisiana took on its own aromas and tastes when the first colonial women, like their English counterparts on the Atlantic Coast, began to adapt the ingredients and some of the methods of New World cooking. Louisiana's French colonists became Spanish subjects only forty years after the settlement of New Orleans, and for another four decades, until the beginning of the nineteenth century, Spanish tastes prevailed among the ruling Creole cooks. New Orleans, as the principal port of the Gulf of Mexico, teemed with traffic in imported goods from Latin America and the islands of the Caribbean. Tropical foods and seasonings suited the city's indulgent climate. Most influential of all were the assertive spices, uncharacteristic of Gallic cooking, but so welcome in Spanish kitchens that Columbus's discovery of the New World had been (as history has so often insisted) a sort of by-product of his search for the Spice Islands. Hot peppers, such as cayenne from the Guiana coast and the fiery *Capsicum frutescens* from the arid plains of Tabasco, were brought north by Spaniards, and today some Louisianans claim that more peppers are raised in their state than in any other section of the United States. The use of peppers, both mild and stinging, in combination with tomatoes became a common way to turn standard recipes into Creole variations. It has become common also to apply the word *Creole* to such Cajun dishes as gumbo and jambalaya. However, although the way of cooking that deserves to be distinguished as Creole rather than Southern is spicy enough, the difference is really a matter of style and attitude on the part of the cook. Included may be *allumettes* of sweet potatoes glazed in syrup, or broiled breast of guinea hen served with thinly sliced country ham and a dressing of tomatoes, green peppers, and green olives.

Rice and Beans—and Color No Matter

The hurried traveler in Louisiana is apt to get the impression that all the best food is traditional French in style, but—as careful preservation of ancient architecture in the Vieux Carré also makes clear—Spaniards left several kinds of permanent changes in gastronomy. Like other Europeans, they planted the seeds and encouraged the appetite for beans, especially the red ones that are often kidney-shaped, or those known in Spanish as *frijoles colorado* or *habichuelas*. Red beans combined with rice comprise a basic dish, as typical of southern Louisiana as Hoppin' John of the Carolinas, the good-luck dish for New Year's feasts. In one form or another, bean dishes are even more intrinsic to Spanish-influenced American food than to that of other parts of the country. The *conquistadores* introduced black beans into Florida from their Caribbean islands, along with more exotic ingredients, such as the oranges that sometimes seem synonymous with the name of the state.

Again in Florida, rice is mixed with beans—black beans and rice are a sobering dish considered by some partygoers in Tampa to be a fine way to mark the witching hour of midnight. The beans are cooked very slowly with a ham hock. Red onions, garlic, and chopped green pepper are added along with bay leaf and a little vinegar to the simmering beans. After about three or four hours, rice is cooked separately to a fine fluffiness. The combination is served with the ham-and-pepper-flavored beans topping the white rice, and on top of all a garnish of finely minced onion and a lacing of oil and vinegar; sometimes chili powder and cayenne pepper are stirred into the beans. And sometimes, among those who haven't forgotten their Spanish history, this combination is still called "Moors and Christians," the pristine rice representing the good guys, of course.[2] Black beans are a variant of *Phaseolus vulgaris*, the botanical family to which kidney, navy, pea, pinto, and other New World beans belong. Their flavor is heartier than most others, tastier in my opinion, but for some reason they are reserved for soup in most parts of the country. Black bean soup may well be, in fact, the best of all bean soups, no matter what region influences the cook. Onion, carrots, celery, and garden herbs are common accents, and in some recipes a ham bone or some chicken broth can add a meaty flavor. In that old Spanish town of San Antonio, Texas, however, sausages floated in the brew of black beans ladled out at the century-old Menger Hotel, and wine, garlic, and the zest of Tabasco underline this soup's south-of-the-border influences. The hairy pods of the pigeon pea have been grown in Florida's warm climate since soon after the beginning of the earliest Spanish settlement, and the peas, fresh or dried, are basic to a stew that is rich with morsels of fresh lean pork, accented by *comino*, or cuminseed, onions, garlic, and tomatoes. The affinity of long-established Florida cooks for the food of island neighbors is clear in the popular dish called "Pigeon Peas with Rice Puerto Rican Style" as well as in *arroz con pollo* or *arroz con carne*, the traditional Spanish styles of serving chicken or beef with rice.

Early in the sixteenth century, a hundred years before the first British settlement, Ponce de León, who was governor of both Florida and Puerto Rico, brought rum to the mainland; there, perhaps inevitably, that distillation of sugar cane, rather than wine, was used to point up the oregano and garlic flavors of baked black beans. In Florida today this recipe is dressed up by sour cream floating on each serving, with ham—smoked or baked fresh—as the accompanying meat. *Spanish beans* is a term that sometimes refers to black beans and sometimes to garbanzos, or chick-peas, and I've

[2] In Louisiana that particular ethnoreligious slur has been forgotten and the combination is called simply "Red and White." It's considered a hearty workingman's meal, and is often accompanied (as at Kolb's, on St. Charles Street, New Orleans) by sliced country ham, garlic bread, and beer. Sometimes the "reds" are mashed with butter, with the ham slices, or salt pork, laid on top and the boiled rice on the side; with a green salad this version is considered a Louisiana favorite.

wondered occasionally why the *conquistadores*, who found the Indians using so many kinds of beans unknown to the Old World, went to all the trouble of shipping garbanzos across the ocean. A story for which I can't vouch has it that the Southwest tribes—who, say anthropologists, have been cultivating beans since the fifth century—developed many varieties; they most valued the yellow, blue, red, white, pinto, and black because they symbolized the six cardinal points, north, east, south, west, zenith, and nadir. The Spanish found the Indian cooks stewing beans, frying them in animal fat, making them into bread and cakes, and even serving them cold in a primitive sort of salad. Still, men who came in search of the Seven Cities of Cibola introduced the chick-pea to the Indians and—as other settlers entered the regions that Spaniards had colonized—to the developing American cuisine.

In Louisiana chick-peas are cooked with various meats seasoned by minced green peppers, chili powder, cayenne, cuminseed, and are proffered with sliced pimiento and plain boiled rice, much like "Moors and Christians." In New Mexico and Arizona, where they give way to the pinto and the red bean in popularity among legumes, chick-peas are mashed and baked as a sort of chili-flavored soufflé, or stewed with lamb shanks and the scent of saffron, or simmered with the hot Spanish type of local sausages, called *chorizo picante*, and a sauce made from red and green chili peppers. A Los Angeles versions, obviously modified for Anglo tastes, combines blander sausages, ground beef, cooked chicken, onions, and tomato paste, but leaves out the hot peppers. A more typical California way with chick-peas makes them a part of a barbecue; the cooked legumes are mixed with green chilis, green onions, and green pepper, all finely minced and tossed with *comino* and seasoned oil and vinegar. When designated as an hors d'oeuvre this delicious concoction is served alone but gets a lettuce cup if offered as a salad. A similar recipe in Florida substitutes Tabasco sauce for the minced chilis, adds oregano, garlic, a goodly quantity of avocado cubes, and shredded spinach. Another combination—served hot this time—mixes cooked chard, cooked tiny new potatoes, and chopped tomatoes, with sautéed onions, garlic, crumbled dried chilis, and grated cheese. In New Mexico where pueblo cooks combine Indian ingredients with twentieth-century cooking styles, chick-peas (or garbanzos, as they say) are mashed, seasoned, and eaten with tostadas, which are thin tortillas fried and broken in small pieces. According to a Tesuque pueblo recipe, four cups of cooked chick-peas call for two tablespoons of sunflower seed oil to be added while being mashed in a blender; the seasoning includes three tablespoons of lemon juice, three tablespoons of farmer cheese, and a half-cup of chopped, seeded green chilis. The resulting spread is garnished with piñon nuts that have been toasted and chopped.

Old-time Cooking of Florida and the Keys

Bolichi is a typical Florida *pièce de résistance* and calls for an eye of beef round to be stuffed with a mixture of piquant Cuban-style sausage (ham or salt pork are sometimes substituted), pimiento-stuffed olives, green pepper, onions, and other vegetables, with accents of lime juice and cuminseed, both influences first brought in by the Spaniards. Also olive-flavored and equally Spanish is *alcoporado*, a Florida beef stew further distinguished by a scattering of raisins to contrast with the piquancy of other flavors. *Piccadillo* is a mélange of minced beef, usually perked up by both raisins and olives—a dish as appreciated on Key West as on the mainland peninsula—and it is characteristically served with rice.

Old Key West residents for generations have referred to themselves as conchs (pronounced "conks"), the name of an iridescently pink spiral-shaped mollusk, as attractive as any edible thing Columbus discovered. Arawak Indians not only thrived on conch but used its shell to make various tools, and American Tories escaping to the Bahamas during the Revolution are said to have protested, "We'd rather eat conch than fight the king." The early settlers along the Florida coast adapted conch meat to traditional Creole recipes, and there are scores of tomatoey chowder recipes as a result; many used bird peppers and thin-but-hot pepper sauce as accents. The natural conch flavor, however, is delicate and therefore excellent in a bland Yankee-style chowder or in egg-batter fritters.

Not only the Florida keys but the interior of the state has developed recipes for making savory dishes with turtle meat as the principal ingredient. Like Louisiana's Cajuns, islanders and Everglades dwellers make superlative gastronomic use of this undomesticated source of sustenance that in the twentieth century became almost exclusively the pleasure of epicures. Floridian turtle cooks have had a choice of five varieties: the sea turtle that becomes scarcer and scarcer, the hard-shell inland turtle, the common land turtle, the "alligator cooter," and the soft-shell. *Carapachio* (the Spanish word for carapace) is an early colonial word for turtle soup that was corrupted into "calipash"—a spicy, peppery, sherry- or rum-laced brew sometimes served in the natural shell with floating islands of cooked turtle eggs and a baked pastry canopy to seal in the flavors.

One spring day my wife and I drove into the panhandle of Florida's Orange County and stopped at a fishing camp eating place where a woman was moving desultorily in her screened-in kitchen. She asked if we would eat turtle and, hardly waiting for the answer, shuffled out to a tree and brought in a covered basket of meat, along with the turtle's calipash, or undershell. She pried out some strips of the shell's thin, tacky jelly, which gives a real turtle soup its character, then cut some of the meat into cubes. She began to boil the calipash pieces in an iron kettle, adding a few deep yellow, shell-less ovarian eggs. The meat pieces were mixed with some of the greenish turtle fat and scraped into a skillet of hot coconut fat, to which was added a chopped Spanish onion and some *pimienta brava*. When the fat was spitting, the cook drained the liquid from the calipash, then added garlic and a little oil and finally the seared meat. The turtle filled our nostrils with a piquant aroma of meat and spice, and soon she warmed some white corn bread in the oven and served us turtle ragout with fried plantains on the side. The green turtle soup that is canned in Florida and shipped everywhere may be good for turning back the pages of time to the era when mock turtle soup, usually prepared at home with veal, was a part of almost every American household's repertoire, but this was the real thing.

Floridians, like all cooks surrounded by water, and with more than their share of inland streams and lakes as well, are resourceful when it comes to fish. The red snapper industry, which made this tropical fish the most popular in the country, started in Pensacola a few years after the Civil War, and snapper is served in many imaginative ways, including the spreading of a whole fish with a Spanish sauce that includes tiny peas and small whole mushrooms—to be added to a strongly lemon-accented mixture of tomatoes and green peppers. Snapper fillets served in a common Floridian style are baked with grated orange rind, a soupçon of juice, and seasoned with pepper and nutmeg. One of the finest of American fish chowders used to be served at a ramshackle pierside restaurant on the southern edge of Everglades National Park, and today with a fresh snapper on hand it can be easily reproduced.

The cut-up meat of a cleaned and boned four-pound fish, along with its skeleton and head, should be simmered in a large pot with a couple of stalks of celery, a few sprigs of parsley, two chopped onions, some bay leaf, salt, pepper, and two quarts of water. After about fifteen minutes, when the fish is cooked enough to flake easily, strain the broth and set aside the flaked fish. Dice a quarter-pound of salt pork, brown it in a skillet, and add a cup and a half of chopped onion, cooking until tender. Pour in the strained broth, two cups of diced raw potatoes, and cook fifteen minutes. Make a light roux of a half-cup of butter and an equal amount of flour, then gradually blend in two cups of cream, seasoning the mixture to taste with salt and pepper and adding oregano and a few drops of a really hot pepper sauce; carefully stir this into the chowder, simmer until all flavors have intermingled, and serve while still bubbling.

Some Like Them Hot

The Spanish first encountered chili peppers, which their descendants and other Americans have learned to use so profusely, when Columbus came upon some of them after his landing at Hispaniola. Mistakenly, the admiral called them peppers, as if they were related to *Piper nigrum*, the Asian plant whose berries are dried and ground and used as seasoning in all kinds of cookery. The peppers of the New World are *Capsicums*, and there is a profusion of them—they vary in color from red to green to yellow, and in flavor from the mildly biting common green or bell peppers to the aggressive heat of a couple of hundred kinds of chili peppers.

Out of all these varieties only green peppers gained full acceptance in northern gardens; the Puritans banned pepper and many other spices on grounds that they encouraged their users toward passionate excitation.

Capsicums have appeared on lists of aphrodisiacs, but no case has ever been proved. The excitement usually occurs, if at all, over the first taste of a dish enlivened by chili peppers. A report of one of the earliest U.S. visitors to Taos, while that region was a part of Mexico, tells us that he and his companions could not eat the first meal offered them because the food was so fiery. Another early pioneer in Brownsville, Texas, wrote that he could "quaff the Rio Grande at a draught" because he found the chili-ignited diet so full of heat.

Theories vary on why anybody tolerates food so hot with spices that the eater thinks his mouth is on fire. One speculation holds that diets based on such things as beans and rice are so bland that enhancement with stronger and stronger seasoning may have been inevitable. History has it that Portuguese circumnavigators found in India a ready market for chili peppers because the average palate there already had a high appreciation of *Piper nigrum*, the black pepper that had become harder for the average Asian to get after that spice became such a prized trade item in Europe.

China's province of Szechwan once was more closely related to India, and because of a somewhat tropical climate it also had a natural affinity for the hot peppers of the New World. Its cooks have used them exceedingly well. The increase in the number of Szechwan restaurants in the United States during the last decades of the twentieth century could be seen as the trail of capsicums come full circle, for many of the distinguishing flavors of this Chinese cuisine originated in the Western Hemisphere. Yet Szechwan food is attractive to American diners-out because of the subtleties and range of the flavors; the spices are not allowed to be domineering. On the other hand, any dish made with the same spices and labeled "chili"—that is, any such dish made in the authentic manner of the Southwest—is apt to be forthright, to say the least.

Used alone, the word *chili*, to most Americans, means *chile con carne*, which translates from the Spanish into "chili peppers with meat," and is rather the wrong emphasis in describing a mixture that is more meat (in canned form usually more beans) than pepper. There are infinite variations in the preparation of chili con carne, but chili cooks can generally be categorized in one of two ways—those who follow the Old Spanish-American recipes calling for chili pepper in pod form and those who insist that no authentic chili—or "bowl of red" as it is known by some Texans—can be made without the mixed seasoning called chili powder.

In its most widely distributed form, chili powder consists of dried chilies ground fine, with cuminseed, oregano, and garlic, also ground—the combination mixed to make a powder that looks a good deal like instant coffee. There is no doubt that the packaging of this formula by Texans toward the end of the nineteenth century helped to maintain the popularity of chili con carne in regions where there was Spanish influence in the kitchen, and across the northern tier of states as well. In the mid-1970s, in fact, Craig Claiborne of the *New York Times* wrote, "We've thought for years that if there's such a thing as a national American dish, it isn't apple pie, it's chili

Chile Sauce

No mild compound of hashed vegetables, sugar, and imported spices is the Southwestern chile sauce. You start with three or four whole, dried, red chile peppers. They go in a pan, preferably enamel or earthenware, with a clove of garlic and a quart of water. When the mixture has boiled until the chiles are pulpy, put it through a sieve to remove the seeds and membranes of the peppers. The sauce can be thickened a little with flour, and it can be salted, but purists object to this tampering with Nature's experiment in spontaneous combustion. They eat it as is, and they eat it on everything. Often chile seems to replace salt in the Southwestern diet.

—Alice Marriott
in *The Valley Below*

con carne. . . . In one form or another, chili in America knows no regional boundaries. North, South, East, and West, almost every man, woman and child has a favorite recipe." Midway in that decade, Americans in a single year consumed eight million pounds of chilies, the vast majority converted into powder that is high in vitamins A and C. Dr. Roy M. Nakayama of the New Mexico State University horticulture department has proved that chilies both preserve meat and break down fibers, making tough cuts more palatable. The hotness of chili, which makes strong men feel stronger, comes from capsaicin, a nitrogen compound secreted in the seeds and membranes. More than two hundred varieties are grown, from the inch-long Bahaman ("denture-melting," in the judgment of a Colorado connoisseur) to a large, comparatively mild type called Sâo Paolo.

Whatever chili variety may supply the flavor, a good argument can be worked up about the ingredients of a bowl of chili con carne wherever it may be concocted. "No living man" an Illinois writer who went east once said, ". . . can put together a pot of chili as ambrosial . . . as the chili I make. . . . That is the way of us chili men. Each of us knows that *his* chili is light years beyond all other chili in quality and singularity." Some recipes call for ripe tomatoes and red peppers, some for green tomatoes and green chilies—Texas purists say that the original San Antonio style rejects tomatoes of any kind, rejects onions and all other vegetables except peppers and garlic. Southwesterners in show business, like Will Rogers, have been known to refuse to travel without a supply of canned chili, and a Texas-born swing band leader of the 1940s went so far as to suggest that Congress, as he wrote to a friend, "should pass a law making it mandatory for all restaurants to follow a Texas recipe."

Most chili is based on beef, which faithful cooks never grind but cut into small cubes instead. In New Mexico lamb or mutton is substituted, and virtually every kind of game has been the base of good chili dishes. In a Dallas recipe fresh ham is diced and mixed with cut-up round steak in a proportion of one to two. There is much argument about the merit of suet, and when Lyndon Johnson was president, there was considerable to-do because the White House version of the Texas hill country recipe called for no beans. To put the matter straight, beans may or may not be included—mixed in or served alongside of the chili concoction. Chili is meat flavored with hot peppers and herbs—and with other embellishments, depending upon the cook. Fresh chili peppers are cultivated, among other places, in California's Ventura and Orange counties, in Texas, Arizona, and New Mexico. Unfortunately, the names vary from place to place. The milder varieties may sometimes be called simply California, or *poblano*, or *ancho*; some of the hot ones are known as *serrano* and *jalapeño* and *pequín*.

In early fall anyone who drives through the upper Rio Grande Valley toward Taos can see brilliantly red *ristras*, or ropes of pepper pods, hung against adobe walls and over roofs to dry in the sun until they are the color of live coals. Around Chimayo and other places, of course, chili peppers are the major crop of the local Spanish-Indian farmers, and part of the harvest is to be found there in markets, often labeled "New Mexico chili pods." Others are ground and packaged without the addition of extra seasonings. (Chimayo takes its name from the wild celery growing nearby, which is a common seasoning for chicken and pork, and gives characteristic flavor, when the root is dried, to the fermented Christmas drink, *mistela de chimaja.)* In the Santa Cruz Valley in southern Arizona both red and green chilies are prepared for shipment, and Santa Cruz chili powder is carefully marked "no spices added."

Cooks whose palates are conditioned to peppery flavors sometimes suspect the nationally distributed powdered chili compounds of being stretched with cornmeal. Whether this happens or not, most chili cooks who opt for pure dried peppers, or the powder derived therefrom, do so because they like to control precisely the amount of cuminseed and oregano—the wild marjoram native to the Southwest—and garlic. Generally speaking, no other spice is acceptable in a traditional chili con carne, yet a Florida cook who proclaimed her own product "as fine a chili con carne as I have ever tasted" included in her formula an amount of paprika equal to the chili powder she used plus a third as much allspice. I have tried this, and while the recipe may seem heresy to the Chili Appreciation Society of Dallas, the International Chili Society of California, or the International Connoisseurs of Green and Red Chili of New Mexico, it results in a superior Spanish-American feast. "Chili heads," as some of the most enthusiastic like to call themselves, have their own assortment of human foibles. They quarrel loudly and publicly over ingredients and techniques. Someone has likened them to "a bunch of wine snobs with their talk of 'nice afterbite' or 'subtle texture,' and they drive the noninitiated to distraction with debates on the merits of hand-cubed or coarsely-ground meat." Hollywood actress Elizabeth Taylor, playing the role of Cleopatra in Rome, underscored her commitment to the recipe of a Hollywood restaurant when she telephoned Dave Chasen and ordered ten gallons of Chasen's chili to be airfreighted immediately to Via Appia Pignatelli, as a source of needed strength, apparently.

Long before this state of affairs developed, the unique chili flavor was introduced in the Spanish style of cooking that prevailed in the Southwest before the region was taken over by the United States. The traditional dishes may not be as numerous as the towns with Spanish names that are scattered from the Mississippi to the Pacific, but the Iberian influence on American cooks has been a major one for a couple of hundred years. (A Texas town where "chili heads" gather annually to compete as creative cooks is named Terlingua, a word that means "three tongues.") A pork tenderloin recipe called lomo that appears in a number of the earliest West Coast cookbooks requires marinating the pork with mild peppers as a seasoning, but it is likely enough that the original cooks used chili peppers, along with oregano and other California wild herbs. *Puchero* is a Southwest boiled dinner sometimes made with chili powder, yet it is at its most *picante* when the vegetables and the chick-peas that give it body are sea-

soned with fresh hot peppers, *comino*, and regional herbs that sometimes include the Southwest's wild mint, which imparts a flavor of pennyroyal.

In the Southwest an average regionally minded cook's repertoire includes dozens of dishes for which the zest of chili is essential. In Santa Fe and its environs (an outdoor lunch at Rancho de Chimayo is memorable) it is common to be served a stewlike dish called *posole*, in which hominy, red chili pulp, oregano, and diced pork are combined. *Carne adobado*, another popular dinner course in Santa Fe—and at Chimayo as well—consists of marinated pork steak baked in a sauce that blends ripe red *pimienta picante, comino,* onions, and garlic into a smooth, unctuous blanket. There are chili sauces—both green and red—in infinite variation. For *mancha manteles* (the name means "tablecloth stainer" and the dish is a combination of pork, chicken, sweet potatoes, apples, bananas, and a touch of pineapple) the sauce is invested with chili powder, almonds, sesame seeds, cinnamon, and cloves; it is no less delicious because it seems exotic. A simple repast for breakfast or lunch is known sometimes as *huevos rancheros*, sometimes as *huevos en purgatorio* or "eggs in hell," the hot sauce providing the poaching liquid for the eggs.

The most internationally noted chili sauce is a chocolate-colored, mysterious-flavored gravy called *mole poblano* and served most frequently to dress up a turkey. *Guajalote en mole poblano*, challenging as it is to produce in the average kitchen, is popular in Arizona, Nevada, New Mexico, and Utah, and in the widening Spanish-speaking enclaves in Colorado. Although *mole*'s chocolate content tends to rouse suspicions in those who have never tasted it, the harmonious blend of dark bitter chocolate (the Aztecs used ground cacao beans), cloves, cinnamon, *comino*, *cilantro*, almonds, peanuts, pumpkin seeds, sesame, garlic, tomatoes, and several chilies is a prescription worth following—like a good mixture of spices with which to make one's own curry. When turkey pieces are simmered in broth thus seasoned, the result defies comparison. "The very thought of it makes your mouth water," a Spanish historian wrote.

Of Seeds and Sauces

There may be fewer chili con carne purists in Florida than in the Southwest, but much of the other peninsula food shows that Florida for centuries has been receptive to newcomers with Spanish leanings. In Ybor City, the cigar-making suburb of Tampa, the black beans and rice may be accompanied by roast beef stuffed with raisins, olives, and bacon that releases a sweetly pungent aroma when carved. Spaniards brought the same idea to southern California, where today roast pork infused with oregano and garlic is covered by thick brown sauce containing as accents sliced ripe native olives, raisins, cuminseed, chopped green pepper, and tomatoes. But there is also an East Coast version that calls for pork roast to be stuffed with rice ornamented with olives and raisins in a piquant tomato sauce.

In Spain the *arroz con pollo* mentioned earlier is a classic—chicken cooked with saffron rice and peas and garnished with either artichokes or young asparagus. In Mexico Spaniards substituted chilies for the milder vegetables, a treatment of chicken-and-rice that moved north with the Dons into California. In Puerto Rico and Key West and South Florida and Spanish Harlem the accents are sometimes olives and capers, and more and more in such places as Ybor City a mélange that is also called *arroz con pollo*, on menus and in homes alike, is dominated by tomatoes and sweet peppers. The classic architecture submits to the materials at hand. *Arroz con pollo a los Estados Unidos*, like the average American citizen, retains its Old World name and an affinity for its origins, but it will never be the same.

Poultry and pumpkin seed sauce is something else again. Indians who met the Spaniards on the Rio Grande included pumpkin seeds among their gifts of peace, and the conquerors of the Pueblo Indian towns soon began adapting Indian ways of using the seeds in cooking. Chicken in a sauce of blanched almonds, pumpkin seeds, cuminseed, popped corn, ground chili, and garlic is one of the legacies of the *conquistadores*. It is exotic, it is delicious, and it is not difficult for anyone who owns a blender to make. Almonds and the two kinds of seeds are stirred in a hot dry skillet until lightly toasted, then spun in the blender along with almost as much popped corn, the chili, and the garlic. This amalgam is incorporated into some chicken stock, sometimes with tomatoes, and simmered until it is the consistency of a thick gravy. Sometimes the chicken is poached, sometimes browned before baking in the sauce. The combination of flavors seems to take this dish beyond its Spanish-Indian beginnings, and the ineffable quality baffles guests—no one ever spots the popcorn flavor.

New Englanders made such dishes as popcorn pudding, saturating the popped corn in milk. Euell Gibbons, who grew up in the Southwest, tells in his *Stalking the Healthful Herbs* of devising a suet pudding that combines a meal made by spinning dry-popped corn in a blender with flour ground from dried roots of the chufa, or earth almond, which grows wild in Florida and the Southwest as well as other regions; Indians ate the roots like nuts, while Spanish soldiers drank *horchata de chufas*, a sweet but refreshing beverage. Gibbons's chufa pudding uses two parts of popcorn meal to one part of chufa flour along with sugar, eggs, and buttermilk. His recipe is, perhaps, an unwitting twentieth-century crossing of Spanish and Indian food lines.

Seeds, nuts and spices distinguish the chili-flavored sauce that makes Turkey Mole a Spanish-American recipe (one so firmly established in California that a company in Rosemead, in the citrus country east of Los Angeles, sells a ready-mixed mole powder). Turkey Mole is rare and delicious enough to need no romanticization, but an apocryphal story about its origin may be worth repeating.

In the early nineteenth century the American Southwest was still under the jurisdiction of the see of Durango, and when any member of the church hierarchy moved north to visit the colonial parishes there was great excitement. Legend has it that the first Turkey Mole was concocted at the Convent of Santa Rosa to mark the arrival of the archbishop. In the kitchen the cooks were inspired, quite naturally, to outdo themselves. They managed to get hold of some chocolate, which the ancient Aztec custom reserved for royalty, and which therefore seemed suitable for the head of the church. They ground the usual variety of dried chilies, added sesame and anise and coriander, cloves and cinnamon, garlic and tomatoes. To this long-brewed mixture, already dark brown from hours on the fire, the nuns decided to add that regal touch; bitter chocolate was certain to mystify His Excellency, as well as to flatter him when he should ask to have it identified. The sauce called *mole*, because the chocolate is mixed with other ingredients, is used in several ways.[3] (A recipe for Turkey Mole is on page 325.)

Once cooks learn the ease with which this seemingly complicated sauce can be made, they frequently apply it to other fowl, and often to pork—sometimes also to game, which might include anything from a roast leg of venison to cottontail rabbits so common in the Southwest. Some Californians say that generally they prefer rabbit to chicken, and those with Mexican tastes stew rabbit or hare with chilies and tomatoes. There are other Spanish-oriented rabbit recipes still hailed in places where missions were once the only signs of civilization. A California dish called *conejo casserole* calls for an herb-wine marination, then slow cooking with sliced mushrooms and at least a cup of sliced ripe olives. Apricots grown and dried by the padres crept into rabbit recipes, and some are a part of current repertoires. One calls for the rabbit to be marinated in white wine and white wine vinegar seasoned with oregano and rosemary. The rabbit pieces are then sautéed and baked in the marinade with dried apricots for about an hour. The resulting flavor is as distinctly suggestive of the Southwest style of cooking as any chili.

On Avocados

The alligator-pear—or let us call it avocado, please—is one of the Creator's masterpieces—what we would call a stroke of genius had a mortal originated it. . . . The avocado was undoubtedly created to serve as a salad. If you cut it in two, lengthwise, and take out the big stone, you have two halves like those of a small melon. The flesh, firm, though soft and custardy, has a most exquisite flavor—a faint flavor which, with oil and vinegar makes a symphony of fragrance.

After writing the above remarks I came across a clipping in which an evident epicure objected to "desecrating" the avocado pear by oil or mayonnaise dressing when served. "Eat it with a spoon slowly," he advises, "to give time for the pleasure it imparts to permeate the very soul, and let who will rail at fate. There are those who give it a slight sprinkling of salt, others who dust it over with a little white pepper, but personally I would as soon think of flavoring my currant jelly with garlic or my chateau Yquem with Trinidad rum."

—Henry T. Finck

The Circuitous Ways of the Avocado

The United States does not owe all the culinary uses of chocolate—or even chili—to pre-Columbian cooks. But guacamole is another matter. The sauce, which predates New World history, is made of avocado and is now so prevalent at cocktail parties that the word itself is accepted by recent American dictionaries as part of the language. In circles less than lexiconic it is not unusual to find the phonetic spelling, *waca molay*, serving to identify a recipe. In the centuries that passed after Hernando Cortés became, perhaps, the first European to taste the avocado at one of Montezuma's banquets, the record indicates that George Washington also had a bite of one when he went to Barbados as a young man. In his journal of that trip in 1751, he wrote that "the Avagado pair is generally most admired," adding that he himself preferred the pineapple.

[3] Since chocolate was considered by Aztecs to be aphrodisiacal, foods made of chocolate were forbidden to women; but a popular drink at the time of Cortés was made of cacao, vanilla, and red pepper chilled by snow.

A traveler from Latin America was responsible for avocados growing in the Hawaiian Islands as early as 1825, and a horticulturalist named Henry Perrine cultivated some south of Miami in 1833. Known more commonly as alligator pears, they were grown as ornamental plants and occasionally were served as fruit at exclusive dining clubs. In fact, the San Francisco financier Henry E. Huntington was so intrigued when his own club offered them that he pocketed a huge pit and had it planted in his garden of exotica. There, so Californians say, that same seed bears fruit today.

"If reliable witnesses do not err," Lately Thomas wrote in his entertaining book about the Delmonico family, 1895 was the year the avocado was introduced to fashionable New Yorkers at the Madison Square hostelry, "Richard Harding Davis was co-sponsor of the delicacy. That Gallahadian idol of the popular press toured Central and South America in 1895, and at Caracas he was served avocados. So intrigued was he with their buttery, musky flavor that he brought a basketful back to New York. He carried them to Delmonico's where 'Charley' [Ranhofer, the chef] peeled one, tasted, and approved. Thereafter a supply was shipped regularly to the restaurant, and the avocado's popularity began."

Less than a decade later, the avocado had been so accepted by gastronomes, the author of a book called *Food and Flavor* went on record:

> The alligator-pear—or let us call it avocado, please—is one of the Creator's masterpieces—what we would call a stroke of genius had a mortal originated it. . . . The avocado was undoubtedly created to serve as a salad. If you cut it in two, lengthwise, and take out the big stone, you have two halves like those of a small melon. The flesh, firm, though soft and custardy, has a most exquisite flavor—a faint flavor which, with oil and vinegar makes a symphony of fragrance.
>
> After writing the above remarks [Henry T. Finck wrote], I came across a clipping in which an evident epicure objected to "desecrating" the avocado pear by oil or mayonnaise dressing when served. "Eat it with a spoon slowly," he advises, "to give time for the pleasure it imparts to permeate the very soul, and let who will rail at fate. There are those who give it a slight sprinkling of salt, others who dust it over with a little white pepper, but personally I would as soon think of flavoring my currant jelly with garlic or my chateau Yquem with Trinidad rum."

In California, however, it was not until 1924 that Anglo farmers took this plant of the Spanish missions seriously enough to organize the Avocado Growers Exchange. That group now raises nineteen of the ninety-nine varieties and ships them—as do equally productive Florida growers—to markets around the world. They do thrive in many other parts of this planet, of course. Somerset Maugham once claimed at a small dinner party in Paris that he personally had been responsible for introducing them to French soil; he had brought seeds from a friend's California avocado ranch and had had his gardener plant and tend them at his villa on Cap Ferrat.

Maugham also confided to a friend that he was the inventor of avocado

Guspacha Salad

Slice *cucumbers* very thin, also *onions* and peel *tomatoes*; fill a glass dish with alternate layers of this mixture with *bread crumbs* (*stale*) sprinkled over each layer. Cover all with *French dressing* and garnish with *lettuce*, and serve icy cold.

—Col. Talbott

ice cream, a claim one might even find justifiable after remembering how often culinary minds hit upon the same ideas. The butterfat texture is as tempting to the palate as rich cream, and the thought of chilling avocados in parfaits or turning them into a frozen dessert with added flavors of nuts or fruit juices comes easily. That texture also seems a natural complement to a simple green salad dressed with good California olive oil and lemon juice; but in a meal in full progress there is surprise, delightful and sprightly on the tongue, when pieces of avocado are tossed at the last minute with hot rice that has steeped in chicken stock flavored with saffron and the essence of garlic.

There are many other Spanish- or Latin-American-influenced recipes for this bland vegetable, which was sometimes called (in days when Britannia ruled the waves) "midshipman's butter." Creamed fish and chicken are considered by many contemporary cooks to be glamorized when served in the hollow of an avocado half. This sort of thing can be as pastily unappetizing as chicken à la king at any businessmen's lunch club, depending on the cook. A hungry man might try instead a baked avocado stuffed with some ground cooked pork stirred into a little chopped tomato and flavored with three capers and a pinch of fresh marjoram; a spoonful or so of beaten egg and some breadcrumbs top things off as the avocado goes into the oven.

In a Spanish colony in Florida chilled avocados are stuffed with marinated and finely minced white onions. I season an omelet with a stirring of cuminseed, coriander, cardamom, ginger, and perhaps some other tropical spices; then as the egg mixture begins to set, I decorate the center with small cubes of avocado. Breaking away from Hispanic influence, the New York chef Albert Stockli invented an avocado bisque that depends on tiny smelts, cooked in wine with mushrooms, onions, and rice; when puréed, this fish mixture is blended with avocado, seasoned with oregano, basil, and thyme, and reheated with enough light cream to make a smooth soup.

Still easily available only to regional cooks—as the avocado was until shortly before World War II—is the chayote, a bland, pale green variety of squash that is called *mirliton* in Louisiana, where it is commonly grown as a decorative vine on fences and porches. It is somewhat pear-shaped and in some places is known as the vegetable pear. It is much admired by Floridians for its dessert propensities, along with the fact that it can be cooked and stuffed in many of the ways that make the avocado good eating. When you want to serve it as a vegetable, make a stuffing of the chayote pulp and mix with garlic-flavored spinach or with green pepper and tomatoes. Some Californians crumble chorizos to mix in the stuffing; and as good as anything of this sort is chayote when it is stuffed with shrimp from any place along the Gulf Coast. One of the elegant Florida desserts consists of chayotes accented by raisins and rum, topped with an almond-sprinkled meringue. Cooked chayote makes good salad when dressed with oil and vinegar.

To start off a meal in any part of the Spanish fringe of this country, the average cook's avocado soup is more likely to be based on chicken stock, and there are dozens of variations—a few that make use of chayotes, too. But in California the start of a meal is as apt as not to be a salad—not the Spanish salad soup, known as gazpacho on both sides of the Atlantic, which usually combines cucumber, tomatoes, and sweet pepper and is aromatically seasoned in an icy broth—but such things as guacamole used as a mayonnaiselike dressing for marinated cauliflower; or pitted ripe olives, chopped green pepper, and mayonnaise tossed with diced dry bread that has been sealed in a jar for several days with a dried chili pod.

Why salad as a first course, instead of cleansing the palate between one course and another with the delicately dressed greens of France? Eastern Americans have been known to sneer at this custom without even wanting to know from whence it sprang. Some gastronomes have surmised that starting a meal with salad was a custom introduced by immigrants who brought the Italian way of eating a few fresh raw things before sailing into the heaviness of *pasta*. But I suspect eating salad as a first course may be related also to the outdoor life of the Dons who came north to a climate that produced abundant fruits and vegetables and who may have savored the raw food as they waited for the meat to sizzle to the right degree of flavor and juiciness on the barbecue rack.

In the Beginning There Was Barbecue

Barbecue is the English adaptation of the Spanish *barbacoa*, a word applied first in the New World to the outdoor grilling of meat by the Indians of Haiti. When Ponce de León and de Soto and Spaniards after them probed the southern Atlantic coast of North America, they found the Indians using crude wooden racks to smoke or dry fish, fowl, and other meat over open fires. The Cherokees and Creeks of the Carolinas and the Gulf Coast continued to apply their techniques of grilling as Spanish cattle and pigs began to thrive, and the colonizers refined the practice when their *ranchos* took root in arid Texas, New Mexico, and Arizona and in the fertile valleys of California. The Spaniards added the sauces that have, for most barbecues of today, the accent of hot peppers and garlic, whether they are the simple marinade bastings of the Old South or the thick tomatoey variations on the *mole* theme that have proliferated in the Southwest and California.[3]

"Way back when the Dons first came to California," Helen Evans Brown wrote in her lively *West Coast Cook Book*, "grilled meat was a part of every festive gathering. A huge fire was made, a freshly killed beef hung in the shade of a tree, and vaqueros and their ladies cut off pieces every time that hunger called, and cooked it over the waiting fire." She added, "It wasn't

[3] Sarah Hicks Williams, a bride who left New York in 1852 to live in Clifton Grove, North Carolina, on the plantation of her husband's family, stressed the culinary differences between North and South in letters to her parents. "They live more heartily," she wrote of her new Carolina relatives. "There must always be two or three kinds of meats on Mrs. Williams' table for breakfast & dinner. Red pepper is much used to flavor meat with the famous 'barbecue' of the South and [the dish] which I believe they esteem above all dishes is roasted pig dressed with red pepper & vinegar."

only charcoal grilling that was practiced by those Californians of the past, they also had their huge pit barbecues even as today."

Traditional community barbecues still bring together people from the ranches, the range, and neighboring towns; and the cordwood piled in the long narrow ditches, dug for the purpose, is apt to burn all the night before. On iron bars and chicken wire stretched across the sunken fire the meat is placed to broil slowly throughout the morning. A cook with a bucket of vinegar and his own special seasoning treks back and forth along the pit's rim, swabbing the meat, occasionally turning it. At serving time, when the juicy slices are carved, there is time for nostalgia: The traditional accompaniments were always homemade bread and baked beans—and freshly churned butter, pickles, preserves, and dozens of kinds of pies and cakes made by wives and daughters.

For years the Spanish-American sheriff of Los Angeles County held an annual barbecue that attracted as many as sixty thousand people. Such enormous affairs ceased to be common, but ranchers still gather in Texas and the Mountain States for old-style range feeds, just as other families gather for community picnics. By the middle of the twentieth century observers of American mores might have been tempted to assess the custom of picnic area or backyard barbecuing as one of the equations of affluence. A good deal of chicken, beef, pork, and chunks of lamb has been charred, scorched, and burned as the result of the availability of a myriad supply of outdoor cooking equipment. And all of this comes naturally to Americans in every part of the country—from the luaus of Hawaii to the cookouts of New England.

Actually, a fair amount of contemporary barbecuing is done—as was equally true in colonial days and on every frontier—because it is pleasanter to cook outside on a hot summer day. In the old days, with open-hearth kitchen fires, it was a warm-weather necessity. Outdoor cooking is in the American blood. At the same time the Dons were establishing the custom in the Southwest, British colonials were adapting the word to the sizable gatherings at which people were fed on meat, game, and other food cooked over well-laid fires. Electioneering and barbecuing became virtually synonymous in the eighteenth and nineteenth centuries. And in the modern Deep South the old lavish alfresco hospitality, made possible by slavery, is emulated in some degree where estates are maintained: Cooking hearths are sheltered by roofs on many contemporary plantations, and the barbecue is frequently served in a summer house.

Chicken, spareribs, tenderloin, and other cuts of pork are still the prevailing choices among Southern barbecuers, even as beef is the preference of most Texans and Californians. But the Spanish also introduced the first sheep and goats to American ranges, and their descendants in the Southwest have enormous appetites for barbecued *borrego*, baby lamb, and *cabrito*, suckling goat. So do the Basque herdsmen who were brought from Spain to the Mountain States toward the end of the nineteenth century. With the exception of a few chophouses in cosmopolitan cities, mutton is easily available only in parts of the Rockies. In Winnemucca, Nevada, at the foot of Sonoma Peak, for instance, nobody waits for barbecue weather—there is Basque family-style dining in restaurants, and oven-roasted mutton or even mutton hash are fixtures on the menus. Basque cooking is straightforward and filling, with few frills—not even simple desserts. Down in the Four Corners country, in sight of the Sangre de Cristos Mountains, lamb is considered fiesta meat, and the older and wiser heads among the Chicanos insist that butchers follow the Spanish way of cutting with the grain to seal in the juices; then they barbecue the roast over a hot fire and slice it thin.[4]

There is no surprise in the fact that Americans have turned barbecues into a business. Lyndon Johnson made it all too clear that a successful feast under the live oaks required the best professional barbecue man in Texas. West of Johnson City there used to be an outfit that showed up annually in such places as Albuquerque with two truckloads of equipment, three cooks, and something like 650 pounds of beef and lamb. Preparing a feast took the professionals from five A.M. to six-thirty p.m., while logs burned down to the right kind of coals and great slabs of meat cooked in homemade barbecue sauce alongside skillets of Texas onions and pots of bubbling pinto beans. In northern New England, far from the incursions of the Spanish Empire, halves of chickens are grilled over coals, and the folks who gather for small-town Fourth of July celebrations salute the traveling barbecue expert as they stand around licking their fingers and biting into broilers that have a taste not to be duplicated outside America. Here there is no palate-burning, vaguely Spanish barbecue, but the principle is the same.

A Meal in the Hand

Literally taking things into one's own hands when it comes to eating has helped to encourage the American penchant for what too many women's magazines choose to call "finger foods"—whether they be vegetables or cracker variants, used to scoop up "cocktail dips," or corn on the cob, or sausages or meat patties slapped between pieces of bread and labeled hot dogs, hamburgers, or Sloppy Joes. Indians showed Puritans and Cavaliers alike how easy the eating of freshly boiled corn on the cob could be. Cortés and his men reported that the Aztecs munched tamales on the street. Other *conquistadores* described how Pueblo tribesmen made their tortillas from ground corn and turned them into tacos by filling the flat cakes with beans or meat sauces and rolling them up by hand. Contemporary Hopi cooks grind meal from the local blue corn for many kinds of bread, including

[4] Like Basque shepherds, Portuguese sailors from the Azores were brought to this country because of their special skills, and many Portuguese families transplanted their culinary customs to the New England shore, on Martha's Vineyard and at Mystic, Connecticut, for instance. Portuguese cooks are known for their baking, and their *massa sovado* is a yeast bread made especially at Easter. They used as much cornmeal as the other Iberians who have influenced Western cooking but insist that the meal must be white, instead of yellow—or blue, as many Southwestern cooks demand.

breakfast pancakes served to travelers who are accustomed to the use of forks. On the Navaho reservation north of Flagstaff, Arizona, I once met a grandmotherly woman who invited me into her kitchen to see the electric grinder with which that morning she turned dried blue corn kernels into fluffy, gray-blue meal. She was justly proud of her machine, but except for this substitute for muscle she had cut no corners. "I roasted the corn first," she said as she scooped up some of the flour—it was really that finely ground. Back in New York it made pancakes that were rich in flavor and indigenously embellished when served with Grade A maple syrup from a Vermont farm.

Floridians, Puerto Ricans, Chicanos of the Southwest, and other Americans of Spanish heritage depend on an excellent European style of bread, but for many Southwesterners the pre-Columbian tortilla is still the staff of life. Except that the dough is made from flour that is ground after dried corn is cooked with lime, it is identical to the *chapatis* of India. A mixture of meal and water is patted into shape between the hands of the cook—or sometimes a final smoothing takes place on the suntanned surface of a bare thigh. Like a maid "setting her cap" in a Yankee springtime, the Chicano girl who finishes a round flat cake in this way is turning out a tortilla that is bound, of course, to cause the youth who eats it to fall in love. Nowadays *tamalina* or *masa harina*, "instant" corn flour mixtures, are available in Spanish groceries, and tortilla presses can be bought by those cooks who aren't concentrating on the way to a young man's heart. In the old days tortillas were always baked on a round, flat *comal*, made of stone or pottery, but they can be cooked as well on a modern griddle.

Spanish Sausages

are made from the fat and lean of the back and loins of a well-fed two-year-old hog, finely minced or pounded together and strongly seasoned with cloves of garlic and green or red capsicums or chilies; but as these cannot always be conveniently procured in this country, cayenne pepper may be substituted. The whole should be covered with any sort of strong, dry wine, until absorbed by the ingredients, which will occupy perhaps a few days, according to the quantity. Fill the largest skins you can get with the meat, fat and lean alternately, occasionally adding some of the wine. Tie up in links, and hang them in a room where they will not get damp or become too dry, and they will keep twelve months.

Like bread, tortillas accompany meat dishes. When they are filled with one of the infinity of stuffings devised over centuries—that is, when they are rolled around a mixture of fish, meat, and sometimes beans—they are properly described as tacos. When a tortilla is fried crisp in fat, it is transformed into a tostada and is folded once to enclose a filling; thus it becomes the Spanish-American Indian version of the sandwich. The process of turning tortillas into enchiladas begins with the dipping of the flat bread in a tomato sauce. Sometimes a delicious filling is made by combining Monterey Jack cheese with sautéed chorizos, the peppery, garlic-and-paprika pork sausages to be found where Mexican and Spanish foods are sold. Sausage and cheese are rolled up in the tortillas, laid side by side in a baking dish, and covered with more sauce, then a sprinkling of grated cheese, before going into the oven. Tamales (the Spanish simply added an *e* to the Indian word) are corn-husk envelopes filled with cornmeal mush or *masa harina* dough, plus chili in one form or another, for flavor. They can be cooked in hot ashes like corn on the cob but are more likely to be steamed.[5]

As cooks from England, in their own good time, found many ways to adapt corn products to Old World recipes, so did those from Spain who

[5] In New York's *El Barrio*, residential center for American citizens who came from Puerto Rico, Cuba, and other Spanish-speaking places, a *chuleta empanada* is a popular snack that encloses a breaded pork chop in a fold of baked dough.

settled in Texas, New Mexico, Arizona, and California. New World hominy, combined with Old World *menudo* (tripe) was for centuries a traditional Christmas breakfast among Spanish-Americans and it is still celebratory fare. In most of the Southwest *menudo* is served on Sunday mornings as a marvelous stick-to-the-ribs soup when the night before has been a late one.

The trouble with tripe may be that Americans who have been caught in the maze of upward mobility think of it as poor man's food; instead, especially when prepared with love and Spanish-Indian ingenuity, it is the kind of delicacy that converts cynics. The Chicano method with *menudo* does not produce as richly gelatinous a result as is *tripes à la mode de Caen*, nor is it dominated by tomatoes, in the style of Italian cooks. Traditionally calling for hominy, or corn in one form or another, it is an americanization of a Castilian dish called *callos a la madrileña*. The *menudo* of the Great West should bubble lazily with a knuckle bone and the characteristic Spanish-American herbs and spices. With the perfume of Alta California in the steam that rises from each bowl, and with plain *tostadas* at the ready, this is a beautifully simple midday meal.

To make it for eight or ten persons, you ought to start with about three pounds of beef tripe and a couple of pig's feet, or a veal knuckle. Cover the meat with salted water, add three cloves of garlic, two cups of chopped onions, some chopped fresh coriander if possible (or two teaspoons of powdered), some minced fresh oregano, chili powder or whole chili peppers, and two to three cups of cooked hominy. Let the pot just barely simmer for four hours or more, then set aside to cool; remove the tripe and cut into small bite-size squares and take away the pork or veal bones. Reheat and serve the *menudo* with thin slices of lemon or lime and a sprinkling of minced chives.

The Good Herbs

In her research into restorative soups and stews, Helen Brown discovered that *sopa de albóndigas* so intrigued nineteenth-century California Anglos that those pioneers from the East recorded variations of a Spanish dish of meatballs under such spellings as *avonigas, abondegas, abondas*—"the early American ladies cooked it better than they pronounced it," Mrs. Brown said. Their successors still cook it, not because the idea of soup with meatballs is so unusual, but because a medley of herbal flavors distinguishes it. The taste of chili peppers is imperative, but broth and meatballs alike may be infused with a variety of herbs—most especially mint if the dish is made in New Mexico or Arizona. In the Southwest mint is found more useful than elsewhere.

Yerba buena, which translates as "good herb," and refers in Spanish to one of the native American herbs, was the name first given to the settlement on San Francisco Bay. It was an herb that ran wild over the hills and it came to add a very special savor to the cooking of meat and other foods

Spanish Friceo

This dish is made from good beef (the same kind as used for beef-steak), lean pork or young mutton. The best is beef and pork in equal quantities. Two pounds of meat is enough for six or eight persons. The meat is beaten till soft and then cut in thin slices; cut raw potatoes in thin slices, washing them before they are cut, but not after, and take two soup plates of them. Mix with potatoes two saucerfuls of onions cut in slices. Take a pudding dish and put the meat and potatoes in layers. Scatter over each layer some pepper, some Jamaica pepper, and salt; put on every layer of potatoes a piece of butter and at least three-quarters of a tablespoonful of thick sour cream. Close the pudding dish well and put it into boiling water, and let it boil for one and one-half hours.

—Hand-written recipe

in the early period. Some modern cooks substitute tarragon mixed with chervil or parsley on the theory that the combination is gentler as well as more civilized than wild *yerba buena*. But ordinary dried mint, available in virtually all food stores, is used in the New Mexico broth brewed from pork neck bones; mint flavors breaded pork chops that are served with fried chili peppers and—again as a balance to chili—is an accent for a braised round steak, popular around Santa Fe, that simmers with onions and tomatoes and Napa Valley Pinot Noir wine. When cooks of this region season lamb, they often used juniper berries, and they insist on the wild ones when they can find them in the field.

The Spanish, with their love of herbs and spices, have influenced the evolution of American cooking more than is generally recognized. The bright orange blossoms of the safflower plant, seen throughout New Mexico and Arizona, are there today because centuries ago seeds from Spain were planted by padres. Now safflower oil is common enough in American supermarkets, but this plant contributes in another way to Southwest cooking. According to a regional authority, local cooks learned early that safflower blossoms could be dried and crumbled to serve as a substitute for the extravagantly priced Old World saffron. Their flavor gives a somewhat more poignant taste to Rio Grande *arrozos* and various soups, and the plants that escaped the cloisters to grow wild continue to remind one of the padres who introduced them to the arid soil.

Three hundred years ago, when the Spanish priests arrived, they found the Southwest Indians making much use of nuts from the piñon, now the state tree of New Mexico. Much like the *pignoli* of southern Europe, the fruits of the piñon were eaten just as were the seeds of other plants, and the Pueblo tribes also added them to stews or ground them for use as thickeners. Spanish-American families (for some of the poorest of whom piñons are more a necessity than a subtle addition to their cuisine) annually gather the nuts wild and store them for the winter or sell them in trade. Among affluent Southwesterners with an interest in distinguished food, sophisticated adaptations of primitive recipes are among the rewards of eating in their homes. A spicy filling for avocado halves mixes piñons with tomatoes and citrus juice. And a delicate soup, compared by some cooks to a deftly seasoned vichyssoise, is made by blending a quantity of pine nuts with chicken broth and light cream redolent of scallions, coriander, and mint.

H. L. Mencken noted that the American language has absorbed more Spanish influences than those of any other European tongue. I am not going to try to prove it, but a similar case can be made for the flavors of Spain in American food. The fancy for peppers, red and green and yellow, hot and sweet, must seem to be the most prosaic of all items. Yet there are many others. Garlic was lifting the flavor of southwestern gastronomy long before the arrival of Italian cooks in so many parts of the rest of the country. Olives were not left to the Greeks who infiltrated the restaurant business. Stuffed or not, the olives so prevalent in American living rooms at the cocktail hour have added piquancy to a new American variety called, appropriately, mission olives. Oil remains the prime use of California's mission olives, and highly developed groves are now in the arid San Joaquin Valley and in Butte County, north of Sacramento. Unfortunately, the most widely distributed American olive is the large black ripe fruit that is canned and often seems to have little more than waterlogged flavor. But vast quantities of Spanish green olives, usually stuffed with bland but colorful cores of pimiento, are also a part of California's contribution to the shaping of American eating habits. Long before the first olive was dropped into a pale mixture of gin and vermouth—undoubtedly to give some color to an otherwise watery-looking drink—American women who swore by Fannie Farmer or Mrs. S. R. Dull (a Georgian who helped to set culinary standards in the South) considered an olive sauce to serve with meats almost commonplace. Mrs. Dull's flourishes included chopped green peppers, pimientos, celery, tomato catsup, and Worcestershire sauce. There are hints here of Creole sauces evolving in New Orleans, where Spanish occupiers had made olives welcome, and where several traditional veal dishes require olives, black or green, as accents. When you drive through the Southwest, you can see olive groves in New Mexico and, along with dates and oranges, in Arizona's Valley of the Sun. Here the Spanish again were responsible for the first figs as well as dates (California's Coachella Valley has more than five thousand acres in date palm orchards) and for numerous other fruits.

The citrus fruits brought by the Spanish to the New World seem to have been planted for medical needs, rather than as colonial crops to be harvested. There is reason to believe that both Ponce de León, who discovered Florida in 1513, and Hernando de Soto, a generation later, planted orange seeds. Soon a Spanish law required every sailor on a ship bound for America to carry one hundred seeds for planting; later because the seeds lost fertility in drying out, Spanish ships were required by law to transport seedling trees that might more readily survive. Some of these thrived and eventually grew wild in southern Florida. The first practicing American naturalist, John Bartram, was glad to find some of these in 1765, and he recorded in his diary that the wild Florida orange made "a relishing morsel" when he pulled some honey from a tree and poured it over the pulp of the uncultivated citrus. The orange juice industry was not to be quite yet, but a market awaited the distribution of the fruit in the colonies. Cooked desserts such as orange pie have been popular in Virginia and other parts of the South since before the Revolutionary War. (By the time the conflict with England was under way, a New Yorker named Jesse Fish had become rich and important running an orange grove near St. Augustine, and in 1776 he shipped sixty-five thousand oranges to buyers in London; two years later he delivered sixteen hogsheads of juice.) A clear Spanish-American influence is evident in the classic Southern dessert called ambrosia, which is a simple layering of orange sections, freshly shredded coconut, sugar, and sometimes sherry, which is well chilled before serving. Louisiana hostesses are known for meals that end with a frothy cooked orange cream made with orange juice, sugar, eggs, rich milk, and the accent of lemon.

San Antonio, like California towns, originated during the mission period, and when settlement began in earnest, people from the Canary Islands—from whence Columbus had brought the first oranges—were resettled there by royal decree. The Spaniards and Mexicans who came later have seen to it that San Antonio remains Spanish in a more easily recognizable way than any other American city. And food is among those recognitions. The city has a Spanish market square, just as Olivera Street remains a landmark in Los Angeles. Along the San Antonio River, with its picturesque stone bridges and Old World buildings, there are sidewalk cafés to add to the effect. Chicano women at curbside stands sell hot tortillas, tamales, and tacos, the way hot dogs are sold under umbrellas in New York and other northern cities. Texas ranchers and farmers who show up in town for breakfast can expect to find tacos and chili on the morning menu, along with refried beans and spicy chorizo served with eggs or hashed brown potatoes. In place of the catsup bottle, which in less Spanish regions is always at hand in public eating places, the ubiquitous tomato sauce of Texas and other parts of the Southwest is called *ranchero* or *serrano*, after the hot chili peppers that inflame the mixture of garlic, raw onions, salt, and cooked tomatoes (*ranchero* sauce demands *comino* as well). *Huevos rancheros*—like "eggs in purgatory"—is a favorite breakfast, and so is steak daubed liberally with hot *ranchero* sauce.

In Zavala County, which lies between San Antonio and the border, the word for breakfast is sometimes *barbacoa*. Much the same way as bean-hole beans are baked in New England, this Rio Grande form of barbecue is cooked in a sealed pit from early evening until breakfast time. The meat is a whole beef's head, wrapped first in foil, then in saturated hemp sacks, set into the mesquite-wood fire at the bottom of a hole dug in the ground; a sheet of tin is put over the beef's head, and the pit is refilled with dirt to prevent the escape of steam. Brains and slices of tongue and head meat are served with a sauce of *jalapẽno* peppers, and on the side refried beans and highly spiced avocado. The method can be traced to Spanish soldiers, and it has been modified by Anglos of the Southwest, who substitute beef brisket for head meat.

When visitors stand before the Spanish cathedral built by Willa Cather's archbishop in Santa Fe—especially, perhaps, in contemplation of the intricate stonework of San Antonio's Mission of San José—wherever remnants of Spain remain in the Southwest, or in Florida or Louisiana, there are reminders of Spanish ways of living. Spaniards established the cultivation of many of the basic ingredients of the American diet, and they left a legacy of style as well—not something to be minimized as "Tex-Mex." The important Spanish gastronomical influences have become so much a part of American cooking that they are all too commonly overlooked.

GEMÜTLICHKEIT AND SERIOUS EATING

The farmers' market in Lancaster, Pennsylvania—established in perpetuity by royal charter of George II in 1742—is as indicative in the twentieth century of German influence on American food as it was in the years before the Revolution. Twice a week in the 1970s the turreted, mansard-roofed red brick building teemed with the dwindling romance and the unabated aromas of food products from hundreds of small farms in and around Lancaster County. Dairy products, vegetables, baked goods, freshly killed poultry, hickory-smoked meats, barrel-aged pickles, honey, apple butter, sauerkraut, Pennsylvania Dutch corn relish, homemade fudge—most of the food taken home by those who browse through Lancaster's central market is raised or wrought by others whose names are German and whose style of cooking has dominated many kitchens in other parts of America, wherever pioneer movements have led.

The Pennsylvania Dutch have no roots in Holland; their ancestors were German-speaking religious refugees who came to the New World by way of the Rhineland and other parts of Germanic Europe. Within a year of the arrival of the first Quakers from England and Wales who established Philadelphia, nearby Germantown was settled by the Mennonites who were to have so much influence in many rural sections of America. As Mennonites were followed by Amish from Switzerland, Bohemian Moravians, Schwenkenfelders, Dunkard Baptists (who helped to fix doughnut dunking in the language), word of the good food to be had in Pennsylvania began to spread to other colonies.

George Washington, as a result of his wartime months in Pennsylvania, is said to have maintained a lifelong appetite for the regional food. He was only one of the founding fathers who ate frequently at the Sun Inn, which

Sausage Scrapple

Bring 1 quart water to a rolling boil and add 1 cup white cornmeal a little at a time, letting pot boil up after each addition; crumble in 1 pound pork sausage, stirring to mix well with cornmeal. Add ½ teaspoon each dried thyme and sage and 1 teaspoon of salt. Cover pot and simmer 1½ hours, stirring frequently. Pour into loaf pan and set aside to cool; put in refrigerator for about 3 hours, until loaf is very firm. To serve, cut in slices about ⅓ inch thick and fry in bacon fat over medium heat, until crisp.

had been opened for business at Bethlehem by Moravians in 1758. It was at this roadside tavern that many colonial Americans first tasted such Pennsylvania Dutch specialties as *Schnitz and Knepp*, raisin pie, sauerkraut, *Schmierkäse*, and many kinds of cake previously unfamiliar to Britishers. An eighteenth-century traveler who stopped at the Sun gave a glimpse of what attracted Americans by reporting he was "constantly supplied with venison, moor game, the most delicious red and yellow bellied Trout, the highest flavoured wild strawberries, the most luxurious asparagus, and the best vegetables I ever saw." Clearly, the self-denial that marked the religious precepts of Pennsylvania's Germans did not apply to cooking and eating—fortunately for American gastronomy in general. Recipes that had originated in the German Alps, or in the Rhineland, or in pastoral Alsace evolved often in new directions when the wives of the early German-speaking farmers began to deal with Pennsylvania bounty and to experiment with new ingredients. "Of all the regional cooking styles," according to José Wilson, a frequent commentator on cookery, "perhaps the most enduring and distinctive can be claimed by the Pennsylvania Dutch." More than most who came to the New World in search of religious freedom, they cherished the value of farm produce because in many cases their European enemies had destroyed their crops, cut down their orchards, and dug up their vines in dead of winter to drive them out. Caring about food, they insisted it be cooked with skill just as they devoted themselves to learning ways to use new ingredients in common with the food of the Old World.

"Better a burst stomach than wasted food" is a Pennsylvania Dutch saying that has been current for generations. In the fieldstone houses they built in southeast Pennsylvania, they made kitchens almost invariably the biggest rooms, large enough not only to serve the whole family at enormous meals three times a day, but also to serve as centers of food preservation. They developed techniques for canning vegetables and fruits, and fundamental to Pennsylvania Dutch cooking are recipes for making preserved food taste at least as delicious as the same fruits, vegetables, and meat when fresh. Their use of spices and herbs, as harmonious additives rather than as seasonings to shock the palate, is unlike any other cuisine.

A MORAVIAN COMMUNAL MEAL

Philadelphia, which was already a cosmopolitan and sophisticated community in the eighteenth century, had been swift to appreciate the culinary art of its rural neighbors, and Pennsylvania Dutch scrapple, an aromatic mixture of Indian corn meal and pork scraps formed into a loaf compactly designed for slicing, became essential to a proper Philadephia breakfast menu very early in colonial history. The acceptance by the Quaker city was such that most renditions of this mealy, sausagelike loaf are still known as Philadelphia scrapple, even though much of it is made on the farms or in such Pennsylvania Dutch towns as Reading.

"One wonders," the Pennsylvania historian Frederic Klees once wrote, "how the Philadelphians got along for a whole year—that of 1682—until the Pennsylvania Dutch arrived and gave them scrapple." Firm loaves of sage-and-marjoram-flavored scrapple are sliced thin and broiled, or fried very crisp, as the *pièce de résistance* of a hearty breakfast. Scrapple goes as well with eggs as does bacon or ham, and some Philadelphians insist upon daubing their sizzling, crisply sheathed slices with catsup. Others dress up scrapple with fried sliced apples, or applesauce, and on many Pennsylvania Dutch farms the accent is either maple or brown sugar syrup. At meals other than breakfast, green peppers and cabbages are stuffed with scrapple, potatoes are scalloped with scrapple, and fragrant croquettes are made by combining cooked rice, hard-boiled eggs, freshly minced parsley, and scrapple in an egg batter. Marylanders make their own scrapple from pork sausage and cornmeal, and Cincinnatians substitute oats for cornmeal, while Germans in St. Louis achieve a similar result by combining pork with oatmeal and rice or barley.

Biddle for Breadfast

In the nineteenth century scrapple gained fame not only among Americans but also among foreigners. Edward VII, then prince of Wales and nineteen years of age, made a North American tour that took him from Canada to Washington, where he was entertained by President James Buchanan, the only chief executive to come from Pennsylvania Dutch country. There is no record that scrapple was on the White House menu (Buchanan had established a French cuisine) for the prince, but he undoubtedly sampled scrapple when he visited Philadelphia. The joke is still told—as one of the hoariest in the Philadelphia repertoire—that the prince remarked, "I met a large and interesting family named Scrapple, and I discovered a rather delicious native food they call biddle." Distinguished bearers of the Biddle family name have handled the matter with aplomb.

In any form, scrapple is apt to be a homely dish, even though more nostalgia-inducing than most, and it is one of the gastronomical divertissements from Pennsylvania that turn up in other parts of the country to underscore the German influence. Emigration from Pennsylvania began a score of years before the Revolution, when Moravians from Bethlehem, on the Lehigh river, pulled stakes and moved along the Blue Ridge to a new settlement in North Carolina. Here they made scrapple from pork liver and called it, as often as not, ponhaws (from the German *Pfann Hass*), as it is still sometimes referred to in Pennsylvania.

Wherever Germans migrated, and they traveled singly and in groups to settle in almost every region of the country, they made lasting contributions, adding zest to plain dishes English colonizers had borrowed from the Indians and enlarging the general American repertoire in ways so subtle that few people today may be aware of how many "standard American" ways with food are German in origin. "The Pennsylvania Dutch [style] strongly influenced this trend," J. George Frederick wrote in an informal history, "because in colonial times it was admittedly superior to all cuisines. English cookery has never been competent, and thus in prevailing English background the Pennsylvania Dutch cuisine shone by contrast."

The national appetite for sausages of all kinds began with the founding of Lebanon, home of the smoked beef hard sausages, almost as famous as frankfurters, which originated in Germany but are considered by most Americans to be as indigenous as baseball. Hamburgers were also named for a German city—one in which chopped beef was popular—and pretzels, invented in Alsace, were so accepted by thirsty travelers in Pennsylvania that it is a rare tavern keeper in any state who permits his stock to run out. So it is with cole slaw in many American restaurants. Delicatessen (which contemporary Americans have shortened to "deli") is a German concept, and much of the food to be bought in such places derives from Teutonic tastes.

Pennsylvania Dutch cooks apparently were as swift to make use of spices and subtropic vegetables brought into the crowded docks of eighteenth-century Philadelphia as were others who lived in such ports as Charleston and New Orleans. Like New England housewives, those in Pennsylvania adapted the basic Indian succotash; inhibited by few if any moral attitudes toward food, they enlivened the mixture of corn and beans with green peppers and other vegetables from the West Indies. Thomas Jefferson's interest in the tomato as a source of food failed to influence the average cook until some time after his death, yet tomatoes were also added to succotash by Pennsylvania cooks early in the nineteenth century, and their variation is a vegetable stew that combines sautéed onions, green pepper, fresh tomatoes, and potatoes cubed with corn and lima beans. On farms in southeast Pennsylvania this version of succotash is topped with featherweight dumplings—sometimes made of potatoes, onions, and bread, or of poached liver and beaten eggs.

There is kinship between this mélange of New World vegetables and the North Carolina recipe for Brunswick stew, which, whatever its true origin, is now claimed as the invention of pioneer cooks in every state south of the Mason-Dixon line. Brunswick stew uses all the vegetables of the Pennsylvania succotash, involving also a good many other items as well as endless arguments about whether or not chicken is a poor substitute for the traditional squirrel meat. (Most North Carolina recipes call for both, as well as beef and sometimes veal. After visiting in Mississippi's uplands, however, the New York chef Louis P. De Gouy reported that he was ridiculed there for even mentioning domestic chicken as an acceptable ingredient.) There also are sotto voce debates as to whether or not to borrow the okra that is organic to most gumbo recipes and makes Brunswick stew, after long hours of simmering, as thick as old-fashioned porridge.

Pepper Pot at Valley Forge

Old-fashioned may be as appreciative a way as any for labeling American food that has German antecedents. These recipes reach deep into the past. One more of this lineage is the classic Philadelphia pepper pot. The folklore insists that this thick soup was invented on the spot when provisions were at their lowest during the Continental Army's desperate winter at Valley Forge, in Pennsylvania Dutchland. As Louis De Gouy once fantasized: "General Washington's soldiers were in rags, shoes had worn thin; misery came unrelentingly; food was ever lacking. Cooks made ends meet where there were nothing but ends, and they met just over the starvation line. Soldiers began to think of home. Why stay to starve and die at Valley Forge? Desertions were frequent. The story is that General Washington took matters into his own hands and called for the head chef of all the Revolutionary armed forces. He explained the seriousness of the hour. He demanded a great dish. The chef protested: 'There is nothing , my general, but scraps in the kitchens. There is only tripe—a few hundred pounds, the gift of a nearby butcher. And there are peppercorns, a gift from a Germantown patriot. All the rest is scraps and more scraps.'

"'. . . From nothing,' said General Washington, 'you must create a great dish.' The chef experimented. The tripe was scrubbed, it was simmered tender. Additions went into the big kettles, all the odds and ends of the kitchens. The peppercorns were ground to add fire to the stew. The early darkness came. Great kettles sent up their heart-warming belly-comforting fragrance to the miserable men. The call of the bugle, and men ate their fill of this fortifying dish. Men laughed again . . . they joked: '. . . Bring on the Red Coats!'

"The general called for the chef: '. . . This dish is the stuff of heroes! What is its name?' 'General, I have conceived it, but not called it,' the chef replied, 'but pepper pot would be my humble suggestion, sir.' . . . 'Call it Philadelphia Pepper Pot,' said Washington, 'in honor of your home town.'"

Whether or not George Washington had anything to do with it, this American peppery stew has never had another hometown—even though it no longer is sold from carts pushed by women through Philadelphia's once-narrow streets, their cries piercing the hoary winter cold:

All hot! All hot!
Pepper pot! Pepper pot!
Makes backs strong,
Makes lives long,
All hot! Pepper pot!

Even in the centrally heated twentieth century the aromatic flavor of Philadelphia pepper pot insures this thick ragout a hearty welcome—psychologically, at least—when the winter seems long. It is a dish to line the ribs and soothe any spirit. It may well derive from another dish, Dutch goose, which is tripe that has been stuffed and which retains its popularity among modern Pennsylvania Dutchmen. Farm cooks still prepare Dutch goose by packing a pig's stomach with ground pork or pork sausage mixed with potatoes and the savory herbs of the kitchen garden, or with shredded cabbage mixed with onions, potatoes, and a spice or two such as caraway or cardamom.

J. George Frederick, who had a scholarly interest in American gastron-

Philadelphia Pepper Pot

Wash 2 pounds fresh tripe under running water, then put in pot with water to cover, bring to boil and simmer 7–8 hours, adding boiling water as necessary to keep meat covered, and 1 tsp. salt. Put a meaty veal knuckle in another pot with a bay leaf, 4 or 5 sprigs of parsley, 1 stalk celery with leaves, a green pepper chopped, 1 onion chopped, and 2 carrots sliced; cover with water, bring to boil and simmer 1 hour. Add ½ tsp. salt with ½ teaspoon each of allspice, marjoram, savory, thyme, and crushed whole peppercorns, and continue simmering 1 hour, until veal falls away from bone. Strain, chill, and remove grease. Remove tripe from its broth, adding broth to clear veal stock. Cut tripe in ½ inch squares and add with veal meat to combined stocks. Add 1½ cups diced potatoes, bring to simmering point, and cook until potatoes are tender.

omy, once pointed out that the average Pennsylvania Dutch farm was more isolated than most and therefore had to be more independent of general stores than other rural homes ever were. "For this reason," he wrote, in 1935, "the Pennsylvania Dutch farm from 1700–1900—two full centuries . . . was made into a food factory of amazing scope and range." Frederick's own boyhood in the state persuaded him that German farmers like his grandparents could not stop at mere self-sufficiency; the Pennsylvania *Hausfrau* mastered "a phenomenally wide range of food manufacturing arts" to such an extent that each farm produced a great surplus of prepared food and transported it to markets as far as fifty miles away, "wagonloads of it to sell each week, winter and summer." Describing what he believed to be his grandmother's "genius with food," he boasted that "no conjurer ever pulled rabbits out of a hat with the facility that she exercised with food from May until December, in preparing and producing an endless variety of things to eat."

Her way of life, still followed by many Philadelphia women who haven't succumbed to convenience foods, helps to explain why so much that is good in American culinary achievement was developed in this region. It is the cooking of artisans, artisans devoted to their craft of making the most of ingredients rather than to epicurean finesse. It is not, however, a kind of cooking to suit everyone's taste. Indeed, it has been said that one must be Pennsylvania Dutch to appreciate all of this regional cuisine. Yet there are dozens of dishes that awaken nostalgia when they are mentioned—or when they are served by cooks with Amish, Moravian, or other German or Middle European backgrounds who live in other parts of the country.

A Sufficiency of Soups

I first had chicken and corn soup when visiting a Midwest farm as a youngster, but many people think one must go to the source to taste the real flavor of this all-American pottage. Chicken and corn soup as made in Pennsylvania is a thick combination of pungent bits of simmered chicken with kernels from freshly picked corn and egg noodles rolled out while the saffron-flavored broth is brewing; it brings tourists from far and near to Lancaster County and other parts of Pennsylvania Dutch country for church suppers and outdoor food festivals. The legendary pepper pot of Valley Forge is simply the best known of a parade of soups, thin and thick, that have become part of culinary lore in America.

Of these the typical Pennsylvania chicken and corn soup is made according to a simple formula. As George Frederick once put it: "Boil chicken until tender, remove bones and shred meat; make a smooth dough of one egg and one-and-one-half cups of flour; roll out and cut into dice; score and cut off corn from six ears; put all into the chicken broth and boil together till corn is soft. Serve with popcorn floating on the soup." In Newton, North Carolina, the Blue Ridge Mountains chicken and corn soup that has brought fame to the annual women's guild supper is produced from a recipe members have pledged to keep secret, but it is known that veal is simmered along with the chicken and that rice is added as a thickener. A Virginia variation on the general theme combines veal knuckle with tripe, potatoes, and butter balls and is known locally as pepper pot.

Perhaps the Pennsylvania Dutch have more affinity for soups than others whose work has taken them outdoors, or who, in the days before central heating, had hearty need of food that would help them withstand the cold. The so-called Amish preaching soup is just such a rib-sticking mélange that belongs to the Old Order of House Amish who hold their Sabbath services in various homes and serve this stewlike combination of beans and ham and smoked pork butts during the interval between the two Sunday preachings. The soup is said to fortify both preacher and the gathered faithful.

Diced country ham also gives pungency to a porridgelike dish in which a cup of dried lentils and a half-cup of split peas are soaked before being stirred into flour-thickened chicken stock that is seasoned with a little salt, some freshly ground pepper, sautéed chopped onion, and a quarter-cup of grated carrots. A recipe for mock oyster, or salsify (oyster plant), soup comes from Salisbury, Pennsylvania, and the German version of eel soup in this part of the country is a fragrant purée of eel fillets, small sweet shrimp, veal, parsley and parsley root, carrots, celery, shallots, mushrooms, and accents of cayenne, thyme, laurel, mace, and basil.

There are other soups of the region that are delicate, and one of the best is cream of clam soup, as prepared at a fishing and cooking club, formally organized in 1732 (it calls itself the oldest club in the world). Officially known as the State in Schuylkill, the circle of gentlemen chefs is referred to most familiarly now as the Fish House, from whence sprang the punch that carries that name. The edifice of the "fish house" is a castle on the Delaware, the urban sprawl of Philadelphia having driven the club to abandon the river whose name it bears,[1] and it is the gathering place of members who pretend that the State in Schuylkill (originally the Colony) is an independent government complete with governor, counselors, sheriff, and even a coroner. Never having accepted the Constitution, although it went on record as joining the union in 1781, the club was never troubled by the years of Prohibition that inhibited other states.

Aside from the Schuylkill club's highly alcoholic punch—a mixture of rum, cognac, peach brandy, lemon, and sugar—there is no limit to the kind

Dutch Chicken Corn Soup

Boil chicken until tender, remove bones and shred meat; make a smooth dough of one egg and one and one-half cups of flour; roll out and cut into dice; score and cut off corn from six ears; put all into the chicken broth and boil together till corn is soft. Serve with popcorn floating on the soup.

—George Frederick

[1] Dr. Charles Browne, who served in Congress and as mayor of Princeton, New Jersey, wrote in 1930: "The dining-room or 'Castle' was floated down the Schuylkill on barges and up the Delaware to the new club site, just below Eddington. The deal dining tables, built in 1748, are still in use and have silver plates in them marking the places where Washington and Lafayette dined." Browne himself presided over Princeton's Gun Club whose members, he said, were not stalkers of game and eaters of wild flesh but only shooters of clay birds who loved to cook and eat. In *The Gun Club Book*, which Browne compiled, he noted: "If an army fights upon its stomach (as Napoleon or someone else has said) the arts of peace also depend upon a well-fed nation." His book, he wrote, eschewed any attempt "to describe the alluring confections of the French cuisine"; it deals, in fact, in many things, including "the great American standby, more fixed than the Constitution and less subject to amendments, 'ham and eggs.' "

of cooking done by members when they don their white aprons and mandarin straw boaters. The club's version of pepper pot is made with meat dumplings that combine bread crumbs with minced veal and salt pork flavored with sherry, marjoram, thyme, cloves, and red and black pepper. Fish House terrapin is flavored with Madeira. The Fish House cream of clam soup, as it was prepared by chef John Wagner, gets its distinctive flavor from celery seeds. Seeming never to tire of kitchens, most of the "citizens" of the State in Schuylkill are also members of a junior cooking club known as the Rabbit—not because Welsh rabbit is a specialty but because the original clubhouse was on Rabbit Lane on the Main Line.

As Smooth as Creamed Oysters

Philadelphia food is by no means, of course, exclusively Pennsylvania Dutch, but much emphasis remains on such things as scrapple and cinnamon buns; the city's fare has been decribed by Nathaniel Burt in *The Perennial Philadelphians* as "rich and smooth, as in creamed oysters, chicken or seafood croquettes, white mountain cake and Philadelphia ice cream." Menus are accented by Jerusalem artichokes cooked in milk, then battered and fried in deep hot fat, by sauerkraut simmered with salt pork and caraway seeds, or by goose stuffed with apples, prunes, and slivered almonds. The custom of accompanying each meal of consequence with a multiplicity of relishes and preserved fruits—referred to as "seven sweets and seven sours"—prevails in certain Philadelphia quarters just as it does in Pittsburgh and, of course, in the "Dutch" cities of Reading, Lancaster, Allentown, and Bethlehem.

Dutch Jerusalem Fritters

Boil and mash 10 Jerusalem artichokes, let cool, and then add the yolk of 1 egg. Mold into cakes, dip in flour and fry in butter on a hot griddle.

—Tulpehocken farmwife

Wherever served, such food cannot be taken lightly. Indeed, it has been pointedly said that the average Pennsylvania Dutch menu is so satisfying and generous that "it has little need for some of the time-killers that are used to clutter menus elsewhere." The regional aphorism, "Fill yourself up, clean your plate," expresses a way of life. From beginning to end, from thick soup through meats, pies, cakes, and sweet desserts, dining in Pennsylvania Dutch tradition requires full commitment and an unreluctant appetite.

The pig in all its forms plays a large part in the cookery shaped by this tradition. Pig's knuckles and sauerkraut with Moravian egg dumplings may not sound like a repast for every man, but when tenderly prepared and lovingly seasoned, the combination rouses appetites in Bethlehem and many parts of Pennsylvania. The richly jellied souse is made with pig's feet or sometimes a mixture of veal shin and pork shoulder. Cooks of this region are also justly renowned for their headcheese, and for the variety of their sausage recipes.

Sausage making is so much a part of the American culinary tradition that even the recipe used by Martha Washington is a matter of record. The craft, as practiced by Germanic cooks, was an important function of the "food factory" described by George Frederick. "With meat grinders, large mixing bowls and sausage stuffing machines," he wrote, "my grandparents would produce, before my astounded young eyes, a wide variety of foods, fresh pork sausage, smoked beef and beef sausage, Lebanon style bologna, highly spiced, liverwurst, and a half dozen other wursts. They would smoke hams and slabs of bacon, tongues and other pieces of meat. . . . The bologna, five inches in diameter [from the Pennsylvania town of that name], is probably over-spiced for most tastes, but it is surely appetizing."

Sausage stuffer

True Lebanon sausage, now as then, is made of nothing but coarsely ground beef precured and aged in barrels, then seasoned with sweet herbs and assertive spices, forced into airtight casings, and smoked over smoldering sawdust for a matter of days. For those who applaud the pungent flavor, pieces of Lebanon sausages are frequently dipped in batter, or in egg and bread crumbs, and served with sauerkraut and mashed potatoes, or in a white sauce to accompany flannel cakes. In recent years, as Pennsylvanians have come to absorb the Italian influence on American cooking, these sausages are sometimes diced, mixed with ground beef and tomato sauce, and served over spaghetti or German noodles. Some fans, I was astonished to learn, slice Lebanon sausage as they would cheese and eat it with apple pie.

Yet this idea is not strange at all to the Pennsylvania Dutch. Every one of the dishes in their multicourse meals is put on the table before the diners first sit down, for it is the custom to enjoy a piece of pie with one of the meat courses. And there is almost always more than one meat course. In the old days a Pennsylvania Dutch hotel dining room or restaurant habitually had forty or fifty dishes set out at mealtime; in private homes the tables are laden with a dozen or more, three times a day. It's no accident that the kitchen is almost always the largest room in the house. Of few people on this earth can the platitude be so accurately applied as to these citizens of the Keystone State: They eat to live, and live to eat. "Probably," one of their historians wrote, "it is the superabundance of pork and pie the Dutch have been eating for generations that turns so many of them into walking mountains of flesh." Rudyard Kipling, at the end of the nineteenth century, was enchanted by Pennsylvania Dutch farmers and their "fat cattle, fat women." The way these Americans lived, he wrote, was "as peacefull as Heaven might be if they farmed there."

A Meal Without Pie May Be No Meal at All

Some social chroniclers seem convinced that fruit pies as Americans now know them were invented by the Pennsylvania Dutch. Let's just admit that it's possible. Potters in the southeastern counties of the state were making pie plates early in the eighteenth century, and cooks had begun to envelop with crisp crusts every fruit that grew in the region. "It may be . . ." Frederic Klees asserted, "that during the Revolution men from other colonies came to know this dish in Pennsylvania and carried that knowledge back home to establish pie as the great American dessert. Why not?" Why

Pennsylvania Spiced Cantaloupe

Six pounds of cantaloupe cut as nearly one size as possible, 4 quarts water, 1 ounce alum; bring to boiling point, drop in your fruit, cook 15 minutes, lift and drain a short while. Then take 1 quart of vinegar, 3 pounds white sugar, 3 tsps. yellow mustard seed, 1 tsp. black mustard seed, 1 tsp. whole mace, 8-inch stick of cinnamon, 9 whole cloves, about a dozen whole allspice. Place the fruit in it and slowly cook until clear; requires about 2 hours.

else would there be no fewer than fifty kinds of dessert pies made today by various Pennsylvania Dutch cooks? Along with standard American apple, berry, butterscotch, chocolate, custard, lemon, mince, pumpkin, rhubarb, *et al.*, the Pennsylvania Dutch certainly originated shoofly pie, really a molasses sponge cake baked in a crust. They also make *rosina*, which is a lemony raisin affair that is always baked when someone dies and therefore is called funeral pie. They make Amish half-moon pies, whose other name is "preaching pies," because they are used to thwart the restlessness of children at long Sunday services.

No matter how many such pies are on the table, other sweet things are always served with a Dutch meal. Applesauce, of course, is a standard accompaniment for many pork dishes, and apple butter, claimed as a Pennsylvania invention, is an everyday spread for bread and toast. Perhaps the most famous of all is the dish still known as *Schnitz und Knepp*. Dried apples soaked until they regain their original size, and then cooked with highly flavored ham, are accompanied by steamed dumplings. Smoked or otherwise, pork is seldom considered complete without a cooked fruit to lend contrast to its bland texture and taste.[2]

Chief accents—indeed, the rhetoric—of this eating style are found in that ancient custom known as "seven sweets and seven sours." Meals are not considered authentic unless meats and vegetables are complemented by jellies, jams, honey, ginger pears, spiced peaches, quince chips (to name a few "sweets"), and by briny pepper cabbage, pickled beets, chow-chow, Jerusalem artichokes in cider vinegar, pickled eggs, unripe green tomatoes, or yellow tomatoes, a variety that is fully ripe when its skin turns a golden yellow (to name a few "sours"). In a properly run Pennsylvania Dutch household no table ever fully represented the family hospitality unless it offered fourteen such preserves and condiments to pass from diner to diner.

Spiced cantaloupe, pungent with the aroma of cinnamon and cloves, is prepared according to recipes kept through generations by many families. One heirloom method calls for six pounds of cantaloupe cut into uniform chunks, simmered fifteen minutes in four quarts of water mixed with an ounce of alum. The drained cantaloupe is then cooked in a quart of vinegar combined with three pounds of sugar, three teaspoons of yellow mustard, one teaspoon of black mustard, a teaspoon of mace, a long stick of cinnamon, nine whole cloves, and ten or twelve allspice berries. It is ready to seal in jars after about two hours on the stove. (Some Lancaster County farmwives substitute oil of cinnamon and oil of clove, bought from a local pharmacist, as a means of preventing discoloration.)

Perhaps the early settlers of William Penn's colony had no greater access

[2] "By the by," wrote the British Captain Marryat in his *Diary in America*, "we laugh at the notion of pork and molasses. In the first place, the American pork is far superior to any that we ever salted down; and, in the next, it eats uncommonly well with molasses. I have tasted it, and '*it is a fact.*' After all, why should we eat currant jelly with venison and not allow the Americans the humble imitation of pork and molasses?"

to spices from abroad than their rural neighbors, but they seem to have had a greater penchant for cinnamon in all kinds of cooking—with the use of ginger, nutmeg, cloves, allspice, even cardamom not far behind. In the collection William Penn, Jr., kept of his mother's recipes, the directions "Too make a Brown hasty puding" call for both cinnamon and nutmeg, sugar and rosemary to season a hasty pudding that mixes bread crumbs instead of cornmeal with eggs and milk. After the pudding has boiled thoroughly, it is put in a serving dish; "then take a fire shovel Red hot and hold it close" until the surface browns.

Philadelphia cinnamon buns, or a variation called sticky buns, are breakfast treats as habit-forming in many parts of the country as Danish pastry. Cinnamon bread with raisins is a Philadelphian's notion of what is needed for the kind of toast to start the day right. The glazed cookies known in Pennsylvania as *Zimsterne*, cinnamon stars, are considered by cookie fans as outstanding as homemade ginger snaps. Pennsylvania Dutch cooks held no patent on the use of such spices, but they have been noted by travelers for numerous specialties such as *Ginger Gapickelti Roata Reeva* (pickled beets) and spiced beef pot roast that has languished in a bath seented with ginger and other aromatics.

A Proprietary Zest

Much of the American appetite for sweet rolls and cakes comes from these specific Germans as well as from the Holland settlements that had so much influence on early New York, New Jersey, and Delaware. All of those colonial cooks made fruity, buttery breakfast or coffee cakes from recipes that vary only slightly from methods used in the twentieth century. They also share some of the responsibility for the national zest for doughnuts—as do New Englanders, who may, as some historians suggest, derive their proprietary interest in fried cakes from the years the Mayflower colonists spent in Holland before their landing at Plymouth Rock. Indeed, the National Gallery of Art in Washington, D.C., has a 1627 still life by the Dutch-Spanish artist Juan van der Hamen y León in which are portrayed two doughnuts in every way similar to those considered ideal for dunking.

There have been claims of all kinds about doughnuts, for they are, after all, a part of American folklore. In 1975, the magazine of the Smithsonian Institution in the nation's capital published a report asserting that the first hole in a doughnut was made by Captain Hanson Crockett Gregory, "from the rugged American seacoast community of Rockport, Maine. . . . This fact was established in what was billed as the Great Doughnut Debate held in New York in late November 1941." Presenting affidavits, letters, and other documents, Captain Gregory won the unanimous vote of the judges. "Young Hanson," the report affirmed, "was in the kitchen of his home watching his mother make fried cakes. He asked her why the centers were so soggy. She said that for some reason they never got cooked. Then the boy decided to poke out the center of some uncooked cakes with a fork. His mother cooked them. They were the first (ring) doughnuts. . . . In 1947, a century after the invention of the doughnut, or doughnut hole, whichever you prefer, a bronze tablet was placed on the home where Gregory resided. The inscription on the plaque read: 'In commemoration. This is the birthplace of Captain Hanson Gregory who first invented the hole in the doughnut in 1847. Erected by his friends, November 2, 1947.' "

Small matter how the hole in the round fried cakes was introduced—doughnuts had become an American symbol of creature comfort before World War I, and when a Salvation Army worker in France was inspired to make a batch for the troops "over there," she unwittingly tapped the national sentiment that soon caused soldiers of the American Expeditionary Force to be called "doughboys," a slang word perhaps more loving than was the term GI's that was used in the next war. In any event, the word *doughnut* is said to have been first used in print by Washington Irving in his Knickerbocker stories of Dutch life in New York, where housewives deep-fried cakes called *oly Koeks*, literally "oily cakes." Because fat was forbidden in Pennsylvania Dutch kitchens during Lent, Shrove Tuesday was marked by making *Fasnachts*, the cakes of potato dough fried in boiling pork fat, as a way of using up what might prove tempting during the six weeks before Easter. Traditional *Fasnachts* are diamond-shaped and have no hole, although they are often slit to expose their centers, and they appear, to the delight of the cognoscenti, on breakfast menus in numerous Pennsylvania highway restaurants.

An enterprising eater named Peter Quimme surveyed the doughnut scene in 1976 to find out why doughnuts had remained "a fad that hasn't faded." He reported that "otherwise fussy gourmets crave the wheel-shaped goodies long after giving up all the other junk food they enjoyed in unsophisticated youth. Ask people about the doughnuts in their past, though, and they'll tell you they weren't junk food. The doughnuts they remember . . . were wholesome and bursting with goodness, warm as a country kitchen in a New England winter. . . . There simply aren't any around today as good as you could get back then, I was assured by all I queried."

The extent to which this comment is true lies in the fact that the appetite that makes doughnuts America's most popular pastry in the twentieth century must be satisfied by machines making just another fast food item from commercial mixes. (Annual sales exceed two billion dollars.) Homemade doughnuts are no more difficult to turn out than in 1886, when a recipe was provided by Mrs. Sarah T. Rorer in her *Philadelphia Cook Book*. Mrs. Rorer called for a half-cup of homemade yeast, which could be produced from grated raw potatoes, sugar, and salt, or half a cake of compressed yeast. With a soft dough that was left to rise overnight, her doughnuts were formed by ring cutters of two sizes and fried in melted suet.

The Shape of Things to Come

Once there was a time when no American kitchen was deemed well equipped unless it had metal forms to shape doughnuts and cookies. Even before the use of metal stamps emigrants from Europe brought with them rolling pins and boards whose surfaces were divided into squares with carved indentations in the shapes of birds, animals, flowers, and human figures; cookies so shaped are still known as *Springerles* ("little jumpers") and are still made by Pennsylvania Dutch as well as many other Americans of German lineage. The word *cookie* itself is an American distortion of the Dutch word *koekje*, which means "little cake"; but the concept of small flat cakes the British still call biscuits has developed so greatly on this side of the Atlantic that cookies as we know them are generic to the U.S. cuisine.

So, in a way, is the dessert we call cake, which has changed in dozens of ways since the first Pennsylvania Dutch mixed stone-ground flour and molasses and sugar and eggs and ginger, and baked a *Küchen*. Early settlers from Moravia, Switzerland, and various parts of the old Austro-Hungarian Empire had inherited a proclivity for cooking with spices from generations back when Crusaders brought exotic condiments from the east, when more than one ruler in Central Europe married a Byzantine princess who made cooking with aromatics fashionable. German-speaking cooks developed a deft hand, so to speak, at combining spices with nuts and fruits and, in Pennsylvania particularly, they came upon a richly endowed land. Their men often chose the acres upon which they settled on the sighting of a stand of black walnut trees, knowing that such woods indicated limestone soil that would guarantee rich harvests; they planted orchards of many kinds of fruit along with their other crops. Cakes and other desserts reflected this bounty.

There are Americans in the twentieth century who have yet to be enchanted by the flavor of black walnuts, but throughout Pennsylvania Dutchland—and in Virginia, West Virginia, Tennessee, the Carolinas, and the Midwest especially—lavish black walnut cakes are perennial favorites. Black John cake is of two layers made from dough that blends brown sugar, molasses, eggs, butter, flour, ginger, cinnamon, buttermilk, and baking soda and has a filling accented by raisins, coconut, and black walnut. The magnolia cake of the Moravian community in North Carolina is made with black walnuts in the dough, instead of the frosting, as is also Alyse Kistler's version of Pennsylvania Dutch black walnut Christmas cake.

Nut cakes and nut breads have been common in American cooking in all periods and in all regions. But the so-called fancy cakes that evolved beginning with the first use of pearl ash (pearly hued potassium carbonate) as a leavener added a new quality to New World cooking. Recipes for sponge cakes, which appeared about the same time, go back to the turn of the eighteenth century, and angel (or angel food) cakes, which some believe evolved as the result of numerous egg whites left over after the making of noodles, may or may not be the brainchild of thrifty Pennsylvania cooks who considered it sinful to waste anything.

Mary Emma Showalter, who received her master's degree for a study of Mennonite cooking in America, gathered material from more than a hundred communities scattered across the country, and she came to the conclu-

Dutch Doughnuts, 1740

About twelve o'clock set a little yeast to rise, so as to be ready at five P.M. to mix with the following ingredients: 3¾ pounds of flour, 1 pound of sugar, ½ pound of butter and lard mixed, 1½ pints of milk, 6 eggs, 1 pint raised yeast. Warm the butter, sugar, and milk together, grate a nutmeg in flour, add eggs last. Place in a warm place to rise. If quite light at bedtime, work them down by pressing with the hand. At nine next morning make into small balls with the hand, and place in the centre of each a bit of raisin, citron, and apple chopped fine. Lay on a well-floured pie-board and allow them to rise again. They are frequently ready to boil at two o'clock. In removing them from the board use a knife, well-floured, and just give them a little roll with the hand to make them round. Have the fat boiling, and boil each one five minutes. When cool roll in sifted sugar.

sion that cake recipes held first place in the "old hand-written notebooks that bear dates prior to the Civil War. . . . These cake recipes were not only the first ones recorded in [the average] book, but they occupied the greatest number of pages." Baking powder had become available in this period, and it undoubtedly added impetus to the urge to succeed at cake baking.

For the Lock-up

One of the cakes that appeared in the study, and a recipe that is still popular, came from the Mennonite community in Rockingham County, Virginia; it is called marble cake—because of the swirling contrast of colors in its interior—and the recipe ends with the admonishment: "This cake will not keep unless it is put under lock and key!" Molasses was called for as the darkening agent in the documentary instructions, but most twentieth-century cooks use chocolate to get a similar effect, and they have similar problems keeping a remnant of the cake once it has been tasted.

Although chocolate was first used in cooking by pre-Columbian chefs south of the Rio Grande, it was a Dutchman who developed powdered cocoa and a century later a Swiss who worked out the formula for milk chocolate. Trading vessels from the West Indies brought the cacao bean to American ports not long after the arrival of immigrants from Holland and central Europe. Although the earliest colonial use was almost exclusively in hot drinks, the making of desserts that were chocolate-flavored followed the establishment of the first American chocolate mill in 1765. The production of chocolate in various forms began soon thereafter in Pennsylvania.

Spiced Chocolate

Grate 2 squares of chocolate. Boil 1 quart of milk, reserving a little cold to moisten the chocolate, which must be mixed perfectly smooth to a thin paste. When the milk boils (in which the cinnamon must be put when cold, and boil in it), stir in the chocolate, and let it boil up quickly, then pour into a pitcher, and grate on a little nutmeg. Rich cream added to the milk, will improve it.

—*Miss Beecher's Domestic Receipt Book,* 1848

Much candy, including fudge, with chocolate as the predominating flavor, is made by housewives, and there is a piquant chocolate sauce from Landsdale, Pennsylvania, that combines unsweetened chocolate with sugar and cornstarch to dress up desserts. Chocolate sauce over ice cream has become unbiquitous in America, and in Strathmore, a Philadelphia commuters' town, a chocolate sauce, accented with coarsely chopped butternuts, combines eight ounces of butter and twelve ounces of semisweet chocolate bits, simmered over boiling water, to serve warm over vanilla ice cream.

It's true that no German in Pennsylvania had anything to do with the invention of ice cream, but the record indicates that Philadelphians were among the first Americans to serve a frozen dessert, and that "Philadelphia ice cream" became a standard of excellence. There were vociferous partisans of the Philadelphia recipe in opposition to New York's method, or even to French ice cream with its base of beaten eggs. Writing early in the twentieth century Cornelius Weygandt, a gallant flag waver for the Germanic influences on American food, said flatly that the best ice cream was to be had in the Germantown section and in Philadelphia proper; he nominated Sauter's Ice Cream Parlor on Locust Street opposite the Academy of Music as setting a standard not to be trifled with and pointed to other sources in Bristol, just up the Delaware, Morristown on the Schuylkill, and one among the hex-marked barns of Bucks County.

"The Dutch Cupboard" in Coatesville serves a dessert of Pennsylvania origin that combines a number of flavors. Layers of vanilla cake with chocolate filling are topped by ice cream and butterscotch sauce, an example of gilding the lily in all-too-characteristic American fashion, but the ice cream itself is not to be faulted if it is the genuine old-fashioned Philadelphia kind.

That kind, according to Mrs. Rorer, writing in her *Philadelphia Cook Book*, could be produced in only one way: "To make good Philadelphia ice cream, use only the best materials. Avoid gelatine, arrowroot, or any other thickening substance. Good, pure cream, ripe fruit, or the best canned in winter, and granulated sugar, make a perfect ice cream. Next, get a good freezer, one working with a crank, and double revolving dasher, making a triple motion." She offered details for every step in a careful process of scalding the cream ("when raw cream is frozen . . . [it] has a frozen, snowy taste"), packing the freezer, and ripening the ice cream to blend the flavors. Mrs. Rorer's firmly worded instructions have been modified over the years, but Philadelphia-style ice cream, without eggs, as opposed to that called French, which has a custard base, is still commercially made, with no compromise on the quality of ingredients, including the use of vanilla beans. And Bassett's in the city of its origin is an old-fashioned ice cream parlor serving a product that draws addicts toward it as if it were a minor Mecca.

In Pennsylvania Dutch homes, where pie is served with the meat and at least one cake dresses the table, the final course—for which any hostess would expect one to make room—is a cooked dessert, a pudding, for instance, or sugar dumplings known as comforts. Fruit dumplings are also served, made with peaches, apples, prunes, rhubarb, and frequently topped with vanilla sauce. Dutch puffs, another common dessert, are made of a yeast dough that rises for four hours before being deep fried and flavored with orange. Dumplings, disguised as slumps and grunts in New England parlance, and puddings with British pedigrees are common enough to Yankee cooks, and the cuisine of the South is plentifully supplied with custards. It takes a German-influenced hostess, however, to make a man feel he hasn't really eaten until he's topped off a meal of a dozen separate items with a rich and—let's face it—heavy dessert.

Sarah Rorer was not in favor of such indulgences. Through her cooking classes, her public appearances across the country, and her food columns, she made certain that few people were ignorant of her ideas, about desserts as about almost everything else. She was heard to say: "Under protest I shall make for you some new desserts which I hope none of you will think of imitating. Remember, desserts are both unhealthy and unnecessary as articles of food." Another time she teased her class with: "Desserts of any sort have very little value as food, so my subject today may be classified as a somewhat dubious one." Producing a charlotte russe with chocolate sauce, she would add, "All these things look so good but they are so deadly."

For a woman born in Bucks County, Pennsylvania, this might be judged as brave talk. Surrounded by accomplished Pennsylvania Dutch rural cooks, Mrs. Rorer made no effort to hide her prejudice against German cooking, including the use of salt and vinegar, which are so much a part of the pickling and preserving characteristic of Pennsylvania kitchens since colonial times. "If salt and vinegar will eat away copper," she once asked, "what will it do to the lining of the stomach?"

A Trace of the Germanic

As author and teacher, Mrs. Rorer may have had more national influence than anyone except Fannie Farmer, but she failed in her efforts to minimize the Germanic contributions to the nation's diet. *Gemütlichkeit* came to American cooking when the first emigrants from Holland opened food shops and shared their baking and sausage making with English-speaking neighbors in New York and New Jersey. Over the centuries there has been persistent migration from countries where the language is basically German. Richard Hofstadter pointed out that the path of German settlement during the colonial period can still be traced from Waldeboro, Maine, southward through the New York towns of Herkimer (once the best known of the cheese-making centers), Mannheim, Newburgh, down through Kutztown, Bethlehem, Emmaus, Ephrata, Gettysburg, and Hanover in Pennsylvania, through Hagerstown, Maryland, and Fredericksburg, Virginia, to New Bern in North Carolina, Orangeberg in South Carolina, and New Ebenezer, just north of Savannah, Georgia. In New Amsterdam pork and cabbage was spoken of as *Speck ende kool*, in Pennsylvania as *sauerkraut und shpeck*; roast duck in colonial New Netherlands was served with pork liver dumplings, in Pennsylvania Dutchland liver dumplings still turn a soup into a meal in itself, and roast duck nests on a bed of sauerkraut. German cooks in Old Salem, North Carolina, are also known for their liver dumpling soup. Migrating Pennsylvania Dutch pickle Jerusalem artichokes, or make "cole slaw" with turnips instead of cabbage, paring and grating raw turnips, then pouring over them a dressing made by combining sugar, salt, vinegar, and sour cream. Poppy seed dressing has been a favorite among Texas cooks since Germans settled the hill country around Austin in the 1840s, and a variation of the mixture of poppy seeds and sweetened oil and vinegar is one of the recipes that helped Helen Corbitt, who grew up in Pennsylvania Dutch country, make the Zodiac Room in Dallas the most famous eating place in Texas. (The Corbitt formula appears on page 400.)

Growing up in the Middle West, I spent my first year away from home as a boarder with two German sisters, who lived with a nephew not much older than I in a small farming community. Nothing but dishes the sisters had learned to make as young girls was ever served. We had noodles often, always homemade. Chicken and noodles began with cleaning and plucking of a fat fowl; it was cut in pieces and cooked until tender in water to cover. Meanwhile the noodles were made by mixing three beaten eggs with enough flour to make a stiff dough, which was then rolled out in a thin

Dutch Slaw

Add sugar to vinegar to make sweet sour taste and heat along with a few celery seeds, stirring to dissolve sugar. Do not dilute vinegar. Remove from heat and cool.

Add chopped green pepper and pimiento as desired to chopped or shredded cabbage in a glass jar. Cover with vinegar solution. Put on lid and let it stand. It may be eaten right away but it is better after a day or so.

—Old Salem Cookery

sheet to be sprinkled with flour. The floury sheet was rolled like a jelly roll and cut in thin ribbons. By this time the chicken would be tender and it was removed from its broth to make room for the noodles. The dish was served on a hot platter, with the chicken pieces and the fragrant noodles inundated by a white sauce conjured out of chicken broth, sweet cream from the top of the morning's milk, and a little flour. It was an evening meal that tasted of chicken as chickens used to taste when they were free running and could feed themselves on anything they liked to eat.

On other occasions I remember, we would have a German chicken stew made with celery root—a vegetable new to me. Cut-up pieces from a fat hen were cooked in enough water to cover, along with a small onion, sliced, a carrot, a bay leaf or two, allspice berries, peppercorns, and salt. Perhaps a half hour before the chicken was tender, a couple of cups of diced celery root were added, and finally celery and chicken were covered with their own gravy, slightly thickened, and a heavy dusting of minced parsley and paprika. Another homely dish whose savory memory comes back to me was noodle pie, made with the usual noodles that were layered with leftover pot roast, onions, cut paper thin, sliced tomatoes seasoned with nutmeg, along with a topping of bread crumbs mixed with grated cheese.

Like thousands of others before and since, I fell in love that year with hot potato salad, a specialty of German cooks in many American communities. Neither my wife nor I has yet perfected a recipe to measure up to my young and impossible memories of how that early taste comforted my sensibilities. Yet that knack with potatoes and seasonings points up a central truth: One way to eat well is to have respect for simple ingredients, but to underscore their natural flavors with seasonings that enhance.

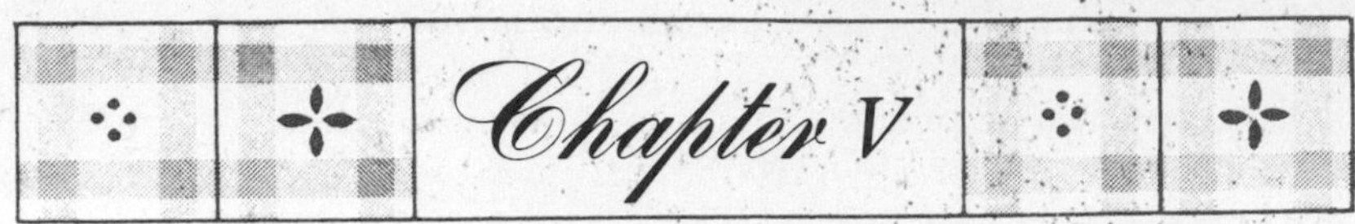

Chapter V

BODY AND SOUL

It is easy enough to find Americans with great nostalgia for the food of childhood. Mark Twain—in Europe and homesick in 1878—said it had been many months since he had had a proper meal, and he wrote out a menu of more than sixty dishes culled from his memory of American kitchens. A half century later Thomas Wolfe sprinkled his novels with his own hunger for good food—any food—but most often for the unpretentious fare of the Carolina hills.

No one, however, has written more eloquently than Ralph Ellison, describing a black youth recently arrived from the South as he chances upon a Harlem street vendor whose specialty is roasted yams: "At home we'd bake them in the hot coals of the fireplace . . . carried them cold to school for lunch; Yes, and we'd loved them candied, or baked in a cobbler, deep-fat fried in a pocket of dough, or roasted with pork and glazed with well-browned fat," Ellison wrote in *Invisible Man*. "I took a bite, finding it as sweet and hot as any I'd ever had, and was overcome by such a surge of homesickness that I turned away to keep my control."

As Ellison's narrator walks along, eating his yam, "the sugary pulp steaming in the cold," his imagination is ignited by thoughts of chitterlings, mustard greens, racks of pig's ears, pork chops, black-eyed peas, hot sweet potato fried pies, and he comes to the realization that he no longer needs to hide his love for his native food.

Twenty years or so after Ellison's book was published, there were few people reluctant to show their enthusiasm for thrifty Southern dishes—a vogue had developed for a distinct branch of American cookery called soul food. Restaurants specializing in black American cuisine were established in white neighborhoods, and cookbooks limited to the subject were issued in large printings by publishers sensitive to the new mood. Soul food, like some contemporary painting, is difficult to explain or analyze but very easy to enjoy. While it may not have made as deep a mark on the national consciousness as did the music given the same label, there developed the realization that soul food was as much a factor to be considered in American regional cookery as any other.

There is no dictionary definition of the term that is wholly satisfactory. Generally, *soul* is used by blacks to imply a naturalness of expression, an openness to life and one's fellows, a sharing of common sorrows, common joys. As there is a lack of inhibition in soul music, there is an absence of snobbishness about ingredients that comprise the basis of soul food. Described by a black restaurateur in historic and sociological terms, soul food evolved from the restricted cooking made necessary by the environment in which Southern blacks lived. Some of the favorite dishes of American blacks are such simply prepared, unsophisticated foods as collards and kale and turnip tops (and the wild greens that all American pioneers often depended upon), as well as the remains of pig meat considered not choice enough for the "big house" on plantations.

The percentage of slaves who were taught to cook in a European style is slight in comparison to the number of black women who were forced to make do for their families—especially in the economic debacle that followed the defeat of the Confederacy—with roots, beans, fish, opossums, and other wild animals. Yet the food that was prepared in the fields or in slave quarters, regardless of the raw materials, had its own style and flavor because the same food had been cooked for generations in Africa. Although field workers were often given nothing but cornmeal or hominy for their midday sustenance, and they were forced to make it edible by boiling it over fires they had to keep alive while they continued to work, the resulting porridges were produced in familiar ways. Corn was only one of the New World foods taken to Africa by traders and explorers, and it had become a staple in the diet of ancestors of most slaves. Dishes combining corn with native African ingredients were easily adapted by blacks in America.

"Soul food, black folk cooking," wrote Pamela Strobel, proprietor of a New York restaurant, "is compassion food"; and she added that the appetite for dishes that have earned the description is sufficiently related "to honest-to-God hunger to impart to food a savor deep enough for joy and solace." The savor comes as a result of combining ingredients that often contrast with one another in flavor or which are complementary—as in the way fat meats are balanced by astringent greens.

Thrifty as the Dutch

There are those who assert that soul food has evolved with little or no European influence. In fact it differs less from other styles of cooking than does jazz from its African and Continental roots. The black musician has not refrained from appropriating (as does all music) the best of certain previous styles, but black cooks were thwarted by a limited range of foodstuffs upon which to draw. To feed themselves, former slaves and their descendants had to learn to be even more frugal than the thrifty Pennsylvania Dutch. Indeed, their appreciation of beans and other plain vegetables and their ways with offal—scorned by some more affluent kitchens—is akin to that of Germanic cooks who moved south through the Valley of Virginia. Again like jazz, which has borrowed rhythmic influences from middle-European gypsy tempos, soul food has echoed Central Europe's way with pig's feet and sauerkraut, adding the accents of African heritage.

Soul food has traveled throughout North America, maintaining its basic integrity. Even in those urban areas where there are no gardens and no wild vegetation within many leagues supermarkets provide frozen greens and black-eyed peas, canned hominy, pork ribs and backbones, hocks and chitterlings.[1] Much of the home-cooked food in Watts is the same as that in the South Bronx or Washington, D.C. In a memoir of childhood in southern Arkansas, Maya Angelou said that the Sunday morning breakfast—a periodic feast—consisted of, among other things, "yellow hominy and crisp perch fried so hard we would pop them in our mouths and chew bones, fins and all."

The cuisine of black cooks when preparing meals for themselves has been described as "full and rich in tastes. What is bland becomes exciting by the addition of our spices—garlic, pepper, bay leaf—hot pepper sauce, either from the West Indies or Louisiana. As a result, we developed a virtuosity in converting chitterlings, ham hocks, and hog maws into some of our most flavorful dishes."

The Importance of Using Pepper

Any palate conditioned in Africa or the West Indies is more than likely to have tolerance for the hottest of spices. An Alabama catfish sandwich begins with bread rolls that are scooped out and toasted, then spread with a mixture of Tabasco, mustard, tomato catsup, and onion slices to make a bed for deep-fried fillets of fresh catfish still sizzling from the hot oil. A proper catfish stew is seldom served by a black hostess without a liberal lacing of Tabasco or sprinklings of cayenne or other red pepper; the tame English-oriented codfish cakes were long ago transformed by slave cooks when the bland basic mixture was lifted out of its rut by seasoning with vinegar, two kinds of peppercorns, and herbs picked wild or from the kitchen garden.

When soul cooks make their versions of souse, or jellied pork, they add

[1] In 1972 James A. Beard wrote in his syndicated column on food: "Chitterlings are the small intestines of the pig and are considered a great delicacy in the South when cooked and served with turnip greens or black-eyed peas. . . . However they are done, they are a welcome change and resemble many European dishes made with the same ingredient. They are as old as history and not entirely exclusive to the South. . . . Recently I stopped at a huge shop in Los Angeles advertising 'Buckets of Chitlin's.' They were wonderful. You can eat them there in the garden or you can literally carry away paper buckets of them."

red pepper with a generous hand; they boil pig's feet until the meat is very tender, pulling it away from the bones and chopping it before forming it into a spicy gelatinous loaf. Their sage-heady sausage is teeming with minced hot pepper pods or seeds. One of their ways with lamb kidneys is to slice and sauté them with onions and deck them with red-peppery gravy in which dumplings are simmered. They make a hog maw salad flavored with celery and green pepper that is so esoteric it is sometimes taken for chicken salad. The spicy touch may have developed as an antidote for the blues, but it certainly is also a vestige of cooking indigenous to much of Africa.

The South owes its penchant for hot sauces to the women in its kitchens who retained a memory of African seasoning. In introducing the surprise of peppery accents to ordinary dishes they sometimes helped to establish new plantation customs. Harriet Ross Colquitt described a way of serving okra soup in antebellum days, when black cooks had their own kitchen dooryard garden patches. "The ritual of the bird's-eye pepper is still observed in the old-fashioned households where the soup comes on steaming in the big tureen, and the host serves it at the table. He asks each guest if he will have one or two of the little green peppers which are picked fresh just before the meal, and he mashes it (or them, if the guest has a hardy palate) in the plate before putting in the soup, so that it permeates the dish. But woe be to the guest who fails to remove the innocent looking little green condiment, for its trail is hot enough for the 'highest' taste, and a touch of the pepper itself is purgatory undiluted."

Along the Ogeechee River in Georgia blacks for generations harvested limes believed to have been first planted by Spanish settlers, and used them in condiments for meat and game. In Key West a native sauce called "Old Sour" is the result of pickling bird's-eye, or datil, peppers, or *chiles piquin*, in lime juice; it is the prevalent seasoning for seafood. Since the seventeenth century, when Captain John Thurber brought the first rice from Africa to South Carolina, plain boiled rice has been as important to Southern kitchens as hominy or grits; and among black cooks rice is considered essential in a variety of soul food dishes, from fluffy rice waffles to "dirty rice," sautéed in peanut oil and combined with minced cooked giblets, onions, celery, and nuts.

Fat for deep-frying fish, meats, and vegetables was rarely difficult for blacks to come by—there was always plenty of lard to be had from their rations of low-grade pig meat. And the cooking style that called for a large pot full of bubbling grease in which various foods might sizzle had been a common African heritage. In tropical regions where there had been no pigs before the European conquest palm oil was habitually used for cooking diced yams, okra, sweet potato leaves, fried rounds of bananas or plantains; so palm oil served African cooks who dipped whole mullet or fillets of shad in cornmeal to be served hot and crackling after frying.

In America catfish, especially, and butterfish, haddock, trout—the catch brought home from the nearest fishing waters—was also cleaned, lightly coated with meal, lowered carefully into a heavy pot filled to within three

Hog Maw Salad

Cook 4 pounds hog maws in salted boiling water about 4 hours, until tender. Remove fat and chop finely. Mix with 1½ cups chopped celery, 1 green pepper chopped, 2 medium onions chopped and 2 cups mayonnaise and season to taste with salt and pepper.

inches of the top with fat hot enough to brown a cube of bread in thirty seconds; in slave quarters such crusty morsels of fish were often eaten sprinkled with cider vinegar highly seasoned with hot pepper.[2] Again, the taste for spices that seem to singe the taste buds was brought to the cooking style of the South from Africa. As a Yoruba proverb has it: "The man who eats no pepper is weak, for pepper is the staff of life."

The Peanut's Progress in America

The Chinese may have been the first to press oil from peanuts, but peanut oil is so commonly used in Africa that it is second only to the orangey-red oil extracted from the palm nut; some black cooks mix it with paprika to give dishes the characteristic color. Only a small percentage of peanuts grown in America is used for oil, and part of the reason for that may be that a black agricultural scientist, George Washington Carver, discovered so many other ways of turning peanuts into a profitable crop for blacks and other farmers in the South. Among the more than three hundred uses for peanuts and their by-products developed by Carver were such boons to the food world as synthetic cheese, coffee, and flour. Enterprising women in the kitchen, without academic help, discovered that pies, cakes, and other desserts as well as candies could be produced when peanuts were at hand, and in 1904 at the World's Fair in St. Louis peanut butter was introduced as a health food.

The sandwich spread that seems so incontrovertibly American is essentially nothing other than ground peanuts, although when purchased in commercial form it usually contains a stabilizer to prevent the oil from separating as well as some added amino acid components not present in the nut itself. A more pleasing version can be made by grinding two cups of dry-roasted peanuts in a blender, adding, a little at a time, about a half-cup of vegetable oil; when the nuts are evenly ground, add a touch of sugar and salt to taste. Soups that begin with peanuts thus ground are daily fare in every African country, and adaptations of the basic recipes have been made in America for hundreds of years.

In her study of Southern food published by the University of North Carolina Press Marion Brown has said that "peanut soup is to Virginia what white bean soup is to Boston." It comes in many styles. "When one does not use meat," as one early-nineteenth-century recipe puts it, "an excellent soup can be made using peanuts as a base." The ingredients, including the addition of tomatoes, correspond with those that African cooks employ. Tuskegee soup takes its name from Tuskegee Institute, the university at which Dr. Carver taught, and is a highly sophisticated bisque so subtle in the blend of its flavors that diners seldom find it easy to define. It begins

[2] Describing twentieth-century plantation life, Lillian Heinsohn seemed unwarrantedly surprised to learn "that not only did our colored people love to fish, but that along about March or April an absolute compulsion for fishing seems to seize them. It's almost like a disease . . . 'catfish fever.' It occurs with unfailing regularity."

with the sautéeing of four or five minced scallions in about three tablespoons of butter; after blending in a like amount of flour, the cook stirs in a half-cup of peanut butter, then adds two cups of chicken stock off heat, stirring well and letting the mixture thicken. Into this smooth soup, a half-cup of cream is mixed along with the juice from a quart of oysters and salt, cayenne pepper, and savory to taste. The soup is finished with two to three tablespoons of sherry, a sprinkling of parsley, and the addition of the oysters about three minutes before it is time to serve.

Tuskegee Soup

Sauté 4 or 5 minced scallions in fat 2–3 minutes, then stir in ½ cup of peanut butter and 3 tablespoons of flour, blending until smooth. Off heat, blend in 2 cups of chicken stock, return to heat and let mixture thicken. Add ½ cup cream and juice from 1 quart of oysters. Season with salt, cayenne and savory, and 2–3 Tbs sherry. Add oysters and let them get hot. Sprinkle each bowl with parsley.

In his years at Tuskegee, Dr. Carver introduced to the dining hall kitchens various neglected natural foods including dandelion greens, chicory, watercress, and pepper grass. To prove how versatile a food the peanut could be, he once whipped up a nine-course lunch for some local businessmen in which everything was created from peanuts: soup, a "chicken" dish, bread, salad, peanuts as a vegetable, ice cream, candy, cookies, and coffee.

Even without his encouragement, the inventiveness of soul cooks goes far beyond the use of peanuts in sandwiches and snacks, far beyond the substitution of peanuts for pecans in the Southland's favorite of all pies. One fertile culinary mind, influenced consciously or otherwise by her African background, was responsible for a dish called "Kay's Yam Peanut Thing," in which equal parts of chopped peanuts and mashed yams (or sweet potatoes) are mixed with eggs, crumbs, and seasonings, formed into small cakes, and stippled with shredded coconut, then fried in deep fat. In Africa peanuts fresh from the garden are served as a vegetable, and in this country soul cooks often prepare dried or roasted peanuts in a cream sauce. Tender young peanuts—or goobers, as Carolinians call them—are shelled, boiled in salted water, and stirred into a creamy white sauce when they have been thoroughly drained. "It is a dish," a Blue Ridge journalist once wrote, "for all the world like creamed chestnuts." Another cream sauce, into which peanut butter is mixed, has devotees who use it as a garnish for steamed cauliflower, cabbage, or onions. Raw peanuts taste like peas; when boiled they are mild of flavor, and their flavor and color become more developed when the nuts are roasted. When George Washington Carver perfected the sauce he called "peanut gravy," he declared it to be "one of the most delicious and economical gravies I have ever eaten."

Aficionados of the peanut recognize few limits. "The fillip of peanut butter spread on barbecued fresh green corn," an affluent sportsman wrote after a sortie with black hunters in the Carolina mountains, "is a touch of genius." More interesting in flavor than spinach salad with crumbled bacon is a "mess o' greens," kale or collards, for instance, seasoned with chopped onions and ground, freshly roasted peanuts. To serve greens in this manner, you need only to cook a package of frozen spinach according to directions, adding a cup of chopped onions that have been sautéed lightly in oil, along with about four tablespoons of peanut bits. Similarly, peanut-flavored boiled dressings are used on fruit salads. And double-roasted peanuts mixed with onions, corn bread, melted butter, and wine accent just one of the innovative stuffings for goose, duck, or other poultry devised by black cooks. They also bake peanut butter bread, biscuits, muffins, and a tasty vegetarian loaf that combines carrots, tomatoes, and peanuts in equal parts. A recipe for sweet potato and peanut croquettes calls for a cup of finely ground parched peanuts to be combined with one cup of mashed sweet potatoes, a tablespoon of flour, and cayenne pepper and salt to taste; the mixture is shaped into croquettes, rolled in bread crumbs, beaten egg, and another coat of crumbs, and is fried in deep fat. (A more basic combination of sweet potatoes and nuts has been credited to American Indian cooks, who baked the sweet potatoes until soft, split them, and filled the opening with flakes of hazelnuts that had been roasted.) The inventiveness of black cooks includes peanut candies, cakes, and other desserts almost too numerous to mention.

Like Arabian Nights

Sesame seeds were not unknown to cooks with European backgrounds, yet South Carolina, and Charleston in particular, developed a proprietary interest because of a local tradition that slaves brought the seeds under a different name (in the Mandingo country on the upper Niger river the plant is known as benne) and used them in their native cooking. The same mystic power invoked by Ali Baba to open the cave of jewels was attached to benne seeds by old slaves who planted sesame in their gardens and sprinkled their doorsteps with seeds to bring luck to the house and to ward off ants. A story that may be apocryphal makes a poignant picture: Slaves hoeing cotton dropped benne seeds at the end of each row of their masters' crops, thus making a border of their own plants from the grains they had smuggled away from Africa.

As Middle Eastern cooks do to make *tahini*, slaves in the Carolina Low Country pounded benne into a paste and mixed it into hominy, knowing instinctively that it added nourishment because it is high in protein. They combined oysters and benne seeds, instead of peanuts, to make a cream soup. In Charleston's twentieth-century cuisine one of the subtly spirited ways of serving chicken recipes suggests shaking pieces in a bag to coat with a mixture of benne seeds, flour, grated orange peel, and seasonings; another South Carolina recipe from the days of slavery coats chicken breasts with grape preserves accented with cayenne and then sprinkled with benne seeds. Oozing with juices after grilling in the broiler, this is served with wedges of hot corn bread.

Sesame catfish is, for true believers, at least as good a dish. For dressed and skinned fish you make a sauce of a half-cup of melted fat, a half-cup of benne seeds, four tablespoons of lemon juice, a teaspoon of salt and a grind or two of peppercorns. Put the fish in greased hinged wire grills, and combine the sesame and other ingredients. Use this sauce to baste the catfish, and grill them about eight minutes over moderately hot coals; turn and continue, grilling other side eight to ten minutes.

The most common soul food ways with benne seeds, however, include various recipes for cookies and one or two for candy, and they come close to serving as trademarks for Charleston. Benne seed cookies (called good-luck cookies up the coast at Myrtle Beach) are wafer thin and the result of combining brown sugar with flour, eggs, butter, and seasonings. In Mount Pleasant, just across the bridge from Charleston, cooks devised an icebox version. And a recipe that found its finishing touches as far north as Winston-Salem uses no eggs but tempers the granulated sugar content with corn syrup. Benne seed candy, as made in Savannah (and once was peddled on the streets by bandannaed vendors) is based on equally simple formulas requiring no flour.

In hard times when candy was made in the kitchens of blacks it was set aside for sale to whites. In Charlottesville, Virginia, one day in conversation a local housewife named Annie Hale told of having candy only when her father paid his bill at the country store. Each month he'd buy a bag for the children and, as it worked out, there would be one piece a night for a week for each child. Growing up on a small farm in the Piedmont, Annie Hale nurtured her sweet tooth on fruits, wild and domestic, fresh from the branches or transformed into cobblers "from all the fruits you could name." From small, dark wild grapes called coon grapes because, Mrs. Hale said, "you had to reach so high to get them," the family made both a sweet wine and the wine jelly so characteristic of the South. And they put up preserves from blackberries, dewberries, huckleberries, apples—and peaches that grew from the seed her father had planted.

One of the simplest of fruit desserts contrived in the Piedmont is called Virginia fried peaches. It is nothing more than fresh pared peaches, cut in half and simmered in butter with brown sugar melting in their hollows; when the peach halves are tender and drooling with thick sugary syrup, they are served with homemade vanilla ice cream. In seasons when nature seemed less generous, black cooks might turn out turnip pies. The fillings combined three cups of cooked mashed turnips, brown sugar, a touch of salt, ginger, cinnamon, nutmeg, and ground cloves with two eggs beaten into a little milk and cream. The result is a rustic dessert equally satisfying but interestingly different in flavor from those based on sweet potatoes or squash.

Owning the land they farmed made little difference in the soul food character of Annie Hale's family diet. From the garden came butter beans, pinto beans, black-eyed peas—to be eaten fresh or canned for winter. Cabbages and turnips were cooked all day, Annie said, with a piece of salted side meat or shoulder. "The turnips would turn real brown," she remembered, "and we'd thicken the stew with flour so it was like gravy." Long, slow cooking was the secret. "We boiled chitlins three hours, then dipped them in flour batter and fried them. We boiled pig's ears until they were tender.[3] We boiled down our own lard, and with the cracklings that were

[3] Delicacies like pig's ears are expensive in regions where good cooks have worked out appetizing recipes. In France, for instance, pig's ears may be served as a first course, or as a treat for the family, allowing one per person. For a simple stew of pig's ears and pig's feet,

Soul Puddin'

Sift 2 cups cake flour, 2 tsps. baking powder, ½ teaspoon salt. Cream 3 Tbs. margarine, gradually adding 1 cup sugar to make a very smooth mixture. Add alternately flour and 1 cup milk, a little at a time; beat after each addition until smooth, adding ½ teaspoon vanilla with last of milk. Pour into 8 by 8-inch rectangular pan and bake at 350° about 1 hour. Serve hot with chocolate sauce.

left we made crackling bread." When sheep were killed anywhere in that part of the Piedmont, Annie's family sometimes got head and neck bones; they were a welcome change from pork and chicken. Raising their own poultry, the family sometimes had fried chicken and gravy, with rolls, for Sunday breakfast, and fried chicken again the same evening. They made their own sausage—"with sage," Annie said, "black and red pepper, salt—the crumbly kind. They were kept by wrapping the sausage in corn husks, packing them in cheesecloth bags, and hanging them. They'd get a little moldy but they never spoiled."

Among the dishes prepared by black cooks that have been classics since Martha Washington presided at Mount Vernon is liver pudding—so basic it was as common in kitchens such as Annie Hale's as on plantation dining tables, and was another way of creating a delectable food while making thrifty use of pork. Liver pudding is produced by long, slow simmering of equal parts of pig's liver and pig's jowl with onion, salt, and pepper, then coarsely grinding the meat with the onion. The mixture is made quite thin by the addition of two cups of the broth in which the pork was simmered, is seasoned with freshly chopped sage and more salt and pepper, and then is baked about two and a half hours at 275°F. in a casserole. After chilling in a refrigerator, liver pudding is sliced and served cold, like pâté.

Food as Celebration

When Annie Hale was growing up, she said, there were nine kids. "Everybody chipped in and we loved doing that." Like most youngsters in large households, she learned to cook by osmosis. She learned to make pancakes with cornmeal, to eat with liver pudding or fried sausage meat. Her mother, she remembered, made batter bread with buttermilk in a hot oven and "would cut it up like brownies." Buckwheat cakes were made up the night before. "They rise in the bowl like something spoiled, but you just pushed it down and when they fried—my goodness, they was good. Sometimes there was sorghum molasses to go with." Naturally the biggest meal of the year was on Christmas Day, the only time ham appeared on the table. With it would be baked spareribs that had been salted down, sliced sweet potatoes that gave off a great scent of nutmeg, yeast rolls made with precious white flour; there would also invariably be four cakes: caramel, chocolate, plain, and coconut, not just for the family but for the neighbors who stopped in for a taste and for a drop of homemade wine.

There are fewer such self-sufficient farms left in the South than in some other parts of the country, and most soul food cooking has become depen-

---

soak the ears overnight in brine before simmering with vegetables until tender. Broiled pig's ears are also cherished by connoisseurs of good food. Put them in a pot, add some vegetables, herbs, salt, pepper, and warm stock to cover; simmer about an hour. Drain, cut the ears in two pieces, brush with melted butter, and spread with fresh bread crumbs pressed on firmly. Sprinkle with more butter and broil. When brown and crisp, serve with Cajun mustard and mashed white potatoes.

dent on the distribution policies of supermarkets. Yet pork is still the basic meat, and greens or beans steaming in a pot are as likely as not to be among the numerous dishes at weekend soul food parties that continue to demonstrate the penchant of blacks for hospitality. It is a custom that comes, according to Ruth Gaskins, a local food historian of Alexandria, Virginia, "from back in the days when we were slaves. For over two hundred years we were told where to live and where to work. We were given husbands, and we made children, and all these things could be taken away from us. The only real comfort came at the end of the day, when we took either the food that we were given, or the food we raised, or the food we caught, and we put it in the pot, and we sat with our own kind and talked and sang and ate."

Often the cooking could be started only when darkness had come and the day's work in the fields had been finished. Instead of collapsing from fatigue, black women found new strength when they poked up the fire, or in later years of tenant farming turned on kerosene or primitive gas stoves. To be able to cook and feed children and friends was more often than not one of the few real pleasures that black families could share. It was also, for many not gifted as professional performers, a way to exercise creative urges, uninspiring as the material available might seem. Mostly, it was a way of feeling free.

A black woman in one Southern community gained fame locally for celebrating the year-end holidays by crowding a buffet table with every dish she possessed that would hold food. All those dishes were kept filled from Christmas Eve until New Year's Day with corn-bread-stuffed turkey and giblet gravy, country ham, fried chicken, collard greens, sweet peas, sweet potatoes, corn pudding, potato salad, lettuce and tomatoes, biscuits, rolls, corn bread, cranberry sauce, pickles, homemade relish, apple, pumpkin and sweet potato pies, caramel and chocolate cake, fruit cakes and pound cakes, cookies, and eggnogs. Through her house, during those days, there was always a constant stream of friends, and strangers, too.

There must be very few black people who think a formal excuse is needed for an open-house gathering. "No matter what his age," Ruth Gaskin wrote without too much exaggeration, "every Negro gives himself a birthday party. It usually starts at nine and ends when someone happens to notice the sun is coming up." It actually begins with a decision about food, she said. "If my birthday falls on a weekend I could spend the day cooking and cleaning chitterlings. If it comes on a week night I could spend the night before frying chicken." It seems apparent that the important thing is to invest the occasion with enough soul to make a lot of people happy. Soul food cooks say that the table for a Saturday night party or for a Sunday dinner is distinguished not so much by what things cost, or how fancy the recipes are, but by the bounty of simple food. "In fact," one of them said, "the foods that are typical of soul food are especially suitable for cooking in quantity—one-pot meals of soups, stews, gumbos, and beans."

Brunswick Stew, Marsh Rabbits, and Barbecue

Catfish stew with a strong accent of onions, tomatoes, and hot red pepper sauce for centuries was as popular among Southern blacks as was catfish briskly fried in cornmeal. Many cooks preferred a version of Brunswick stew in which a pig's head, or tails, ears, feet, and hocks simmer with beans, tomatoes, hot peppers, and corn. Others, however, insisted upon what they considered to be authenticity. "One thing about Brunswick stew," a woman told her daughter, who was collecting recipes, "it's a pretty pale imitation if it hasn't got squirrel. In other words, if it ain't got squirrel, it ain't got soul." (A black Virginia cook is said to have established this rule in 1828.)

Squirrel pie has got soul in good measure when the meat is simmered with celery, onions, seasoned with both black and red pepper, then baked between layers of hard-boiled eggs in a pie shell. Squirrel is sometimes fricasseed and is considered a festive meal when served with grits, hot biscuits, and honey. For frying, a good cook would prefer rabbit to squirrel, and the result is apt to be as tender and delicate as Southern fried chicken.

Well into the twentieth century in the rural South, a possum hunt remained a favorite cold-weather sport, and roast possum and sweet potatoes was always cause for celebration. Sometimes the cleaned and dressed possum simmered with garlic, thyme, allspice, cloves, laurel, parsley, celery, salt, and red pepper until very tender, then went into the oven with the potatoes or yams cut in slices and flavored with lemon.

A soul food cook could always do similar things to raccoon, and in South Carolina and Georgia particularly some of the soul brothers who hunt bring back from an autumn trek along coastal creeks and inlets braces of marsh hens. These birds are traditionally skinned rather than picked and are kept under refrigeration for a couple of days before cooking, sometimes in deep fat. "Marsh rabbit" is an Eastern Shore euphemism for muskrat, a fine-flavored meat that, after marinating overnight, is coated with flour and fried, then served up with currant jelly and beaten biscuits.

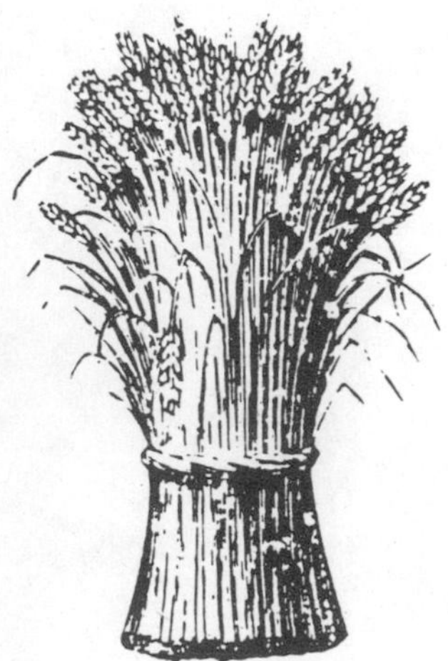

True beaten biscuits are made without leavening of any kind, and they have the virtue of keeping absolutely fresh for at least a week, although they are never either tender or light. They are about the size of a half-dollar and only about a quarter of an inch thick. In texture and taste they are a cross between a soda cracker and an ordinary biscuit. Traditionally the dough—a mixture of winter wheat flour, salt, leaf lard, and ice water—was wrapped by the black cook in a clean towel and beaten mercilessly with a hatchet, flat iron, hardwood stick, or rolling pin. In Maryland, according to old-timers, one could tell when it was eight A.M. by the sound of beaters thumping into dough—long enough for the biscuit mixture to snap and crackle (it must blister, they say) before the paste was shaped into small rounds to be pricked on top with the tines of a fork. In plantation parlors beaten biscuits were frequently proudly served with sherry or port, but it was at least as common, considering the effort involved, to reserve the production of beaten biscuits for occasions when special meats were on the menu.

Perhaps no Americans know more than skilled blacks about the cooking of wild game for festive meals, or, for that matter, the barbecuing of meat of any kind. "When we think of barbecue and soul together," Pearl Bowser and Joan Eckstein wrote in their book *A Pinch of Soul*, "ribs are what come to mind." Seldom able when cooking for themselves to get their hands on so-called luxury meats, "few of our grandparents indulged in a whole pig or side of beef cooked on an open fire," these writers pointed out. Yet techniques were perfected when slaves did the indoor and outdoor cooking for their white families. Small black boys kept the spit turning in the enormous fireplaces of colonial houses, and some of them became specialists at outdoor cooking when they grew up.

Bob Jeffries, who began cooking on an Alabama farm and who became a caterer and *chef de cuisine* in New York, put on paper his memory of what he called a "true" barbecue: "Back home we used hickory logs . . . and when the coals were just right to lay the chicken or ribs on, you could smell the fragrance for miles around." The meats, he said, were carefully arranged, "close together on the grill so that the smoke was trapped under them and not lost in the air. The fats will drip down into the hot ash and steam back up into the meat which also adds flavor."

The Jeffries instructions for barbecuing T-bone steaks begin: "Rub each steak with confectioner's sugar (no, you are not going to be eating a sweet steak, so read on before you decide this is not for you.)" He made gashes close to the bone to insert garlic slivers and let the meat absorb room temperature until the dissolved sugar glistened on the surface. At six inches from very hot coals the surface was turned into a dark crust in about one minute for each side; the juices were sealed in while the steaks continued to cook.

Most barbecue sauces that permeate the surfaces of soul food spareribs, beef, or chicken are devised with a base of tomato catsup; they're really not much different from commercial sauces. Pamela Strobel, however, puts together a sweet-and-sour mixture she calls "Sauce Beautiful," which includes peach preserves, sugar, lemon, vinegar, paprika, oil, and commercial steak sauce. It has been served to restaurant patrons on baked ribs and over chicken dipped in egg and coated with seasoned flour and cornmeal. A more traditional formula, used by the black cook at a plantation on the Georgia-Florida border, calls for spiced peaches to accompany fried chicken seasoned with cinnamon. For barbecued spareribs, an inspired amateur cook added to the soul food style a few flourishes he had learned from observing the preparation of ribs in Chinese kitchens: "I used honey instead of sugar, which the Chinese prefer, because of its more exciting texture and flavor," he wrote. He also added a hot sauce from Jamaica because "it contains the flavor of tropical fruits," disclaiming any intention

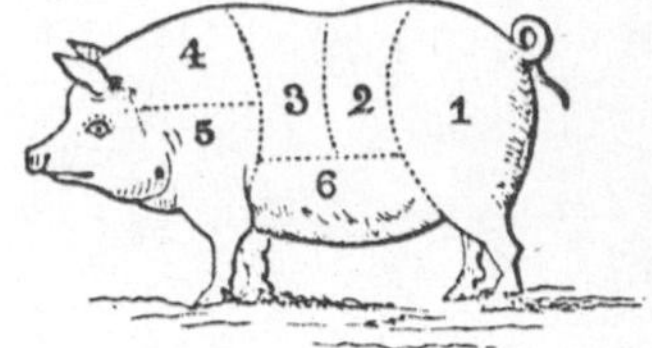

of making "a really hot barbecue sauce, but only a suggestion of it." The dominant fruit in this recipe is diced pineapple, added along with a jigger of Cointreau just before serving.

Perhaps it is obvious that there should be likenesses between soul food and that of the more affluent South. There are records to indicate that many recipes were written down by mistresses of plantations in an era when slaves who had not been taught to read or write were nevertheless inventive. The authors of *A Pinch of Soul* touched the heart of the matter when they wrote, "We had to rely on momma's and grandma's experience and what we could learn by watching as they went about their chores in the kitchen. The advantage of learning at grandmother's elbow is discovering things which are not in any book." Their conclusion was that the unsung, unrecorded soul food cook deserved as much praise as did any of her creations.

Soul in the Southern Repertoire

Just as it has been true that much of the soul food knack was never written down, there are also some records that prove that dishes now considered standard in the southern repertoire evolved from the black cook's skill at improvising. Marion Brown, in her *Southern Cookbook*, published a recipe she copied verbatim, she reported, from "a faded little copybook of penciled recipes" that she found on a Raleigh, North Carolina, plantation: "7 cup chicken, 2 quort creem. Make creem dressing 1 tablespoon to each cup, 5 pound mushroomes, 2½ cup celery, 1 green pepper, 1 tablespoon salt in creem dressing, 1 stick butter in creem dressing, 1 stick in mushroomes." Mrs. Brown offered this, she said, because "I have discovered some rich old recipes created by Negro cooks."[4]

Other documentary examples are not hard to find. Slave cooks adapted the tradition of simmering turnip and other greens with hog jowl, developing variations drawn from their African backgrounds. One of these, called "herb gumbo," is the recipe of a woman who served as cook for forty years in the same family. As recorded by her mistress, it incorporates fresh spinach, beet tops, radish leaves, mustard greens, a head of lettuce, and the wild greens known as patience or spinach dock. The directions call for boiling the vegetables and chopping them "altogether on a nice clean board. . . . Fry a dozen small pieces of ham cut in pieces an inch long and half an inch wide, and also half a chicken cut in pieces, or a piece of veal, say half a pound. Add a cup of water [to the meat] and let it simmer three quarters of an hour or until all are soft. Then add your herbs. Let them simmer together for a quarter of an hour. If it looks too thick add a few tablespoons of water. It must have the consistency of a thick purée. To be served hot, and eaten with dry rice."

[4] In her book on Savannah cookery Harriet Ross Colquitt asserted that black cooks "are extremely modest about their accomplishments, and they cannot believe that the everyday dishes which they turn out with so simple a twist, can be what we really admire."

Lacking okra or sassafras, this is really not a gumbo but is a "mess o' greens" as slaves contrived the dish under the influence of the vegetables found in antebellum Louisiana. With the choice of greens skillfully balanced, so the taste is neither too acidulous nor too bland, this can be a delectable concoction. In most of the twentieth-century South it is known simply as greens and pot likker, and no soul food restaurant bill of fare would be considered complete without it.

"A type of cooking made necessary by the environment in which southern blacks lived" is the phrase one soul food restaurateur used to describe his cuisine. In 1969 Bob Jeffries put it this way: "To begin with, soul food is honest. It is easy to cook but does not adapt well to 'Let's-get-out-of-the-kitchen-fast' shortcuts. It is delicious food, but does not allow for any frills. Sauces, for example, are used only because they taste good, never just to dress up a dish. Finally, it is sincere—because the good cooks who traditionally prepared it always worked with their whole heart, doing the best they could with what they had on hand to make sure their dishes would be enjoyed by all who sat down to eat. . . . In addition, Negroes have always had an understanding and knowledge of herbs, spices, and seasonings and have known how to use them. It is only recently that soul food is being discovered, and I consider that good news."

THE HARVEST CENTURY

The good news most often hailed in the nineteenth century was the prevailing bounty. Out of this same gastronomical chauvinism native food, like everything else American, was considered finer in quality and quantity than that of any other part of the world.

European visitors who criticized were often dismissed as snobbish and pretentious. Easterners who showed a liking for foreign manners and tastes were branded by provincial Americans as misguided if not disloyal. With field and garden crops so abundant no need existed (so the prevailing attitude seemed to make clear) for inventive ways in the kitchen. While the backwoodsman became transformed, as the public saw things, into homesteader, the cooking of the average nineteenth-century farmwife went through many changes for the better as a new American style evolved that was based on plenty—plenty of meat and fish, wild or domesticated, plenty of good things direct from the good earth, plenty of eggs and cream.

The vastness of the continent, the seeming inexhaustibility of the forests—along with the new stretches of virgin land to be homesteaded over the horizon—has had happy and unhappy influences on American individuals as well as on the national character. Plenty of food is as much a natural resource as mineral wealth, and accessible wild provender continues as an important part of the consciousness of plenty. Whether cooked outdoors in a pot over open fires or in an organized kitchen, game is essential in defining American gastronomy. The early dependence on wildlife for food, and firearms for protection on the frontiers, created a lasting mood. Twentieth-century Americans are said to go hunting at the rate of fourteen million annually, and the roster of males and females with active fishing licenses in both fresh water and seawater regions is more than twenty-two million.

That percentage of the population, one in ten, used to be closer to one hundred. To get Englishmen to come to live in the New World, indeed, the first promotional material suggested that game was every man's right—in the new social order that America represented it was no longer the prerogative of an upper class to be able to hunt, to keep a deer park, and to prosecute poachers. In the colonies poaching became obsolete, a man helped to provide for his family as a free hunter, and colonial women adapted all they knew of cooking game to the vast amounts of food to be found in field and forest and open water. During an era in which Americans tamed one westward frontier after another, they became increasingly dependent on firearms and more and more certain of a God-given right to meat for essential sustenance. Nineteenth-century newcomers believed that the bounty was really unending, illimitable. There was little reason to scrimp and scamp in the many farming regions, where it seemed there was no end to good eating. Appreciation of such good eating makes many old cookbooks a delight to read and has marked many memoirs with a thread of wistfulness.

Sometimes the wistfulness was declamatory if no less affectionate. "My family dumplings are sleek and seductive, yet stout and masculine," Robert P. Tristram Coffin wrote on his Maine saltwater farm. "They taste of meat, yet of flour. They are wet, yet they are dry. They have weight but are light. Airy, yet substantial. Earth, air, fire, water; velvet and elastic! Meat, wheat, and magic! They are our family glory!" Simple food, untampered-with food, in the words the Maine man chose, was without doubt on his part one of the components in ancient Olympic feasts which, he said, gave rise to the phrase "food for the gods."

Olympic or otherwise, the words are full of honest hunger for home cooking. So is the memory of a Kentucky hill country repast: "Venison steak, bass fried in corn meal, mast-fattened bacon cured with hickory wood fire, snap beans cooked with green corn, pone bread from the skillet on the hearth." In New England a man born at the end of the century remembered, "My grandmother was celebrated for her homemade sausage meat, her root and spruce and ginger beer, her mead and her currant, grape and gooseberry wines, made according to recipes of her mother, my great-grandmother." He said that his mother was "acknowledged to be, in the local language of understatement, 'a good cook' of baked beans and brown bread and Indian pudding, of chicken and veal pot pies with feathery dumplings." And he couldn't resist adding, "Her chicken pies with a crust melted in one's mouth."

Meals that include dishes whose ingredients are undisguised were dominant in the nineteenth century. "The meal was bountiful," a reminiscence of a Minnesota pioneer says of his first invitation to a frontier dinner. "I had a helping of meat, very juicy and fine flavored, much like tenderloin today, a strip of fat, a strip of lean." He had smiled up from his plate to compliment the cook on "the finest roast beef I have ever tasted." But he was wrong. "This is what we call 'boss' of buffalo," he was told, "and is the

To Fatten a Turkey, Make the Dressing, and Roast It.

Get your turkey six weeks before you need it; put him in a coop just large enough to let him walk, or in a small yard; give him walnuts—one the first day, and increase every day one till he has nine; then go back to one and up to nine until you kill him, stuffing him twice with corn meal dough each day, in which put a little chopped onion and celery, if you have it. For the dressing, use bread, picked up fine, a table spoonful of butter, some sage, thyme, chopped onion, pepper, salt, and the yolks of two eggs, and pour in a little boiling water to make it stick together; before putting it in the turkey pour boiling water inside and outside, to cleanse and plump it; then roast it in a tin kitchen [portable oven put on top of stove], basting all the time. It will be splendid, served with a nice piece of ham and cranberry sauce.

—*Los Angeles Cookery: 1881*

hump of the back of a young male." On the table was also a heaping plate of what was taken for dried beef. "No," the guest again was admonished. "This too is something you have never tasted before—it is boned dried beaver's tail." Nostalgia brings back visions of tables stretching, as a Wisconsin writer recalled, "vast and white, crammed with two or three roasts and a dozen relishes and vegetables for an ordinary supper—and yet Aunt Dell moaning that she had nothing in the house."

Wilderness and Bounty

Nothing to eat in the house? "Frequently," a Missourian reported of his family's covered-wagon move to the frontier, "my father killed three deer before breakfast." Old diaries are full of praise for the wilderness bounty. "We lived the first winter in Wayzata on fish, venison and corn meal and I have never lived so well." Flights of pigeons "so thick they darkened the sky" were common as settlers began to build new homes. "Geese and ducks, too, were in enormous flocks. In season they seemed to cover everything. We used the eggs of prairie chickens for cooking." Recipes, like the various formulas for Brunswick stew, also followed the horizon, and cooks were told in books they consulted when available that the "large grey and fox squirrels are the best for eating," especially in that classic American stew of cut up squirrel meat simmered with corn, butter beans, and tomatoes, usually highly seasoned by cooks in the South, where it was first adapted from Indian recipes. "A good Brunswick stew," someone once said, "is made of practically everything on the farm and in the woods, including chicken, beef, veal, squirrels, okra, beans, corn, potatoes, tomatoes, butter-beans, vinegar, celery, catsup, sugar, mustard, and enough red pepper to bring tears to your eyes."

Longing for food like this was just what overcame Mark Twain while in Europe in 1878, and he wrote, only slightly tongue in cheek, toward the end of *A Tramp Abroad*, that after the long months since he had eaten what he termed a nourishing meal, he was soon to have one—"a modest, private affair, all to myself. I have selected a few dishes, and made out a bill of fare, which will go home in the steamer that proceeds me [across the Atlantic], and be hot when I arrive—as follows."

Radishes. Baked apples, with cream.
Fried oysters; stewed oysters. Frogs.
American coffee, with real cream.
American butter.
Porter-house steak.
Saratoga potatoes.
Broiled chicken, American style.
Hot biscuits, Southern style.
Hot wheat-bread, Southern style.
Soft-shell crabs. Connecticut shad.
Baltimore perch.
Brook trout, from Sierra Nevadas.
Lake trout, from Tahoe.
Sheep-head and croakers, from New Orleans.
Black bass from the Mississippi.
American roast beef.
Roast turkey, Thanksgiving style.
Cranberry sauce. Celery.

Small Cucumber Pickles

Wash and wipe one hundred small cucumbers and place them in jars. Cover them with boiling brine, strong enough to bear an egg; let stand twenty-four hours. Then take them out, wipe, place in clean jars, and cover with hot vinegar, spiced with an onion, twelve whole cloves, one ounce of mustard seed, and three blades of mace. They will be ready to use in two weeks.

—Mrs. S. T. Rorer, 1886.

Hot buckwheat cakes.
American toast. Clear maple syrup.
Virginia bacon, broiled.
Blue points, on the half shell.
Cherry-stone clams.
San Francisco mussels, steamed.
Oyster soup. Clam soup.
Philadelphia Terrapin soup.
Bacon and greens, Southern style.
Hominy. Boiled onions. Turnips.
Pumpkin. Squash. Asparagus.
Butter beans. Sweet potatoes.
Lettuce. Succotash. String beans.
Mashed potatoes. Catsup.
Boiled potatoes, in their skins.
New Potatoes, minus the skins.
Early rose potatoes, roasted in the ashes, Southern style, served hot.
Sliced tomatoes, with sugar or vinegar. Stewed tomatoes.
Green corn, cut from the ear and served with butter and pepper.
Oysters roasted in shell—Northern style.
Roast wild turkey. Woodcock.
Canvas-back-duck, from Baltimore.
Prairie hens, from Illinois.
Missouri partridges, broiled.
'Possum. Coon.
Boston bacon and beans.
Green corn, on the ear.
Hot corn-pone, with chitlings, Southern style.
Hot hoe-cake, Southern style.
Hot egg-bread, Southern style.
Hot light-bread, Southern style.
Buttermilk. Iced sweet milk.
Apple dumplings, with real cream.
Apple pie.
Apple fritters.
Apple puffs, Southern style.
Peach cobbler, Southern style.
Peach pie. American mince pie.
Pumpkin pie. Squash pie.
All sorts of American pastry.

Cream and Butter Without Sham

Mark Twain ran a gamut, from Boston beans to Southern-style peach cobbler, from steamed San Francisco mussels to Lake Tahoe trout to Connecticut River shad, roast wild turkey, woodcock, canvasback ducks from Baltimore, prairie hens from Illinois—and he mentions no adornments or sauces except "real cream," "clear maple syrup," and "American butter," which he said was not the "sham" that Europe's was because it was properly salted. As a Missourian of the late nineteenth century, he had a special appetite for Southern food. (Note that he cites opossum and coon, which have been relished in the South, along with Brunswick stew, since it was discovered that a possum brought home live and fattened on persimmons made succulent eating.) He also liked Saratoga potatoes, or french fries, and sliced tomatoes with sugar and vinegar, green corn sliced off in kernels to be seasoned with running butter and freshly ground pepper. A postscript he added to the list of foods that made him homesick points up a philosophy he shared with his contemporaries: "Fresh American fruits of all sorts [should include] strawberries which are not to be doled out as if they were jewelry, but in a more liberal way."

There is no better word than liberal for the way American cooks indulged in cream and butter—indeed for many it was easy to ignore the sense of thrift which inspired the inventiveness of much provincial cooking in Europe. With thriving farmlands providing so much, there seemed no reason for culinary creativity to turn meager ingredients into the semblance of plenty. Americans like Mark Twain coveted the luxury of naturally rich comestibles more than anything else.

Nothing is more American than strawberries freshly picked and drenched in thick cream skimmed from the morning's milk, unless it is strawberry shortcake. There are variations—sometimes this earthy Americanism has been gussied up by the employment of layers of airy white cake, or a bread dough enriched with sugar and eggs, as in old Nantucket kitchens—but an unimpeachable strawberry shortcake needs a baking powder biscuit dough lavishly mixed with butter and cream. Baked to flaky perfection, this is carefully split into two layers, the lower of which is usually slathered with butter before accepting its burden of berries with sugar to make a filling that drips in rivulets down the sides. The top half is buttered, still hot, and covers the crushed berries, and in its turn is capped with more berries. Some cooks put their strawberry shortcakes back in the oven to ripen for a minute or two and then serve the dessert with a pitcher of cream.

Desserts like this have become as common as the names applied to some of them in the nineteenth century were uncommon. Shortcakes made of berries were limited only by their creator's imagination. Southern cooks devised a combination of raspberries and peaches as a luscious filling for a shortcake finished with a meringue topping. In the blueberry country of New England the berries were combined with a baking-powder cake-flour dough to produce blueberry buckle, served warm under a blanket of nutmeg-flavored blueberry sauce. The more sophisticated sweet called Lalla Rookh was named for the heroine created by the Irish poet Thomas Moore in 1817; this dessert in its New York version consisted of half a cantaloupe filled with orange sherbet and a dram of liqueur. (In Philadelphia the same poetic name was applied to a frozen punch in which sugar and egg yolks cooked together were mixed with brandy, rum, stiffly beaten egg white, and grated nutmeg, then packed in ice like ice cream.) Apple pie à la Virginia is composed of two pie shells filled with applesauce and stacked one on top of the other. "To serve," this yellowing recipe says firmly, "cut in sections and put a spoonful of whipped cream on top with a sprinkle of nutmeg. The crust *must* be crisp, and the sauce *cold*." Piping hot apple pie was dished up in New Hampshire "swimming in maple syrup." On dairy farms from New England to Oregon pies of all kinds were served so thickly coated with whipped cream there often seemed no way of knowing what filling lay within.

Centers of Family Life

The unassuming honesty of such confections still conjures up kitchens in farmhouses or in frame dwellings with porches opening to elm-shaded streets. What we tend to think of as American cooking reached its zenith in those nineteenth-century kitchens. They were centers of family life, often doubling as dining rooms three times a day, as a place to sew by the fire, to whittle a new household gadget, to do homework assigned by a schoolteacher, or just to hang around in while food was produced to suit seemingly insatiable appetites.

The Wisconsin novelist Edward Harris Heth wrote of his mother's kitchen: ". . . it was a kind of holy place from which she ministered lavishly to her family via stove and sink and cupboards and flour bins. There were rag rugs on the floor; usually wild white daisies or goldenrod stuck in a milk bottle, or garden flowers (her favorite bunch was of snow-on-the mountain and small deep red dahlias); and almost always a rolling pin or flour sifter or earthenware mixing bowl was in sight. . . . She would have looked with smiling placidity, but inward scorn and despair for her sex, at today's housewives, who are helpless without packaged pie crust and canned potato salad and precooked rice and who deem it a chore to simmer day-long an honest soup, depriving themselves of its aromatic pleasure. Good cooking," Heth continued, "was a way of life and enjoyment. You did not save time but spent it recklessly, proudly, and with a full reward inside these four spotless walls."

In addition to cooking, much time was devoted to preserving food, with results that include such classic American fare as New England boiled dinner. It was originally a meal-in-one-dish of salt beef cooked at the open fire where meat and vegetables could be combined in a single pot hanging from a crane and bubbling gently for hours while the housewife pursued her dozens of other chores. It remains a meal for the heartiest appetites, still in the repertoire of many women whose ancestors migrated across the country. The average Yankee recipe calls for corned brisket, flank, or beef rump to be simmered with a variety of root vegetables. As preparation, some Maine cooks rub a three- or four-pound piece of beef with coarse salt, then cover it with water so heavily salted it will float a potato or an egg. They may take an old-fashioned iron doorstop to weight down the meat while it absorbs the brine for several weeks.

Served as a midday meal on farms, a traditional boiled dinner goes to the stove soon after breakfast when corned beef and a piece of salt pork, along with a head of cabbage, are covered with water and simmered very slowly. In about three hours there may be added a dozen whole peeled potatoes, an equal number of scraped carrots, and six to eight peeled white onions; well-scrubbed beets are usually cooked separately. When the meat has simmered about four hours, the beef is drained and put on a hot platter, surrounded by the vegetables and garnished with parsley. Some Yankees call for a sprinkling of cider vinegar, but the most common accents are homemade horseradish sauce or strong mustard.

Greens from the Garden and from the Woods

In Maine and other parts of New England, and throughout the South of course, greens are basic ingredients, whether they come from the garden, the supermarket, or from the woods in the spring of the year. Boiled fresh pork ribs, backbone (chine), or loin with greens, potatoes, and cornmeal dumplings are commonly cooked together and called boiled dinner by country cooks of North Carolina. But the concept of boiled meat, green leaves, and other vegetables is more formally related to Old World customs when smoked ham hock (instead of corned beef) is simmered until tender and combined with cabbage, corn on the cob, carrots, and other root vegetables, then finished off with dumplings that are formed of cornmeal batter and dropped around the edge of the boiling pot.

Potlikker, the vitamin-rich liquid that remains in the cooking vessel after vegetables and greens are boiled, spiced up the political shenanigans of Huey Long when he was governor of Louisiana. Long began to extol the dietary virtues of this pungent broth, and he caused such a stir that potlikker became widely known in parts of the country where such "down home" cooking had previously been scorned. Long said corn pones—patties of cornmeal, hot water, and salt, fried in a greased skilled—were a necessary accompaniment to sipping the soup, and he added that they must be dunked. There then developed a national argument between those who dunked and those who insisted on crumbling the corn pone into the potlikker. Among the latter was Franklin D. Roosevelt, then a hopeful candidate for the presidency, who mock-seriously suggested referring the issue to the platform committee of the 1932 Democratic National Convention.

Using dock greens and salt pork, cooks in New England sometimes offer in spring a dish that has the liquid drained off before it is served—as a sort of wild spinach—with new potatoes rolled in garden parsley and melted butter, and hot johnnycake on the side. Dandelion greens (fiddleheads, too) are popular enough among Yankees so that a small factory in northern New England cans them every year. Fresh dandelion buds add tantalizing flavor when added to an omelet just before it is folded, and so do the blue flowers of chive plants.

Turnip tops and kale, and dandelion greens as well, may be simmered with salt pork, but such delicate wild greens as fiddlehead ferns are simply steamed when they have been freshly picked in a poplar grove, say, in early May. When fiddleheads are dressed with melted butter, hot cream, or thin white sauce, traditional Maine cooks often serve them on fingers of toast. Fiddleheads, when steamed and finely chopped, seasoned with salt, pepper, lemon juice, and some minced onion, can make a soufflé of delicate flavor that seems the essence of a Yankee spring. A fiddlehead pie, as served in Maine, is much like a quiche. To prepare one, beat a cup of milk, a cup of cream, two egg yolks, a teaspoon of salt, a half-teaspoon of sugar, and four teaspoons of minced green onion. Chop enough fiddlehead greens to make about one and a quarter cups, add them to the seething butter, and cook

Grandma's Muffins

(A hand-written recipe pinned into a page of *Miss Beecher's Receipt Book*, published by Harper & Brothers in 1848.)

" 4 Eggs
2 Pints sweet milk
1 Table spoon full of butter melted. A little salt
4½ Pints of flour
4½ Tea spoons full of Yeast Powder.

Bake in rings that have been well greased.

May 29 1874"

about three minutes; then combine with the milk-cream mixture. After it has set for about a half-hour, pour the fiddlehead custard into a partly baked pie shell, baking at 350°F. about thirty minutes.

In Maryland I once encountered a subtly flavored bisque that was enhanced by adding a cup or so of lightly-simmered fiddleheads to a couple of quarts of egg-and-lemon soup. More rustic, in the hills of West Virginia and other Appalachian places there are annual feasts for which the wild food of honor is the oniony green-leaved plant called ramp, an Elizabethan word for wild leeks.[1] Like fiddleheads, ramps are a regional tradition among some rural cooks. Chopped and parboiled, fried in hot bacon fat, the assertive ramps are frequently served with frizzled ham and sausage, home-fried potatoes, white and brown beans, and corn bread. In other kitchens they may be prepared like fiddleheads and served under a cheese sauce.

Cherry Pie

Seed the cherries first, then scald them in their own juice. Sweeten liberally and pour into a deep pie plate lined with a rich paste. Dredge with flour, cover with a top crust and bake. Scarlet or short-stem cherries are best. It is necessary to scald most fruits, as otherwise the pastry will burn before the fruit is thoroughly done.

—*Housekeeping in Old Virginia*, 1879

Away with Dead Vegetables

So ingrained were British culinary habits in the lives of early New England colonists that cooked vegetables for generations were referred to as garden sass, that is, garden sauce to be served in side dishes to accompany meat and fish and to be eaten with a spoon. The word stems from the Latin *salsa*, meaning salted, and its origin is the same as that for salad. Garden sass, however, suggests all too accurately vegetables cooked to a mushy consistency and deprived of their natural texture and much of their nourishment. It was common enough for Yankees to cook green peas for thirty minutes, and small wonder, perhaps, that such leftovers might be mashed and combined with flour and eggs to produce pale green griddle cakes or transformed into a bisque with an addition of minced clams. Mrs. N. M. K. Lee, who signed herself "a Boston housekeeper" when she published *The Cook's Own Book*, stressed that vegetables "should be brought in from the garden early in the morning; they will then have the fragrant freshness, which they lose by keeping." Her recipe for stewed celery, nevertheless, would disappoint modern vegetable lovers who aim not only for produce recently harvested but for genuine garden flavor. Mrs. Lee cooked her celery in veal stock and masked it with sauce made of cream and eggs flavored with lemon and nutmeg. Somehow she could write that "I should as soon think of roasting an animal alive as of boiling a vegetable after it is dead," yet encourage cooks to blanket overdone vegetables with floury mixtures. Everything from roots such as sweet potatoes and Jerusalem artichokes to broccoli and spinach were thus prepared. Even the delicately exotic flavor of palmetto or swamp cabbage (frequently served in Charleston, where some think it tastes like chestnuts) was commonly covered with cream sauce, or—in Florida, where it is commercially canned—has often been stewed with tomatoes and bacon.

[1] In Cosby, Tennessee, on the edge of Great Smoky Mountains National Park, the local citizens celebrate the rites of spring with a "ramp feed" that draws thousands of visitors. In addition to "the vilest smelling and sweetest tasting vegetable that grows," the menu includes barbecued chicken, baked beans, cornbread, and sassafras tea.

In the century before vitamins were known to exist, vegetables weren't eaten with enthusiasm but as an accompaniment to meat and fish (as applesauce traditionally has been served with pork). Vegetables of the period were reduced to purée, of saucelike consistency, and overcooked by Americans in the characteristic British way—even those food plants considered exotic. Hearts of palm, as the edible part of the palmetto is called in most markets, is rare simply because it is the core of a young palm tree, and its cutting means the death of the tree. It is harvested in South Carolina as well as Florida, and enough of it is put up in hermetically sealed containers to make hearts of palm salad seem a festive course—limited as the supply of palmetto trees may be. Maple trees, though not destroyed when their sap is harvested, have less effect than they once did on American gastronomy because so many trees were destroyed in the lumbering era. In northern New England sugar maples are still annually tapped, and this natural sweetener of the nineteenth century continues to aid farm cooks in the Midwest, northern Maryland, Virginia, and West Virginia.

"The Preference of Every True American"

Wherever maple trees grow, farmers slash the bark along about Washington's Birthday to encourage sap to drip, and then settle into the arduous procedure of boiling nature's product into the liquid sugar that the *Old Farmer's Almanac* in 1798 predicted, too optimistically, "will ever have the preference of every true American." It became, in fact, a luxury product that all too often has been robbed of its true excellence by dilution at the rate of 90 percent cane syrup to 10 percent maple.[2] In its pure state it invests food with a unique flavor, and its uses are surprisingly diverse. Outside the United States and Canada, one seldom comes across a recipe calling for maple syrup; for only in Germany and Japan have the trees been planted in appreciable numbers, and it takes forty years before a sugar maple can be tapped.

But American cooks have created all kinds of maple syrup combinations, spiking cream cheese modified by sour cream, for instances with maple flavor, then serving this sauce with a topping of mashed strawberries accented by a drop or so of applejack. New Englanders, including President John F. Kennedy, have maintained the "preference" for maple sugar (as the *Old Farmer's Almanac* predicted) over any other kind on cinnamon toast. Thousands of others have never reconciled to any substitute syrup on buckwheat cakes; in fact it is difficult to think of the traditional American breakfast without conjuring up the flavor of maple. In Antigo, Wisconsin, northwest of Green Bay, a "Maple Syrup and Pancake Festival" is celebrated every month of May in proof of this sentiment. In southern Wiscon-

How to Sugar-Off for Maple Syrup

Use a caldron deeper than it is wide and never fill it more than half full to allow room for boiling up. Prepare a thick bed of faggots for fast, hot kindling. Since few people have the new sugaring-off houses, pile some brush to break the wind. He who figures to get more than one gallon of syrup from less than 35 gallons of sap is not good at figuring nor at making maple syrup.

[2] Pure maple sap contains much iron and phosphorous and is considered a good tonic. In northern Michigan, where U. P. Hendrick grew up, "Our syrup was dark brown. Its flavor was not delicate but robust; darkened by smoke . . . [with] a smoky taste like Irish bacon, Scotch whisky or Souchong tea."

sin an enterprising farmwife devised what may be the ultimate morning meal in the ancient Yankee sugary mode: Her maple dumplings were prepared with a baking powder batter and cooked very slowly under cover in a mixture of maple syrup and butter, then served with more maple syrup and powdered sugar. For a more common old-fashioned breakfast treat, maple biscuits are baked when there is easy access to maple sugar. The soft baking powder dough is cut in four-inch rounds, and a topping of raisins, chopped nuts, and maple sugar is pressed into the upper surface before baking in a hot oven. A version of corn muffins sweetened with maple syrup is a less ornate way to start the day.

There are dozens of maple pies, cookies, cakes, ice creams, mousses, puddings—including maple Grape Nut pudding, which is given extra distinction by the addition of a breakfast cereal. And early-nineteenth-century cooks in Kentucky developed a maple salad dressing much recommended for Bibb lettuce (which Kentuckians claim to have been propagated in the Blue Grass country by John B. Bibb of Frankfort). The sweet dressing, with its lacing of olive oil, vinegar, and hint of mustard and Tabasco, is spicier than most of its kind and adds a purely American zest to fruit salads.

Maple syrup, bringing a distinctive flavor to country ham when it is added to the liquid in which the meat is boiled, also gives an American accent when used in sauces to serve after the ham is cooked. Maine cooks mix two tablespoons of vinegar with a couple of teaspoons of dry mustard and about three-quarters of a cup of syrup to blanket a thick slice of corncob-smoked ham as it bakes. In the South maple flavor attaches a little mystery to a superlative combination of fried chicken and broiled Virginia ham on crisp waffles that is served with a thin but rich sauce of fresh cream and syrup.

When many nineteenth-century Wisconsin farmers tapped sugar maples, an inspired Scandinavian farmwife substituted the flavor of maple for molasses in preparing an old-country pot roast, and the result is a subtle taste at which guests usually can only guess. At the annual maple festivals of Chardon, Ohio, the barbecued spareribs have been maple-flavored for generations. In various regions, maple sugar sprinkled generously on tart apple slices distributed evenly over a pastry shell and covered in heavy farm-fresh cream produces an indisputable New World pie.

1832 *"Apple Fraze"*

Cut Apples into thick slices, and fry them a clear light brown; take them from the pan, and lay them to drain; they may be pared or not; then make a batter. Take five eggs, leaving out two whites, beat them up with cream or flour, and a little white wine, make it of the consistency of pancake batter; pour in a little melted butter, mixed with nutmeg and sugar. Let the batter be hot, and drop in the fritters, laying on every one a slice of apple, and then a spoonful of batter on each. Fry them of a pale brown, when taken up, strew double-refined sugar all over them.

A Scattering across the Nation

Without help from various quarters, however, apple pie might never have become the legendary American dessert that it is. It took a man named John Chapman to scatter apple seeds—perhaps a little like the scattering of colonial recipes—as he moved westward in the Ohio Valley. "Among the pioneers," a regional historian wrote in 1864, "was an oddity called Johnny Appleseed. . . . The trees from his nursery are bearing fruit in a dozen different counties in Indiana, and thousands are enjoying the fruit who never heard of Johnny Appleseed."

Warren, R.I. Apple Fritters

Sift together 3 cups of flour, ½ teaspoon of nutmeg, 1 cup of sugar and ½ teaspoon of salt. Dissolve ½ teaspoon of soda in ½ cup of milk and stir into sifted flour. Beat 2 eggs, adding ½ cup of milk, and stir into batter, blending until very smooth. Peel and core 6 tart apples, then slice them about ¼ inch thick and fold into batter so apple rings are completely covered. With long-handled fork carefully dip rings into deep fat (370°F.). Brown lightly, drain on absorbent paper, and sprinkle with mixture of sugar and cinnamon. Serve with maple syrup or honey.

The seeds retrieved from cider mills by this early ecologist were planted and grew into small orchards to which John Chapman returned again and again to care for the trees that offered "pie timber"—as nineteenth-century cooks referred to ingredients for fillings—for many generations to come after him. He was a vegetarian whose preferred food, they said, was buttermilk and beebread (the pollen substance in honeycombs upon which bees feed); but for all the noncomformism in his own diet, he helped to bring apples to pioneer kitchens from the Alleghenies to the Mississippi, and seeds from trees he had nurtured went farther west when women accompanied their men on the Oregon Trail.[3] East of the Mississippi and in the Pacific West, wild crab apples provide an indigenous, if sour, crop, and they make the best of jellies; but Johnny Appleseed did more, in his eccentric way, than anyone else to make most of America apple country.

Varieties of U.S. apples now are almost numberless, and some of the older types have been so pushed to the background that an orchard "museum" was established in North Grafton, Massachusetts, where one hundred old-time apples, such as Sterlings, Yellow Newtowns, and Roxbury Russets, are tenderly encouraged to continue producing. Twenty-five percent of the nation's crop continues to come from large highly organized orchards in Washington State, but there are still rugged individualists among apple growers. Some family orchards, such as that of Pine Tree Farm in Minnesota, have harvested as many as fifteen varieties annually. In western Michigan, where orchardists have concentrated on McIntosh, Northern Spy, Jonathan, Delicious, and Wealthy, the wives of fruit growers in the 1950s toted up 120 different apple dishes made with local apples, including apple salad, apple meatloaf, apple bread, relishes, desserts, apple punch, apple fritters fried in deep fat and dusted with sugar, candied caramel apples, apple butterhorns, apple potato salad, sweet potatoes baked with apples, and an uncounted number of apple pie variants.

Seventy-five percent of America's McIntoshes are grown in the New York–New England area. How much of this crop goes into pie is anyone's guess. But the way a McIntosh pie is seasoned is a matter of debate. Some insist the fruit must be pure—unadulterated by spices—to insure a pervasive taste of apple. In Kent's Corners, Vermont (and many other places, too), cinnamon, nutmeg, and the zest of lemon accent the juicy McIntosh essence.

"My mother's pie was beyond description," Della Lutes' memoir of nineteenth-century Michigan says. "The crust was flaky, crisp, and tender. She used lard, and she mixed this with flour until it 'felt right.' She poured in

[3] Narcissa Whitman, the first of these, wrote her family in 1836 of sumptuous meals she had at Dr. John McLaughlin's Columbia River trading post that ended in "a nice pudding or an apple pie," made with fruit from a tree McLaughlin grew; he had received seeds from a sea captain who, when requested to dress for dinner, as was McLaughlin's habit, found in his long-unused pocket the pits from a dessert apple give him by a young lady at a farewell dinner in London. McLaughlin had the tree so well attended that it not only forecast the arboricultural future of the Northwest but it thrived for more than a hundred years and was still alive at this writing.

water with a teacup, or the dipper, or whatever was at hand, but she never poured too much or too little. She laid on to the lower crust a bed of sliced apples to exactly the right height for proper thickness when the pie was done. It was never so thick that it felt like biting into a feather bed, nor so thin that your teeth clicked. It never ran over, and it had just the proper amount of juice. She sprinkled sugar over it with neither mete nor measure, and allspice and cinnamon from a can. But when the pie was done (crimped around the edges and golden brown on the humps, with an 'A' slashed in the top crust) it was a masterpiece of culinary art. With the edge of the oven's heat taken off, but never allowed to chill, and a goodly piece of cheese from the neighboring factory alongside, here was a dish which the average citizen of any country rarely meets."

Surely that Lutes' masterpiece was an apple pie for Mark Twain, and just as surely it was a glowing example of the nineteenth-century gastronomy that depended equally on the love and skill of the cook and the simple quality of readily available ingredients. For such an apple-pie ending, a formal meal of the period might have begun with watercress and Jerusalem artichoke soup, made from the cress to be gathered at the farm spring and the artichoke that is really the delicately flavorful root of a member of the sunflower family, first noted by Samuel Champlain when he explored Indian gardens on Cape Cod in 1605. This is an elegant soup—rich with butter, homemade chicken stock, milk, cream, egg yolk, and the fragrance of nutmeg, the verdant tartness of parsley—beautifully blending the combined flavors of watercress and the American sunflower root from the cuisine of Narragansett Indians.

The Unyielding Appetite for Beef

In Europe Mark Twain pined for a porterhouse steak, which might have been the *pièce de résistance* of a meal with this beginning and this ending. Although, once back in New York, the writer might have ordered such a steak at a chophouse that specialized in them, the average housewife more often than not had to make do with beef as tough as saddle leather.[4] Very little beef was raised for meat alone until late in the century, and butchers dealt mostly with cuts that came from animals that had worked hard, rather than lazily grazing the plains before final weeks of eating corn to enrich the flavor and tenderness of the meat. Cooks learned to solve the problems of toughness, sometimes by simply marinating a steak for a dozen hours in clarified butter and pounding it flat before frying in a cast-iron skillet; sometimes a sirloin was soaked in a mixture of highly spiced vinegar and wine, then rolled up around a stuffing of suet and seasoned breadcrumbs to be roasted on a spit. A man with a twentieth-century palate and a lifelong indulgence of the world's best beef pales at the thought, and he is even

[4] Porterhouse steak takes its name from the saloons that once specialized in dark brown malt beer for neighborhood porters and is the cut of beef that comes between sirloin steaks and those called tenderloin.

more appalled at one sirloin recipe's title: "Rolled Beef That Equals Hare."

Many twentieth-century cooks have looked askance at rabbit or hare, not realizing how good that meat tastes when skillfully prepared, and their way of treating tender porterhouse or T-bone, which is the smaller version of tenderloin steak, calls for the simplicity of broiling, by indoor or outdoor means. A good beef roast is likely to be cooked at home in the oven rather than on a fireplace spit, but it still comes to the table accompanied by a sizzling, egg-rich Yorkshire pudding as often as it did when English colonists saluted Hanoverian princes. The first published recipe appeared in a cookbook, issued in Manchester by a Yorkshire woman in 1762, which was bought by a number of Virginia homemakers before the Revolution. An old New England collection of recipes cautions that "Rare done is the taste of this age" when it comes to beef, and it directs that a roast be accompanied by cranberry sauce as well as Yorkshire pudding.[5] Beef, adorned or otherwise, has always been central to the notions most Americans have of a meal uninhibited by cost—or, for that matter, by Continental kickshaws. Not surprisingly, the appetite for red meat was sufficient to inspire editorial writers. "We are essentially," asserted one frontier newspaper in the middle of the century, "a hungry *beef-eating* people, who live by eating."

Still, the nineteenth-century economy that limited the availability of top-grade beef widened the horizons of inventive cooks. A four-pound piece of chuck might be browned in bacon fat, salted, peppered, its top spread with prepared mustard and the juice of half a lemon, then covered with thin onion slices and five or six branches of dill and allowed to simmer several hours in a small amount of red wine under a very tight cover. Or in the spring of the year a housewife might turn to veal, which was available only in that season, or to freshwater fish.

Not the So-called Baby Beef

As is true of most food in the twentieth century, there is no longer a limited season for veal, but traditionally the best meat from calves was available in the spring of the year. The youngest and most delicate was called milk veal and came from animals born late in the winter; grass veal, found in butcher shops during the summer, came from animals that had left their mothers to feed in pastures during summer months. In spite of the fact that veal (not the so-called baby beef that has gone from milk-feeding to corn) is the flesh of calves from three to twelve weeks old and therefore tender, this young meat has for years been considered indigestible by many Americans who failed to understand how to cook it. But there was a time on Southern plantations and Midwestern farms when, during the annual season, veal was so abundant that keeping the meat was a problem because of lack of

1832 Veal Pie

Take two pounds of veal cutlets, cut them in middling-size pieces, season with pepper and a very little salt; likewise one of raw or dressed ham cut in slices, lay it alternately in the dish, and put some forced or sausage meat at the top, with some stewed mushrooms, and the yolks of three eggs boiled hard, and a gill of water; then proceed as with rump-steak pie.

N.B.—The best end of a neck is the fine part for a pie, cut in chops, and the chine bone taken away.

[5] Settlers from Maine who founded Portland, Oregon, americanized the pudding from Yorkshire by cooking the batter in custard cups lubricated with drippings from the roasting beef (or sometimes pork); another modification was the use of garlic and, frequently, herbs. The result is called Portland popover pudding, individual balloons of crusty meat-flavored pastry.

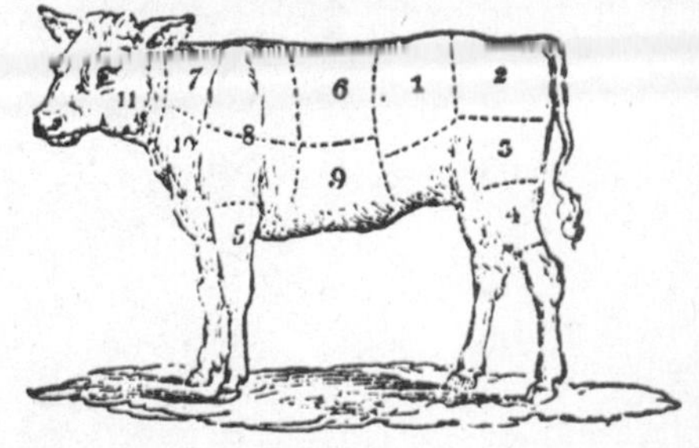

ice machines and freezing equipment; as a result much imagination was exercised by willing cooks to create a great variety of veal dishes.

In Delaware a recipe for veal pot roast called for the very slow simmering of a good-size piece of rump with garden vegetables, the meat to be served in slices with a sauce made by puréeing the vegetables. Some New Englanders cut veal in collops, cook them gently, and dress them with a sauce that is a simple mixture of young cucumbers and rich cream. California's traditional veal rolls are stuffed, flavored with onion, green pepper, and fresh herbs and topped with a sauce dominated by sliced black olives from orchards begun when Father Serra arrived in 1769. Some Floridians use olives and lime juice to accent veal served with a tuna fish sauce, and in some Louisiana kitchens veal steaks are cut in pieces, marinated in rum and fruit juice, braised in olive oil, and embellished with a combination of pineapple juice, raisins, and ripe olives over which capers are sprinkled when this veal dish is served atop boiled rice. But at least as genuinely rural-American as any of these is a stew using a thick slice of veal from the leg that is simmered in stock with chestnuts.

When such dishes were commonly cooked, the chestnuts came from trees that grew on the home place, and the vegetables that added their separate flavors to the stew were from seeds planted by the cook herself, most likely, or by a member of her family. The combination of imaginative cooking and the products of one's own farm made it easy to eat affluently at the cost of almost no cash at all. In other countries few "common people" possessed farms of their own and few had as various a horn of plenty from which to choose.

Hands to Work, and Mouths to Feed

In this country, the operation of farms—before the late-nineteenth-century arrival of mechanization—required the help of many hands, and most farmers had numerous children; their wives, thereby, had many mouths to feed. As their share in earning the food they ate, young boys did chores without question, and young girls helped in the cooking, gardening, dairying. Not long ago I read a childhood memory of a former airline stewardess who had retired to run a restaurant. "All of the Nortons old enough to read," she said of her family, "had sugar to measure and spice bags to assemble. All of the Nortons old enough to be careful with a knife had cutting and peeling chores to do. This was 'togetherness' before it became a magazine fad. We all felt we were part of our winter provisions, and we all knew this was the economy that made bicycles and doll carriages and patent leather Mary Janes a possibility." It was the nineteenth-century home economy that had carried over into pre–World War II days, reflecting a time when as many as a dozen heads might be counted around the table daily.

Cooking for so many on a regular basis, cooking for even larger appetites when the harvest season brought in helpful neighbors and hired hands to be

Fried Green Tomatoes

Slice ¼ inch thick firm large tomatoes, green throughout. Sprinkle with salt, pepper and sugar. Dip in cornmeal and fry in a skillet containing enough bacon drippings to cover skillet ¼ inch deep. Have fat hot when tomatoes are added, then reduce heat and brown on one side. Turn with pancake turner and brown on the other side. Serve with hot homemade chili sauce.

—Old Kentucky recipe

fed as a part of the cost of bringing in the crops—these occasions were not only challenges in terms of logistics, but times of rivalry when good cooks showed how really good they were. When hungry threshers sat down at a harvest table, they found it burdened with good things: relishes, cottage cheese, pickles, beets, hot baking powder biscuits, sliced fresh bread, two or three roast meats, fried chicken, a platter laden with pork chops, steaming greens, several kinds of potatoes, fried green tomatoes, sliced red tomatoes in oil and vinegar, assorted pies, and, yes, very likely, a cake or two as well.[6]

The plenty burdening a farmhouse table for harvesters is, I suppose, symbolic of the period's foremost attitude. The land was fertile, much of it never tilled by any other than the residing family. Providence smiled. In years of church-going, of candles and oil lamps and no electronic distractions, no easy travel to far places, home was a place where contentment prevailed, or at least was encouraged. What better way of encouraging it than by serving bountiful meals that reflected the success of the home place? The holiday rhyme that recalls the pleasure of going "over the hills to Grandma's house" is implicit with the promise of a family gathering and abundant good food, a table laden (throughout the year, not just at harvest time) with relishes, preserves, condiments, fragrant roasts, every vegetable grown in the garden, desserts that might be either rustic or sophisticated, hot coffee with every course, homemade bread and rolls, and nuts to eat at hearthside later.[7] It all brings memories of coming home from church to be met by smells of chicken roasting in the cast-iron stove's oven, of family reunions in days before calorie counts, when Americans lightened their spirits with the pleasure of good food more often than with alcohol. Nineteenth-century diary entries often underscore this pleasure: "May 5th, 1837, and another real summer day! Last evening a number of the Brethren went fishing in Lake Erie. Toward noon today they brought home their catch—except the small ones which they always cast into their mill-pond on their way home. They had enough for all three Families; there were several muskies, a fine haul of white fish, a number of pike along with a lot of catfish and yet other kinds. They are all splendid eating. This evening we had a good supper of boiled catfish with herb-sauce, fried potatoes, boiled greens, pickled peppers, hot bread and lemon pie and tea."

The lemon pie was simple: "Slice two lemons as thin as paper, rind and all. Place them in a bowl and pour over them 2 cups of sugar. Mix well and let stand for 2 hours or better. Then go about making your best pastry for 2 crusts. Line a pie dish with same. Beat 4 eggs together and pour over lemons. Fill unbaked pieshell with this and add top crust with small vents

[6] A twentieth-century Indiana menu for ten, recorded after a corn harvest, included "roast guinea, fried fish, roasting ears, potato salad, baked macaroni and cheese, baked beans, glazed sweet potatoes, green beans, celery, sliced onions in vinegar, sliced tomatoes red and yellow, homemade rolls with butter and blackberry jam, three kinds of cookies, pumpkin pie, milk, iced tea, coffee with endless cream and sugar."

[7] Itemizing her baking for the year 1877, a Vermont housewife counted 152 cakes, 421 pies, 1,038 loaves of bread, 2,140 doughnuts.

cut to let out steam. Place in a hot oven for 15 minutes and then cut down heat and bake until a silver knife inserted into custard comes out clean."

Bountifully laden tables were perceived as a better sign of a woman's culinary ability than any finesse she might have developed in the kitchen. In small towns and cities, as well as in the countryside, meals designed to fill the stomach were more important than those that might be described as "fancy." Mrs. Rorer preached such ideas in her cookbook. The peripatetic author once told a Minnesota audience that "well fed people never mind the weather," adding that thoughtfully prepared food not only could add "an inch of healthy fat on the body," but was "worth more in keeping warm than a sealskin coat." As an example of her philosophy, Mrs. Rorer gave users of her cookbook three pages of menus for "small and less pretentious families":

BREAKFAST

Oat Meal Mush with Whipped Cream
Broiled Steak *Stewed Potatoes*
Quick Muffins
Coffee
Fruit

BREAKFAST

Fried Indian Mush, Maple Syrup
Cecils of Cold Meat *Saratoga Potatoes*
Flannel Cakes
Cocoa
Fruit in Season

BREAKFAST (SPRING)

Small Hominy Boiled in Milk
Lamb Chops, Broiled *Lyonnaise Potatoes*
Gems *Coffee*
Orange Salad

BREAKFAST (SPRING)

Flannel Cakes *Coffee*
Fried Chicken, Cream Sauce
Scalloped Potatoes
Salad with French Dressing

BREAKFAST (SUMMER)

Strawberries Without Stemming
Broiled Tomatoes, Cream Gravy *New Potatoes, Boiled*
Cheese Ramekins
Rolls
Coffee

LUNCHEON

Bouillon
Orange Sherbet Served in Orange Skins
Fish à la Reine in Paper Cases
Chicken Croquettes French Peas
Terrapin with Saratoga Potatoes
Boned Chicken
Wafers Montrose Pudding Cheese
Black Coffee

LUNCHEON

Roman Punch Served in Ice Tumblers
Sweetbreads à la Crème Served in Paper Cases
Partridges on Toast
Salmon Croquettes, Sauce Hollandaise
Cheese Ramekins
Charlotte Russe
Black Coffee

DINNER (WINTER)

Oysters on the Half Shell
Consommé
Cream Macaroni
Boiled Leg of Mutton, Caper Sauce Currant Jelly
Mashed Potatoes Peas Cauliflower
Lettuce with French Dressing
Water Crackers Neufchâtel
Lemon Sponge
Black Coffee

Menus like these are worth a searching glance because they vouch for the prevailing recognition of all kinds of bounty. Terrapin for lunch never used to seem exotic—any more than did beefsteak for breakfast; and partridges served on toast was a common dish when the game season was on. In fact, as cooks found more time to spend on varying the preparation of readily available ingredients, they looked for cookbooks containing new methods of serving sweetwater fish and game. "No market in the world is so abundantly supplied with this species of food as the American," said the Ohio women who compiled soon after the Civil War *The Buckeye Cook Book* for "Plucky Housewives Who Master Their Work Instead of Allowing It to Master Them." Like other kitchen guides, including Mrs. Rorer's, this devoted pages to game recipes—how to smoke venison hams, how to roast bear meat, appetizing ways to prepare raccoons and skunks, as well as possums and such fish as sturgeon. A traditional Virginia way of serving partridges calls for steaming the birds first, stuffing them with fresh oysters, and, after broiling, covering them with a butter sauce in which the oyster juice has been amalgamated.

The central flyway of the Mississippi Valley still brings thousands of wild ducks to Texas coastal regions, where some cooks simmer the birds in tomato sauce spiced with cinnamon, cloves, and a little onion, then bake the ducks another hour and a half. A nineteenth-century recipe popular in St. Louis begins with a five-to-six-pound dressed goose sprinkled with salt and paprika; it is roasted under a coating of sour-cream-and-mushroom sauce seasoned with rosemary and thyme. Some Viriginia cooks soaked the wild goose several hours in salted water, then stuffed it with chopped celery, chopped eggs, mashed potatoes, raw grated turnip, bits of fat pork, and pepper vinegar.

When Oysters Were in Season

Virginia colonists in 1609 were kept from starving to death when sent to the oyster beds on the Elizabeth River with no other food than ground corn rationed at a pint a week per person. But by the middle of the nineteenth century, far from being used to stave off starvation, oysters were eaten as a between-meal snack and they were at least as popular as hot dogs a hundred years later.

Even Americans who had never visited coastal regions knew and loved their taste. Entrepreneurs set up "oyster expresses," which in one instance started oysters off in Baltimore, in a packing of seawater-soaked bags. Driven in fast wagons to Pittsburgh, barrels of the Baltimore oysters were loaded on Ohio steamboats for the next leg, which took them to Cincinnati; there they were kept alive in saltwater tanks in retail stores. Chicago is reported to have celebrated its first oysters in 1848, when mollusks that had arrived alive in Ohio were boiled, packed in ice, and shipped by rail to the head of Lake Michigan. And Vermonters a hundred years ago could sit down to a supper in Montpelier, St. Johnsbury, or Burlington and eat oysters that had spent the day in barrels of ice on the train from Boston. Even earlier, oysters had traveled similar distances in saddle bags or packed in kegs of flour or meal. At hinterland taverns they were kept alive, along with clams, buried in beds of sea sand and Indian meal that was faithfully watered twice a week or so. Oyster caravans, the spring wagons rattling along unpaved roads, served upper New York housewives, who swapped butter, cheese, homespun, or their own carded yarn for some of the sea's bounty.

Such things helped to change the character of American cuisine more quickly from regional to national. Here's a diary entry of a late-nineteenth-century St. Louis girl that tells us that "oysters and other shellfish come by boat from New Orleans in barrels, and when a family is fortunate enough to get a barrel, all their friends are invited for the evening . . . what a treat this is considered!" The word treat only begins to suggest the enthusiasm virtually all America had for oysters while the great plenty lasted. People bought and ate them on the street from wheelbarrows and wagons. Men, sometimes a little sneakily perhaps, went downstairs into cellars to purchase their fill of bivalves in smoky places called oyster saloons. Some were fancy enough to cause a British visitor to note "the pleasant addition of curtains to inclose you in your box." With amenities like that, some of these oyster rendezvous were called parlors.

Such places developed some fancy ways of serving oysters. For instance, in St. Louis when oysters and other shellfish came up river regularly in barrels, a dozen of the finest bivalves might be dipped in an egg batter and a mixture of delicately seasoned, shredded crab meat before they were sautéed in butter and served as an after-theater snack. In a similar opulent mood, St. Louis hostesses of the period combined oysters with sweetbreads, and it is easy enough to do today if you have a half-gallon of small oysters, two pairs of blanched sweetbreads, some sautéed mushrooms—you make a cream sauce, enriching it with oyster liquor, add the principal ingredients, and when the oysters are plump, season the combination with salt, pepper, and lemon juice; stir in seven well-beaten egg yolks, and serve in warmed patty shells.

In the late nineteenth century almost every town of any size was a likely stop for the traveler interested in good eating; there was apt to be somewhere to sit and consume oysters prepared in a variety of ways, and a note of elegance in the decor—in that Victorian age—usually indicated that ladies would be welcome. In San Francisco a place called Gobey's proudly advertised its "Ladies and Gents Parlor," perhaps to dispose of rumors that such hostelries may have been illicitly inclined. During the Gold Rush, in other places in that town, the company was overwhelmingly male as oysters were greedily eaten at twenty dollars a plate—and the greed was still there during the 1890s, when a dozen on the half shell, along with a small steak and a cup of coffee, could be had for a quarter. A Philadelphian recalled a time when few blocks in his home city were without oyster cellars, and he added, somewhat longingly, that he was born too late "to have been taught that oyster eating, especially the eating of raw oysters, was the indulgence of low taste." He remembered that in that era of active temperance societies there were people who thought the eating of raw oysters was a form of cruelty to animals.

It is apparent that few Americans paid attention to such hard criticism—even when William Makepeace Thackeray, dining at Boston's Parker House and eating his first Wellfleet oyster, was widely quoted as having said that he felt as if he had just swallowed a baby. Another Englishman said that "a first rate American oyster is as big as a cheese-plate" and he added that a half-dozen—"their flavor undeniable"—were enough for a complete dinner. Captain Marryat, who had commented admiringly on Boston lobsters, was not so keen on oysters, which he found insipid. "As the Americans assert that the English and French oysters taste of copper," the British naval officer wrote, "that's the reason why we do not like American oysters, copper being better than no flavor at all."

Nevertheless, the enthusiasm in this country for home-grown oysters expanded every year. There are reports that complete meals of nothing but oysters were not infrequent in New England; presenting them in several ways could and did result in a menu of variety. Community suppers, prepared by women with Yankee inventiveness, might go something like this:

Oysters on the Half Shell with Lemon and Horseradish
Pickled Oysters *Pigs in Blankets*
Oyster Stew, Montpelier Crackers or Oyster Crackers
Escalloped Oysters, Brown Bread Sandwiches
Oyster Pie *Fried Oysters*
Creamed Oysters with Pastry Diamonds
or Oyster Patties
Potato Salad
Apple Pie, Hot or Cold *Mince Pie, Hot or Cold*
Cheese *Coffee*

Even during the Depression oyster suppers in Philadelphia were considered a "universal" way of gathering with the neighbors, and a surviving menu for one such affair afforded each diner, at one sitting, five raw oysters, a dish of oyster stew, turkey with scalloped oysters, and mashed potatoes. Not a choice, mind you, but all the courses—and with healthy American appetites present, one can believe there were those who went back for seconds.

It is doubtful that any country ever went as crazy over oysters as the United States seemed to do in those years between the Revolutionary War and the end of westward expansion. Dozens of ways of cooking them were devised, many of them bearing an undeniably American stamp. Many were traditional, such as the method of making "beef and oyster sausages" by combining finely chopped oysters with minced beef and mutton, seasoning with cloves and mace, and binding with egg yolks; shaped like breakfast sausages, the mixture was dipped in egg and crumbs and fried. The plenitude of oysters made them a natural addition to the stuffing that filled birds and turned various combinations of oysters and turkey—whether in pies or appetizingly stuffed buckwheat pancakes—into Yankee dishes. They have inspired closely guarded recipes, such as those for oysters Rockefeller and cream of squash soup. They have even caused the invention of a new kind of cracker. For special oyster use, two New Jersey brothers, John and Adam Exeter, in 1847 devised a tiny biscuit one-and-one-quarter inches in diameter and three quarters of an inch thick—just the right size to be accepted universally as "oyster crackers."

The oysters native to the San Francisco Bay Area, until their popularity caused them to disappear, were tiny ones, with a greenish copper color. They inspired chef Ernest Arbogast of the Palace Hotel to create an omelet of such unforgettable flavor that it attracted visitors to the Bay City for no other reason. It was a specialty of the hotel's "Ladies Grill," but its popular-

ity infected both men and women. Now the Arbogast omelet is flavored by the West Coast's small Olympia oysters. A home version can be made if you heat up a cup of cream sauce based on the best available cream, adding a cup of the small bivalves, salt, pepper, and a touch of sherry. Make a French omelet of four eggs and spoon into it half of the cream sauce and oysters before folding. Turn it out then on a hot platter and garnish with the remaining oysters and sauce.

Oyster stew produced from the Olympia variety is a West Coast favorite, often accented with a dash of Tabasco sauce. During what might be called the "oyster century" a stew made from any of various oysters was often a supper in itself when Sunday evening came for families in every region. The enthusiasm coincided with the wide acceptance of the chafing dish, which, for a couple of generations or more, proved to be not only a boon to bachelors but to households left to their own resources when the cook had a day of leisure. In chafing dish cookery, more often than not, the man of the family presided over the alcohol lamp and its heating pans, and equally often he was apt to consider oyster stew the finest, if not the only, dish in his repertoire. To judge by the memories of some who have written about such Sunday suppings, paterfamiliases may well have been talented.

"It is more than a quarter century," says one of these tributes, "since I have had an oyster stew comparable to those Father used to do on the chafing dish on the table. He had a properly heavy hand with the sherry and a properly light hand with the red pepper." Less adventurous Yankees were likely to have a proper hand with paprika and nutmeg, or even celery salt. In my own boyhood it was the butter that got the very proper attention, being cut into a thin pat that was dropped into each dish at the last edge-of-boiling minute, so that it was a disappearing golden island as the first sip was taken.

Most oyster stew recipes produce essentially uncomplicated soups; one I found some years ago evolves into a real stew, if you are a stickler for the dictionary definition of a stew as a mixture of meat or fish with vegetables and liquid. This, then, is stew à la June Platt, which she has said "was the specialty of a colored chef on the private railroad car *The Bright Star*, who taught it to a very famous banker, who then taught it to my pretty mother, who taught me how to make it at the age of twelve." It is a combination of chopped turnips, carrots, onions, and hearts of celery to which she added cream and oysters (see the recipe section).

If oyster stew is a dish for family suppers at home, roast oysters are for larger celebrations, and, like clambakes in New England, oyster roasts gather big crowds below the Mason-Dixon line. Along the southern Atlantic and Gulf coasts, oysters thrive by clinging to rocks, mangrove roots, and anything else. They are harvested commercially near Mobile; indeed, along with catfish, oysters are among important "pop foods" of Alabama. (A twentieth-century eater in a Mobile seafood restaurant consumed nineteen dozen raw oysters in twenty-five minutes.) And at Biloxi—where there are streets once paved with oyster shells and shaded by moss-draped oaks—

"oyster bakes" are the local tradition. In between those two Gulf cities the Old Spanish Fort at Pascagoula, Mississippi, has original moss-mud-and-oyster-shell walls. Oysters are also harvested at Apalachicola in the Florida panhandle and at Fernandina, northeast of Jacksonville; at Naples, Florida, the oysters considered great delicacies are about the size of a fingernail.

On North Carolina's coastline the sea-hemmed-in village of Roadanthe year after year has boasted of having the world's greatest oyster roast. Plantation owners on such rivers as South Carolina's Combahee still entertain with oysters by the bushel freshly dredged from local streams. (One bushel for fifteen guests is the rule.) They are washed and scrubbed and shoveled onto iron mesh, or grills, or sheet iron over a hot crackling fire made of brush. A blanket of wet gunnysacking provides steam, and when the oysters pop and are spread out on a great table, the hungry fall to and devour them in typically informal American style.

Feasting on Crabs

Outdoor "crab feasts" are common enough on Maryland's Eastern Shore, the live hard-shell crabs being forced into a makeshift container (giant lard cans are popular) to be steamed in hotly spiced vinegar vapor. Picnic tables are spread with newspapers in thick layers and each guest is provided with a sturdy paring knife or nutcracker to break into the shells, washing the white meat down with beer. The oceanside crab houses specializing in newspaper-covered tables and all-you-can-eat servings of crabs are disappearing, but among those left at this writing is one at Wilmington, Georgia, not far from Savannah. In addition to steamed blue crabs, the place prepares giant Alaskan claws, Dungeness, snow crabs (a working fisherman's name for spider crabs), and claws from the stone crabs that can be found from the Carolinas to Florida.

Charleston and Savannah both lay claim to the invention of she-crab soup, one of the most delicious of the region's springtime specialties. Spring also brings the traditional dinner parties in such places as Mobile, on the Gulf Coast, at which she-crabs are celebrated. The soup is based on a combination of the meat and roe of the female blue crab, which is recognizable by its broad "apron" on the underside of the shell. In its simplest form, Charleston she-crab soup begins with a dozen boiled crabs, the eggs of which have been carefully set aside. Sauté a half-cup of chopped onion in butter, stir in the crab, the roe, a couple of cups of milk, and a quarter as much cream; and while this heats, season it with salt, pepper, and a dash or so of Worcestershire sauce. As a thickener, mix a little flour with water and blend it in, cooking until you get a smooth-silky texture. Add a tablespoon or so of sherry—some cooks insist on Manzanilla—and simmer over very low heat about thirty minutes. Particular cooks are also inclined to use chicken stock as part of the base and to include some minced celery with the onion, and when they can't get she-crabs, they cheat a little by crum-

bling into the soup the yolks of two hard-boiled eggs as a substitute for the roe. In the South crab roe is canned, and in South Carolina, especially, such eggs are added when necessary to soup made with male crabs, for they give the same flavor.

She-crab soup used to be perpetually on the menu of Charleston's Fort Sumter Hotel, and it was a strikingly different dish—rich and quite thick, it had the pale color of the green lima beans and yellow corn kernels which were added to the crabmeat and roe, making it almost a meal in itself. A tomatoey nineteenth-century version with green peas is served in Alabama, the lump crab meat supported by an equal amount of lobster meat; a discerning palate sometimes recognizes a hint of ginger and cayenne pepper, and the servings are frequently garnished with a spoonful of whipped cream. This last pinkish soup evolved shortly after the end of the eighteenth century, when tomatoes were finally accepted as an edible vegetable, rather than as a decorative fruit that some considered poisonous. Another bisque of crab meat was developed in recent years after avocados became a crop in Florida; it employs a base of puréed potato soup that is combined with milk, a large peeled and pitted avocado that is mashed, and lump crab meat, with accents of Tabasco and chili powder, and avocado slices floating on top.

Crabs—in greater variety than on any other continent—were found by settlers on both coasts of North America. Stone crabs, common from North Carolina to Texas, remain abundant in Florida and the Keys, and are trapped around Beaufort, North Carolina, and Charleston, South Carolina. There antebellum cooks used to stew them in white wine laced with vinegar; then with a seasoning of nutmeg and anchovy the cook would heat the crab with a good deal of butter and egg yolks, serving it in a large crab shell as a second course. A similar dish can be made with lobster, or with the meat of the blue crabs from Chesapeake Bay and other waters, available canned or frozen almost everywhere.

To reach the world market, the live crustaceans go into dockside packing plants and are pressure-cooked before the white flakes of succulent meat are picked by hand and graded. Backfin lump is the best grade; next comes the so-called white crab meat, the middle grade; and next the claws, the meat slightly darker and marketed for easy serving as cocktail tidbits. Away from the shore, crab is almost always canned or frozen, and it is expensive. Yet the fact there is no waste helps.

In whatever way it comes to the kitchen, crab meat moves inventive cooks to improvise and sometimes to include extenders among the ingredients for a crab dish. An uncommon combination, called crab meat with walnuts, comes from a cook who spent a lifetime summering on Peconic Bay. Her method was to mix two cups of crab meat with a half-cup of chopped walnuts, a minced hard-boiled egg, two tablespoons of parsley, salt and pepper to taste, a teaspoon of Worcestershire sauce, a half-teaspoon of prepared mustard, and a dash of Tabasco. She spooned this into four crab or scallop shells, spread three-quarters of a cup of her own mayonnaise

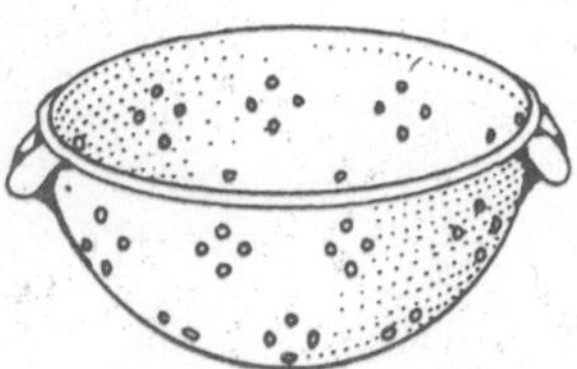

evenly over each portion, then baked the shells in a hot oven for about a half-hour.

The flavor of crab is delicate enough to need enhancing rather than smothering. A common recipe in the Chesapeake Bay area is crab Norfolk, a method of baking the finest lump meat in butter, seasoned with salt, pepper, lemon juice or vinegar, and a dash of Tabasco or other hot sauce; sometimes crab Norfolk is broiled in individual ramekins. On the West Coast legs of Alaska's king crab, first anointed with hot lemon butter, are broiled over charcoal; or they are sometimes the heart of a famous salad that originated generations ago at the Palace Hotel and is a presentation made colorful by artichoke hearts, carrots, peas, and Thousand Island dressing.

Soft-shell crabs are another matter. They are the blue crabs of Long Island Sound, the Eastern Shore, or of the Gulf of Mexico in that biological state when they have molted one shell and have not yet grown a new one. In this period of about forty-eight hours crabs seek peace and protection in vegetation-sheltered water near the shoreline. For the she-crab this idyll is the moment when she may welcome love. She waits for a hard-shell male and then, after whatever ecstasies, she develops a new carapace and moves on toward maturity. When such soft-shell crabs are caught, they should be kept alive until they are put into the vessel in which they are to cook. An expert at shellfish cooking told me, "The only good crab is a live one. Hard crabs should be fighting their grim end when they are dropped into the pot of boiling water, and soft-shell crabs should be alive through their last-minute preparation for the skillet or the broiler."

Crab meat may *seem* edible when bought frozen or canned, but none can compare with that fresh from the water. The blue crabs of the Eastern Shore that turn so brilliant a red when boiled alive are the basis of a considerable variety of cooked dishes. Sometimes this variety increases when a hero passes through town, inspiring the creativity of local chefs. (This happened often enough in the nineteenth century, when the world seemed more heroic.) When Admiral George Dewey returned from his Spanish American War victory, the chef of the Maryland Yacht Club dipped into his French culinary background and devised crab meat Dewey—white mushrooms, black truffles, shallots, crab, all in a white wine sauce finished with thick, scalded cream glazed under the broiler.

The crab I remember best was not done à la George Dewey; it had no French sauce at all. It was just plain steamed Dungeness crab, a good deal bigger than crabs of the Atlantic coast. Named for a promontory just off the Strait of Juan de Fuca, Dungeness are found all the way from the Aleutians to Mexico, and I doubt that any were ever better in flavor than the great piles from a Palo Alto fish man that we had on a Thanksgiving Day in a California ranch house, vaguely Spanish, midway up the Sonoma Valley. Our hostess was a California native for whom this arched room with its beams and its stippled walls and its expansive, open-doored, warming Franklin stove had been designed. She sat at the end of the massive refec-

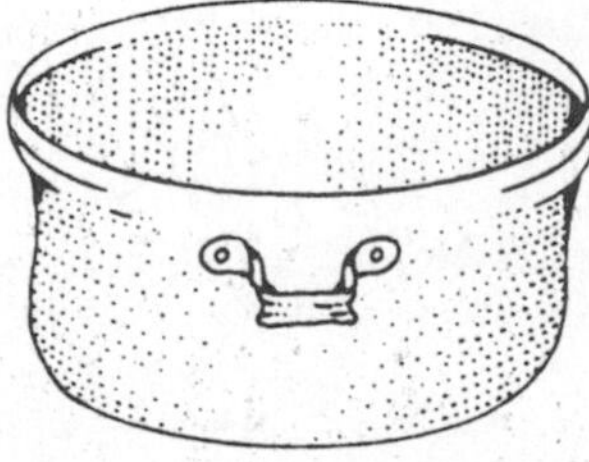

tory table delicately stripping away shells, and piling fat shreds of crab meat neatly on her plate before she began to eat. Most of the guests were less dignified—there were small sounds of shells being cracked by impatient teeth, of fingers licked, and monosyllables of appreciation. This had no hot pepper, as in Louisiana, nor hint of nutmeg common in Charleston and on the Carolina coast. The meat was so sweet and delicately pungent that it seemed to me to need nothing, not even the lemony melted butter with which it was served. What little it needed may have been the cool, dry Napa Valley Johannisberger Riesling—which was amply provided.

Wines Preserved the Bounty

During the nineteenth century—when the temperance movement was steadily gaining momentum—cooks on farms and in small towns annually bottled a comforting amount of homemade wine. Early colonists had fermented many gallons of cider and wine because they were convinced that much bad health could be traced to drinking water. But as the frontiers moved west, fruit wines and vegetable beers were important because they comprised another way of preserving the bounty of the land. Wine was sometimes made after gathering bushels of blossoms from dandelions or elderberries, which had no other nutritive use. More often than not, however, the berries remaining after all the jams and jellies had been put up were mashed and their juices fermented, to serve medicinal or celebratory purposes. Gooseberries, raspberries, cherries, and currants were turned into popular sweet wines, as were wild and domestic grapes of which there were many varieties. A recipe for blackberry wine, as made by General Robert E. Lee's wife in the kitchen at Arlington, overlooking the national capital, was preserved by her daughter just as the Confederate commander's lady wrote it down:

> Fill a large stone jar with ripe fruit and cover it with water. Tie a cloth over the jar and let them stand three or four days to ferment; then mash and press them through a cloth. To every gallon of juice add three pounds of brown sugar. Return the mixture to the jar and cover closely. Skim it every morning for more than a week, until it clears from the second fermentation. When clear, pour it carefully from the sediment into the demijohn. Cork it tightly, set it in a cool place. When two months old it will be fit for use.

Robert E. Lee Blackberry Wine

Fill a large stone jar with ripe fruit and cover it with water. Tie a cloth over the jar and let them stand three or four days to ferment; then mash and press them through a cloth. To every gallon of juice add three pounds of brown sugar. Return the mixture to the jar and cover closely. Skim it every morning for more than a week, until it clears from the second fermentation. When clear, pour it carefully from the sediment into the demijohn. Cork it tightly, set it in a cool place. When two months old it will be fit for use.

—Mrs. Lee in *Housekeeping in Old Virginia*

In virtually every region delicious and potable beers were brewed at home with roots or bark or buds as a base. Homemade root beer in the twentieth century has been a simple matter of using a factory-made extract, but the real thing, which was one of the pleasures of the nineteenth century, was brewed from sarsparilla roots, sometimes sassafras bark, molasses, and maybe some wintergreen leaves. Ginger beer is a compound based on ginger root or powdered ginger, and the spruce brew gets its distinction from essence of spruce or from boiling outer sprigs of the spruce fir.

Edward Everett Hale described the street sale of these forerunners of modern soft drinks: "Ginger beer and spruce beer were sold from funny little wheelbarrows, which had attractive pictures of the bottles throwing out their corks. . . . You might have a glass of spruce beer for two cents, and, to boys as impecunious as most of us were, the dealers would sell half a glass for one cent." In fact, the word *pop* derives from the effervescent quality of these drinks; a New England aphorism describes a clever man "as full of wit as a ginger-beer bottle is of pop."

New World roots such as Jerusalem artichokes did not make their way into the wine cellar, but were instead pickled, as were so many other vegetables and fruits, in one of the many processes employed for making use of—that is, not wasting—any of the plenty that came from the good earth. Methods of producing ketchup which English cooks had adapted from a sauce brought back from Asia, were borrowed and changed by American cooks (some of them changed the spelling of the word, too) to create walnut catsups first, then cranberry, elderberry, gooseberry, and grape catsups when sugar became plentiful. The earliest of these sauces, based sometimes on nuts, sometimes on mushrooms, had been made without sugar, resulting in spicy and tart concoctions in somewhat the manner of Worcestershire sauce. Early tomato catsup recipes are similarly tart: Mrs. Randolph's specifies only onions, mace, and black pepper as seasonings; a generation later Catherine Beecher, the sister of Mrs. Stowe, in her *Domestic Economy and Receipt Book*, gave a tomato catsup recipe that required only cloves and nutmegs, pepper, and a little wine as seasonings.

I suspect the evolution of catsup may help to explain a rather important national characteristic. The writer and historian Kenneth Roberts wrote that Maine sea captains "brought tomato seeds from Spain and Cuba, their wives planted them, and the good cooks in the families experimented with variants of the ubiquitous and somewhat characterless tomato sauce of Spain and Cuba." Without resorting to the use of sugar, those Maine essays in making catsup, Mr. Roberts said, were so successful that the new tomato mixture came to be "considered indispensable with hash, fish cakes and baked beans." He himself became, he added, "almost a ketchup drunkard; for when I couldn't get it, I yearned for it. Because of that yearning I begged the recipe from my grandmother when I went away from home; and since that day I have made many and many a batch," none of which was sugary, for a sweetened catsup "is regarded as an offense against God and man, against nature and good taste." The Roberts family catsup recipe had the tang of red and black pepper, allspice, mustard, cloves, and "sharp vinegar." Sharpness also distinguished the taste of tomato catsup in antebellum Charleston, that regional gastronomical capital where *bon gout* was more than an epigram. But soon, across the country, the American appetite for sugar had its way.

In the period immediately after the Civil War, Joshua Davenport was manufacturing and selling vinegar, pickles, and catsup in the Berkshire Hills of Massachusetts. According to the recipe handed down (the story goes) in the Davenport family, Joshua added two cups of sugar to a mixture

Mary Randolph's Tomato Catsup

Gather a peck of tomatos, pick out the stems, and wash them; put them on the fire without water, sprinkle on a few spoonsful of salt, let them boil steadily an hour, stirring them frequently; strain them through a colander, and then through a sieve; put the liquid on the fire with half a pint of chopped onions, half a quarter of an ounce of mace broke in small pieces; and if not sufficiently salty, add a little more—one table-spoonful of whole black pepper; boil all together until just enough to fill two bottles; cork it tight. Make it in August, in dry weather.

—*The Virginia Housewife*, 1831

of a gallon of tomato stock and a half-pint of vinegar flavored with cinnamon, cayenne, and salt. Chances are he was not the first man to sweeten the pot, but by the time Mrs. Rorer's cookbook began to influence a wide public in 1886 the sugary tomato sauce was firmly established. Catsup began to vie with mustard as the acceptable condiment for frankfurters and hamburgers—even for french fries and mashed potatoes—and before the nation was two hundred years old, it had gone from having a president who believed in a cuisine of high standards for the United States, as did Jefferson, to one whose taste ran to cottage cheese and sweetened red catsup for lunch, according to White House reports.

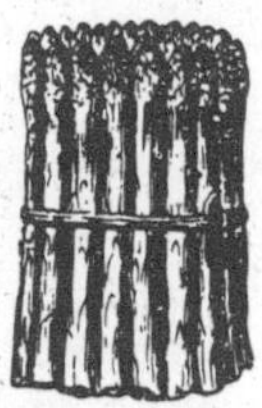

Fannie Farmer's Sweetbreads and Asparagus

Parboil a sweetbread, split, and cut in pieces shaped like a small cutlet, or cut in circular pieces. Sprinkle with salt and pepper, dip in crumbs, egg, and crumbs, and saute in butter. Arrange in a circle around Creamed Asparagus Tips.

—*The Boston Cooking-School Cook Book,* 1896

In the twentieth century weight consciousness helped to explain some gustatory aberrations, but a hundred years earlier most Americans ate as much or more for lunch as they did for breakfast or supper; dinner was, of course, properly served at midday when, in town or city, a man came home from his job. Like the farmer, the urban male knew a lot about food, and many of them were more familiar with the stalls in their local market buildings than were their wives.[8]

"My grandfather," wrote Margaret Rudkin, who earned fame with her Pepperidge Farm bread, "often did a bit of shopping on his way home, and when he stopped at the slaughterhouse on First Avenue where the United Nations building now stands, he would bring home a treat—'the liver and lights.' That meant calves were being killed that day and he bought fresh calf's liver and sweetbreads. . . . The calf's liver was left whole, larded with thin strips of salt pork, sprinkled with herbs and spices, covered with strips of bacon, and roasted, being basted often with the bacon fat and plenty of melted butter. It was heavenly," Mrs. Rudkin remembered almost a half-century later, adding that the accompaniment for the baked liver was a purée of dried peas, and that it was often served cold next day with rye bread and mustard pickles.

The nostalgia here is not unlike that of Mark Twain, adrift in Europe among cooking styles he thought too pretentious or not sufficiently respectful of high-quality ingredients. After all, the homesick writer from Hannibal, Missouri, wanted to return to such straightforward kitchen masterpieces as "apple dumplings with real cream. . . . Apple fritters, Apple puffs, Southern style, Peach cobbler, Southern style. . . . All sorts of American pastry." American cooks of the nineteenth century transformed mere abundance into a way with food that had its own style. Mark Twain's longing for real cream and American butter could be answered by many recipes common in various regions. Southern-style peach cobbler is simply a deep dish pie of peaches previously simmered with plenty of sugar, then layered in the crust with dots of butter. A whipped-cream pie of the period,

[8] Daniel Webster, in Washington, found surcease from the demands of statesmanship—and a great variety of provender—on his early-morning market tours to make his choice of Maine salmon, New Jersey oysters, Florida shad, Kentucky beef, Delaware canvasbacks, Virginia terrapin, South Carolina ricebirds, as well as the best of the fruits and vegetables brought into the district.

often served at the White House, consisted of a prebaked pastry shell filled with stiffly whipped sweet cream sweetened with powdered sugar and sometimes topped with flakes of chocolate.

A spicy confection, often called black cake, was the pride of many American cooks—from Martha Washington to the New England poet Emily Dickinson. In 1977, when the play *The Belle of Amherst* was performed by Julie Harris, the recipe for a cake requiring two pounds of flour, two pounds of sugar, two pounds of butter, nineteen eggs, five pounds of raisins, one and a half pounds of citron, one and a half pounds of currants, a half-pint of brandy, one-and-a-half pints of molasses, two nutmegs, grated, and three teaspoons of cloves was offered to the audience nightly by Emily Dickinson reincarnated:

> Beat butter and sugar together. Then you add the nineteen eggs, one at a time. Without beating—this is very important. Then you beat the mixture again, and add the brandy, alternately with the flour, soda, salt and spices that you sifted together. Then the molasses. Then take the five pounds of raisins, and your three pounds of currants and citron and sprinkle in all three pounds. Bake about three hours, and if you use cake pans or if you use a milk pan, as I do, you'd better leave it in the oven six or seven hours. . . . Sometimes I bake it for a neighbor and enclose a short poem.

The recipe, along with manuscript copies of Miss Dickinson's more formal compositions, is preserved in the Harvard archives set aside for the poet's work. Like so many women of her generation, she was as proud of her culinary achievements as of other accomplishments.

When I was a child, my mother often left her own writing and editing to cook in ways she had learned before the turn of the century, and she maintained the best of those ways as her repertoire widened with travel and a developing taste. Along with many of her contemporaries, she never submitted to so-called convenience foods as a way of life. She believed in the best of ingredients. On one of the end papers of one of her numerous volumes of recipes there appears this way of using fresh fruit, with comment, in her handwriting:

RASPBERRY SHERBET
(I originated. June 1931, 102°)

2 c. raspberries, mashed
with 2 c. sugar.
1 qt. milk (whole)
juice of 1 orange
Partly freeze, then stir in 2 stiffly beaten
egg whites, finish freezing & pack.
Best if left packed several hours.

It is a simple recipe, typical of many "originated" by women in every part of the country where there were cooks respectful of the quality of the materials at hand. It proves, if anything, that there was a time when nothing, not even the hottest day of a Midwest summer, was permitted by earnest cooks to interfere with the serving of good food.

SHAKERS, BAKERS, BREAKFAST FOOD MAKERS

American food styles changed unalterably as a result (indirect if you will) of a chain of events that began early in the nineteenth century. It might be said, in fact, that there is a traceable line from early Shaker cooking through the preachments of a man whose name is now coupled with whole wheat flour to the breakfast menus of most twentieth-century American homes. It is doubtful that the sounds of cornflakes ever would have been heard in the land had it not been for cooks who became convinced that good health is just as important as good food.

By the middle of the nineteenth century there was a massive reaction to a malaise that was usually described as dyspepsia but was aptly rechristened "Americanitis" by Marion Harland, a Virginia novelist who discovered a wider audience when she turned to writing books about food and household management. Thousands were in need of guidance. Those sedentary city dwellers who indulged in breakfasts of steak and pie, and greasy foods at every meal, belonged to a segment of the citizenry only too willing to listen to miraculous cure-alls.

An era of reform and revival had settled on the country—there was almost incessant talk of utopia, and many societies were formed to make the concept a reality, some in religious ways and some as socialistic panaceas. One of the earliest was the United Society of Believers in Christ's Second Coming, a spin-off from the Society of Friends whose members became known (there was a great deal of movement in their services) as the Shaking Quakers.

As a celibate sect, the Shakers established isolated communities dedicated to regular and simple living habits. Plain, wholesome food eaten in moderation was, they said, a preventative against indigestion and was cen-

Shaker Haying Water

Put 4 cups sugar or 3 cups maple syrup, 2 cups molasses, 2 teaspoons powdered ginger, and 2 gallons cold water together and stir until thoroughly blended. Pour into large jug, and chill. Serves 30.

—North Union Shaker Village

tral to the Shaker faith. Shakers were among the first to advocate greater use of vegetables and fruit as well as the use of whole grain in making flour. They considered their communities "Heavens on earth" in which they devoted themselves to thrift yet at the same time to standards of living far above the average. They created their own excellent architecture, designed furniture that is much coveted in the twentieth century, devised methods to increase productivity of soil and livestock, and became superior mechanics, responsible for inventions that helped improve the lives of many outsiders.

When travelers had to be put up in a Shaker village because there was no nearby hostelry, they were fed cheerfully enough in a separate dining room but admonished to "eat hearty and clean out the plate," for Shakers could not tolerate waste of any kind. They stopped short of so dividing their visitors that men and women dined at different tables, as was required of themselves, but cards were placed in visitors' bedrooms asking that "marital privileges" be foresworn during the stay in the community.[1]

Vegetarianism was not strictly enforced among the Shakers, but because the sect's leadership believed in a future in which all mankind would accept a meatless diet, the women who cooked together in the large community kitchens perfected recipes that were often published in the Shaker *Manifesto*, a periodical that circulated in each of the separate Shaker compounds. "It does not seem to be generally known that the cucumber is one of the most valuable vegetables we raise," announced one issue of the *Manifesto*. "It can be dressed in more palatable and suitable ways than most any other vegetable except tomatoes. It is far better than squash and more delicate than eggplant . . . and is most delicious when made into fritters in a dainty batter."

Another issue admonished: "One of the first signs of spring is the tiny sawlike leaf of the dandelion sticking its leaves above the thawing earth. Before they have a chance to burst into bloom, have the children gather these succulent plants. This furnishes you with a tasty dish and at the same time rids your dooryard of weeds." Shaker cooks also saluted winter's departure by making "Spring Vegetable Soup," a combination of chicken broth, fresh parsley leaves, and scraped parsley roots, slices of tiny young carrots, new potatoes, leeks and celery, sautéed in butter; to these were added chopped green pepper and shredded leaves of Boston lettuce. They devised a seasonal salad by combining three cups of diced ripe pears, three cups of diced peaches, one cup of diced tart apples, one cup of white grapes with a cup of mayonnaise, freshly made, and a cup of fresh cream, served on a bed of shredded lettuce.

Shaker Indian pudding, usually sweetened with maple syrup, was based

Cucumber Salad

Select 2 tender young cucumbers; peel one but leave the other unpeeled. Slice very fine. Sprinkle with salt and let stand just three minutes, thus removing any bitter taste of the skin. Mince ½ onion and add to cucumbers. Mix dressing of ½ cup sour cream, ½ cup vinegar, ½ teaspoon salt, ¼ teaspoon pepper, 2 tablespoons sugar, and ¼ teaspoon mustard; pour over cucumbers. Serve at once for full flavor.

—Amelia's Shaker Recipes

[1] A sample of Shaker versifying given to dining room guests: "We found of these bounties / Which heaven does give, / That some live to eat, / And that some eat to live– / That some think of nothing / But pleasing the taste, / And care very little / How much they do waste." Outsiders can still visit Shaker communities at Sabbathlake, Maine, and Canterbury, New Hampshire, as well as museums open at defunct villages near Hancock, Massachusetts, and Old Chatham, New York, and the Shaker Historical Society in Cleveland.

on methods many native cooks habitually used to make the most of wild produce as it became available. You can make one such cornmeal dessert by soaking a cup of white cornmeal in two cups of water and adding to it four tablespoons of nut butter (natural peanut butter from a health food store will do), then slowly cooking the mixture, stirring constantly until it thickens in about fifteen minutes. Stir in a cup of blackberry, raspberry, or blueberry juice, two cups of the berries you choose, and a teaspoon of grated nutmeg; bring to a boil. Stir in three-quarters of a cup of heavy cream and the same amount of maple syrup, blending thoroughly. Beat three eggs lightly; remove the fruit mixture from the heat and stir in the eggs. Serve with whipped cream.

Shaker Herbade

Combine ½ cup lemon balm, cut fine, ½ cup mint, chopped fine, ½ cup regular sugar syrup, and ½ cup lemon juice, and let stand 1 hour. Then add 4 quarts of Shaker gingerade or ginger ale. Serves 16.

—Canterbury Shaker Village

The Doing of Inventive Things

Shaker men found time to develop a mechanical apple parer, a pea sheller, a water-powered butter churn, an automatic cheese press, a superior woodburning stove, matches, and a revolving oven for baking dozens of pies at a time.[2] The women charged with the community cooking did inventive things with all kinds of ingredients. Shakers perfected a way to produce dried corn—and thereby helped provide Americans generally with year-round supplies that would not spoil easily. They made of the normal growing season "a rotation of crops of beans, peas, spinach, beets and turnips . . . in order to have crisp, fresh vegetables almost until the snow flies."

"Cucumbers want herbs!" cried the *Manifesto*, and growing them, drying, grinding, and packaging them provided some communities their chief source of income. They also were among the first to market wild roots and other herbaceous plants that grew naturally on the frontiers. They may have been the first to use advertising to guide other cooks toward improving the flavor of the food served in average homes, pointing out in leaflets that herbs "stimulate appetite, they give character to food and add charm and variety to ordinary dishes."

Shakers may never have heard of such infusions as the *tisanes* prepared by the French in the interest of health, but they were expert at such summer necessities as "haying water" to quench the thirst of field workers. And long before soft drinks were bottled commercially, "Shaker herbade" was regularly produced in hot weather from herbs especially picked for the occasion. Lemony herbade results from combining one-half cup each of finely cut lemon balm and mint leaves with an equal amount of sugar syrup and lemon juice, then stirring the mixture into four quarts of homemade gingerade or ginger ale. The result will soothe sixteen guests on a summer afternoon.

[2] The history of one of the earliest ventures in wholesale pie making was described in a 1963 issue of the New Haven *Register*. Amos Munson opened a factory in New Haven in 1844 to make and ship "Connecticut pies" via steamboat to New York, where, he had been told by his own homesick son, there were many people who longed for "old-fashioned pies." Within five years Munson's cooks were producing a thousand pies a day, and his steamboat costs were so high that he opened a plant in New York.

Maple Wheaten Bread

Scald 1 cup milk and add 1 tablespoon salt, 4 tablespoons maple syrup (or honey), and 3 tablespoons butter, and ¾ cup warm water and stir well. Let cool to lukewarm. Dissolve 1 cake of yeast in ¼ cup warm water and add to other liquid mixture. Add 2 cups of flour and 4 cups of whole wheat flour gradually and knead into a smooth ball. Proceed as usual in kneading. When well risen in loaf pans, bake in moderate (350°) oven for 50 to 60 minutes. Yields one very substantial loaf of extremely wholesome bread.

—Eldress Clymena Miner, North Union

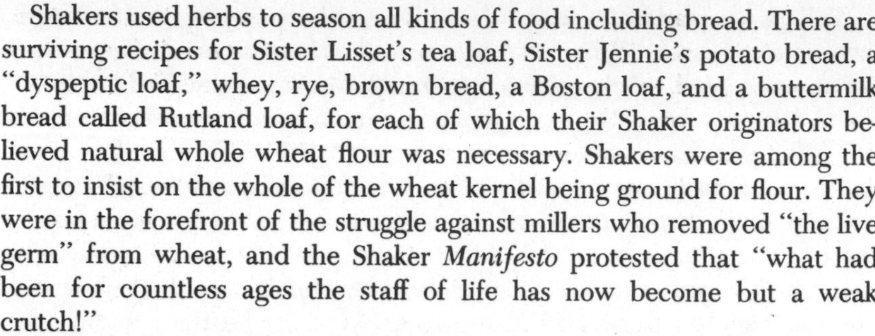

Shakers used herbs to season all kinds of food including bread. There are surviving recipes for Sister Lisset's tea loaf, Sister Jennie's potato bread, a "dyspeptic loaf," whey, rye, brown bread, a Boston loaf, and a buttermilk bread called Rutland loaf, for each of which their Shaker originators believed natural whole wheat flour was necessary. Shakers were among the first to insist on the whole of the wheat kernel being ground for flour. They were in the forefront of the struggle against millers who removed "the live germ" from wheat, and the Shaker *Manifesto* protested that "what had been for countless ages the staff of life has now become but a weak crutch!"

A Shaker loaf called "Maple Wheaten Bread" may be as satisfying and as nourishing as any produced by home bakers in the twentieth century, and it can be easily turned out in modern kitchens. Scald one cup of milk and add one tablespoon of salt, four tablespoons of maple syrup (or honey), and three tablespoons of butter in three-quarters cup of warm water and stir well. Let the mixture cool to lukewarm. Dissolve one cake of yeast in one-quarter cup of warm water and add to the milk mixture. Stir in two cups of white flour and four cups of whole wheat flour, then knead into a smooth ball. Butter a bowl and put dough in it, cover and let rise in a warm place until doubled in bulk. Punch dough down and knead about five minutes. Shape to fit a loaf pan and let rise again. When doubled in bulk, bake in 350°F. oven about one hour.

The Shaker protests about bread reached the susceptible mind of a young man from Connecticut in search of a cause. Labeled a "mad enthusiast" in his college days at Amherst, Sylvester Graham had been expelled on a charge trumped up by his classmates. As a result, he had had a nervous breakdown, and he suffered from incipient tuberculosis. But he was determined to be a leader and to emblazon his name—as he saw things—"in the skies of posterity." He became a Presbyterian minister in New Jersey, and, after appointment as general agent of the Pennsylvania State Society for the Suppression of the Use of Ardent Spirits, he came into contact with members of a vegetarian church in Philadelphia. The emphasis of this group was on a puritan life sustained by plain, wholesome food.

After such exposures, Graham studied the physiological aspects of the vegetarian church doctrines and became convinced that a great many Americans abused their bodies with bad food as well as with the evils of drink and other excesses. On the lecture platform he inveighed against salt, condiments, pork, hot mince pie, heavy clothing, corsets, and feather beds—the latter on the grounds that they led to behavior considered less than puritan. He seems to have convinced himself that the fall from grace resulted when men "began to put asunder what God joined together"—specifically, to mill the bran out of wheat flour. One of his publications, *The Graham Journal of Health and Longevity*, asserted: "Every farmer knows that if his horse has straw cut with his grain, or hay in abundance, he does well enough. Just so it is with the human species. Man needs bran in his bread."

While a vegetarian leader of the Shakers was asking, in the forthright rhetoric of the sect, "Why make a graveyard of your stomach, when there are so many good, wholesome things to eat?" the Reverend Graham told a friend, "I *feel* I know the mind of God." To Graham it was clear that the only good bread was that made from the whole kernel of the wheat. Further, he preached that all bread should be made in home kitchens, and only by the wife and mother, not by any servant, for in his belief the least a housewife owed her family was the shaping—with her own hands—of dough made from the whole kernel flour, investing it with all the love and care she gave to nursing a child when sick.

His accusations against commercially made bread (and against the health-threatening practices of butchers in unsanitary abattoirs) aroused so much animosity in Boston that the mayor refused police protection for a Graham meeting, hoping to persuade the health food leader's followers not to appear. Instead, some of them waited until the protesting butchers and bakers had gathered, then set about routing them; they flung shovelfuls of lime on the bakers, refusing to be deterred until the enemy was as white and unappetizing-looking as the Grahamites considered the factory-made bread to be.

Graham's platform eloquence in the interest of a better national diet so aroused some cooks and their families that Grahamite societies were organized, and there were grocery stores that specialized in items recommended by the master. Some temperance hotels, which had been content to attract clients who were teetotalers, turned themselves into Graham hotels with strictly regulated dining rooms.[3] At one, Horace Greeley paid court—while consuming meals limited to Graham bread, baked beans, rice, and the blandest of puddings—to his future wife. Bronson Alcott, the father of Louisa May and other little women, may not formally have been a Grahamite, but he went even farther than the strictest Shakers when he and Charles Lane established the colony called Fruitlands (on a farm not far from a Massachusetts Shaker village), where he ordered his seventeen resident adherents to put their bodies under "utter subjugation"; they were to live on native grains, fruits, herbs, and roots—no fish, fowl, flesh, butter, eggs, milk, cheese, nor any drink but spring water to pass their lips.

More fanatic even than Graham in submitting to the charm of his own ideas, Bronson Alcott had gone too far in setting the rules for Fruitlands. The regime was too much for a young woman, an assistant to Mrs. Alcott in preparing the spartan diet in the commune's kitchen. She admitted, upon discovery, to having eaten fish once at the house of a neighbor and to have hidden cheese in her trunk. Summarily, she was drummed out of the house of idyll.

[3] Graham said his diet of unsifted flour and vegetables would cure alcoholism. A century later, the redoubtable Vrest Orton of Weston, Vermont, reported in his treatise on whole grains that he received much mail from those who benefited from products of his gristmill. One letter that pleased him, he wrote, was from a young lady who began eating whole grains twice and sometimes three times a day after remaining childless five years. Ten months later she wrote Orton to announced the birth of twin sons.

Dr. Kellogg and the U.S. Diet

Mrs. Kellogg's Cereal Crust
(for 9-inch pie plate)

Blend 1 to 3 tablespoons sugar into 1½ cups cereal crumbs, then add 6 tablespoons melted butter. Mix thoroughly. Use your fingers if necessary. Turn out into a pie plate and press firmly against sides and bottoms. Place in warm oven (325°) and bake for 5 to 8 minutes.

Neither the Grahamites nor the Shakers carried matters of diet to the extreme espoused by a woman leader of the Seventh-Day Adventists, whose world headquarters had been established at Battle Creek, Michigan. She was Ellen White, wife of Elder James White, who had adopted Graham's ideas about food; Mrs. White was constantly receiving spiritual messages, and on Christmas Day 1865, she became convinced that the Adventists, who were frequently troubled by dyspepsia, should be treated in a sanitarium of their own. Not long after her vision became a reality, Mrs. White and her husband awarded a medical scholarship to a young Seventh-Day Adventist names John Harvey Kellogg, and the influence of Battle Creek on the American diet was set in motion.

While pursuing his medical studies in New York, young J. H. Kellogg breakfasted daily on seven graham crackers and an apple—once a week allowing himself a coconut as well, and occasionally including potatoes or oatmeal in the menu. Kellogg did his own cooking, and the chore increased his interest in developing a healthier diet for the patients he was being trained to serve back in Battle Creek.

"The breakfast food idea," he once recalled, "made its appearance in a little third-story room on the corner of 28th Street and Third Avenue, New York City. . . . My cooking facilities were very limited, [making it] very difficult to prepare cereals. It often occurred to me that it should be possible to purchase cereals at groceries already cooked and ready to eat, and I considered different ways in which this might be done." But it was two years later, after he had been put in charge of the Seventh-Day Adventist health sanitarium, that he hit upon a workable formula and, as he put it, "prepared the first Battle Creek health food which I called Granola." And in the following years, Kellogg told an interviewer, "I invented nearly sixty other foods to meet purely dietetic needs."

Granola may have been the first of the Battle Creek products that led to such twentieth-century breakfast items as Kellogg's Special K, but it was only one of the experimental precooked cereal products flooding the market before the turn of the century. Shredded wheat resulted from work done by Henry Perky, a dyspeptic who became an apostle of the wheat berry as the perfect food. He ran a vegetarian restaurant in Denver as well. His heart, however, was in the cooked grain product he developed and made famous as shredded wheat.[4]

[4] It's unlikely that Perky imagined all the ways that eventually developed for using shredded wheat. Henry Wallace, who served as Franklin D. Roosevelt's least conventional vice president, seems to have relished a shredded wheat meal so unusual that it should, perhaps, remain unique: "The Wallace farm was an egg farm," Lillian Hellman wrote in *Scoundrel Time*, "and Ilo's dinner consisted of two poached eggs for Henry put on two shredded wheat biscuits, a horrid sight, made more insulting by one egg on shredded wheat for me and one for Ilo. It was the sight of this stingy, discourteous supper that made me say that I had already eaten and didn't wish anything else. . . . Ilo was undisturbed—what could disturb a woman who put eggs on shredded wheat?"

A woman who can make a baked pudding of two shredded wheat biscuits is in another

Corn flakes are two words even better known internationally, and they acquired their specific meaning at the end of the century, when Dr. Kellogg and his brother Will perfected a method of flaking, which they first used on wheat kernels. Grape-nuts, so christened because the dextrose contained in the kernels was called grape sugar and because the new product had a nutty flavor, were developed by C. W. Post, who had come to the Battle Creek sanitarium as a patient of Dr. Kellogg.

In all their great variety, dry, precooked breakfast foods revolutionized menus for the morning meal. They helped to increase the consumption of milk and to minimize the high cost of living. Ironically, products that originated in the interest of improving health have undergone so many modifications to provide sweetness and other pleasant flavors that their once-vaunted nutritional values have been all but lost. A study conducted in 1970 indicated that forty out of sixty dry cereals may "fatten but do little to prevent malnutrition."

Still, may other uses have been found for breakfast foods since Mrs. J. H. Kellogg, author of *Science in the Kitchen* and *Every-Day Dishes*, published her recipe for "Cereal Pie Crust" made from her husband's products. Commenting on the "dietetic evils of Pastries," she said that "the very name had become almost synonymous with indigestion and dyspepsia," and she worked out her recipe for a crumb crust not so much to increase sales as to steer cooks away from butter and lard. She stipulated one and a half cups of cereal crumbs in making a crust for a nine-inch pie; the crumbs, mixed with one to three tablespoons of sugar and six tablespoons of melted butter stick to the pie dish when pressed firmly against sides and bottom and should be prebaked at 325°F. for five minutes or a little longer.

Dr. Kellogg had said that the "original purpose in making the toasted flaked cereal was to replace the half-cooked, pasty, dyspepsia producing breakfast mush." In the considerable writing his wife did, she agreed, and she recommended that the newfangled flakes would provide "the very best capital upon which people who have real work to do in the world can begin the day." I would be surprised if she entertained the possibility of pancakes or waffles based on corn flakes, but such recipes were to come along nevertheless. For pancakes, corn flakes may be mixed with a buttermilk or sour cream batter and should be cooked at once to maintain their crunchy texture. Corn flakes also make interesting cookies. But Mrs. Kellogg might not have thought these innovations to be worthy enough. She was not one to gild the lily, for she advocated temperate eating in general. "A great variety of foods at one meal," she wrote, "creates a love of eating as a source of pleasure merely, and likewise furnishes temptation to overeat. Let us have well-cooked nutritious, palatable food, and plenty of it," she added, "but not too great a variety at each meal."

category. Ruth Wakefield, who established a famous Massachusetts restaurant called the Toll House Inn, served her shredded wheat dessert with a hard sauce. Her recipe calls for crumbling the biscuits and mixing with a cup of milk, a slightly beaten egg, three-quarters of a cup of dark molasses, a teaspoon of cinnamon, and a little salt. The batter is dotted with butter and baked at 350°F. for three-quarters of an hour.

Toll House Shredded Wheat Pudding

Crumble in baking dish 2 shredded wheat biscuits.

Mix in a bowl 2 eggs, slightly beaten, 2 cups milk, ¾ cup dark molasses, 1 teaspoon cinnamon, ¼ teaspoon salt.

Pour mixture over shredded wheat. Dot with butter. Bake in 350° oven for 45 minutes. Serve with Hard Sauce or whipped cream. Serves 4.

—Toll House Inn,
Whitman, Mass.

Mrs. Kellogg's Corn Puffs

Add ⅞ cup of milk and 1 teaspoon melted butter to 2 beaten eggs; then stir gradually into ½ cup flour, 4 level tablespoons yellow cornmeal, and ¼ teaspoon salt, which have been sifted together. Beat the batter with an egg-beater until full of bubbles. Fill well-buttered hot muffin pans two-thirds full. Bake 15 minutes at 450°; reduce heat to 375° and bake for another 15 to 20 minutes. This quantity will make 10 popovers in 2½-inch muffin tins. Be sure tins are preheated.

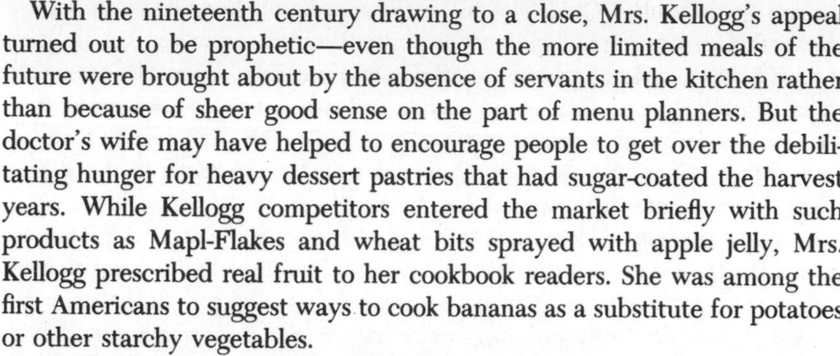

With the nineteenth century drawing to a close, Mrs. Kellogg's appeal turned out to be prophetic—even though the more limited meals of the future were brought about by the absence of servants in the kitchen rather than because of sheer good sense on the part of menu planners. But the doctor's wife may have helped to encourage people to get over the debilitating hunger for heavy dessert pastries that had sugar-coated the harvest years. While Kellogg competitors entered the market briefly with such products as Mapl-Flakes and wheat bits sprayed with apple jelly, Mrs. Kellogg prescribed real fruit to her cookbook readers. She was among the first Americans to suggest ways to cook bananas as a substitute for potatoes or other starchy vegetables.

And through her experimental cooking in the Kellogg factory, Ella Kellogg developed great enthusiasm for cornmeal, devising many ways to make use of it in a well-balanced diet, including a recipe for corn puffs that can be served, like popovers, with the main course of dinner. Her husband said of her contribution to the diet revolution: "Without the help derived from this fertile incubator of ideas, the great food industries of Battle Creek would never have existed. They are all direct or indirect outgrowths of Mrs. Kellogg's experimental kitchen."

A Doctor's Name for Wheat

There were parallel developments in cities far from Battle Creek. In Baltimore the Ralston Club, founded by a local physician, blossomed into a national membership said to consist in 1898 of 800,000 persons. It was so influential that manufacturers of various food products sought the endorsement of Dr. Ralston, who—for a small fee—would recommend that his members use the selections he approved. The story is that when the product known as Purina Wheat was developed in St. Louis, it so pleased the Baltimore health man that he endowed the Purina company with his name.

The name of Horace Fletcher became at least as immortal when it found its way into dictionaries as "Fletcherism." A man who late in life did a double back somersault into the Battle Creek sanitarium pool, Horace Fletcher was a friend of the Kelloggs, who supplemented their whole-grain philosophy by writing such tomes as *The ABC of Nutrition, Glutton or Epicure,* and *Fletcherism: What It Is.* What it was was a businessman's theory that the more one chews, the less one needs to eat. "Nature will castigate those who don't masticate," he wrote, making a palatable rhyme of his instructions for what he termed "mouth thoroughness." It was this thoroughness that threw philosopher William James for a loss. "I had to give it up," he said after chewing assiduously for three months. "It nearly killed me."

Lethal or not, Fletcherism wasn't really so very new. Prime Minister William Gladstone, who had died before Fletcher's first book was published, had already put himself on record: "I have made it a rule to give every tooth of mine a chance, and when I eat, to chew every bite thirty-two times. To this rule," Gladstone wrote, "I owe much of my success in life." Nevertheless, the same theory was called Fletcherism when practiced by John D. Rockefeller, Upton Sinclair, Thomas A. Edison, and the cadets of West Point.

The possibility of charlatanism was ever-present, but at Battle Creek the initial belief in whole grains and mastication for improved nutrition was sincere—in spite of the fact that it made money. Not nearly so much money would have flowed in, however, had it not been for the promotion and sales genius demonstrated by W. K. Kellogg and C. W. Post particularly. Both died immensely rich, and Post said frequently, "All I have I owe to advertising." The same could be said for the whole breakfast food industry and its impact on American eating and cooking habits. The advertising slogan "Breakfast of Champions" is not such a far cry from the precepts of the Shakers; to insure the superiority of their lives and their contributions to the world over those of outsiders they stuck to diets so healthful that the Shakers set records for longevity.

Cults that satisfy cravings to be in fashion, to attract attention, to be different, to be better—zealotry attached to any such desire happens all the time in all countries. But only in America, perhaps, could the yearnings of several generations of dissatisfied eaters be turned into a vast commercial success that has endowed every little eater and his parent with a new kind of meal altogether—in flavor, texture, and sound.

Stillwater Corn-Flake Pancakes

Put together 1 cup corn flakes (preferably Post Toasties), 1½ cups white flour, ½ teaspoon salt, ½ teaspoon soda, and 1½ teaspoons baking powder, and sift over corn-flakes in mixing bowl. Add 1 egg, beaten light, 1 cup sour milk or buttermilk, 1 tablespoon melted shortening, and mix thoroughly. Bake a try-cake, and if too thick, thin with a little sweet milk. These are delicious if you use sour cream and no shortening.

—Parish Guild, Ascension Church, May, 1923

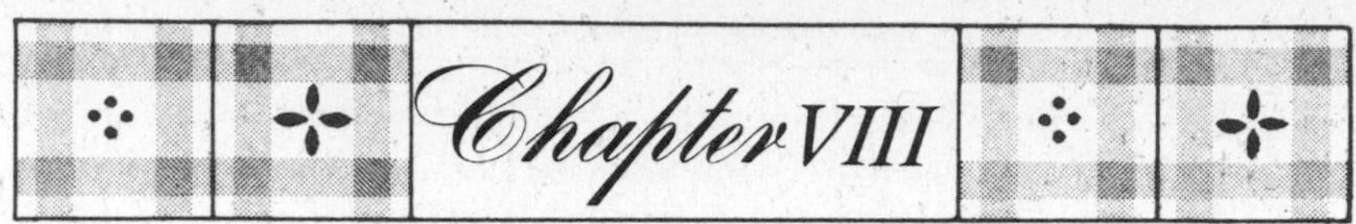

Chapter VIII

MELTING POT?

By the 1950s few Americans were still aware that only a generation previously the style of cooking that a bride might bring to her new house could represent ethnic differences. For some it seemed hard to believe that a girl from several generations of American background might once have had to learn to cook all over again if she married a demanding man with—for instance—Mediterranean antecedents.

Of almost countless examples, I know of one such marriage in which the lady sprang from a line of Yankees, her husband from an Italian metropolis. Only as she set up housekeeping did this young wife of the years before the Great Depression face the fact that her heirloom recipes—which ignored garlic and scarcely admitted the existence of olive oil—needed drastic overhauling if she were to feed her new husband in the style to which he was accustomed. Happily, she managed the trick, and along with others whose spouses had been reared on the cuisines of Middle Europe, Scandinavia, Greece, or one of the other Americas, her horizons widened, as did those of the rest of the gastronomical U.S.A.

This happened—there is no doubt about it. But other things were happening, too, some of them in direct opposition to infusions of new tastes. As many immigrant names were anglicized to help their bearers blend more easily into the New World landscape, the menus of some immigrant families—those who could afford it—were also anglicized, ridding kitchens of fragrances that ranged from the puckery atmosphere created by boiled cabbage or fried onions to the scented air thrown off by dishes in which herbs exercised their ineffable spells. Much was lost as new families, striving to be accepted, determined to make their meals as bland as those of neighbors who had lived longer in America.

However, the unavoidable fact is that much good food survived to become a part of an American cuisine because many people were too poor to have neighbors to keep up with. There were Dutchtowns, Jewish ghettos, and Little Italys in large cities, and in the unsettled West fledgling communities sprang up that were sometimes almost entirely populated by newcomers from, say, Scandinavia, Bohemia, or Holland. In neighborhoods dominated by one or another group from Europe the meals eaten by even the most economically depressed were, in any general assessment, more edible, more appetizing, than those of middle-class families who felt themselves more directly related to johnnycake and red meat.

The Italian Revolution

What everybody learned early about families arriving from Italy was that they seldom had a meal that failed to include spaghetti, a kind of food that, for some reason, seemed more exotic (read foreign!) than the noodles of the Pennsylvania Dutch or the macaroni that had been common enough—at least as a part of the American vocabulary—since it had been first imported by Thomas Jefferson.

Indeed, certain things about Italian meals had sturdy, if somewhat snobbish, champions. "Macaroni, as an article of food," Mrs. Rorer wrote in 1886, "is rather more valuable than bread, as it contains a larger proportion of gluten. It is the bread of the Italian laborer. In this country, it is a sort of luxury among the upper classes; but there is no good reason, considering its price, why it should not enter more extensively into the food of our working classes." Mrs. Rorer recommended Italian "spighetti," as she spelled it, as "the most delicate form of macaroni that comes to this country."

And there were other noticeable influences. Italians were in evidence as restaurant proprietors and cooks as early as the Gold Rush of 1849, when every California mining town had at least one hostelry dealing in tomatoey sauces. It was also about this time that a Genoan sailor named Giuseppe Buzzaro, as San Francisco legends say, "invented" a fish stew that later became known as *cioppino*—perhaps a distorted version of *ciupin*, a Ligurian mariner's fish soup found by twentieth-century travelers on menus in Genoa. A delicious and "genuinely Californian" *cioppino* may include every fish found in San Francisco waters along with tomatoes, green peppers, and several herbs, but pasta is one thing it does not include.

Spaghetti, nevertheless, became as "naturalized" as did any Italian-American between the end of the nineteenth century and the beginning of World War II. It became a repast first accepted by nonconformists. Certainly its bohemian reputation was solidified by proximity: Greenwich Village's art colony (and this was true in San Francisco and other cities) was next door to New York's Little Italy, where a spaghetti dinner was cheap, filling, and redolent of good flavors not to be found elsewhere. The good word spread. American "bohemians" joined Italians in preparing spaghetti in their own kitchens, buying the pasta from immigrant grocers in whose solidly stocked shops they also found imported cheeses and ingredients for sauces.

Two facts brought about the making of pasta in myriad forms by Italians in the United States. Dr. Mark Carleton, a Department of Agriculture agronomist, got farmers in Kansas and other plains states to grow durum wheat that had the necessary hard quality for good pasta dough; and World War I cut off imports and pushed the manufacture in this country that led gradually to distribution regionally and finally on a national scale. At about the same time, canning companies began to seal tomatoes hermetically, then developed canned tomato sauces that housewives had only to heat before serving a meal. Soon there were such ready-to-eat products as meat- or cheese-filled ravioli put up in glass jars filled with sauce.

By the middle of the twentieth century dry pasta was being manufactured in 150 shapes and sizes, according to the National Macaroni Manufacturer's Institute. In the 1970s, specialty stores with such names as Pasta, Inc. and Pasta and Cheese were offering their customers a variety of spaghetti and other pastas made fresh each day. And for those Americans who had become *fanatici* there were portable machines for the shaping of doughy ribbons of linguini and fettucine, as well as forms in which to make ravioli pouches at home. Catering services discovered the appetite for Italian meals, and in Washington, D.C., Pasta, Inc., augmented its freshly made *tagliatelle* and *cappelli d'angelo* (prepared with a choice of eggs, whole wheat flour, spinach, or tomato) by adding a line of custom-made *pesto* and other sauces to take home and heat up with the fettucine. The final touch for Pasta, Inc., was the "in-home pasta man," who for $150 took over private kitchens when guests arrived for fashionable dinners.

Camarillo Salad

Peel the largest ripe tomatoes that can be found, and slice them rather thick. Arrange flat or just slightly overlapping on a large platter or tray, and sprinkle with salt. Now take orégano and, rubbing it between your hands, powder it in a thin dust over the tomatoes. A drizzle of olive oil will finish this salad. Vinegar is *not* necessary because of the acid in the tomatoes, and the orégano eliminates the need for pepper. Serve very cold.

—*Crumbs from Everybody's Table*, 1910

Changing the Character of U.S. Cookery

Long gone were the days when Italian grocers supplied only immigrant fellow countrymen and their offspring. The shoppers who had first started coming in search of imported pasta also had found for the first time in their experience not only such dry sausages as *coppa* and *mortadella* but also salamis and bologna. (The latter became so standard in American life that it doubles, in its anglicized spelling, as one of the sturdiest words in American slang.) The new Italian accent to American food was due to newcomers who clannishly had refused to abandon the delicacies of their native tables even though they lived far from Atlantic ports. They had seen to it that no tiny frontier village where Italians settled was too remote from a mail-order house through which they could purchase olive oil, Parmesan and other cheeses, and various kinds of pasta.

The West Coast attracted many Italians with an extraordinary talent for making the soil produce, and they introduced fruits and vegetables that did much to change the character of American cookery. Californians sometimes say that artichokes, which came to cover so many acres around Half

Moon Bay, were rejected as too much trouble to *eat* until Italians not only grew them better but showed how tastily they could be cooked. (Today in Santa Clara county a restaurant called the Giant Artichoke serves artichoke soup, deep fried artichoke hearts, and a sweet-artichoke cake for dessert.) Californians also learned far more about the appetizing qualities of squashes from the Italians than they had from the Indians. A recipe that proves the point, a method of enhancing the flavor of several vegetables, is called *taglierini alla* Sonoma. To make this you need two small zucchini that have been diced, one small unpeeled diced eggplant, one chopped onion, and a diced carrot. Melt a little butter in a skillet and fry three slices of bacon cut in squares. When the bacon is crisp, stir in the vegetables and cook about three minutes. Add a half-cup of Pinot Chardonnay, cooking until it evaporates. Add a cup of tomato sauce, eight sliced mushrooms, and a half-cup of grated Parmesan cheese. Cook a pound of taglierini and serve with the vegetable sauce, a sprinkling of minced parsley, and more cheese.

In California they trace the commercial growing of many vegetables, such as bell peppers, eggplant, broccoli, Savoy cabbage, cauliflower, and fava beans, to Italians; the western tomato industry began with Camillo Pregno, who improved growing techniques and opened a factory for canning tomato purée to appease the burgeoning demand for pasta sauces outside the Italian communities.

A Hungarian, Agoston Haraszthy, is still sometimes referred to as the father of California's modern wine industry. Spanish vintners, who had been well established in the eighteenth century, were joined by French, Alsatian, German, and other European wine makers. But thousands of Italians worked the vineyards, and some of their countrymen set up large, now famous wineries of their own. In addition, newly arrived *contadini* grew almonds and lemons in California; apples and peaches on the slopes of the Ozarks; watermelon, sugar cane, rice, and cotton in the southwestern states. They husbanded gardens that thrived in cities and sold their produce from door to door in nonimmigrant neighborhoods.

They did more, perhaps, than any other ethnic group to expand the American cuisine. Even the antipasto, the vegetable-studded introduction to an Italian meal, has been blamed for the American habit of serving a garden or fruit salad before the entrée instead of as a light punctuation mark to cleanse the palate between one course and another.[1] Unlike the course of empire, the salad-as-appetizer syndrome has moved inexorably east from the Pacific Coast, bringing with it the fruit concoctions and gelatines and sweet salad dressings that are peculiar to the United States. Among West Coast salad exports with a justifiable and increasingly international reputation, however, is one created by Caesar Cardini, an Italian

[1] Rather than blame the Italians, it should be noted that U.S. eating places prepare salads in advance and offer them as a stopgap for impatient diners while they await their steaks—or whatever entrée they may order. In the 1970s restaurants across the country successfully promoted the "salad bar," an American variation of Scandinavian "cold tables," with the emphasis on green salads accented by tomatoes, shrimp, and so on.

immigrant, whose Tijuana restaurant attracted hundreds of diners from nearby San Diego as well as other parts of the United States.

With its Italian accents, Caesar's salad itself attracted imitators in home kitchens as well as in public eating places. The original recipe calls for romaine lettuce (brought to America by gardeners from the Mediterranean), anchovies, and imported Parmesan cheese. Shortcut methods result in many recipes with Worcestershire sauce (which contains a hint of anchovy) substituted for anchovy fillets. But an authentic Caesar salad is a work worthy of an Italian-American artist. It should be made at the table, with real olive oil in which a crushed clove of garlic has rested overnight. It also needs two cups of croutons, made from stale sourdough French loaves and cooked in a little of the garlic oil, and two eggs cooked one minute only. Put six to eight romaine leaves in a large bowl and season with salt and freshly ground pepper, add the oil, then carefully turn the leaves to coat them thoroughly. Break in the eggs and squeeze over the salad a juicy lemon. Continue mixing the leaves to incorporate eggs and lemon, and add six or eight anchovy fillets as you snip them into bits. Toss in a half-cup of freshly grated Parmesan, and add the croutons before the final mixing of the salad.

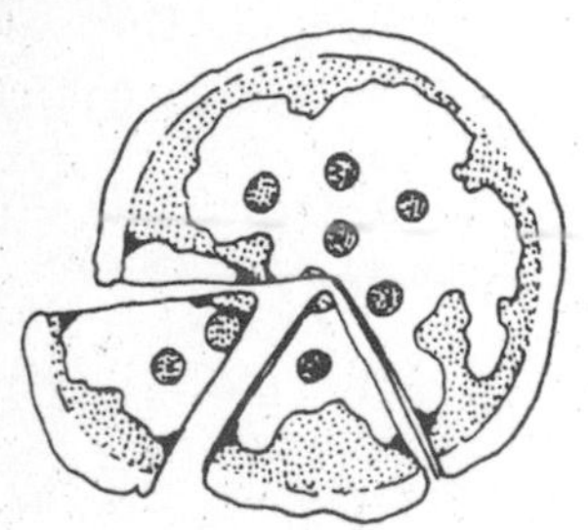

Even more Italian and even more popular is the pie called pizza, which was charted by a 1970 Gallup poll as the favorite snack of Americans over twenty-one and under thirty-four. A wedge of tomato-covered bread dough with the savor of oregano along with a briny anchovy tang misting upward, or the texture and taste of mushrooms nestled in one or more kinds of bubbling cheese, can be marvelous informal food. Neapolitan-style pizzas with all their American modifications became as readily available as any common sandwich. *Pizza rustica*, Italy's "deep dish" cheese-and-meat conglomerate, is made in American homes, but only a few restaurants specialize in the pie that has crisp crusts top and bottom, sort of like a fruit cobbler. In Chicago one such place developed such a reputation that it attracted stalwart pizza fans willing to travel regularly as far as forty-five miles for a rustic snack gooey with mozzarella, sausage, and tomato sauce; and others came even from such distant places as Chattanooga, Tennessee.

Still, neither the best of pizzas nor the average Italian restaurant meal (most of which are tempered to New World tastes) accounts for the permanence of the Italian accent on American gastronomy. The strongest influence—aside from Neapolitan sauces—has come from somewhat more elegant dishes. In California, for instance, those fields of artichokes were put to good use when cooks from Italy combined artichokes with tomatoes, oregano, Livermore sherry, and pounded veal cutlets. By the 1970s *scallopini*, the word for such pale pink pieces of calves' meat, had entered the language and even U.S. dictionaries. And cold *vitello tonatto* had been translated as veal with tuna-fish sauce to become a standby for summer hostesses across the country.

Not the least of the reasons for the gradual increase in Italian dishes on

American menus is due to Italian butchers who have prided themselves on being among the best. More than some others, they built reputations for knowing a good deal about the art of good plain cooking; equally important, they often guided customers in transforming leftovers and inexpensive cuts of meat into dishes seldom attempted in other kitchens. Some Italian butchers made it a habit to pass along recipes. In Barre, Vermont, for instance—where a lot of northern Italian stone quarriers settled—it became common to order a roast preseasoned with herbs by the butcher. Almost necessarily many American cooks adopted Italian ways with meat and poultry; results seemed equally good whether they simmered marrowbones with tomatoes and called it *osso buco*, or uttered Tuscan incantations when simmering one of the many variations of hunter-style chicken in a sauce fragrant with garlic and mushrooms.

Long ago a friendly Manhattan butcher named Luigi Trianni gave me his thoughts about cooking veal knuckles. Having cut four three-inch slices from the shank, he directed that they be washed in water mixed with a little lemon juice. "Dry them and dredge in seasoned flour," he said. "Melt a couple of tablespoons of butter and two of good Italian olive oil in a heavy pot and sear the meat on all sides. After removing the shanks, put into the same pot two well chopped onions, two carrots, two stalks of celery, two strips of bacon, and two slices of Italian prosciutto, all finely chopped. Cook these slowly about ten minutes, and add a bay leaf, some chopped Italian parsley, a little basil, and a little thyme. Put back the veal pieces and cover them just barely with chicken stock, tomato juice, and dry white wine in equal parts. Put a lid on the pot and simmer two and a half to three hours. Take out the meat and put it on a hot platter while you strain the sauce, which you pour over the meat. Sprinkle on some chopped parsley and grated lemon rind, and serve with risotto."

Some time after World War II risotto (rice cooked in stock with the addition of meat or vegetables) became as acceptably American as San Francisco's Ghirardelli Square; a similarly popular one-dish meal, eagerly admired by mothers with a kitchen full of children and no domestic help, combined rice and sweet Italian sausage. Something called "Italian seasoning" was packaged commercially to seduce cooks whose herb shelves were otherwise bare. In American kitchens the gastronomy that had originated in southern Italy seemed simpler either than Paris's *haute cuisine* or the best provincial recipes of France; savory, colorful dishes like many-splendored, many-layered lasagna became widely accepted party fare among young people and in those middle-class circles where dieting was not the norm.

I learned some fine points about one of the simplest foods of this kind—the egg dish called *frittata*—in the Seattle kitchen of Angelo Pellegrini, distinguished university teacher and also an authority on Tuscan food and wine. His backyard garden, hedged in by berry vines, a thicket of tall artichokes, and a bushy row of hydrangeas and dahlias, furnished the Pelle-

An Italian Butcher's Way with Marrow Bones

Wash 4 veal knuckles (1 for each person) in water to which you have added a little lemon juice. Dry them and dredge in seasoned flour. Melt 2 tablespoons of butter and 2 of olive oil in a heavy stewing pan or kettle and sear the veal knuckles. Remove them from the pan and set aside. Now add to the fat in the pan 2 onions, 2 carrots, 2 stalks of celery, 2 strips of bacon, and 2 slices of prosciutto (Italian ham), all finely chopped. Cook slowly for 10 minutes, then add a bay leaf, some chopped Italian parsley, a little basil and a little thyme. Return the veal knuckles to the pot and add enough liquid to just cover them; the liquid should be chicken bouillon, tomato juice, and dry white wine in equal parts. Cover the pan and cook slowly for 2½ to 3 hours. When done put the veal knuckles on a hot platter, strain the sauce, pour it over the meat, sprinkle with chopped parsley and a little grated lemon rind. Serve with risotto.

—Luigi Trianni,
New York meatman

grini family with fruit, herbs, and vegetables from early spring to the end of the following winter. Fresh from this garden, the family's favorite *frittati* often were based on diced zucchini braised with zucchini blossoms.

Like French omelets, a *frittata* can be made with many kinds of vegetables, meats, or fish, to add texture, flavor, and body. In fact, it is so plausible a way to combine eggs with other foods that at our house we had been duplicating Angelo's virtuosity with these flat, thick omelets without knowing they had an Italian name. Our "egg pie," cooked very slowly on top of the stove and finished under the broiler, long ago became a favorite way of proving the worth of the refrigerator's cache of leftovers. And though we now call it a *frittata* (see recipe section), neither I nor any of my relatives by blood or law have any Italian heritage.

It is easy to forget that all so-called American food has some foreign influence (British or otherwise) and that many dishes that bear titles in English fail to honor the place of their origin. In the past when demographers assured the world that the melting-pot theory would prevail, that all traces of ethnic differences could be homogenized, names and regions of origin were often dropped along with many distinguishing flavors—in cookery as well as other customs. The formality of giving credit was easily overlooked. A contemporary cookbook includes a recipe for lamb patties with lemon sauce without admitting that the initial conceit was Greek; indeed it had become commonplace to consider Italy's macaroni to be as indigenous to America as Yankee Doodle.

Ethnic Recognitions

The difference between the Greeks and the Italians is that the latter opened restaurants to serve the kind of food they themselves preferred. The Greeks, for many decades, foreswore their own culinary tradition in the ubiquitous "Greek restaurants" that sprang up in every city; the food served in these places dominated by overhead fans was largely characterless. Not until air travel had given millions a chance to sample the best of Greek food in its native habitat did such delights as shish kebabs begin to turn up on American barbecue menus. And when that happened, some of these food styles "discovered" abroad were accepted quickly and widely, just as cola drinks have become ingrained in the folkways of other countries.

Greeks first came to the east coast of Florida in the eighteenth century, and on the west coast of the peninsula, at Tarpon Springs, a colony of sponge fishermen in the 1880s began to adapt New World ingredients to ancient Hellenic methods. The "*cioppino*" of Tarpon Springs is an oil-based soup dominated by red snapper from the Gulf that is seasoned with wild marjoram, onions, green peppers, tomatoes, and lemons; beaten eggs are added at the end, along with fine strands of pasta. In Tarpon Springs tradition remained strong. Celebrating Greeks continued to stuff spring lamb with pecans and rice; their recipe for garden salad combined briny feta cheese, lettuce, celery, cucumbers, tomatoes, onions, green peppers and avocados with the flavors of anchovies, olives, and oregano. The Florida version of the classic Greek *avogolemono*, or lemon soup, differed from that of the home islanders only in using beef broth instead of chicken broth.

Greek cooks did as much as those of Italy or any other Mediterranean country to increase the number of uses of eggplant in American kitchens. For instance, when chopped and combined with garlic, onion, herbs, spices, oil, and lemon, it was transformed into something Americans call eggplant cavier. Closer to real caviar, however, is the Mediterranean *taramasalata*, a paste made from the roe of gray mullet or carp, now popular among some U.S. hostesses. (When asked why real caviar was so expensive, Chicago hotelkeeper Ernie Byfield once replied, "After all, it's a year's work for the sturgeon.")

America has absorbed many good things from the Middle East. Eggplant layered with minced lamb and seasonings under a blanket of baked custard—known all over the Middle East as moussaka—became a common U.S. buffet supper entrée. In a fifty-year period after the first edition of Fannie Farmer's cookbook was published in 1896, the number of eggplant recipes jumped from two bland suggestions to more than a dozen in the seventh edition; included was a prevalent Mediterranean way of mixing eggplant with rice so seasoned that provincial Americans considered it fit only for immigrants. By 1979, when Miss Farmer had been dead for sixty-four years (although not her influence—a revised version of her book sold about 300,000 copies that year), her recipes included an eggplant quiche that combined culinary nuances from France and the Middle East. "Learning to make quiches," according to Fannie Farmer precepts, was a good way to add variety to a cook's repertoire; her attitude had done much to minimize prejudice about unfamiliar recipes.

Another thing that helped chase away such disdain was the effort of immigrant offspring to preserve the best of their ethnic backgrounds through folk festivals celebrating their heritage in food, as well as in music, arts, crafts, songs, dances, and pageantry. Of twenty-four ethnic groups celebrating annually in Pittsburgh, the Lebanese-Americans cut up scores of legs of lamb for *kibbi* and shish kebab, and cooks from Israel have helped to make falafel popular as a snack to be eaten on the street. At this festival Slovene women prepare kielbasa sausages under the gaze of passers-by, while in a neighboring booth cabbage leaves are stuffed the Hungarian way. Often these celebrations, in Pittsburgh and elsewhere, combine the atmosphere of a village market day and the midway of an American county fair.

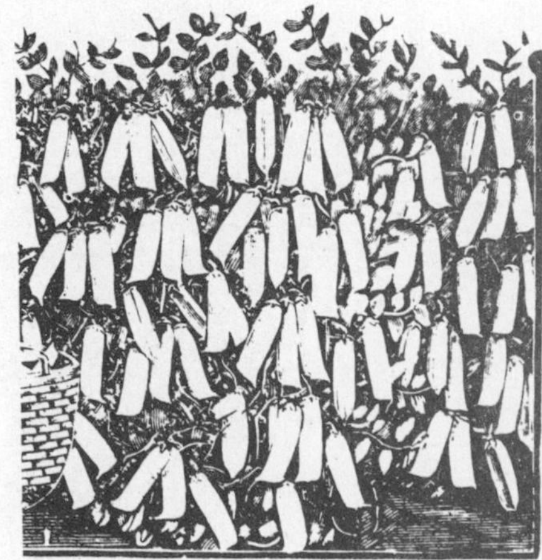

Relatively few people, however, are aware of the fetes of ethnic groups like those who come from such modest countries as Portugal. In Stonington, Connecticut, the Sunday before Labor Day is observed as the Feast of the Holy Ghost—an occasion marking the end of a great famine in the time of Queen Isabella. The seaside town is filled with continuous music and dancing, a neighborly parade, and a festive meal of strong Portuguese marrowbone soup, along with ice cream that is free to all. Families of Portuguese-American fishermen in New Bedford, Massachusetts, celebrate with fado singing and dancing and provide curious festival visitors with dried codfish in spicy sauces that originated in Portugal.

People from the Atlantic coast of the Iberian peninsula fished the Grand Banks of the American continent, probably earlier than the "discovery" by Columbus, but not until a generation before the Civil War did they make a strong impression in New England. Coming as sailors and fishermen, they began to settle on the coast in such places as Stonington, Falmouth, New Bedford, and Martha's Vineyard, bringing the culinary ways and other customs of the Azores and Cape Verde. Now in Gloucester every spring (sixty days after Easter), they stage an annual Portuguese Fish Festival. In Provincetown, on Cape Cod, an everyday Portuguese specialty called quahog pie is a combination of clams and a local version of *linguiça* sausage that has been seasoned with cuminseed, cinnamon, garlic, and red pepper, pickled in vinegar, and heavily smoked. Portuguese sausage not only is found on the breakfast menu of New Bedford's Orchid Diner but is the base of a meat pie, and it gives an Iberian touch when used in the diner's roast turkey stuffing. At least as common is a sausage soup made with *chouriços*, an even hotter sausage, which these New England fishermen's wives often simmer with kale. They also stuff squid with either shrimp or *linguiças*, and either of the two Portuguese sausages may be sliced and added to a dish of lentils, onions, garlic, and tomatoes.

There are gifted bakers among Portuguese-Americans who have their own way of mixing white cornmeal and white flour to produce round loaves of bread to accompany hearty soups, and the bread is also matched with salad as a simple lunch menu. A sweet bread served on Sundays and often called Easter bread may require a dozen eggs, seven pounds of flour, four cups of sugar, three yeast cakes, a half-pound of butter, and more shortening in equal amount, and two extra egg whites. The result is a half-dozen big loaves of which slices are toasted and spread with cream cheese and homemade beach plum jelly when served at the coffee hour. The Portuguese bakery, all by itself, has made Stonington a mecca for connoisseurs of ethnic food.

For almost half a century "Kolacky Day" has been celebrated in Montgomery, Minnesota, with music by polka bands and eating contests centered on *kolaches*, the Bohemian fruit-filled pastries flavored with poppy seeds. Similarly, in New York's Little Italy members of the San Gennaro Society annually stage a street fair lining the length of Mulberry Street with booths and the aroma of Italian sausages and barbecued sweetbreads. The fair also offers as many opportunities to nibble such barbecued food as *chawarma*, or lamb cooked on a gyro in the Greek style. Or for other palates, Cantonese delicacies are served by Little Italy's neighbors from adjacent Chinatown.

A Symbol of the Blood of Life

There was once an effort to establish a Little Poland, not as a ghetto in a city, but as a large geopolitical area in the Middle West, and though this dream of certain Poles proved unavailing, it did encourage a wave of immigration that, incidentally, brought more subtle accents to the food of America. Few Polish contributions are as elegant as the dish that combines fish with lobster and cheese sauce, known as sole *à la Waleska*, but generally speaking, many of the recipes that account for the abundant use of sour cream in the twentieth century—originally characterized as in the style of *Smetana*—were developed by Poles.

Perhaps borscht is the best known of them all. This luxuriantly red soup, a French chef said, "is national in Russia and in Poland, and in Russia you must swear on your life that it's Russian, but in Poland you must salute it as a symbol of Poland's life blood." In America many cooks consider borscht to be kosher, brought here by Jews from both countries. No matter—when it is spelled "barszcz," it is as authentic as any memory of the Vistula River.

Borscht polonaise, as some menus would have it, can be brewed from a broth of one whole duck, a large beef bone, and a chunk of bacon flavored with beets, carrots, leeks, laurel, thyme, parsley, celery, onions, garlic, and a grating of nutmeg. It takes hours. It is skimmed, sieved through cheesecloth, beaten with egg whites and their crushed shells, sieved again, and served very hot or very cold—always with plenty of sour cream to make a topping for an ideal soup to soothe a summer day.

With borscht available in cans and jars, few Americans continue to make the soup from scratch, but those of Polish extraction have helped to popularize another mélange they called *chłodnik*—a cold cucumber soup based on sour cream, of course, with the flavor of beets, dill, onion, and sometimes hard-cooked eggs. In the twentieth century all kinds of Americans have gone overboard for sour cream on baked potatoes and as the basis for many sauces, to be used for desserts or otherwise. Sour cream provides the sauce for meat balls simmered with onions and mushrooms, in a recipe again attributed to both Russian and Polish immigrants, and known as *bitki*.

The recipes of Hungarian-Americans are perhaps at least as lavish in the use of sour cream. *Goulash* is an American cookbook term borrowed from Austria where, in turn, it is a Teutonic spelling of the Hungarian *gulyás*. As a kind of generic stew it became popular in the Middle West at the time of the great immigration from Central Europe. By 1969, according to a Gallup poll, when Americans numbered it among their five favorite meat dishes, it had lost much of its original definition and was considered satisfactorily

Northern Pike with Polish Sauce

Place one Minnesota Northern pike in saucepan with 2 cups white wine, 1 cup vinegar, a generous pinch of saffron and ½ cup seedless raisins; simmer slowly ½ hour. Blend 1 tablespoon flour with 1 tablespoon butter and stir into sauce, cooking until it thickens.
—Polanie Club, Minneapolis

prepared as long as it was adorned with paprika and, for preference, sour cream.[2] Among purists, the Hungarian gastronomical specialist George Lang has written that only in Transylvania was sour cream considered an authentic goulash ingredient. But all things appear to change in American kitchens, and an appetite for sour cream increased enormously after the mid-century introduction of the cultured product. The lower calorie count of manufactured sour cream added many new culinary uses and boosted the popularity of salads dressed with cultured cream instead of mayonnaise. Chicken paprika, another internationally accepted Hungarian ragout, requires an abundance of sour cream and is a mainstay of many American menus, including those of Hungarian steelworkers in such places as Gary, Indiana, and East Chicago.

A Nod from Escoffier

Paprika, as the powdered form of the New World *Capsicum* is known, became identified with Hungarian cooking in the nineteenth century, according to George Lang. In his long research for *The Cuisine of Hungary* he determined that chicken paprika was accepted as a national dish by the Magyars in 1844, when it first appeared on the menu of the exclusive parliamentary dining room. Thirty-five years later the French chef Auguste Escoffier, visiting the city of Szeged, tasted paprika-flavored *gulyás* and chicken in a rosy sour cream sauce, and soon thereafter he introduced *gulyás hongrois* and *poulet au paprika* to international travelers who ate his classic food at Monte Carlo. The recipes traveled with Escoffier after he joined Cèsar Ritz, when he and the chefs he trained set up kitchens on both sides of the Atlantic.

Aside from loyalty to paprika, Hungarian-American cooks also preserved old traditions by using tomatoes and green peppers as creatively as Italian-Americans, or the cooks of the Southwest and the Gulf Coast. Dozens of Hungarian stuffings for peppers continued to be used in American kitchens, and wonderful mixtures were concocted of sliced smoke sausages, onions, green peppers, and boiled eggs—layered in a casserole to provide one of the meals-in-a-dish that Americans like. Another Hungarian recipe calls for fresh mackerel to be put on a layer of potato slices in a buttered baking dish; then diagonal slashes in the fish are filled with juliennes of green pepper, tomatoes, onions, and bacon. Covered with sour cream or yogurt, the fish is baked just long enough to be beautifully flaky, and the vegetables maintain both tang and texture.

And like all the cooks of Central Europe, Hungarians spurred Americans to outdo even Vienna in emphasizing desserts. Joseph Wechsberg, who

Grandma's Debricina Goulash

Dice 4 pounds of well aged round steak. Peel and cut up enough onions to make half as much as beef. Brown the meat in a deep, heavy metal pot. Push the meat aside; add the onions and cook, stirring, until golden brown. Add salt, pepper, and 2 tablespoons paprika. Mix well, cover and simmer for about 30 minutes. Cover with one No. 2½ can sauerkraut, being careful to keep meat and kraut in separate layers. Spread one cup sour cream over the kraut, being careful to keep this, too, separate. Cover and cook over low heat (at a simmer) for one hour. In the inns around St. Louis, this was served right from the pot, at the table.

—Mrs. Estelle Umbright, St. Louis

[2] Something of the same thing happened to beef Stroganoff, which had a slightly more elegant popularity after World War II. *Boeuf à la Stroganoff*, a combination of tenderloin juliennes, shallots, mustard, broth, and sour cream, was created in a Paris restaurant for Count Paul Stroganoff, a nineteenth-century Russian diplomat. In the United States, every modish cook, professional or amateur, developed his or her own "refinements."

grew up in what had been the Austro-Hungarian Empire, once wrote that he never heard of a dessertless meal, even among the very poor. That tradition was reinforced in the United States when immigrant women assuaged lean days by adding something sweet to their menus. The availability of cream of tartar in the 1850s, to be followed later by baking powder, made lighter, better cakes possible, but the lists of them in cookbooks remained largely confined to such colonial recipes as Shrewsbury cake and sponge cake and Boston cream pie until late in the nineteenth century. Newly arrived cooks helped to change the picture, and among them were professional pastry chefs who were often quick to find occasions for bringing attention to themselves and their knack for creating rich desserts. Kossuth cake is a result of a cook and an occasion coming together at the right moment, and it remains a favorite of Baltimore hostesses. The sponge cake is the size of a large cream puff and is filled with whipped cream and topped with chocolate sour cream icing in a thick layer; it was created in honor of the Hungarian patriot General Lajos Kossuth on his visit to Baltimore in 1851. Popular as Kossuth cake still is in Maryland, it is considered by some hostesses to be the sort of challenge best left to local bakery shops. American housewives nevertheless have been unabashed in turning out pastries worthy of Austro-Hungarian chefs, including such luscious creations as Dobostorte (chocolate filled with caramel frosting and originated by Josef Dobos, a great Hungarian pastry master); indeed an anonymous Midwest woman gave proof of this when she devised her own five-egg, three-layer cake known now as Minnesota fudge cake. In similar tradition, Wisconsin cooks bake a seven-layer cake and spread a filling of different flavor at each level.

"Bake sales" sponsored by women's church groups or schools—or other efforts for one or another worthy cause—encouraged the competition that once put U.S. women among the best dessert makers in the world. So did agricultural fairs at which their husbands showed off crops and livestock in pursuit of blue ribbons; blue ribbons were also handed out to cooks who in many cases were demonstrating the worth of recipes their mothers or grandmothers had brought from abroad. At the Guadalupe County Fair in Seguin, Texas, for instance, Viola Schlicting won first prize for her carrot cake in the 1960s. This fact alone may not have been responsible for the sudden popularity of carrot cake throughout the country—vegetarian partisans helped to spread the news—but creative cooks were inspired to produce many variations once they discovered the carrot's potential as the basis of dessert. Many carrot cakes have frostings of cream cheese; Mrs. Schlicting's gilds the carrot-colored batter with an orange glaze, and with its addition of Texas pecans it is a dessert lover's delicious variation of carrot-nut bread as it was originally made in Germany.

As the historian Arthur M. Schlesinger, Sr., put it after a half century of scholarly attention: "The European newcomer, although ever the chief gainer in the matter of food, atoned in some degree by enriching the national menu with his own traditional dishes. In this sense the melting pot was also the cooking pot." In the Midwest and far Northwest especially, menus were enriched by Scandinavian cooks whose cuisine may not have been as rich as that of the old Austro-Hungarian empire but was distinguished by variety that helped make the style of eating known as smorgasbord a part of the gustatory experience of many Americans.

Eye Appeal for Informal Dining

In her *West Coast Cook Book*, the definitive treatise on gastronomical mores between the Rockies and the Pacific, Helen Evans Brown pointed out that "the smorgasbord, that fabulous feast of good food, has won the complete and enthusiastic approval of the entire West Coast. It's really a natural for us," she wrote in the 1950s "—it's perfectly adapted to informal entertaining, which is what most of us go in for." Smorgasbord dining also came naturally to several midwestern states, such as Minnesota, where Scandinavians outnumbered all other immigrants. It was introduced to other Americans at Scandinavian church suppers, and it became so modified by various informalities that a committee of women of the Swedish Institute in Minneapolis was moved in the middle of the twentieth century to issue a brief dissertation cautioning Americans on the proper approach to serving a smorgasbord. "It should be noted that every effort is made toward an attractive and well-balanced effect. 'Eye-appeal' is stressed, rather than a mere attempt to serve the largest assortment of foods," the ladies said.

They stipulated the possibility of assembling on the table as many as twenty-five cold dishes and a dozen or more hot ones that might include pickled and smoked fish, jellied meats, roasts with fruit, sausages, hot meat balls, escalloped herring, sweetbread omelet, vegetables, cheeses, stewed fruit. "The smorgasbord can be the most simple form," it was emphasized, "or it can be an elaborate culinary masterpiece." In its simplest form it provided (along with the old-time saloon "free lunch") inspiration for the array of appetizers, canapes, or hors d'oeuvre served at cocktail parties or with preprandial drinks.

The Swedish Institute's meat ball recipe is worth noting, for it is simple to follow and easily accomplished:

SMORGASBORD MEAT BALLS

Soak one-half cup fine dry bread crumbs in one-half cup cream. Grind one-half pound beef, one-quarter pound veal, and one-quarter pound pork three times, using fine blade. Mix crumbs and meats thoroughly; add one-half cup milk, two egg yolks, beaten slightly, two tablespoons minced onion, three teaspoons salt, one-third teaspoon pepper, one-half teaspoon allspice. Blend well, form into tiny balls and brown on all sides in four tablespoons fat. Keep warm over hot water.

Most Swedes, Norwegians, and Danes who came to America were led to parts of the country where the weather was similar to the climate of their homelands, and the meat and fish dishes that bolstered the traditional smorgasbord supplied—along with aquavit with which to wash them down—energy and warmth that helped to mollify winter temperatures. In the upper Midwest, largely settled by Scandinavian farmers and lumbermen who spend much of their lives outdoors, meals are often measured by quantity and heartiness, and along the shores of the western Great Lakes the "fish boil" is not only symbolic but has become a classic church supper and attracts hundreds of trenchermen to lakeside resorts. It is simply fresh-caught whitefish or lake trout boiled with potatoes and served with fish steaks, cabbage slaw, homemade rye bread, cherry pie, and endless coffee—an unpretentious "feed" cooked with care by good cooks. But Scandinavians are also gifted culinary artists who draw on their heritage to create decorative open-face sandwiches, skewered combinations of cold meats and cheese and fruits, and many other jewellike tidbits, as well as the more filling dishes that have, for generations, made a smorgasbord a square meal in itself.

More than that, Scandinavians were perhaps more responsible than anyone else for making America as coffee-break-conscious as it is, and for perfecting the kind of food that goes well with coffee. German women had already brought the *Kaffeeklatsch* to their frontier communities, but it was in the kitchens where there was always a pot brewing on the back of the stove that Scandinavian hospitality and coffee became synonymous. There, also, began the average American's habit of having coffee with or without food, at virtually any hour of the day. The term *coffee klatch* became part of the language, and its original meaning—a moment that combined gossip with coffee drinking—was changed to define the American version of England's tea, a midmorning or midafternoon gathering at which to imbibe and ingest. From these social hours in homes evolved the worker's "coffee break," an office ritual so firmly established that it became in many cases a matter of union contract, or of law.

Like the cooks from Central Europe, most Scandinavian cooks have prided themselves on the simple forms of pastry making that include so-called coffee breads, coffee cakes, coffee rings, sweet rolls, and buns. Danish pastries became so popular that no more was needed than the single word *Danish*, in any short-order eating place, to order any of a number of light, bready confections. Of a richness somewhere between coffee cake and fine pastry, they might be either Danish, Swedish, or Norwegian in origin, but they have become as authentically a fixture on American breakfast menus as French toast. A Danish can be a fat envelope of pastry containing sugary spices or something fruity; it can be crescent-shaped or molded like a comb with tines the thickness of a thumb. Its chief characteristic is the flakiness of the superbly light crumb. After World War II it became almost as popular at stool-and-counter breakfasts as the doughnut.

From the Counters of Delicatessens

The Scandinavians brought their own versions of cooked-food shops to America, but it was in the German delicatessens, which cropped up in cities large and small toward the end of the nineteenth century, that many German foods began the process of Americanization. There one could find pumpernickel, zwieback, bauernbrot, sauerkraut, sauerbraten, leberwurst (which became liverwurst), wienerwurst (which brought about the corruption of the name of Austria's capital to weenie), and *lager* and *bok* as two kinds of beer. H. L. Mencken has pointed out that such words "mirror the profound effect of German migration upon American drinking habits and the American cuisine." He also said in *The American Language* that as late as 1921 he had found *sourbraten* (*sic*) on the menu at Delmonico's and, "more surprising still, *'braten* with potato salad.' " Another German-Americanism, the hot dog, was mated with a roll shaped to fit a Frankfurt-style wurst at the St. Louis World's Fair of 1904, but its nickname came along when a sports cartoonist created a dachshund with a body that looked like a sausage.

By the last third of the twentieth century the delicatessens that once sold a good many frankfurters had changed as had most other food emporiums; most were run by Jews who were not necessarily of German background. By that time a "hot pastrami on rye" had become a favorite sandwich of Americans, few of whom knew that *pastrami* was a Rumanian word for beef that had been pickled and smoked and made popular by New York kosher delicatessens. *New York* magazine conducted its "first Pastrami Olympics" early in 1973, lining up a jury of experts to taste and test sandwiches from eighteen delicatessens. Prices ranged from a $2.45 high to a low of $1.50 per sandwich; the amount of meat in each varied from three ounces to six ounces. The winner chosen by the six jurors weighed 3.75 ounces, cost $1.75, and was judged on the quality, flavor, and texture of the smoked beef. The most expensive of the lot also had the most meat, but its general quality rated it no better than sixteenth place.

Sweet Potato Tzimmes

Put 4 unpeeled sweet potatoes and 4 carrots in boiling water, cook until tender. Drain and peel, then put in bowl and mash until smooth. Cook 1 cup prunes in water to cover 15 minutes; drain, reserving 1 cup liquid. Pit and chop prunes and add to potato mixture with reserved liquid, ¼ cup honey, salt and pepper to taste. Place in baking pan in oven preheated to 350° F. for 15 minutes.

A Reuben sandwich, another New York Jewish creation that joined corned beef, sauerkraut, and cheese under a broiler, could be successfully ordered at eating places across the country and had been miniaturized for serving as a cocktail snack. As a part of American food folklore, the Reuben has been claimed as the invention of a sandwich chef who was made famous by Damon Runyon and whose Broadway restaurant bore his name. The first Reuben special, so this story goes, was made in 1914 for an actress playing the lead in a Charlie Chaplin film, but it employed Virginia baked ham instead of corned beef. The National Kraut Packers Association, however, has given the credit to the version that evolved during a weekly poker game in Omaha in 1955. Among the players who fixed their own sandwiches was Reuben Kay, a wholesale grocer who devised the combination of sauerkraut, corned beef, and Swiss cheese on sourdough pumpernickel bread. To make the sandwich named for Reuben Kay of Omaha, kosher corned beef is piled on one slice of pumpernickel and Emmenthaler cheese on another. Sauerkraut is mixed with Russian dressing and added. The bread is buttered on the outside and the sandwich is grilled, to be served with a hot exterior and a cold interior, preferably with crunchy dill pickle slices as a garnish.

Less publicity may have been accorded to chopped chicken liver, but it is a ghetto contribution no less worthy of acclaim. Chopped liver so captured the hearts of the Jews' fellow Americans that a Methodist woman in a North Carolina town won a cooking competition with her nonkosher recipe and earned lengthy comment from Harry Golden, editor of the *Carolina Israelite*. Golden wanted a statue erected in Washington to the Jewish immigrant mother whose talent for turning meager ingredients into food that evoked nostalgia made her, he thought, unique. Throughout his writing life, this former New Yorker was moved to cite his own mother's cooking. Golden was forever mentioning "Mother's potato latkes (pancakes) and holishkas (chopped beef and spices rolled in cabbage leaves and cooked in a sweet-and-sour raisin sauce)." He referred those who said Jewish food is nothing more than German, or Rumanian, or Russian to the Declaration of Independence. Jefferson knew about Magna Carta, didn't he? In other words, Golden argued that Jewish food may have links to someone else's past, but it becomes different as it becomes a part of the Jewish experience. The same logic applies to the whole of American gastronomy.

Kreplach in the San Hsien T'ang

There are interesting duplications among many ethnic cuisines. Jews for centuries have spoken reverently of their own kreplach, which are small airy pouches of dough, usually filled with minced meat and put into chicken soup. When many Jews—in the United States particularly—became addicted to dining out in Chinese restaurants, they found won ton soup "with kreplach," as some of them said in surprise; actually the soup contained the Oriental version of tiny envelopes laden with meat. Similarly, those Jews who lived in Italy in the Middle Ages might have been surprised at their first encounters with ravioli, or with *agnolotti*, the meaty Italian pasta plumped with minced ham, sausage, and sweetbreads that are also served in soup. It is not true, however, that the Western world, including makers of kreplach, had to wait until Marco Polo returned from Cathay with the first "spaghetti." Ravioli, the pasta dumpling usually filled with cheese, was a popular Roman dish before the Italian trader headed toward the Orient; ravioli was served then, as in the twentieth century, as a dish by itself, the way many Bronx and Brooklyn housewives often served kreplach after browning it in hot fat.

Had Jews or Italians gone after culinary secrets in China, they might have come back with many. Chinese cooking ranks with the cuisine of France at the top of international gastronomy. It is because it is different—rather than because of a few look-alikes such as kreplach and won ton—that Oriental food in general was slow in finding acceptance among most Americans. But there were Chinese dishes that were exceptions, of course.

Some of the simplest, such as eggs foo yung, sweet and sour spareribs, fried shrimp, and fried rice, were considered indigenous to the West Coast before half of the twentieth century had slipped away.

A century earlier, in 1847, the first Chinese immigrants settled in San Francisco and were followed by thousands who helped to build the transcontinental railways. The meals of hundreds of California families were influenced by cooks who were Chinese and had been hired as housemen in middle-class homes. They seldom were permitted to prepare Oriental meals, but they held to their art of serving vegetables that do not lose their crispness or color. Perhaps a modest contribution, but it eliminated the English way of overcooking that had been habitual among Americans of British heritage. Vegetable cooking on the West Coast was never again categorically as bad as in some other regions.

Other Chinese were cooks for the work gangs, and one of these, I am willing to believe, invented the sandwich that is called a "western" in states east of the Mississippi and a "Denver" in most of the rest of the country. When a hungry cowboy asked for a sandwich between meals, the story goes, the Chinese cook prepared eggs foo yung by making the traditional Oriental omelet from meats and vegetables at hand—in this case the green pepper that was grown by early Spanish in the West, along with onions and some chopped ham. Put between slices of bread, this hasty Chinese creation became the prototype of one of the most American of all sandwiches.

There are similar stories about the origin of chop suey—which translates ignominiously as "miscellaneous odds and ends"—first served, some say, to a party of non-Oriental Americans who liked it enough to return to the same Cantonese eating place repeatedly. Chow mein, a term often confused with chop suey, is an admitted part of the Chinese food lexicon and means, literally, soft-fried noodles; it is a dish utterly different from the chow mein noodles invented to please Occidental tastes and sold in retail food stores everywhere.

In the early California Chinese restaurants there was a willingness to cater to customers—some proprietors served their non-Chinese clients only what they thought those diners wanted, that is, chop suey and fried steak. Better restaurants gained fame on San Francisco's Grant Avenue, on or near New York's Mott Street, in Los Angeles, and every other American city of consequence, and the developing taste for genuine Chinese food resulted in a vogue for home delivery of such easily portable items as egg rolls and chicken chow mein in paper buckets. But it wasn't until after World War II that Americans began consciously to augment their Oriental kitchen repertoires by attending classes in Chinese cooking and avidly sampling new tastes that became available in restaurants specializing in Mandarin, Hunan, Fukien, and Szechwan dishes in addition to those from Canton.

This influence on American eating habits came after new political relationships encouraged interest in largely unknown regions of the People's

Republic, and many more Chinese entrepreneurs arrived to join what had been dominantly a Cantonese population in the United States. Increased interest in Japanese food, on the other hand, was due to air travel that took thousands of Americans on vacations that heightened their appreciation of the food they ate in such cities as Tokyo and Kyoto. Recipes for sukiyaki had already entered American cookbooks, and the Japanese ceremony in which guests could share in the tabletop cooking of beef, mushrooms, bamboo shoots, and other more colorful vegetables had become as much the raison d'être for a party as had the Swiss fondue.

Tastes of the Fiftieth State

Much earlier, the Japanese had had a tremendous effect on food in the Hawaiian Islands, but it did not take Hawaii's statehood to make mainland Americans practitioners of island cookery. Bananas and pineapples had become important in the kitchens of New England women whose seafaring men had brought the tropical fruits back from various ports of call. They were much favored in Charleston's market square in the early nineteenth century. But the Spanish-American War and the consequent exploitation of the tropical fruit canning business did as much as anything to embellish meals in every state with fruit salads, upside-down cakes, and baked hams adorned with pineapple slices.

The fiftieth state acquired a cuisine as international as any of its sisters. Hawaii was characteristically Polynesian until the nineteenth century, and its diet of fish and fruit remained unmodified until the coming of the missionaries and clipper ships from New England. Dried meat and salted fish had fed American sailors, and these foods became a part of Hawaiian tradition—as *pipikaula*, the jerked beef that is broiled in tiny pieces and served with a sweet-sour sauce, and as *lomi lomi*, thin fillets of salted salmon that some New Yorkers have described as better in its indigenous way than lox (smoked salmon) from their own favorite delicatessens. Mixed with chopped onions and tomatoes, *lomi lomi* is habitually served as a salad. Salmon, to the early Hawaiians, was common enough to be known as "the pig in the sea." Other fish were used after the coming of the missionaries to produce such things as fish chowder in basic Yankee fashion, and Scots who came to the islands as technicians and plantation overseers added their native scones and shortbreads to the daily fare of thousands of Hawaiians who generations before had adopted the Portuguese sweet bread of the first European immigrants. Cornmeal and red bean soup, also brought by the Portuguese, have been accepted as Hawaiian by islanders of all ethnic roots, and rather than submitting to a single style, island cooks have incorporated many European dishes, along with those from Chinese, Japanese, and Korean sources, developing a culinary tradition that may be among the most festive in the world.

The traditional Hawaiian feast called the luau is the ultimate of American picnics, cookouts, and barbecues, and it has added much to the variety

Hawaiian Pipikaula

Combine 1 cup soy sauce, juice of ½ lemon, 1–2 tablespoons of rock salt, freshly ground pepper and 1 teaspoon of sugar. Have 2–3 pounds of steak cut 1–1½ inches thick. Cut beef into strips about 1½ inches wide, and pound strips slightly before marinating them in soy mixture; run the sauce into meat and let stand 1 hour. Then dry in hot sun about two days (be sure not to let it stay out in the night air). Broil, turning until nicely browned. It is delicious with poi or baked sweet potato.

—Hilo Woman's Club

of outdoor feasting on the American mainland, especially in California. Yet the great Hawaiian influences on American food may be forgotten in the haze of too many cocktail parties. A chunk of pineapple broiled in a wrapping of bacon, for instance, may be known as a *pupu*, and the same word is used for parties at which food is limited to appetizers. *Pupus* can be anything and everything from cubes of barbecued pork to Chinese spring rolls or teriyaki. From island *pupu* parties came *rumaki*, the Hawaiian bacon-wrapped kebabs of chicken livers and water chestnuts that turn up at parties in Charleston, St. Louis, or Pasadena, once blessed by the *New York Times* as "almost as popular as pizza pie in metropolitan America."

In urban and rural areas as well, many Americans in the 1970s began to be interested in the nation's inherent cookery. Natives who traced their ancestry back to the Old Dominion or whose pedigrees were rich with *Mayflower* stock had learned to embrace the onion, to dally even with garlic. Anyone who loved good food had become aware that in the eclectic style that had developed there was included—although often in modified form—a bill of fare with origins of the highest order.

Many Americans continued to be culinary chauvinists, of course. A man could write with feeling about Down East food, as Haydn S. Pearson did in a newspaper column: "It is unfortunate that the word hash has fallen into some disrepute. . . . it is good, solid, everyday grub. Red-flannel hash, however, is on a different plane. It is an Oriental-looking, taste-tantalizing dish. Its color is exciting. It has allure and snap. A frying pan full of it on the kitchen stove sends a nostril-tickling aroma through the room. As a man comes through the woodshed with the milk pails on his arm, he inhales the smell and a smile lights his face. What better reward for a long day's work digging potatoes or picking apples?

"How to make it? Heat an old spider iron on a wood-burning stove. Fry a few slices of bacon until they are crisp and break into small bits. Chop a dozen cooked beets into small pieces; mix in two or three boiled potatoes and two chopped onions. The countryman, who is meticulous regarding certain culinary points, says that correct red-flannel hash is 85 per cent beet, 10 per cent potato, 3 per cent onion, and 2 per cent bacon; and that never under any circumstances should it include meat (other than bacon), gravy, or extraneous vegetables. Serve it piping hot with yellow corn-meal muffins and green tomato pickles. For dessert, a wedge of deep-dish apple pie, a piece of old sharp cheese, and a glass of cold, creamy milk are acceptable."

Such American palates considered, the Yankee bride nonetheless had learned a lot from her Italian husband. "The culinary arts of all countries were our birthright," Irma Goodrich Mazza wrote in *Herbs for the Kitchen*, adding, "England, Holland, Italy, France, Spain, Scandinavia, Germany, and other lands, both Occidental and Oriental, merged their kitchen secrets within our borders to give us richer, fuller food consciousness than any other single people." She thought that added up as "a legacy to treasure."

Chapter IX

BEGINNINGS REVISITED

Gustave W. Swift took his wife and six children to Chicago's freight yards one day in 1877 to witness a family triumph. As a train began to move, he is reported to have turned to his wife with a smile. "There are gigantic days in every man's life, Annie," Swift's biographers tell us he said. "This," he added with obvious pleasure, "is one of mine."

The day was also a big one for everyone else interested in American food. The Swift family had been gathered to watch the first train equipped with effectively refrigerated cars head east with tons of freshly butchered meat that was virtually guaranteed against spoilage. After years of persistence Swift had devised the system that was to make beef, veal, pork—all kinds of perishables—available to Americans regardless of season and without dependence on local conditions.

A half century later, Clarence Birdseye, a Department of Agriculture naturalist, quit the government to try to prove that a method of food preservation he had learned from the Eskimos could revolutionize the marketing of many kinds of food. Birdseye worked out fast-freezing techniques to attain the solid effect caused in an instant by Labrador winter weather. His methods and equipment, later perfected to preserve vegetables, fruit, meat, and poultry, as well as fish, did more than Swift's refrigerated cars to change the American attitude toward food.

Most of what is bad and much of what is good about American cookery has been governed by industrial enterprise. The fifty states might never have evolved into a nation of steak eaters had not refrigerated transportation become important so early in the history of the country. Railroads did much to revolutionize the supply system for fruits and vegetables, as well. Gustave Swift's competitor, Philip D. Armour, also invested heavily in refrigerator cars and, in order to use them fully, looked for products other than meat to carry. He encouraged farmers in the South to grow large quantities of normally perishable fruits and berries that would require refrigerated shipping to cities in the North.

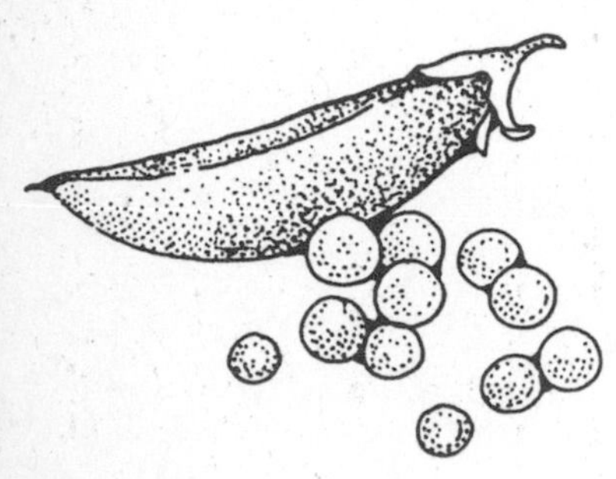

Railroad promoters transported green peas from Louisiana to Chicago, and others ran a special train, known as the "Pea Line," to bring produce across the Hudson from New Jersey's garden region to New York. Vegetables and fruits were shipped north from the rail center established at Norfolk, Virginia. The new transportation ended the era in which New Yorkers had to pay $1.50 for strawberries while housewives in Baltimore, for instance, could have all the berries they wanted for ten cents a quart. Food seasons got longer in metropolitan areas, for such garden vegetables as tomatoes became readily available all year round as the result of the new efficiency, instead of being limited to the old season of four months. In the rest of the world, cooking styles that developed because of regional limitations retained their principal characteristics through the maintenance of market days on which farmers gather at appointed places in villages and towns to sell the raw produce indigenous to the region. In the United States, even before World War I, lettuce, asparagus, watermelons, cantaloupes, and tomatoes grown in irrigated fields of California's Imperial Valley were transported three thousand miles by refrigerated cars to markets across the continent. By the 1930s the average distance between the fields where fruits and vegetables were grown and the markets in which they were sold was fifteen hundred miles. Fresh fruits and vegetables were no longer considered a luxury in off-seasons for the average American family.

At the same time, the commercial process of canning various foods had been introduced in France, and the system was applied in the United States to such an extent that larger amounts (and many more different kinds) of food were being packed in American plants than in all other countries combined. The effects on American menus were such that one historian of the canning industry felt entitled to wax lyrical:

> Canning gives the American family—especially in cities and factory towns—a kitchen garden where all good things grow, and where it is always harvest time. There are more tomatoes in a ten-cent can than could be bought in city markets for that sum when tomatoes are at their cheapest, and this is true of most other tinned foods. A regular Arabian Nights garden, where raspberries, apricots, olives, and pineapples, always ripe, grow side by side with peas, pumpkins, spinach; a garden with baked beans, vines and spaghetti bushes, and sauerkraut beds, and great caldrons of hot soup, and through it running a branch of the ocean in which one can catch salmon, lobsters, crabs and shrimp, and dig oysters and clams.[1]

Like the frozen food industry that followed it, commercial canning had advanced the process of turning American women into short-order cooks.

[1] James H. Collins, *The Story of Canned Foods* (New York, 1924).

So did the food departments of women's magazines, whose pages were loaded with luring appeals for the use of factory-packaged and manufactured foods—advertisements and recipes replete with simplified methods of cooking that included such shortcuts as substitution of various canned creamed soups for freshly made sauces. And national advertising created national rather than regional appetites and tastes.

The Oranging of America

Skillful national advertising, for instance, transformed Americans from a population that occasionally ate oranges as fresh fruit to one more apt than not to begin the day with a glass of orange juice. The technical factor that made the market almost universal was the perfection of a process to condense and squeeze juice; as a result, a consumer who added water to orange juice concentrate could have a fresh-tasting, mellow drink, free of seeds, pulp, and bitter oil. The idea needed financial backing as well as advertising and promotion.

In 1948, John Hay Whitney, a heavy investor in the company that developed the frozen concentrate process, one day offered a glass of Minute Maid orange juice to his golf partner, who happened to be Bing Crosby. The singer liked what he tasted. He bought twenty thousand shares and began to exploit orange juice on his radio shows and later in television commercials. The business of reducing fruit juices to frozen concentrate form skyrocketed, and the demand for Florida oranges increased fourfold, Floridians themselves became so partial to frozen juice that there were times when a traveler could not buy a glass of freshly squeezed orange juice. The state that produced more oranges than even California succumbed to the argument that natural juice might be either too sour or too sweet. On the other hand, it was thought that reconstituted frozen orange concentrate could be skillfully blended after a good harvest to produce a winelike beverage—so good, some orange men said, it had vintage years that reflected the seasonal climate.

Many of the advertising approaches that helped to put frozen juice in virtually every active kitchen had been used much earlier; promotion had helped to addict Americans to the patented mixture of powdered gelatin, sugar, imitation fruit flavors, and fake colors that was packaged with recipes for desserts (easily made by the addition of such ingredients as berries or chunks of pineapple). Even more threatening to honest cooks, the persuasive advertising depicted colorful gelatin "salads" bobbing with marshmallows, dates, diced fruits and vegetables, and the saturation exploitation in periodicals touching every American home resulted in meals often designed around such aberrations.[2]

[2] One called "candlelight salad" is described in *The Fannie Farmer Cookbook*: "a hideous concoction of a lettuce leaf with an upright banana sitting on it (the candle), topped with a dribble of mayonnaise (melting wax), a shred of coconut (the wick), and a dot of pimiento (to simulate the flame)."

"The Six-Year-Old Palate"

To measure the influence of advertising, one had only to travel the country to experience the blandness of public food as one of the results of skillful commercial persuasion. National advertising and standardization combined to reduce quality. As the Iowa novelist Vance Bourjaily told an interviewer, "people in the United States don't eat for pleasure," and he added that for most people "eating is just something done in response to advertising." And James Beard, author of a score of cookbooks and the dominant culinary influence on thousands of home cooks in the decades after World War II, succinctly defined the lowest common denominator of public feeding as "the six-year-old palate," a mass market that was unable to recognize—regardless of age—the adventure implicit in trying food that differs from the customary fare of the average American.

Advertising combined with television programming made an instant success of packaged "TV dinners" accurately aimed at the six-year-old palate. At the same time those meals-in-a-lap did terrible things to the reputation of traditional cooks, whose abilities were somewhat scornfully ignored in the push to sell precooked foods that needed nothing but heating before they were served. The only good thing to be said about many such products was that they were labor-saving. And in many cases advertising compounded deception. Hams, for example, were promoted as "tenderized" when the simple fact was that they had been put through a steaming process that filled them with water—adding to the weight for which the consumer must pay. They were "ready to eat," as the ads said, but they robbed home cooking of the tang, texture, and old-fashioned honesty of smokehouse products.[3]

Away from home, advertising and its allied arts were combined to produce the unprecedented success of a food chain known as McDonald's, "a great machine [in the words of James Beard] that belches forth hamburgers." McDonald's is also a brain trust of exploitation practices. The string of hamburger emporiums that has been spun in the last third of the twentieth century promises the public that each of its licensees or operators is a graduate of Hamburger University, and it set up an inspection system to insure that its graduate hamburger makers pursued the corporate policies. (The computerized recipe stipulates ten hamburgers to the pound of meat.) Its gimmickry proved so successful that it did more than had been done before to establish American fast-food tactics abroad. McDonald's hypnotized many traveling European youths. But a Parisian friend who tried a

[3] In the 1970s the number of cooks unwilling to accept the "tenderized" hams increased—and so did the availability of country hams cured in the old ways, which brought on bouts of nostalgia when their flavor was tasted by gastronomes who had felt deprived for years. Smokehouses once again functioned in hill-country regions to make traditional hams easy to order by mail. Some of these reflected the proverbial urge of the city man to return to simple rural life: In Wolftown, Virginia, a former New York Yankees player, Jim Kite, Jr., settled down to turn out what food authority Craig Claiborne called "conceivably the finest ham produced in America."

Big Mac for lunch in New York said cheerfully to my wife and me, "This is not food—this is a vector for communication." And as if to prove himself a genuine Parisian, he added that he found in the McDonald atmosphere "a *complaisance* that might be considered a national myth."

The myth had long before become an overbearing reality. The hamburger originally was a nineteenth-century import from Germany, a meat dish of chopped (not ground) beef known as a Hamburg steak, after the teeming port city on the Elbe River. The term *hamburg steak* first appeared in English in 1884 in the Boston *Journal.* Around the turn of the century a version known as Salisbury steak became popular on both sides of the Atlantic when broiled chopped beef was prescribed for his British patients by Dr. J. H. Salisbury—indeed the name still clings as a restaurant meat course. At the same time the "hamburger" gained wide acceptance as a classic American sandwich after being introduced at world's fairs in St. Louis and elsewhere. In this form it later became known throughout England as the Wimpy, sold by a chain bearing the same name (a monicker which had originated in "Popeye," the American comic strip drawn by Seegar). The funny papers could not be "credited with the popularity of the hamburg sandwich," etymologist Arnold Williams wrote, but he added that the cartoon endowed the snack "in the character of Wimpy . . . with a mythos." It did not take scholars, however, to recognize that it was the automobile and a nation constantly on the move that made the hamburger the prime example of fast food and an international institution. In addition, a quick meal of minced beef became so integrated in the American diet (easy to cook, easy to digest) that a young Midwest mother dubbed it "the Daily Grind."

Prepared at home or in a roadside kitchen, the most common variant of the ground beef sandwich is the purely New World contribution to gastronomy, the cheeseburger. It does not have to be a gooey contrivance of greasy, nearly tasteless granules and tacky processed cheese squeezed between halves of a bun that reminds you of cotton batting. It can, for instance, be a "Cheddar Ground Round," as it has been called at the Little Cottage Café in Bismarck, North Dakota; in making this unusual snack a ten-ounce pat of minced beef is wrapped with bacon, and liberally seasoned with Cheddar, Emmenthaler, and Parmesan cheese before it is broiled. Other variations abound. Unadorned by cheese of any kind, a satisfying hamburger can be made by mixing a pound of ground round steak with one egg, four tablespoon of catsup, a dash or two of milk, a small onion minced, and salt and pepper. Formed in four equal patties and dipped in flour, a hamburger variation is made by broiling to taste and serving on fresh tomato slices. Why so many cooks fail to use their own inventive imaginations to rid even fast food of ill repute is worth investigating.

Charles Kuralt, sent forth by the Columbia Broadcasting System to shed light on American foibles—including eating habits—appeared on home screens with his hamburger report in the fall of 1970. Against a changing tapestry of scenes showing carhop service along highways and city streets in many parts of the country, Kuralt delivered himself of the following observations on the great American snack:

> Americans ate forty billion hamburgers last year, give or take a few hundred million, and on the road you tend to eat more than your share. You can find your way across this country using burger joints the way a navigator uses stars. . . . We have munched Bridge burgers in the shadow of Brooklyn Bridge and Cable burgers hard by the Golden Gate, Dixie burgers in the sunny South and Yankee Doodle burgers in the North. The Civil War must be over—they taste exactly alike. . . . We had a Capitol burger—guess where. And so help us, in the inner courtyard of the Pentagon, a Penta burger. . . . and then there was the night in New Mexico when the lady was just closing up and we had to decide in a hurry. What'll it be, she said, a whoppa burger or a bitta burger? Hard to decide. . . .
>
> But this is not merely a local phenomenon. The smell of fried onions is abroad in the land, and if the French chefs among us will avert their eyes, we will finish reciting our menu of the last few weeks on the highways of America. We've had grabba burgers, kinga burgers, lotta burgers, castle burgers, country burgers, bronco burgers. Broadway burgers, broiled burgers, beefnut burgers, bell burgers, plush burgers, prime burgers, flame burgers . . . dude burgers, char burgers, tall boy burgers, golden burgers, 747 jet burgers, whiz burgers, nifty burgers, and thing burgers. . . .

Kuralt wound up as the camera showed a hamburger stand surrounded by nothing but endless desert, and said that he wondered if the last American to survive the holocaust were to leave a single monument (like the unexplained giant sculptures of Easter Island), whether or not it would be a shack with a blazing hamburger sign.

The Survival of Pop Food

He might have picked an equally frail edifice dedicated to production of fried chicken, an American pop food for which sales equal to those for hamburgers have often been claimed. Colonel Sanders' Kentucky Fried Chicken combines "finger-lickin' good" as an advertising slogan and a secret mixture of herbs he said came from an old family recipe. He opened an international field of food-on-the-run that was soon entered by franchising firms with names like Chicken Delight, Kansas Fried ("with a touch of soul"), and Chicken Lickin.

Harland Sanders transformed the concept of Southern fried chicken into a success story characteristic of individual American enterprise, but the pattern he established for fast-food chains has done nothing to maintain reputations that once made Southern cooks proud. Forced out of the restaurant business in rural Kentucky at the age of sixty-six, Colonel Sanders took to the road with his method of cooking and seasoning fried chicken in a mere eight minutes, thus eliminating the usual half-hour wait. "Let me prepare fried chicken my way," he told restaurateurs. "If you agree that it's the best you've ever tasted, I'll sell you my mixture of herbs and spices and teach you how to use my special pressure cooker. You pay me four cents on every chicken you sell." In eight years he had franchised more than six hundred Kentucky Fried Chicken operations, and thousands of Americans were converted to the notion that food served with speed was more important than a meal carefully prepared. (Twenty years later the colonel's formula was employed in more than six thousand stores in almost fifty countries throughout the world—carrying new notions of American food abroad.) On the other hand, Chicken Maryland, dredged in flour and/or bread crumbs, or in a batter, and sautéed, then served with corn fritters or cornmeal mush, has escaped being overly popularized; it was accepted and refined by France's great chefs, including Escoffier and Henri Pellaprat, who established it as something of an international classic.

The taste for chicken as take-away food, as is obviously true of the appetite for hamburgers, is prevalent everywhere in the country. In New England, along Atlantic shores, road food for generations has acquired, in the popularity of lobster rolls, something akin to elegance. It has been reported that the buttery, uniquely American bread roll stuffed with unadulterated lobster meat was invented at Palisades Park at West Haven, Connecticut. "Served warm, with a side order of onion rings, it is the undisputed top-of-the-line of carry-out food," according to a bulletin issued in 1977. Grilled sandwiches filled with variable lobster stuffings can be found on New England's coast as far north as Maine, and many versions are produced in private kitchens. (Slowly toasted frankfurter rolls, fastidiously buttered, are filled with cooked, finely chopped lobster meat that has been mixed with minced celery, lemon juice, mayonnaise, grated onion; shredded lettuce is strewn over all.)

A claim is made in Essex, Massachusetts, that a local seafood maestro named Lawrence Woodman in 1916 was the first to dip a clam in bread crumbs and then to fry it in deep fat, thereby inventing an even earlier genre of portable American seafood. Woodman's place, perched on the edge of a salt marsh, today is one of many small businesses specializing in crisp, puffy fried clams, and it may have set a pattern that helped to make Howard Johnson a famous name in the franchise food industry. When this chain of restaurants was founded, the house specialty of fried clams brought in as many people off the road as did the chain's orange tile roofs. But, alas, fresh fried clams seem to have become unprofitable, and in most franchise eating places they were replaced by a processed substitute.

Pop food, like pop art, scorns many of the traditions of creativity, but its survival has been assured by the disappearance of help in home kitchens as well as an economy in which affluence has become persuasive. For middle-income families it is easier and almost as inexpensive to feed the children at the local hamburger joint; a bonus may be found in the fact that the jaunt can also be considered entertainment. Among average women who have children—and frequently a job as well—culinary creativity had narrowed down by the 1960s to such *chef d'oeuvre* as casseroles made with preseasoned mixtures referred to as Hamburger Helper and "homemade" desserts that might be conjured from packaged cake mixes and other processed ingredients sure to turn out exotic puddings in minutes.

The nation's cooking had become worse only to take a turn for the better. During the same time period at least some of all those post–World War II travelers had been learning to take the act of eating as something more than stoking up. Accepting the food of other cultures, they increased their appreciation of life in general. Unhappily the meaning of the word *gourmet* became distorted as it was misused, but the distortion signified, at least, a generally healthy respect for excellence in the kitchen. "What originally began as a gastronomic expedition of a few Idle Rich and Serious Epicureans has become a widespread phenonemon of mass travel," the gastronomic critic Joseph Wechsberg wrote in 1967.

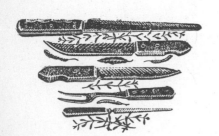

Tourists who went on those gustatory romps multiplied alarmingly. Among them, perhaps, were some who once might have been considered idle rich but who in the 1970s were paying, instead, for the privilege of working as menials in *les hautes cuisines*. Americans attended Paris cooking schools, then wrought what seemed to them to be wonders in their own kitchens with new enthusiasm for culinary techniques, savoring their classic recipes like blue-chip stocks and bonds. Some of those who went abroad managed to arrange stints as apprentices to three-star chefs. Cookbook writers such as Marcella Hazan, on her own ground in Italy, drew hundreds of eager students from the States. Many of these novice gastronomes used this kind of experience to serve impressive food to guests back home; others founded cooking schools in their communities—to augment their incomes or more, perhaps, to establish culinary careers for themselves.

"These days," a report in *Bon Appetit* asserted in 1977, "the food pages of newspapers all over the country list thousands of cooking schools every spring and fall. It almost seems as if everybody who ever belonged to the Shallot of the Month Club or owns a butcher's block table or has some remote ethnic presumption has proclaimed himself dean of his own cooking college." Nevertheless, local culinary classes influenced trends in American food in encouraging ways. In just one instance during midwinter 1978, an Iowa City cooking teacher invited as a special attraction from New York the author of *The Fine Art of Italian Cooking*, Giuliano Bugialli. During his visit, the Iowa classes in cookery drew students from as far away as St. Louis and helped to prove, Bugialli said, that "the standard of eating is improving all around the country. The meat-and-potatoes image is going to become completely forgotten." Bugialli certainly had found reason for his optimism, but other observers did not ignore the problems inherent in improving the quality of American cookery. Few in this country have really discriminating palates, a French-born cooking school teacher in Wisconsin noted, because they haven't been taught culinary theory. Living in unsophisticated communities, married to an American, Liane Kuony told acquaintances she couldn't believe the food she saw her neighbors eating;

among them she recognized victims of clever merchandising. "Imagine!" she cried. "Marshmallows and gelatin in the salads!" In Fond du Lac, Wisconsin, Mrs. Kuony was so depressed by the American diet that she opened a restaurant soon after World War II, "to show people what good food tastes like."

She proved, when she established the Postillion Restaurant and School of Culinary Arts, that Chicagoans not only would drive six hours just to dine well but others would fly across the country to enroll in her cooking classes. "They don't come *here*," said Mrs. Kuony, "to learn to fix a meal just to impress their friends." If they weren't interested in learning culinary theory, she rejected applicants. Neither would she have anything to do with "cooking instructors who stay just one lesson ahead of their students." Still, she found that there were Americans willing to try anything in order to master the right way of doing things. "If you learn to be honest with food," she repeatedly admonished all who listened, "it spills over into your whole life."

As a pioneer in leading American housewives away from the perils of "domestic science" and "home economics," Mrs. Kuony was also in advance of the whole-foods movement of the 1970s. She persuaded neighboring farmers to raise meat to her specifications on feed containing no chemicals. She helped to create sources for milk-fed veal and chickens made plump and tasty by a diet of sunflower seeds and corn instead of manufactured feeds. She insisted on whitefish freshly caught in deep waters of Lake Michigan, wild rice from the Menominee Indian Reservation, and naturally grown domestic geese. She preached that American foods have "valor and worth" that can be recognized by anyone sufficiently interested to develop a palate. "Wisconsin sour cream," she said with pride, "cannot be excelled. Nor can homemade greengage jam and tarts, or hand-churned ice cream with hickory nut brittle." Throughout the country people who never heard of Liane Kuony began accepting the essence of her message from numerous sources.

Gastronomy and Revenge

Perhaps for the first time among middle-class Americans there was understanding of cooking as an art form, of dining as a social grace to be taken seriously. General readership magazines in the United States probed the mysteries of great cuisines and great chefs. The subject of food had been taken over by the cognoscenti. And wine—that, too, became a subject to be mastered by one and all. The whole spirit of the 1970s may have been summed up one day in October 1973, when the weekly called *New York* (itself a guidon in the prevailing winds) adapted an acerbic Spanish proverb by captioning an issue devoted entirely to food and drink: Eating Well Is the Best Revenge.

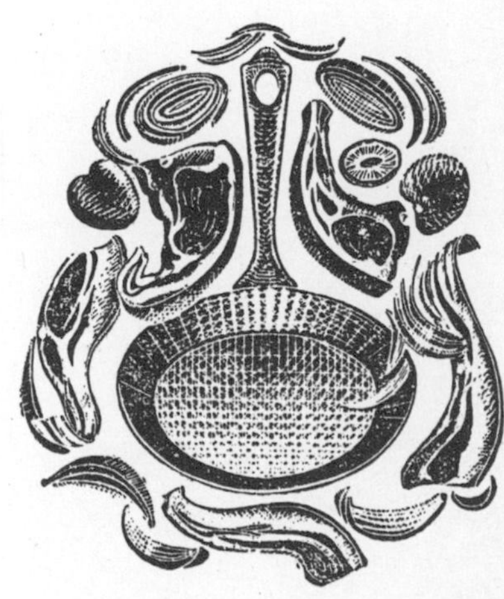

Food had become a central factor in living well, in pursuing a stylish life. Mastering the art of the cuisine had evolved into something more than a fad. To this end the return of an unknown woman named Julia Child from years of living abroad had been fatefully timed. While an expatriate in France she had collaborated in the writing of *Mastering the Art of French Cooking*, a cookbook that changed the lives of thousands after its publication in America in 1961. No previous U.S. culinary manual had been so detailed and yet so encouraging to those hesitant to try complicated procedures. Its chief effect was to persuade connoisseurs and neophytes alike that sophisticated recipes could be mastered and that really good classic food could be readily prepared in home kitchens. It proved to be a necessary guidebook for those who were caught in the culinary renaissance. Mrs. Child's ensuing television performances—first as "The French Chef" and later in programs that widened the scope of the American kitchen and expounded ideas for entertaining—also helped convince those intent on cooking well that almost anyone could turn out epicurean meals. Her gift as a performer entertained earnest cooks as well as other kinds of viewers, and most of all, it seemed, she showed by example that good cooks could make mistakes and still avoid disaster. Her unassuming demonstrations were not without *faux pas*—it may be that her audience multiplied after she dropped a chicken while the cameras were rolling and blithely observed that such things could happen to anyone. Her message seemed to be that *haute cuisine* techniques could be adapted to all kinds of kitchen productions and that cooking could be fun. She so touched the mood of the country that she became a celebrity in small towns as well as cosmopolitan gathering places.

James Beard, without the regularity of television exposure but whose column appeared in many newspapers and who crisscrossed the country making local appearances, became as recognizable as a home-run hitter among baseball fans. Frequently spotted when eating in restaurants, Beard was implored one day in Chicago to write a good-luck message for his waitress to pass on to her son about to graduate from a school for chefs. Mrs. Child, strolling a midwestern street with her husband, the painter Paul Child, was accosted by a woman who followed her television show and recognized Mrs. Child's distinctive voice. The admirer stopped her and asked, "What will we be having tonight, dearie?" (Unlike most celebrities of the entertainment world, the "superstars" of food are perceived by many admirers as members of their families.)

In the 1960s the character of the best American cookbooks changed from catch-all collections of recipes to skillfully written books that had themes, vibrancy, and eclecticism. The proliferation of published volumes on the subject of food did not by any means exclude tomes devoted to notions about what to feed your cranky husband, your weekend guests, your finicky children, or to special recipes for microwave ovens and other kitchen gadgets. Most of these opportunistic ventures, Anne Mendelson pointed out, contained "not very good advice, and some of it is downright laughable. The people who chiefly benefit from it are those who write, edit, publish, and sell cookbooks—certainly not those who buy them." The best of the mixed bag, however, were highly successful because they were serious, well-written treatises rather than mere conglomerations of recipes. *The Food of France* and *The Food of Italy* by Waverley Root made clear to Americans the origin and refinement of cooking styles in those two countries and, without supplying formal recipes, offered the cook practical understanding of culinary diversity unavailable elsewhere. Claudia Roden's *A Book of Middle Eastern Food* was not only the first presentation of authentic recipes of the region but a delight to read even for Americans with limited interest in the act of cooking. In addition, books such as *From My Mother's Kitchen* by Mimi Sheraton and *The Taste of Country Cooking* by Edna Lewis were personal testaments invoking the living style of another time. And among writers interested in regional food, the gifted June Platt published her *New England Cook Book* in 1971 as the last of several volumes that made her, as James Beard said, "undoubtedly one of the most important gastronomic authorities this country has produced."

Beard himself summed up a lifetime of kitchen mastery and accumulated knowledge of this country's gastronomy in his *American Cookery* and *Theory and Practice of Good Cooking*. The twelfth edition of *The Joy of Cooking* by Irma S. Rombauer and her daughter Marian Becker expanded its command of the American kitchen by including such ethnic dishes as couscous and *rijstafel*. American publishers had issued 49 cookbooks in 1960, and a dozen years later the annual total, according to *Publisher's Weekly*, had jumped to 385 new titles (not to mention paperbacks and reprints). The most surprising publishing event was the revision of *The Fannie Farmer Cookbook* by Alfred A. Knopf, Inc., in 1979. In the revised version all the makeshift recipes that successors had accumulated in the half century after Fannie's death were banished. There were no more suggestions for using canned soups instead of making sauces from scratch, and the number of tips for tremulous gelatin salads coagulating around chunks of canned fruits was minimal. As Fannie Farmer had set out to do in 1896, her revised masterwork (a compendium of more than two thousand recipes) catalogued the best of American food as it had evolved from colonial influences and reflected ethnic contributions made almost indigenous through common usage.

As better cookbooks were issued, much of what was affecting the changes in American food was noted by readers of *Gourmet*, a monthly paean to the art of cooking and eating triumphantly. Established before World War II and much before widespread popular interest in culinary arts had been aroused, its circulation could be seen as a barometer of what was about to happen. In the five years beginning in 1967 readership had increased at the rate of fifty thousand a year, and the mail received by the editors often indicated the increasing interest in serious cooking among men, a surprising percentage identifying themselves as doctors of medicine.

On every economic level, however, the interest among the young was most noticeable of all. There were in most American communities wives of servicemen who had lived abroad, and many had learned about foreign food by doing their own marketing in addition to mastering recipes that were new to them. The appreciations they brought back and shared with one another in suburban and small-town gourmet clubs proved contagious. In such places as Burlington, Vermont, where there is an air force base and where numerous young academics live, young couples took turns planning and executing dinners for club members on a monthly schedule. Cosmopolitan cities such as New York and New Orleans had their Chevaliers du Taste-Vins, but there were even more groups in such cities as Minneapolis and St. Paul, which organized as "societies of amateur chefs"—not simply gatherings of fledgling connoisseurs but of men who found more joy in the act of cooking than in spectator sports.

Cooking as a Life-Style

"The absolute status symbol of the New York apartment," a fashionable decorator told the *New York Times* in 1973, "is the kitchen." With few people hiring cooks or dining room maids, more and more festive meals were served in kitchens transformed into rooms that echoed an American past when the center of the house was a fireplace used for cooking as well as heating. Kitchen work tables, often made of laminated butcher-block wood, once again served first in the preparation of a meal and were then rearranged as dining tables in rooms no longer reminiscent of chemical laboratories. Utensils of copper and other decorative materials were recognized as suitable objets d'art to hang on walls. Hosts or hostesses, admitting guests to the scene of the evening's culinary activity, devised a new kind of party described by some as a "come-help-cook" dinner. This social wrinkle thrived because of developing interest in meals that include a large number of separate dishes. Any hostess preparing an exotic meal calling for the chopping of various condiments, herbs, vegetables, and other ingredients—like that of India, Japan, China, or any of the Middle Eastern cultures—may urge guests to join in the preparation.

In the culinary world the signs of the coming "revolution" were being slowly recognized by the 1970s. The previous decade had been accented by only a scattering of enterprises with special commitments to food. Cheese stores were rare throughout the country. In California, for instance, cooks who bought esoteric ingredients did so mostly through mail orders. Only Orientals cooked with woks, and few American natives knew the meaning of tofu. Stores making and selling fresh pasta were unheard of.

In describing the California upheaval, Ruth Reichl wrote in *New West*: "Suddenly you can't walk down the street without bumping into cheese stores that stock eight kinds of blue cheese and ten varieties of chèvre. Coffee, freshly roasted, of course, is tenderly brewed in all kinds of contraptions, and the home espresso machine is quite commonplace. Pâté is purchased at the corner store. Not so long ago few of us were fond of fish; we now eat it raw. Our tastes have changed."

Among young people throughout the country an important extension of this fascination with food became evident in the increasing number who abandoned successful careers to become cooks in their own restaurants. One of the highly praised French restaurants opening in Manhattan in 1979—facing competition from chefs professionally trained in France's best kitchens—was established by a youthful Boston couple who had given up careers in the milieus of finance and advertising; they wanted more than anything else to cook for Americans who had become devotees of what some Europeans might call *cuisine par excellence*. The most admired restaurant in the San Francisco area had been created a few years before by a former Montessori teacher who abruptly changed the course of her life after a trip abroad. With scholarly dedication, insatiable curiosity, and unstinting energy in her search for ingredients, Alice Waters set such standards at Chez Panisse (starting as a neighborhood eating place in Berkeley) that critics asserted she and her restaurant had more influence on northern California cuisine than any other factor. As far away as Vermont, a handful of country inns, opened in the 1970s, were run by young people devoted to equally high aims—Perley Fielders, for instance, left his government job in Washington for a new life as *chef-patron* a few miles south of the Canadian border. As the world of food metamorphized, the ability to cook well seemed at last to have become honorable, and there were hundreds of young travelers who returned from abroad with burgeoning pride in their appreciation of culinary accomplishment.

Waterwheels Begin to Turn

The exposure to other cultures transformed some visitors to the Middle East and the Orient into vegetarians and even more into devotees of natural foods. Again there was an echo of the past as so-called health food stores sprang up throughout the country. In New England and the South especially, waterwheels that had been still for generations began to turn again to grind whole grains into flour. Farms devoted to raising unadulterated foodstuffs increased as the demand for organic food mounted—many crops were raised by those who relied on such age-old pest repellents as garlic, nasturtiums, praying mantises, and tansy and yarrow plants instead of commercial pesticides and chemical fertilizers.

Thousands of people in the 1970s went back to preparing some of the same kind of food their ancestors had eaten, and the number practicing a meatless diet in the United States in the 1970s was estimated to be as high as five million. Others seemed to emulate food faddists of the nineteenth century by refusing to eat anything injected with antibiotics or hormones, or anything contained in packages whose labels followed the letter of the law by admitting in fine print the use of synthetic sweeteners, preservatives, emulsifiers, dyes, and stabilizers. Thousands were moved to reject the ersatz convenience foods that often substituted the chore of heating for the craft of cooking.

Evidence of the growth of vegetarianism could be found in the increased availability of vegetarian alternatives for meals served in campus dining rooms and other campus eating places. There were young people who had served in the Peace Corps and had learned overseas that interesting and appetizing food need not be luxurious. In addition, as Janet Barkas wrote in *The Vegetable Passion*, the appeal of a crusade was recognized: "Vegetarianism offers idealistic youth a chance to show their parents that there *is* a way for each person to fight the unharnessed aggression and violence association with earlier generations. . . . Furthermore, vegetarianism offers a way of returning to nature, an aspect of human existence that is quickly disappearing from the large urban areas of contemporary America."

"Anything Fake Is Deplored"

Without the fanaticism of an earlier time, the health-minded young were reassured that natural food, untampered with by manufacturers, was good food. Also the interest in what one ate was for some an expression of the growing affinity for Eastern philosophies, and those peripatetic youths who explored Asian cultures often drew parallels between idealistic thought and diet. As gurus became fashionable, many highly educated young people became earnest students of culinary matters. They learned, for instance, that no true Indian dish is made with ready-mixed curry powder, but that flavor comes from the cook's initiative in blending spices like coriander, cuminseed, ginger, garlic, nutmeg, or turmeric. They learned what various foods taste like when they are grown naturally and how they can be turned into appealingly aromatic dishes when seasoned with herbs or unmixed spices and not embellished with synthetics. This trend was identified by Madhur Jaffrey in her *Invitation to Indian Cooking*, published in 1973. Young Americans, she wrote, "seem to have a great desire to experience the 'real' thing, an authentic taste, a different life style. Anything fake is deplored, fake foods included."

For some the impetus to find a different way of life was rebellious. Many of those young Americans—reacting against adult life and everything "fake" it represented to them—discovered they didn't have to visit Asia or the Middle East to learn to appreciate the cracked-wheat dishes that were known variously as kasha or *burghul* and were not so very different from the American Indian samp, once a mainstay of New England diets.[4] In their spiritual quests these young people gathered in communes not unlike

[4] The worth of a diet based on cereal has been proved again and again, of course. In her marvelous book, *How to Cook a Wolf*, M. F. K. Fisher tells of a California college student who lived for two years during the Depression on about seven cents a day. "He would buy whole ground wheat at a feed-and-grain store, cook it slowly in a big kettle with a lot of water until it was tender," Mrs. Fisher wrote, "and eat it three times a day with a weekly gallon of milk which he got from a cut-rate dairy. Almost every day he stole a piece of fruit from a Chinese pushcart near his room." Perhaps in contrast to the mores of the 1970s, Mrs. Fisher added: "After he graduated he sent the [pushcart] owner a ten-dollar bill, and got four dollars back, with an agreeable note inviting him to a New Year's party in Chinatown in San Francisco. He went."

Brook Farm, Fruitlands, and the Shaker villages of a century earlier; and those of them who cooked sometimes dished up fine things after simmering pots of groats to which mushrooms, herbs, and seasonings might be added. In their rejection of ersatz values, they consumed brown rice by the carloads, sat down to simple meals that sometimes included dandelion soup or green peppers stuffed with savory lentils, salads of carrots and raisins, herbal infusions, bread they made from whole-grain flour and often sold to outsiders to provide themselves with income. In the process, a message was reaching a widening audience, and the rewards inherent in cooking with whole grains were recognized by thousands unswayed by communal thinking.

Not many communes lasted. Some young idealists, leaving the land, or finding pure democracy an impossible dream, moved into New England hill villages, mountain towns in the Rockies and the Southwest, and elsewhere, to set up stores specializing in natural foods and elixirs. Some established public restaurants to share their dedication. In the *Moosewood Cookbook*, published in 1977, Mollie Katzen explained a restaurant established in Ithaca, New York, by a small band of young vegetarians. "The reasons are various, ranging from simplicity of one sort (health, lightness, purity) to simplicity of another (convenience, economy). We also want to spread the notion that protein and aesthetics need not be sacrificed when you leave meat out of a meal," she wrote. "Cheese, eggs, nuts, grains, beans and bean curd are the staples on which this cuisine is designed. . . . The cooking styles have been handed back and forth. . . . The result is an eclectic cuisine, with vegetarian, international emphases."

Other young vegetarians noticed that outsiders appreciated the superiority of organically grown vegetables and sold their bumper crops to average consumers. The general appetite for unpackaged garden produce free of preservatives resulted in a revival of farmer's markets in large and small communities throughout the nation. Again, young people refusing to conform set in motion a trend that elicited grateful speeches from oldsters who had been deprived since childhood of the taste of organically nurtured food. In New York and other metropolises parking lots were transformed into "Green Markets" on summer shopping days—the hunger for fruits and vegetables fresh from their growing plots was no longer to be dismissed as a cultist notion. In fact, here was new evidence of the inclination on the part of young and old alike to enjoy food for its natural qualities.

There was also evidence that some cooks in the 1970s could thank inflation for their realization that cooking could be fun, in addition to being economical and a way of improving the quality of diets. Shortages in beefsteaks and other high-priced cuts of various meats combined with rising food costs in general to persuade cooks with hungry families to try recipes long ignored as too taxing or complicated. Some agreed when columnist Harriet Van Horne wrote during critical weeks in 1973, "Some of the best meals I have ever eaten have been savory blends of inexpensive meats,

simmered gently with vegetables and herbs." That thought didn't convince the worshipers of red meat, of course, but it may have helped in varying the menus of others.

"The silent revolution of the American palate," as it has been called, occurred as a reaction to problems of ecology as well as of economy. Young people were specifically concerned about pollution that affected the availability of food. They worked to clean up dead rivers like the Hudson, a source for past generations of such favorite American fish as shad and striped bass. Many who were not necessarily formal vegetarians were keenly interested in meat substitutes, but not in the commercial analogues, the meatless meats analogous to beef, ham, chicken, and seafood served in some eating places to unwary customers. The vanguard, instead, accepted soybeans without pretense. Their soybean croquettes may look like hamburgers, but they are served without euphemism. Broiled patties are sometimes quite delicious mixtures of soybeans, wild rice, and vegetable seasonings; they make soybean chili, and festive combinations of the Oriental legume with tomatoes, squash, garlic, garden herbs, and grated cheese. Not very different, really, from the South Union, Ohio, Shakers of a century age who baked for dinner a meatlike loaf that combined succulent lentils, grated onions, and their own tangy cheese, and served it with a sauce made from fresh tomatoes, garlic, and fragrant herbs.

There were, here and there, other signs of a return to beginnings. Rejecting the factory product that had lost any connection with traditional bread, thousands of ordinary women—and men, too—turned to baking their own. If young health enthusiasts in search of karma made dark and aromatic loaves, others, returning to apartment life after gastronomical travels, proved that Julia Child's recipe for French bread was, as one of them averred, infallible. *Beard on Bread*—a volume that brought together all the styles of baking contributed by Americans of every ethnic background—demonstrated the author's thesis that well-made bread "is the most fundamentally satisfying of all foods." There was no accurate tally of homemade breads in 1974, but twentieth-century cooks are proving that more efficient ovens are no deterrent to emulating their grandmothers. "The smell of good bread baking, like the sound of lightly flowing water," M. F. K. Fisher wrote in 1968, "is indescribable in its evocation of innocence and delight." The smell of good bread baking, evoking the past, is one of the compensations for Americans rediscovering the general satisfactions of the kitchen.

In its fourth century America may have developed no distinctive cuisine to set it wholly apart from other nations, but in many ways Americans with appreciative interest in food could find inspiration and renewal in looking back into the past. And the most committed of them might say, with Thomas Jefferson, "I too am an Epicurian."

(in collaboration with Judith B. Jones)
A personal gathering of recipes
from various periods in
U.S. history, various regions, and
various ethnic influences.

APPETIZERS AND HORS D'OEUVRE

AVOCADO-HAZELNUT DIP

Used by American cooks more than those of any other country, avocados are probably more versatile than most fruits. They may be transformed into appetizers, soups, entrées; they are basic to a variety of salads, and they make desserts that provide just the right accent for certain menus. One of the simplest of the desserts popular in the avocado orchard country northwest of Los Angeles is a mixture of avocado pulp, rich cream, and a touch of sugar that is smoothly blended and chilled (see Avocado Ice Cream, p. 485).

1 large ripe avocado
1/2 cup cottage cheese
few drops of lemon juice
2 Tbs. chopped hazelnuts
2 Tbs. finely chopped sweet red pepper
2 Tbs. finely chopped green pepper
1 scallion, minced (white part only)
2 Tbs. minced parsley
salt
freshly ground pepper (optional)
shredded fresh basil or parsley sprigs for garnish
dip-size tacos

Peel and mash avocado and blend with cottage cheese and lemon juice until smooth. Mix in nuts, peppers, scallion, and parsley. Add salt and pepper only if needed. Serve in a mound garnished with strips of purple basil (if available) or green basil or parsley and surrounded by tacos.

MAKES ABOUT 2 CUPS.

GUACAMOLE WITH CLAMS

1 large ripe avocado
1 garlic clove
1/2 tsp. salt
1/4 tsp. chili powder
1 tsp. lemon juice
4 Tbs., or more, minced clams

Peel avocado and garlic. Cut garlic into halves and rub it into serving bowl, then discard. Mash avocado in serving bowl, adding salt, chili powder, lemon juice, and minced clams. Chill for 1 hour.

MAKES ABOUT 1 1/2 CUPS.

LAKE MICHIGAN BLINIS

Whitefish caviar from Port Washington, Wisconsin, needs no comparison with Beluga, Sevruga, or Osetra from the Caspian Sea. It has its own virtues. The roe of sturgeon caught in American waters may be another story. As the cost of imported caviar rose to as much as $400 a pound at the end of the 1970s, caviar from the West Coast appeared on menus of fine restaurants in New York and elsewhere, and there were signs that the best domestic product was to be found in the Hudson River; the price in retail shops was about 25 percent of that brought from abroad. American caviar can be good enough to serve alone, or the whitefish variety is highly acceptable as part of this Nashville recipe for buckwheat cakes with a filling of roe and sour cream.

1 recipe buckwheat pancakes (p. 214)
1/2 cup warm water
2 cups sour cream
1/2 cup whitefish caviar

Thin batter with water to make cakes about 5 inches in diameter. Mix sour cream with caviar and quickly spread half of mixture on hot cakes; roll up cakes and top with remaining caviar mixture.

MAKES ABOUT 8 SERVINGS.

AUNT ROSE'S CHEESE AND PIMIENTO SANDWICH SPREAD

Devised in Durand, Wisconsin, and making use of the state's best Cheddar, this is a Welsh-American cook's variation on the ancient Cymric standby, Welsh rabbit; it is also good hot (Cambrian Baked Eggs with Cheese Sauce, p. 423).

2 Tbs. butter
1 cup shredded Wisconsin Cheddar cheese
1 cup milk
3 eggs, well beaten
1/2 tsp. salt
1/4 tsp. dry mustard
5 canned pimientos, chopped

In the top part of a double boiler, over simmering water, melt butter, then blend in cheese, stirring until free of lumps. Stir in milk and add eggs, continuing to stir over low heat as mixture thickens. Stir in salt and mustard. Do not let boil, or eggs will tend to scramble. Remove from heat and stir in pimientos. Cool in refrigerator overnight.

MAKES ABOUT 2 CUPS.

CHILES RELLENOS

Chiles rellenos, or stuffed chili peppers, were popular on California's Spanish ranchos before Yankees and Southerners arrived from the East, and they were so appreciated by the newcomers that they began to appear immediately in local cookbooks. They are often served with refried beans, a salad, tortillas, or immersed in tomato sauce.

1/2 lb. Monterey Jack or Cheddar cheese
6 to 8 canned whole green chilies
4 eggs, separated
1/4 cup flour
1/2 tsp. salt

SAUCE:

1 onion, chopped fine
1 garlic clove, minced
2 Tbs. vegetable oil
2 cups tomato puree
2 cups chicken stock
1 tsp. salt
freshly ground pepper
1/4 tsp. dried oregano
1/4 tsp. dried basil

Cut cheese into pieces to fit chilies. Slit one side of chilies and remove seeds unless you like things very spicy-hot. Wrap chilies around cheese pieces. Beat egg yolks until fluffy, then gradually stir in flour and salt. In a separate bowl beat whites until peaks form, then fold into batter. Fill skillet to depth of 2 inches with corn oil and heat. Dip stuffed chilies into batter, one at a time, coating thoroughly. Slide into hot oil, turn immediately, cook for 5 minutes, then turn and cook other side, for about the same time. Drain on paper towels. *Chiles rellenos* may be cooked any time ahead if they are served with sauce.

Make the sauce: Sauté onion and garlic in oil, then add tomato puree and stock. Stir in salt, a few turns of pepper grinder, oregano, and basil; let simmer for at least 30 minutes. Drop in stuffed cooked chilies and let simmer just long enough to heat. If chilies are cold, continue simmering for 5 to 10 minutes. Serve piping hot.

MAKES 6 TO 8 SERVINGS.

HOT CHILI-TOMATO DIP

2 to 3 Tbs. butter
2 large onions, chopped fine
2 garlic cloves, minced
3 Tbs. minced green chili peppers
1 Tbs. Worcestershire sauce
1 cup grated Monterey Jack cheese
2 1/2 cups canned tomatoes, drained and chopped
1 Tbs. cornstarch dissolved in water
corn chips

Melt butter in a saucepan and sauté onions, garlic, and peppers about 4 minutes; add Worcestershire sauce. Melt cheese in top part of a double boiler over simmering water; stir in tomatoes and cooked onion mixure. When this begins to bubble, stir in cornstarch mixture; stir until sauce thickens. Pour into top of chafing dish and keep hot while serving with corn chips as dips.

MAKES 8 SERVINGS OR MORE.

COACH HOUSE CRAB WITH PROSCIUTTO

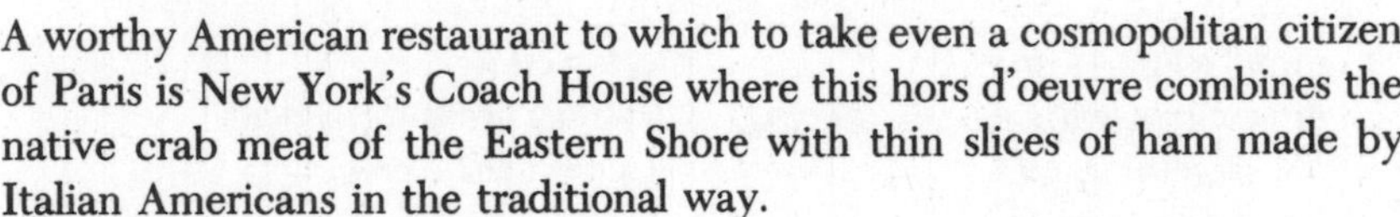

A worthy American restaurant to which to take even a cosmopolitan citizen of Paris is New York's Coach House where this hors d'oeuvre combines the native crab meat of the Eastern Shore with thin slices of ham made by Italian Americans in the traditional way.

24 thin slices of prosciutto
12 oz. fresh lump crab meat
3/4 cup (1 1/2 sticks) butter
1 tsp. Worcestershire sauce
1/2 tsp. Tabasco or Louisiana hot sauce
1 lemon
2 Tbs. minced parsley
freshly ground black pepper

Arrange 4 slices of prosciutto on a flat surface, each slice slightly overlapping the other. Place in the center a heaping tablespoon of crab. Roll ham slices over filling cigar-style; repeat with remaining prosciutto and crab. Heat butter in a large skillet; when it foams, add the 6 rolls. (The ham will cling to the crab when heated.) Turn rolls once and cook until ham starts to frizzle and crab is heated through; transfer to a hot serving dish. Add Worcestershire and Tabasco to skillet and squeeze in juice of lemon. Heat for about 30 seconds and pour over ham. Sprinkle each roll with parsley and pepper.

MAKES 6 SERVINGS.

INDIVIDUAL CRAB SOUFFLÉS BAKED IN SHELLS

3 Tbs. butter
3 Tbs. flour
3/4 cup milk
2 egg yolks
1/2 tsp. salt
1/2 tsp. minced chives
1/2 tsp. minced parsley
1/2 tsp. dried savory
1 or 2 dashes of Tabasco
2/3 cup grated Wisconsin asiago cheese
2 Tbs. Madeira
12 oz. fresh crab meat
1 tsp. lemon juice
1 Tbs. butter, softened
5 egg whites

Preheat oven to 425° F.

Melt butter in a saucepan over low heat, then stir in flour, eliminating lumps. Let mixture bubble for about 1 minute, then remove from heat and stir in milk with a wire whisk, mixing briskly. Return to heat and keep stirring constantly until sauce thickens to a pastelike consistency. Off the heat, beat in egg yolks, one at a time, then add salt, chives, parsley, savory, Tabasco, 1/2 cup cheese, and the Madeira. Let cool. Remove any hard bits from crab meat and sprinkle with lemon juice. Butter 4 scallop shells. Beat egg whites until they form peaks, then fold into cooled sauce. Put a spoonful of soufflé mixture into each shell, then gently distribute one-quarter of crab meat over each one. Divide remaining soufflé mixture among the shells, mounding neatly on top, but do not let them overflow. Sprinkle with remaining cheese. Bake for 10 minutes; reduce heat to 375° and bake for 10 minutes more.

MAKES 4 SERVINGS.

COLD CRAB IN BASIL SAUCE

6 to 7 oz. cooked fresh crab meat
4 water chestnuts
12 large basil leaves, minced
2 Tbs. minced parsley
1 whole egg
1/2 tsp. salt
1 Tbs. wine vinegar
1/2 tsp. Dijon mustard or 1/4 tsp. dry mustard
1/2 cup olive oil
1/2 cup vegetable, walnut, or peanut oil
lemon juice

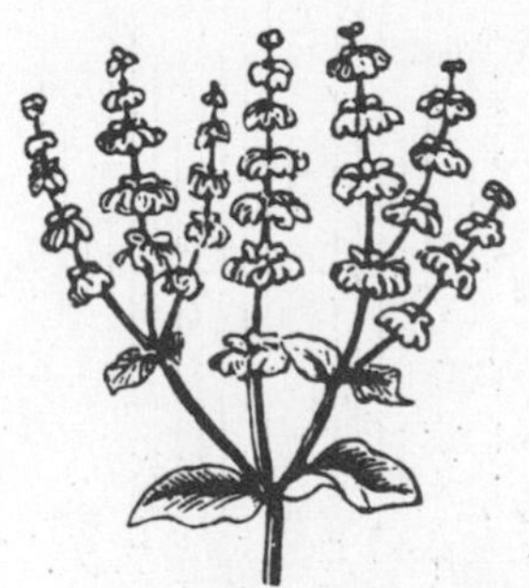

Remove any bits of bone from crab meat. Drain water chestnuts and slice thin. Spin basil and parsley in a blender or food processor for about 50 seconds; add egg, salt, vinegar, mustard, then slowly pour in both oils mixed together while continuing to blend. If mixture becomes stiff before using all of oil, add a few drops of lemon juice. When sauce is thoroughly blended and oil is completely used, taste for seasoning and add a few drops more of lemon juice. Mix this sauce into crab meat and stir in sliced water chestnuts. Serve with tomato and cucumber slices as an hors d'oeuvre. Or serve as lunch for 4 in avocado halves.

COCKTAIL FRANKFURTERS IN PASTRY

1 recipe Basic Piecrust (p. 459)
3/4 lb. cocktail-size frankfurters
1 to 2 Tbs. mustard (old-fashioned whole-seed preferred)
1 egg beaten with 1 Tbs. water

Preheat oven to 450° F.

Prepare dough and divide into 2 pieces. Roll out thin. Arrange half of frankfurters on 1 sheet of dough so that each sausage has enough dough to wrap around sides and ends; cut dough accordingly. Brush each frankfurter on all sides with mustard, then pull sides and ends of dough upward, painting inner seams with egg wash. Tuck in ends and seal main seam, pressing edges firmly together. Arrange packages seam side down, about 1 inch apart on a buttered cookie sheet. Repeat with second half of franks and remaining dough. Brush all tops and sides with remaining egg, then prick tops with a fork. Chill for 10 minutes before putting in oven. Bake for 10 minutes, or until golden.

MAKES 12 SERVINGS OR MORE.

ALL-AMERICAN HOT HORS D'OEUVRE

Crisp, bacon-wrapped hot mouthfuls are made in American kitchens in every state. Angels on horseback—oysters wrapped in bacon—have been known as *ostras ángeles* in Spanish California, and they become *angelenos* when an anchovy fillet encircles the oyster underneath the wrapping of bacon. Broiled bacon also encircles chicken livers, cocktail sausages, lobster chunks, mushrooms, scallops, shad roe, shrimps, and water chestnuts. Put them under the broiler and keep turning until done.

Bacon pinwheels are made by trimming the crust from an unsliced loaf of fresh white bread, then cutting it into 1/4-inch lengthwise slices. Each slice is spread with cream cheese softened at room temperature and rolled like a jelly roll. Cut the rolls into 2 or 3 pieces and wrap each in sliced bacon, tying with a thread. Toast under moderate broiler heat, turning often until bacon is cooked.

LIVER SPREAD

1 to 1 1/2 cups cooked beef, veal, or chicken liver
2 eggs, hard-cooked and sieved
1 small onion, minced very fine
8 anchovy fillets, mashed to a paste
3 to 4 Tbs. butter, softened
freshly ground pepper
3 Tbs., more or less, heavy cream
1/4 cup minced parsley

Put liver through the fine blade of a meat grinder, then mash through a sieve. Mix in eggs, onion, anchovies, and butter. Add pepper to taste and stir in cream, a little at a time, using either more or less, according to desired consistency. Shape mixture into a mound on a suitable serving dish and sprinkle with minced parsley or use as a sandwich spread.

MAKES 8 SERVINGS OR MORE.

COLD MUSSEL COQUILLE WITH GREEN SAUCE

1/2 bunch of watercress, blanched for 1 minute
3 sprigs parsley
1 whole scallion
1 egg
1/2 tsp. prepared mustard
1/2 tsp. salt
1 lime
2/3 cup olive oil
2/3 cup peanut oil
2 lb. fresh cooked mussels removed from shells, or 1 can (12 oz.) mussels
1/2 lb. small cooked shrimp, shelled, or 1 small can (7 oz.) tiny shrimps
3 shallots, minced fine
1 Tbs. minced parsley
1 Tbs. minced chives

Make green sauce by spinning in blender the watercress, parsley, scallion, egg, mustard, salt, and 1/2 Tbs. lime juice; save half of lime to slice for garnish. Add oil, a little at a time, to achieve mayonnaise consistency; if too thick, add a little more lime juice as spinning continues. Drain mussels and shrimps and mix with shallots; fold in one-third of green sauce, then divide to fill 8 scallop shells. Top with remaining green sauce and sprinkle with parsley and chives.

MAKES 8 SERVINGS.

SCALLOPED SHRIMPS IN SOUR CREAM

1 lb. uncooked shrimps
4 Tbs. (1/2 stick) butter
1/3 lb. fresh mushrooms, sliced
1 cup sour cream at room temperature
1/2 tsp. salt
freshly ground white pepper
1 tsp. soy sauce
paprika
1/4 cup grated Parmesan cheese

Shell and clean shrimps. Melt butter in a skillet and stir in sliced mushrooms; sauté for 5 or 6 minutes, then stir in shrimps and sauté until they turn pink, about 3 minutes. Put sour cream in a saucepan and heat slowly, stirring in salt, pepper, soy sauce, and enough paprika to make sauce pink; do not let boil. Stir into shrimps and mushrooms and cook just long enough so sauce is thick and well blended. Spoon into 4 scallop shells and sprinkle cheese over tops. Put under broiler until cheese turns golden.

MAKES 4 SERVINGS.

HOT OYSTER COCKTAIL

1/2 cup chili sauce
1/2 cup tomato catsup
1/4 cup finely chopped celery
1 tsp. Tabasco
1/2 tsp. lemon juice
2 Tbs. butter
24 very fresh large oysters, drained

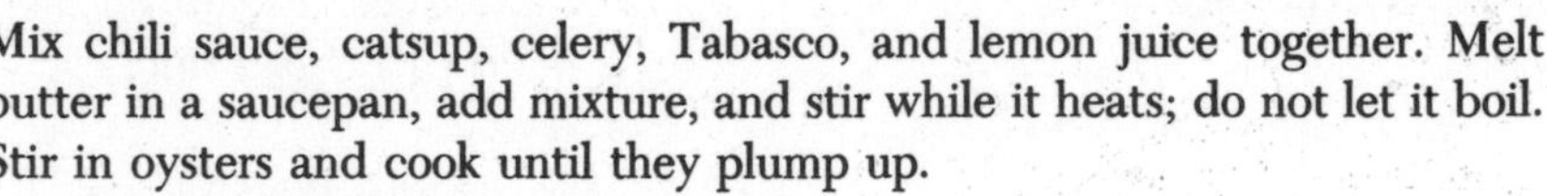

Mix chili sauce, catsup, celery, Tabasco, and lemon juice together. Melt butter in a saucepan, add mixture, and stir while it heats; do not let it boil. Stir in oysters and cook until they plump up.

MAKES 6 SERVINGS.

SHRIMPS DE JONGHE

Years ago, when we first tasted this dish or one very similar to it, it was called shrimps Boveri and was served in a Chicago restaurant of that Italian name. Versions of the formula, which vary in the number of herbs used, are popular in St. Paul, and in many parts of the Midwest and the South. In Louisville, Kentucky, not long after World War II Marion Flexner reported that this hors d'oeuvre had been the specialty of a Belgian couple named de Jonghe, who ran a Chicago restaurant, and that their nephew had taken over the business, "although he refuses to divulge the secret family recipe. However, he does insist that his version has twelve herbs in it." In that respect it is somewhat like oysters Rockefeller: The recipe is under lock and key, and outsiders can only trust their taste memories.

2 garlic cloves, minced
1/2 tsp. each of finely minced parsley, scallion, shallot, chives, chervil, tarragon, thyme
1/4 lb. (1 stick) butter, softened
1 cup fresh bread crumbs
1/4 cup dry sherry
dash of Tabasco
pinch of grated nutmeg
pinch of ground mace
salt
freshly ground pepper
1 lb. raw shrimps

Preheat oven to 400° F.

Stir garlic and herbs together, then work into butter until evenly distributed. Add bread crumbs, sherry, Tabasco, grated nutmeg, and mace. Taste, adding salt if necessary and several turns of the pepper grinder. The mixture will improve if left to mature in refrigerator. Shell and clean shrimps and cook in boiling salted water for 3 minutes, then divide into 4 piles. Put a layer of herbed butter-crumb mixture in the bottom of each of 4 scallop shells. Arrange shrimps spoon-fashion in a single layer, pressing into butter-crumb mixture. Divide remaining herbed butter into 4 parts and spread over tops of shrimp. Bake for 10 to 15 minutes, or bake for 10 minutes, then put under broiler until tops brown.

MAKES 4 SERVINGS.

CHARLESTON SHRIMP PASTE

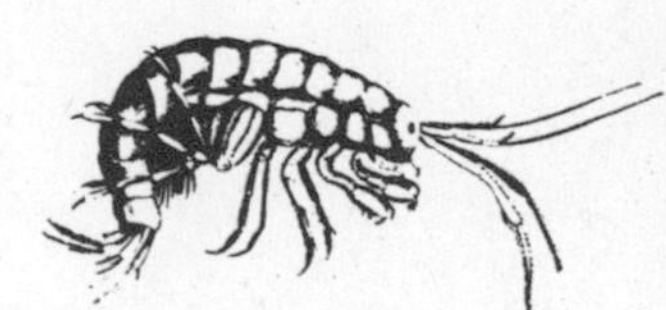

1 lb. cooked shrimp
4 Tbs. (1/2 stick) butter, softened
Worcestershire sauce
lemon juice
Tabasco
grated nutmeg
salt
freshly ground pepper

Put shrimp through a meat grinder, then grind again. Stir in butter, blending well, and add seasonings to taste. Chill 2 hours or more. Serve on sesame crackers or Melba rounds.

MAKES 8 TO 10 SERVINGS.

COCKTAIL POPCORN

1/2 cup popcorn kernels
2/3 cup (1 stick plus 2 2/3 Tbs.) butter or 1/3 cup butter and 1/3 cup corn oil
1 1/2 tsp. salt
1 small garlic clove
1/4 cup minced chives

Put corn in a skillet large enough so that kernels can be spread over bottom in 1 uncrowded layer. Put another skillet over low heat and melt 1/3 cup butter or heat oil; after 2 minutes test by dropping in 1 kernel. If kernel pops immediately, add remaining corn and cover skillet. Shake back and forth to keep kernels moving. In a separate pan melt remaining butter; add salt, garlic, and chives; pour over popped corn and toss.

MAKES 3 QUARTS.

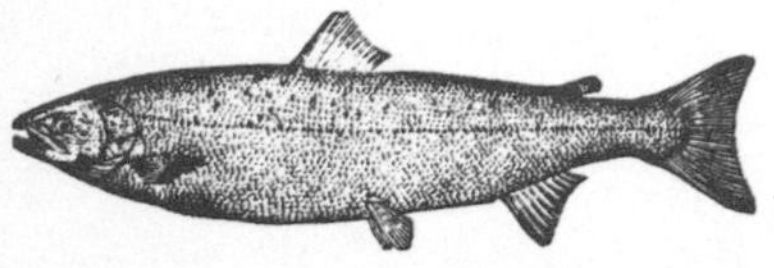

SALMON-CAVIAR HORS D'OEUVRE

2 cups flaked cooked salmon
4 cup-shaped lettuce leaves
1/2 cup red caviar, chilled
1/2 cup fresh Homemade Mayonnaise (p. 400)
1/2 cup stiffly whipped cream

Arrange flaked salmon in lettuce cups. Carefully fold caviar into mayonnaise, then fold in whipped cream. Spoon this sauce over salmon.

MAKES 4 SERVINGS.

LOUISIANA SHALLOT PIE

In some regions, especially the South, the word *shallot* is used for scallions (or tiny green onions) instead of for the somewhat garlic-shaped cloven brown onion that in France is known as *éschalote*. Although the flavors are quite different, scallions and shallots are often used interchangeably. In this ham-flavored pie, as in a Bayou cornmeal pie, the subtlety is the result of mincing both white and green parts of scallions. In the latter, 2 cups of minced scallions and the same amount of grated cheese are cooked in butter to make a filling between 2 layers of cornmeal mush, then baked in a hot oven for 30 minutes. Because it is so rich and tasty, we have found the scallion-ham-cream filling particularly delicious in bite-size pastry shells served piping hot as a cocktail snack.

3 egg yolks, beaten
1/2 tsp. salt
pinch of cayenne pepper
1 tsp. flour
freshly ground white pepper
1 cup sour cream
3 Tbs. butter
1 cup minced whole scallions
1/2 cup minced ham
16 to 20 prebaked small pastry shells (see p. 459)

Preheat oven to 350° F.

Mix egg yolks with salt, cayenne, flour, one or two turns of pepper grinder, and the sour cream. Cook in the top part of a double boiler over simmering water for about 20 minutes, or until thick; let cool. Melt butter and sauté scallions for 2 or 3 minutes. Stir in ham and cook for 1 minute more, then mix well with custard. Pour into prebaked pastry shells and bake for 7 to 8 minutes.

MAKES 8 TO 10 SERVINGS.

BROILED MUSHROOMS WITH HAM STUFFING

12 medium-size fresh mushrooms
1/4 cup olive oil
1 Tbs. lemon juice
1 garlic clove, minced
2 Tbs. butter
1 medium-size green pepper, chopped fine
2 large shallots, chopped fine
1/2 tsp. dried chervil
1/2 tsp. dried oregano
1/2 cup minced ham
toast points

Remove stems from mushrooms and set aside. Use a sharp knife to slash mushroom caps, then put in a bowl with mixture of oil, lemon juice, and garlic for 30 minutes. Meanwhile melt butter and sauté green pepper, shallots, and herbs. Chop mushroom stems very fine, mix with ham, and stir into green pepper mixture, cooking over very low heat for about 10 minutes; add marinade from mushroom caps. Broil caps for 3 minutes on each side. Put caps on toast points and spoon stuffing over.

MAKES 2 SERVINGS.

JERUSALEM ARTICHOKE AND CELERY ROOT SALAD

1 large celery root
3/4 lb. Jerusalem artichokes
2/3 cup country ham, cut into match-size strips
1 cup Lemony Mustard Sauce (p. 445)
lettuce cups
1/4 cup minced parsley

Peel celery root, cut into halves, then parboil for 7 minutes. Wash artichokes very thoroughly but do not peel; boil for about 10 minutes. Cut blanched celery root into match-size strips. Trim all hard, knotty areas from cooked Jerusalem artichokes along with a little of the skin, although some skin should be left for texture and flavor; slice lengthwise, then into 3 or 4 strips. Toss ham and vegetable strips gently with mustard sauce. Distribute equal portions over lettuce leaves and top with parsley. Serve as a first course.

MAKES 4 SERVINGS.

LITTLE CANADA RABBIT TERRINE

1 rabbit (3 lb.), marinated for several days
1 lb. lean pork, ground
1 lb. pork fat, ground
2 medium-size onions, chopped fine
3 Tbs. lard
2 garlic cloves, minced fine
½ cup applejack or other brandy or Madeira
2 eggs
2 to 3 tsp. salt
freshly ground pepper
2 Tbs. minced parsley
1 tsp. dried savory
½ tsp. dried thyme
2 or 3 whole allspice, ground
½ lb. salt pork, sliced thin
1 lb. country ham, cut into ⅓-in.-thick strips
1 large bay leaf

Preheat oven to 350° F.

Strip well-marinated rabbit meat from bones. Use best pieces (about half of total) to cut into long strips ½ to ⅓ inch thick. Grind less-tender pieces and scraps of rabbit and mix with ground pork and ground fat. Sauté onions in lard until translucent, then stir into ground meat; add garlic, applejack, eggs, and seasonings. Test flavor by frying a small sample of mixture; it should be heartily seasoned but not oversalted if country ham is as tangy as it should be.

Blanch salt pork slices 5 minutes in 2 quarts water; drain and pat dry, then use them to line a 2-quart terrine, letting edges just meet. Spread one-third of ground meat mixture over bottom, then lay over it alternating strips of rabbit meat and ham, using half of total. Repeat layer of ground meat, rabbit and ham strips, finishing with ground meat. Put bay leaf in the center, then cover top with salt pork slices, tucking down into sides so that mixture is well wrapped. Set terrine in a pan with hot water that comes about halfway up the side of the terrine; bake for 2 ½ hours. Let cool, weighting top surface with an old flatiron or other heavy object. When cool, chill for several days. Serve from the terrine.

MAKES 12 SERVINGS.

MARINADE FOR RABBIT:

1 ½ cups red wine
¾ cup wine vinegar
1 onion, chopped coarse
1 carrot, cut into chunks
2 stalks celery, cut into short pieces
1 garlic clove, crushed
½ tsp. dried dillweed
½ tsp. mustard seeds
½ tsp. whole coriander, bruised
½ tsp. peppercorns, bruised

Mix all ingredients with about ¾ cup water, or enough to cover meat. Marinate meat for 24 hours or more, turning occasionally.

SMOKED WHITEFISH COCKTAIL APPETIZER

The availability of smoked whitefish from the Great Lakes led to the development of this party tidbit. Members of the Society of Amateur Chefs in Minneapolis found it so popular that they received hundreds of requests for the recipe after it was described on a television program.

2 lb. smoked whitefish or other smoked fish
1 cup Homemade Mayonnaise (p. 400)
1 Tbs. dry mustard
1 Tbs. minced chives
1 large tomato, peeled, seeded, and diced
1 Tbs. dry sherry
freshly ground black pepper

Several hours ahead, bone and flake fish and refrigerate. Mix mayonnaise with mustard, chives, and tomato dice. Fold in chilled flaked fish, then blend with sherry and add several turns of pepper grinder. Salt should not be necessary, but it may be added if fish is bland. Serve on Melba rounds.

MAKES 12 SERVINGS.

Chapter 11

BREADS, PANCAKES, DOUGHNUTS

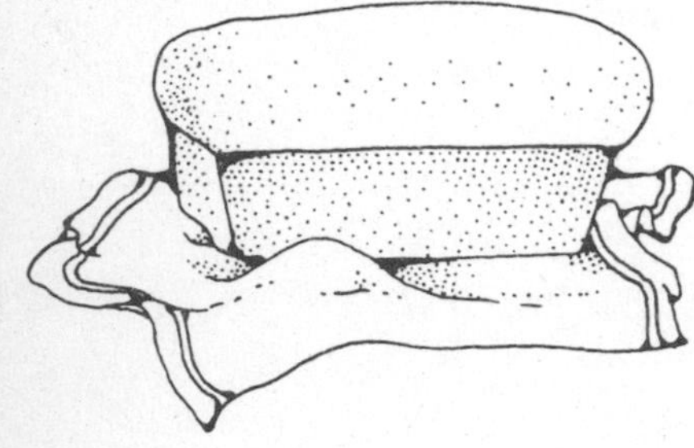

BEATEN BISCUITS MADE IN A FOOD PROCESSOR

A beaten biscuit has been described as a cross between a soda cracker and a baking powder biscuit. "It is neither tender nor light," a Southerner wrote affectionately, "but is food for those with strong jaws and good teeth." Frequently served at fancy afternoon gatherings with thin, small slices of aged country ham, beaten biscuits, during the days of slavery in the South, were the products of husky cooks who beat the dough until blisters of air formed—purists maintained that an hour of beating by hand was needed to do the job right. When fewer kitchen workers were available, some families acquired "beaten biscuit machines," some of which consisted of a marble slab on iron legs with a set of metal rollers at one end. The dough was fed through the rollers many times to approximate the two hundred whacks considered necessary for beating by hand. In Winston-Salem a versifier of the Whatsoever Circle, Kings Daughters, described the old process, never dreaming that a twentieth-century kitchen food processor would make beaten biscuits easy to serve:

> About the 'gredients required I needn't mention dem;
> Of course you knows of flour an' things, how much to put an' when.
> But soon as you is got dat dough mixed up all smooth an' neat,
> Den's when yo' genius gwine to show, to get dem biscuits beat!
> Two hundred licks is what I give for home folks, never fewer,
> An' if I'm spectin' company in, I gives five hundred sure!"

With a food processor the procedure is less taxing.

2 cups flour
1 tsp. salt
8 Tbs. cold, hard butter, cut into small pieces
1/2 cup ice water

Preheat oven to 350° F.

Put flour and salt in a food processor container and spin blade to aerate mixture. While processor is running, add cut-up butter and slowly pour water through processor funnel, spinning until dough forms a ball. Continue for about 2 minutes, then turn dough out onto a lightly floured surface. Roll dough into a rectangle about 1/8 inch thick. Fold dough to make 2 equal layers. Cut with a 1 1/2-inch biscuit cutter, then arrange these rounds on an ungreased cookie sheet. Bake for about 30 minutes, or until biscuits turn golden brown. When split, they should be crisply firm inside.

MAKES ABOUT 1 DOZEN.

BUTTERMILK BISCUITS

2 cups flour
2 tsp. baking powder
2/3 tsp. baking soda
3/4 tsp. salt
1/4 cup vegetable shortening
3/4 cups buttermilk

Preheat oven to 450° F.

Sift flour, baking powder and soda, and salt together 3 times. Cut in shortening until mixture is crumbly, then gradually add buttermilk, mixing until smooth. Knead dough lightly on a floured surface. Roll to 1/8 inch thick and cut into circles. Bake for 10 to 12 minutes on a buttered cookie sheet.

MAKES ABOUT 2 DOZEN SMALL BISCUITS.

APPLE-CHEESE MUFFINS

4 Tbs. (1/2 stick) butter, softened
1/2 cup sugar
2 large eggs
1 1/2 cups sifted flour
1 tsp. baking powder
1 tsp. baking soda
1/2 tsp. salt
3/4 cup rolled oats
1 large tart apple
2/3 cup grated Cheddar cheese
1/2 cup chopped walnuts
3/4 cup milk
1 or 2 large apples
4 Tbs. (1/2 stick) butter, melted
2 Tbs. sugar mixed with 1 Tbs. ground cinnamon

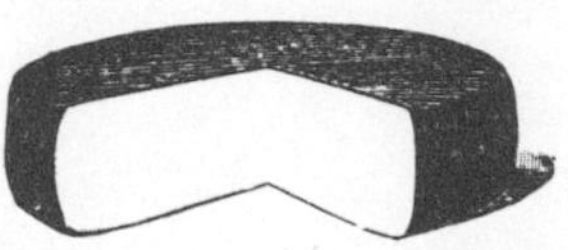

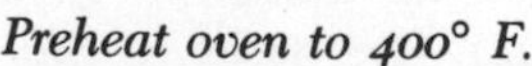

Preheat oven to 400° F.

Cream butter and sugar together. Add eggs and beat well. Sift together flour, baking powder, baking soda, and salt, then stir into butter-sugar mixture; stir in oats. Chop tart apple into 1/8-inch dice; add to mixture, along with cheese and walnuts. Gradually stir in milk, mixing lightly. Fill well-buttered muffin tins two-thirds full. Cut remaining whole apples into 12 thin slices the same diameter as muffin tins; brush slices with melted butter and coat with cinnamon-sugar mixture, then top batter in each muffin tin with 1 apple slice. Sprinkle remaining cinnamon-sugar mixture evenly over muffins. Bake for about 25 minutes. Let cool on a wire rack.

MAKES 12.

BACON AND PEANUT BUTTER MUFFINS

2 cups sifted flour
1 Tbs. baking powder
2 Tbs. sugar
1 tsp. salt
2 Tbs. bacon fat or butter, melted
1 egg, well beaten
1 cup milk
3 bacon strips, chopped fine
about 1/4 cup peanut butter

Preheat oven to 400° F.

Sift flour, baking powder, sugar, and salt together. Blend bacon fat or butter, egg, milk, and bacon, then stir in flour mixture, but do not beat; mixture should be just moistened. Pour a little batter into each well-buttered muffin tin, then drop about 1/3 teaspoon peanut butter into each before filling tins three-quarters full. Bake for 20 to 25 minutes. Let cool on a wire rack.

MAKES 12.

BLUEBERRY MUFFINS

2 cups flour, sifted twice
1 brimming cup blueberries, washed and hulled
2 Tbs. sugar
1/2 tsp. salt
1 Tbs. baking powder
2 Tbs. butter, melted
1 egg, well beaten
3/4 cup milk

Preheat oven to 375° F.

Be sure flour measures 2 cups after sifting; mix 1/2 cup with blueberries and set aside. Add sugar, salt, and baking powder to remaining flour and sift 3 times. Stir together butter, egg, and milk, then add this mixture alternately with berries to flour mixture, tossing lightly, just enough to moisten flour. Do not overmix. Grease a cast-iron gem or muffin pan. Pour batter to three-quarter point in 10 cups of gem pan and half-fill remaining cups with water (this keeps muffins from scorching). Bake for 25 minutes. Let cool on a wire rack.

MAKES 10.

BRAN AND HAM MUFFINS

1 cup bran
1 1/4 cups milk
1 egg, beaten
2 Tbs. butter, melted
1 cup flour
1 Tbs. sugar
1/2 tsp. salt
2 1/2 tsp. baking powder
1 cup ground ham
1 scallion, minced fine (white part only)
1 to 2 Tbs. minced parsley
freshly ground black pepper

Preheat oven to 400° F.

Let bran soak in milk for about 5 minutes, then stir in egg and butter. Sift together flour, sugar, salt, and baking powder; blend this lightly into milk mixture, just enough to dampen the flour. Stir in ham (country-cured ham will give muffins real character), scallion, parsley and 3 or 4 turns of pepper grinder. Divide among well-buttered muffin tins and bake for 25 to 40 minutes. Let cool on a wire rack.

MAKES 12.

HOMINY MUFFINS

3 Tbs. hominy
5/8 tsp. salt
2 tsp. dry yeast
2 Tbs. warm water
4 Tbs. (1/2 stick) butter
1 Tbs. sugar
1/2 cup milk, scalded
1 1/2 to 1 3/4 cups flour

Preheat oven to 375° F. *

Cook hominy by sprinkling it into 1 cup boiling water. Add 1/8 teaspoon salt, reduce heat, cover, and let simmer, stirring occasionally, for 25 minutes; it should make about 1/2 cup cooked. Dissolve yeast in water. In a larger bowl mix still-warm cooked hominy with butter, sugar, milk, and remaining salt, making sure to break up any lumps. When cool, add dissolved yeast and enough flour to make a moist dough, mixing well. Turn out onto a floured surface and knead for a few minutes, adding a little more flour if necessary. Cover and let rise in a warm place until the dough has doubled in bulk. Punch down. Butter gem pans for 12 muffins, fill two-thirds full, and let rise, uncovered, for 1 hour.* Bake in top third of the oven for 25 to 30 minutes. Let cool on a wire rack.

MAKES 12.

PUMPKIN MUFFINS

2 cups white flour
2 cups yellow cornmeal
2 Tbs. baking powder
1 tsp. baking soda
2 tsp. salt
3 eggs
1 cup cooked pumpkin
1/2 cup honey
1/2 cup light molasses
2 cups buttermilk
1/4 lb. (1 stick) butter, melted

Preheat oven to 425° F.

Sift dry ingredients together. Beat eggs thoroughly, then add pumpkin, honey, molasses, and buttermilk. Combine with dry ingredients and mix well. Stir in butter. Grease muffin tins and fill two-thirds full with batter. Bake for about 20 minutes, or until golden brown. Let cool on wire racks.

MAKES ABOUT 2 1/2 DOZEN.

EVERYDAY CORN BREAD

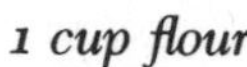

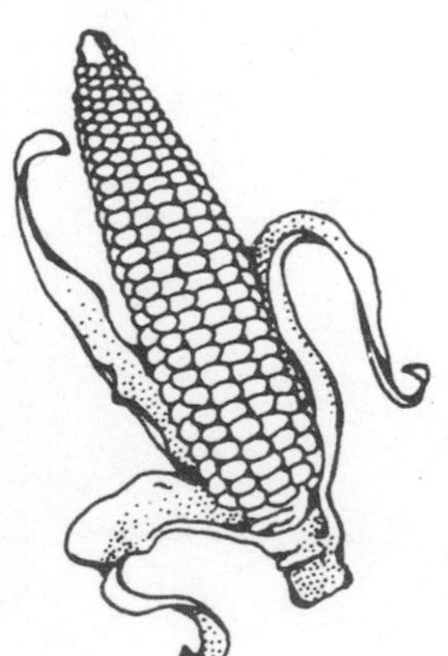

1 cup flour
1 Tbs. sugar
3/4 tsp. salt
5 tsp. baking powder
1 cup yellow cornmeal
3 Tbs. butter, melted and cooled
1 cup milk
1 egg, slightly beaten

Preheat oven to 425° F.

Sift together flour, sugar, salt, and baking powder, and stir in cornmeal. Mix butter, milk, and egg together. Combine with dry ingredients and beat for about 1 minute. Pour into a buttered 8-inch square baking pan and bake for 25 minutes. Let cool on a wire rack.

MAKES 8 SERVINGS.

SOFT-AS-PIE TEXAS CORNBREAD

1 thin bacon strip
3/4 cup coarsely ground yellow cornmeal
1 cup boiling water
2 Tbs. butter mixed with 2 Tbs. sausage or bacon fat, melted
3 medium-size eggs, beaten
2 tsp. baking powder
1 cup buttermilk
1 Tbs. molasses
3/4 cup cooked corn kernels (optional)
4 Tbs. (1/2 stick) butter, melted (optional)
1 or 2 chili peppers, chopped

Preheat oven to 350° F.

Put a 7- or 8-inch cast-iron skillet containing the bacon in a preheated oven and let bacon sizzle while preparing remaining ingredients. Scald cornmeal with boiling water and let it steep for 5 minutes. Then add melted butter and fat and mix well; stir in eggs, baking powder, buttermilk, and molasses. (If you are serving this as a kind of spoon bread with meats, you might add corn kernels and more butter.) Add chili peppers to give a hot accent. When well blended, pour mixture on top of bacon in skillet and bake for about 30 minutes. Let cool on a wire rack.

MAKES 6 SERVINGS.

EDNA'S SPOON BREAD

Spoon bread, sometimes called batter bread, has distinguished American tables since colonial times, and it has been a common twentieth-century substitute in the South for mashed potatoes. The recipe below belongs to Edna Lewis, author of *The Taste of Country Cooking.* Mrs. Lewis's family still lives in the Virginia region in which their forebears once were slaves and where the style of cooking, she believes, still shows the influence of Jefferson's commitment to *haute cuisine.* Spoon bread isn't French—it is sometimes accented with fresh corn kernels, whole hominy, or rice—but it was prepared regularly in the Monticello kitchens.

1 cup white water-ground cornmeal
1/2 tsp. salt
2 tsp. sugar
1/3 tsp. baking soda
1 tsp. baking powder
3 medium-size eggs, beaten
2 Tbs. butter
2 cups buttermilk

Preheat oven to 400° F.

Use an 8-inch-square baking pan, or a 1 1/2-quart soufflé dish. Sift cornmeal, salt, sugar, baking soda, and baking powder together in a mixing bowl, making a well in the center. Pour in eggs. At this point set baking pan in oven with butter to heat. Stir eggs vigorously into cornmeal mixture. Pour in buttermilk and stir well again. Remove hot pan from oven, tilt it around to butter surface of pan, pour excess butter into cornmeal batter, stirring quickly, then pour batter into hot baking pan. Bake for 35 minutes. Serve right from oven with loads of fresh butter.

MAKES 8 SERVINGS.

BOSTON BROWN BREAD

1/2 cup rye flour
1/2 cup whole wheat flour
1/2 tsp. baking soda
1/2 tsp. baking powder
1/2 tsp. salt
1/2 cup yellow cornmeal
1 1/2 cups buttermilk
1/2 cup molasses, warmed†

Preheat oven to 300° F. *

Sift flour with baking soda, baking powder, and salt into a large bowl. Add cornmeal. Make a hollow in the sifted ingredients, then mix buttermilk and molasses and pour into hollow; beat mixture thoroughly. Butter a 1-quart melon mold, including inside of lid, and pour in mixture. See that it is covered tightly, then set on a rack in a kettle and pour in boiling water to a point about halfway up mold. Cover kettle and steam for 3 hours.* Remove lid from mold and put bread in oven to dry for 6 or 7 minutes. Best when served warm.

MAKES 6 SERVINGS.

†To make pouring easier, put container of molasses in warm water while measuring the flour and cornmeal.

GRANDMA McLEOD'S GINGERBREAD

1/4 cup shortening
1/2 cup sugar
3/4 tsp. baking soda
1/2 cup molasses
1 1/2 cups flour
3/4 tsp. baking powder
1 tsp. ground cinnamon
1 tsp. ground ginger
1/4 tsp. ground cloves
pinch of salt
3/4 cup boiling water
1 egg, beaten

Preheat oven to 325° F.

Cream together shortening and sugar. Beat 1/2 teaspoon of the baking soda into molasses until fluffy and light; add to shortening and sugar. Sift together flour, baking powder, cinnamon, ginger, cloves, and salt; mix boiling water and remaining 1/4 teaspoon baking soda, then gradually add liquid, alternating with dry ingredients, to molasses mixture. Stir until well mixed, then stir in egg. Butter and flour an 8-inch square baking pan and pour in gingerbread mixture. Bake for about 20 minutes. Let cool on a wire rack.

MAKES 8 SERVINGS.

PUMPKIN BREAD

3 1/2 cups sifted flour
1 tsp. salt
2 1/2 cups sugar
2 tsps. baking soda
2 cups pumpkin purée
1 cup vegetable oil
1/2 cup water
4 eggs, beaten
3/4 tsp. ground cinnamon
1/2 tsp. grated nutmeg
1 cup chopped nutmeats (optional)

Preheat oven to 350° F.

Sift flour, salt, sugar, and baking soda together. Mix pumpkin, oil, water, eggs, and spices together and combine with dry ingredients, but do not overmix. Add nuts if desired. Bake in well-buttered loaf pans (9 by 5 by 3 inches) for 45 minutes to 1 hour, or until a straw comes out clean. Turn out and let cool on wire racks.

MAKES 2 LOAVES.

CASPIAN POND SUNDAY CORN BREAD

2 pkg. dry yeast, or 1 oz. fresh yeast cake
1/2 cup warm water
2 Tbs. honey
3 Tbs. chicken or goose fat
1 cup hot water
1 tsp. salt
3 to 3 1/2 cups unbleached flour
1 cup yellow cornmeal

*Preheat oven to 350° F.**

Proof yeast in warm water mixed with honey. Put fat into a large bowl; add hot water and salt; set aside to cool; then stir in dissolved yeast and enough flour to make a moist dough. Turn out onto a floured surface and work in cornmeal, kneading for about 10 minutes. Place dough in a buttered bowl and turn to coat with butter all over; cover with a cloth and let rise in a warm place until doubled in bulk. Punch down, knead a little more, then divide and form into 2 round loaves; place in 8-inch buttered pie pans, cover, and let rise until once more doubled in bulk.* Bake for 45 minutes, or until loaves sound hollow when tapped. Let cool on wire racks.

MAKES 2 ROUND LOAVES.

ANADAMA BREAD

At Rockport, Massachusetts, on Cape Ann, they used to tell a story that may have given this New England bread its name: Anna was a lazy wife whose bread was so much like her character that her Yankee husband devised his own recipe while he muttered, "Anna, damn 'er!"

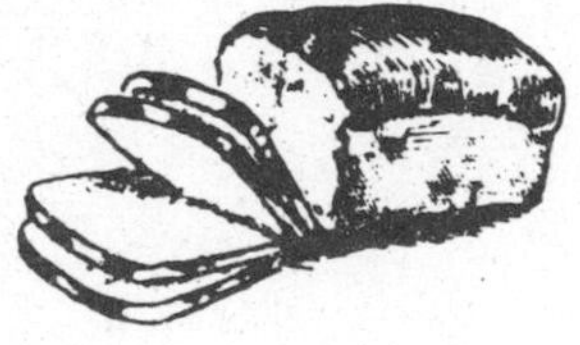

1 pkg. dry yeast
1/2 cup warm water
2 Tbs. butter or other shortening
1/2 cup molasses
2 cups hot water
about 5 cups unbleached flour
1/2 cup cornmeal
2 tsp. salt

Preheat oven to 400° F.

Dissolve yeast in warm water. Melt butter and molasses in hot water. Cool to lukewarm and stir in yeast mixture, then mix 4 cups of flour with cornmeal and salt; blend with yeast-molasses liquid, 1 cup at a time. Continue to add flour until dough is stiff. Turn out onto a floured surface and knead for 10 minutes, adding more flour as necessary. When dough is smooth and elastic and springs back, place in a well-buttered bowl and turn to coat with butter all over; cover with a cloth and set in a warm place until doubled in bulk. Punch down, knead again for a minute or so, then form into 2 loaves. Put loaves in buttered 8-inch loaf pans. Cover and let rise again in a warm place until dough has risen over tops of pans by about 1/2 inch. Bake loaves for 15 minutes, then reduce heat to 350° and bake for 25 to 30 minutes longer, or until loaves sound hollow when tapped. Let cool on wire racks.

MAKES 2 LOAVES.

CHALLAH (JEWISH EGG BREAD)

This light, airy yeast bread is common in Jewish delicatessens and is even more delicious when made at home every week for the Sabbath. Gertrude Berg, who created the famous radio heroine Molly Goldberg, wrote that in making challah when her children were small, "I would always make enough dough so that they could each make their own loaves," according to the child's size. She added, "Before you knew it, they were making loaves of challah as big as mine." The chief bread baker at our house said, "Until you've made your own, you have little idea of how delicious, tender, and spectacular looking challah can be, to say nothing of how much fun it is to make."

1 1/4 pkg. dry yeast, or .7 oz. fresh yeast cake
3/4 cup warm water
1 Tbs. sugar
2 tsp. coarse salt
2 eggs, slightly beaten
2 Tbs. vegetable oil
3 1/2 to 3 3/4 cups flour

GLAZE:
1 egg yolk mixed with 1/2 tsp. water
poppy seeds

*Preheat oven to 400° F.**
Dissolve yeast in warm water in a large bowl. When dissolved, add sugar, salt, eggs, oil, and, 1 cup at a time, as much flour as can be stirred into liquid. Turn out onto a floured surface and knead for at least 10 minutes, adding more flour as wanted, until dough is smooth and elastic. Put dough into an oiled bowl and turn to coat with oil all over; cover and leave in a warm place until doubled in bulk. Punch down, knead in a little more flour if too moist to handle, then divide into 2 portions. Portion 1: cut into 3 equal parts, rolling each into ropes about 10 inches long. Pinch one end of each rope together, then braid and pinch together other ends to make one braided piece. Portion 2: divide into 2 pieces, one larger than the other; make braids of each piece in same manner as with portion 1. Now take first large braid and place on an oiled cookie sheet; place next largest braid on top of first; then the smallest on top. Pinch here and there where the 3 portions touch to help them sit firmly in place. Cover and let rise at room temperature until doubled in bulk.*

Brush loaf with egg yolk mixture, covering surfaces thoroughly, and sprinkle liberally with poppy seeds. Bake for 10 minutes, then reduce heat to 375° and bake for 35 to 40 minutes more. Let cool on a wire rack.

MAKES 1 LARGE LOAF.

SALT-RISING BREAD

Difficulty in finding commercial yeast and the unreliability of the yeast produced at home once made salt-rising bread popular, and rural and small-town cooks like Grace Goodspeed of Pen Yan, New York, carefully preserved recipes they found to work well. Her method is here followed by a slightly more detailed formula:

"To set rising overnight, take two-thirds of a cup of hot water (not scalding), a pinch of salt, a pinch of soda, and thicken with graham flour or corn meal. This must be kept warm and will ferment and become light in twelve hours or less. In the morning scald one pint of milk and put it into the bread pan or mixer, also one pint of cold water, one teaspoon salt, pinch of soda. Thicken with bread flour and add the cup of rising, stirring thoroughly. Keep in a warm place until doubled in bulk. Stir down, adding a little more salt and a bit of soda and flour to make out. This will make about three loaves. Put into tins and keep very warm until light. Bake forty-five minutes. This bread will sour very easily if allowed to become chilled at any stage, or if any of the utensils or dishes used are not immaculately clean."

1 cup milk, scalded
2 Tbs. sugar
1 1/2 tsp. salt
1/4 cup cornmeal
1 cup lukewarm water (100°)
2 Tbs. vegetable shortening
4 1/2 cups flour, sifted
2 Tbs. butter, melted

*Preheat oven to 375° F.**

Combine milk, 1 tablespoon sugar, salt, and cornmeal. Turn into a 2-quart jar or pitcher and set in a pan of hot water (110 to 115°). Let stand in a warm place for 6 to 7 hours, or until it ferments. When gas escapes freely, stir in lukewarm water, the remaining sugar, the shortening, and half the flour. Beat this mixture thoroughly. Put jar or pitcher of "risin'" in pan of hot water (115°) and let rise until sponge is very light and full of bubbles. Empty mixture into a thoroughly greased warm bowl and gradually blend in the remaining flour to make a stiff dough. Turn out onto a floured surface and knead until smooth. Shape into 2 loaves and put into well-greased loaf pans. Brush with melted butter, cover with a cloth, and put in a warm place to rise. It should gain 2 1/2 times its original bulk.* Bake for 10 minutes, then reduce heat to 350° and continue baking for about 25 minutes, or until loaves sound hollow when tapped.

MAKES 2 LOAVES.

GOOD EARTH BREAD

2 1/4 cups boiling water
2 cups rolled oats
1/2 cup cracked wheat
1/4 cup wheat germ
3/4 cup blackstrap molasses
2 Tbs. butter, melted
1 1/2 Tbs. salt
2 pkg. dry yeast, or 1 oz. fresh yeast cake
1 cup milk, warmed
1 tsp. sugar
3 cups stone-ground whole wheat flour
2 to 3 cups unbleached flour
1 egg white mixed with water

*Preheat oven to 375° F.**

Pour boiling water over rolled oats, cracked wheat, and wheat germ. Add molasses, butter, and salt; mix well, let cool to body temperature. Meanwhile dissolve yeast in milk, add sugar, and let stand until mixture swells. Now add whole wheat flour and 1 cup unbleached flour to yeast mixture; then add steeped oats and mix well. Turn out onto a floured surface. Let rest for a few minutes, then start kneading, adding some of the rest of the flour to achieve a firm, pliable consistency; it will be sticky, so don't do much kneading at this time. Place in a well-buttered bowl and turn to coat with butter all over; cover with a cloth and let rise in a warm place until doubled in bulk. Punch down, turn out onto a floured surface, and knead well this time—for 8 to 10 minutes—adding more flour as necessary. Divide into half and form 2 loaves; place in buttered (9 by 5 by 3 inches) loaf pans; dough should fill pans about two-thirds full. Let rise again until almost doubled; dough should swell over tops of pans.* Brush with wash of egg white mixed with water. Bake for 15 minutes, then reduce heat to 350° and continue baking for 30 to 40 minutes, or until bread sounds hollow when tapped. Remove loaves from pans and return them to oven. Turn off heat and let bread cool in oven.

MAKES 2 LOAVES.

WHOLE WHEAT BREAD

1 1/2 pkg. dry yeast
1/2 cup warm water
2 cups skim milk
3 Tbs. butter
2 Tbs. molasses
2 tsp. salt
2 to 3 cups unbleached flour
3 cups stone-ground whole wheat flour
1/2 cup wheat germ

*Preheat oven to 425° F.**

Dissolve yeast in warm water. Meanwhile warm milk just enough to dissolve 1 tablespoon butter, the molasses, and the salt. In a large bowl mix 2 cups unbleached white flour with all whole wheat flour and wheat germ. Stir in yeast and warm milk mixture, blending thoroughly. Turn out onto a floured surface and knead, adding as much unbleached flour as necessary to keep dough from sticking as you knead. After about 10 minutes, dough should be smooth and elastic; place in a buttered bowl and turn to coat with butter all over; cover with a cloth and let rise in a warm place until doubled in bulk. Punch down, knead for a few seconds, then shape into 2 loaves and place in buttered loaf pans (9 by 5 by 3 inches). Cover loaves and let rise under towel until dough has swelled over tops of pans.* Bake for 10 minutes, then reduce heat to 400° and bake for approximately 15 minutes more, or until loaves sound hollow when tapped. Let cool on wire racks.

MAKES 2 LOAVES.

HERB-WHEAT BREAD

1 cup milk, scalded
2 Tbs. sugar
1 Tbs. salt
2 pkg. dry yeast
1 cup warm water
3 Tbs. chopped parsley
2 Tbs. chopped fresh basil, or 1 Tbs. dried
1 Tbs. chopped chives
1 tsp. dried oregano
1/4 tsp. dried thyme
3 1/2 cups unbleached flour
1 cup stone-ground whole wheat flour

Preheat oven to 375°F. *

Put milk into a bowl with sugar and salt and let cool. Empty yeast into a large bowl and cover with warm water, letting yeast dissolve completely. Stir in milk mixture, herbs, 3 cups of unbleached flour, and all the whole wheat flour. Mix well and beat with a wooden spoon for about 1 minute. Let rest, then turn out onto a floured surface and knead, working in remaining 1/2 cup of unbleached flour; dough is ready when it is smooth and shiny. Rinse out bowl with warm water, butter it, and return dough, turning it so that it picks up butter and is coated all over. Cover with a cloth and let rise in a warm place for about 1 hour, or until doubled in bulk. Turn out of bowl and knead again briefly. Butter a shallow 1 1/2 quart casserole (this will make 1 large loaf; butter smaller casseroles to make 2 loaves), and put dough in it. Let rise for 45 minutes or until dough swells to make a rounded dome on the casserole.* Brush or spray with cold water just before putting casserole in oven; repeat twice during first 10 minutes of baking. Bake for about 1 hour for the large loaf, 50 minutes for the smaller loaves. Turn off oven, take out bread, and return to oven rack for 10 minutes to give bread a glorious crust.

MAKES 1 LARGE OR 2 SMALL LOAVES.

CINNAMON BUNS

1 oz. fresh yeast cake
1/4 cup sugar
1 cup milk, scalded and cooled to lukewarm
4 cups flour
1/4 cup vegetable shortening
1/4 lb. (1 stick) butter, softened
1 cup brown sugar
3/4 tsp. ground cinnamon

Preheat oven to 375° F. *

Dissolve yeast cake in a little warm water in a large mixing bowl. When yeast is a milky liquid, add sugar and milk; stir until smooth, then stir in flour. Melt shortening and blend into dough. Put dough into a buttered bowl, and turn to coat with butter all over. Cover with a cloth and let dough rise in a warm place for 1 hour, or until doubled in size. Turn out onto a floured surface and roll flat to about 1/4-inch thickness; spread with half of the butter. Mix brown sugar and cinnamon and sprinkle half over buttered dough, then roll dough like a jelly roll and slice into 1 1/2-inch sections. Mix remaining butter with remaining brown sugar and cinnamon and scatter over bottoms of 2 buttered 8-inch cake pans. Place rolls on top and let rise, covered, until doubled their size.* Bake for 25 to 30 minutes. Let cool on wire racks.

MAKES ABOUT 20.

DINNER ROLLS

1 pkg. dry yeast
2 Tbs. sugar
1/4 cup warm water
1 cup sour cream, slightly warmed
2 Tbs. butter, melted
1 tsp. salt
1/8 tsp. baking powder
3 cups flour

*Preheat oven to 425° F.**

Dissolve yeast and sugar in warm water. Add sour cream, melted butter, salt, baking powder, and 2 1/2 cups flour. Mix well. Turn out onto a floured surface and knead, incorporating the rest of the flour as needed. When smooth—after about 5 minutes—place in a buttered bowl, turn once to coat the dough, cover with a cloth, and let rise in a warm place until doubled in bulk. For small rolls butter two 8-inch cake pans and form the dough into rolls the size of golf balls, pinching the dough together at the bottoms. Place rolls in pans almost touching each other. For larger rolls form into balls about twice that size and place almost touching each other in a buttered round 10-inch pan or dish. Let the rolls rise, covered, in a warm place until doubled in size.* Brush tops with softened butter. Bake for a little less than 15 minutes for the smaller size, about 18 minutes for the larger, or until golden. Serve still warm.

MAKES 24 SMALL ROLLS OR 12 LARGE ROLLS.

PARKER HOUSE ROLLS

Harvey D. Parker opened the Boston hotel that bore his name in 1856, after several years of running a restaurant that may have been the first to serve food at any hour instead of at fixed times for breakfast, lunch, and dinner.

1 pkg. dry yeast, or 1 oz. fresh yeast cake
1/4 cup lukewarm water
3/4 cup (1 1/2 sticks) butter
2 Tbs. sugar
1 tsp. salt
2 cups milk, scalded
5 1/2 to 6 cups unbleached flour, sifted

Preheat oven to 375° F. *

Dissolve yeast in lukewarm water. Stir 4 tablespoons butter, the sugar, and the salt into milk. When milk has cooled to lukewarm, mix in with dissolved yeast. Stir enough flour into milk mixture to make dough just stiff enough to handle. Turn out onto a floured surface and knead for 5 to 10 minutes, then put in a large buttered bowl. Melt another 4 tablespoons butter and lightly brush over top of dough; cover and put in a warm place to rise, about 2 hours, until doubled in bulk. Meanwhile allow remaining butter to soften. Dust your hands with flour and shape risen dough into 2 1/2-inch balls. Flatten balls slightly and crease tops with floured rubber spatula. Brush half of top with softened butter and fold other half over it. Place an inch apart on buttered cookie sheets. Cover with a cloth and set aside to rise in a warm place for about 45 minutes.* Brush tops with melted butter and bake for about 25 minutes.

MAKES 4 DOZEN.

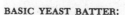

BUCKWHEAT PANCAKES

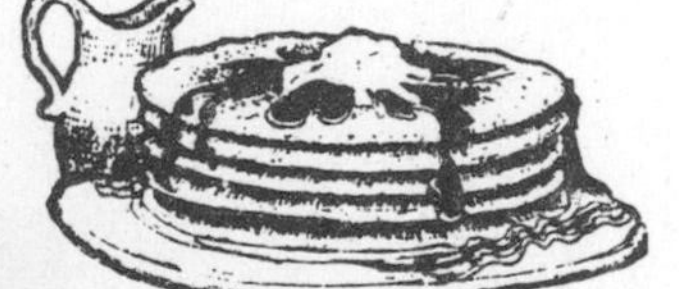

Wrote Mrs. Rorer: "This grain is inferior to wheat in nutritive value, containing more heat-producing food, and not half the muscle or brain-food." The source of this prejudice is unknown, and the truth is that buckwheat—aside from its wonderful flavor—is especially rich in B vitamins.

BASIC YEAST BATTER:
1 pkg. dry yeast, or .5 oz. fresh yeast cake
2 cups, or more, warm water
1 cup buckwheat flour
1 cup unbleached flour
1 tsp. salt
1 Tbs. butter, melted
1/4 tsp. baking soda
3 Tbs. butter, softened

FOR SWEET CAKES:
2 Tbs. molasses

About 12 hours before cooking time, dissolve yeast in 2 cups warm water in a large bowl, then stir in both flours and salt. Cover and set aside in a warm place. Just before cooking add butter and baking soda (and, if you are making sweet pancakes, the molasses). You may need to thin batter with up to 1/3 cup more warm water. For blini and stuffed pancakes, omit molasses and add enough water to give batter about the consistency of heavy cream. To bake, rub a large, heavy skillet with softened butter. Heat until almost smoking, then pour in 2 tablespoons batter to form 3 or 4 cakes, not touching. Turn when bubbles appear on the surface and bake until lightly browned on the other side. For stuffed pancakes, use a 6- or 8-inch skillet and fill pan, swirling around to make a thin layer.

MAKES ABOUT 20 SMALL CAKES OR 10 LARGE CAKES.

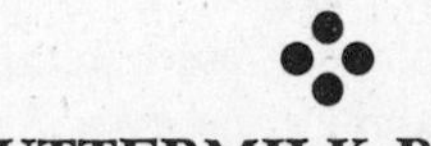

BUTTERMILK PANCAKES

2 cups sifted flour
3/4 tsp. baking soda
1 tsp. salt
2 eggs, separated
2 1/2 cups buttermilk
2 Tbs. butter, melted
grated cheese

Sift together flour and baking soda and stir in salt. Beat egg yolks, then add to flour mixture with buttermilk and butter; beat until smooth. Beat egg whites stiff enough to form peaks and fold into batter. Drop spoonfuls of batter onto a hot greased griddle, making 12 pancakes; turn and brown on the other side. Sprinkle with cheese.

MAKES 12.

THIN PANCAKES

1 cup flour
1/2 cup milk
1/2 cup water
3 eggs
3 Tbs. melted butter
1/4 tsp. salt

Spin all ingredients in a blender for at least a minute. Let batter stand several hours before using. To bake: brush butter or oil over cooking surface of a hot skillet. (Pan may be 4, 6, or 8 inches, depending on size you want to make.) Pour in just enough batter to coat the bottom, and tip pan to distribute evenly. Cook over medium-high heat until bubbles appear on surface, then flip pancake over and cook about a minute on the other side. Stack the cakes and cover with foil to keep warm in a low oven. Extra pancakes may also be refrigerated or frozen, then warmed up again in foil.

CORNMEAL GRIDDLE CAKES

3 cups milk
2 eggs
1 cup yellow cornmeal
1/2 cup all-purpose flour
1 1/2 tsp. sugar
1 tsp. baking powder
1/2 tsp. salt
1/2 cup lard, melted

Pour milk into a large mixing bowl and beat in eggs until well blended. Mix cornmeal, flour, sugar, baking powder, and salt in another bowl, then gradually stir this dry mixture into milk and eggs. Add lard and blend until a smooth batter is formed. Heat a cast-iron griddle and brush it with bacon fat or butter. Drop batter, 2 tablespoons at a time, onto hot griddle and cook until bubbles break in center and edges are slightly crusty. Turn cakes and brown for about 1 minute on the other side. Hold in oven or in covered warm dish until ready to serve.

MAKES ABOUT 16 TO 18 SMALL CAKES.

CORNMEAL AND RICE GRIDDLE CAKES

1 1/2 cups white cornmeal
1/2 cup flour
4 tsp. baking powder
1/2 tsp. salt
1 Tbs. sugar
1 egg, beaten
3/4 cup milk
3/4 cup water
1 Tbs. butter, melted
1 cup cooked rice

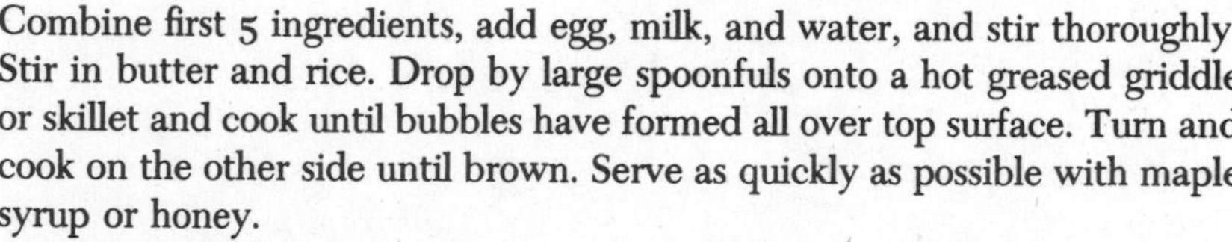

Combine first 5 ingredients, add egg, milk, and water, and stir thoroughly. Stir in butter and rice. Drop by large spoonfuls onto a hot greased griddle or skillet and cook until bubbles have formed all over top surface. Turn and cook on the other side until brown. Serve as quickly as possible with maple syrup or honey.

MAKES ABOUT 12.

WILD RICE AND CORNMEAL CAKES

6 Tbs. cornmeal, either white or yellow
2 cups boiling salted water
1 tsp. salt
2 cups cooked wild rice
coarse salt
freshly ground black pepper
1 cup bacon fat

Dribble cornmeal into water and stir constantly until smooth; lower heat and cook, stirring occasionally. After about 10 minutes, when mixture is very thick, remove from heat and let cool. Stir in wild rice, salt to taste, and several turns of the pepper grinder. Form into 4 large cakes, or 8 smaller ones. Chill for 20 to 30 minutes. Heat bacon fat to sizzling point in a griddle or heavy skillet and fry cakes, turning after 3 or 4 minutes to brown the other side.

MAKES 4 SERVINGS.

BLUE CORN PANCAKES

Blue cornmeal is not easy to come by in most of the country, but it can be one of the rewards of a tour of the Southwest to stop at Second Mesa or to visit a Navaho home on the reservation near Cameron, Arizona. These pancakes were first produced after buying meal ground that morning (almost as fine as wheat flour) by an Indian grandmother who was preparing to entertain at a family reunion later in the day. The texture of the cakes is less grainy than those made with yellow cornmeal, and the flavor is also unusual.

1 egg, slightly beaten
3/4 cup milk
2 Tbs. butter, melted
1/2 cup blue cornmeal
1/2 cup white flour
2 tsp. baking powder
2 Tbs. sugar
1/2 tsp. salt
2 to 3 Tbs. water (optional)

Mix egg with milk and butter. Combine dry ingredients and stir into the liquid just enough to mix. If batter seems too thick and you want a thinner pancake, add 2 to 3 tablespoons water. Lightly grease a griddle or heavy skillet and heat almost to smoking; then drop batter in, 2 to 3 tablespoons for each cake. Cook until tops bubble; the bottoms should be slightly browned when turned. Cook for about 1 minute more. Stack cakes and keep warm. Serve with softened butter and maple syrup.

MAKES ABOUT 8 GOOD-SIZE CAKES.

DOUGHNUTS

Good rules to follow:

1. Don't overmix the dough.
2. Don't add too much flour. Dough should be slightly sticky, and by letting it rest at least 30 minutes in the refrigerator it will be manageable.
3. After you've shaped the doughnuts, let them rest for about 10 minutes before frying.
4. Use fresh oil for frying, keeping the oil at 365° F., and have at least 3 inches in your frying kettle.
5. Don't crowd doughnuts. Fry only 3 or 4 at a time. If you turn them several times during the cooking, you'll have fewer breaks.

6. To thaw frozen doughnuts, be sure to remove them from their wrapping and heat in a moderate oven; otherwise they'll be soggy.

PLAIN DOUGHNUTS

1 cup milk
1 cup sugar
4 tsp. baking powder
1 tsp. salt
1 egg, beaten
2 Tbs. butter, melted
½ tsp. freshly grated nutmeg
3 ½ cups flour
Oil for deep frying: fresh pure pork fat, vegetable oil, or shortening.
confectioner's sugar

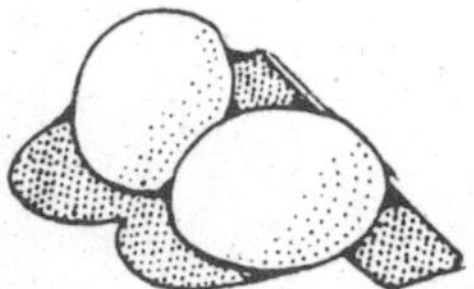

Combine milk, sugar, baking powder, salt, egg, butter, and nutmeg. Stir in just enough flour to mix and form a soft, barely handleable dough. Cover bowl and refrigerate for 30 minutes to 1 hour. Roll or pat out dough on a floured surface. When dough is ½ inch thick, using a well-floured doughnut cutter cut out doughnut shapes and let them rest on a lightly floured surface (remove the holes, but save them to fry along with the doughnuts—they're delicious). Heat enough fat or oil to fill your frying kettle at least 3 inches. When fat reaches 365° (or, as old-fashioned cooks would say, "when it is hot enough to set a match aflame"), drop in 3 or 4 doughnuts. As soon as they float to the surface and are holding their shape, turn them. Fry until golden brown on both sides—about 2 to 3 minutes. Drain on paper towels and dust with confectioner's sugar after they have cooled a little.

MAKES ABOUT 16.

BUTTERMILK DOUGHNUTS

2 eggs
1 egg yolk
1 cup sugar
1 cup buttermilk
4 cups flour
1 tsp. baking powder
½ tsp. baking soda
½ tsp. salt
½ tsp. freshly grated nutmeg
1 Tbs. butter, melted
oil for deep frying

Beat eggs and yolk together, then gradually add sugar and buttermilk. Sift flour, baking powder, baking soda, and salt together, and stir into egg mixture; add nutmeg and butter. This batter should not be refrigerated, so cut doughnut shapes, let them rest for about 5 minutes on a lightly floured surface, and then fry as in the preceding recipe.

MAKES ABOUT 16.

BROWN SUGAR DOUGHNUTS

2 cups brown sugar
2 cups cake flour
1 cup all-purpose flour
3 tsp. baking powder
1/4 tsp. grated nutmeg
1/4 tsp. ground cinnamon
1/2 tsp. salt
1 cup milk
2 eggs
1 egg yolk
4 Tbs. (1/2 stick) butter, melted
oil for deep frying

Sift all dry ingredients together. Whisk milk, eggs, and yolk together until well blended and light. Combine dry and liquid ingredients, then add butter. Let dough rest and proceed as in plain doughnuts.

MAKES ABOUT 16.

RAISED DOUGHNUTS

2 Tbs. butter
1/2 cup milk
1 pkg. (1 Tbs.) dry yeast
1/3 cup sugar
1/4 cup warm water
2 1/4 to 2 1/2 cups white flour
1 egg, lightly beaten
1/2 tsp. salt
1/4 tsp. cardamon
1/4 tsp. cinnamon
1/4 tsp. mace
oil for frying
confectioner's sugar

Heat butter with milk, bringing it just to the boil, then let cool. In a medium bowl dissolve yeast and sugar in the water. When milk mixture has cooled to lukewarm, stir it in. Beat in 2 1/4 cups of the flour, the egg, salt and spices. You should have a soft manageable dough; add a little more flour if necessary. Turn out and knead lightly on a floured surface for 1 minute. Clean and grease bowl and return dough to it. Cover with plastic wrap and let rise until double in volume or overnight in refrigerator. Turn out on lightly floured surface and pat or roll out dough to 1/2-in. thickness. Cut with doughnut cutter, cover lightly with a towel and let rise to almost double—about 25 minutes. Heat 3 inches of frying oil in a kettle to 375°. Slip in doughnuts one by one, but do not fry more than 4 at a time. They will rise to the surface almost immediately; separate if they drift together. In 2 minutes turn with a spatula and fry 2 minutes more. Remove and drain on paper toweling; keep warm in slow oven. Be sure fat remains at 370° while you finish frying. Sprinkle warm doughnuts with confectioner's sugar, and serve immediately.

MAKES 1 1/2 DOZEN.

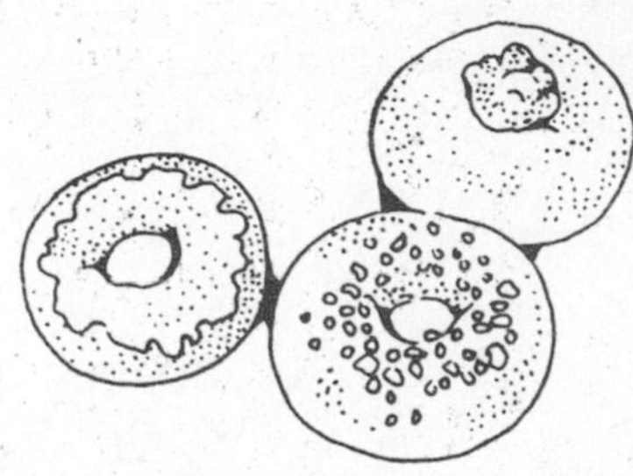

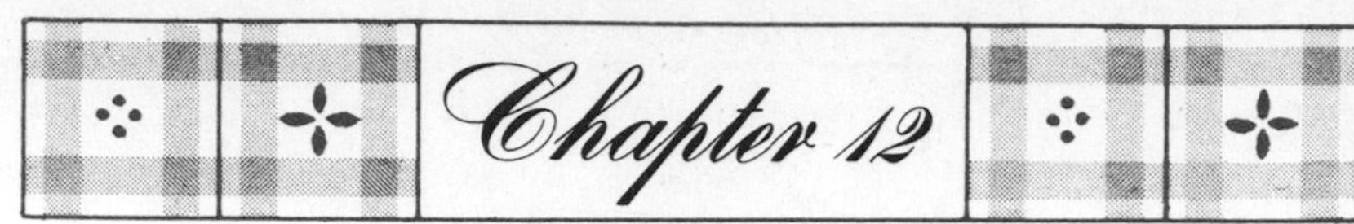

SOUPS

COLD ARTICHOKE SOUP

1 pkg. (9 oz.) frozen artichoke hearts
1 medium-size white onion, chopped
1 medium-size potato, peeled and diced
2 Tbs. butter
3 cups chicken stock
1 cup heavy cream
1 Tbs. mixed chopped parsley and chopped fresh basil

Thaw artichokes enough to chop coarsely, then put in a heavy saucepan with onion, potato, and butter, and sauté for about 5 minutes. Add stock, cover, and let simmer for 40 minutes; let cool. Purée in a blender, then refrigerate for about 3 hours. Beat in cream and serve soup in chilled bowls, garnished with chopped herbs.

MAKES 4 SERVINGS.

HELEN'S AVOCADO SOUP

Helen Corbitt, a transplanted Pennsylvanian, created one of Texas's great cuisines at the Neiman-Marcus Zodiac Room in Dallas; she also created this soup and gave us the recipe one pleasant afternoon.

4 Tbs. (1/2 stick) butter
1/4 cup flour
2 cups milk
2 cups light cream
3 ripe avocados
1/4 tsp. ground ginger (optional)
grated rind of 1 orange
salt

Melt butter, stir in flour, and cook until bubbly. Off the heat, add milk and cream, stirring, then cook until thickened and smooth; let cool. Peel and mash avocados, reserving enough to make 1 cup of avocado cubes for garnish. Stir mashed avocado into cream sauce along with ginger and orange rind, then spin in a blender until smooth as velvet. Add salt to taste. Chill for several hours. Serve very cold with garnish of avocado cubes.

MAKES 8 OR 10 SERVINGS.

CANTALOUPE-TOMATO COLD SOUP

3 cups tomato juice
2/3 cup sour cream
1 small white onion, grated
1 Tbs. lemon juice
1 tsp. grated lemon rind
salt
freshly ground white pepper
2/3 cup diced peeled cucumber
1 1/2 to 2 cups cantaloupe melon balls
4 strips bacon
4 tsp. minced fresh basil
1 Tbs. minced fresh rosemary

Pour tomato juice into a medium-size bowl and stir in sour cream, onion, lemon juice, and lemon rind; season with salt and pepper to taste. Cover and refrigerate for 3 to 4 hours. Lightly mix cucumber dice and melon balls and refrigerate for 3 hours or longer. Chill 4 soup bowls. Meanwhile sauté bacon until crisp and crumble into small bits. Immediately before serving combine tomato and sour cream mixture with cucumber and melon balls. Sprinkle with minced herbs. Divide among soup bowls and scatter crumbled bacon over each.

MAKES 4 SERVINGS.

LONG ISLAND CORN AND LOBSTER SOUP

4 ears of fresh corn, shucked
1 lobster (1 1/2 lb.), cooked
2 cups plus 2 Tbs. heavy cream
dash of sherry
salt
cayenne pepper

At least 1 hour ahead of serving, cook corn for 3 minutes in boiling water. Score each row of kernels with a sharp knife and press corn pulp into a bowl. Shred lobster meat and add to corn with 2 tablespoons cream and the sherry; set aside to marinate for at least 1 hour. Combine with remaining cream and season to taste with salt and cayenne pepper. Chill thoroughly.

MAKES 6 SERVINGS.

COLD CARROT SOUP

3 Tbs. butter
2 Tbs. grated onion
1 lb. carrots, cleaned and grated
1 cup ground almonds
2 tsp. puréed chervil, or 1/2 tsp. dried
1/4 tsp. grated nutmeg
salt
dash of Creole or cayenne pepper
2 1/2 cups chicken stock
1/2 cup buttermilk
1 egg, hard-cooked and minced
1 1/2 to 2 Tbs. minced parsley

Melt butter in a saucepan and in it cook grated onion over very low heat for 1 minute. Stir in grated carrots and ground almonds, cover, and braise for 20 minutes. Stir in chervil, nutmeg, salt to taste, Creole or cayenne pepper, and stock. Let simmer for 15 minutes; let cool. Stir in buttermilk and chill. Sprinkle with egg and parsley before serving.

MAKES 6 SERVINGS.

POLISH CUCUMBER AND BEET SOUP

This is an important soup called *chłodnik* that was Americanized by Polish women of Minnesota, who adapted recipes from their mothers.

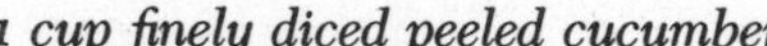

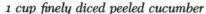

1 cup finely diced peeled cucumber
1 cup finely diced cooked beets
2 cups sour cream
1 cup yogurt
1 Tbs. finely minced fresh dillweed
1 Tbs. finely minced scallion (white part only)
2 eggs, hard-cooked and minced
4 bacon strips, cooked crisp and crumbled
2 Tbs. minced parsley

Scald cucumber dice with boiling water, rinse in cold water, then chill for at least 3 hours. Chill all other ingredients, drain beets if necessary, and stir together everything except eggs, bacon, and parsley; return to refrigerator until just before serving. Stir in bacon bits and sprinkle each serving with eggs and parsley.

MAKES 4 SERVINGS.

CHILLED CUCUMBER-YOGURT SOUP

3 cucumbers
1 qt. chicken stock
2 Tbs. minced whole scallion
1/2 cup chopped celery
1/2 tsp. dried dillweed
1/2 tsp. dried mint leaves
1 tsp. grated lemon rind
2 cups yogurt
3 to 4 Tbs. minced parsley

Peel cucumbers, cut into halves, and remove seeds; dice enough to make 3 cups. Bring chicken stock to a boil, add cucumbers, scallion, celery, dillweed, and mint, and let simmer for 10 minutes. Let cool; spin in a blender until smooth or put through a food mill. Add lemon rind and stir in yogurt. Chill for 3 to 4 hours. Sprinkle each serving with parsley.

MAKES 6 TO 8 SERVINGS.

PASADENA GAZPACHO

1 clove garlic, cut into halves
2 firm, ripe tomatoes
1 cup thinly sliced peeled cucumbers
1/2 cup minced green pepper
1/2 cup minced onion
2 cups light chicken stock
6 to 8 Tbs. chopped fresh herbs: parsley, chives, basil, marjoram, tarragon
1/3 cup olive oil
2 Tbs. lemon or lime juice
1 tsp., or more, salt
Creole or cayenne pepper

Rub salad bowl with cut halves of garlic clove. Peel tomatoes; if cores are pithy, cut them out. Chop tomatoes; put the small chunks into the salad bowl and strain juice into bowl, thus eliminating seeds. Add cucumber, green pepper, and onion. Sprinkle in herbs and toss. Gradually pour in olive oil and lemon or lime juice, adding salt and pepper to taste. Chill for 2 hours or more and serve with ice cube in each soup plate.

MAKES 4 SERVINGS.

SCANDINAVIAN FRUIT SOUP

Throughout the Midwest there are cooks who learned from their grandparents the art of making summer coolers and sweet soups to get a good meal off to a tempting start. Fruit soups may be concocted of almost anything in season, and they may be served either hot or cold. In Minnesota in the nineteenth century, sago, a popular starch of the period, was often used as a thickener for a cinnamon-flavored black cherry soup in addition to other sweet bisques. At the Old Rittenhouse Inn in Bayfield, Wisconsin, near the

Apostle Islands, innkeeper Mary Phillips serves a dish she calls strawberry consommé, using the following method.

1 1/2 cups coarsely chopped red rhubarb
1 1/2 cups hulled strawberries
3-in. cinnamon stick
3/4 cup sugar
1/3 cup good red wine
1/3 cup club soda
1/2 cup sliced strawberries

In a large saucepan place rhubarb, strawberries, cinnamon stick, and sugar; add water to cover, bring to a boil, and let simmer for 5 to 7 minutes, or until rhubarb is tender. Remove from heat and mash through sieve into a bowl. Liquid should be rosy pink. Add wine and soda and chill thoroughly. Serve with sliced strawberries on top.

MAKES 6 SERVINGS.

JERUSALEM ARTICHOKE BISQUE

Lately the term *bisque* has been narrowly used in *haute cuisine* to identify creamy shellfish soups, but it really has a wider meaning, and American cooks have been making vegetable bisques at least since Fannie Farmer published her first book, in 1896. This recipe and the one that follows richly deserve to be included among the best of bisques.

1/2 lb. Jerusalem artichokes
1 small onion
2 Tbs. butter
2 1/2 cups chicken stock
1 cup heavy cream
Freshly ground pepper and salt
2 Tbs. mixed chopped parsley and watercress
paprika for garnish

Scrub and peel Jerusalem artichokes; peel and slice onion. In a heavy pot melt butter and sauté vegetables slowly for about 5 minutes. Add stock and let simmer for 30 to 40 minutes or until vegetables are soft. Let cool. Put through food mill or spin in blender for just a few seconds. Return to the pot, add cream and salt and pepper to taste. Serve hot with chopped greens on top and a dusting of paprika.

MAKES 4 SERVINGS.

CELERY-FENNEL BISQUE

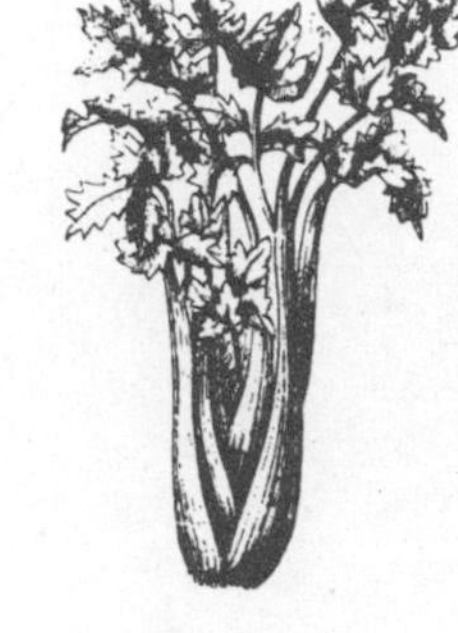

2 Tbs. butter
1 cup finely chopped celery
1 cup finely chopped fennel
1 medium-size onion, chopped
1 qt. beef stock
1/2 tsp. salt
1/4 tsp. cayenne pepper
1/4 cup sour cream
2 to 3 Tbs. minced chives

Melt butter and sauté celery, fennel, and onion for about 3 minutes. Add stock, bring to a boil, and let simmer over low heat for about 4 minutes, or until vegetables are soft; let cool. Put in a blender and spin for 30 seconds, then strain or put through a food mill. Return to pan and reheat; add salt and cayenne. Divide soup among 4 soup bowls, top each with a dollop of sour cream, and sprinkle with chives.

MAKES 4 SERVINGS.

LOBSTER BISQUE

1 small live lobster (about 1 1/4 lb.)
1/4 lb. (1 stick) butter
1 large carrot, diced
2 heaping Tbs. chopped onion
1/2 cup white wine
6 cups fish or chicken stock
bouquet garni
1/4 cup uncooked rice
salt
freshly ground pepper
cayenne pepper
1/2 cup heavy cream
1/4 cup brandy
3 to 4 Tbs. minced parsley

Cut live lobster into large pieces, reserving coral (lobster roe) and liver. Melt half of the butter in a skillet and sauté carrot and onion until golden. Add lobster with its shell and cook until it turns bright red, about 5 minutes. Add wine, boiling until liquid is reduced to half; add enough stock to cover lobster pieces, then let simmer for 5 minutes. Remove lobster, reserving meat, and put shells into a large saucepan; cover with liquid in which lobster was cooked, including carrot and onion. Add remainder of stock, the bouquet garni, and the rice. Cook for 20 minutes, then remove lobster shells and herbs; let cool. In a food mill or blender, purée remaining butter, the coral, liver, contents of saucepan, and reserved lobster meat, reserving 1 or 2 pieces for garnishing tureen. Strain to remove any particle of shell. Wash saucepan and return soup to it; reheat. Sprinkle with salt, pepper, and cayenne, then stir in cream and brandy; cut reserved lobster pieces into neat slices and float in the bisque, which must be served very hot, with a sprinkling of parsley in each soup dish.

MAKES 6 TO 8 SERVINGS.

COLD GUMBO BISQUE

This beautiful summer soup developed when we had in the freezer a stock made of the skeleton of a pike and about a cup of crab claws from which crab meat had been extracted. Lacking such a stock, a base for the bisque can be made by simmering for at least an hour 1 quart chicken bouillon, 1/4 cup of apple cider, and the remnant claws of one 13-ounce can of crab claws. But for best results save your next large fish skeleton.

FISH STOCK:

1 can (13 oz.) crab claws (meat removed and reserved for gumbo)
1 fish skeleton with head (from baked pike or other large fish)
1/4 cup apple cider
1 celery rib
1 medium-size onion
1 carrot
1 bay leaf
1/2 tsp. dried thyme
3 qt. water

GUMBO:

3 Tbs. butter
1 cup diced celery
1 cup chopped onion
1/2 cup chopped green pepper
1 1/2 cups sliced fresh okra, tips removed
2 cups canned tomatoes, chopped
1/2 cup uncooked rice
salt
freshly ground pepper
flaked crab meat (reserved from crab claws)

Make the stock: Combine ingredients in a large saucepan and let simmer until liquid is reduced by about half.

Melt butter in a large pot and cook celery, onion, and green pepper until onion is transparent; add okra and tomatoes and bring to a boil. Strain fish stock and stir into vegetables, then add rice. Cover the pot and let simmer, stirring frequently, for about 1 1/2 hours. Taste, adding salt and pepper only if needed; let cool. Spin about 1 cup at a time in a blender until soup is very smooth. Refrigerate overnight to meld flavors. Serve in chilled soup bowls garnished with meat reserved from crab claws.

MAKES 6 TO 8 SERVINGS.

BISQUE OF FROZEN PEAS AND CORN

1 pkg. (10 oz.) frozen corn kernels
1 pkg. (10 oz.) frozen peas
1 medium-size onion, chopped
2 Tbs. butter
1 cup chicken stock
3/4 cup heavy cream
salt
freshly ground pepper

Cook corn and peas separately according to package directions; drain. In a 1 1/2-quart saucepan, sauté onion in butter until soft. Put corn through a food mill, squeezing out hard skins; or spin in a blender, then strain out skins. Put peas in blender, add sautéed onion, using rubber spatula to scrape out all of butter, then spin until very smooth. Return to saucepan and stir in pureed corn, stock, and cream; let simmer for 3 or 4 minutes. Add salt and several turns of pepper grinder to taste.

MAKES 6 SERVINGS.

U.S. SENATE BEAN SOUP

A favorite for more than half a century in the Senate restaurant, this method for preparing soup from dried beans is a variation on a very American theme; it's the mashed potatoes that caused Senator Henry Cabot Lodge, Sr., to urge the Massachusetts specialty on his peers.

2 cups dried pea beans
3 qt. cold water
hambone with meat still clinging
3 potatoes, peeled, cooked, and mashed
3 onions, chopped fine
2 garlic cloves, minced
3 medium-size celery ribs, chopped
1/4 cup minced parsley

Soak beans overnight. Drain, then cover with boiling water and cook for about 2 1/2 hours, or until tender. Drain thoroughly, then return to pot with 3 quarts of cold water and hambone. Bring to a boil and let simmer for 2 hours. Stir in potatoes, onions, garlic, and celery. Cover and continue cooking over low heat for about 1 hour. Remove hambone but scrape meat into soup. Stir in parsley and serve very hot.

MAKES ABOUT 12 SERVINGS.

BAKED BEAN SOUP

3 cups baked beans
1 qt. water or stock
2 Tbs. minced onion
2 to 3 Tbs. finely chopped celery
4 uncooked frankfurters, or 1/4 cup diced salt pork or hard sausage
1 tsp. instant coffee (optional)
2 Tbs. sherry
1 lemon, sliced
2 eggs, hard-cooked and chopped fine

Combine beans, water or stock, onion, and celery, divide into 3 or 4 batches, and spin each batch in a blender until smooth. Let this resulting purée simmer over low heat for about 30 minutes, adding a little liquid only if it seems too thick. (One Vermont cook adds a teaspoon of instant coffee to give her soup a deeper color; the flavor blends in to the point of mystery.) Cook frankfurters or fry salt pork until crisp; if using sausage, cut into small dice. Add meat to soup and heat; add sherry just before ladling soup into hot dishes. Put a lemon slice in each serving and sprinkle in bits of chopped egg.

MAKES 6 SERVINGS.

BLACK BEAN SOUP

1 lb. dried black beans
2 qt. water
1 lb. veal, cubed
1 veal knucklebone
3 onions, chopped
1 lemon, quartered
4 whole cloves
1/4 tsp. ground allspice
freshly ground black pepper
3 Tbs. salt
1/2 to 1 cup dry sherry
8 lemon slices

Cover beans with cold water and soak overnight; drain. Put water into a soup kettle with beans, veal, knucklebone, onions, lemon quarters, spices, and salt. Bring to a boil, then let simmer for about 5 hours, or until beans are very soft. Take out meat and bones and set aside. Discard lemon and cloves. Put 2 or 3 cups of beans in a blender and spin until smooth; repeat until all beans are puréed. Return to kettle and shred veal into purée; stir in sherry gradually, according to taste. Let simmer for 5 minutes. Center a lemon slice in each bowl when serving.

MAKES 8 SERVINGS.

LANCASTER RED BEAN SOUP

1 cup dried kidney beans
1 hambone with some meat
1 leek
1 large carrot
2 onions, unpeeled
4 qt. water
2 Tbs. bacon fat
1/2 cup chopped celery
1 medium-size onion, chopped
2 tomatoes, chopped (about 1 cup), or 1 cup canned tomatoes
1 tsp. dried basil
Tabasco
1/2 cup cooked rice

Put beans into a bowl and pour over enough water to cover by about 1 1/2 inches; soak overnight; do not drain. Put hambone, leek, carrot, and whole onions into a pot and add 4 quarts water; bring to a boil and let simmer for about 4 hours. In another large pot melt bacon fat and sauté celery and chopped onion. When ham stock has reduced by about one-third, strain it over celery and onion. Add the soaked beans and their soaking liquid and bring to a boil; let simmer for 3 hours. Add tomatoes, basil, and Tabasco to taste and continue simmering for 15 minutes. Add cooked rice about 5 minutes before serving.

MAKES 6 TO 8 SERVINGS.

CHESTNUT SOUP

No one likes to peel chestnuts; it's one of the world's most torturous chores. However, this potage has made such a splendid beginning to some of our Thanksgiving feasts that it seems worth that initial effort.

1 lb. chestnuts
vegetable oil
4 Tbs. (1/2 stick) butter
4 1/2 cups chicken stock
1 1/2 cups heavy cream
1/2 tsp. salt
1/2 tsp. sugar
dash of cayenne pepper
2 egg yolks
3 Tbs. minced parsley

Preheat oven to 350° F.

Use a very sharp knife to make a large X on rounded side of each chestnut. Put them in a shallow pan with enough oil to coat them and shake well. Put in oven until shells and skins split; then peel off. Melt butter and sauté nuts for 4 or 5 minutes, or until soft. Add 1 cup of the stock and let simmer for 1 minute; let cool. Purée nuts and stock in a blender. Stir purée into remaining stock, add cream, salt, sugar, and a few grains of cayenne. Let simmer for a few minutes. Beat egg yolks, then add some hot soup, a little at a time; when beaten eggs are warm and very fluid, stir into soup and heat for 2 minutes without boiling. Garnish with a dash of cayenne and parsley.

MAKES 6 SERVINGS.

KANSAS HAZELNUT SOUP

1/2 lb. (2 sticks) butter
2 carrots, chopped
2 celery ribs, chopped
1 leek, chopped
1 garlic clove, minced
1 1/2 cups finely chopped hazelnuts
2 qt. chicken stock
2 Tbs. flour
freshly grated nutmeg
dash of cayenne pepper
2 bay leaves
1 cup heavy cream
salt
freshly ground pepper

Melt 1/4 pound of the butter in a saucepan and sauté chopped vegetables, garlic, and 2/3 cup hazelnuts; turn heat very low, cover, and cook for about

30 minutes. When vegetables are softened, let cool and puree in a blender, using a little of the stock if necessary. Return to saucepan, sprinkle in flour, and blend thoroughly. Cook for about 2 minutes and stir in stock; season with several gratings of nutmeg, the cayenne, and the bay leaves. Let simmer for about 1 hour. Just before serving add cream, remaining butter in small bits, and remaining hazelnuts. Add salt and pepper to taste. Heat soup but don't let it boil.

MAKES 8 SERVINGS.

CHICKEN SOUP WITH MATZOH BALLS

1 chicken (5 to 6 lb.) with giblets (also feet and neck, if possible)
3 qt. cold water
1 Tbs. salt
1 large onion
2 carrots
4 celery ribs
1 parsnip
1 bay leaf
4 parsley sprigs
1/2 tsp. dried dillweed

MATZOH BALLS:

4 eggs, separated
1 cup matzoh meal
1 tsp. salt
freshly ground pepper
1/8 tsp. grated nutmeg
1 Tbs. minced parsley
2 Tbs. melted chicken fat from soup

Cut up chicken, put it into a large pot, and cover with cold water. Add salt and bring to a boil, then let simmer, covered, skimming as necessary. In 30 minutes add vegetables and herbs, continuing to cook, covered, for 2 to 2 1/2 hours, or until chicken is tender. Strain and chill. Skim off fat, reheat, and serve with matzoh balls (or kreplach).

Make the matzoh balls: Beat egg yolks and stir in matzoh meal along with 3 or 4 tablespoons of the soup, the seasonings, and the chicken fat. When thoroughly mixed, fold in stiffly beaten egg whites. Chill for about 40 minutes. Wet hands to shape chilled mixture into walnut-sized balls. Drop into boiling soup, cover, and let simmer for about 15 minutes.

MAKES 8 SERVINGS.

SAGE AND PIMIENTO CHICKEN SOUP

1/4 cup minced fresh sage
1/4 cup chopped canned pimiento
2 cups diced cooked chicken
1 qt. chicken stock
2 Tbs. lemon juice
salt
freshly ground pepper

Combine sage, pimiento, chicken, stock, and lemon juice in a saucepan, then season with salt and pepper to taste. Let simmer for 10 minutes.

MAKES 6 SERVINGS.

PENNSYLVANIA CHICKEN-CORN SOUP WITH NOODLES

This has been described as the favorite summer soup in Lancaster County and for generations the *pièce de résistance* of Sunday school picnic suppers and other outdoor gatherings.

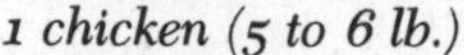

1 chicken (5 to 6 lb.)
4 qt. water
1 Tbs. salt
1 medium-size onion
1/2 tsp. saffron shreds
2 eggs, beaten
freshly ground pepper
2 pkg. (10 oz. each) frozen corn kernels, thawed
1/4 cup minced parsley
1/4 cup minced celery leaves

NOODLES:
2 eggs
1 1/2 cups, more or less, flour
1/2 tsp. salt

Cover chicken with water, add salt and onion, and bring to a boil; cover and let simmer over low heat for about 2 hours, or until tender.

Meanwhile, make the noodles: Beat eggs in a large bowl; stir in flour and 1/2 eggshell of water to make a stiff dough; season with salt. Knead for 10 to 15 minutes, or until smooth and elastic. Roll out on a floured surface, making dough as thin as possible. Cut into pieces 1/2 inch by 1 1/2 inches; set aside to dry.

Remove chicken from broth and let it cool. Skin chicken, remove meat from bones, and cut meat into small dice; return meat to broth. Stir in saffron. Bring chicken broth to a boil, add noodles and several turns of pepper grinder, then cook for 5 minutes. Add corn, return broth to a boil, and let simmer for 3 minutes. Stir in beaten eggs, then parsley and celery leaves. Test noodles, which should now be firm but not too chewy.

MAKES 6 TO 8 SERVINGS.

CHICKEN-SQUASH SOUP WITH OYSTERS

3 Tbs. butter
1/2 cup minced celery
1/2 minced onion
6 Tbs. flour
1 1/2 cups mashed cooked squash
1/2 tsp. salt
freshly ground pepper
3 cups chicken stock
1 cup heavy cream
1 cup fresh oysters with liquor

Melt 2 tablespoons butter and stir in celery and onion; let simmer for 10 minutes. Stir in remaining butter and the flour, a little at a time, blending well with vegetables. Add squash, salt, and pepper to taste. Off the heat, gradually blend in stock. When perfectly smooth, return to heat and add cream, cooking until soup thickens to desired consistency. Add oysters with their liquor and continue cooking until oysters plump up.

MAKES 6 SERVINGS.

EASTERN SHORE TERRAPIN SOUP

4 Tbs. (1/2 stick) butter
1 Tbs. flour
2 cups milk
salt
freshly ground pepper
3 eggs, hard-cooked
2 lb. cooked terrapin meat, cubed
1/2 cup heavy cream
1/4 cup dry sherry
cayenne pepper

Melt butter in a good-size saucepan and blend in flour; off the heat, gradually stir in milk, then add salt and pepper to taste. Chop whites of eggs very fine; mash yolks. Stir chopped egg whites, terrapin meat, and mashed yolks into white sauce; let simmer for 5 minutes. Stir in cream as soup cooks for 5 minutes more; blend in sherry. Dust each bowl with cayenne before serving.

MAKES 6 SERVINGS.

MENEMSHA CLAM CHOWDER

50 soft-shell clams, well scrubbed
1 cup water
1/4 lb. salt pork, chopped fine
1 small onion, chopped fine
3 cups diced potatoes
1/2 tsp. minced fresh thyme
1 bay leaf
1 whole clove
1 parsley sprig
2 cups boiling water
1 qt. milk
2 Tbs. butter
salt
freshly ground pepper

Steam clams in 1 cup water; remove from shells, separating hard and soft parts. Chop hard parts fine. Strain clam liquor through a fine cloth. Sauté salt pork and onions in a good-size pot; when onions are golden, drain excess fat. Add potatoes, thyme, bay leaf, clove, parsley, and boiling water. Let simmer for about 15 minutes, or until potatoes are tender. Add clams and set aside to cool, then refrigerate. Next day stir in reserved clam liquor, milk, butter, salt to taste, and several turns of pepper grinder; heat and serve.

MAKES ABOUT 4 SERVINGS.

CREAM OF CLAM SOUP

1/2 cup white wine
4 dozen clams, well scrubbed
1 small onion, minced
3 Tbs. chopped celery
6 Tbs. minced parsley
1 tsp. dried sage
1/2 tsp. dried chervil
1/2 tsp. dried thyme
1/2 tsp. peppercorns
6 whole allspice
2 cups heavy cream
1 cup half-and-half
1 cup milk
1/4 tsp. baking soda
1 Tbs. cornstarch
freshly ground black pepper
sprinkling of cayenne pepper
1 egg yolk
3 Tbs. dry sherry

Put white wine into large pot and add enough water to cover bottom to depth of 1 inch; add clams, cover tightly, and steam for about 10 minutes, or until all are open. Strain out clams, reserving liquid, and put clam meat through medium blade of meat grinder. Combine vegetables, 1 tablespoon of parsley, the sage, chervil, thyme, peppercorns and allspice, with clams and their liquid and simmer very gently for about 1 hour. Allow broth to settle, then draw off broth from sediment very carefully and add enough water to make 1 quart. Combine cream, half-and-half, and milk and heat; add clam broth and stir in baking soda. Mix cornstarch with enough water to make a thin paste and stir into soup; watch carefully so that soup thickens without boiling. Season with several turns of pepper grinder and cayenne. Beat egg yolk until creamy, then add some of hot soup, a little at a time, stirring continuously; when this mixture is warm, stir it carefully into rest of soup and heat gently for 4 or 5 minutes without letting it boil. Add sherry when soup has thickened. Serve in heated bowls with a sprinkling of reserved parsley.

MAKES 8 TO 10 SERVINGS.

MARTHA'S VINEYARD RAZOR CLAM SOUP

40 to 50 razor clams, freshly dug
1 cup cornmeal
¼ cup white wine
2 cups half-and-half
2 Tbs. butter
salt
freshly ground pepper
paprika
1 Tbs. minced parsley

Take home the clams in a quantity of seawater. Wash them thoroughly, put them back in the seawater with a handful of cornmeal, and leave them alone in refrigerator overnight, long enough to free themselves of ingested sand. Put cleaned clams and wine into a large pot, cover, bring to a boil, then lower heat and steam for 10 minutes. Remove clams with a slotted spoon and set aside to cool. Strain liquid through cheesecloth and reserve. Remove clams from shells and chop coarsely. Combine half-and-half, clam liquid, and butter in the top part of a double boiler over simmering water; add chopped clams and heat just to boiling point. Season to taste with salt and pepper. Garnish each serving with a dusting of paprika and minced parsley.

MAKES ABOUT 4 SERVINGS.

CRAB CLAW SOUP

When Franklin D. Roosevelt was president, the food he and his family were served was in the hands of Henrietta Nesbitt, who published her *White House Diary* in 1948. "All the Roosevelts like fish and soup," she wrote, "so the crabmeat was a special treat, made from an old American recipe that had been a favorite of George Washington. Whenever I wanted to do something especially nice for Mrs. R., I'd order this soup, just the way Martha Washington used to have it fixed at Mount Vernon. It calls for a pound and a half of crab meat in nice chunks and you can use the claw meat. . . ."

2 Tbs. butter
1 Tbs. flour
2 eggs, hard-cooked and sieved
1 tsp. grated lemon rind
2 cups cream
2 cups milk
1 ½ lb. crab meat from claws, cut into chunks
1 tsp. Worcestershire sauce
½ cup sherry
salt
freshly ground pepper
4 Tbs. minced parsley

Blend butter and flour in the top part of a double boiler over simmering water. Stir in eggs and lemon rind. Stir in cream and milk alternately, a little at a time; continue stirring until smooth and slightly thickened. Add crab meat and let simmer for 5 minutes. Stir in Worcestershire sauce and sherry, then season to taste with salt and pepper. Serve in heated soup plates with a sprinkling of parsley.

MAKES ABOUT 6 SERVINGS.

PENNSYLVANIA DUTCH EEL-SHRIMP SOUP

3 lb. eel, filleted
4 Tbs. (1/2 stick) butter
cayenne pepper
1 tsp. salt
1 tsp. lemon juice
2 Tbs. minced parsley leaves
1/2 cup sherry
1 1/2 cups chopped carrots
1 medium-size celery rib, chopped
2 shallots, minced
2 whole scallions, minced
1/4 cup minced parsley stems
1 cup chopped fresh mushrooms
1/2 tsp. dried thyme
1/2 tsp. dried basil
1/2 tsp. ground mace
1 1/2 qt. chicken stock
1 1/2 lb. raw shrimps, peeled
freshly ground pepper
8 egg yolks
3 to 4 Tbs. minced parsley

Cut filleted eel into 1 1/2- by 2-inch pieces. Melt half the butter in a large saucepan; add eel, a liberal sprinkling of cayenne, the salt, lemon juice, and minced parsley leaves. Cook over low heat for about 20 minutes, stirring frequently. Add sherry, bring to a boil, let simmer for 2 minutes, then set aside. In another saucepan melt remaining 2 tablespoons butter, stir in chopped vegetables, herbs, and spices and sauté for 5 minutes. Add chicken stock and let simmer for 30 minutes. Meanwhile, return eel mixture to heat, stir in shrimps, and cook for about 5 minutes, or until shrimps turn color. Combine fish with vegetable broth and cook for about 3 minutes; add a few turns of pepper grinder. Beat egg yolks; stir into them, a little at a time, enough hot broth to raise temperature without curdling eggs; stir immediately into soup. Serve garnished with parsley.

MAKES 6 TO 8 SERVINGS.

SCALLOP SOUP

2 bottles (8 oz. each) clam juice
1 Tbs. butter
1/2 tsp. Worcestershire sauce
1/2 tsp. dry mustard
1 Tbs. minced celery leaves
salt
freshly ground white pepper
3/4 lb. scallops (preferably tiny bay scallops, or sea scallops cut into small pieces)
2 egg yolks
1 cup heavy cream
1/4 cup dry white wine
2 Tbs. minced parsley

Put clam juice and butter in a saucepan and let simmer, adding Worcestershire, mustard, celery leaves, a little salt if needed, and a turn or two of pepper grinder. When mixture is just about to boil, add scallops; let simmer for 3 or 4 minutes. Meanwhile, beat egg yolks with cream, then stir into them a little hot broth; then stir egg-cream mixture into soup and continue simmering for 1 or 2 minutes more. Add wine, bring just to boiling point, and serve with parsley sprinkled into each bowl.

MAKES 4 LARGE SERVINGS.

FISHY CREAM OF CELERY SOUP

American cooks have traditionally been inventive about leftovers, and many good soups have resulted from the use of a fish carcass in making stock. Keeping fish stock in the freezer is highly recommended as a base for such soups as this.

1 Tbs. butter
1 cup chopped celery
1 medium onion, chopped
2 cups fish or seafood stock
1 1/2 Tbs. cornstarch
2 cups milk
2 Tbs. minced parsley

Melt butter in a saucepan and stir in celery and onion; cook over low heat for 3 or 4 minutes. Add half of fish stock, bring to a boil, and let simmer for 10 to 12 minutes. Let cool, then spin in a blender until smooth. Return to saucepan with remaining stock and let simmer. Stir cornstarch into 1/2 cup milk until it is smooth, then blend into soup. Cook slowly until soup thickens. Off the heat, add remaining milk; return to heat and cook for 5 minutes. Serve with parsley sprinkled over each serving.

MAKES 4 SERVINGS.

DOUBLE MUSHROOM SOUP

Gatherers of wild mushrooms—and there are growing numbers of them in America—often combine two kinds in a soup when the day's hunt has been particularly good, using one variety for the purée and a rarer, fine-textured kind for the garnish. The inventive Michael Field put this trick to work with the commercially grown species that appear in supermarkets. In our kitchen double mushroom soup is made as follows.

5 or 6 scallions (including some of green part), minced
3 Tbs. butter
1 Tbs. flour
2 1/2 cups stock (chicken, turkey, or goose)
1 lb. fresh mushrooms
3/4 cup heavy cream
salt
freshly ground pepper

Sauté scallions in butter over very low heat for about 15 minutes. Stir in flour and cook for several minutes. Remove from heat and slowly stir in stock, eliminating all lumps. Set aside 4 large mushrooms of uniform size and mince remainder very fine. Stir minced mushrooms into soup; bring to a boil, and let simmer gently for 10 minutes. Put soup through a food mill or strainer. Return to stove, add cream, and heat. Season with salt and pepper. Meanwhile slice reserved mushrooms very thin and put them in a warm soup tureen or individual soup dishes. Pour in hot soup and serve. MAKES 4 SERVINGS.

SOUTHERN SCALLION VICHYSSOISE

Louis Diat, chef of New York's Ritz-Carlton, is said to have served the first *crème vichyssoise glacé* in 1910, having chilled the kind of leek and potato soup his mother had made and named it in honor of the fashionable French watering place. By then French-speaking Louisianians had been making "shallot porridge" for generations, combining potatoes with sautéed scallions instead of leeks. In Louisville, Kentucky, a version similar to the one below is made with eggs instead of potatoes as a thickener. Diat's creation, at one time as popular a party dish as beef Stroganoff, just missed entering history as *crème Gauloise* in 1941, when a group of chefs in America voted to change the name because they were offended by the wartime Vichy government. Too many people, however, were addicted to the original term, which is now ingrained in the American language.

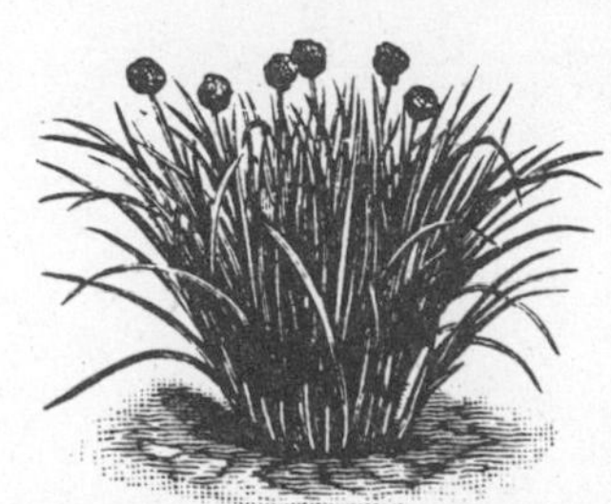

8 large whole scallions
1 qt. chicken stock
1/4 tsp. dried tarragon
4 to 5 Tbs. chopped celery leaves
salt
freshly ground white pepper
3 egg yolks
2 cups heavy cream
3 Tbs. minced chives

Cut scallions into thin rings, including all of the green part that is fresh. Add to chicken stock along with tarragon and celery leaves and let simmer for 20 to 25 minutes. Season to taste with salt and white pepper as necessary. While soup cools, beat egg yolks with cream. Strain soup; stir some into egg-cream mixture, a little at a time, then combine in the top part of a double boiler over simmering water; stir constantly until soup coats spoon. It must not boil. Chill in refrigerator for several hours. Sprinkle each serving with chives.

MAKES 6 SERVINGS.

JOE TILDEN'S SAN FRANCISCO CREAM OF ONION SOUP

A *bon vivant* famous in the Bay Area at the turn of the century, Major Tilden perfected his own versions of many dishes, American and otherwise. We make his creamy soup this way:

3 to 4 Tbs. butter
4 medium-size onions, sliced thin
2 cups beef stock
2 cups milk
1 tsp. dried chervil
1 tsp. dried savory
4 egg yolks, well beaten
1/2 cup grated Monterey Jack cheese

Melt butter in a heavy cast-iron pot and stir in onion slices over low heat; cook slowly for at least 15 minutes, stirring often. Onions should be rich brown in color, without being burned. Stir in stock, milk, and herbs. Cook for at least 5 minutes to marry flavors. Just before serving, add soup, a spoonful at a time, to egg yolks; when this mixture is warm and well blended, stir into soup and cook for 3 or 4 minutes to thicken. Cheese may either be added just before ladling out soup or be served separately.

MAKES 4 SERVINGS.

ONION SOUP WITH HAMBURGER AND MOZZARELLA

2 Tbs. butter
4 small onions, sliced thin
1/2 tsp. sugar
1/2 lb. beef round, ground
6 cups boiling water
1/4 tsp. dried oregano
1/4 tsp. dried basil
1/2 tsp. salt
freshly ground pepper
4 slices of rye bread
2 Tbs. corn oil
4 large, thin slices of mozzarella cheese

Preheat oven to 375°F.

Melt butter in a saucepan and sauté onion slices over low heat for about 20 minutes, stirring occasionally, until they turn brownish. Stir in sugar and let it caramelize before adding beef; continue stirring and scrape up bits from pan bottom until meat has lost its redness. Pour in boiling water, add seasonings, and let simmer, covered, for 10 minutes. Fry bread slices quickly in sizzling oil, then put them in bottom of 4 individual heatproof casseroles. Put a slice of cheese on top of each slice of bread, pressing down to make it adhere to bread. Pour piping-hot soup into each casserole; cheese and bread will rise to surface. Put in oven for 20 minutes. Finish, if you wish, by putting casseroles close to broiler heat to brown cheese.

MAKES 4 SERVINGS.

OJIBWAY BUTTERNUT SQUASH AND CORN CHOWDER

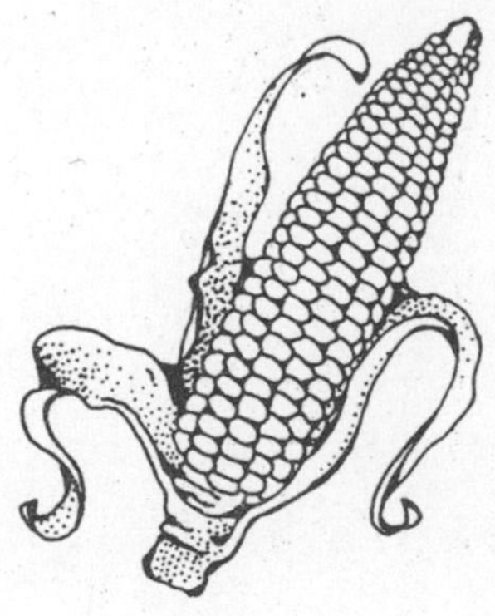

Most recipes developed originally by Indian cooks became fixed as part of American culinary lore centuries ago. Nothing about this way of producing a vegetable chowder is startlingly new, but the recipe is a contemporary Ojibway woman's adaptation of a traditional method used by her ancestors in their villages in the Upper Mississippi River country.

1 medium-size onion, chopped
2 Tbs. butter
1 lb. butternut squash, peeled, seeded, and chopped
3 ears of corn, scraped (about 1 1/2 cups)
1 qt. water
3/4 cup heavy cream
salt
cayenne pepper
12 bacon strips, cooked crisp and crumbled

Sauté onion lightly in butter, then add squash, corn, and water. Bring to a boil, then let simmer, partially covered, for about 1 hour, or until the squash is very soft. Whisk well to blend, then add cream; season with salt to taste. Serve the soup garnished with a dash of cayenne and a sprinkling of bacon over each bowlful.

MAKES ABOUT 4 SERVINGS.

EAST CRAFTSBURY PUMPKIN OR SQUASH SOUP

1 pumpkin or winter squash (about 8 in. in diameter and 6 to 8 in. high)
2 Tbs. butter, softened
1/2 cup coarse salt
freshly ground pepper
1 medium-size onion, sliced thin
1/4 cup uncooked rice
1 qt. boiling chicken stock
pinch of freshly grated nutmeg

GARNISH:
4 bacon strips, cooked crisp and crumbled
2 Tbs. grated mozzarella cheese

or

1/2 cup heavy cream, warmed
1 tsp. minced chives

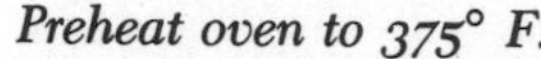
Preheat oven to 375° F.

Cut a lid out of pumpkin or squash, as if making a jack-o'-lantern, then scrape out all the seeds and fibers. Rub walls with butter, salt, and grind in a few turns of pepper. Sprinkle onion slices and rice on bottom, then pour in boiling stock. Put pumpkin lid back on, put pumpkin in pan, and bake for 2 hours. Before serving, scrape some of tender pumpkin pulp from walls into broth. Correct seasoning, add nutmeg, and serve. Garnish either with bacon and cheese or with warm cream floated on top of soup, then sprinkled with chives. Be sure each serving gets a generous portion of scraped squash pulp.

MAKES 4 SERVINGS.

SQUASH-APPLE CREAM SOUP

3 cups chicken stock
1 medium-size butternut squash, seeded and chopped coarse
2 small tart apples, peeled, seeded, and chopped
1 small onion, chopped
2 tsp. minced fresh rosemary
4 Tbs. (1/2 stick) butter
1/4 cup flour
1/2 cup heavy cream
salt
freshly ground pepper
1 small red apple, cubed, for garnish

Put stock, squash (it need not be peeled), tart apples, onions, and rosemary in a saucepan; cover and let simmer for about 25 minutes, or until squash is tender. Force through a strainer or purée in a food processor or blender.

In a separate pan melt butter, blend in flour to make a smooth paste, and cook slowly for 2 to 3 minutes, stirring constantly. Stir in puréed squash-apple mixture, blending thoroughly; let simmer for about 15 minutes. Just before serving, stir in cream and heat without boiling. Season to taste with salt and pepper. Garnish with cubes of red apple and serve hot.

MAKES ABOUT 6 SERVINGS.

SWEET POTATO SOUP

2 cups diced sweet potatoes
1 cup mixed chopped onions and leeks or shallots
1/2 cup chopped carrots
1/2 cup chopped celery
1/4 cup coarsely chopped parsley
2 Tbs. butter
1 qt. chicken stock
1/2 tsp. dried tarragon
1/2 to 3/4 cup cream
salt
freshly ground pepper
2 Tbs. finely minced parsley

In a heavy 2-quart saucepan sauté chopped vegetables in butter for 5 minutes, stirring occasionally. Add stock and tarragon, bring to a boil, and let simmer, covered, for about 1 hour. Put through a food mill, return to saucepan with cream, blend well, and season with salt and pepper to taste. Serve sprinkled with minced parsley.

MAKES 4 TO 6 SERVINGS.

JELLIED WATERCRESS SOUP

1 qt. rich chicken or other poultry stock
1/2 tsp. unflavored gelatin (optional)
1 Tbs. Madeira
1 bunch of watercress
salt
freshly ground white pepper
lemon juice
4 thin lemon slices

If stock is not quite firm enough to jell, blend gelatin with Madeira and add to heated stock, otherwise simply add the wine. Finely chop watercress or, if you choose, shred the sprigs coarsely and spin in a blender with 1 cup of stock for a couple of seconds, just enough to mince but not mash. Add chopped watercress to heated stock and season with a little salt, pepper, and lemon juice to taste. Divide among 4 soup dishes and chill until firmly set. Garnish with lemon slices.

MAKES 4 SERVINGS.

ZUCCHINI SOUP

4 medium-size zucchini (about 2 lbs.)
6 cups chicken or turkey stock
1 medium-size onion, sliced
1/4 tsp. dried chervil
salt
freshly ground pepper
1/2 cup fresh or frozen peas
1/4 to 1/2 cup sour cream
2 to 3 Tbs. mixed fresh basil and tarragon or parsley and chives (optional)

Cut washed zucchini into chunks and set aside. Heat stock in a saucepan; add onion and chervil, and season with a little salt and pepper, depending on taste of stock. Bring to a boil, add zucchini, and let simmer for 20 minutes. Add peas, return to boil, and let simmer for 5 minutes. Put one-third of soup at one time into a blender and spin for 2 or 3 seconds, retaining some of vegetable texture. Garnish soup with sour cream and a sprinkling of fresh herbs if available.

MAKES 6 SERVINGS.

VEGETABLES

BRAISED ARTICHOKES

4 small to medium-size globe artichokes
1/2 lemon
1/2 cup olive oil
1 large onion, chopped fine
2 garlic cloves, chopped fine
1 carrot, chopped fine
1 large tomato, peeled, seeded, and chopped fine
1 cup chicken stock
1/2 tsp. salt
freshly ground pepper
2 to 3 Tbs. mixed chopped fresh parsley and basil

Trim the tops and stems from the artichokes, snip the thorny tips from the leaves, and remove small, tough outermost leaves. Split into halves and, with a sharp knife, cut out the chokes. Rub all the cut surfaces with lemon; reserve lemon. Coat the bottom of a heavy pan with some of the oil and arrange artichokes in 1 layer, cut side up. Spoon chopped vegetables over, filling up the scooped-out centers. Pour stock around, season well with salt and pepper, and cover the pan tightly. Let simmer about 45 minutes, or until flesh can be easily pierced. With a slotted spoon, remove artichokes to a serving dish and distribute chopped vegetables over tops. Pour remaining oil over top, and sprinkle with juice from reserved lemon, garnish with chopped parsley and basil. Serve either tepid or chilled.

MAKES 4 SERVINGS.

ARTICHOKES STUFFED WITH PEAS

4 artichokes
1 can (10 1/2 oz.) condensed beef bouillon
juice of 1 lemon
salt
1/2 cup cooked small peas
2 Tbs. minced chives
freshly ground pepper
4 thin slices of mozzarella cheese
4 tsp. fresh bread crumbs
4 thin squares of butter

Cut artichoke stems off evenly, so that vegetables will sit nicely. Level off the tops and cut away the thorny tips of leaves. Remove small, tough outermost leaves. Cook artichokes in boiling bouillon diluted with an equal amount of water, plus the juice of 1 lemon and about 1/2 teaspoon salt, for about 25 minutes, or until a leaf pulls out easily. When done, remove the small leaves in the center and then with a teaspoon scoop out the fuzzy part (the choke) over the heart. Mix peas with chives, season with salt and pepper to taste, and fill each artichoke with equal amounts. Place a slice of mozzarella on top of each, cover with bread crumbs, then dot with a square of butter. Broil for 10 minutes.

MAKES 4 SERVINGS.

JERSALEM ARTICHOKES IN LEMON SAUCE

1 lb. Jerusalem artichokes
6 to 8 Tbs. vinegar

SAUCE:
4 Tbs. (1/2 stick) butter
juice of 1 lemon
rind of 1 lemon
3 Tbs. minced parsley
salt
freshly ground pepper

Wash and peel artichokes, dropping them into 1 quart of water to which vinegar has been added to prevent darkening. Drain, then cook in boiling water for about 25 minutes, or until soft.

Make the sauce: While artichokes are cooking, melt butter in a saucepan, stir in lemon juice, lemon rind, parsley, very little salt, and freshly ground white pepper to taste. When artichokes are done, drain and serve covered with lemon sauce.

MAKES 4 SERVINGS.

BARLEY BAKED WITH MUSHROOMS AND GREEN PEPPER

1/2 lb. fresh mushrooms
3 to 4 Tbs. bacon fat
1/4 cup chopped green pepper
1 cup uncooked barley
2 beef bouillon cubes
1 qt. boiling water
1 tsp. salt

Preheat oven to 350° F.

Wipe mushrooms with a damp cloth, trim off tough ends of stems, and slice. Melt fat in a flameproof 1 1/2- to 2-quart casserole and sauté mushrooms with green pepper for about 5 minutes. Stir in barley, coating it with fat, then add bouillon cubes dissolved in boiling water, and the salt. Bake, uncovered, for 1 1/2 hours, stirring occasionally, then cover casserole and continue baking for 30 minutes more.

MAKES 4 SERVINGS.

GREEN BEANS WITH CHEESE

1 lb. green beans
3 Tbs. butter
2 small onions, chopped
1 1/2 cups milk
2 eggs, beaten
1 1/2 cups 1/2-in. fresh bread cubes
1/2 cup grated Parmesan or Cheddar cheese
1/2 tsp. salt
freshly ground pepper
1/2 tsp. each of dried basil, oregano, and rosemary

Preheat oven to 350° F.

Trim beans and cut on bias; cook in boiling salted water for about 10 minutes; drain. Butter a 1 1/2-quart casserole. Melt remaining butter and sauté chopped onions for about 4 minutes. Off the heat, add milk, eggs, bread cubes, cheese, salt, and several turns of pepper grinder; add herbs and stir well before adding drained beans. Transfer to buttered casserole. Bake for 40 minutes.

MAKES 4 SERVINGS.

BARBECUED BEANS

Westerners sometimes call their version of baked beans barbecued when they are seasoned with hot peppers or chili and tomatoes. In the South barbecued beans can mean either butter beans (baby limas) baked and highly seasoned or string beans in an assertive "sweet and sour" sauce. Either choice produces a characteristic American accompaniment to hamburger or sausages cooked on an outdoor grill.

1 lb. green beans, cut into sections
salt
4 Tbs. (1/2 stick) butter
1 Tbs. chopped onion
1 tart apple, peeled, seeded, and sliced
1 Tbs. flour
2 Tbs. brown sugar
1 tsp. dry mustard
1 tsp. curry powder
1/4 cup cider vinegar
cayenne or red pepper

Cook beans in salted water until tender. Drain, reserving 1 cup of cooking water. Melt butter in a large skillet and cook onion for about 3 minutes; stir in apple slices. Sprinkle in flour, brown sugar, mustard, and curry powder, and stir thoroughly, adding reserved cooking water and vinegar. Add drained beans, mix well, and reheat. Season to taste with hot pepper and serve hot.

MAKES 4 SERVINGS.

POLISH-STYLE RED CABBAGE

The immigrant Poles who settled in various parts of the United States named this dish *Kapusta Czerwona*. It goes well with either steak or game and is a perfect accompaniment for roast venison.

2 medium-size red cabbages
2 Tbs. salt
2 cups red wine
2 tsp. sugar
freshly ground black pepper
1/2 tsp. ground cloves
2 1/2 Tbs. butter
3 Tbs. flour
1 cup rich beef stock
2 Tbs. vinegar

Cut cabbages into halves, then cut vertically into thin shreds and put in a stainless steel or enameled bowl; mix with salt and let stand for 10 minutes. Turn into a colander to drain, pressing out as much liquid as possible. Put the cabbage into a stainless steel pot and barely cover with boiling water, then gently cook for about 6 minutes, or until almost tender. Add wine, sugar, several turns of pepper grinder, and cloves; cook for 2 to 3 minutes more. In a large skillet, brown butter and blend in flour to make a rich brown paste, then stir in 2 cups or more of cabbage cooking liquid, continuing to stir until you have a thinnish, silky brown sauce. Add the vinegar. Drain cabbage or lift out with a slotted spoon and mix into sauce. Serve hot.

MAKES 6 TO 8 SERVINGS.

PUEBLO CAULIFLOWER WITH PUMPKIN SEEDS

Indians of the Southwest ate a lot of pumpkin seeds, even if they didn't grow cauliflower until after white men took over the territory. Nobody knows which good New Mexico cook first arrived at this combination or adapted the idea from Mexico.

1 head of cauliflower
1/2 cup pumpkin seeds, toasted
1/4 cup almonds, blanched
1/2 tsp. cuminseed
3 small green Tabasco peppers, seeded
1 large clove garlic, minced
1/4 cup minced parsley
1 cup chicken stock
1/3 cup grated Monterey Jack cheese

Preheat oven to 350° F.

Put cauliflower into boiling salted water and cook for about 20 minutes. Drain, cool, and break into flowerets. Put pumpkin seeds, almonds, and cuminseed into a blender; spin until gritty. Add green Tabasco peppers to contents of blender along with garlic and parsley and spin long enough to make a smooth paste. Put this into a saucepan and add stock, a little at a time, while bringing mixture to a boil. Let simmer for about 5 minutes, then add drained cauliflower. Mix well and turn into a baking dish; top with cheese. Bake for 10 minutes, or until cheese bubbles.

MAKES 4 SERVINGS.

ARIZONA BAKED CORN

1 Tbs. lard
1 onion, minced
1 Tbs. finely chopped celery
2 Tbs. butter
2 Tbs. chili powder
2 cups tomato purée
3 cups raw, tender corn cut from cobs
salt
freshly ground pepper
1/4 cup grated Monterey Jack cheese

Preheat oven to 350° F.

Heat lard and sauté minced onion without browning; then stir in celery and cook for 5 minutes more. Add butter and stir in chili powder, then tomato purée and corn. Season to taste with salt and pepper. Pour into a casserole, top with cheese, and bake, covered, for 45 minutes. Remove the cover and continue baking for 15 minutes more.

MAKES 4 SERVINGS.

BRUCE YOUNG'S CORN OYSTERS

Not everybody can count on freshly picked ears from Bruce Young's Vermont garden, but this recipe was developed with that head start. The important thing is to have corn that is as fresh as possible.

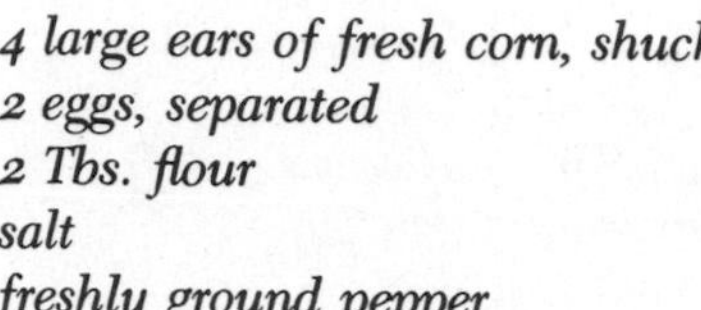

4 large ears of fresh corn, shucked
2 eggs, separated
2 Tbs. flour
salt
freshly ground pepper
1 tsp. finely chopped green pepper (optional)
1/2 tsp. chopped chives (optional)
fat for deep frying

Use a very sharp knife to cut kernels from cobs. Beat egg yolks and stir in flour, 1/2 teaspoon salt, several turns of pepper grinder, and green pepper and/or chives if you choose. Stir in corn. Beat egg whites with a pinch of salt until they form soft peaks; fold into corn batter. In 2 batches, drop spoonfuls of batter, about the size of oysters, into deep fat heated to 375° F. Corn oysters brown quickly. Turn once, remove to drain on paper towels, and serve immediately.

MAKES 4 SERVINGS.

CORN ON THE COB POACHED IN MILK

2 qt. milk
2 qt. water
12 ears of fresh sweet corn, shucked
melted butter
salt
freshly ground pepper

Fill a good-size pot with milk and water, add corn, then bring to the boiling point. Remove from heat, leaving corn in liquid for 10 minutes if freshly picked, otherwise about 15 minutes. Serve with plenty of melted butter, salt, and pepper.

MAKES 6 SERVINGS.

CREAMED CORN AND GREEN PEPPERS

4 bacon strips
4 ears of fresh corn, shucked
2 medium-size green peppers, or 1 green and 1 sweet red pepper
3 or 4 whole scallions
4 Tbs. (1/2 stick) butter
1/2 cup heavy cream
salt
freshly ground black pepper
1 Tbs. minced parsley
1 canned pimiento, cut into strips (optional)

Cook bacon in a medium-size skillet until crisp; drain on paper towels. Meanwhile cut kernels from corn cobs with a sharp knife. Cut peppers into 3/4-inch squares. Mince scallions, including some of green part. Remove bacon fat from skillet and melt butter in same pan to sauté vegetables. After cooking for about 1 minute, add cream and a little salt and pepper. Let simmer, covered, for 30 minutes, or until corn is tender. (Corn that is not very fresh will be tough and take longer to cook.) When vegetables are done, cream should be almost absorbed. If it has cooked away, add a little extra cream and let it cook down; the dish should be moist but not liquid. Just before serving, crumble bacon and sprinkle it over the top with a scattering of parsley and the pimiento strips.

MAKES 4 SERVINGS.

VIRGINIA CORN PUDDING

2 cups corn kernels
1 Tbs. flour
1/2 tsp. salt
cayenne pepper
freshly grated nutmeg
2 eggs, well beaten
1/2 cup heavy cream
1/4 cup milk
3 Tbs. butter
2 Tbs. minced parsley

Preheat oven to 350° F.

Drain corn if canned. Mix with flour, then add salt, a little cayenne, and a few gratings of nutmeg. Stir in eggs, cream, and milk. Butter a 1 1/2-quart baking dish and melt remaining butter, stirring it into corn mixture; pour corn into baking dish and sprinkle top with parsley. Set dish in a pan of hot water and bake for about 50 minutes.

MAKES 4 SERVINGS.

CORN SAUTÉED WITH WALNUTS

6 ears of fresh corn, shucked
2 Tbs. walnut oil or other oil
1/4 cup ground black walnuts
salt
freshly ground pepper

Cook corn until just tender, then cut kernels from cobs with a sharp knife. Heat oil in a skillet, add corn and nuts, and sauté for about 5 minutes, stirring frequently. Add salt and pepper to taste.

MAKES 4 SERVINGS.

PENNSYLVANIA DUTCH FRIED CUCUMBERS

2 cucumbers, 7 to 8 inches long
salt
1 cup loosely packed fresh bread crumbs (see preparation)
1 egg
1/4 tsp. dried savory
1/4 tsp. dried thyme
salt
freshly ground pepper
6 Tbs. corn oil
juice of 1/2 a lemon

Peel cucumbers and cut into 1/4-inch slices. Sprinkle with salt and let them rest for about 20 minutes, then drain and pat dry. Prepare bread crumbs by removing crusts from a couple of slices of firm white bread, tearing bread into pieces, and spinning in a blender for a moment until you have 1 cup of quite fine crumbs. Dip the cucumber slices into egg, then into the crumbs seasoned with the herbs, salt and pepper. Fry the slices gently in oil for about 15 minutes, turning once to give even color. Sprinkle with lemon juice. Serve with flank steak and sautéed mushrooms or stuffed pork tenderloin.

MAKES 4 SERVINGS.

SAUTÉED CUCUMBERS

2 medium-size cucumbers
2 tsp. coarse salt
1 tsp. vinegar
3 or 4 whole scallions
2 Tbs. butter
1 Tbs. vegetable oil
salt
freshly ground pepper
1 Tbs. each of minced fresh parsley and dillweed or basil
1/4 cup heavy cream (optional)

Peel cucumbers, split lengthwise, and scoop out seeds; split lengthwise once or twice again and cut into pieces 1 inch long. Toss in a bowl with salt and sprinkle with vinegar. Let stand for at least 30 minutes, then drain and pat dry with paper towels. Chop white part of scallions; reserve tenderest part of green leaves. Heat butter and oil and sauté chopped scallions until they begin to take on color; add cucumber pieces and cook over very low heat, covered, for 20 to 30 minutes, depending on how crunchy you like them. Taste and add salt only if needed; sprinkle with pepper, then toss with herbs. Mince reserved green scallion leaves, add, and toss again. For a richer dish, add heavy cream and boil down slightly to thicken.

MAKES 4 SERVINGS.

STUFFED CYMLING (PATTYPAN SQUASH)

4 pattypan squashes (about 6 oz. each)
4 shallots, or 2 to 3 Tbs. minced onion
½ cup chopped green pepper
1 Tbs. minced fresh basil, or ½ tsp. dried
2 to 3 Tbs. minced parsley
1 Tbs. bacon fat
butter
½ cup white wine or hard cider

Preheat oven to 350° F.

Carefully cut off tops of squashes and scoop out centers with a melon ball cutter, discarding pith and seeds. The remaining shell should be no more than ¼ inch thick. Coarsely chop squash flesh. Mince shallots or onion and mix with green pepper, basil, and parsley and cook for about 3 minutes in bacon fat. Spoon mixture into squash shells, dotting surface with a little butter; replace lids cut from squashes. Put squash into a shallow baking pan and bake for 30 to 35 minutes.

MAKES 6 TO 8 SERVINGS.

EGGPLANT AND CORN IN SKILLET

1 medium-size eggplant
3 ears fresh corn, shucked
3 Tbs. oil
12 to 15 cherry tomatoes, cut into halves
3 Tbs. butter
salt
freshly ground black pepper
3 Tbs. mixed minced fresh herbs (parsley, chives, basil)

Do not peel eggplant, but cut into ¾-inch slices, then chop into neat cubes. Cut corn kernels from cobs. In a good-sized skillet with a close-fitting lid heat oil to almost smoking. Toss in eggplant and turn several times until cubes brown on all surfaces. Reduce heat and add corn kernels and tomatoes. Break butter into small pieces and scatter over top of vegetables. Sprinkle with a little salt and a few turns of pepper grinder, then cover tightly and cook over gentle heat for about 20 minutes; shake pan from time to time. Taste to see if eggplant is cooked but still firm and if corn is tender; cook for 5 minutes more if needed. Sprinkle with minced herbs before serving.

MAKES 6 TO 8 SERVINGS.

EGGPLANT KENTUCKY-STYLE

1 medium-size eggplant, or 2 or 3 very small ones
1 Tbs. coarse salt
6 Tbs. vegetable oil
1 large onion, sliced
2 Tbs. minced parsley
freshly ground pepper
½ cup heavy cream
1 egg
6 slices (1-in. thick each) of French bread or dry rolls, soaked in enough milk to cover
1 Tbs. butter
1 Tbs. grated Parmesan or other sharp, dry cheese

Preheat oven to 350° F.

Slice eggplant into ½-inch slices and toss in a bowl with coarse salt; let sweat for about 30 minutes. Heat some oil in a large skillet. Pat dry pieces of eggplant and fry in several batches, not crowding, until browned on both sides, adding more oil if necessary. Remove to brown paper or paper towels, then fry onion slices until translucent. Spread half the eggplant on the bottom of a 1 ½-quart casserole, cover with the onions, sprinkle with parsley and pepper, then top with rest of eggplant. Beat cream and egg together and pour over all. Finally make a layer of soaked bread. Dot the surface with butter and cheese. Bake for 30 minutes; increase heat to 450° for last 5 minutes to brown, or slip under the broiler.

MAKES 4 SERVINGS.

SCALLOPED EGGPLANT

1 large eggplant
½ cup chopped green pepper
¼ cup chopped onion
1 Tbs. vegetable oil
½ tsp. salt
freshly ground pepper
½ tsp. dried tarragon
1 large egg, beaten
½ tsp. Worcestershire sauce
2 Tbs. butter
3 Tbs. dry bread crumbs

Preheat oven to 375° F.

Peel eggplant and cut into ½-inch cubes. Put into a saucepan and cover with boiling water; gently boil, covered, for about 15 minutes, or until soft and no longer pale in color; drain. Meanwhile sauté green pepper and onion in oil for about 5 minutes, without browning. Mash cooked eggplant thoroughly. Stir in green pepper-onion mixture, salt, several turns of pepper grinder, and tarragon. When well mixed, stir in egg and Worcestershire sauce. Melt butter, stir in bread crumbs. Put eggplant mixture into buttered

1 1/2-quart baking dish, spreading buttered crumbs evenly over top. Bake for 30 minutes.

MAKES 4 TO 6 SERVINGS.

FENNEL BAKED WITH CHEESE

Fennel is a member of the celery family, but it has the flavor of anise; it was not well known in America until after gardens were planted by Italian immigrants, but it became more and more popular after World War II, both in cooked dishes and in salads.

3 medium-size heads of fennel
4 Tbs. (1/2 stick) butter
2 Tbs. flour
2 cups milk
1/2 tsp. salt
freshly ground white pepper
1/4 cup grated Parmesan cheese
2 to 3 Tbs. fresh bread crumbs

Preheat oven to 350° F.

Trim leaves and tough outer ribs from fennel. Boil bulbs in salted water for about 20 minutes, or until they feel barely tender when tested with a fork. Drain thoroughly, then cut into 1/2-inch slices. Melt butter in a skillet and sauté slices over brisk heat, turning to avoid burning. When just slightly colored, stir in flour, smoothing out all lumps. Off the heat, stir in milk, a little at a time, until mixture is smooth. Return to heat and stir while sauce thickens. Add salt and 2 or 3 turns of pepper grinder. Turn into a baking dish, sprinkle top with cheese, then with bread crumbs. Bake for 15 minutes to brown bread crumbs.

MAKES 4 SERVINGS.

FIDDLEHEADS

Ferns with heads that curl like the head of a violin have been cooked and eaten by Americans since colonial days, and there are twentieth-century devotees in places like Maryland and Maine where communities gather together to hunt them in the spring. Of three types, the most popular is the ostrich fern, which thrives in lowlands and comes to life when spring freshets recede. Faneuil Hall Market in Boston used to be famous for its shipments of fiddleheads; today the ferns are available in cans, and they can be cooked in delicious ways when frozen. They have a delicate flavor when boiled (see recipe) and are sometimes used in a soufflé, in salads with oil and vinegar dressing, or served hot with a cheese sauce.

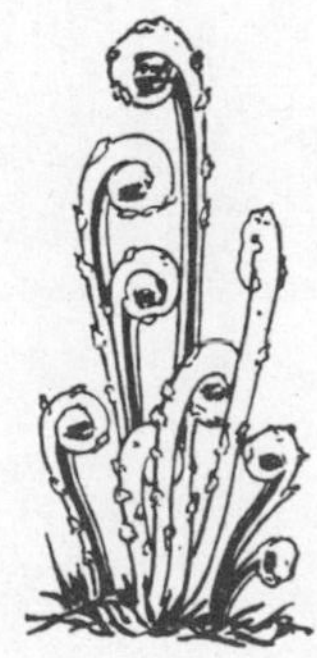

2 lb. fresh fiddleheads
1 cup boiling water
2 Tbs. butter
1 tsp. lemon juice
1/2 tsp. salt
freshly ground pepper

Cook fiddleheads in boiling water for 10 to 15 minutes, or until they can be easily pierced with a sharp-tined fork. Drain well. Toss while hot with butter, lemon juice, and seasoning to taste; serve on toast.

MAKES 6 SERVINGS.

BAKED HOMINY GRITS WITH CHEESE

2 cups cooked hominy grits, cold
1/4 lb. (1 stick) butter
2 garlic cloves, minced
1 1/2 cups grated Cheddar cheese, plus 1/4 cup additional (optional)
1 cup milk
4 eggs, well beaten
salt
freshly ground pepper

Preheat oven to 350° F.

Break up cold grits with a fork. Melt butter with minced garlic. Add cheese, milk and eggs; stir well and combine with cold grits until mixture is very smooth. Taste and add salt if needed and a few turns of pepper grinder. Pour into a buttered 2-quart casserole and bake for about 45 minutes. If you like, sprinkle the top with additional cheese and bake for 15 minutes more.

MAKES 4 SERVINGS.

WATER STREET CREAMED MUSHROOMS

There are natural caves under the business district of St. Paul, Minnesota, where French frontiersmen, down from Quebec, began growing mushrooms a century ago. This is a Minnesota version of the classic recipe.

2 lb. fresh mushrooms
4 to 5 Tbs. butter
1/2 cup heavy cream
2 Tbs. flour
2 Tbs. canned puréed chervil
salt
freshly ground white pepper

Wipe mushrooms with a damp cloth and trim stems close to undersides of caps. Melt butter in a large skillet and stew mushrooms, uncovered, for 10 minutes. Put cream and flour into a jar with a screw cap and shake until flour is absorbed. Pour into skillet with mushrooms and cook for several minutes to thicken sauce. Add chervil. Add salt and pepper to taste.

MAKES 6 TO 8 SERVINGS.

OKRA WITH CHEESE MINNESOTA-STYLE

1 Tb. butter
1 cup diced Cornhusker or Cheddar cheese
1 cup diced Monterey Jack cheese
1 pkg. (10 oz.) frozen chopped okra, defrosted
2 cups halved cherry tomatoes
1 cup chopped green pepper
2 cups cream-style corn, drained
3–4 scallions, green part chopped, white part minced
Salt
Freshly ground black pepper

Preheat oven to 350° F.

Butter well a 2-quart casserole. Toss the two cheeses together. Lightly mix the okra, cherry tomato halves, green pepper and corn. Make a layer on the bottom of the casserole of one-third of the vegetable mixture, sprinkle one-third of the scallions over, season with salt and several grinds of pepper. Cover with one-third of the cheese. Repeat twice, and bake the casserole for 40 minutes. Serve bubbling hot with boiled rice.

MAKES 6 TO 8 SERVINGS.

BAKED ONION-PEAS CASSEROLE

8 small white onions, cooked
1 Tbs. butter
1/2 cup fresh bread crumbs
2 cups fresh peas
salt
freshly ground pepper
1/2 tsp. dried basil
1/2 cup milk or half-and-half
2 Tbs. minced parsley

Preheat oven to 350° F.

Put half the onions in the bottom of a greased baking dish. Melt butter and in it brown bread crumbs; sprinkle half the crumbs over onions. Pour in peas, sprinkle with salt and pepper, and add remaining onions. Sprinkle in basil. Cover vegetables with milk, then spread with remaining crumbs and the parsley. Bake for about 10 minutes.

MAKES 4 SERVINGS.

CREOLE-BAKED PARSNIPS

This is very good as a separate dish and really first-rate when baked in the same pan with roast pork.

6 medium-size parsnips (about 2 lb.)
1 1/2 tsp. salt
1/4 tsp. grated nutmeg
3 Tbs. sugar
4 eggs, slightly beaten
1/2 cup chopped green pepper
4 Tbs. (1/2 stick) butter
1/2 cup raisins

*Preheat oven to 350° F.**
Cook parsnips in boiling salted water for 40 minutes. Plunge into cold water, peel, and cut out hard fibers at core. Mash until smooth, adding salt, nutmeg, sugar, and eggs.* Meanwhile sauté green pepper in butter for about 6 minutes; stir into mashed parsnips along with raisins. Bake in a buttered 1 1/2-quart casserole (or along with roast pork) for about 15 minutes.

MAKES 4 TO 6 SERVINGS.

POTATO-CARROT PUDDING

3 Tbs. butter
2 cups grated potatoes
1 cup grated carrots
1 cup minced whole scallions or grated onion
2 tsp. salt
freshly ground pepper
2 Tbs. cream

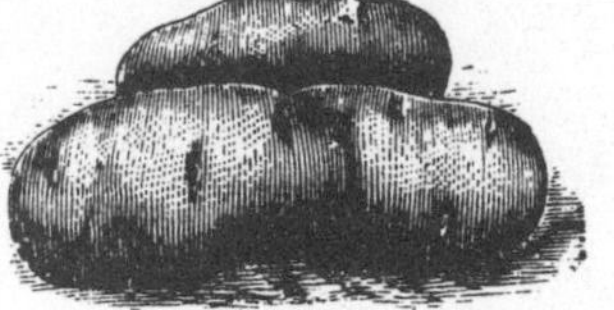

Preheat oven to 350° F.
Lightly butter a 1 1/2-quart casserole and divide remaining butter into small dollops; mix these into combined vegetables along with salt, pepper, and cream. Cover casserole and bake for about 40 minutes; remove cover and continue baking for 5 to 10 minutes more, or until crisp on top.

MAKES 6 TO 8 SERVINGS.

BRAISED POTATOES AND CELERY

4 medium-size potatoes
4 celery ribs
1/4 cup olive oil
1 1/2 tsp. salt
2 Tbs. lemon juice
freshly ground black pepper

Peel potatoes, cut into 1/2-inch slabs, and cover with water. Clean and trim celery and cut into 1/2-inch semicircles, reserving leaves for other use. Put oil into a skillet along with celery and 1/2 teaspoon salt; cover and let simmer over low heat for about 30 minutes. Add potato slabs, lemon juice, about 1 teaspoon salt, and a few turns of pepper grinder. Continue cooking for about 30 minutes, or until celery and potatoes are soft but still firm. Remove with a slotted spoon. Good with Cheese-Breaded Lamb Chops (p. 283).

MAKES 4 SERVINGS.

HASHED BROWN POTATOES

Hashed brown potatoes are a classic American side dish from Maine to San Diego County, California, and there was a time when short-order cooks in roadside eating places took great pride in their mastery of the techniques necessary to serve potatoes in this omelet form. Short-cut versions are commonly listed on breakfast menus in the West, and California cooks with more ornate notions sometimes mix in chopped almonds, filberts, walnuts, or sesame seeds.

8 medium-size potatoes, or 6 large
6 Tbs. bacon or other fat
coarse salt
freshly ground black pepper
chopped parsley

Boil potatoes in skins until just barely done through. Let cool and peel. Chop coarse. Heat half of fat in a large, heavy skillet. Add potatoes, press down with spatula, and fry over medium heat. Salt and pepper liberally. Turn half of potatoes over on top of other half, then add more fat to empty side of pan; when fat is sizzling, turn potatoes over onto fat. Break up, mix around, add salt and pepper, and again press down with spatula. Repeat twice more. (This way you should get all the pieces of potato really brown, which is the secret of good hashed browns.) After the last turn let potatoes get a good solid crust. Fold one side of potatoes over the other, sprinkle with parsley, and serve like an omelet.

MAKES 8 SERVINGS.

RUTABAGA SOUFFLÉ

Often called yellow turnips, which they are not, rutabagas (*Brassica Napobrassica*) frequently were the first root vegetable to be planted in newly broken soil of Plains States homesteads, and they were cooked sometimes as a substitute for potatoes, sometimes in combination with them. Scandinavian-Americans are particularly adept at various rutabaga dishes.

4 cups diced peeled rutabaga
1 tsp. salt
1 tsp. sugar
2 Tbs. butter
freshly ground pepper
1 Tbs. minced onion
3 eggs, separated
2 Tbs. grated Colby cheese
1 Tbs. minced parsley

Preheat oven to 325° F.

Put diced rutabaga, salt, and sugar in a large saucepan and add enough boiling water to cover by 1 inch. Boil for 3 minutes. Cover pan and reduce heat so that water boils very gently while rutabaga cooks for about 15 minutes more. Drain when soft, then whip until fluffy, adding butter, several turns of pepper grinder, and minced onion. Taste and add a little salt only if needed. Beat egg yolks until lemony and stir into vegetable mixture; beat whites until stiff, then carefully fold in. Pour mixture into a greased 1 1/2-quart casserole and bake for about 55 minutes. Sprinkle with grated cheese and bake for 5 to 8 minutes more, or until cheese melts. Sprinkle with parsley.

MAKES 6 TO 8 SERVINGS.

SAUERKRAUT AND APPLES

This dish is particularly good as an accompaniment to goose, either wild or domestic, or roast pork or sausages.

1 lb. sauerkraut
3 Tbs. fat, preferably goose or chicken fat
1 cup apple cider or white wine
1/2 cup chicken stock
1 small onion, chopped
3 large tart apples
2 tsp. brown sugar
1 tsp. caraway seeds
salt
freshly ground pepper

Preheat oven to 350° F.

Drain sauerkraut and rinse slightly; 1 cup of cold water poured over is sufficient. Melt 1 tablespoon fat in a heavy saucepan that can go into the oven; add sauerkraut and stir well over medium heat to coat the kraut. Pour cider and stock over and let simmer, covered, while preparing additional ingredients. Sauté onion in remaining fat. Peel and core apples and chop into 3/4-inch dice. Add to onion, turn, and brown slightly. Sprinkle on 1 teaspoon brown sugar to glaze. Add this mixture to the sauerkraut. Mix in caraway seeds, salt and pepper to taste, and sprinkle remaining brown sugar over the top. Bake for 30 to 40 minutes.

MAKES 4 SERVINGS.

BAKED SPINACH AND TOMATOES

2 pkg. (10 oz. each) frozen leaf spinach, cooked according to directions
1 Tbs. lemon juice
1/4 cup sour cream
1/4 lb. fresh mushrooms
2 Tbs. butter
2 large ripe tomatoes
5 to 6 Tbs. grated Cheddar cheese
1 tsp. salt
freshly ground black pepper
thin slices of mozzarella cheese

Preheat oven to 375° F.
Sprinkle cooked spinach with lemon juice and stir in sour cream; set aside. If mushrooms are very small, leave them whole; if large, remove stems and quarter heads. Melt butter in a skillet and sauté mushrooms for 5 minutes, just long enough to soften. Fold into spinach. Slice tomatoes about 1/4 inch thick. Put spinach-mushroom mixture into a 1 1/2-quart casserole. Sprinkle lightly with cheese. Cover with a layer of tomato slices, half of the salt, a few gratings of pepper, and more cheese. Repeat, using all of tomatoes and all of remaining cheese. Top with enough mozzarella to seal. Bake for about 30 minutes, or until vegetables bubble and mozzarella is golden.

MAKES 4 TO 6 SERVINGS.

BAKED SQUASH IN CINNAMON AND CREAM

1 medium-size butternut squash
butter
cinnamon
salt
freshly ground pepper
1 1/4 to 1 1/2 cups heavy cream

Preheat oven to 350°F.
Split squash and scoop out fibers and seeds; peel and grate or chop into small pieces in a food processor. Butter a 1 1/2-quart casserole; add a layer of squash, sprinkling it with cinnamon, salt, pepper, and cream. Repeat until all squash is used. Dot with butter and bake for 1 1/2 hours, or until all the cream is absorbed and the top is slightly browned.

MAKES 6 SERVINGS.

ACORN SQUASH STUFFED WITH APPLES AND CHUTNEY

2 acorn squash
1 cup diced tart apple
1/2 cup chutney (mango, apricot, or green tomato)
2 Tbs. butter

Preheat oven to 350° F.
Cut squashes into halves and scoop out fibers and seeds. Fill each half with diced apple mixed with chutney in equal quantities; top each with ½ tablespoon butter. Put in a shallow pan with about ½ inch water in bottom. Bake for about 1 ½ hours, or until squash is tender.

MAKES 4 SERVINGS.

SPAGHETTI SQUASH

Americans tend to think carelessly that all squashes are indigenous, passed on to colonists by Indian gardeners. Not so with *Cucurbita ficifolia*. This smooth-skinned gourd with a loose, fibrous interior that looks like linguine seems to have been discovered in Japan and was introduced to British gardeners in 1964. "Easy to grow, easy to cook, good to eat," was the verdict of Jane Grigson after the new veg was publicized in the *Times* of London. "Break off the stalk and push in a skewer to make a hole," she wrote in *Jane Grigson's Vegetable Book*, published in New York in 1979. "Boil the vegetable spaghetti whole in plenty of salted water. It should be ready in about 30 to 45 minutes." She recommended cutting the squash vertically in half and filling the cavity "with some delicious mixture such as buttered peas or sweetcorn, or creamed chicken." Spaghetti squash has become a successful commercial crop in California and elsewhere in this country and can be bought at specialty vegetable and fruit markets. Craig Claiborne of the *New York Times* has recommended baking it whole for 1 ½ hours. "You scrape out the spaghetti-like strands," he told readers of the *Times*, "and serve according to your whim. The label said it was good served with spaghetti sauce. We served it instead with butter and grated parmesan cheese, and it was excellent." To eat, swirl the strands onto a fork, spaghetti-style. "It spoils the entertainment to cut up the strings," says Mrs. Grigson. We also find it delicious cold, tossed with plenty of chopped scallions, some chopped red pepper, and a dressing of vinegar and oil with salt and sesame oil to taste.

GRATIN OF SWEET POTATOES AND ORANGE

3 large sweet potatoes
4 Tbs. (½ stick) butter
grated rind of 1 orange
1 cup orange juice
salt
2 to 3 Tbs. brown sugar

Preheat oven to 400° F.
Steam or boil sweet potatoes until just barely tender. Peel and cut into ½-inch slices. Butter a fairly shallow casserole. Make a layer of potatoes, salt

lightly, sprinkle a little of the orange rind on, and dot with butter. Repeat until potatoes are used up. Pour orange juice over and top with brown sugar. Bake for about 20 to 25 minutes.

MAKES 4 TO 6 SERVINGS.

GREEN TOMATO STEW

4 bacon strips, cut into squares
1 small onion, chopped
1/2 cup chopped celery
6 large green tomatoes
3/4 to 1 cup grated medium-sharp Cheddar cheese
salt
freshly ground black pepper
1/4 cup shelled peas

Fry bacon pieces until almost crisp, then add onion and celery and cook for 3 or 4 minutes more. Slice tomatoes, add, and cook for 15 minutes. Stir in cheese (the exact amount depending on how strong cheese is, or to taste), a few turns of pepper grinder, and the peas. Continue to cook for about 5 minutes, or until peas are just tender. Serve on buttered toast.

MAKES 6 SERVINGS.

TURNIPS BAKED WITH MAPLE SYRUP

1 1/2 lb. white turnips
3 Tbs. butter
2 Tbs. prepared mustard (old-fashioned mustard with whole seeds preferred)
3 Tbs. maple syrup
salt
freshly ground pepper
1/2 cup fresh bread crumbs (whole wheat preferred)

Preheat oven to 400° F.

Peel turnips and slice about 1/3 inch thick, then drop into boiling salted water and cook for about 8 minutes. Meanwhile melt butter in 1-quart shallow ovenproof dish. Stir in mustard, using less if mustard is hot. Drain turnips and pat dry; toss slices in butter-mustard mixture; add maple syrup, a sprinkling of salt, and a few turns of pepper grinder. Sprinkle bread crumbs over top. Bake for 10 minutes, or set dish 8 to 10 inches from broiler heat and broil until browned.

MAKES 4 SERVINGS.

MASHED TURNIPS WITH RICE

2 medium-size white turnips
3/4 cup chicken stock
2 cups cooked rice
1/2 tsp. dried chervil
salt
freshly ground pepper

Peel and dice turnips, then cook in boiling water for about 15 minutes, or until tender; drain. Spin in a blender with stock just long enough to remove lumps. Combine with rice and chervil and add salt and pepper to taste. Return to heat and cook over brisk heat, stirring constantly, to reduce excess liquid and blend flavors.

MAKES 4 SERVINGS.

VERMONT ZUCCHINI-POTATO CASSEROLE

4 medium-size zucchini
3 medium-size potatoes
1/4 cup minced parsley
4 or 5 large fresh basil leaves, minced
2 garlic cloves, minced
4 Tbs. (1/2 stick) butter
1 cup grated Vermont Cheddar cheese
1 cup fresh bread crumbs
salt
freshly ground pepper
1 Tbs. olive oil

Preheat oven to 350° F.

Slice zucchini 1/8 inch thick. Peel and slice potatoes as thin as possible. Mash herbs and garlic to a paste. Butter a 1 1/2- to 2-quart casserole. Make a layer of zucchini slices, sprinkle with some cheese, bread crumbs, dots of butter, and a little of garlic-herb mixture; sprinkle with salt and pepper. Make a layer of sliced potatoes and sprinkle with cheese, bread crumbs, garlic-herb mixture, salt, and pepper. Continue in alternating layers until all is used up, ending with crumbs, cheese, and butter. Sprinkle with about 3 tablespoons water and dribble olive oil over top; cover and bake for 1 1/2 hours, removing cover after 1 hour and 10 minutes so that top browns.

MAKES 6 SERVINGS.

ZUCCHINI WITH BLACK WALNUTS

1 lb. zucchini
1 large onion, sliced
3 to 4 Tbs. corn oil
1 cup chopped black walnuts
¼ cup Zinfandel wine
1 Tbs. lemon juice

Clean zucchini and cut into ½-inch slices. Sauté onion in oil for about 1 minute, then add sliced zucchini and nuts and cook over low heat for 15 minutes, turning occasionally. Add wine and lemon juice, bring to a boil, and let simmer for 5 minutes more.

MAKES 4 SERVINGS.

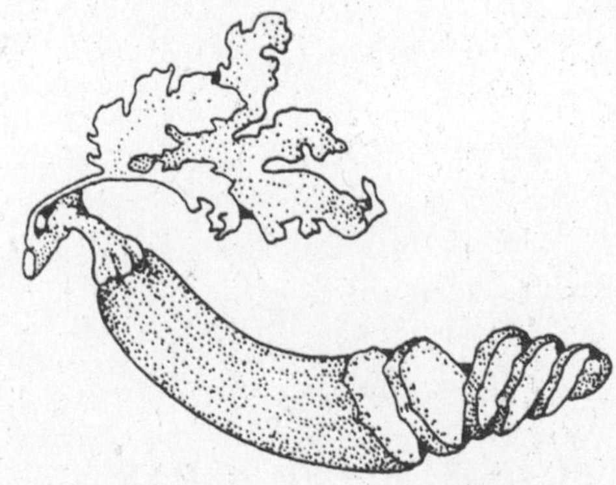

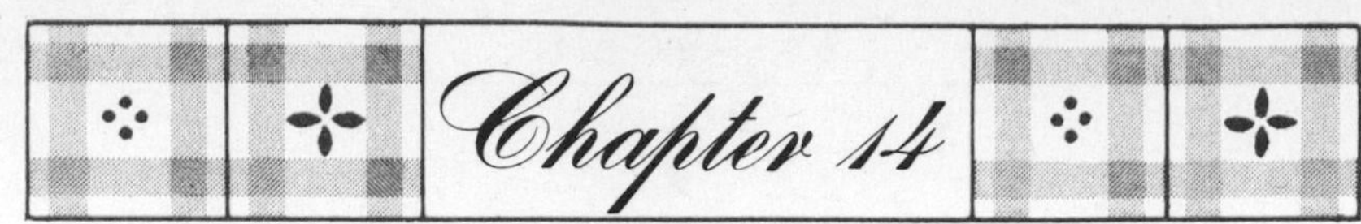

MEAT

BRAISED BEEF CALIFORNIA

4 bacon strips, diced
1 large onion, chopped
Flour, seasoned with salt and freshly ground pepper
2 lb. beef chuck, cut into small cubes
1 cup California red table wine
1 can (8 oz.) tomatoes
1 bay leaf, crumbled
1/2 tsp. dried thyme
1/2 tsp. dried marjoram
1 cup pitted olives, cut into halves
2 Tbs. chopped parsley

Cook bacon and onion together in a heavy flameproof casserole or Dutch oven. Remove bacon and onion with a slotted spoon and set aside. Dredge the meat in the seasoned flour. Brown meat in 4 separate batches in the fat in the casserole; brown on all sides, taking care not to crowd. When the last batch is done, return all the meat, bacon, and onion to the casserole; add wine, tomatoes, and seasonings. Cover and let simmer gently for 2 1/2 hours, stirring now and then and thinning with a little water if the sauce gets too thick. Add olives 5 minutes before serving, and at the last minute sprinkle parsley over all.

MAKES 4 SERVINGS.

MARINATED BEEF BRISKET

3 1/2 to 4 lb. beef brisket in 1 piece

MARINADE:

1 cup vinegar
1 cup water
8 whole cloves
6 parsley sprigs
2 bay leaves
2 sprigs celery leaves, chopped
1/2 tsp. dried thyme
1/2 tsp. dried rosemary
1/2 tsp. dried basil
2 juniper berries, crushed
1 medium-size onion, sliced
2 garlic cloves, minced
1 tsp. salt

SAUCE:

1 to 2 Tbs. bacon fat
1 cup tomato purée
1 1/2 cups beef stock
1 Tbs. brown sugar
1 Tbs. lemon juice
1 tsp. thin slivers of lemon rind
8 gingersnaps, crushed
1 Tbs. Worcestershire sauce
2 beef bouillon cubes

Preheat oven to 325° F.°

Put meat into an earthenware dish large enough so that beef lies flat and fits snugly; pour vinegar and water over and add remaining marinade ingredients. Cover and put in lowest part of refrigerator, turning twice daily for 4 days.

At least 4 hours before mealtime, drain meat thoroughly and reserve marinade. Put bacon fat into a large roasting pan and sear meat on all surfaces over high heat.° When meat is browned, pour marinade over it, then stir in tomato purée, stock, brown sugar, lemon juice, rind slivers, gingersnaps, Worcestershire sauce, and bouillon cubes; mix well. Cover and bake for about 4 hours. When meat is very tender, put it on a platter to rest. Strain sauce, reheat it, and serve it over sliced meat.

MAKES 6 TO 8 SERVINGS.

NEW ENGLAND BOILED DINNER

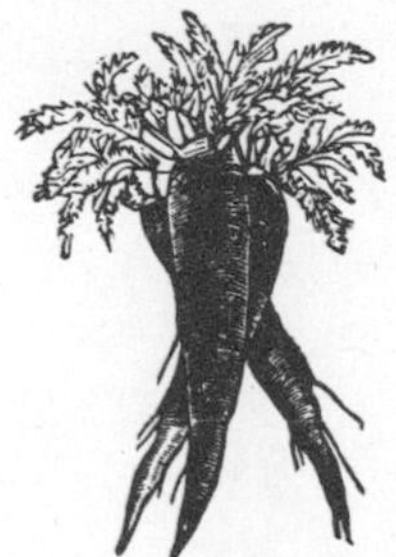

3 1/2 lb. corned beef brisket
6 turns of freshly ground pepper
1 bay leaf
1 parsnip
1/2 rutabaga
3 large carrots
4 medium-size potatoes
1/2 cabbage
6 small beets, preboiled and peeled
1 Tbs. horseradish
2 Tbs. sour cream
2 or 3 dashes of Tabasco

Cover corned brisket with fresh water, add pepper and bay leaf, and bring to a simmer over medium heat. Let simmer for a total of 4 hours. Before the last hour add parsnip, rutabaga, carrots, and potatoes. Before the last 20 minutes add cabbage, and before the last 10 minutes add beets. Remove corned beef and slice thin. Remove vegetables with a slotted spoon and distribute around beef slices, breaking larger ones into 4 servings. Prepare accompanying sauce by mixing horseradish, sour cream, and Tabasco together; serve sauce separately.

MAKES 4 SERVINGS (with some corned beef left over for red flannel hash).

FLAMING BEEF COLLOPS

MARINADE:

2 onions, sliced thin
1 garlic clove, crushed
1 cup Burgundy wine
1/2 cup olive oil
2 Tbs. vinegar
2 tsp. salt
freshly ground pepper
pinch of cayenne pepper
1/4 tsp. dried oregano
1 bay leaf, crushed

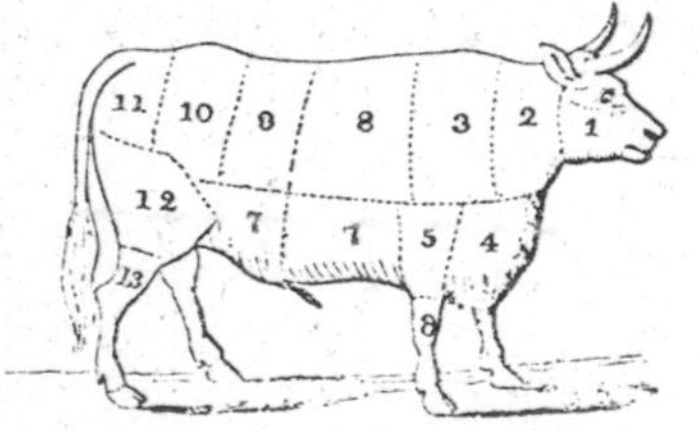

SKEWERS:

1 1/2 lb. beef, sirloin, or prime chuck, cut into 1 1/2-in. cubes
12 fresh mushroom caps
1 green pepper, seeded and cut into 1 1/2-in. squares
12 cherry tomatoes, or 3 small tomatoes, quartered
1 lemon, quartered
1/4 cup brandy

Mix the marinade ingredients in a bowl and steep the meat for 3 to 4 hours or overnight. Drain, but reserve the marinade. Arrange meat cubes on 4 skewers, alternating with mushroom caps, pieces of green pepper, and tomatoes. Place a lemon quarter at the end of each skewer. Broil slowly, turning often and brushing several times with reserved marinade. Warm the brandy and soak 4 cotton balls in it. Test meat for doneness by slicing into a chunk; the sirloin can be as rare as desired, but the chuck should be done a bit longer and moistened frequently while broiling. When the meat is ready, bring skewers to the table aflame by sticking a cotton ball on the end of each one and setting alight.

MAKES 4 SERVINGS.

ALFRED LUNT'S POT ROAST

During his long acting career with his wife, Lynn Fontanne, one of Alfred Lunt's favorite relaxations was cooking, often done in the kitchen of his Swedish farmhouse near Genesee Depot, Wisconsin. His recipe for pot roast, given to many friends, reflects a Scandinavian influence common in the use of native bounty in the Midwest.

3 ½ lb. rolled rump of beef without fat
fat from beef
¼ cup cider vinegar
2 Tbs. pure Wisconsin maple syrup
2 medium-size onions, chopped fine
16 peppercorns
12 whole allspice
2 bay leaves
3 anchovy fillets
2 cups beef stock
arrowroot starch

Have butcher trim fat from meat and include it with roast. Try out fat in a cast-iron pot; brown roast on all surfaces, then drain off all but 2 tablespoons of fat. Add vinegar, maple syrup, onions, spices, and anchovies. Pour in stock, bring to a boil, and let simmer over low heat for 2 ½ hours, or until roast is tender. Thicken the broth with a teaspoon or more of arrowroot mixed with a little water.

MAKES 6 SERVINGS.

BEEF SHANK WITH VEGETABLES

1 beef shank, chopped into pieces about 2 ½ in. thick
½ cup flour
1 tsp. dried savory
1 Tbs. salt
freshly ground pepper
3 Tbs. bacon fat
2 celery ribs, chopped
12 whole allspice
1 ½ cups diced carrots
1 ½ cup diced turnips
2 cups tiny onions
2 Tbs. butter, softened
3 Tbs. port

Wash shank pieces and pat dry. Mix flour with herbs, salt, and pepper, and dredge meat pieces thoroughly; reserve remaining seasoned flour. Brown meat, a few pieces at a time, in hot bacon fat, then put into a large pot or casserole. Add enough water to cover meat by 1 inch; bring to a boil and skim the surface. Add celery and allspice, reduce heat and cover. Let simmer very slowly for 2 ½ to 3 hours, or until meat is tender. Remove meat pieces from pot and set liquid aside to cool until fat rises on top. When it can be easily skimmed off, remove it and strain the liquid. Return meat to the pot with liquid, add carrots, turnips, and onions, and cook until they are just tender, about 30 minutes. With your fingers mix ¼ cup of the reserved seasoned flour with the softened butter and add, in small bits, to the pot, stirring constantly over medium heat to incorporate; use just enough of the butter-flour to thicken to a gravylike consistency. Add port, correct seasoning, and let simmer for another 5 minutes.

MAKES 4 SERVINGS.

SHORT RIBS WITH APRICOTS

5 to 6 Tbs. flour
1 tsp. coarse salt
3 lb. beef short ribs
2 Tbs. goose fat or other flavorful shortening
1 1/2 to 2 cups beef stock
6 whole allspice
6 cloves
1/4 tsp. ground cinnamon
1 cup dried apricots
2 Tbs. brown sugar
2 Tbs. vinegar

Mix flour and salt and dredge meat with it thoroughly. Brown in hot fat in a heavy pan large enough to hold ribs flat in 1 layer; don't crowd; brown only half at a time. When ribs are crusted and brown, drain off fat, return ribs to pan, and cover them with stock mixed with spices. Bring to a boil on top of stove, then reduce heat so that sauce barely simmers when pan is covered. Cook very slowly for 2 1/2 hours. Add apricots, brown sugar, and vinegar, and let simmer for another hour. Remove from heat, let cool, and refrigerate until fat congeals at top and can be easily removed. Then reheat and serve.

MAKES 4 SERVINGS.

SHORT RIBS RANCH-STYLE

3 lb., or more, short ribs of beef
1/4 cup flour
salt
freshly ground pepper
3 to 4 Tbs. fat
1/2 cup chopped onion
1/2 cup chopped celery
1/2 cup chopped, green pepper
1 large garlic clove, minced
1 tsp. ground cuminseed
1/2 tsp. chili powder
1 cup chili sauce
1 cup red wine
1/2 cup brown sugar
1 cup beef consommé

Roll beef ribs in flour seasoned with salt and pepper, then sear in hot fat in a cast-iron pot. Add chopped vegetables and garlic and sauté for 5 minutes or so; sprinkle in cuminseed and chili powder. Add chili sauce, wine, and brown sugar and stir well. Cover with consommé diluted with some water, just enough to cover, and let simmer for 2 1/2 to 3 hours, stirring from time to time and adding a little more consommé and water if sauce condenses too much; it should have the consistency of thick gravy. The dish is not done until meat is about to fall off bones. Correct seasoning, adding more salt and pepper if necessary. The final sauce should be a subtle blend of flavors with only a slight sweet-sour taste, and just fluid enough to pour over rice served as the accompaniment.

MAKES 4 SERVINGS.

PENNSYLVANIA SHORT RIBS WITH PARSLEY DUMPLINGS

2 1/2 lbs. beef short ribs, cut up
2 cups canned tomatoes
1 1/2 cups water
1 Tbs. vinegar
1 Tbs. Worcestershire sauce
2 medium-size onions, sliced
3 bay leaves
1 Tbs. sugar
4 tsp. prepared horseradish
2 Tbs. strong spicy mustard
dash of Tabasco
1 tsp. salt
freshly ground pepper

For best results make this a day ahead of time. Put ribs in bottom of a large flat-bottomed bowl. Mix remaining ingredients and pour over meat, coating well; keep in refrigerator overnight. On the following morning turn meat and marinade into a heavy cast-iron pot. Cover tightly, bring to a boil, then let simmer for about 2 1/2 hours, or until meat is very tender. Chill during afternoon and skim off fat shortly before mealtime. Reheat short ribs in their sauce and serve with parsley dumplings (recipe follows).

PARSLEY DUMPLINGS

2 cups sifted flour
4 tsp. baking powder
1 tsp. salt
pinch of dried thyme
pinch of ground sage
freshly grated nutmeg
3 cloves, ground fine
1/3 cup minced parsley
1 Tbs. butter
1/2 to 1 cup boiling water

Return sifted flour to a sifter and add baking powder, salt, thyme, sage, a liberal grating of nutmeg, and the cloves. Sift on top of parsley in a large bowl. Cut in butter, then mix in boiling water, using just enough to give a stiff consistency. Drop by teaspoonfuls into short-rib stew (preceding recipe), or into soup, chowder, or fricassee.

MAKES 4 SERVINGS.

WEST RIVER COLONIAL BEEF AND KIDNEY PIE

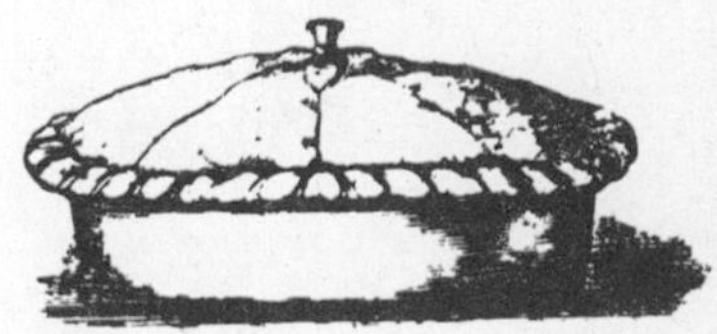

There was no starving time in colonial Maryland, and the rich food served in the homes of lords of manors on both sides of the Chesapeake was royalist in style. Stewed beef kidneys have remained a favorite Sunday breakfast throughout the twentieth century, and more than one house along the Severn River serves claret-braised lamb or veal kidneys with buttermilk-rice waffles. This pie can also be topped with baking powder biscuits.

1 beef kidney (about 1 lb.)
2 lb. lean beef chuck, cut into 1- to 1 1/2-in. cubes
flour
6 Tbs. (3/4 stick) butter
1 medium-size onion, sliced very thin
1/2 lb. fresh mushrooms, sliced
1 cup boiling water
2 tsp. salt
freshly ground pepper
1 tsp. dried rosemary, bruised
1 cup red wine
1 Tbs. flour, mixed with enough water to make a thin paste
1 recipe Basic Piecrust (p. 459)

*Preheat oven to 350° F.**
Cut beef kidney into halves, and freeze 1 part for future use. Soak the other in salted water for 1 hour. Trim any fat from beef cubes, then dredge with flour. Melt the butter in a large, heavy skillet at least 12 inches in diameter; sauté onion over low heat for about 10 minutes, then push to one side. Sear beef cubes quickly, stirring in a few at a time and turning so that surfaces are evenly browned. Drain kidney, trim away fat and gristle, cut into thin slices, and pat dry with paper towels.* In a large heatproof casserole melt remaining 3 tablespoons butter and add sliced mushrooms and kidney, stirring over low heat for about 5 minutes. Turn seared beef cubes and onion into casserole. Rinse the skillet with some of the boiling water to get all the beef and onion juices and pour into casserole. Add remaining boiling water, salt, a few turns from pepper grinder, and the rosemary. Cover, bring to a boil on top of stove, and put in oven for 1 hour. Remove casserole from oven and stir in flour paste to thicken sauce. Return to the oven for 10 minutes more. Meanwhile make pastry dough. Remove casserole from oven, and replace cover with pastry rolled out to fit top of casserole. Or roll out pastry and cut to size and bake separately for about 15 minutes, to place over beef and kidney pie just before serving.

MAKES 6 SERVINGS.

EAST CHICAGO BEEF STEW WITH DILL

4 Tbs. (1/2 stick) butter
3 medium-size potatoes, peeled and cubed
2 medium-size onions, sliced thin
2 Tbs. vegetable oil
1 lb. beef chuck, cut into 1/2-in. cubes
salt
freshly ground pepper
2/3 cup beef stock, hot
1 bay leaf
1/3 cup dry red wine
1 cup sour cream
1 Tbs. chopped fresh dill
1 Tbs. chopped parsley

Preheat oven to 350° F.

In a large skillet melt 3 tablespoons butter and sauté potatoes, turning frequently, until they have turned golden brown. Remove with a slotted spoon and reserve. Add remaining butter, and in the same pan sauté the onions until translucent and golden; remove them too and reserve. Finally add oil to skillet, increase the heat, and sauté meat cubes, a handful at a time, until nicely browned. Now arrange in a casserole first the meat, seasoning it well with salt and pepper, then the onions, and then the potatoes. Pour beef stock over and add bay leaf and wine. Bake, covered, for 1 hour. Shortly before serving pour sour cream over and top with dillweed and parsley. Return to the oven just long enough to warm through and serve from the casserole.

MAKES 4 SERVINGS.

SHIN BONE STEW

5 to 6 lb. beef shinbone or shank
1/4 lb. salt pork
3 medium-size onions, chopped coarse
2 medium-size carrots, chopped coarse
3 garlic cloves, chopped coarse
salt
freshly ground pepper
1/2 tsp. dried thyme
1 bay leaf
about 2 dozen small white onions
12 baby carrots
6 parsnips, cut into halves, thick part into quarters
2 Tbs. butter
1 tsp. sugar
1 lb. fresh peas, or 1 pkg. (10 oz.) frozen
2 tsp. cornstarch dissolved in 1 Tbs. cold water

Cut shinbone about 2 inches thick through the bone with a generous portion of meat surrounding it; you should have 4 ample pieces if cut where there is plenty of meat; set aside. Cut salt pork into small dice and fry in a large, heavy-bottomed casserole or skillet. When browned and crisp, remove to drain on paper towels. Remove all but 1 tablespoon fat. Add shinbone to remaining pork fat and brown on all sides, then pile to one side and lightly brown the chopped onions and carrots. Add garlic and distribute the vegetables around meat, which should now about fill the pan in 1 layer. Add water to cover and sprinkle well with salt, pepper, and thyme. Put bay leaf on top and cover securely. Let simmer very gently for at least 3 1/2 hours. When tender, remove meat, skim off fat (it may be easier to do if you chill for a while first), then reduce liquid by rapidly boiling down to half its volume. Meanwhile, in large skillet, toss whole onions, baby carrots, and parsnips in butter; sprinkle with sugar and keep stirring until nicely glazed. Add a little water, cover, and cook gently for about 10 minutes, then add peas (you may need a little more water) and cook for a few minutes, or until just tender. Stir dissolved cornstarch into reduced meat liquid. Now return meat to pan, scatter vegetables on top, and let simmer for a few minutes. Before serving, sprinkle salt pork over top.

MAKES 8 SERVINGS.

CLUB STEAKS WITH GREEN PEPPERCORN SAUCE

American cooks, apt to try the newest of anything, particularly if it has been featured as the latest rage in Paris, in the 1970s welcomed pickled green peppercorns when they became available here in small glass jars; numerous new ways of cooking with them evolved. This recipe is one of the versions of peppercorn-seasoned beef.

4 individual club steaks (about 1/3 lb. each)
2 tsp. pickled green peppercorns, drained
3 Tbs. butter
coarse salt
1/4 cup dry red wine
3/4 cup rich beef stock or leftover gravy†
2 Tbs. chopped parsley

Trim steaks and melt fat to grease the bottom of a large skillet big enough to hold the 4 steaks comfortably without crowding (otherwise use 2 skillets). Mash peppercorns into butter, crushing each one. Discard any extra fat from the skillet and sear steaks in hot fat, frying for 3 or 4 minutes on each side. Remove to a warm platter and sprinkle with coarse salt. Quickly pour wine into hot skillet; let it sizzle, and reduce by more than half. Add stock and continue to boil until reduced to about 1/3 cup, then swirl in butter-peppercorn mixture. Spoon this sauce over the steaks, sprinkle on parsley, and serve.

†We used some from a beefsteak and kidney pie leftover.

SALT-BROILED STEAK

A Hollywood restaurateur named Dave Chasen derived some extraterritorial notoriety for delivering his own version of chili by air to movie stars on location in foreign parts. Chasen, who spent some time in vaudeville, may have drawn more on his show-biz background when he exploited the method of encasing sirloin in damp salt before submitting it to intense heat. Although his salt-broiled beef is referred to as hobo steak, the sentimentality is no guarantee of anything special; a serious butcher is not apt to recommend the treatment, in spite of its all-American dramatics. The salt doesn't spoil the taste, it simply prevents the development of a charred exterior. What follows is Chasen's method.

2 sirloin steaks (2 in. thick each)
freshly ground pepper
4 cups salt
1 cup water
8 to 12 thin slices of white bread
½ lb. (2 sticks) butter

Liberally sprinkle steaks on both sides with pepper. Put them into a broiler pan, fat edges out. Tie each steak with string running crosswise and dividing each steak roughly into thirds. Put salt into a mixing bowl and add enough of the water to make a soft mush, then spread half of this thick mixture over tops of steaks, making a crust 1 ½ inches thick. Place broiler pan 3 inches below heat and broil for 15 to 20 minutes, or until salt casing begins to heave upward. Remove casing with a spatula and turn steaks. Cover uncooked surface with remaining salt mixture. Return to broiler for 15 to 20 minutes, or until salt begins to separate from meat. Meanwhile toast bread slices and keep warm. Melt butter in a large skillet, but keep it from browning. When meat is broiled on second side, cut into ¼-inch slices and add to hot butter. Sauté very quickly and serve on toast slices.

MAKES 4 TO 6 SERVINGS.

DONN PIERCE'S FIFTIETH STEAK

The late Donn Pierce was a gentleman chef who developed his repertoire in many places, including a ten-year hitch in Hawaii, where he adopted many an Island way with American ingredients. As we do, he believed that flank steak has the best of all beef flavors, and he left this admonishment: "Flank steaks should be treated gently. They can be completely wrecked by overcooking." It reminds one of the cowboy named Ray Pugh, who was in London in 1885 with a Wild West show. When Ray ordered a rare beefsteak, his waiter brought him one so rare that it jerked about on the plate, and Ray drew his piece and fired several shots into the flopping sirloin to kill it dead. The *Breeder's Gazette* reported to its American readers that fifty London bobbies were called to arrest Mr. Pugh, who persuaded them to let him finish devouring the beef that by this time had had just enough exposure to fire.

1 flank steak (about 3 lb.)
1 cup soy sauce
¼ cup sugar
½ cup sherry
1-in. piece of gingerroot, grated fine
1 garlic clove, minced

Cover steak with soy sauce, sugar, sherry, gingerroot, and garlic and set aside to marinate for about 2 hours. Drain, reserving marinade for future use. Broil steak for 5 minutes; turn. Broil other side for about 3 minutes, depending on your own taste and the thickness of the meat.

MAKES 8 SERVINGS.

STUFFED MARINATED FLANK STEAK

1 flank steak (about 2 lb.)
2 medium-size tomatoes, peeled and chopped
1 medium-size onion, chopped
2 garlic cloves, minced
1 tsp. prepared mustard
1 tsp. Worcestershire sauce
1/2 tsp. dried thyme
1 bay leaf, crumbled
1 Tbs. minced parsley
salt
freshly ground pepper
about 1 cup dark beer
about 1 cup beef stock
melted butter
bread crumbs

*Preheat oven to 400° F.**

Trim flank steak of excess fat. Mix tomatoes, onion, garlic, mustard, Worcestershire sauce, and herbs; add salt to taste and several turns of pepper grinder. Spread this mixture on side of meat; roll carefully and tie in 3 places. Put into a bowl just large enough to hold rolled steak and pour over equal amounts of beer and stock. Marinate in refrigerator for at least 8 hours, turning several times. Put roll and marinade into a pot and let simmer for about 2 hours, or until meat is tender.* Remove meat to a baking pan and brush with butter, then sprinkle on bread crumbs. Bake in a hot oven for 15 minutes, or until crumbs are browned. Meanwhile boil down marinade to little more than 1 cup; serve as sauce for meat.

MAKES 4 TO 6 SERVINGS.

FLANK STEAK GRILLADES WITH ORANGE SAUCE

1/2 cup flour
1 Tbs. coarse salt
1 Tbs. paprika
dash of freshly ground black pepper
1 flank steak (about 2 lb.), cut into quarters
3 Tbs. beef fat
1/2 cup chopped green pepper
1 cup chopped shallots or whole scallions
1 cup chopped tomatoes
1/2 cup orange juice
2 cups beef stock
1/4 tsp. dried rosemary
1/4 tsp. dried thyme
2 bay leaves

Mix flour with salt, paprika, and pepper. Pound this mixture into the pieces of steak. Melt fat in a heavy skillet large enough to hold the meat in 1 layer. Sear steaks, then add green pepper, shallots, and tomatoes, orange juice, stock, and herbs. Bring to a boil, then let simmer gently, covered, for 3 hours, or until meat is tender enough to cut with a spoon.

MAKES 4 SERVINGS.

CHICKEN-FRIED STEAK

Dating back to times when beef was not nurtured with tender, loving care, steak identified as chicken-fried or country-fried, or sometimes "smothered," can be prepared with any cut of beef but is obviously no better than the quality of the piece chosen. It is still popular in the South and West, especially at roadside eating places.

2 lb. round steak, cut 1/2 in. thick
2 eggs, lightly beaten
2 Tbs. milk
1 cup flour
1 1/2 tsp. salt
freshly ground pepper
1/2 cup vegetable oil
1 cup heavy cream
1 tomato, peeled and chopped
Worcestershire or hot sauce

Sprinkle steaks with flour and pound with the side of sturdy plate, beating flour into meat and breaking down fibers. Mix eggs with milk, and season remaining flour with salt and pepper. Dip steak in milk mixture and then in seasoned flour. Heat oil to about 400° in a heavy skillet and slide meat in when a slight haze can be seen over the skillet. When well browned on both sides, cover the skillet and let simmer for a few minutes, then transfer to a hot plate or platter. Drain off all but 3 tablespoons fat, and stir in 3 tablespoons remaining flour, scraping up any brown bits left in the skillet. Stir in, a little at a time, about 1 cup cream to make gravy, adding the chopped tomato as the mixture thickens. Season to taste with Worcestershire sauce or hot sauce.

SWISS STEAK

3 lb. beef round (preferably top round) in 1 piece
1/4 cup flour
salt
freshly ground pepper
2 Tbs. bacon fat
2 cups boiling water
1 large onion, sliced thin
1 garlic clove
2 bay leaves
6 to 8 parsley sprigs
1 celery rib
2 whole cloves
8 canned tomatoes, drained, or 1 cup puréed
1 Tbs. prepared mustard
1/2 tsp. ground ginger
1/2 tsp. celery seeds
1/2 tsp. ground cinnamon
1/2 tsp. ground cloves
1/2 tsp. ground allspice
1/2 tsp. grated nutmeg
1/4 tsp. hot pepper sauce
2 tsp. sugar
3 Tbs. vinegar

Rub steak with flour seasoned with salt and pepper, pounding flour into meat as thoroughly as possible. Melt fat in an enameled cast-iron pot large enough to hold meat flat; slash sides of meat to prevent curling, then brown well on both sides. Add water, onion slices, garlic, bay leaves, parsley, celery, and whole cloves. Cover pot and let simmer very slowly for 1 hour. Purée canned tomatoes in a blender and pour over meat along with mustard and all of spices; add sugar and vinegar. Continue simmering for at least 1 hour more, or until meat can be cut with a spoon. Serve with carrots and mashed potatoes.

MAKES 6 TO 8 SERVINGS.

PENNSYLVANIA DUTCH BRAISED ROUND STEAK

2 lb., or a little more, round steak in 1 piece
1/2 tsp. sugar
1/2 lemon
1/2 cup flour
1 Tbs. dry mustard
1 tsp. salt
freshly ground pepper
1/4 cup bacon fat
2 medium-size onions, chopped
2 large celery ribs
1 green pepper, chopped
1/4 lb. fresh mushrooms, chopped
1 cup beef stock

Preheat oven to 275° F.

Rub surface of steak with sugar, then squeeze a few drops of lemon over it and rub with cut side of lemon; repeat on other side. Mix flour, mustard, salt, and several grindings of pepper; sprinkle on meat and pound in, using edge of a heavy plate or meat pounder; use as much flour mixture as meat will absorb. Melt bacon fat in a large cast-iron pot (oval shape is best) and sear meat over brisk heat for about 2 minutes on each side, tending carefully so that flour does not burn. Lift out, letting fat drip back into pot; set meat aside. Sauté vegetables together in the same pot for 3 or 4 minutes, stirring constantly. Return meat to pot and scatter vegetables over. Pour in beef stock, cover tightly, and bring to a boil on top of stove. Then bake for 3 hours. Serve with noodles.

MAKES 4 TO 6 SERVINGS.

SOUTHWEST ROUND STEAK

1/2 cup flour or masa harina
1 1/2 tsps. salt
freshly ground pepper
2 1/2 lb. beef round steak
2 Tbs. beef fat, oil, or lard
6 canned green chilies, chopped
1 Tbs. dried mint
1 green pepper, cut into strips
1 medium-size red onion, chopped
2 cups tomato juice
1 tsp. brown sugar
1/2 tsp. fennel seeds
1/2 cup dry red wine

Season the flour or *masa harina* with salt and pepper and pound this into meat, using the edge of a plate. Heat fat in a heavy skillet or cocotte and brown meat on all sides. Add all the rest of the ingredients. Bring to a boil, then let simmer, covered (there should be the barest burbling of liquid) for 3 to 4 hours. Serve with chick-peas or grits.

MAKES 4 SERVINGS.

SALISBURY STEAK

2 lb. beef round, chopped
5 Tbs. finely minced onion
2 1/2 Tbs. buttermilk
2 Tbs. minced parsley
2/3 cup fresh bread crumbs
freshly ground pepper
salt
2 bacon strips, chopped

Bring chopped beef to room temperature. Add onion and buttermilk and mix lightly but thoroughly with hands. Combine parsley and bread crumbs. Shape meat into a flat oval about 1 1/4 to 1 1/2 inches thick and sprinkle all surfaces evenly with parsley-crumb mixture and several turns of the pepper grinder. Put meat on foil or in a shallow pan, and broil about 3 inches from heat for 3 minutes. Take out and salt cooked side, then turn over and press bacon bits into uncooked side; return and broil 4 inches from heat for about 5 minutes if you like it rare in the center. Season very lightly with salt on bacon side, along with a few turns of the pepper grinder.

MAKES 4 TO 6 SERVINGS.

BEST HAMBURGER EVER

4 large fresh mushrooms
2 Tbs. (1/2 stick) butter
4 scallions, including some of the green part, chopped
2 lb. chuck, freshly ground
1 Tbs. strong mustard
few drops of Worcestershire sauce
1 Tbs. coarse salt
freshly ground pepper
3 Tbs. chopped parsley
1/3 cup dry red wine

Wipe mushrooms with a damp cloth; trim off tough ends of stems and separate stems from caps. Sauté mushroom caps in 1 tablespoon butter. Chop mushroom stems and add. Remove with a slotted spoon when just cooked through, about 5 minutes. In the same skillet sauté scallions gently in remaining butter until limp and translucent. Meanwhile spread out ground meat, smear mustard over, add Worcestershire, and season well with salt and pepper. Add the scallions and most of the butter they were cooked in, leaving only a thin film of fat in the skillet. Toss 2 tablespoons parsley into the meat and mix all gently with your fingers. Divide into quarters and shape 4 large hamburgers, keeping the meat light, *never* slapping it down. Heat the skillet and sauté the hamburgers over quite high heat for about 3 minutes on each side, more if you like them well done. Remove hamburgers and pour the wine into the skillet, cooking over high heat for about 1 minute and scraping up pan juices; add mushrooms and caps to heat through. Serve hamburgers topped with mushroom caps, with winy pan juices poured over and remaining parsley.

MAKES 4 SERVINGS.

BURGERS WITH HAM AND CHEESE

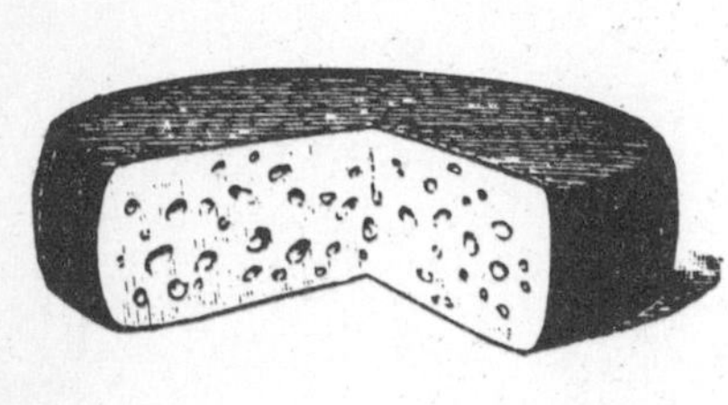

1 1/2 lb. top round or chuck, ground
1/4 cup minced country ham or prosciutto
1/2 cup grated sharp Cheddar cheese

Shape ground beef lightly into 4 hamburgers and broil for 1 minute on each side. Remove from broiler and put 1 tablespoon country ham or prosciutto on top of each burger; top this with 2 tablespoons cheese spread evenly over the ham. Return to broiler and leave for 2 minutes, or until cheese has melted and browned. Very little salt is needed because of the salty ham. Serve freshly ground pepper at the table along with mustard and pickles and other condiments.

MAKES 4 SERVINGS.

CHINATOWN MEATBALLS

1 lb. ground beef
1/2 cup chow mein noodles
1/2 cup sour milk
2 Tbs. coarsely chopped onion
2 garlic cloves
freshly ground pepper
1/2 cup soy sauce
1/4 cup sherry
1 Tbs. sugar
1 tsp. grated gingerroot
2 Tbs. vegetable oil

Put ground beef into a mixing bowl. In a blender spin noodles, sour milk, onion, and garlic until you have a smooth paste, then mix this into meat, adding several turns of pepper grinder. Shape meat mixture into 24 small balls and put them into a large, flat pan. Mix soy sauce, sherry, sugar, and gingerroot and pour this over the meatballs. Let them marinate for about 1 hour, using a bulb baster to saturate the meat from time to time. Drain, reserving the sauce. Heat oil in a skillet and sear meatballs. Add marinating sauce and cook for about 15 minutes, turning 2 or 3 times. Serve with sauce poured over.

MAKES 4 SERVINGS.

LAMB BLANKETED WITH DILL SAUCE

1 large bunch of fresh dillweed (about 1/4 lb.)
5 cups water
8 peppercorns
1 1/2 bay leaves
1 Tbs. salt
3 lb. shoulder of lamb, cut into good-size pieces with bone left in
1 cup uncooked rice
3 Tbs. butter
3 Tbs. flour
1 1/2 Tbs. vinegar (preferably white wine)
1 1/2 tsp. sugar
2 egg yolks

Preheat oven to 375° F.

Mince about 2 tablespoons dill tips and set aside; let remainder simmer in water along with peppercorns, bay leaves, and salt for about 20 minutes; let cool to lukewarm before adding lamb pieces to steep for 30 minutes. Bring to a boil, remove scum, and let simmer for 1 1/2 hours or a little more, or until meat is tender. Meanwhile remove 2 1/2 cups hot broth and strain; put rice into a heatproof dish, pour broth over rice, cover tightly, and bake for 20 to 25 minutes. Let lamb cook for 10 minutes more; remove and keep warm. In a saucepan melt butter, stir in flour, and cook for 2 or 3 minutes. Add remaining lamb broth, stirring until all lumps are eliminated, then add vinegar and sugar. Beat egg yolks lightly, then stir a little hot broth into them, blend this warm mixture into hot lamb sauce; add meat. Adjust seasoning. Serve on a hot platter and sprinkle with reserved minced dill, with baked rice spooned around the meat.

MAKES 4 SERVINGS.

ROAST LEG OF LAMB, BREADED

1 leg of lamb (6 to 7 lb.)
2 to 3 Tbs. vegetable oil
1 tsp. dried thyme leaves
1/4 cup minced parsley
1 1/2 Tbs. minced whole scallions
1 cup tightly packed fresh bread crumbs
1 scant tsp. salt
freshly ground pepper
2 to 3 lemons
parsley sprigs

Preheat oven to 450° F.

Wipe meat with a damp cloth, then with oil. Thoroughly mix thyme, parsley, scallions, bread crumbs, salt, and several turns of pepper grinder. Spread mixture on oily surface of meat, pressing gently so that crumbs will adhere. Put lamb on a rack in a shallow baking pan, sprinkle with the juice of 1 lemon, and roast for about 10 minutes; reduce to 350° and continue roasting until interior temperature is about 145° (160° for well done). Baste occasionally with pan juices and more lemon juice. Let rest a few minutes on a hot platter. Line top of roast with a slice of lemon for each guest and surround meat with a few sprigs of parsley. Parboiled peeled potatoes may be roasted with lamb in the meat juices for last 45 minutes; if this is done, arrange potatoes between parsley sprigs on platter. Carve and serve sliced lamb with lemon quarters.

MAKES 6 TO 8 SERVINGS.

LEG OF LAMB, BUTTERFLIED AND BARBECUED

1 leg of lamb (6 to 7 lb.)
1 garlic clove
1 tsp. dried rosemary
1 cup olive oil
1 celery rib with leaves
1 small bunch of parsley
1 tarragon sprig with leaves

Have butcher remove bone from leg of lamb, so that meat opens out flat, in 1 piece. It will vary in thickness, allowing you easy opportunity to serve well-done pieces to those who like them, rare pieces to others. Mince garlic and add, along with dried rosemary, to oil; put this mixture into a wide, open-mouthed vessel. Find a suitable stick to use as handle and tie celery, parsley, and tarragon securely to one end. Use this as a mop to brush meat with herbed oil at frequent intervals while grilling. Grill 15 minutes over very hot coals, then turn and grill other side about 12 minutes or until done the way you like it.

MAKES 8 SERVINGS.

PUERTO RICAN LEG OF LAMB

When Ponce de Léon abandoned his colony of Puerto Rico in 1513 to search for the Fountain of Youth, he left behind a Spanish community that has maintained a strong gastronomical influence not only on the island but on mainland United States, especially in the lively herbal seasoning that make such dishes as this one a memorable dining experience. In addition, although it must be marinated for 24 hours, this is one of the simpler ways of preparing roast lamb.

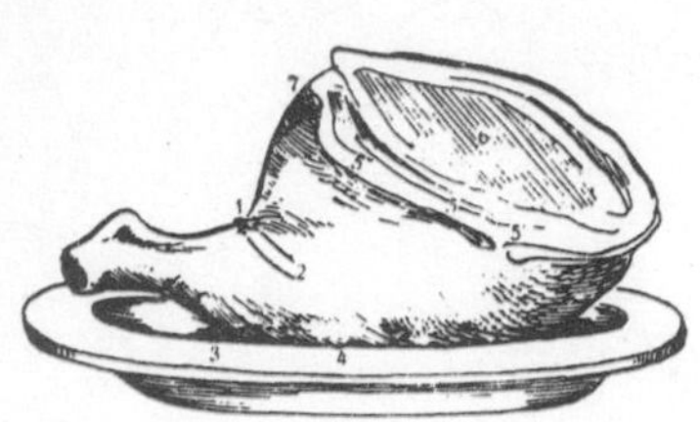

1 leg of lamb (6 lb. or smaller)
2 large garlic cloves
1 1/2 tsp. coarse salt
1 to 2 Tbs. dried oregano
1 tsp. freshly ground black pepper
3 Tbs. olive oil

*Preheat oven to 350° F.**

Use a sharp knife to score fat side of leg of lamb, forming a diamond pattern. The day before serving, mince garlic very fine and put into a mortar, along with coarse salt, oregano, pepper, and olive oil, and mix with a pestle, bearing down hard to bind ingredients into an oily paste. Spread this over all surfaces of meat. Put roast into a shallow container and cover with butcher paper, tucking edges down around meat (foil or plastic wrap may be used); put into lower part of refrigerator. Remove about 3 hours before roasting and let meat come to room temperature.* Put meat on a rack in a shallow roasting pan and roast for about 1 1/2 hours, or 15 minutes per pound. Serve with lamb juices as sauce.

MAKES 8 SERVINGS.

MUSSEL-STUFFED SPIT-ROASTED LAMB

3 lb. fresh mussels
1 1/2 cups cooked rice
1 1/2 cups cooked chopped spinach (10-oz. pkg. frozen or 2 lb. fresh)
1 medium-size onion, or 4 whole scallions, chopped fine
1 garlic clove, minced
1/4 cup minced parsley
2 Tbs. minced fresh basil (purple leaf if available)
1 tsp. minced fresh rosemary
salt
freshly ground pepper
1 leg of lamb (6 to 7 lb.) with shinbone intact, but larger bone removed to leave pocket for stuffing

Scrub mussels under running water, them steam open over a small amount of water in a heavy pot, covered, for 2 or 3 minutes. Remove mussels from shells, mix with rice, spinach, onion, garlic, herbs, salt to taste, and several turns of pepper grinder. Stuff mixture into pocket in lamb made by removal of bone; sew up, sprinkling salt and pepper over outside. Fix lamb on spit and roast close to source of heat for about 2 hours.

MAKES 8 SERVINGS.

BRAISED LAMB SHANKS

Lamb and mutton are far more popular in certain parts of the West and Southwest than in most other regions—not simply because sheep are raised in mountainous areas, but because traditions of early Spanish life are not forgotten. Lamb shanks are often barbecued outdoors in Texas, and they can be prepared in numerous ways in the kitchen to provide an especially succulent meat course; in this case there are hints of Latin-American influences.

4 lamb shanks, about 1 lb. each
1 lemon
1/2 tsp. dried tarragon
1/2 tsp. dry mustard
salt
freshly ground pepper
2 to 3 Tbs. olive or vegetable oil
3 garlic cloves, minced
1 cup freshly brewed strong black coffee
1/2 cup lamb or chicken stock
1/2 cup California red wine
1/3 cup red currant jelly or other fruit preserve
1 tsp. cornstarch dissolved in 1 Tbs. water

Cut lemon in half and rub meat with it; sprinkle meat with tarragon, mustard, salt, and pepper. Brown shanks in oil in a pot large enough to hold them snugly side by side. Add garlic and pour coffee, stock, and wine over meat. Cover pot and let simmer over lowest possible heat for about 2 1/2 hours, turning several times during cooking. Test for doneness—meat should be very tender, so cook longer if necessary. Brush meat with jelly, then glaze under broiler. Thicken meat juices by stirring in cornstarch-water mixture. Put shanks on a hot platter and pour sauce around them.
MAKES 4 SERVINGS.

CURRIED LAMB STEW

"I like a *basic* curry," a British actor in Hollywood said a little edgily, "and not those things you are served in this country that contain a teaspoon of curry powder and are full of fruit and are called curry." Nevertheless, American cooks use a great deal of seasoning that has been described by manufacturers as curry since colonial days. The following recipe calls for curry powder to be augmented by additional spices, and it is a formula for which the old British Empire need not apologize.

2 1/2 Tbs. vegetable oil
4 medium-size onions, chopped
3 Tbs. curry powder
1 tsp. ground coriander
1 tsp. ground cumin
1 tsp. ground allspice
2 lb. lean lamb stew meat, cut into 1 1/2-in. cubes
1 cup chicken stock
3 Tbs. grated gingerroot
3 Tbs. coarsely chopped preserved gingerroot
3 sour apples, peeled and cut into eighths
juice of 1 lemon, more or less
1/4 cup freshly grated coconut (optional)

Trim fat from lamb. Heat oil in a large skillet and cook onions slowly, about 5 minutes. Stir in curry powder, coriander, cumin, and allspice, coating onions; stir in lamb pieces, blending well. Add stock, gingerroot, and preserved gingerroot. Cover skillet and let simmer slowly for about 2 hours. Add apple pieces the last few minutes of cooking—you want them to hold their shape—and stir in lemon juice to taste just before serving. Freshly grated coconut may be sprinkled on top of stew, with chopped egg and sliced bananas served separately as accompaniments.

MAKES 4 TO 6 SERVINGS.

TARPON SPRINGS LAMB STEW WITH PASTA

1 Tbs. olive oil
1 1/2 to 2 lb. lamb in 2-inch cubes
2 onions, chopped
1 1/2 cups tomatoes, peeled and chopped
1 tsp. salt
freshly ground pepper
1/4 tsp. ground cinnamon
1 Tbs. minced fresh mint leaves
1 Tbs. lemon juice
1 qt. boiling water
1 cup small pasta (orzo or riso)
1 cup grated Parmesan cheese

Heat oil in an enameled pot and brown lamb and onions for 10 minutes, stirring to sear meat on all sides. Stir in tomatoes, salt, a liberal grinding of pepper, cinnamon, mint, and lemon juice. Add 2 cups boiling water and let simmer for 1 1/2 to 2 hours, or until lamb is falling off bones. Add remaining 2 cups boiling water and the pasta and cook for about 15 minutes (or according to package directions). Serve with grated cheese.

MAKES 4 SERVINGS.

CHEESE-BREADED LAMB CHOPS

4 lamb chops (about 1 in. thick each)
2 lamb kidneys, cut into halves
1/3 cup grated Parmesan cheese
1 egg, beaten
1 cup fresh bread crumbs
vegetable oil
salt
freshly ground pepper

Trim excess fat from chops and wrap tail of meat around kidney halves, skewering securely. Put cheese on wax paper and press chops into it, covering all surfaces. Dip chops into egg, then into crumbs. Cover the bottom of a skillet large enough to hold all chops flat with about 1/2 inch of oil; heat. Carefully place chops in hot oil and let them brown. Watch closely so that they do not burn; turn after about 4 minutes. Sprinkle top with salt and pepper and cook for about 4 minutes. Reduce heat, cover skillet, and cook for 20 minutes. Drain and serve very hot.

MAKES 4 SERVINGS.

SMITHFIELD OR OTHER COUNTRY HAM

Some country hams come with instructions attached, but generally speaking they require little or no scrubbing, whereas those bearing the Smithfield lable should be well cleaned before cooking. It isn't necessary to bake a ham after it has been boiled, yet there is a certain festiveness in a decorated ham, and there is a added flavor when the following recipe is used.

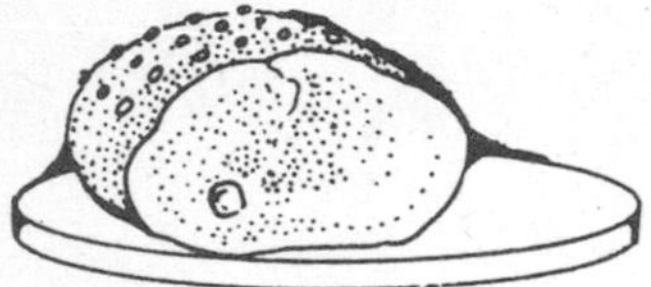

1 Smithfield ham
2/3 cup brown sugar
1/3 cup prepared mustard
1 Tbs. ground allspice
1 tsp. ground cloves
2 cups champagne, scuppernong, or other white wine

Preheat oven to 350° F.

Soak ham for 24 hours if possible, no less than 12 hours, changing water at least 3 times. Scrub soaked ham in hot water with a stiff brush, then wipe with a damp cloth. Put it in a kettle or boiler large enough so that it can be thoroughly covered with water. Let simmer slowly, 18 minutes per pound, or until the shank bone comes out easily. Skin and rub with some of the brown sugar. Mix together remaining sugar, mustard, allspice, cloves, and half the wine, and spread this paste over fatty surface of ham. Bake for 1 hour, pouring remaining wine into bottom of roasting pan. Let cool, then serve by slicing paper thin.

MAKES 8 TO 10 SERVINGS.

SOUTHERN HAM STEAK

6 whole cloves
1 slice country ham, 1 in. thick
freshly grated nutmeg
1/4 cup water
1/2 cup honey
1 cup sliced cooked parsnips
1/2 cup sliced cooked sweet potatoes

Preheat oven to 325° F.

Press cloves into ham surface and sprinkle with grated nutmeg; put in lightly greased baking dish just large enough to hold ham. Mix water and honey and pour over ham. Cover and bake about 45 minutes. Remove from oven and spread parsnips and sweet potatoes over ham. Increase heat to 350° and bake uncovered about 10 minutes, until vegetables are slightly brown.

MAKES 4 SERVINGS.

LIME-ANGOSTURA HAM GLAZE

juice of 1 ½ limes
2 Tbs. currant jelly
1 cup honey
2 Tbs. Angostura bitters

Mix all ingredients in a small saucepan and heat slowly until mixture begins to boil. Remove and keep at room temperature. About 20 minutes before ham finishes baking, increase oven heat to 425° F. and paint ham sides with glaze. Repeat at 5-minute intervals.

MAKES ENOUGH FOR HALF A HAM.

STUFFED HAM SOUTHERN-STYLE

1 whole country ham, boiled
1 ½ cups ground biscuit crumbs
½ cup minced celery
½ cup minced onion
crushed red pepper, to taste
heavy cream

Preheat oven to 425° F.

Use a sharp knife to cut incisions at intervals into meaty part of ham. Spread open these cuts and push in stuffing made by mixing other ingredients to a sticky consistency. Sprinkle remaining stuffing over ham, then bake until golden brown.

SCALLOPED COUNTRY HAM

4 Tbs. (½ stick) butter
3 Tbs. flour
1 ½ cups milk
freshly ground pepper
½ lb. fresh mushrooms, sliced
2 scallions or shallots, minced
2 Tbs. Madeira
2 to 3 Tbs. chopped parsley
½ tsp. dried tarragon
¾ cup crumbled buttered soda crackers
1 ½ cups coarsely ground country ham
3 eggs, hard-cooked and chopped

Preheat oven to 350° F.

Make a white sauce: Melt 3 tablespoons butter, then stir in flour, cooking gently for a few minutes. Remove from heat, then add milk, whisking well. Return to heat until thickened. Season with pepper (avoid salt, as good country ham is apt to be very salty) and set aside.

In a separate pan melt remaining butter and cook mushrooms, scallions or shallots, and Madeira for 3 to 4 minutes. Add parsley and tarragon. In the bottom of a one-quart casserole sprinkle half the cracker crumbs, then add eggs, ham, and cooked mushroom mixture. Pour white sauce over and sprinkle remaining cracker crumbs on top. Bake for about 30 minutes, or until bubbly and browned on top.

MAKES 4 SERVINGS.

MAPLE-FLAVORED HAM STEAK

1-in.-thick slice of corncob-smoked ham (about 1 lb.)
3/4 cup maple syrup
2 Tbs. cider vinegar
2 tsp. dry mustard

Preheat oven to 350° F.

Put ham into a baking dish only slightly larger than the ham slice. Mix remaining ingredients and pour over ham. Cover and bake for 45 minutes.

MAKES 3 TO 4 SERVINGS.

HAM À LA KING

baked country ham
1/4 lb. mushrooms
4 Tbs. butter
1 green pepper
pimiento
1/3 cup milk
1/3 cup chicken broth
1 Tbs. arrowroot
1/3 cup light cream
Madeira
1 egg, separated

Cut enough ham in thin 1 1/2-in. rectangles to make 1 cup. Slice mushrooms and sauté in 2 tablespoons butter with green pepper cut into a half-dozen short strips. Cut pimiento in a few short strips and cook with other vegetables about 1 minute. Make cream sauce by heating in a saucepan the milk and chicken broth and 1 tablespoon of butter. Mix arrowroot and cream to a smooth paste and stir into milk-broth; cook until mixture thickens. Combine sauce with ham, mushrooms, green pepper and pimiento. Stir in 2 tablespoons Madeira and, off heat, add beaten egg yolk.

HAM HOCKS AND GREENS

4 fresh pigs' knuckles
2 qt. cold water
½ tsp. crushed red pepper
1 tsp. salt
freshly ground black pepper
½ lb. salt pork, diced
1 lb. collards, chopped
½ lb. kale, chopped
½ lb. mustard greens, chopped
½ lb. turnip greens, chopped
¼ lb. watercress, chopped
splash of vinegar (optional)
2 eggs, hard-cooked and sliced
4 whole scallions, minced

Put pigs' knuckles into a large pot with a cover and pour in cold water. Add crushed red pepper, salt, and a few turns of pepper grinder. Bring water to a boil, then let simmer, covered, for about 30 minutes. Add salt pork dice to pot and continue simmering, covered, for about 30 minutes more, or until meat is soft and beginning to fall away from bones. Add greens, return to the boil, cover, and let simmer for about 1 hour. Taste and add more salt and freshly ground pepper and vinegar if desired. Use a slotted spoon to put greens and meat onto a serving plate, topping with egg slices and scallions. Serve pot liquor in separate cups, with hot corn bread on the side.

MAKES 4 SERVINGS.

CUMBERLAND HAM LOAF

2 cups ground Tennessee country ham
2 cups ground lean pork
2 eggs, slightly beaten
1 small onion, chopped fine
½ green pepper, chopped fine
½ tsp. dried chervil
½ tsp. dried rosemary
freshly ground pepper
1 cup milk
¾ cup brown sugar
1 tsp. dry mustard
¼ cup cider vinegar
3 slices of fresh pineapple
1 Tbs. red currant jelly

Preheat oven to 375° F.

Combine ham, pork, eggs, onion, green pepper, chervil, rosemary, a few turns of pepper grinder, and milk; mix well. Mix sugar, mustard, and vinegar and spread on bottom of a well-greased 9-inch bread pan. Trim pineapple slices, cutting out core, and press them into sugar mixture in loaf pan; fill holes with jelly. Fill pan with ham mixture. Bake for about 1 ½ hours; if loaf browns too fast, reduce heat to 350° and cover top of meat with greased paper.

MAKES 4 SERVINGS.

DAN OKRENT'S STUFFED FRESH HAM

1 fresh ham (12 to 15 lb., with bone in)
3/4 cup coarsely chopped pistachios, with some whole ones
3/4 cup sultana raisins, presoaked in sherry
1 cup chopped Italian parsley
5 garlic cloves, minced
1/4 cup coarse salt
freshly ground black pepper
1 tsp. dried sage

BASTING SAUCE:
1/3 cup butter, melted
1/3 cup dry sherry
1/3 cup apple jelly

Preheat oven to 325° F.

Wipe ham with a damp cloth. Make stuffing by mixing pistachios, raisins, parsley, and garlic. Rub outside of ham with salt mixed with plenty of pepper and sage, then use a sharp knife to cross-hatch fat on top of pork; stick knife into lean parts of meat, twisting and turning to open up deep holes; stuff these tightly with nut-raisin mixture. Bake for 25 minutes per pound, or until internal temperature is 170°.

Meanwhile make basting sauce by blending sauce ingredients. Baste meat frequently during the last hour of cooking.

MAKES 10 TO 12 SERVINGS WITH LEFTOVERS.

HAM STEAK WITH FRIED APPLE RINGS

1 thick center-cut slice of country ham
1 to 2 Tbs. applejack or hard cider
1 egg, well beaten
3/4 cup milk
1/4 tsp. salt
6 to 8 Tbs. flour
4 tart cooking apples
bacon fat (optional)
brown sugar
ground cinnamon

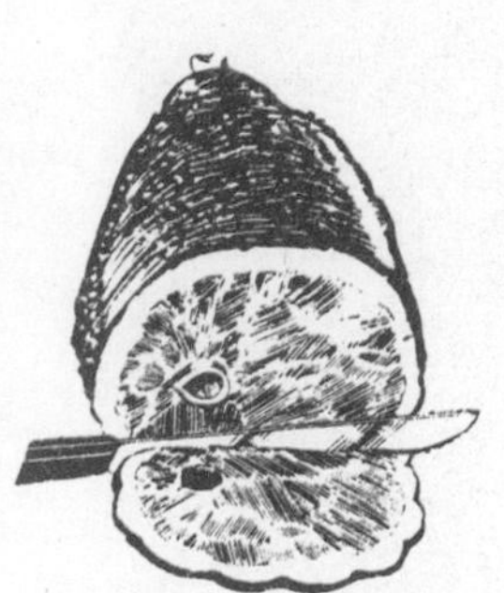

Trim fat from ham and render enough of it to film the bottom of a skillet; reserve the rest. Brown ham on both sides and pour the applejack or cider over. Cover skillet and cook over low heat for 30 minutes, turning several times. Meanwhile beat together egg, milk, salt, and enough flour to make a medium-thick batter. Core unpeeled apples and cut into horizontal slices about 1/3 inch thick. In another skillet melt enough ham fat, or, if there is not enough, bacon fat to cover bottom about 1 inch deep and heat until almost smoking. Dip apple rings into batter and fry a few at a time until golden brown on each side. Arrange ham steak on a platter with a ring of apple slices sprinkled lightly with brown sugar and cinnamon.

MAKES 4 SERVINGS.

CHITLINS

At Salley, South Carolina, near the South Fork of the Edisto River, travelers gather from all over on the late fall day when "Miss Chitlin Strut" is crowned, and they crowd in at long tables outdoors to devour platefuls of this tidbit that is considered a great delicacy by all kinds of people in the South. Chitlins (chitterlings) are boiled and eaten with greens and sometimes dipped into batter and deep-fried. They are best when fresh, as they are at Salley's annual bash, but they can be bought year-round in frozen 10-pound containers (follow package directions for preparation).

10 lb. frozen chitlins, thawed
1/2 cup water
1 medium-size onion
2 celery ribs
3 Tbs. salt
6 whole peppercorns
2 whole garlic cloves
1 tsp. crushed red pepper
1 cup vinegar

Soak chitlins in running water and remove all bits of fat, if necessary—a job that takes a couple of hours. Drain, then rinse again in fresh cold water. Put into a large pot; add remaining ingredients, and let simmer for 3 to 4 hours, or until very tender. Serve with potato salad, greens, corn bread, maybe a turnip pie made in squash or pumpkin pie style, beer, and/or iced tea.

MAKES 8 SERVINGS.

CHINESE-AMERICAN PORK

This easily prepared combination of meat and vegetables can be cooked in either a skillet or a wok, the efficient Oriental concave pan used for stir frying. Few diners will guess that leftover pork may have been used.

3 Tbs. vegetable oil
3 or 4 whole scallions, sliced fine
1 garlic clove
2 slices of gingerroot, the size of quarters
1 cup fresh or dried mushrooms, cut into narrow strips
3 cups julienne strips of cooked lean pork
1/2 tsp. salt
1/2 tsp. sugar
1/4 cup soy sauce
1/4 cup chicken stock
1 tsp. cornstarch mixed with 2 Tbs. water

Heat oil and stir in scallions, the whole garlic clove, and slices of gingerroot; fry for about 1 minute. Add mushrooms (soaked for 20 minutes and drained, if you are using dried), pork, salt, sugar, soy sauce, and stock; cook for about 5 minutes over medium-high heat, stirring and tossing. Stir in cornstarch mixture and heat, stirring, until the sauce has thickened. Serve on boiled rice.

MAKES 4 TO 6 SERVINGS.

FLORIDA PORK BACK RIBS

3 lb. pork back ribs, cut into pieces
2 tsp. salt
3/4 tsp. Tabasco
1/2 cup finely minced onion
3/4 cup orange juice
1/2 cup water
1 lemon, sliced thin
2 tsp. arrowroot starch

Preheat oven to 300° F.

Parboil meat for 15 minutes; let cool. Rub salt and Tabasco into meat. Place fatty side down in skillet and cook over low heat to render some of fat; pour off all but 3 tablespoons fat. Add onion and continue cooking for 3 or 4 minutes. Transfer meat and onion to a shallow baking dish, add orange juice and water, and bake, uncovered, for 2 hours, basting frequently. Skim off fat (or drain most of juices into a shallow dish, put into freezing compartment of refrigerator, then skim when fat has congealed). Meanwhile put lemon slices on top of meat pieces and return to oven for 30 minutes. Blend the defatted juices with arrowroot starch by shaking together in a covered jar; mix this with meat juices in baking dish and let thicken in oven for 5 minutes more. Serve with baked tomatoes.

MAKES 4 SERVINGS.

ROAST PORK WITH APPLES AND APPLEJACK

Some cooks in apple-growing regions began developing unique recipes flavored with applejack soon after this American version of apple brandy was first produced in New Jersey in the late seventeenth century. Pork lends itself well to variations, and this roast with apples and potatoes is a very successful main course at our house.

5-lb. pork loin roast, chops cracked
3/4 cup applejack
1 Tbs. coarse salt
freshly ground black pepper
freshly grated nutmeg
1/4 tsp. ground cloves
2 or 3 allspice berries, crushed
6 medium-size potatoes
6 large tart apples
1/2 cup brown sugar
1/4 tsp. ground cinnamon

Preheat oven to 325° F. *

Marinate pork in applejack for at least 4 hours (or overnight), spooning liquid over meat several times. About 3 hours before dinner, drain and save marinade. * Rub pork on all surfaces with salt, a generous amount of pepper, a liberal grating of nutmeg, the ground cloves, and allspice. Put the meat on a rack in a roasting pan and roast for 2 hours. About 1 hour before serving, peel potatoes and boil in salted water for about 5 minutes. Drain, cut into quarters, and pat dry. Pour off fat from roasting pork into a shallow metal pan, toss potatoes in fat, then spread them out in roasting pan and let them roast in oven beside pork. Peel and core apples, then slice. Remove pork from its pan and spread apples around bottom of pan; sprinkle them with brown sugar and cinnamon. Warm the marinade, add a little extra applejack if you choose, set it aflame, and pour over apples. Return pork to bed of apples and continue roasting for 45 minutes or more, or until pork is very tender. If meat seems to be getting dry, cover with foil. Turn potatoes about 30 minutes after they begin to roast; if they are not really crisp, increase heat to 500°, remove tender roast and apples, and cook potatoes for about 5 minutes while pork rests.

MAKES 8 SERVINGS.

SOUTHWESTERN-STYLE PORK ROAST

5 to 6 lb. pork loin roast
2 tsp. salt
1 tsp. dried oregano
1 1/2 tsp. dried oregano
1 1/2 tsp. cuminseed
3 cloves garlic, minced
1/4 cup flour
2 cups puréed tomatoes
2 tsp. chili powder
1 cup water
1/2 cup sliced black olives
1/2 cup raisins
1/2 cup canned green chili peppers, chopped

Preheat oven to 350° F.

Wipe pork with a damp cloth, then pound salt, oregano, 1 teaspoon cuminseed, and the garlic with a mortar and pestle and spread over pork on all sides; let stand at room temperature for 1 to 2 hours. Roast about 2 1/4 hours, or until internal temperature is 165°.

Remove pork to a hot platter in a warm place. Pour off all but about 1/4 cup fat in roasting pan and stir in flour, cooking over medium heat long enough to thicken slightly; stir in tomatoes, chili powder, and water. When sauce is smooth, add olives, raisins, chili peppers, and remaining 1/2 teaspoon cuminseed; serve on the side.

MAKES 8 SERVINGS.

STUFFED PORK CHOPS

1 large onion, chopped
6 Tbs. butter
1/2 green pepper, seeded and chopped
2 cups fresh bread crumbs
3 Tbs. chopped parsley
salt
freshly ground pepper
1/2 tsp. thyme
1 tsp. dried crushed rosemary
1 Tbs. cooking oil
4 thick pork chops
cayenne pepper

Preheat oven to 300° F.

Sauté onion in butter until translucent but still firm. Add chopped pepper and sauté one minute more. Toss the bread crumbs with the sautéed onions and peppers and cooking butter. Add parsley, salt and pepper to taste, thyme, and rosemary. Sauté the pork chops in just enough oil to film the bottom of the pan, browning quickly on each side. Transfer to an oiled baking dish that will hold chops in a single layer. Distribute even amounts of the stuffing on top of each chop, covering all over and pressing lightly to adhere. Cover loosely with foil. Bake in a 300° oven for almost 2 hours until very, very tender. Remove foil for last 10 minutes of baking.

MAKES 4 SERVINGS.

PORK TENDERLOIN WITH HERBS

2 Tbs. minced fresh rosemary
3 large basil leaves, minced
1/4 tsp. dried oregano
1 tsp. dried sage leaves
1 Tbs. minced Italian parsley
3 Tbs. finely chopped pancetta or bacon
2 garlic cloves, minced
2 lb. pork tenderloin
salt
freshly ground pepper
2 Tbs. olive oil
3 bay leaves

SAUCE:

3 Tbs. olive oil or butter
3 Tbs. chopped onion
3 Tbs. flour
1 Tbs. minced fresh tarragon
1 tsp. minced Italian parsley
1/4 tsp. freshly grated nutmeg
cayenne pepper
paprika
1/2 cup cream
salt
freshly ground pepper
1/2 cup dry white wine
3/4 cup Marsala

*Preheat oven to 400° F.**

Combine first 7 ingredients, spread mixture over pork and put into a baking dish. Cover and set aside for about 3 hours.* Add oil and bay leaves to baking dish. Roast pork, uncovered, for 45 minutes, reducing heat to 375° immediately. Baste every 10 minutes or so.

While meat is roasting, make sauce: Heat oil or butter in a saucepan, then add onion and cook gently until golden. Stir in flour and cook until it begins to turn light brown. Stir in herbs and spices, add cream, and cook long enough to thicken mixture. Season to taste with salt and pepper. Add white wine and Marsala, blend well, and continue cooking over very low heat for about 10 minutes. When pork is done, remove to a hot platter and pour sauce over it.

MAKES 4 TO 6 SERVINGS.

PORK TENDERLOIN WITH SAGE AND TURNIPS

1 tsp. dried sage leaves
2 tsp. coarse salt
freshly ground pepper
2 garlic cloves
2 pork tenderloins
4 Tbs. (1/2 stick) butter
1 large onion, sliced
1 carrot, sliced
1/2 cup water
18 small white turnips, peeled
1 tsp. brown sugar

Preheat oven to 375° F.

Use a mortar and pestle to pound sage, salt, pepper, and garlic, then coat tenderloins thoroughly. Melt butter in a flameproof dish large enough to hold pork. Sauté onion and carrot for about 2 to 3 minutes, then add pork, turning it in butter to coat all over. Add water, cover loosely with foil, and bake about 45 minutes; baste 2 or 3 times. Parboil turnips in boiling salted water for about 15 minutes, or until barely tender; drain, then sprinkle with brown sugar. Add turnips to pork for the last 10 minutes of cooking. When pork reaches an internal temperature of 160°, reduce liquid over high heat, slightly turning turnips in the remaining juice until golden. Slice pork and turnips thinly and serve in the baking dish, topped with pan juices, along with panfried potatoes and applesauce seasoned with cinnamon and nutmeg.

MAKES 4 TO 6 SERVINGS.

CRUST-WRAPPED PORK TENDERLOIN

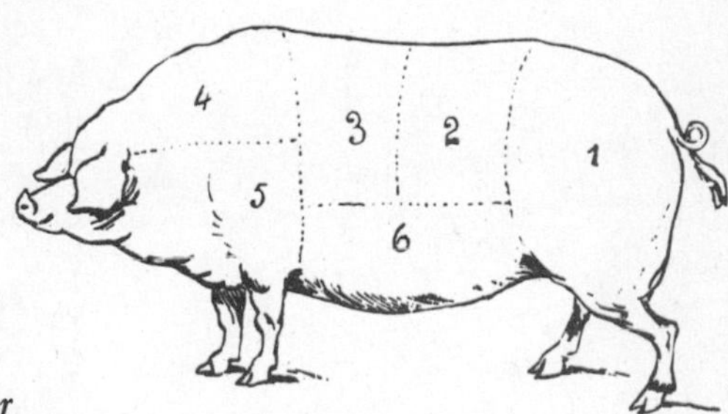

1 pork tenderloin
2 tsp. coarse salt
freshly ground pepper
2 tsp. finely minced fresh rosemary
2 garlic cloves, chopped
3 Tbs. butter
1 egg, beaten with 1 tsp. water
branches of rosemary for garnish

PASTRY:

2 cups flour
1 tsp. salt
2/3 cup shortening
1/3 to 1/2 cup water

Preheat oven to 375° F. *
Sprinkle all surfaces of tenderloin with coarse salt, a liberal dusting of pepper, the rosemary, and the garlic. Set pork aside to marinate for 2 to 3 hours or longer; drain. *

Meanwhile make the pastry: Combine flour, salt, then cut in the shortening. Add water a little at a time to make a pastry that can be easily rolled to less than 1/4 inch thickness.

Melt butter in a skillet and carefully brown all surfaces of pork. Put browned meat on rolled-out pastry, bringing edges together to enclose meat and sealing with water. Put the roll, seam side down, into a flat baking dish. Brush pastry with beaten egg and water. Bake for 45 minutes, or until internal temperature of pork is 160°. Garnish with rosemary branches.

MAKES 4 SERVINGS.

PORK RIBLETS BILOXI

1 lb. pork riblets
about 2 Tbs. oil
salt
freshly ground pepper
2 dried hot red peppers
2 onions, chopped
2 celery ribs, chopped
1 green pepper, chopped
1 1/2 cups canned plum tomatoes, with juice
2 Tbs. brown sugar
2 Tbs. cider vinegar

Preheat oven to 300° F.
Trim riblets of excess fat and sear in just enough oil to film the skillet. When browned on all sides, remove. Sprinkle on salt and pepper liberally and place in a casserole dish. Add remaining oil and, when good and hot, drop in dried red peppers, frying until they turn black. Reduce heat to moderate and sauté onions, celery, and green pepper for about 5 minutes, turning frequently. Add tomatoes and their juice, brown sugar, and vinegar. Taste and correct the seasoning, bring to a boil, then pour this sauce over the meat in the casserole. Cover and bake for 45 minutes. Remove hot peppers before serving and have warm corn bread on the side.

MAKES ABOUT 4 SERVINGS.

CALIFORNIA SWEET AND SOUR PORK

1 ½ lb. pork tenderloin, cut into 1-in. cubes
¼ cup vegetable oil
salt
freshly ground pepper
¼ cup brown sugar
½ cup cider vinegar
1 small tomato, peeled, seeded, and mashed
3 Tbs. soy sauce
3 Tbs. cornstarch dissolved in ½ cup water
2 small onions
1 green pepper
1 cup fresh pineapple chunks
2 firm tomatoes, cut into wedges

Put pork cubes into a saucepan, cover with boiling water, and let simmer for about 5 minutes; drain until almost dry. Heat oil in a large skillet and brown meat on all surfaces, adding a little salt and pepper. Remove pork with a slotted spoon and put on paper towels to drain; reserve oil in skillet. Mix sugar, vinegar, mashed tomato, soy sauce, and cornstarch mixture in a saucepan; bring to a boil, stirring constantly until sauce is smooth and shiny. Peel onions and cut into quarters, then cut quarters in half horizontally and put these curled pieces into the skillet used for the pork. Cut green pepper into similar pieces and add to skillet along with browned pork. Stir to coat with oil and cover, cooking for about 5 minutes. Add pineapple chunks and stir thoroughly; continue cooking for about 10 minutes. Stir in tomato wedges just before serving and let them heat.

MAKES ABOUT 4 SERVINGS.

RABBIT WITH HAM AND HERB SAUCE

1 rabbit (about 2 lb.), cut up
2 Tbs. butter
2 Tbs. oil
1 medium-size onion, minced
1 garlic clove, minced
1 rabbit liver, chopped
½ cup minced country ham or Italian-style ham
1 Tbs. flour
½ tsp. dried rosemary
½ tsp. dried thyme
½ tsp. grated lemon rind
1 cup chicken stock
½ to ¾ cup dry white wine
1 Tbs. chopped mint
toast points for 4 persons
2 Tbs. minced parsley

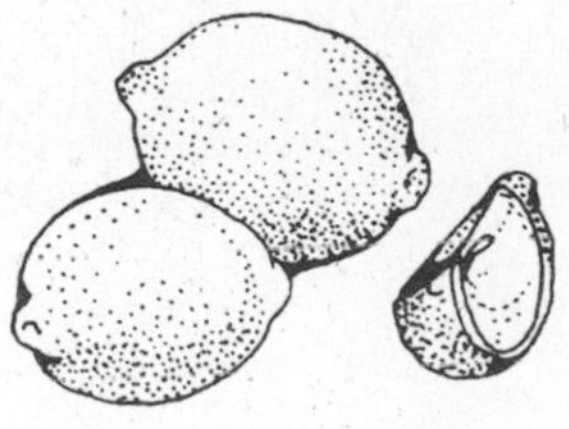

Wipe rabbit pieces with paper towels. In a skillet large enough to fit the meat side by side in a single layer, melt butter and add 1 tablespoon oil. Brown meat in several batches on all surfaces; remove and keep in a warm place. Add remaining oil to skillet and sauté onion and garlic for about 2

minutes. Stir in liver and ham, sprinkle in flour, and continue stirring over heat for about 2 minutes, sprinkling in herbs and lemon rind. Add stock and wine and stir until sauce is smooth and thickened. Now return rabbit pieces to skillet, turning pieces to cover well with sauce and regain heat. Cover skillet and let simmer over very low heat for about 1 1/2 hours, or bake in preheated 325° F. oven. About 15 minutes before serving, stir mint into sauce. Make toast or fry bread triangles in butter. Top with rabbit pieces and their sauce, and sprinkle with parsley.

MAKES 4 SERVINGS.

SOUTH ST. LOUIS RABBIT STEW

Domestic rabbit tends to be a little bland, tasting more like chicken. Twenty-four hours or a couple of days in this bath gives the meat of rabbits raised as a crop a "gamy" flavor.

MARINADE:

1 1/2 cups red wine
3/4 cup water
3/4 cup wine vinegar
1 medium-size onion, chopped coarse
1 carrot, cut into chunks
2 celery ribs
1 garlic clove, crushed
1/2 tsp. dried dillweed
1/2 tsp. mustard seeds
1/2 tsp. coriander berries, bruised
1/2 tsp. peppercorns, bruised

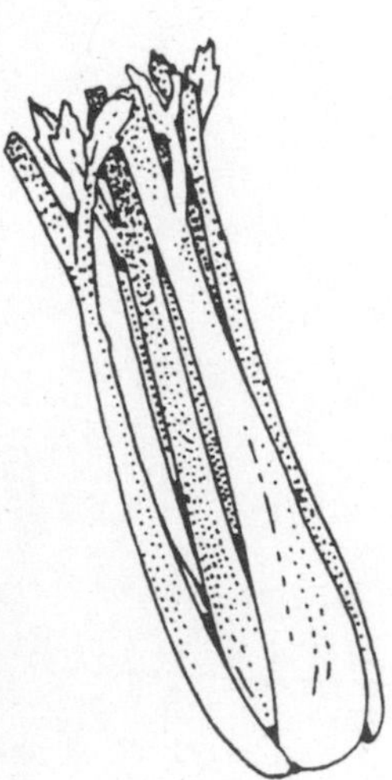

STEW:

1 rabbit (3 to 4 lb.), cut into pieces
1/4 lb. bacon, diced
1 Tbs. butter
1/2 lb. fresh mushrooms, sliced
8 small white onions
2 Tbs. flour
1 cup beef stock
1 cup red wine
1 Tbs. minced parsley
2 carrots, sliced
1 small bay leaf
salt
freshly ground black pepper

Mix marinade ingredients in a large bowl, adding about 3/4 cup of water, which should be enough to cover 4 pounds of rabbit cut in pieces. Turn rabbit occasionally so meat steeps evenly.

Put bacon and butter into a heavy pot and cook until bacon browns. Add rabbit pieces and sauté, browning all surfaces; stir in mushrooms and onions and sauté until onions brown. Add flour and blend into fat. Off the heat, stir in stock and wine, parsley, carrots, and bay leaf. Return to the heat and let simmer gently for about 2 hours, depending upon tenderness of rabbit.

MAKES 6 SERVINGS.

SWEETBREADS CALIFORNIA-STYLE

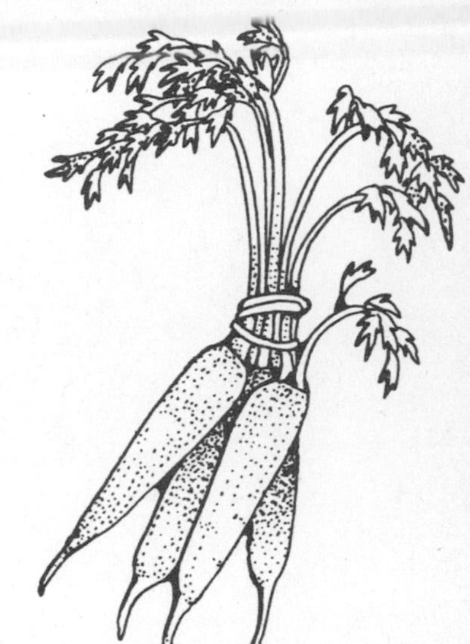

1 lb. sweetbreads
2 Tbs. butter
2 Tbs. olive oil
1 medium-size onion, chopped
1 carrot, chopped
1 celery rib, chopped
3 oz. country ham, chopped (about 1/3 cup)
1/3 cup white wine
1/2 cup chicken stock
2 anchovy fillets, cut into small pieces
3 parsley sprigs
1 bay leaf
1/4 tsp. dried thyme
1/4 lb. fresh mushrooms, sliced
1/4 cup almonds, blanched and sliced
1 1/2 Tbs. flour
1/4 cup Madeira
1/4 to 1/2 cup milk
1/3 cup green olives, sliced

Preheat oven to 300° F.

Blanch the sweetbreads by covering with water acidulated with lemon juice—1 tablespoon to a quart; let simmer for 20 minutes, then plunge into cold water. When cool, remove outer membranes and cut into rough pieces. Heat 1 tablespoon butter and 1 tablespoon oil, and sauté onion, carrot, and celery for about 3 minutes, then add ham and sweetbreads. Toss over heat for a few minutes until lightly browned; add wine and stock. Put mixture into a baking dish along with anchovies and seasonings, and bake, covered, for 45 minutes. A few minutes before removing, sauté mushrooms in remaining olive oil; add to the casserole, then toast almonds lightly in the same pan. In a small saucepan melt remaining 1 tablespoon butter, stir in flour, cook for a few minutes, then add Madeira, the liquid from the casserole, and enough milk to make a lightly thickened sauce; taste and correct the seasoning. Pour this over the sweetbreads, add olives, and top with toasted almonds. Heat through and serve with toast croutons or rice.

MAKES 4 SERVINGS.

STUFFED VEAL BREAST

Among some Midwestern cooks, veal was never considered acceptable in the days before the Depression. But Polish cooks who settled in Minnesota, Wisconsin, and Illinois adapted Old World recipes, including those that called for wine, which was not easily available during the Prohibition period; the recipe below was sometimes zipped up with homemade vodka, and the delicate flavor of veal was enhanced by herbs.

4 lb. breast of veal
5 Tbs. butter
2 medium-size onions, chopped
6 garlic cloves, minced
2 cups dry bread cubes
salt
freshly ground pepper
½ tsp. dried savory
½ tsp. dried marjoram
½ cup milk
1 egg
4 Tbs. chopped parsley
1 bay leaf
1 Tbs. vegetable oil
½ cup white wine or half vodka and half water

Preheat oven to 325° F.

Wash meat and wipe dry. Cut pocket next to ribs with a sharp knife. Melt 3 tablespoons butter in a skillet and sauté half the onions and half the garlic for about 3 minutes without browning. Toss in bread cubes and stir well, then let cool. Season to taste with salt and pepper and add herbs. Beat milk and egg together and stir into bread cubes. Fill pocket and fasten with a skewer. Sprinkle top with half of the chopped parsley, then put veal in a roasting pan along with the remaining parsley, remaining onion, the bay leaf, remaining garlic, the oil, butter, and the wine or vodka. Bring to a boil on top of the stove. Roast veal, uncovered, for about 1 ½ hours, basting every 15 minutes (add a little water to keep enough liquid). Cover and continue roasting for 1 ½ hours more.

MAKES 6 TO 8 SERVINGS.

SANTA CRUZ VEAL RAGOUT WITH ARTICHOKES AND TOMATOES

6 Tbs. olive oil
3 lb. veal shoulder with some bone, cut into 2-in. cubes
2 medium-size onions, chopped
4 garlic cloves, minced
2 bay leaves
2 tsp. dried rosemary
1 tsp. salt
freshly ground pepper
¾ cup Pinot Chardonnay white wine
¼ cup minced parsley
2 pkg. (9 oz. each) frozen artichokes
1 large can (28 oz.) Italian plum tomatoes, chopped coarse

Heat oil in a large cast-iron pot and brown veal on all surfaces. Stir in onions and garlic and cook for 5 minutes, scraping onions from bottom of pot. Add bay leaves, rosemary, salt, and several turns of pepper grinder; pour in wine. Cover tightly and let simmer over very low heat for 1 hour. Add parsley, artichokes, and tomatoes and most of their juice and cook for 30 minutes or more, until veal is very tender.

MAKES 6 SERVINGS.

ROAST VEAL WITH KIDNEYS

In many parts of the country, especially Saint Louis (which began as a French outpost, then became American, and later acquired a very strong German character during the nineteenth century), a kidney-veal roast was a favorite of housewives, who sometimes flavored it with nasturtium seeds.

4 to 5 lb. veal roast with veal kidney
12 to 15 canned anchovy fillets, drained
2 Tbs. butter or oil
1 garlic clove, minced
1/4 cup applejack
1 3/4 cup cider or white wine
2 carrots, sliced
2 medium-size onions, chopped
1 large onion, unpeeled
salt
freshly ground black pepper
chopped parsley

Preheat oven to 375° F.

Spread out meat for stuffing. Place kidney on veal and distribute anchovies evenly; roll kidney up and tie. Heat butter or oil in a large cast-iron pot and in it brown all surfaces of roast; stir garlic into hot fat. Add applejack and cider or wine, and stir in carrots and chopped onions. Cover the pot and bake for 2 to 2 1/2 hours. At the same time, put an unpeeled onion in the oven to bake. After 1 hour reduce heat to 350° and add salt and pepper to taste. By this time the onion should be charred and soft; remove skin, mash soft interior, and add to veal and vegetable juices in pot. Continue cooking until meat can be cut with a spoon. Sprinkle finished roast with chopped parsley.

MAKES 8 SERVINGS.

VEAL SCALLOPS WITH CRAB MEAT

It is not uncommon to find various cuts of veal served in combination with seafood in the Middle West. Veal steaks, encased in egg, minced mushrooms, and cornflake crumbs, sometimes go to the table with asparagus spears and a sherry-flavored lobster sauce. Veal chops are served with crab and asparagus. None of these recipes is better than this way with thinly pounded scallops.

8 veal scallops, pounded thin
flour
1 1/2 tsp. salt
freshly ground pepper
1 tsp. dried marjoram
3 Tbs. vegetable oil
2 to 3 Tbs. minced parsley

CRAB-MEAT SAUCE:

3 Tbs. butter
2 Tbs. flour
1 1/2 cups milk
1 tsp. salt
cayenne pepper
1/2 to 3/4 cup crab meat
1 tsp. lemon juice
2 Tbs. sherry
1 egg yolk
2 to 3 Tbs. minced parsley

Dust each piece of veal thoroughly in seasoned flour, then sauté quickly over brisk heat for about 1 minute per side.

Make crab-meat sauce: Melt butter and stir in flour until smooth, then gradually add milk off the heat, stirring constantly to make a well-blended mixture; return to heat to thicken, adding salt and a dash of cayenne. Flake crab meat and stir into sauce. Just before serving, add lemon juice, sherry, and egg yolk, stirring over low heat for about 1 minute. Before serving, cover veal with sauce and sprinkle with parsley.

MAKES 4 SERVINGS.

VEAL COLLOPS WITH CUCUMBER SAUCE

Earlier American cooks seem to have found many delicious ways to serve cooked cucumbers, as a single hot vegetable or as an integral accompaniment to meat or fish. One rule of thumb asserted that cucumbers must be served "under meat and over fish." An affinity for veal was established long ago by New England cooks, and this recipe breaks the rule by topping the meat with cucumbers.

2 cucumbers (6 to 7 in. long), peeled and sliced thin
6 Tbs. butter
8 or 9 medium-size shallots, sliced
1/2 to 3/4 cup sour cream
1/2 tsp. dried thyme
salt
freshly ground pepper
1 1/2 lb. leg of veal, cut and pounded into thin collops about 2 by 3 in., at room temperature

Cover sliced cucumbers with boiling water and parboil for 10 minutes; drain. Melt 3 tablespoons butter in a saucepan and sauté shallots over low heat for 10 minutes. Stir in cucumbers, sour cream, thyme, and salt and pepper to taste. Let simmer over lowest possible heat for 10 minutes.

Meanwhile, trim veal of any remaining fat or gristle. Melt remaining 3 tablespoons butter and sauté collops for about 4 minutes on each side. Season with salt and pepper to taste, and serve topped with cucumber sauce.

MAKES 6 SERVINGS.

BAKED VEAL STEW WITH CHOW MEIN NOODLES

Poet Louis Untermeyer and his wife for years had an Ohio farmwife named Clara as a cook. "Though she was never out of her county," Untermeyer once wrote, "Clara has learned to cook in any language; the more exotic, the more brilliant." Clara's wine-baked veal is another example of Americanism in the kitchen—a touch of *blanquette de veau*, a little *zöldpaprika*, and crisp so-called chow mein noodles invented by Chinese Americans. The combination of contrasting flavors and textures is unusual and a delight to the palate.

1 1/2 lb. lean veal (leg preferred), trimmed and cut into 1 1/2-in. cubes
1/4 lb. (1 stick) butter
1 Tbs. flour
1 1/2 cups milk
1/4 cup chopped green pepper
1/4 tsp., or more, salt
freshly ground pepper
5 to 6 Tbs. California white wine
1 can (3 oz.) chow mein noodles

Preheat oven to 350° F.

Make sure veal cubes are free of gristle. In a heavy skillet melt butter, add meat, and cover tightly to steam over very low heat for about 20 minutes. After 10 minutes turn meat pieces so that all sides are exposed to butter. Increase heat, remove cover, and let moisture evaporate; then fry veal, stirring frequently, so that cubes brown lightly on all surfaces. Add flour and stir constantly, letting it brown lightly and scraping the bottom of the pan. Remove pan from heat and continue stirring and scraping while adding milk. Return to heat and cook slowly until sauce thickens and is smooth. Stir in green pepper, salt, and a few turns of pepper grinder. Pour into a 1 1/2-quart casserole, cover with foil, and bake for 45 minutes. Remove foil, add wine, a little at a time, and spread noodles over top. Increase heat to 500° and leave dish in oven for 5 minutes more to turn noodles very crisp, being careful not to burn them or boil sauce hard. Serve very hot.

MAKES 2 TO 4 SERVINGS.

BEEF LIVER HILO-STYLE

The Hawaiian way of combining livers, spices, soy sauce, and water chestnuts, then broiling them with bacon, is a favorite cocktail nibble in most of the fifty states. The version below is a meal, very rich and moist and not for those who like liver cooked dry.

1 lb. beef liver, cut into 4 slices
1/2 cup soy sauce
1/2 cup peanut oil
1/2 cup applejack
2 Tbs. sugar
1/4 tsp. ground ginger
1 tsp. minced lemon rind
1 can (6 oz.) water chestnuts, drained and sliced
4 bacon strips, cut into squares
4 Tbs. (1/2 stick) butter
1/2 cup bread crumbs
2 bananas, sliced

Preheat oven to 350° F. *
Wipe liver with a damp cloth. Stir together soy sauce, oil, applejack, sugar, ginger, and lemon rind. Marinate meat and water chestnuts in the mixture for 2 hours. About 30 minutes before serving time, sauté bacon pieces, then drain on paper towels.* In a saucepan melt most of butter and stir in bread crumbs. Butter a shallow baking dish. Drain liver and water chestnuts thoroughly and put into the baking dish; arrange banana slices on top and spread with buttered crumbs. Bake for 20 minutes.

MAKES 4 SERVINGS.

BEEF LIVER IN HERBED WINE

1 to 1/2 lb. beef liver, cut into 1/2-in. slices
3 Tbs. butter
3/4 tsp. dried rosemary
1/2 tsp. dried sage
2 large whole scallions, minced
3 Tbs. dry sherry
2 Tbs. port
salt
freshly ground pepper

Cut sliced liver into rectangles 1 by 1 1/2 inches. Melt butter in a skillet and stir in herbs and scallions. Add liver pieces and sauté, turning to brown evenly on both sides. Add sherry and port over brisk heat, bringing wine to just below boiling point. Season to taste. Serve immediately over hot rice.

MAKES 6 SERVINGS.

CALF'S LIVER WITH JUNIPER-BUTTERMILK SAUCE

1 1/2 cups buttermilk
4 thick slices of calf's liver
4 Tbs. (1/2 stick) butter
1/4 cup bouillon
1/2 cup fresh bread crumbs
8 juniper berries, well crushed
1 Tbs. flour
1 tsp. salt
freshly ground pepper

An hour before cooking time, pour buttermilk over liver slices and set aside. Drain when liver has soaked for at least 1 hour; reserve buttermilk which will have absorbed some of the meat juices, and warm over very low heat. Melt 1 tablespoon butter in a skillet and brown liver carefully over moderate to high heat, then turn very low and cook for 10 minutes, basting with bouillon. Meanwhile in a small pan melt remaining 3 tablespoons butter, then stir in bread crumbs, juniper berries, flour, salt, and several turns of pepper grinder. When flour has absorbed butter smoothly, remove pan from heat and whisk in warmed buttermilk. Pour over liver slices and cook for 4 to 5 minutes, or until sauce thickens slightly. Serve with sautéed mushrooms.

MAKES 4 SERVINGS.

CREOLE CALF'S BRAINS

3 pairs of calf's brains
1 Tbs. lemon juice
salt
4 Tbs. (1/2 stick) butter, melted
1/2 lb. fresh mushrooms, sliced
2 Tbs. minced shallots or white part of scallions
2 Tbs. flour
1 cup chicken stock
2 to 3 Tbs. minced celery
2 Tbs. minced parsley
1/2 tsp. dried savory
1/2 cup heavy cream
2 Tbs. Madeira
freshly ground pepper
bread crumbs

Preheat oven to 425° F. *

Soak brains in cold water for 30 minutes, changing water 2 or 3 times; drain. Put into a saucepan and cover with boiling water; add lemon juice and about 1 teaspoon salt. Let simmer gently for 20 minutes. Drain and plunge into cold water. Meanwhile place 2 tablespoons butter in a saucepan and sauté mushrooms and shallots or scallions for 5 minutes. Stir in flour, mixing well, and cook for another minute or two. Off the heat, pour in chicken stock, celery, and herbs, then return to heat and cook slowly, stirring constantly, until sauce is thick and smooth. Add cream and Madeira, blend well, and season to taste with salt and pepper.* Now remove membranes from the cooled brains and slice them about 1/3 inch thick. Place them in a shallow casserole, pour the sauce over, and sprinkle bread crumbs on top, dribbling over them the remaining 2 tablespoons butter. Bake the casserole just until it bubbles and has browned on top, about 5 minutes.

MAKES 4 SERVINGS.

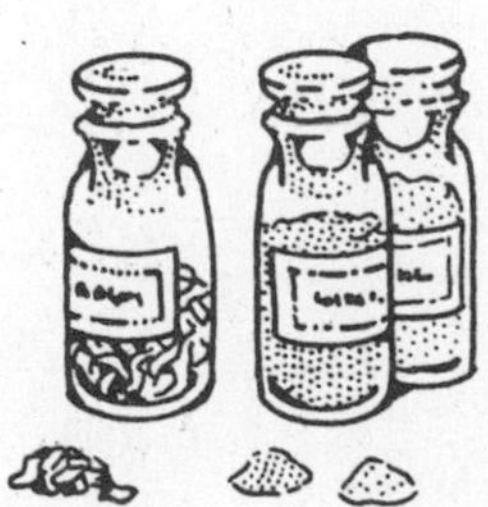

CAROLINA LOW-COUNTRY OXTAIL STEW

2 lb. oxtail, cut into 2-in. pieces
1 Tbs. butter
1/4 lb. bacon, cubed
16 small white onions
1/2 lb. fresh mushrooms, sliced
2 to 3 Tbs. flour
2 cups boiling water
3/4 cup Madeira wine
1 celery rib, chopped coarse
1/2 bay leaf
1/2 tsp. dried thyme
salt
freshly ground pepper
2 small white turnips, peeled and quartered
4 small carrots, quartered
4 squares of cold cooked hominy grits
2 Tbs. bacon fat
1 Tbs. minced parsley

In a large, heavy pot put oxtail pieces, butter, bacon cubes, onions, and mushrooms. Stir constantly over brisk heat until meats are seared and vegetables take on color. Stir in flour and let it brown while stirring. Stir in boiling water and wine, then add celery, bay leaf, thyme, a little salt, and several turns of pepper grinder. Cover and let simmer over low heat for 3 hours or more, until meat is tender. Meanwhile boil turnips in salted water until just tender; drain. When oxtail has cooked for 2 1/2 hours, add carrots and turnips and continue to cook until tender. Just a little before serving fry the cold squares of grits lightly in bacon fat. Serve the stew on top of the grits, sprinkled with parsley.

MAKES 4 SERVINGS.

WALNUT-STUFFED MEAT LOAF

1 1/4 lb. lean beef, ground
1/2 lb. veal, ground
1/4 lb. lean pork, ground
1/3 cup milk
1 egg
2 Tbs. minced shallots or white part of scallions
1 1/2 tsp. salt
freshly ground pepper
1/2 tsp. dried sage leaves
1 cup beef bouillon

THE STUFFING:

2 cups fresh bread crumbs
2 Tbs. minced shallots or scallions
1 tsp. salt
freshly ground pepper
1 1/2 cups very finely chopped celery
1/4 tsp. dried thyme
1/4 tsp. dried basil
1/2 cup red wine
3/4 cup chopped walnuts (black preferred)

Preheat oven to 375° F.

Mix meats in a large bowl if butcher has not ground them together; be sure they are well blended. Beat together milk and egg and stir this into meat along with shallots, and seasonings. Reserve bouillon. Combine stuffing ingredients. Turn meat mixture out onto wax paper and roll into a flat rectangle, about 12 by 15 inches by 3/4 inch thick. Spoon stuffing along widest edge of meat, shaping into a smooth roll. Lift wax paper and roll meat over stuffing, joining two edges of meat rectangle and covering stuffing. Carefully slide rolled meat loaf off wax paper and into a shallow baking pan. Pour about 1/4 cup bouillon over length of loaf. Bake for 1 hour, basting frequently with bouillon.

MAKES 6 SERVINGS.

THREE-MEAT PAPRIKA STEW

1 Tbs. butter
2 large onions, sliced thin
1 tsp. salt
1 Tbs. cider vinegar
1/2 lb. each of beef round, lean lamb, and pork shoulder, cut into strips 1/2 in. by 2 in.
1 1/2 cups beef stock
1 medium-size carrot, cut into match-size strips
1 leek, cut into match-size strips
1 medium-size white turnip, cut into match-size strips
3 medium-size potatoes, diced
1 Tbs. rose paprika
1/2 tsp. Worcestershire sauce
2 Tbs. red horseradish sauce
1/4 tsp. dried marjoram
1 egg yolk
1/4 tsp. cornstarch

Melt butter in a large pot and sauté onions over low heat for about 5 minutes. Stir in salt, vinegar, and beef strips, then cover tightly and let simmer over very low heat for 25 minutes, stirring occasionally. Add lamb and pork strips and beef stock, cover again, and let simmer for about 1 hour. Add vegetables, paprika, Worcestershire, horseradish, and marjoram, and continue simmering for about 30 minutes, or until everything is tender; remove pot from heat. Stir egg yolk and cornstarch together in a small bowl; add some liquid from stew little by little. Stir this mixture into stew and return to heat, letting stew liquid thicken for about 5 minutes. Do not let it boil.

MAKES 4 SERVINGS.

DRIED BEEF AND SWEETBREADS

1 pair of sweetbreads
3 oz. dried beef
lemon juice
1/2 lb. fresh mushrooms, sliced
2 Tbs. butter
2 Tbs. flour
1 cup milk, warmed
1 tsp. chopped fresh rosemary, or 1/2 tsp. dried
salt
freshly ground pepper

Soak sweetbreads in cold water for 20 to 30 minutes. Run cold water between leaves of dried beef. Parboil sweetbreads in 1 quart water with a few drops of lemon juice for 20 minutes; let cool, then remove membranes. Cut into 1-inch dice. Sauté mushrooms in butter for 5 or 6 minutes, turning occasionally. Sprinkle in flour and blend well. Slowly add milk, stirring constantly until sauce thickens. Add diced sweetbreads, dried beef, and rosemary. Season to taste with a little salt, pepper, and a few drops of lemon juice.

MAKES 4 SERVINGS.

PICKLED TONGUE WITH SWEET AND SOUR SAUCE

1 pickled tongue (about 4 lb.)
1 large onion, sliced
2 cups canned tomatoes, chopped coarse
juice of 2 lemons
5 Tbs. brown sugar
1 tsp. salt
6 peppercorns
4 whole cloves
1 garlic clove
1/2 cup raisins

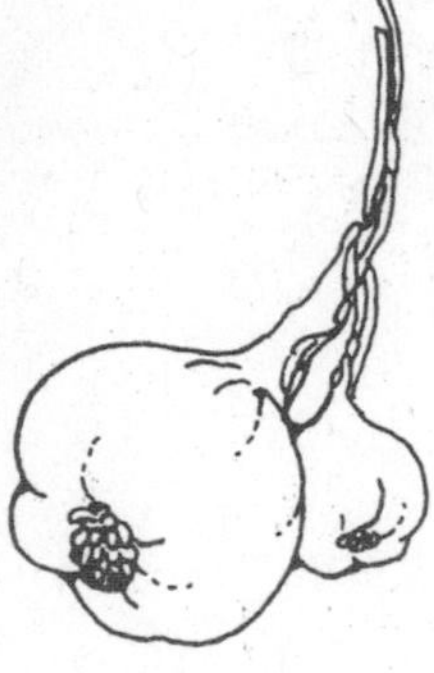

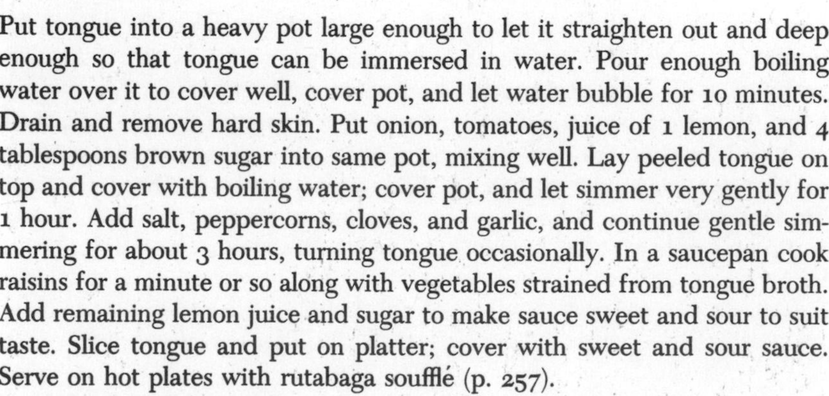

Put tongue into a heavy pot large enough to let it straighten out and deep enough so that tongue can be immersed in water. Pour enough boiling water over it to cover well, cover pot, and let water bubble for 10 minutes. Drain and remove hard skin. Put onion, tomatoes, juice of 1 lemon, and 4 tablespoons brown sugar into same pot, mixing well. Lay peeled tongue on top and cover with boiling water; cover pot, and let simmer very gently for 1 hour. Add salt, peppercorns, cloves, and garlic, and continue gentle simmering for about 3 hours, turning tongue occasionally. In a saucepan cook raisins for a minute or so along with vegetables strained from tongue broth. Add remaining lemon juice and sugar to make sauce sweet and sour to suit taste. Slice tongue and put on platter; cover with sweet and sour sauce. Serve on hot plates with rutabaga soufflé (p. 257).

MAKES 6 TO 8 SERVINGS.

DELICIOUS TRIPE CROQUETTES

1 lb. boiled tripe
1 egg
½ cup fresh bread crumbs
2 tsp. grated onion
1 tsp. lemon juice
1 tsp. salt
freshly ground black pepper
bacon fat or butter

Grind tripe with the finest blade of a food grinder and mix with other ingredients. Grease bottom of a skillet with bacon fat or butter. Shape mixture into flat patties and sauté over medium heat until well browned.

MAKES 4 SERVINGS.

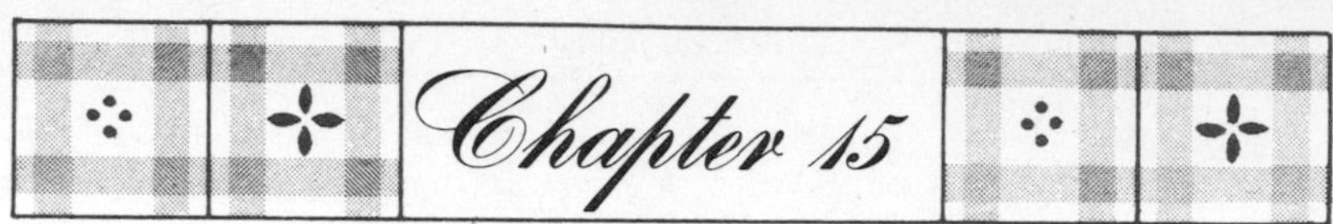

Chapter 15

POULTRY

ROAST CAPON STUFFED WITH PENNSYLVANIA DUTCH STUFFING

1 capon (6½ lb.) with giblets
salt
3 medium-size potatoes
2 onions, chopped
½ cup chopped celery
2 to 3 Tbs. cider or white wine
1 egg, beaten
freshly ground pepper
½ tsp. ground savory
½ tsp. dried thyme
½ tsp. ground sage
1 cup cubed stale bread
4 Tbs. (½ stick) butter, melted

Preheat oven to 375° F. *

Rinse capon inside and out and pat dry before rubbing salt into cavity and over skin; remove fat deposits around opening of cavity and render, then reserve. Scrub potatoes and boil in salted water for 40 to 45 minutes, or until easily pierced by fork; let cool. Cover capon neck, gizzard, and heart with water (reserve liver), bring to a boil, and let simmer for about 1 hour. Break potatoes up with a fork, tossing as lightly as possible. In rendered capon fat, sauté onions and celery for about 5 minutes. Chop uncooked liver and add to vegetables, stirring; sauté just long enough for liver to change color. Toss this mixture with potatoes; deglaze pan with cider or wine, scraping up bits of liver, and add to stuffing. Stir in egg, a little salt, several turns of pepper grinder, savory, thyme, and sage and toss again with bread cubes.* Remove gizzard, heart, and neck from broth. Chop meat finely and stir lightly into stuffing. Spoon stuffing into capon cavity without

forcing, and put any extra into a buttered casserole to bake, along with capon. Put capon on a rack in a shallow roasting pan and bake for 25 minutes. Reduce heat to 325° and bake for about 1 ½ hours more. Baste frequently with melted butter and pan juices.

MAKES 6 SERVINGS.

CAPON WITH WILD RICE AND PECAN STUFFING

1 capon (6 to 7 lb.)
1 cup cooked wild rice
1 cup pecans, chopped fine
1 small onion, grated
1 egg, well beaten
1 tsp. salt
freshly ground pepper
2 to 3 Tbs. chicken fat or butter, melted
¼ cup chopped parsley
½ tsp. ground savory
4 Tbs. (½ stick) butter, softened
1 cup heavy cream, scalded
2 to 3 tsps. flour

Preheat oven to 425° F.

Remove fat from inside capon, render, and reserve. Mix cooked wild rice with pecans, onion, egg, salt, a little pepper, and enough of the melted chicken fat or butter to moisten; then stir in herbs. Pack the stuffing loosely into the bird, sew up, and truss. Rub all over generously with butter, then place on a rack in a roasting pan and roast for 15 minutes; reduce heat to 350° and continue roasting for another 1 ½ hours, basting at intervals with cream. When done, remove bird and make gravy: Sprinkle flour into bottom of roasting pan, scraping up all browned bits, and blend in any remaining cream and a little water if too thick; serve in a separate gravy boat.

MAKES 6 SERVINGS.

CAPON BREASTS WITH ORANGE AND BLACK-WALNUT SAUCE

breast of 5- to 6-lb. capon, or 2 whole chicken breasts
3 Tbs. butter
salt
freshly ground pepper
4 thin slices of country ham or prosciutto
2 Tbs. flour
juice of 2 oranges (about ¾ cup)
¾ cup chicken stock
julienne strips of orange rind
½ cup chopped black walnuts

Remove breast meat from bones in 4 uniform pieces. Melt butter in a large skillet, skim off foam, then sauté breast pieces, being careful to keep butter from turning brown; use tongs to lift pieces when turning them, and cook on all surfaces, basting regularly with butter, for 5 to 6 minutes. Sprinkle all sides with salt and several turns of pepper grinder. Remove meat from skillet and keep warm. Put ham slices in skillet and warm them in remaining butter, then lift them out, letting butter drip off, and put 1 slice on each piece of breast. Stir flour into skillet to absorb remaining butter and cook for about 2 minutes before stirring in orange juice, a little at a time; stir in stock. When thickened, add orange-rind strips and nuts. Spoon sauce over ham and breast pieces.

MAKES 4 SERVINGS.

CHICKEN BREASTS WITH OYSTER STUFFING

STUFFING:

2 Tbs. butter
3 Tbs. minced scallions (white parts only) or shallots
4 slices of stale, firm white bread, crusts removed, diced coarse or crumbled
1/4 cup finely chopped celery
2 Tbs. chopped parsley
1/4 tsp. salt
freshly ground white pepper
1/2 tsp. paprika
1/8 tsp. grated nutmeg
1 pt. oysters, drained but liquor reserved

4 whole chicken breasts (less than 3/4 lb. each)
salt
2 Tbs. butter, softened
Oyster Sauce (p.445)

Preheat oven to 375° F.

Make the stuffing: Heat butter and sauté scallions over gentle heat until soft. Meanwhile mix all the other stuffing ingredients except oysters and liquor. Toss with butter and scallions, cooking for a few minutes until thoroughly coated; if too dry, add a little oyster liquor. Meanwhile, chop oysters into 3 or 4 pieces, depending on size, and set aside.

Split chicken breasts and flatten each half by opening up the area where there is a natural fold. Place each one between two pieces of wax paper and pound to make a fairly thin scallop. Salt and pepper each piece. Place about 1/3 cup of stuffing in the center, fold chicken over, and roll, securing with a piece of string tied at each end and in the center if there is a loose flap. Butter a shallow pan that will hold the breasts comfortably (there should be a little space between), rub softened butter over meat, and cover loosely with foil. Bake for 30 minutes. Remove with a slotted spoon and coat with a little of the oyster sauce, serving the rest in a sauceboat.

MAKES 4 SERVINGS.

CHICKEN BREASTS WITH PEARS AND CIDER CREAM SAUCE

This dish is a very American delicacy—pears were among the first fruits grown by the colonists—when served with parboiled okra that has been fried with a coating of egg and fine soft bread crumbs.

2 chicken breasts, cut into halves
4 Tbs. (1/2 stick) butter
2 or 3 scallions (white parts only), minced
2 fresh pears
3/4 cup cider or apple wine
1/4 cup applejack or bourbon
salt
freshly ground pepper
1 cup heavy cream

Wipe chicken breasts with a damp cloth. Melt butter in large skillet and sauté chicken and scallions over low heat for about 10 minutes. Meanwhile peel pears and core, cutting 4 uniform slices 1/2 inch thick (use the rest for something else). Cover slices with cider or apple wine in an enameled pan and poach for about 20 minutes, or until soft but not mushy. Pour applejack or bourbon over chicken and ignite, letting it burn out. Sprinkle with salt and pepper, then add cream and the cider or wine in which pears were poached; stir and let mixture cook down until reduced by almost half. Lift out chicken pieces and put on a heatproof platter with 1 slice of pear on each piece; pour reduced sauce over and glaze under broiler for about 2 minutes, just long enough to brown.

MAKES 4 SERVINGS.

CHARLESTON BENNE CHICKEN

1/2 cup sesame seeds
1/2 cup flour
1 Tbs. salt
1/4 tsp. cayenne pepper
1/4 tsp. black pepper
2 oranges
1 frying chicken (2 1/2 to 3 lb.), cut into serving-size pieces
2 Tbs. bacon fat
2 Tbs. butter
1/2 cup heavy cream
1 1/2 cups chicken stock

Preheat oven to 325° F.

In a paper bag combine half the sesame seeds, the flour, salt, cayenne, and black pepper. Grate rind from oranges and add to flour-sesame mixture. Shake 1 piece of chicken at a time, coating thoroughly with contents of bag. Over low heat brown chicken pieces in bacon fat. Meanwhile melt butter in a saucepan and stir in 2 tablespoons of the flour-sesame mixture remaining in the bag, then gradually add cream and stock, making sure no lumps form. Squeeze juice from the oranges and slowly add to sauce; when sauce is thick and smooth, add remaining 1/4 cup of sesame seeds. Transfer browned pieces of chicken to ovenproof casserole. Pour off all but 2 or 3 tablespoons fat from skillet, then scrape up browned bits and add to them the orange sauce from saucepan; blend well before pouring over chicken. Cover and bake for 45 minutes; remove cover and bake for 15 minutes more.

MAKES 4 SERVINGS.

FLORIDIAN CHICKEN FRICASSEE

1 frying chicken (about 3 lb.), cut into serving-size pieces
1/2 cup flour, seasoned with salt and pepper
2 to 3 Tbs. bacon fat
2 medium-size onions, chopped
1 medium-size green pepper, chopped
2 garlic cloves, minced
3 or 4 tomatoes, peeled and chopped
1/2 tsp. dried thyme
1/2 tsp. dried oregano
1 bay leaf
large pinch of saffron
1 cup water
1/2 tsp. salt
freshly ground pepper
1/2 cup raisins
2 Tbs. capers, drained
1/2 cup slivered almonds, blanched

Wipe chicken with a damp cloth, dredge with seasoned flour, and brown all surfaces in some of the bacon fat; set aside and keep warm. Sauté onions and green pepper for about 4 minutes, using more bacon fat as needed, then add garlic, tomatoes, herbs, water, salt, and a few turns of the pepper grinder. Add chicken, cover, and let simmer over very low heat for 1 hour, spooning sauce over chicken occasionally. Add raisins, capers, and almonds and cook for about 15 minutes more.

MAKES 4 SERVINGS.

SOUTHERN FRIED CHICKEN

1 frying chicken (2 to 2 1/2 lb.) with giblets
bacon fat
1 cup unbleached flour
1 Tbs. coarse salt
1 tsp. freshly ground black pepper

GRAVY:
1 1/2 Tbs. flour
1 1/2 cups, more or less, milk
1 Tbs. minced parsley
salt
freshly ground pepper

Divide chicken into pieces, separate thighs from legs, remove backbone, divide breast into 2 pieces, and detach wings. Use a skillet just large enough so that pieces will lie flat and fit snugly. Heat enough bacon fat to cover bottom of skillet to a depth of 1 inch. While fat is heating over moderate to high heat, put flour, salt, and pepper into a sturdy brown bag, then drop in chicken pieces (but reserve giblets) 1 or 2 at a time, and give bag a good shake. By that time fat will be sizzling, but not quite at smoking point, so gently place a few floured chicken pieces, no more than 4 at a time, into skillet; preferably use long-handled tongs, because there is bound to be a good deal of splattering. Brown chicken quickly on all sides over high heat, then remove to platter. Repeat the process until all chicken pieces have been browned golden crisp on outside even though not cooked on inside. Now reduce heat to moderate and put back all chicken pieces, tucking them in snugly (which is the secret of keeping them from drying out during their interior cooking). Cook for about 40 to 45 minutes; turn frequently with tongs, moving pieces around from center to edge and vice versa. About 10 minutes before they are finished, add heart, and then liver for the last 5 minutes. When done, chicken should be fork-tender and still crisp; put pieces in warm oven while making cream gravy.

Make the gravy: Chop cooked heart and liver and set aside. Pour off all but 1 ½ tablespoons of fat and remove some of the overly browned bits of flour that may have accumulated. Stir in 1 ½ tablespoons flour, mix well, and let brown. Then add the milk (more or less, depending upon how thick you prefer gravy), and chopped heart and liver. Stir mixture until it thickens, scraping up brown bits from pan and eliminating lumps, then let simmer for about 10 minutes. Finally add parsley and salt and pepper to taste.

MAKES 4 SERVINGS.

FRIED CHICKEN WITH WAFFLES, HAM, AND MAPLE-CREAM SAUCE

1 frying chicken (3 ½ lb.), quartered
1 cup heavy cream
1 cup flour
1 Tbs. butter
1 Tbs. olive oil
salt
freshly ground pepper
1 Tbs. maple syrup
4 waffles, hot and crisp
4 slices of country ham

Preheat oven to 300° F.

Sprinkle chicken with a little cream and rub flour into surfaces. Heat butter and oil in a large skillet and sauté chicken for about 20 minutes, turning at intervals, until golden. Remove to casserole, cover with foil, and bake for 30 to 40 minutes, or until very tender. Meanwhile stir cream into juices remaining in skillet, scraping up coagulated bits; gently boil to reduce liquid by half. Stir in maple syrup and pour mixture over chicken, blending with juices in casserole. Meanwhile, prepare waffles and fry ham slices. Place 1 ham slice on top of each waffle and top with hot chicken quarter. Pour maple-cream sauce over and serve very hot.

MAKES 4 SERVINGS.

NEW ENGLAND CHICKEN AND CLAM PIE

2 Tbs. butter
1 bunch of scallions (white parts only), minced
2 Tbs. flour
1 cup chicken stock
1 can (6 1/2 oz.) clams with juice
salt
freshly ground white pepper
1/2 tsp. ground summer savory
1 1/2 cups diced cooked chicken
3/4 cup diced cooked carrots
1 recipe Buttermilk Biscuits (p. 201)

Preheat oven to 375° F.

Melt butter and sauté scallions for 2 or 3 minutes, then stir in flour. Blend in stock and juice drained from clams. Stir in a little salt, depending on saltiness of stock and clam juice, and a few turns of pepper grinder; add savory, chicken, carrots, and clams. Prepare biscuit dough and line an 8-inch-square shallow baking dish with dough rolled out about 1/8 inch thick. Into this dough pour the chicken-clam mixture. Place an upturned metal cup in the center; arrange remaining rolled-out dough across top, crimping edges and slashing to permit steam to escape. Bake for about 30 minutes.

MAKES 4 SERVINGS.

CHICKEN LOUISIANA

1 large onion, chopped
1 green pepper, chopped
2 Tbs. butter
1 large garlic clove, minced
2 cups canned tomatoes with juice
6 black olives, pitted and quartered
Creole or cayenne pepper
1/2 teaspoon dried thyme
1/2 teaspoon dried oregano
2 bay leaves
2 Tbs. minced parsley
salt
freshly ground black pepper
1 frying chicken (2 1/2 to 3 lb.), cut into quarters
3 Tbs. olive oil
1 Tbs. flour
3/4 cup white wine

Cook onion and green pepper for 5 minutes in butter. Add garlic and cook for 5 minutes more; do not let brown. Stir in tomatoes, olives, and seasonings to taste. Continue cooking, covered, over very low heat for about 25 minutes. Brown chicken in oil, turning frequently; when pieces are uniformly golden, set aside in a warm place. Stir flour into oil in pan and let it turn light brown. With heat very low, stir in wine, a little at a time, and let mixture thicken; stir in the hot sauce, add the browned chicken pieces, and spoon sauce over them. Cover and cook slowly for 45 minutes, or until chicken is tender.

MAKES 4 SERVINGS.

ROAST CHICKEN WITH ORANGES

1 roasting chicken (5 lb.)
salt
1 garlic clove, cut into halves
2 oranges
1 1/2 cups bread cubes, toasted
1 cup thinly sliced celery
4 Tbs. (1/2 stick) butter, melted
freshly ground white pepper
3 sprigs each of fresh tarragon and rosemary, or 1/2 tsp. each dried
1/4 cup wine vinegar
3 Tbs. sugar
2 cups chicken stock
1 Tbs. cornstarch dissolved in 2 Tbs. water
watercress for garnish

Preheat oven to 375° F.

Sprinkle inside of chicken with salt and rub garlic halves well into skin, then sprinkle outside with salt; secure wings at back. Use a vegetable peeler to remove as thinly as possible the orange-colored rind from 1 orange only; cut these peelings into slivers and set aside, then squeeze peeled orange. Remove skin and pith from second orange and divide fruit into segments. Mix bread cubes, celery, butter, about 1/2 teaspoon salt, several turns of pepper grinder, and half of herbs. Toss this mixture with orange segments, then spoon into cavity of chicken and tie legs. Roast on a spit, if you have one, for about 2 hours; if not, roast in oven for about 2 1/2 hours (30 minutes per pound). Meanwhile put vinegar and sugar into a saucepan, bring to a boil, and stir until sugar dissolves. Stir in stock and remaining herbs and let simmer for 10 minutes; stir in orange juice and let simmer for 10 minutes more. Stir cornstarch-water mixture into sauce, cooking for 1 minute or so, then add slivered orange rind. Serve in sauceboat. Garnish the bird with watercress.

MAKES 4 TO 6 SERVINGS.

CHICKEN RAPHAEL WEILL

Among Californians of nostalgic bent, two epicureans who liked the kitchen stand out; both were members of the Bohemian Club, which began encouraging the art of eating well in 1872. Major Joseph Tilden's recipe for onion soup appears on p. 238. Raphael Weill was founder of a great San

Francisco department store, but it was more pleasing to him to be known as an amateur chef of real talent. The chicken dish that bears his name, braised in cream and wine and flavored with shallots, still appears on San Francisco restaurant menus; and thirty-three years after his death, it has been said, Paris's Tour d'Argent still honored him on its *carte*.

4 Tbs. (1/2 stick) butter
4 plump shallots
1 frying chicken (3 lb.), cut into serving-size pieces
salt
freshly ground pepper
1 Tbs. brandy, warmed
1/2 cup chicken stock
1/2 cup Pinot Chardonnay
1 Tbs. minced fresh rosemary
1/2 tsp. dried thyme
1 1/2 cups heavy cream
3 egg yolks
2 Tbs. dry sherry

Melt butter in a heavy skillet and add shallots; add chicken pieces and sauté, turning frequently, for about 10 minutes, or until golden. Season with salt and pepper. Flame brandy and spoon over chicken; add stock, wine, and herbs. Cover and let simmer for about 10 minutes, or until tender. Remove chicken and keep warm. Blend cream and egg yolks together, and stir into pan juices; when this begins to thicken, blend in sherry. Serve sauce on hot platter over chicken.

MAKES 4 SERVINGS.

RIO GRANDE SIMMERED CHICKEN

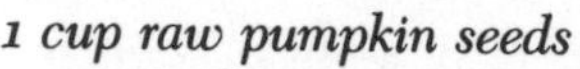

1 cup raw pumpkin seeds
1 cup fresh popcorn, preferably homemade and unsalted
6 cuminseeds
1/4 tsp. ground coriander
1 Tbs. chili powder
1 garlic clove, minced
1 frying chicken, (3 1/2 lb.), cut into 8 pieces, with giblets
1 qt. water
3 cups canned chicken stock (optional)
2 medium-size tomatoes, peeled and chopped
salt

Spin pumpkin seeds in a blender until pulverized; do the same with popcorn, then combine and stir in cuminseeds, coriander, chili powder and garlic. Pull chicken fat away from meat and render in a pot large enough to hold chicken; pour off all but about 2 tablespoonfuls. Remove wing tips and tail and put them into a saucepan along with heart, gizzard, and neck; cover with 1 quart water and let simmer for 1 hour or more, seasoning as desired. (Or have on hand 3 cups canned chicken stock.) Brown chicken pieces in rendered fat. Spin chopped tomatoes in a blender and stir into seed mixture; add 3 cups of chicken stock, a little at a time, until a smooth sauce results. Pour this over browned chicken pieces and cook, covered, for about 30 minutes over low heat; sauce should barely bubble. Chicken will be ready to serve when fork easily penetrates drumstick. Watch out for commercial popcorn saltiness; taste and stir in salt only if needed, just before serving.

MAKES 4 SERVINGS.

STEAMED CHICKEN WITH WATERCRESS SAUCE

1 roasting chicken (3 to 4 lb.)
1/2 lemon
1 Tbs. salt
freshly ground pepper
2 whole cloves
1 celery rib, diced
1/2 cup water
1/2 cup California dry vermouth
1 fresh tarragon sprig
2 bunches of watercress
2 cups boiling water
1 cup heavy cream
2 egg yolks
1 tsp. capers, drained

Carefully remove skin from chicken, chop skin very coarsely, and put in bottom of a heavy cast-iron pot with a tight-fitting lid. Rub flesh of chicken briskly with cut side of lemon (then reserve lemon) and sprinkle on salt and freshly ground pepper. Toss cloves and diced celery in on top of chopped skin, pour in water and vermouth, and bring to a boil. Twist wings to lock at back of chicken, and tie legs. Place a rack in pot over skin and broth and put chicken, breast side up, on rack. Cover breast with tarragon leaves. Cover pot tightly and let simmer for about 30 minutes; time will depend on chicken, so watch carefully so as not to overcook. Cook watercress in boiling water for 20 minutes, keeping tightly covered; drain, and puree in a blender. When chicken is done, remove from pot and keep warm. Remove skin, celery, and cloves from broth with slotted spoon. Off the heat, stir in cream and beat in 1 egg yolk at a time; cook over very low heat until mixture thickens. Add capers and a few drops of lemon juice and blend in pureed watercress. Garnish chicken with some of this sauce and serve remainder in a sauceboat.

MAKES 6 SERVINGS.

CHICKEN TETRAZZINI

Of the many American chicken dishes, two have been served so often in public that they are looked upon as clichés. Chicken à la King, sometimes perceived as the bane of luncheon club life and hotel banquets, is believed to have been created by chef George Greenwald at New York's Brighton Beach Hotel for Mr. and Mrs. E. Clark King III. It is a pretty dish of cut-up chicken in a thickened cream sauce, ornamented with strips of pimiento. The more substantial Chicken Tetrazzini takes its name from an internationally acclaimed coloratura who was the toast of San Francisco where, it may be, the combination of chicken, cheese, and spaghetti was first devised for Luisa Tetrazzini. "She had an astounding girth as well as a thrilling voice and was famous as a gourmande," James Beard once wrote. "As is true of most Italians, she was devoted to pasta." She loved her audiences as much as she loved to eat, and her romance with San Francisco was sealed on Christmas Eve 1910, when she appeared on an outdoor platform at the intersection of Market, Geary, and Kearny streets and led 100,000 of her idolators in singing "Auld Lang Syne."

3 cups cooked chicken breast, cut in strips
2 1/2 cups white sauce made with heavy cream
3/4 lb. freshly cooked spaghetti, drained
1/3 cup sherry
butter
1/2 cup dry bread crumbs
1/2 cup freshly grated Parmesan cheese

Combine chicken and cream sauce and heat; stir in sherry. Arrange pasta in a buttered baking dish. Spread hot chicken mixture over pasta. Sprinkle with crumbs and cheese and brown under broiler.

MAKES 4 TO 6 SERVINGS.

RUM-FLAVORED BAKED CHICKEN

Ethan Allen, hero of the Republic of Vermont, was one of many early Americans with a taste for rum. He favored a hot toddy concocted of butter the size of a black walnut, maple sugar the size of a large hickory nut, a gill of rum, and a small amount of boiling water, sprinkled with nutmeg. Rum has been described as the first central heating of New England, and even straitlaced cooks found ways to use the local liquor distilled from molasses in the seventeenth century and later. Here is an old method of baking chicken under a coating of rum and honey.

1 chicken (about 3 1/2 lb.)
1 medium-size onion
1 bay leaf
1 1/2 Tbs. butter, softened
salt
freshly ground pepper
6 Tbs. rum
1/4 cup chicken stock
1/4 cup clover honey

Preheat oven to 425° F.

Split chicken, trimming out back and neck, and cut each half into equal parts. Cover back and neck with water, add onion and bay leaf, and let simmer 1 hour to make stock. Rub chicken with butter and sprinkle with salt and pepper. Put the pieces, skin side down, into a shallow baking dish and put in center of oven. Bake for 20 minutes, then reduce oven to 400° and invert chicken pieces; return to oven for 15 minutes. Mix 4 tablespoons rum, stock, and honey and baste chicken frequently while continuing baking for about 20 minutes more, or until chicken legs move easily. Remove chicken to hot plates or platter and keep hot. Put baking dish over open flame and scrape up the juices while cooking for 2 to 3 minutes. Heat rum. Spoon juices on chicken; serve after pouring over it remaining 2 tablespoons rum and igniting.

MAKES 4 SERVINGS.

BARBECUED DUCK IN SOY SAUCE

Summers in New York can be more tolerable if space to cook outdoors is available. This recipe was developed on the terrace of a poor man's penthouse equipped with a charcoal-fired spit, but it works equally well with a kitchen rotisserie.

1 Long Island duckling (about 5 lbs.)
salt
1 small onion
1/2 lemon
1/4 cup blackstrap molasses
1/2 cup sour mash bourbon
1/2 cup soy sauce
2 Tbs. honey
1 garlic clove, minced

Wipe duck inside and out with a damp cloth, sprinkle salt into opening, then drop in onion and lemon. Push wing tips into duck's spine and tie securely; tie legs together. Combine molasses, sherry, soy sauce, honey, and garlic in a saucepan, bring to a boil, then let simmer gently for about 5 minutes. Insert spit rod so that weight of duck is well balanced and prongs hold it firmly. Paint with warm barbecue sauce as rotation begins. Roast for about 3 hours, depending upon quality of heat. Paint with sauce at least every 15 minutes to build a glossy, dark carapace over duck skin; delicious. Duck is done when thigh moves easily and juices run clear of blood.

MAKES 4 SERVINGS.

CRUSTY BAKED DUCKLING

1 Long Island duckling (about 5 lb.) with giblets
2 tsp. salt
freshly ground pepper
1 egg
2 Tbs. milk
1/2 tsp. ground savory
2 cups fresh bread crumbs, seasoned
2 Tbs. flour

Preheat oven to 350° F.

Peel all skin from duck except on wings. Remove as much fat as possible and reserve. Use a very sharp knife or poultry shears to cut out backbone and neck; put these pieces into a pot with giblets, about 1 teaspoon salt, a few turns of pepper grinder, and water to cover amply. Let simmer for a couple of hours to make stock for sauce. Remove legs, dividing into drumsticks and second joints; remove wings and divide breast into 4 pieces, easing meat away from ribs; add bones to stock pot. Cut skin and fat into small pieces and render over low heat. Beat egg with milk, remaining 1 teaspoon salt, several turns of pepper grinder, and savory. Dip duck pieces into this mixture, then roll in seasoned bread crumbs, and brown in 2 or 3 tablespoons of duck fat. Transfer to a shallow casserole in which all the pieces can lie flat. Cover and bake for about 50 minutes. Put another 2 tablespoons of duck fat into a saucepan, stir flour into it, and add enough of the stock to make a sauce, stirring to eliminate any lumps.

MAKES 4 SERVINGS.

LONG ISLAND DUCK STEW

1 duck (about 5 lb.)
1 Tbs. flour
1 cup water
1 medium-size onion, finely chopped
1 Tbs. minced fresh mint
1 Tbs. minced fresh sage
1 1/2 tsp. salt
freshly ground pepper
1 small rutabaga, peeled and diced

Pull away as much fat from duck as possible and render fat. (You may pull off skin and the layer of fat underneath it and discard.) Cut duck into serving-size pieces and brown in rendered fat in an enameled cast-iron pot with a tight-fitting lid. Turn pieces occasionally, searing all surfaces. When well browned, pour off all but about 2 tablespoons of the fat and stir in flour; off the heat, stir in water, add onions, herbs, salt, and a few turns of the pepper grinder. Cover pot and cook over low heat for 40 to 50 minutes. Stir in rutabaga dice, cover, and cook over low heat for 30 minutes more. Let cool; put in refrigerator and let fat congeal. Scrape off fat, then reheat stew to serve.

MAKES 4 SERVINGS.

ROCK CORNISH GAME HEN WITH BLACK-WALNUT SAUCE

4 Rock Cornish game birds, cut into halves, with giblets
1 sprig of celery leaves
1 shallot or small onion
3 cups water
salt
freshly ground pepper
3 Tbs. butter
1/4 cup broken black walnuts
1 Tbs. flour
1 cup sour cream
paprika

Cut off wing tips and put with necks, gizzards, hearts, celery leaves, and shallot or onion into a saucepan; add water and let simmer for about 40 minutes, or until stock is reduced to about 1 1/2 to 2 cups; season to taste with salt and pepper. Meanwhile wipe birds with a damp cloth and rub with salt and pepper. Melt 2 tablespoons butter in a skillet large enough to hold birds without crowding; brown them as evenly as possible. When stock is ready, strain it, setting giblets aside; pour stock over browned birds and let simmer, covered, for about 30 minutes. Spin nuts in a blender until pulverized. Use a sharp knife to mince giblets very fine. Melt remaining 1 tablespoon butter in a saucepan and stir in flour to make a roux. Pour stock from simmered chicken, a little at a time, into roux, stirring constantly while sauce thickens; stir in nuts and giblets, then sour cream, blending well without boiling. Pour over birds, cover pan, and heat very slowly for about 15 minutes. Sprinkle with paprika just before serving.

MAKES 4 SERVINGS.

ROAST GOOSE WITH CORN-BREAD STUFFING AND APPLE-ONION SAUCE

1 goose (10 to 12 lb.) with giblets
salt
3 to 4 cups crumbled corn bread
1 Tbs. ground sage
12 juniper berries, bruised
1 medium-size apple, chopped fine
1 medium-size onion, sliced
freshly ground pepper
1 egg, separated

SAUCE:

2 large apples, peeled, cored, and chopped
1/2 cup good beer, ale, or stout
1 small onion, chopped
2 Tbs. sugar
2 tsp. vinegar
2 Tbs. fresh bread crumbs
1/2 tsp. dry mustard
1/2 tsp. ground cinnamon
2 Tbs. flour

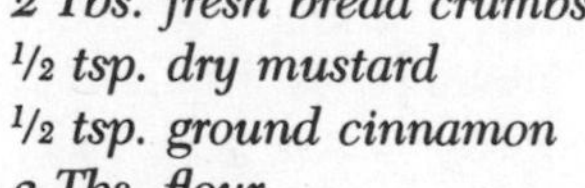

Preheat oven to 400° F.

Wipe goose with a damp cloth and rub salt inside and out. Set aside liver and cook giblets and neck in water to cover, simmering for 30 to 40 minutes. Set giblet stock aside. Put crumbled corn bread into a large bowl and toss with sage, juniper berries, apple, sliced onion, 1 tablespoon salt, and a few turns of pepper grinder. Chop liver and add to mixture with beaten egg yolk. Beat egg white until frothy and fold into stuffing mixture. Spoon stuffing into goose and sew up openings. Roast for 20 minutes, then reduce oven to 325° and roast for 20 minutes per pound, basting frequently with a little water and drawing off fat with a bulb baster; reserve fat.

Make the sauce: Let apples simmer with beer, ale, or stout, chopped onion, sugar, vinegar, bread crumbs, mustard, and cinnamon for about 20 minutes. Meanwhile heat 3 tablespoons of fat drawn from goose and stir in flour. When smooth, stir in reserved giblet stock to make a thinnish gravy, then combine with apple-onion mixture.

MAKES 8 SERVINGS.

SCALLOPS OF TURKEY BREAST WITH CREAM AND SESAME SEEDS

At a time when milk-fed veal was generally almost impossible to find in supermarkets, the idea of slicing turkey breasts in scallop-size pieces and freezing them proved a boon to adaptable cooks. This recipe and the one following suggest two of many imaginative American ways to make one of the so-called convenience foods palatable. Of course the same instructions can be applied to slices of fresh turkey—either cut from the breast or from the thigh.

12 frozen turkey breast scallops (about 1 1/2 lb. altogether)
1/4 cup flour
salt
freshly ground pepper
3 Tbs. butter
3 Tbs. vegetable oil
2 Tbs. minced shallots or whole scallions
1/4 cup dry white wine
1/2 cup heavy cream
2 Tbs. sesame seeds
1/4 to 1/3 cup chicken stock

Defrost turkey scallops, pat dry, and dust with flour well seasoned with salt and pepper. Place between pieces of wax paper and pound each 2 or 3 times. Heat butter and oil to sizzling; brown scallops 3 or 4 at a time to avoid crowding, turning each once. Then return all scallops to pan and cook for 5 minutes. Set aside and keep warm. In same pan cook shallots or scallions until browned, add wine, and cook down quickly, scraping up braised bits, then add cream and boil it down to a syrupy thickness. Turn down heat and return scallops to pan. Meanwhile heat sesame seeds in a small, heavy skillet, shaking pan until they are toast colored; turn off heat. Thin sauce in scallop pan with stock, adding a little at a time to obtained desired consistency. Sprinkle scallops and sauce with toasted sesame seeds and serve.

MAKES 4 SERVINGS.

SCALLOPS OF TURKEY BREAST STUFFED WITH DRIED BEEF

8 frozen turkey breast scallops (about 1 lb. altogether)
1/2 lb. smoked dried beef, chopped
3 medium-size onions, chopped fine
2 1/2 cups fresh bread crumbs
2 Tbs. minced parsley
2 Tbs. minced fresh basil
2 Tbs. minced fresh thyme
1/2 tsp. dried oregano
1 tsp. salt (optional)
freshly ground black pepper
1/4 cup grated Parmesan cheese
2 eggs, beaten
3 to 4 Tbs. butter

Bring turkey scallops to room temperature and put between pieces of wax paper; pound to increase their size about 1 1/2 times. Mix dried beef, onions, 1 1/2 cups bread crumbs, and the herbs. Beware of salt; if beef is very salty do not use any salt. Mix in several grindings of pepper and the cheese. Place about 2 tablespoons of this stuffing on top of each pounded scallop, then roll, turning in ends; lace each one together with a skewer. Dip rolls into eggs, then into remaining bread crumbs. Brown in butter, turning frequently. Cover pan, reduce heat as low as possible, and cook for about 30 minutes, checking frequently.

MAKES 4 SERVINGS.

COUNTRY CAPTAIN

One of the earliest compilers of American recipes, Eliza Leslie, told her readers that Country Captain got its name from a British army officer, stationed in the hinterlands of India, who brought home this method of currying chicken or other fowl. But some Georgians assert it is a Savannah recipe developed when ships sailed the spice routes. Strangely, a twentieth-century Tarheel historian believed it had originated with a famous Columbus hostess for Franklin D. Roosevelt, and he added that General George S. Patton once sent word ahead when he was to visit Columbus briefly: "If you can't give me a party and have Country Captain, put some in a tin bucket and bring it to the train." It is usually made with uncooked chicken and belongs among the curry dishes brought to America by English colonial cooks.

4 bacon strips
1 green pepper, chopped
1 medium-size onion, chopped
2 garlic cloves
3/4 cup chopped celery
6 canned tomatoes with juice
1 cup orange juice
2 Tbs. curry powder
1/4 to 1/2 tsp. dried thyme
8 slices of uncooked chicken or turkey breast
1/2 to 1 cup dried currants
1/2 cup almonds, toasted
1/4 cup minced parsley

Sauté bacon until crisp, set aside, and drain all but 2 tablespoons fat from pan. Stir in green pepper, onion, garlic, and celery and sauté for 5 minutes. Chop tomatoes coarse and add, along with a little of their juice and the orange juice; season with curry powder and thyme. Bring to a boil and let simmer for 5 minutes. Put in slices of turkey and spoon hot sauce over them; continue simmering, covered, for 30 minutes. Garnish with a scattering of crumbled bacon, currants, almonds, and parsley. Serve with rice. MAKES 8 SERVINGS.

THANKSGIVING TURKEY

No Thanksgiving holiday arrives without much discussion of ways old and new to cook the American bird. Turkeys have changed greatly since ancestral family providers took a firing piece from the wall and went into the woods in search of a fowl large enough to feed a houseful of relatives. Nowadays many turkeys come with explicit cooking instructions attached. No treatise on American food, however, would seem complete without some thoughts on this very American subject. In *Los Angeles Cookery* (1881) the fattening process was an important part of the recipe. The cook was advised to "Get your turkey six weeks before you need it; put him in a coop just large enough to let him walk, or in a small yard; give him walnuts—one the first day, and increase every day one until he has nine; then go back to one and up to nine until you kill him, stuffing him twice with corn meal each day, in which you put a little chopped onion and celery, if you have it."

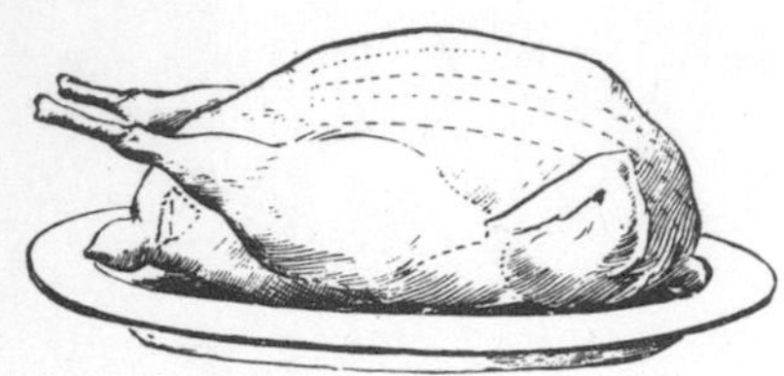

10-lb. turkey
stuffing (see following recipe)
1/4 lb. (1 stick) butter
1 large onion, sliced
2 medium-sized carrots, chopped
1 stalk celery, coarsely chopped
1/2 cup water
1 cup chicken or turkey stock
salt
freshly ground pepper

Preheat oven to 350° F.
Fill prepared turkey with stuffing and close cavities with skewers. Rub all over with about 3 tablespoons butter. Put vegetables and water in bottom of roasting pan. Sprinkle turkey with salt and several turns of pepper

grinder and place on rack in roasting pan. Cut a piece of cheesecloth large enough to drape over turkey and spread it liberally with butter before covering turkey. Put in preheated oven for 3 1/4 hours, basting frequently with juices in bottom of pan. Be sure to lift off cheesecloth each time turkey is basted, add stock as necessary to pan juices. Discard cheesecloth about 40 minutes before bird is done so it will brown on top, but continue basting.

MAKES 8 SERVINGS.

TENNESSEE COUNTRY SAUSAGE STUFFING FOR TURKEY

1 lb. raw chestnuts
2 Tbs. butter
1 1/2 cups chicken or beef stock
2 Tbs. Madeira
1/2 lb. Tennessee smoked country sausage or other pork sausage, preferably but not necessarily smoked
4 onions, chopped
1 to 2 cups chopped celery
1 tsp. dried thyme
1/2 tsp. dried sage leaves
1/4 cup minced parsley
6 cups cubed stale bread
salt
freshly ground pepper

Prepare the chestnuts by cutting a cross in each, covering with cold water, and bringing to a boil for a minute or two. Remove a few at a time and peel inner and outer skins while still warm. Place chestnuts in a heavy saucepan and add butter, stock, and Madeira. Let simmer for 30 to 40 minutes, or until liquid is absorbed. Meanwhile crumble sausage meat and sauté slowly for about 10 minutes; pour off all but about 1/4 cup fat and sauté onions and celery in it for about 10 minutes. Combine with thyme, sage, parsley, bread cubes, and cooked chestnuts, adding salt and pepper to taste (amount of seasoning depends on seasoning of sausage).

MAKES ENOUGH FOR A 10-LB. TURKEY.

TURKEY MOLE À LA MICHAEL FIELD

It has been said that the ambition of every Spanish American is to be served turkey mole on his or her birthday. Part of the trouble in achieving such a wish is that a great deal of grinding (the word *mole* suggests the Spanish word for "mill" and derives as well from the Aztec *molli* for "sauce") was necessary in the old days. Now the efficiency of modern blenders makes this recipe for Turkey Mole à la Michael Field† worth bringing to fruition in any American kitchen.

†From *All Manner of Food*, by Michael Field (New York: Alfred A. Knopf, 1970).

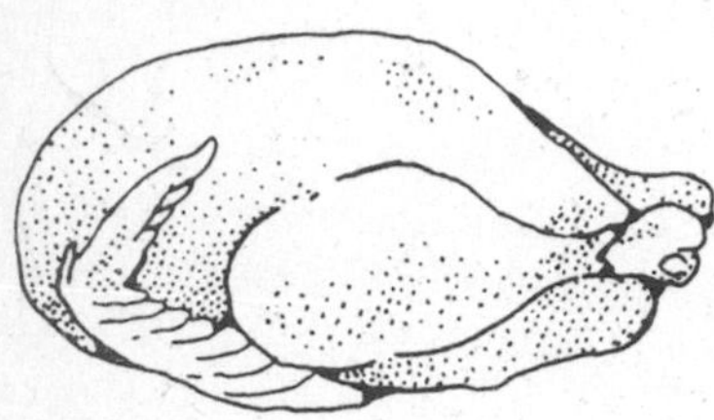

TURKEY AND STOCK:

1 turkey (9 to 10 lb.), cut up, with giblets
2 medium-size onions
2 medium-size carrots
3 celery ribs with leaves
1 large bay leaf
7 to 8 qt. water
1 Tbs. salt
about 20 black peppercorns

MOLE SAUCE:

6 Tbs. chili powder
5 Tbs. sesame seeds
3/4 cup almonds, blanched
1 tortilla, torn into pieces, or 1/4 cup crumbled corn chips
1/2 cup raisins
2 medium-size garlic cloves
1/2 tsp. aniseed
1/2 tsp. ground cinnamon
1/2 tsp. ground cloves
1/2 tsp. coriander seeds or ground coriander
3 medium-size ripe tomatoes, chopped coarse
3 medium-size onions, quartered
2 tsp. salt
1/2 tsp. black peppercorns
1 1/2 oz. unsweetened chocolate, grated
1/4 to 1/2 cup lard

In a 10- to 12- quart soup pot combine turkey pieces, gizzard, heart, onions, carrots, celery, and bay leaf. Pour in water to cover by 2 inches, bring to a boil, and skim off foam and scum. Lower heat, adding salt and peppercorns, then cover and let simmer as gently as possible for about 45 minutes, or until turkey is almost but not quite tender. (A leg or thigh should show slight resistance when pricked with a fork.) Put turkey pieces on board and cut meat away from bones in fairly large serving-size pieces; leave as much skin intact as possible; set aside. Return bones to pot and let stock cook fairly briskly over moderate heat, uncovered, while you make mole sauce.

In a large mixing bowl combine chili powder, 3 tablespoons sesame seeds, almonds, tortilla or corn chips, raisins, garlic, aniseed, cinnamon, cloves, coriander, tomatoes, onions, salt, peppercorns. Strain stock and add 2 cups to dry mixture; mix. (Save remaining stock.) Blend 2 cups of this mixture at a time until all is thoroughly pureed and smooth. Pour into a 4-quart casserole and stir into it 2 more cups stock; bring to a boil, then lower heat and stir in grated chocolate while mixture simmers.

Melt 1/4 cup lard in a 10- to 12-inch skillet and add turkey pieces, skin side down, without crowding. Cook for 3 or 4 minutes, turning frequently, until all pieces are golden; add lard as necessary. As each piece is finished, add it to mole sauce. Let simmer, covered, for about 20 minutes, or until turkey is tender, but do not let mixture boil. Taste for seasoning, then serve sprinkled with remaining sesame seeds.

MAKES 10 TO 12 SERVINGS.

STUFFED TURKEY LEGS

4 large turkey drumsticks
1/2 lb. sweetbreads, blanched and diced
1/2 lb. fresh mushrooms, chopped
3 bacon strips, blanched and cut into squares
3 Tbs. chopped parsley
1 small yellow onion, chopped
3 scallions, chopped (white part only)
1/2 tsp. dried marjoram
1 tsp. salt
freshly ground pepper
1 egg yolk
1/2 cup dry white wine
1/2 cup chicken stock
1 Tbs. butter
1 Tbs. flour
1 Tbs. lemon juice

Preheat oven to 400° F.

Bone drumsticks, carefully taking out tendons and thin bones and leaving a roughly fan-shaped piece of turkey. Mix sweetbread pieces, mushrooms, bacon, parsley, onion, scallions, and marjoram in a bowl and season with salt and pepper, then mix in egg yolk. Pour wine and stock into an oval baking dish just large enough to hold 2 pieces of turkey flat. Spread sweetbread and mushroom mixture evenly over meat and top with remaining turkey pieces. Bake, covered, for about 30 minutes; reduce heat to 350° and bake for 1 to 1 1/2 hours more, or until tender. Baste 2 or 3 times with pan juices. When turkey is well done, melt butter in a small saucepan, stir in flour, then carefully blend in cooking liquor from turkey. Correct seasoning, adding lemon juice to taste. Pour this sauce over cooked turkey and serve.

MAKES 4 SERVINGS.

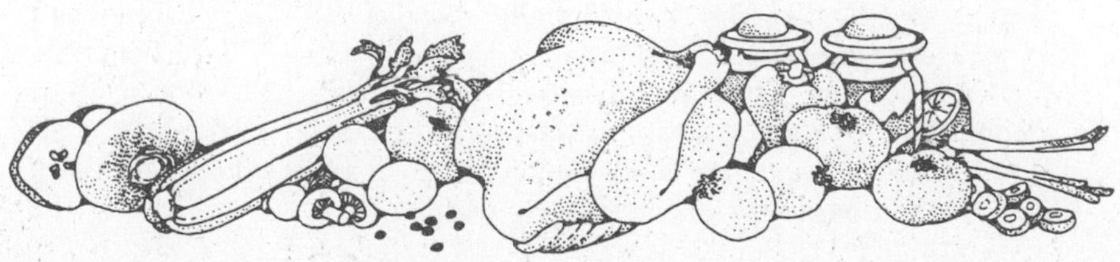

Chapter 16

FISH AND SEAFOOD

WEST COAST ABALONE STEAK

Abalone is considered a great treat in California, where it can be bought fresh, although the supply is limited. Abalone farms at Monterey and Ensenada have been developed, and there is therefore a prospect of greater culinary use of this exceptional univalve meat. In addition to the meunière style, adapted below, abalone makes a delicious chili-flavored salad when cubed, seasoned, and mixed with lime juice, tomatoes, and onion, or it may be prepared in a wok with water chestnuts and served over rice.

1 1/2 lb. abalone steaks (about 1/2 in. thick each)
1/2 tsp. salt
freshly ground pepper
flour
2 eggs, beaten
1/2 cup (1 stick) sweet butter
1/3 cup California olive oil
juice of 1/2 lemon
2 Tbs. minced parsley
4 lemon wedges

If abalone has not been previously tenderized, it must be well pounded with a wooden mallet until soft but not mushy. Season the steaks with salt and pepper; dredge them with flour, dip into eggs, then dredge again with flour. Heat half the butter and the oil in a skillet and brown abalone quickly on each side; overcooking will make fish tough. Put steaks on a warm serving platter. Pour off fat from skillet and add remaining butter; let it get brown but not burned, then add lemon juice and parsley. Pour sauce over abalone and serve with lemon wedges.

MAKES 4 SERVINGS.

DR. RAY'S CHINESE BASS

When Dr. Carleton Ray was one of the directors of marine life at the New York Aquarium, he was also a champion of fish as food for mankind, and his earlier acquaintance with Chinese in San Francisco had made him a devotee of Oriental ways of cooking. One day in his Coney Island office he gave us this recipe for cooking striped or black sea bass, carp, red snapper, or Pacific Coast rockfish with vegetables.

4 dried Chinese mushrooms
8 dried Chinese lichen
2 whole scallions
12 snow pea pods
6 slices of fresh or pickled gingerroot (1/8 in. each)
4 water chestnuts (preferably fresh)
2 fish (about 2 lb. each)
flour
vegetable oil

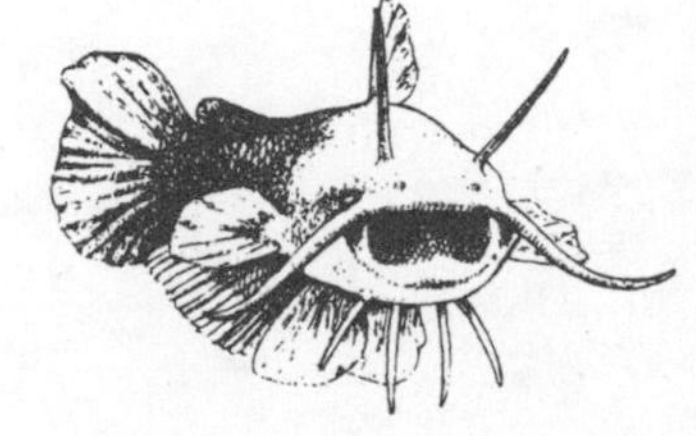

SAUCE:
1/4 cup soy sauce
1/4 cup sherry
1/4 cup white vinegar
1 Tbs. sugar
2 Tbs. cornstarch
2 tsp. salt
1 1/2 cups water

Cover mushrooms and lichens with water in separate containers and soak for 2 hours. Cut scallions into thin slices, including tenderest part of green leaves. Trim ends from snow peas; cut gingerroot into 1/8-inch cubes and chestnuts into 1/6-inch slices; set aside. Meanwhile combine sauce ingredients, eliminating any lumps of cornstarch. Clean fish; chop off fins but leave head and tail on; slash sides at 3/4-inch intervals from gills to tail; dust with flour. Heat enough oil to come up to about middle of fish. When oil is sizzling, fry fish for 1 minute on each side. Turn heat low and cook for 3 minutes more on each side. Outside should be crisp while interior is tender and moist. Remove fish and keep warm. Pour off all but 2 tablespoons oil. Drain mushrooms and lichen, pat dry, and cook with scallions, snow peas, gingerroot, and chestnuts in remaining oil; stir fry over high heat for 1 to 2 minutes so that vegetables are barely cooked. Stir in sauce mixture and cook about 3 minutes until it thickens and becomes clear. Reduce heat and add cooked fish, spooning sauce over it for 1 to 2 minutes. Serve immediately with rice.

MAKES 4 SERVINGS.

FLAMING BLUEFISH FILLETS WITH FENNEL

4 bluefish fillets (about 8 in. long each, approximately 3 lb. altogether)
1 cup flour
1 tsp. salt
freshly ground pepper
2 tsp. whole fennel seeds
4 Tbs. butter
1 to 2 Tbs. minced fresh herbs: thyme, savory, or combination of chives and parsley
1/3 cup brandy

Wipe fish with a damp cloth. Season flour with salt, several turns of pepper grinder, fennel seeds, and dust over both sides of fillets. Melt butter, heating until sizzling but not browned. Put in fillets, skin side up; turn after 3 minutes and sauté other side for 3 to 5 minutes, depending on thickness. Sprinkle top with a little salt, pepper, and the fresh herbs. Heat brandy, pour over fish, and set aflame; spoon over fish until flames die out.

MAKES 4 SERVINGS.

HERMAN DEUTSCH'S CATFISH (OR FLOUNDER) PAUPIETTES

Catfish are not easy to buy in markets, but they make delicious eating when dusted with white cornmeal and fried in bacon fat or when baked in a garlicky Creole sauce of lemon and thyme-flavored tomatoes and green peppers. A New Orleans friend, the late gastronome and newspaper columnist Herman Deutsch, developed a stuffing for catfish fillets that, in the absence of the real thing, is sometimes made in our kitchen with flounder and with a high respect for the cuisine of the Crescent City.

8 small fillets (1 1/2 by 5 in. each)
salt
2 Tbs. capers, drained
18 pecans, chopped fine or pulverized
2 cups dry white wine
2 Tbs. butter
1 Tbs. minced white onion
1/4 cup minced fresh mushrooms
1/2 tsp. dried basil
18 oysters
1 egg, beaten
1 tsp. cornstarch dissolved in 1 Tbs. water
freshly ground pepper

Wipe fillets with a damp cloth and sprinkle with salt. Mash the capers and the ground pecans together and spread this paste evenly over the center of the fillets, then roll them up, securing them with a toothpick or thread. Place them in a saucepan snugly in 1 layer, cover with wine, bring gently to a boil, and let simmer for 3 or 4 minutes. Remove with a slotted spoon and keep warm, covered with foil, while preparing the sauce. Melt butter; add onion, mushrooms, basil, and 1 cup of wine in which fish was cooked, bring to a boil, and let cook down for about 10 minutes. Meanwhile drain oysters and add oyster liquor, no more than ½ cup, to simmering wine. Combine egg with cornstarch-water mixture, gradually blend in some of the hot liquid, then turn egg mixture into the wine sauce and warm, but do not boil, stirring until smooth and thick. Add oysters, correct seasoning, and warm just until oysters curl at the edges. Pat the paupiettes dry, then pour the oyster sauce over them and serve.

MAKES 4 SERVINGS.

FRIED RAZOR CLAMS

Razor clams thrive on both the Atlantic and the Pacific coasts and acquired their name because they so closely resemble a folded straight-edge razor of the kind so common in the past. On the West Coast razor clams are a sentimental favorite, especially the larger clams that are found in chilly waters off Oregon and Washington; these are ideal for frying. New England cooks steam razor clams, use them in chowders and sauces for pasta, or stuff them and sometimes bake them under a pastry crust. Here is a way of panfrying, as practiced in the Northwest.

40 razor clams
½ cup flour
1 tsp. salt
freshly ground pepper
1 egg, well beaten
½ cup fine dry bread crumbs
4 Tbs. (½ stick) butter
chopped chives

Put clams into a frying basket and plunge into boiling water. As they open, remove and plunge into ice water. Remove clams from shells, cut off necks, and trim black spots with a sharp knife. Split clams through the foot and down the front and drain them on paper towels. Season flour with salt and several turns of pepper grinder and dredge clams with it; then dip in egg and dust thoroughly with bread crumbs. Melt butter in a skillet over medium heat. Fry clams for 3 minutes, or until golden, then turn and fry for 2 minutes more. Drain briefly on paper towels, then serve, sprinkled with chives, as hot as possible.

MAKES 4 SERVINGS.

BAKED HERB-STUFFED CLAMS

32 medium-size clams
1/2 cup water
2 scallions, minced (white part only)
1/2 cup minced parsley
1/4 cup minced fresh basil and/or thyme and/or tarragon
1 1/2 Tbs. butter
1 1/2 Tbs. flour
1/3 cup milk
salt
freshly ground pepper
5 or 6 drops of Tabasco
2 Tbs. dry sherry
1/3 cup fresh bread crumbs
4 Tbs. (1/2 stick) butter, melted

Preheat oven to 500° F.

Place clams in a heavy pot with the water, cover tightly, and steam over high heat until shells open, about 5 minutes. Scrape clams from shells and set shells aside. Chop clams very fine and combine with scallion, parsley, and other herbs. Melt 1 1/2 tablespoons butter in a saucepan, stir in flour, and cook for 1 or 2 minutes. Off the heat, beat in milk; return to heat and stir until smooth and thickened. Add salt to taste, several turns of pepper grinder, and Tabasco; stir in sherry. Stir minced clams into sauce, then fill reserved clam shells, using about 20 shells. Sprinkle with bread crumbs, dribble melted butter over, and run under broiler or bake until browned and sizzling.

MAKES ABOUT 6 SERVINGS.

FRIED CLAMS

The first time we tasted a "clamburger" was in an unprepossessing café in Coos Bay, Oregon, but fried clams, in or out of a sandwich, are characteristic of New England. (A good place to try them is The Cove, near the Sea Coast Museum at Mystic, Connecticut.) A claim is made in Essex, Massachusetts, that a local seafood maestro named Lawrence Woodman in 1916 was the first to dip a clam into bread crumbs and then to fry it in deep fat, thereby inventing a new genre of portable seafood. Woodman's place, perched on the edge of a salt marsh, today is one of many specializing in crisp, puffy fried clams, clam cakes, clam fritters, and lobsters and other fruits of the ocean. Down on the Connecticut shore an uncommon clam special consists of a dozen littlenecks cooked in the shell, then split open and broiled with a coating of hot sauce. A more ornate regional sandwich is called a poor boy and is stuffed with fried clams, crab meat, shrimp, or scallops.

24 to 30 clams, shucked
1 cup cracker crumbs, bread crumbs, or cornmeal
2 eggs, beaten
1/2 tsp. salt
1/2 cup milk
2 cups corn oil

Dip clams into crumbs or meal, then into eggs seasoned with salt and mixed with milk, then again into crumbs or meal. Preheat oil to about 385° F. and fry coated clams, not too many at a time, until golden brown. Drain on paper towels and serve piping hot with tartar sauce.

MAKES 4 SERVINGS.

SEATTLE CLAM HASH

An old story maintains that New Englanders who came to settle in the Northwest resorted to making their traditional hash with clams when they had no corned beef.

1 1/2 cups peeled and chopped baked potatoes
2 cups chopped cooked clams
4 Tbs. (1/2 stick) butter
1/4 cup finely minced onion
salt
freshly ground pepper
1/2 cup heavy cream

Toss potatoes with clams. Melt about 2 tablespoons butter in a heavy skillet and lightly sauté onion for about 1 minute. Stir onion into potato-clam mixture. Season to taste. Melt remaining butter in skillet and spread hash over bottom, pressing down evenly, then let it brown. After about 10 minutes pour cream over and let it sink in. Let hash cook over very low heat for about 30 minutes; fold like an omelet.

MAKES 4 SERVINGS.

NEW ENGLAND CODFISH BALLS

1/2 lb. salt cod
4 potatoes
1 celery rib
1 small onion
1 small carrot
3 peppercorns
1 Tbs. butter
1 egg, well beaten
freshly ground pepper
1/2 cup vegetable or peanut oil

Soak fish under running water for 24 hours, or change water several times. Drain and flake. Peel and slice potatoes to make 2 1/2 cups and put into a saucepan with codfish, celery, onion, carrot, and peppercorns; add enough water to cover fish and vegetables by 1 inch. Bring to a boil and let simmer until potatoes are soft, about 20 minutes. Discard celery, onion, carrot, and peppercorns. Drain water off fish and potatoes, then shake saucepan over heat until all moisture has evaporated. Off the heat, mash mixture until potatoes are free of lumps; stir in butter, egg, and pepper. Heat oil in a skillet. When almost smoking, drop spoonfuls of mixture into fat, taking care not to crowd the pan. Turn balls when underside has browned and fry until crisp. Drain on paper towels and keep warm. Make 12 balls in this manner or shape mixture into flat cakes and fry the same way. Serve with catsup or tomato sauce.

MAKES 4 SERVINGS.

CAPE ANN CODFISH PIE

1/2 lb. frozen codfish, thawed
6 Tbs. (3/4 stick) butter
1 Tbs. finely minced onion
1 garlic clove, minced fine
3 Tbs. flour
3/4 cup chicken stock
3 Tbs. heavy cream
2 Tbs. lemon juice
1 tsp. salt
1/2 tsp. white pepper
1/2 tsp. dried thyme
1/4 cup white wine
3 egg yolks
3/4 cup mayonnaise
1 pie shell (9 in.), prebaked for 8 to 10 minutes (see p. 459)

Preheat oven to 375° F.

Bring fish to room temperature and grind very fine. Melt 4 tablespoons butter in a saucepan and sauté fish, onion, and garlic, stirring constantly, for about 3 minutes. Remove with a slotted spoon, then melt remaining butter in same pan and blend in flour. Off the heat, stir in stock; when free of lumps, return to heat and cook until sauce thickens, then stir in cream. Mix fish mixture into sauce along with lemon juice, salt, white pepper, thyme, and wine. Beat egg yolks with mayonnaise until smoothly blended, then fold into sauce with fish. Pour into prebaked pie shell and bake for 35 to 40 minutes, or until golden brown.

MAKES 6 SERVINGS.

FALMOUTH CODFISH WITH SHRIMPS

1 lb. salt cod
2 Tbs. bacon fat
1 small green pepper, chopped
5 or 6 shallots, chopped
2 garlic cloves, minced
1/2 cup chopped celery
1 cup sliced fresh mushrooms
several dashes of Tabasco
salt
1/4 lb. raw shrimps, peeled
butter
2 small potatoes
1/4 cup grated Cheddar cheese
1/4 cup fresh bread crumbs

*Preheat oven to 375° F.**

Soak fish under running water for 24 hours, or change water several times. About 1 1/2 hours before serving, melt bacon fat in a skillet and sauté green pepper, shallots, garlic, celery, and mushrooms.* Flake soaked fish and drain well, then stir into vegetables. Add Tabasco, and a little salt if necessary. Stir in shrimps and heat. Butter a 1 1/2-quart casserole and put half of fish mixture in it. Peel potatoes and slice with vegetable peeler very thin; spread potatoes over fish mixture. Sprinkle in cheese and cover with rest of fish. Melt 1 tablespoon or more of butter and stir in crumbs, then sprinkle crumb-butter mixture on top. Bake for about 1 hour.

MAKES 4 SERVINGS.

CODFISH STEAKS IN ORANGE SAUCE

1/2 cup flour
1 tsp. salt
1/2 tsp. cayenne pepper
4 codfish steaks (about 1/3 lb. each)
3 garlic cloves, minced
1/2 cup minced parsley
3 to 4 Tbs. olive or corn oil
1 to 1 1/2 Tbs. lemon juice
3/4 cup freshly squeezed orange juice
2 Tbs. slivered almonds or crushed hazelnuts

Preheat oven to 475° F.

Mix flour, salt, and cayenne and dredge cod steaks with the mixture. Stir together garlic, parsley, oil, and lemon juice and saturate all surfaces of fish, letting steaks marinate for at least 1 hour. Put them into a baking dish with orange juice and bake for about 25 minutes, basting at least twice with juices; when done, most of juices will have been absorbed. Sprinkle nuts over fish before serving.

MAKES 4 SERVINGS.

SOFT-SHELL CRABS NEWBURG

2 doz. soft-shell crabs
1 recipe sauce Newburg
flour
salt
freshly ground pepper
1/2 cup (1 stick) sweet butter
slices of toast, freshly made and buttered

Wash and drain crabs, cleaning them well, then season flour with salt and pepper. Dredge crabs thoroughly with seasoned flour. Heat Newburg sauce and keep warm. Heat butter in a large skillet and sauté crabs, turning occasionally, until golden brown. Drain on paper towels, add to sauce, and serve on toast.

MAKES 4 SERVINGS.

SAUCE NEWBURG

3 Tbs. butter
3 tsp. flour
1/4 tsp. dry mustard
1/4 tsp. salt
freshly ground pepper
1 1/2 cups light cream
2 egg yolks, beaten
1/4 cup sherry
2 drops Tabasco
Cayenne

Melt butter in top of a double boiler over boiling water. Sprinkle in flour and stir until smooth while you add dry mustard, salt and several turns of pepper grinder. Over medium heat stir in cream and cook about 2 minutes, blending thoroughly. Remove from heat and cool. Meanwhile, beat egg yolks until foamy, then stir in cooled sauce and add Tabasco and a pinch of cayenne. Return mixture to top of double boiler, add sherry and heat 1 minute. Serve very hot with shellfish added.

TRED AVON CRAB CAKES

1 lb. fresh crab meat
1 cup fine fresh bread crumbs
1/2 tsp. salt
freshly ground pepper
1 tsp. dry mustard
1 tsp. Worcestershire sauce
1/4 cup minced whole scallions
1 egg
3 Tbs. mayonnaise
oil for deep frying
1 lemon

Flake crab meat, removing cartilage and shell bits. Stir in half of bread crumbs, the salt, a few turns of pepper grinder, mustard, Worcestershire sauce, scallions, and egg. When well blended, stir in mayonnaise. Use hands to shape into 8 cakes, then coat with remaining crumbs. Place cakes on top of wax paper on a platter and chill for at least 1 hour. Heat 1/2 inch of oil in a skillet until a haze develops. Fry cakes until browned; then turn and brown bottom sides. Cut lemon into wedges to garnish plates; tartar sauce may also be served.

MAKES 4 SERVINGS.

HOT CRAB GRATINÉ

4 Tbs. (1/2 stick) butter
1 whole shallot or scallion, minced
4 large fresh mushrooms (about 1/4 lb.), sliced
2 Tbs. white wine
2 Tbs. flour
1 cup milk
1 cup fresh lump crab meat (about 1/4 lb.)
salt
freshly ground pepper
1 tsp. dried tarragon
2 Tbs. dry sherry
1 egg yolk
1 Tbs. heavy cream
4 tsp. mixed grated cheese and bread crumbs

In a small enamelware saucepan melt 2 tablespoons butter and sauté shallot for 1 minute. Add mushrooms, then stir in wine and let simmer for 5 minutes. Remove vegetables to a dish and keep warm. In same pan melt remaining 2 tablespoons butter and blend in flour; off the heat, stir in milk, eliminating all lumps before returning to heat; stir constantly until sauce thickens. Scrape mushrooms, shallots, and juices from warming dish into sauce. Stir in crab meat, salt, and pepper to taste, tarragon, and sherry. While this gets hot, beat egg yolk with cream, adding to it a bit of hot sauce; whisk again, then add more hot sauce. Now pour all of yolk mixture into hot sauce, stirring constantly. Do not let it boil. Divide crab-mushroom mixture among 4 scallop shells or small baking dishes and sprinkle each with cheese and bread crumb mixture. Slide under broiler to brown.

MAKES 4 SERVINGS.

EEL STIFLE

In places as distant as Japan and Italy, eels are honored among cooks, and in Bridgeport, Connecticut, there is an Eel Institute, which, among other efforts in behalf of anguillaphiles, has developed numerous methods of serving them, some as sophisticated as eel soufflé, others no more pretentious than this colonial stifle.

3/4 lb. fat salt pork, cut into 1/2-in. dice
2 lb. thick eels, unskinned, cut into 2-in. slices
3 large onions, sliced
freshly ground pepper
3 cups water
salt
3 medium-size potatoes, cut into 1/2-in. dice
3 Tbs. flour
2 Tbs. very dry sherry

Fry salt pork dice in a skillet until crisp, then remove and keep warm in a heated oven; pour off and reserve half the fat; leave remainder in skillet. Set aside tails and skinny end pieces of eel and sear the other chunks in fat in skillet; remove, put in metal bowl, and keep warm in oven. Sauté onions in fat that remains in skillet, sprinkling with pepper. Turn heat as low as possible and cover skillet. Meanwhile, put end pieces of eel in a separate pot, cover with 3 cups lightly salted water, and bring slowly to a boil; let simmer for 10 minutes. Remove eel pieces, replace with diced potatoes, and boil gently for 10 minutes. Meanwhile add some reserved salt pork fat to skillet containing onions and stir in flour. Drain cooked potatoes and stir potato water into onions and flour to make a thin sauce; when this is smooth and creamy, add potatoes and the eel pieces from the oven. Cover skillet and let eels and potatoes simmer gently in sauce for 15 to 20 minutes. Add salt to taste and blend in sherry. Serve in hot soup plates with crisp salt pork dice scattered in each. Knives and forks are as necessary as spoons.

MAKES 6 SERVINGS.

HALIBUT WITH AVOCADO AND MUSHROOM STUFFING

4 halibut fillets
salt
freshly ground pepper
lemon juice

STUFFING:

1/8 lb. fresh mushrooms, chopped fine
4 scallions, chopped fine (white part only)
3 Tbs. butter
2 Tbs. flour
1 fresh tomato, peeled and chopped, or canned tomato
1 large ripe avocado, mashed
1/2 cup dry white wine
1/2 cup chicken stock
salt
freshly ground pepper
2 egg yolks

Preheat oven to 400° F.

Wipe fish with a damp cloth and season with a little salt, pepper, and a liberal sprinkling of lemon juice. Put mushrooms, scallions, and butter into a skillet and sauté for 5 minutes. Stir in flour and cook for 2 or 3 minutes more. Add tomato and avocado; stir in wine, stock, and salt and pepper to taste. Off the heat, stir in egg yolks. Cook over low heat as stuffing thickens. Put 2 fillets into a greased baking dish and cover with half of stuffing. Top with 2 more fillets and remaining stuffing. Bake for about 20 minutes.
MAKES 4 SERVINGS.

HALIBUT FILLETS IN ASPIC

1 lb. halibut fillets
2 1/2 cups fish stock
3/4 cup white wine
1 1/2 envelopes unflavored gelatin
1 cup seedless white grapes, peeled
1/2 tsp. salt
1 tsp. minced fresh tarragon
watercress for garnish

Wash fish fillets, fold in half, and put in an enamelware pan or heatproof baking dish just large enough to hold them comfortably. Pour stock and 1/2 cup wine over fish. Bring to just below the boiling point and let simmer gently, covered, for about 5 minutes, or until fish is flaky. Remove fish and set aside to cool. Strain stock through several layers of cheesecloth lining a strainer or colander into a clean pan. Stir gelatin into remaining 1/4 cup wine; when completely dissolved, add to stock and bring liquid back to boiling point. When all traces of gelatin have vanished, remove stock from heat. Meanwhile chill a fish-shaped (or other) mold that holds at least 1 1/2 quarts. When aspic mixture is cool, fill bottom of mold to 1/2 inch in depth; chill in freezer for 15 minutes, until aspic is jelled. Spread a decorative layer of peeled grapes over and return mold to freezer for 5 minutes. Spoon in more stock and let set. Flake cooked fish and make 1 layer in mold, sprinkling with salt and tarragon leaves. Repeat layers of stock, grapes, and fish, finishing with stock. Let set in refrigerator for 4 to 5 hours. Turn out onto a chilled platter and decorate with watercress.

MAKES 4 SERVINGS.

PONTCHARTRAIN JAMBALAYA

One of the greatest of American dishes, jambalaya is one of the most instantly recognizable of Creole creations. Recipes vary from one household to another; this one we have found has delighted guests many times.

1 Tbs. bacon fat or rendered ham fat
2 medium-size onions, chopped
6 highly seasoned pork link sausages
1 Tbs. flour
1/2 lb. country ham, diced
3 medium-size tomatoes, peeled, seeded, and chopped
1 cup uncooked rice
1 large garlic clove, minced
2 cups chicken stock
1 1/2-in. piece of dried red pepper pod, crushed; or 1/4 tsp., or more, Creole or cayenne pepper
1/2 tsp. dried thyme
1 medium-size green pepper, diced
3 Tbs. minced parsley
1 1/2 lb. raw shrimps, peeled
1 1/2 pt. raw oysters, drained

Use a heavy pot with a tight-fitting lid and in it melt fat. Add onions and sausages and stir over moderate heat until sausages brown a little and onions are translucent. Stir in flour and cook slowly, stirring constantly until the "roux" has turned the color of peanut butter. Add ham and tomatoes and cover tightly; let simmer over low heat for about 30 minutes. Add rice, garlic, stock, seasonings, green pepper, and parsley. Cover tightly and let simmer over very low heat for 40 minutes or more, or until rice is cooked but not mushy; do not stir. Stir in shrimps and cook for 2 minutes. Stir in oysters and cook for 3 minutes. Country ham should eliminate the need for salting; taste, and adjust seasoning as desired.

MAKES 6 SERVINGS.

LONG ISLAND JAMBALAYA

1 Tbs. butter
1 medium-size onion, peeled and chopped
2 garlic cloves, minced
1 green pepper, chopped
1 Tbs. flour
1 bay leaf
6 fresh thyme leaves, or 1/2 tsp. dried thyme
1 tsp. Saucier beef glaze
1 cup stewed tomatoes or tomato purée
1 dried red pepper pod, seeded
1 tsp. sugar
salt
freshly ground pepper
3 doz. clams
1/2 cup water
3 doz. raw shrimps
1 cup uncooked rice
1 Tbs. chopped parsley

Melt butter in a large saucepan, stir in onion, garlic, and green pepper, and cook slowly for about 5 minutes. Stir in flour, eliminating lumps, and add bay leaf, thyme, Saucier, tomatoes, and red pepper pod. Bring to a boil and let simmer very slowly, adding sugar and salt and pepper to taste. Steam clams in about 1/2 cup water for about 10 minutes, or until all are open; reserve liquor. Cover shrimps with boiling water, return to a boil, and cook for about 3 minutes. Shell clams, cut away soft parts, and add hard parts to tomato sauce; shell shrimps. Stir in half of clam liquor and rice. Cover and cook so that mixture is bubbling, adding remaining clam liquor a little at a time, for about 30 minutes, or until rice is soft but not mushy. Add reserved clams and shrimps and heat just long enough to heat shellfish. Remove pepper pods. Serve on a platter sprinkled with chopped parsley.

MAKES 6 TO 8 SERVINGS.

CHARLES SCOTTO'S LOBSTER AMERICAINE

This version of a fabled dish—given verbatim—is attributed to Chef Scotto of New York's Hotel Pierre, who was regarded as Escoffier's favorite pupil. Imprecise though they are, these instructions may be followed by experienced cooks. The technique here avoids cutting up live lobsters, but it does not go as far as some older American variations, which call for removing the shell from the lobster pieces in the kitchen.

lobster
salt
pepper
1/3 cup olive oil
10 Tbs. butter
2 shallots, chopped
1 clove garlic, minced
2 Tbs. Chablis
2 Tbs. fish stock
1/4 cup burned-off brandy
1 Tbs. meat glacé
3 small tomatoes, chopped and pressed
pinch of minced parsley
few grains of cayenne
2 or 3 sprigs fried parsley
boiled rice

Plunge lobster into rapidly boiling water for 5 minutes. Remove and drain. Sever and slightly crush the claws; cut tail into sections; split into halves lengthwise; remove the green tomally. Remove intestines and coral, and season lobster with salt and pepper. Then place lobster pieces, still in shells, into a saucepan with olive oil and 2 tablespoons butter, melted and hot. Fry, covered, until meat has stiffened, then tilt pan to empty grease while holding lid. Sprinkle lobster with shallots and garlic, add wine, fish stock, burned-off brandy [heated and set aflame], meat glaze, tomatoes, parsley, and cayenne. Cover and cook in oven for 18 to 20 minutes. Then turn out lobster pieces onto a dish; take meat from sections of tail and claws and put it in a timbal, along with larger pieces still in shells. Keep hot. Now reduce volume of cooking sauce of the lobster to 2/3 cup. Add intestines and chopped coral together with 2 tablespoons butter; cook for a moment and strain. Put this into a pan, heat it without letting it boil, and add, away from fire, remaining butter, cut into small pieces. Pour sauce over pieces of lobster and garnish with fried parsley. Serve with rice.

DELMONICO'S LOBSTER NEWBERG

Ben Wenberg was a sea captain whose ship regularly brought in Cuban fruit. In 1876 he brought something else to his favorite eating place. Home from a cruise, he entered Delmonico's and called for a blazer in which to demonstrate his new method of preparing lobster, then offered the result to his friend Charles Delmonico. The restaurateur was so pleased that he added the dish to his menu and called it Lobster à la Wenberg. He was as quick to strike it from the bill of fare after a falling-out with Wenberg, and when popular demand forced him to compromise, he reversed the spelling of the first syllable of Wenberg's name. The misspelling of the second syllable came later. Here is Delmonico's recipe, adapted for use at home.

2 live lobsters (2 lb. each)
6 Tbs. (3/4 stick) butter, clarified
1/2 tsp. salt
1 cup, more or less, heavy cream
2 Tbs. Madeira wine
3 egg yolks, well beaten
1/4 tsp. cayenne pepper

Cook lobsters in boiling salted water for 25 minutes. Remove and let cool. Cut lobster meat into slices and put slices into a saucepan along with most of the butter, making sure that each piece lies flat; season with salt and sauté lightly on both sides without coloring. Moisten to their height with cream, and reduce liquid quickly to half. Add Madeira and boil once more only. Remove from heat and thicken sauce with egg yolks. Reheat without boiling, incorporating a little cayenne and remaining butter. Arrange lobster pieces in a serving dish and pour sauce over.

MAKES 4 TO 6 SERVINGS.

MACKEREL GRILLED WITH BUTTERMILK

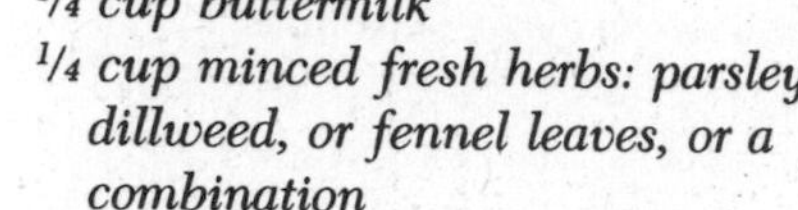

2 mackerel (1 to 1 1/2 lb. each), beheaded and split
3/4 cup buttermilk
1/4 cup minced fresh herbs: parsley, dillweed, or fennel leaves, or a combination
coarse salt
freshly ground pepper

Wipe fish with a damp cloth. Into a flameproof baking dish large enough to hold fish in 1 layer pour enough buttermilk to cover bottom to 1/8 inch deep. Put in fish, skin side down, cover with remaining buttermilk, then sprinkle with herbs, coarse salt, and pepper. Turn on broiler and put in baking dish, about 5 to 6 inches from source of heat. Grill for 12 to 15 minutes, basting with the liquid once or twice.

MAKES ABOUT 4 SERVINGS.

MONKFISH WITH TOMATOES AND PIMIENTOS

Known also as anglerfish or goosefish, monkfish has been neglected by American fishermen, and therefore by cooks. But the firm, white meatiness of its tail—which makes it an essential ingredient in a good French *bouillabaisse* and a fish used regularly by imaginative Spanish cooks—has begun to appeal to Eastern seaboard cooks, who have been known to compare it to lobster. When the tail (the most edible part of this fish) is cut into uniform steaks, monkfish may be salted and baked in a 350° F. oven for about 20 minutes, then cooled, cut up like lobster tail, and served cold in a salad. It may also be prepared in the same way as Lobster à l'Américaine. It is delicious when cooked as indicated below—an American method with a Spanish accent.

2 lb. monkfish, cut into 1 ½-in. steaks
salt
fresly ground pepper
1 cup flour
olive oil
1 large onion, chopped
1 large tomato, chopped
2 large potatoes, sliced into rounds ⅛ in. thick
½ tsp. dried thyme
1 large bay leaf
2 canned pimientos, cut into strips
¼ cup chopped watercress

Season fish with salt and a few turns of pepper grinder. Dredge with flour, then sauté in enough oil to coat bottom of skillet thoroughly. Remove when fish is lightly browned on both sides and set aside. In the same pan cook onion and tomato for about 5 minutes, then stir in potato slices, thyme, and bay leaf and add enough hot water to barely cover vegetables. Cook very slowly for about 30 minutes. Meanwhile drain pimientos on paper towel, sprinkle with salt, dip in olive oil, and arrange the strips on top of sautéed fish pieces; place these in pan with vegetables, spooning mixture over fish. Continue cooking, covered, for 25 minutes. Add watercress and cook just long enough to wilt, about 3 to 4 minutes. Serve on a hot platter.

MAKES 4 TO 6 SERVINGS.

MONKFISH TAIL WITH PEPPERS

¼ cup olive oil
1 dried hot red pepper pod
1 green pepper, chopped
1 large onion, chopped
2 celery ribs, chopped
¼ lb. fresh mushrooms, chopped
2 tomatoes, peeled, seeded, and chopped, or 6 canned plum tomatoes, drained
1 monkfish tail, bone removed and cut into chunks
flour
salt
freshly ground pepper
½ cup dry white wine
8 to 10 black olives, sliced
½ tsp. dried thyme
2 Tbs. chopped parsley

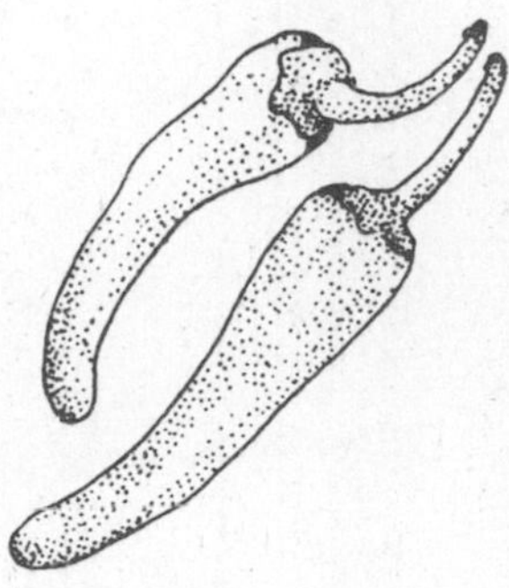

Heat half the olive oil in a large skillet, and when almost smoking, drop in hot pepper and stir around until it begins to darken. Add green pepper, onion, celery, and mushrooms, and cook, stirring, for about 5 minutes. Add tomatoes and cook another minute more. Dredge monkfish pieces with flour seasoned with salt and pepper. Push the vegetable mixture to the side of the skillet, add the remaining olive oil in the center, and turn up the heat. Quickly sear monkfish pieces for a few minutes, turning on all sides. Add olives, wine, thyme, and parsley; taste and correct seasoning; then cover and cook at a moderate heat for about 10 to 15 minutes, or until fish is tender. Remove the dried pepper before serving.

MAKES 4 SERVINGS.

SOUL-FRIED MULLET WITH SAUTÉED ROE

Mullet is a popular fish along the Atlantic coast, the Gulf of Mexico, and especially in bayou country—mullet roe makes a prized breakfast for many hunting parties in the South when it is served with scrambled eggs or with heart of palm salad. The fish makes good stew, and it is often stuffed and baked. Soul-food cooks, for their part, love deep-fried mullet, with the roe cooked separately.

4 lb. mullet with roe
salt
freshly ground pepper
1 egg
1/2 cup milk
1 cup mixed flour and cornmeal
3 Tbs. butter

Remove backbones and cut each fish into 2 pieces. Sprinkle with salt and pepper and set aside. In about an hour beat egg and milk together, dip fish pieces into mixture, then dredge with flour-cornmeal mixture. Heat fat to about 375° F. and fry fish for 3 to 5 minutes, or until golden brown. Season roe with salt and pepper and sauté for about 5 minutes in butter. Serve mullet and roe very hot.

MAKES ABOUT 4 SERVINGS.

EASTERN SHORE BAKED OYSTERS AND CRAB

The Robert Morris Inn at Oxford, Maryland, is famous as the ancient home of one of America's founding families and as an inn preserving the elegance of eighteenth-century life. One of the remarkable dishes created in its kitchen combines two of the seafood delicacies from Chesapeake Bay and is now served at the inn as Oysters à la Gino.

2 dozen oysters, shucked, with shells reserved
1 1/2 cups lump crab meat
salt
freshly ground pepper
2 cups sauce Newburg (p. 336)
3 bacon strips, cooked crisp and crumbled
dash of Worcestershire sauce
1/2 cup sherry
1/4 lb. (1 stick) butter
1 small garlic clove
1 Tbs. paprika
1 cup fresh bread crumbs
6 bacon strips, uncooked and cut into 4 squares each

Preheat oven to 300° F.

Arrange oysters on half shells on a baking tray. Put crab meat into a mixing bowl and season with salt and pepper to taste. Combine sauce Newburg, crumbled bacon, Worcestershire sauce, and sherry; stir into crab meat and spread some of mixture on top of each oyster. Melt butter with garlic; remove garlic and stir butter and paprika into bread crumbs. Spread each oyster with seasoned crumbs and top with bacon square. Bake for 10 to 15 minutes, or until hot and crumbs are delicately browned.

MAKES 4 TO 6 SERVINGS.

OYSTERS BAKED WITH BLUE CHEESE SAUCE

6 oz. blue cheese
6 Tbs. (3/4 stick) butter
6 Tbs. finely chopped celery
4 tsp. Worcestershire sauce
1/2 cup sour cream
1 qt. oysters, drained
juice of 1/2 lemon
2 eggs, hard-cooked and chopped

Preheat oven to 400° F.

Crumble cheese and melt with butter in top part of a double boiler, stirring; add celery; cook for about 5 minutes. Stir in Worcestershire sauce and sour cream. Divide oysters among 6 individual ramekins and sprinkle with lemon juice. Stir eggs into cheese sauce and pour over oysters, dividing evenly. Bake for about 10 minutes and serve piping hot.

MAKES 6 SERVINGS.

OYSTER STEW

5 Tbs. butter
2 small carrots, minced
1 young white turnip, minced
2 small white onions, minced
2 celery hearts, minced
2 Tbs. flour
1 cup milk, scalded
12 oysters, shucked, with their liquor
salt
freshly ground pepper
1 cup heavy cream
paprika
2 Tbs. chopped parsley

Melt 2 tablespoons butter in a skillet and gently sauté vegetables, stirring constantly, for about 20 minutes, or until they just begin to take color. In a saucepan melt 2 tablespoons butter, stir in flour, and when this mixture is smooth and has cooked for about 2 minutes, stir in milk, blending well to make a smooth sauce. In an enamelware saucepan, melt remaining 1 tablespoon butter and turn oysters into it, letting them plump up over heat before adding their liquor. Season with salt and pepper. Add cream to white sauce and stir in cooked minced vegetables, then mix with oysters. Bring stew to point just below boiling, stirring constantly. Pour into a hot soup tureen and sprinkle with parsley.

MAKES 2 SERVINGS.

OCEAN PERCH WITH LOBSTER TAIL, CHERVIL SAUCE

Rosefish, redfish, sea perch, and red perch are all apt to be sold under the name of ocean perch, and they are easily found frozen in most supermarkets. The delicate flavor is enhanced in this recipe because of the contrast with the texture of the lobster tails and the flavor of chervil and sour cream. The fillets run about six to a pound.

1 1/2 to 2 lb. frozen ocean perch
2 cups fish stock or diluted clam juice or chicken stock
4 Tbs. (1/2 stick) butter
1/4 cup minced red onion
1 Tbs. minced parsley
1/2 cup diced lobster tail or crab meat
2 Tbs. flour
salt
freshly ground pepper
1/4 to 1/2 tsp. dried dillweed
2 Tbs. minced fresh chervil leaves or canned puréed chervil, drained
3 to 4 Tbs. sour cream, at room temperature

Thaw fillets in refrigerator overnight or at room temperature for 3 to 4 hours. Poach in simmering stock for about 8 minutes. Meanwhile melt butter in a saucepan, stir in onion, and sauté briefly; stir in parsley and lobster tail; cook for 5 minutes. Remove fillets from stock and keep warm while reducing stock to 1 1/2 cups. Sprinkle lobster and onion with flour, stir over heat for 2 to 3 minutes, then gradually add reduced stock, blending to make a smooth sauce. Add salt only if necessary, and a little pepper. Stir in dillweed, chervil, and sour cream; heat but do not boil before pouring over fish.

MAKES 4 SERVINGS.

SAUTÉED POMPANO IN CHERVIL BUTTER

Some Americans consider pompano to be one of the most elegant of fishes on which to dine, yet it is easy to find in Florida, as well as in other markets near the Gulf of Mexico. It is good enough when broiled and excellent with herbed butter.

2 pompano, (1 1/4 to 1 1/2 lb. each), split and boned
1/4 lb. (1 stick) butter
coarse salt
freshly ground pepper
3/4 cup dry vermouth
3 Tbs. chopped fresh chervil, or 2 tsp. canned puréed chervil, drained

Wipe fish with a damp cloth. Melt about 6 tablespoons butter in a skillet large enough to hold pompano fillets. When butter has foamed, skim off white froth, turn heat to medium high, and saute fillets, flesh side down, for 3 minutes; turn, sprinkle with a little salt and pepper, and sauté on other side for 5 minutes, spooning hot butter over fish. Remove, and keep warm on a serving plate. Sizzle vermouth in hot skillet, boiling down to reduce by half; then add chervil and swirl in remaining butter. Pour sauce over fish just before serving.

MAKES 4 SERVINGS.

ANTOINE'S POMPANO EN PAPILLOTE

From the late Roy Alciatore, grandson of the founder of one of New Orleans' most famous watering places, there came the inscribed recipe on which this is based. The spelling is that used in the Vieux Carré.

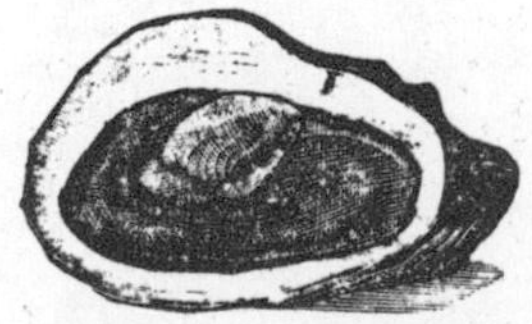

3 medium-size pompano
1 small carrot, chopped coarse
1 celery rib
1 small onion, chopped coarse
2 cups water
2 finely chopped shallots or scallions (white part only)
1 3/4 cups dry white wine
salt
freshly ground pepper
6 Tbs. (3/4 stick) butter
3 or 4 drops of Tabasco
2 cups cooked small shrimps
2 cups crab meat
1 garlic clove, minced fine
pinch of dried thyme
1 bay leaf
2 Tbs. flour
vegetable oil

Preheat oven to 450° F.[*]

Clean pompano and cut into 6 fillets. Use head and bones to make a fish stock, simmering them with carrot, celery, and onion in water and 1 cup wine for about 30 minutes, or until stock is somewhat reduced. Strain stock and pour over fillets, seasoning them with salt and pepper and adding 1/2 cup of the wine. Let fish simmer very gently, covered, for about 8 minutes, then let them rest in the stock. Meanwhile make the sauce: cook shallots or scallions in 3 tablespoons butter for a few minutes, then add Tabasco, shrimps, crab meat, garlic, thyme, and bay leaf. In a separate pan melt remaining butter; blend in flour, and cook slowly, stirring constantly, for a minute or two, then blend in 1 cup of the warm stock and remaining 1/4 cup wine. Combine with the shrimp and crab-meat mixture and correct the seasoning.[*] Now cut 6 pieces of parchment paper in the shape of hearts 8 by 12 inches and oil each piece well. Remove fillets from poaching liquid with a slotted spoon, saving remaining stock for another purpose. Place 1 fillet in the center of each piece of parchment, top with one-sixth of the seafood sauce, and fold the oiled paper over. Seal the edges by making a tight, firm rolled fold all around the open edge. Don't rub oil on the outside. Place parchment hearts on a baking sheet and bake for 15 minutes, or until the paper has browned. Serve immediately in the paper hearts, the *papillotes*.

MAKES 6 SERVINGS.

PORGY BAKED WITH HERBS AND TOMATOES

4 porgies
3 Tbs. peanut oil
1 medium-size onion, chopped
2 Tbs. minced fresh basil
1 bay leaf
coarse salt
4 small ripe tomatoes
freshly ground black pepper
1/2 cup water
2 to 3 Tbs. minced parsley

Preheat oven to 350° F.

Run cold water over fish and pat dry. Put oil, onion, basil, and bay leaf into a saucepan and let simmer for 3 or 4 minutes, stirring occasionally. Salt fish lightly inside and out. Prepare a shallow casserole, large enough to hold fish flat, by straining enough oil from saucepan to cover bottom. Lay fish side by side and scrape onion, seasonings, and remaining oil on top of them. Cut tomatoes into 1-inch-thick slices and arrange around fish. Sprinkle fish and tomatoes with 8 to 10 turns of pepper grinder. Pour water into bottom of casserole, then bake for 30 minutes. Fish should flake easily when done. Sprinkle tomatoes with parsley and serve.

MAKES 4 SERVINGS.

PAN-FRIED PORGY

4 porgies (about 3/4 lb. each) or small trout, sea squabs, flounders, or soles
1 cup cornmeal
1 Tbs. coarse salt
1/2 tsp. freshly ground pepper
1/2 cup corn oil
1/4 lb. (1 stick) butter
1/4 cup minced shallots or whole scallions
2/3 cup dry white wine

Clean porgies but leave whole; rinse and pat dry. Mix together cornmeal, salt, and pepper and dredge fish with mixture. In 1 very large or 2 medium-size skillets heat oil until almost smoking. Fry fish for 5 minutes on each side, then remove and keep warm. Wipe pan clean of any burned bits, then melt 3 to 4 tablespoons butter and sauté minced shallots or scallions until soft and slightly browned; turn up heat, pour in wine, let sizzle and reduce to half. Swirl in remaining butter and pour over warm fish.

MAKES 4 SERVINGS.

SMOKED SALMON ON BED OF SPINACH

½ to ¾ lb. smoked salmon, sliced, at room temperature
2 pkg. (10 oz. each) frozen spinach, or 1 lb. fresh
1 ½ cups Lemony Mustard Sauce (p. 445)
2 to 3 Tbs. minced parsley

Prepare frozen spinach according to package directions or cook fresh spinach in usual fashion until tender, then drain and chop. Heat (or prepare if not on hand) mustard sauce. Reheat drained spinach, placing salmon slices on top to heat also. Put spinach on hot platter, topping with salmon slices and sauce; sprinkle with parsley.

MAKES 4 SERVINGS.

POACHED SALMON STEAKS WITH DILL SAUCE

4 salmon steaks (about ½ lb. each)
1 bunch of fresh dillweed
4 onion slices
½ cup dry white wine
1 to 2 cups fish stock, or half clam juice, half water
2 Tbs. butter
2 Tbs. flour
½ cup light cream or milk
1 egg yolk
salt
freshly ground pepper
dash of grated nutmeg
1 Tbs. minced parsley

Put salmon steaks into a flameproof dish or skillet and top each with 1 dillweed sprig and 1 onion slice. Pour in wine and stock. Bring slowly to a boil and let simmer gently, covered, for 10 minutes. Meanwhile melt butter in a heavy saucepan, stir in flour, and cook over low heat for 1 or 2 minutes. Off the heat, stir in hot stock ladled from fish; when smoothly blended, cook, stirring constantly, until thickened. Beat a little cream or milk with egg yolk, add to it a little of the hot sauce and the remaining cream, and stir into sauce; bring to just below boiling point. Add a little salt and pepper, 1 tablespoon minced dillweed, the nutmeg, and parsley. Drain salmon steaks, scraping off cooking vegetables, and distribute hot sauce over them

MAKES 4 SERVINGS.

SAND DABS GOLDEN GATE

A West Coast member of the flounder family that only Californians enjoy regularly, sand dabs have an indescribable, delicate flavor when sautéed quickly in butter as we first tasted them; or they can be baked in the oven in paper hearts.

2 sand dabs or rex sole, filleted
salt
freshly ground pepper
4 slices of boiled ham, cut slightly smaller than fish pieces
3 to 4 Tbs. butter
8 fresh mushroom caps
1 ½ Tbs. minced fresh chives and parsley

Preheat oven to 450° F.
Sprinkle fillets with salt and pepper and put a slice of ham on top of each. Melt 1 ½ tablespoons butter in a skillet and cook mushroom caps lightly, turning often. Cut each of 4 sheets of bond writing paper (8 ½ by 11 inches) into the shape of a heart, folding lengthwise; butter one side thoroughly and place on it a fillet and ham slice topped by 2 mushroom caps and a sprinkling of mixed chives and parsley. Bring edges of heart together and crimp well to hold in juices. Bake in hot oven for 10 minutes, or until paper browns and puffs up.

MAKES 4 SERVINGS.

MARTHA'S VINEYARD SCALLOPED SCALLOPS

1 qt. fresh bay scallops
4 medium potatoes, peeled and sliced thin
4 medium-size onions, sliced thin
1 cup finely crushed cracker crumbs
salt
freshly ground pepper
milk
4 Tbs. (½ stick) butter

Preheat oven to 350° F.
Butter a 2 ½-quart casserole and cover bottom with a layer of scallops, then a layer of potatoes, then onions, then cracker crumbs. Sprinkle lightly with salt and freshly ground pepper. Repeat layering until all ingredients are used. Pour in enough milk to barely cover, then dot surface with butter. Bake for about 1 hour, or until potatoes are tender.

MAKES 4 SERVINGS.

BROILED SCROD

Pollock, haddock, or other fish are often sold as scrod, but the uniquely American scrod is really a young, small cod, weighing between 1 and 2 pounds, to be broiled as a strictly New England dish. Kenneth Roberts wrote, "State-of-Maine and Boston gourmets, confronted with such fish delicacies as pompano, Great Lakes whitefish or broiled scrod, are as apt to take the scrod as the whitefish or pompano." When the young cod is split wide open and the head, tail, and bones removed, it becomes a scrod;

nothing else will do, nor can anything else duplicate the fresh flavor of this Yankee specialty.

2 whole scrod (1 to 1 1/2 lb. each), split and boned
1/4 lb. (1 stick) butter, melted
salt
freshly ground pepper
1 Tbs. lemon juice

Brush scrod with melted butter and sprinkle with salt and pepper. Place on a greased grill and broil about 3 inches from high heat for 8 minutes. Serve with a sauce made of the remaining melted butter, adding more if desired, to which the lemon juice has been added.

MAKES 4 SERVINGS.

SCROD WITH MINCED MUSHROOMS AND ARTICHOKES

2 lb. scrod
3 cups fish stock, or half clam juice, half water
1/4 cup white wine
1 cup finely chopped fresh mushrooms
2 shallots, minced
4 Tbs. (1/2 stick) butter
1 cup finely minced, cooked, artichoke (see below)
salt
freshly ground pepper
2 Tbs. flour
1/2 cup heavy cream
2 Tbs. dry sherry
3 Tbs. grated aged Cheddar or Parmesan cheese

Place scrod side by side in a Teflon or enamelware skillet; pour in stock and wine and bring to a boil. Cover and let simmer gently for 5 minutes, or until fish flakes easily. (Be careful not to overcook.) Sauté mushrooms and shallots in half the butter for 3 or 4 minutes. Scrape edible pulp from bottoms of artichoke leaves and combine with minced hearts, or mince frozen parboiled artichokes. Mix with mushrooms and shallots to warm, adding salt and pepper to taste. Spread mixture on bottom of a shallow casserole large enough to hold fish pieces in a single layer. Lift fish from cooking liquid with a slotted spoon, pat dry, and lay on vegetable bed, sprinkling with a little salt and pepper; reserve cooking liquid. In a saucepan melt remaining butter, stir in flour, and cook slowly for 2 or 3 minutes. Off the heat, stir in 1 cup cooking liquid from fish, beating to eliminate lumps; stir over heat until thickened, then add cream and sherry. Taste and add salt and pepper if needed. Pour sauce over fish in casserole and top with sprinkling of cheese. Put under broiler to brown. (This can be made ahead of time and brought to room temperature, then baked at 450° F. for 10 minutes before serving.)

MAKES 4 SERVINGS.

FLORIDIAN SEA SQUAB

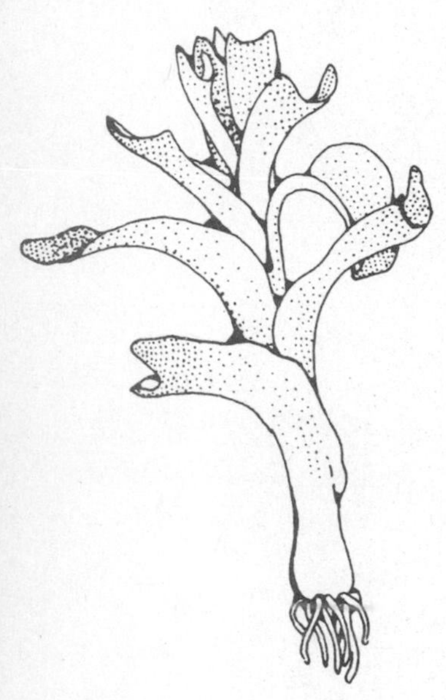

12 to 16 sea squabs (3 or 4 per serving, depending on size)
1/2 cup flour, seasoned with salt and pepper
3 to 4 Tbs. butter
3 Tbs. olive oil
1/2 cup dry white wine
1/4 cup minced shallots or whole scallions
1 garlic clove, minced
1 can (28 oz.) plum tomatoes
1 pkg. (9 oz.) frozen baby artichokes, blanched for 10 minutes
12 pitted black olives
2 Tbs. minced parsley

Rinse sea squabs (sometimes called blowfish), pat dry, and roll in seasoned flour; shake off excess. Heat 1 1/2 tablespoons butter and equal amount of oil in a large skillet until sizzling, then sauté fish 6 to 8 at a time, for 5 minutes on each side. Remove to a heated platter and keep warm; add more butter and oil before cooking remaining fish. When all fish have been removed from skillet, add wine and boil down quickly, scraping up brown bits. Stir in shallots or scallions and brown lightly, adding extra butter if necessary. Stir in garlic and drained tomatoes with about 1 tablespoon tomato liquid; cook down. Add artichokes and olives; when warmed through, put in sea squabs and spoon tomato mixture over them. Taste to correct seasoning. Serve piping hot with sprinkling of parsley.

MAKES 4 SERVINGS.

BROILED SHAD WITH LEMON-CRESS BUTTER SAUCE

The name of this member of the herring family derives from a Latin term meaning "most delicious." The European shad has little culinary significance, but in America the shad season is hailed from the end of December, when the fish begin to appear in the St. Johns River of northern Florida, until the decline in their abundance in the Hudson and Connecticut rivers in May. It takes real skill to bone a shad (a problem solved by machinery in most markets), and fillets of the sweet white meat are considered a traditional American delicacy.

2 lb. boned shad fillets
1/4 lb. (1 stick) butter, melted
1 tsp. salt
freshly ground pepper
1/2 cup finely chopped watercress
juice of 1 lemon

Brush fillets on both sides with butter, sprinkle with salt and pepper, then place on foil and broil, skin side down, 3 inches from heat source, for about

10 minutes, or until fish flakes easily. Meanwhile, combine remaining butter with watercress and lemon juice. Remove cooked fish to a hot platter and pour sauce over. Serve immediately while very hot.

MAKES 4 SERVINGS.

SHAD STUFFED WITH SORREL SAUCE

2 pairs of shad roe
2 Tbs. butter
2 Tbs. minced shallots or whole scallions
3/4 cup white wine
salt
freshly ground pepper
1 shad (4 lb.), cleaned, boned, and split
1 tsp. cornstarch
1 1/4 cups heavy cream
1/3 cup puréed cooked fresh sorrel or canned sorrel

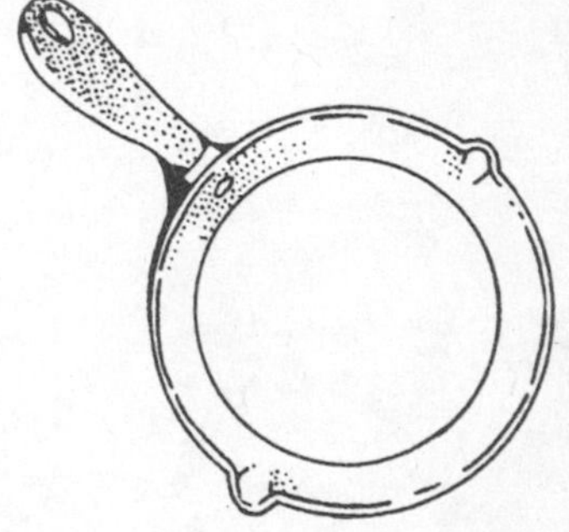

Preheat oven to 375° F.

In an enamelware pan, sauté roes in butter along with shallots or scallions for about 2 minutes on each side; add wine and let simmer for 10 minutes. Remove roes with a slotted spoon, sprinkle generously with salt and pepper, then break up and stuff into the flaps on the two sides of shad. Butter a baking dish just large enough to hold fish; put stuffed fish into it and cover loosely with foil. Bake for about 30 minutes. Meanwhile reduce by one-third the pan juices from the roe, cooking over brisk heat. Dissolve cornstarch in a little of the cream, mix with remainder, and stir into boiling juices. Let simmer until sauce has the consistency of cream, then add sorrel and stir until sauce is hot again. Test fish to see if it flakes easily. If so, it is done; if you like it a little drier, bake for another 5 minutes. Remove to a platter, pour some hot sorrel sauce over, and serve remaining sauce in a sauceboat.

MAKES 6 SERVINGS.

SHAD WITH MUSHROOM AND CORNBREAD STUFFING

1 shad (about 3/4 lb.), boned
3 Tbs. butter
1 Tbs. chopped shallot or scallion (white part only)
1 Tbs. chopped green pepper
3 or 4 medium-size fresh mushroom caps, chopped fine
1/3 cup crumbled corn bread
1/3 cup crumbled baking powder (or commercial water) biscuits
salt
freshly ground pepper
1 tsp. chopped fresh dillweed
1 Tbs. minced parsley
2 to 3 Tbs. water
1 lemon, cut in wedges

Preheat oven to 375° F.

Wipe shad with a damp cloth and put into a lightly buttered shallow baking pan. Make the stuffing: Melt 2 tablespoons of butter in a skillet, add shallot or scallion, green pepper, and mushrooms, and cook slowly for about 5 minutes. Stir in crumbled corn bread and biscuits; sprinkle generously with salt, pepper, and herbs. When well mixed, spread stuffing on inside of fish, fold top piece over, and tie with string in 2 or 3 places. Dot with remaining butter and sprinkle with salt and pepper. Pour water into baking pan and cover fish loosely with foil. Bake for 30 minutes. Remove strings, cut fish into halves, and garnish with lemon wedges.

MAKES 2 SERVINGS.

CHESAPEAKE BAY SHAD ROE

In Maryland shad roe is frequently cooked with mushrooms, sometimes being baked instead of poached or sautéed. After much waiting for spring to come and the shad to run, this is one of the ways we like to prepare this delicacy.

4 pairs of shad roe
3 Tbs. butter
6 to 8 shallots, minced
3 to 4 Tbs. minced parsley
½ lb. small fresh mushrooms
1 cup dry white wine
1 cup heavy cream
1 Tbs. flour

Wipe shad roe with a damp cloth. Melt butter in a large skillet, stir in shallots and parsley, and cook slowly for 1 minute. Stir in mushrooms and cook for 5 minutes more, shaking pan frequently. Carefully add shad roes, cover with wine, and let simmer, covered, for 15 minutes, letting steam escape occasionally. Put cream and flour into a jar and shake until free of lumps. Remove roes from pan and reduce liquid to half, then stir in cream and flour mixture and cook to thicken slightly. Put roes on a flameproof platter, pour sauce over, and broil for 3 or 4 minutes.

MAKES 4 SERVINGS.

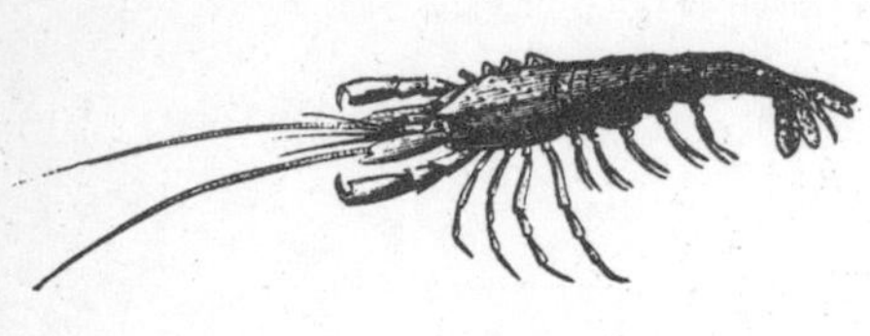

CREOLE SHRIMPS

2 medium-size red onions, chopped fine
2 Tbs. butter
3 tomatoes, peeled and chopped
2 cups chicken stock
1 bay leaf
1 fresh thyme sprig
1 tsp. salt
cayenne or Creole pepper
dash of Tabasco
1 ½ lb. raw shrimps, peeled

Sauté onions and green pepper in butter for about 4 minutes. Add tomatoes, stock, bay leaf, thyme, salt, and cayenne or Creole pepper to taste. Bring to a boil and let simmer for 45 minutes. Add Tabasco, then stir in shrimps and cook for 5 minutes. Serve on hot, fluffy rice.

MAKES 4 SERVINGS.

SOUTHERN SHRIMP PIE

Shrimp is one of the traditional favorites on Southern menus, including breakfast dishes. In Charleston shrimp pie is made with bread crumbs, which are replaced by boiled rice in Savannah. Sometimes a pastry crust is used, sometimes not.

2 lb. raw shrimps
4 slices white bread
1 1/2 cups white wine
1/8 tsp. ground mace
freshly grated nutmeg
salt
cayenne pepper

Preheat oven to 400° F.

Put shrimps into boiling salted water and cook for about 3 minutes. Tear up bread, spin in blender for 1 or 2 seconds, then soak in wine. Peel shrimps and add to wine and crumbs, seasoning with mace, liberal gratings of nutmeg, salt, and cayenne (enough cayenne so that one can taste it). Turn into a buttered baking dish and bake for about 5 minutes.

MAKES 6 SERVINGS.

SPICED LAGOON SHRIMP FLAMBÉ

1 lb. large raw shrimps
3 Tbs. olive oil
1/2 tsp. ground cinnamon
1/4 tsp. freshly grated nutmeg
3 whole cloves
salt
freshly ground pepper
1/4 cup rum
juice of 1/2 lemon

Peel shrimps but leave tails on. Rinse under running water; drain. Heat oil in a skillet large enough to hold shrimps in 1 layer. Pat shrimp dry with paper towels, then sauté in oil until they turn pink; remove from heat. Stir in cinnamon, grate nutmeg over, and stir in cloves. Sprinkle with a little salt and a turn or two of pepper grinder, then let shrimps steep, covered, for 30 minutes or more. Reheat shrimps when ready to serve and warm up rum. Set rum aflame and pour over shrimps in pan, stirring until flames are extinguished. Squeeze on lemon juice and serve hot. Creamed pearl onions makes an interesting side dish.

MAKES 4 SERVINGS.

SPICED SMELTS

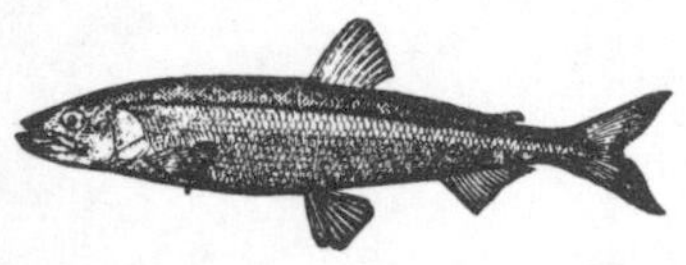

These scaleless silvery fish run in spring and fall in many coastal streams, in Lake Champlain, and in tributaries of the Great Lakes. Smelts of the Pacific Northwest are a fatter variety, and so rich in oil when found in the Columbia River that the Northwest Indians used them, after drying, as candles. Seasonal smelt runs—when the fish are so numerous they can be scooped up with bushel baskets—are traditionally celebrated in places like Michigan and New England. The silver splinters are cooked very simply, often deep-fried, baked, or broiled. In Maine panfuls are crisscrossed with strips of salt pork and baked into a solid slab of matchless crispness with a subtle blend of flavors. The following unusual preparation is a favorite of James Beard.

2 lb. smelts
1 large onion, sliced thin
1 garlic clove, minced
1 large bay leaf
6 peppercorns
1/2 lemon, sliced
1/3 cup olive oil
1/4 cup vinegar
2 tsp. salt
1/2 tsp. paprika
4 whole allspice
1/2-in. cinnamon stick
4 whole cloves
1 cup water
1/2 cup dry white wine or cider

Preheat oven to 400° F.
Make sure you have 3 or 4 smelts per person. Combine all other ingredients in a saucepan and bring to a boil, then let simmer for 15 minutes. Meanwhile wash and clean smelts, leaving heads on. Dry them and arrange in a single layer in a large baking dish; pour simmered liquid over them, cover with a tight lid or with foil pinched around the edges, and bake for 15 minutes for good-size fish, 10 to 12 minutes for small. Let them cool in the spicy liquid, then chill in refrigerator for several hours.

MAKES 4 SERVINGS.

RED SNAPPER WITH WILD RICE STUFFING

Of the fifteen kinds of snapper found in U.S. waters, the red snapper is the most popular and is common from North Carolina to Florida and in the Gulf of Mexico. It is often served with a Creole sauce or stuffed with shrimps, oysters, and other seafood. We like it with this savory wild rice mixture.

1 red snapper, (4 to 5 lb.)
salt
freshly ground pepper
butter, softened
½ cup uncooked wild rice, washed
5 or 6 bacon strips
⅓ cup minced shallots
½ tsp. dried chervil
½ tsp. dried savory
½ cup chopped black walnuts

Preheat oven to 350° F.

Wash and clean fish, season inside and out with salt and pepper, and rub with butter. Boil wild rice for about 30 minutes, or until tender; drain. Sauté 3 strips of bacon, then chop; pour off all but 2 tablespoons fat and sauté shallots for 8 to 10 minutes. Combine rice, bacon, shallots, herbs, and nuts in a mixing bowl, stirring thoroughly. Season to taste with salt and pepper and stuff fish. Bind opening in fish with skewers or thread and place on buttered baking dish. Slash skin of fish to prevent buckling, and lay 2 or 3 bacon strips on top. Bake for about 45 minutes, or until fish flakes readily at touch of a fork. Baste often with pan juices; serve on hot platter.

MAKES 4 TO 6 SERVINGS.

PETRALE SOLE WITH CALIFORNIA CHAMPAGNE

A large Pacific flounder, petrale sole is fished from Alaska to southern California and is deemed to be the most acceptable of West Coast flatfishes. Jamie Davies, who helps her husband, Jack, operate Schramsberg Vineyards in the Napa Valley, shared this recipe during a visit shortly after Schramsberg champagne had been selected to represent the United States during Richard Nixon's rapprochement with the People's Republic of China.

4 large fillets of sole
⅓ cup milk
¼ cup flour
salt
freshly ground pepper
4 Tbs. (½ stick) butter
2 cups cooked spinach, hot
freshly grated nutmeg
8 fresh mushrooms, sliced
1 Tbs. minced parsley
½ cup champagne

Dip fish pieces into milk and dredge with flour; season with salt and pepper. Melt butter in a pan large enough to hold fillets flat, and sauté for about 3 minutes on each side. Season spinach to taste with salt, pepper, and nutmeg and spread on a hot platter. When fish is evenly browned, arrange on top of spinach and keep warm. Sauté mushrooms in pan with butter remaining from cooking sole. Sprinkle with parsley, add champagne, and heat, but do not boil. Pour sauce over fish and spinach and serve very hot.

MAKES 4 SERVINGS.

STURGEON BAKED WITH NEW ENGLAND HARD CIDER

1 1/2 lb. sturgeon steak (1 1/2 to 2 in. thick)
4 very thin slices of salt pork
1 cup finely chopped onion
2 cups very dry cider or dry white wine
5 Tbs. butter, softened
3 Tbs. flour
1/2 cup heavy cream
salt
freshly ground black pepper
1/4 tsp. dried thyme
1/4 tsp. dried basil
1 Tbs. applejack
1 tsp. minced parsley

Cover bottom of an 8-inch baking dish with onion, laying fish steak on top and covering steak with salt pork slices. Pour cider (or wine if only sweet cider is available) over fish. Cut brown paper slightly larger than top of baking dish, saturating it well with about 2 tablespoons butter, then tuck paper in around edges of baking dish to enclose fish and onion. Bake for about 35 minutes, removing from oven when fish flakes easily. Meanwhile knead the flour with remaining 3 tablespoons butter. Remove fish and set aside to keep warm. Put baking dish over direct flame and slowly stir cream into onion-cider sauce; when hot but not boiling, blend in butter-flour paste. Taste as sauce thickens and add seasonings. Stir in applejack and cook for about 1 minute. Pour sauce over hot fish and sprinkle with chopped parsley.

MAKES 4 SERVINGS.

SWORDFISH CHOWDER

Impressive as swordfish can be when broiled, it is so good a fish that it deserves to be used in other ways too. This stew is so delicious that it ought to have a less prosaic title.

1 1/2 lb. swordfish, cut 2 in. thick
1 qt. fish stock, or half clam juice, half water
1 cup diced celery
2 tomatoes, peeled and chopped, or canned tomatoes, drained
1 Tbs. tomato paste
1/2 green pepper, chopped
1 medium-size onion, chopped
1/2 cup chopped carrot
1/2 tsp. dried thyme
1/2 tsp. dried basil
1 tsp. salt
freshly ground black pepper
4 bacon strips, cut into squares
2 small potatoes, diced
2 Tbs. minced parsley

Wipe fish and cut into 2-inch cubes. Heat stock in a 3-quart pot and add celery, tomatoes, tomato paste, green pepper, onion, carrot, herbs, salt, and several turns of pepper grinder; let simmer for about 30 minutes. Meanwhile sauté bacon squares, drain fat, and, when crisp, add squares to chowder. Add potatoes, continue cooking for 10 minutes, then add swordfish chunks and cook for about 20 minutes, or until potatoes are tender but firm. Sprinkle with parsley before serving.

MAKES 4 SERVINGS.

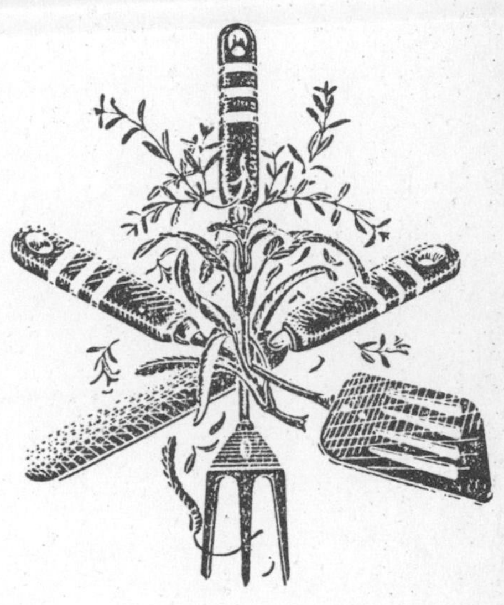

MENEMSHA SWORDFISH WITH FENNEL SPRIGS

3 lb. swordfish, cut 1 1/2 in. thick
4 Tbs. (1/2 stick) butter, melted
salt
freshly ground pepper
2 medium-size fennel heads

When fish is at room temperature, rub with butter, covering top and bottom thoroughly. Season with salt and pepper. Remove leafy sprigs from fennel and save bulbs for other use. Cover bottom of broiling pan with sprigs, put fish on top, and cover with more fennel. Broil about 4 inches from heat for 10 to 20 minutes, depending on thickness of fish; the flesh should flake easily when tested with a fork. Serve fish on a hot platter, arranging fennel sprigs around it.

MAKES 6 SERVINGS.

BROILED TILEFISH WITH WHITEFISH ROE

It was reported in the late 1970s that tilefish (a deep-dwelling creature with firm white flesh sometimes offered in place of lobster meat) was first commercially fished a century earlier, when a good haul was brought up off Nantucket Lightship in 1879. When more than four thousand miles of the Atlantic were covered with their floating bodies three years later, and when tilefish were no longer seen, fishermen assumed they had been wiped out. In the twentieth century, however, commercial fishing has harvested millions of pounds of tilefish annually, and big-game fishermen, angling in 400-foot waters off the New Jersey coast, go after specimens that weigh from twenty to fifty pounds. Whether brought home by sportsmen or found at a fishmonger's shop, tilefish can be cut into good-size slices for broiling; whitefish caviar from Wisconsin accents the rather bland, moist flesh.

5 Tbs. butter
4 slices of tilefish (about 1/2 inch thick each)
coarse salt
freshly ground pepper
1 lemon
4 tsp. whitefish caviar
2 Tbs. minced parsley

Smear about 1 tablespoon butter on the bottom of a baking pan just large enough to hold fish slices in one layer. Place fish in, season with salt and pepper, and squeeze several drops of lemon juice over each piece. Broil under high heat for 3 to 5 minutes, depending on the heat of your broiler, then turn fish over and broil for 3 or 4 minutes more. While broiling, cream remaining butter, then blend in caviar. Now spread equal amounts of this mixture on fish steaks, spoon hot juice over, and run under broiler for another minute to heat through. Spoon juice over again, sprinkle parsley on top, and serve with slices of lemon.

MAKES 4 SERVINGS.

FILLETED TROUT WITH MACADAMIA NUTS AND FRIED CAPERS

This was a dish featured one day during the Christmas holidays at the Four Seasons restaurant, and it was so good that we immediately tried to duplicate it at home.

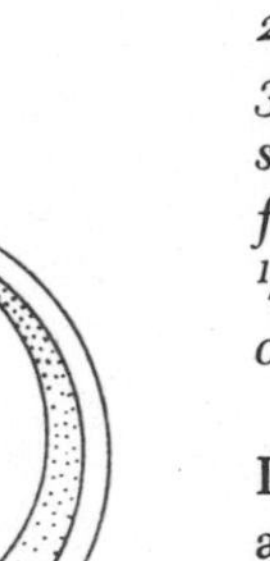

2 trout, filleted
3 to 4 tablespoons butter
salt
freshly ground pepper
1/4 cup macadamia nuts, sliced
oil for deep frying
2 Tbs. capers
splash of dry white wine
1/4 cup fish stock, or half clam juice, half water
3 Tbs. heavy cream
1/8 tsp. tomato paste

In a skillet large enough to hold the fillets melt about 3 tablespoons butter and, when almost sizzling, add trout. Sauté on one side for about 3 minutes, turn, cover for a minute, and then sauté the other side. Season well with salt and pepper. A total of 6 to 7 minutes should do it. Remove to a warm place, add nuts for a moment to toast, then toss over the trout fillets. Meanwhile in a separate small, sturdy pan heat enough oil to that a small strainer can be lowered into it. Let capers drain in the strainer. Returning to the trout pan, splash in a tablespoon or two of wine, then add stock and cream and boil down rapidly, stirring in just a taste of tomato paste and a little more butter. When reduced and slightly thickened, spoon this little bit of pan sauce over the fillets. Now quickly lower the capers into the almost smoking oil. Let them splutter and sizzle a few seconds, then remove the strainer and shake free of oil. Distribute fried capers in neat piles at either end of the fillets and serve immediately.

MAKES 2 SERVINGS.

CALIFORNIA FISH FILLETS IN RED WINE

2 1/2 Tbs. butter
2 white onions or shallots (white parts only), minced
4 fillets of rex sole or flounder
salt
freshly ground white pepper
3/4 cup Pinot Noir or other red wine
2 Tbs. minced parsley

Preheat oven to 350° F.

Use a baking dish just large enough to hold fillets that can also be used on top of stove. Melt 1 1/2 tablespoons butter in it, and cook onions or shallots for 2 or 3 minutes. Lay fillets on onions, sprinkle with salt and pepper, and pour in wine. Bring to a boil, then put baking dish into oven and bake 12 to 14 minutes, basting frequently. When sauce reduces to about 1/4 cup, remove dish from oven, sprinkle fish with parsley, and serve with buttered and parsleyed new potatoes.

MAKES 4 SERVINGS.

CUTCHOGUE FISH STEW

2 lb. fish fillets: sea bass, haddock, flounder
1 eel, skinned and cut into 2-in. pieces
1 Tbs. wine vinegar
1/4 cup olive oil
2 garlic cloves, minced
3 Tbs. minced fresh sorrel leaves, or 1 Tbs. puréed cooked fresh sorrel
1 bay leaf
2 Tbs. minced parsley
1/3 cup chopped onion
1 1/2 cups Muscadet or other dry white wine
2 tomatoes, peeled and chopped, or 1 cup canned
1 tsp. salt
freshly ground pepper
2 lb. fresh mussels
6 slices of stale bread

Put fillets and eel pieces into a mixing bowl and cover with vinegar and oil seasoned with garlic, sorrel, bay leaf, parsley, and onion; add wine, tomatoes, salt, and several turns of pepper grinder. Refrigerate for 2 hours or more.

Wash mussels under running water, using a brush to scrub thoroughly. When ready to cook, put fish and marinade into a heavy pot and spread mussels over; cover tightly and bring to a boil, then let simmer for 12 to 15 minutes. Stew will be done when eel is tender. Do not overcook. Put slices of bread in hot soup plates and pour stew on top.

MAKES 6 SERVINGS.

PINEBARK STEW

On the coast of the Carolinas fish stews have colloquial names. Along Albemarle Sound people get together outdoors to cook a kind of chowder famous in those parts as a "muddle." Some recipes start out with fifty pounds of rockfish and ten pounds of bacon. Even larger amounts have been needed when the annual Mullet Festival at Swansboro has drawn as many as five thousand persons. In the South, mullet is also combined with yams and onions to make a stew "unjustly ignored by cookbook makers," according to a South Carolinian. Pinebark stew is another local delight. "Since seasonings were unavailable during Revolutionary War days," a Carolina newspaper asserted, "the small tender roots of the pine tree (found by digging about 20 feet from the trunk of the tree) were used for flavoring. With homemade ketchup as a base, the only other seasoning was red pepper." Bacon is important to make a good pinebark stew, and the Carolinian cook would use blue bream, redbreast, bass, trout, or even such saltwater fish as sheepshead.

4 bacon strips
1 cup chopped onions
1 1/2 cups finely diced potatoes
1 qt. boiling water
2 tsp. salt
1/2 tsp. dried thyme
1/2 tsp. dried marjoram
2-in. piece of dried hot red pepper pod
1 1/2 lb. bass
1 lb. perch
4 or 5 small tomatoes, peeled, or equivalent canned

Cut bacon into squares and sauté for 13 to 15 minutes over very low heat. Drain off all but about 3 tablespoons fat. Stir in onions and cook for about 5 minutes. Stir in potatoes, cover with boiling water, and season with salt, herbs, and dried pepper pod. Let simmer for 15 to 20 minutes. Add whole fish and continue to let simmer for 10 minutes. Add tomatoes and cook for 5 to 10 more, or until fish flakes easily. Remove pepper pod before serving.
MAKES 4 SERVINGS.

SEA MARSH STEW

This is a fine example of cooking in Cajun kitchens, where *crawfish* is the only word for what much of the rest of the world calls crayfish. If you can't get crayfish, use about 10 ounces of canned tiny Pacific shrimps, but do not add them until the end; cook just long enough to heat through, or they may disintegrate.

1 onion
1 lb. medium-size raw shrimps
1 lb. crayfish
1 ½ cups water
2 cups heavy cream
2 tsp. Worcestershire sauce
pinch of dry mustard
salt
pinch of cayenne pepper
1 tsp. hot sherry pepper sauce, if available
¼ tsp. fennel seed
1 pkg. (10-oz.) frozen small peas, or 1 ½ cups fresh shelled
paprika for garnish
toast rounds

Slice the onion very thin and distribute over the bottom of a heavy pan. Add 1 cup water and bring to a boil. Scatter shrimps on top, then crayfish, and cover tightly. Let steam for 5 minutes. Remove shellfish (but reserve water) and, when cool enough to handle, pull off shells. Add cream and seasonings to reserved shrimp water. Heat, blend well, and return shellfish to the pot. Let simmer for about 5 minutes. Meanwhile blanch the peas in remaining ½ cup water until barely tender, then add to the pot. Now taste carefully and add more seasoning if desired. A true Louisianan would want the liquid to leave a burning sensation on the lips. Turn the stew into warm bowls, dust with paprika, and tuck in a round or two or three of dry toasted bread.

MAKES 6 TO 8 SERVINGS.

SEAFOOD GUMBO

Happiness for a cotton factor or rice planter of the Old South has been defined as a midday meal with a long mint julep to begin it, a slice of iced watermelon to end it, and a thick pottage based on okra as the *pièce de résistance*. Varying as they do throughout the South, such gumbos are often mixtures that include two or more kinds of shellfish and one or more kinds of meat. Lafcadio Hearn, whose *La Cuisine Créole* was published in 1885, recommended enriching a beef or chicken gumbo with oysters, crab, or shrimps, "as all improve the gombo [*sic*]." Goose, or waterbirds (*poule d'eau*) may be used in Louisiana, and in Tennessee some cooks make the cabbage gumbo of the central hills, which leaves out poultry and seafood in favor of tangy country ham, Tennessee pork sausage, and milk.

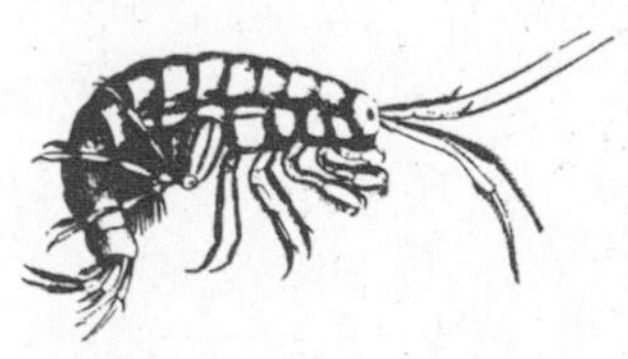

½-lb. piece of ham
1 ½ lb. raw shrimps
1 garlic clove, minced
4 white onions, chopped
¾ lb. fresh okra, trimmed and sliced
2 ½ cups chopped peeled tomatoes
1 can (6 oz.) tomato paste
3 cups chicken stock
several dashes of Tabasco
1 Tbs. Creole seasoning† (optional)
1 green pepper, chopped
1 lb. crab meat
1 lemon
1 Tbs. filé powder
18 fresh mussels, well scrubbed

†Creole seasoning may be found in specialty food stores.

Trim fat from ham, cut lean meat into cubes, and render enough fat to make about 2 tablespoonfuls in bottom of a heavy skillet; reserve remainder. Peel and wash shrimps; pat dry. Sauté garlic, onions, and okra in ham fat, adding shrimps after 10 minutes; continue to cook for 5 minutes more. Remove shrimps and okra to refrigerator. Stir tomatoes into skillet and add tomato paste, stock, Tabasco, and Creole seasoning. Let simmer for 2 hours or more. Add reserved okra 30 minutes before serving. Heat some of reserved ham fat and sauté green pepper and crab meat for about 10 minutes, then add to gumbo. Grate lemon rind and add. Stir in filé powder and reserved shrimps, then top with mussels. Cover tightly and let steam until mussels open. Serve over hot rice.

MAKES 6 TO 8 SERVINGS.

SEAFOOD PILAU

Pilau is probably originally a Turkish word, but the kind of food described is known all over the Middle East, often as *pilav*, or *pilaf*; in India the usual spelling is *pullao*. Recipes arrived in the United States some time after rice was first planted in Carolina, perhaps brought by Charleston trading vessels, and both the spelling and the pronunciation were soon distorted. In places like Savannah and New Orleans it is still frequently referred to as purloo, and spelled sometimes "perlew," sometimes "purlow." Southerners consider a variety of combinations to be their own, from okra or tomato pilaus to those made with lamb, pork, chicken, fish, or shellfish.

2 Tbs. bacon fat
1/4 cup chopped shallots or whole scallions
1/4 cup chopped green pepper
1/2 cup uncooked rice
1 cup fish or chicken stock
1/2 canned red pepper, drained and minced
1/2 tsp. dried thyme
salt
1 cup canned or fresh oysters
1 cup minced clams
1 cup canned or fresh crab meat, drained
1 cup sliced cooked okra
1 cup diced country ham

Melt fat and sauté shallots or scallions and green pepper for 3 or 4 minutes, then stir in rice, coat rice with fat, and cook for 2 or 3 minutes. Add stock, bring to a boil, then let simmer under tight-fitting cover for 20 to 25 minutes, until rice is fluffy and rather dry. (You may use half chicken or other white stock and half liquid from oysters and/or clams; or you may add seafood liquids if rice absorbs stock before it is done.) Season with red pepper, sage, thyme, and very little salt if using country ham. Mix in oysters, clams, crab meat, okra, and ham. Flavors meld better when this dish is made early so it can be set aside to steep under a tight cover; heat carefully just before serving.

MAKES 4 SERVINGS.

GAME

CORNMEAL PANCAKES STUFFED WITH GAME

This is a delicious dish made with leftover game—Canada goose, mallard duck, teal, or any wild-bird dinner of which enough might be left so that by assiduous picking the cook may have 2 cups of finely minced meat. The carcass and separate bones must be stewed for several hours to make a broth first.

STOCK:

2 or 3 game bird carcasses, or other poultry parts
2 carrots
2 onions, unpeeled
2 celery ribs
6 cups water
salt
freshly ground pepper

PANCAKES:

1/2 cup yellow cornmeal
1 tsp. salt
1/2 cup boiling water
1/2 cup flour
1 Tbs. baking powder
1/2 cup milk
1/4 cup water
1/4 cup corn oil
1 egg, well beaten

FILLING:

2 Tbs. butter
1/4 cup finely chopped shallots or whole scallions
1 cup coarsely chopped fresh mushrooms
2 Tbs. flour
2 Tbs. Madeira
2 cups finely chopped game bird meat
salt
freshly ground pepper

SAUCE:

2 Tbs. butter
2 Tbs. flour
salt
freshly ground pepper
1 Tbs. Madeira (optional)
3 Tbs. chopped parsley

Preheat oven to 400° F.

Make the stock: Break and flatten carcasses, put them into a pot with vegetables, and cover with at least 6 cups of water. Add seasoning after letting simmer for 3 hours or more, during which time stock should have considerably reduced; it must be rich in flavor. You should have about 3 cups to use in filling and sauce.

Make the filling: Melt butter in a skillet and sauté shallots or scallions for 4 to 5 minutes. Add mushrooms and cook for about 7 minutes. Stir in flour and let it brown slightly. Off the heat, stir in 1 cup freshly made game bird stock, returning to heat when flour is absorbed; stir until it comes to a boil, then add wine and let simmer for 5 minutes. Add meat and seasonings to taste, and let it heat.

While this meat filling is simmering, make the pancakes: Mix together cornmeal, salt, and boiling water; beat well, then add flour, baking powder, milk, water, oil, and egg, blending thoroughly. Brush an 8-inch skillet with a little butter, heat until almost smoking, and pour in enough batter to cover bottom of pan thinly after pan is tipped to spread batter evenly to edges. Cook over medium heat, turning when bubbles appear on surface; cook other side until lightly browned. Repeat, making 8 pancakes in all.

Divide filling into 8 portions; spread 1 portion in a line in middle of each cake, turn up edge nearest, and roll. Put in buttered ovenproof dish just large enough to hold 8 stuffed rolls. Bake for 15 minutes. Reserve skillet in which filling was cooked.

Make the sauce: Melt butter in skillet in which filling was cooked, scraping brown bits and letting butter turn almost brown without burning. Blend in flour. When bubbles appear, add 2 cups freshly made hot game broth. Cook, stirring constantly as sauce thickens, and add salt and pepper to taste and optional Madeira. When stuffed pancakes are piping hot, spoon sauce over them and sprinkle with parsley.

MAKES 4 SERVINGS.

GAME BIRD CROQUETTES WITH MUSHROOM SAUCE

3 Tbs. butter
1/3 cup flour
1 cup game bird stock or chicken stock
2 cups minced meat from roasted partridge or other game birds
salt
freshly ground pepper
flour
1 egg, well beaten
3/4 cup fresh bread crumbs
1 qt., or more, oil for deep frying
Simple Mushroom and Madeira Sauce (p. 444)

*Preheat oven to 350° F.**

Melt butter in a saucepan, stir in flour, and cook slowly 2 to 3 minutes. Off the heat, stir in stock, a little at a time, then return to heat and stir constantly, eliminating lumps, for about 10 minutes as sauce cooks and thickens. Stir in partridge or other meat; season with salt and pepper. Let cool, then chill for 1 hour or more. Shape chilled partridge mixture into 4 cylindrical croquettes; roll them first in flour, then in egg, then in bread crumbs. Chill overnight.

Heat oil to 375° to 385° F.* Immerse croquettes. In 2 minutes turn them over and fry for 1 or 2 minutes more. Remove with a slotted spoon and drain on paper towels; keep warm in oven. Serve with mushroom sauce.

MAKES 2 TO 4 SERVINGS.

WISCONSIN BEAR STEAK

MARINADE:

3 medium-size onions, chopped
1 1/4 cups chopped shallots
1 1/2 cups chopped carrots
3/4 cup vinegar
2 tsp. salt
5 cups dry white wine
2 garlic cloves, minced
1 tsp. peppercorns, cracked
2 bay leaves
1 tsp. minced fresh tarragon
2/3 cup chopped celery

1/4 lb. (1 stick) butter, melted
1/4 cup minced chives
2 Tbs. prepared mustard
2 Tbs. tomato paste
1/2 tsp. Worcestershire sauce
1 garlic clove, minced
2 bear steaks (2 1/2 lb. each, 2 in. thick)
salt
freshly ground pepper

Combine marinade ingredients in a saucepan, cover, and cook for 5 minutes. Marinate steaks in cooked marinade for 2 to 3 days. Drain, and dry on paper towels. Combine butter, chives, mustard, tomato paste, Worcestershire sauce, and garlic; warm over low heat. Broil steaks for 6 to 8 minutes, then turn and broil for about 7 minutes more; baste constantly with butter mixture and season with salt and pepper before serving.

MAKES 6 TO 8 SERVINGS.

BARBECUED BUFFALO STEAK WITH WILD RICE DRESSING

2/3 cup uncooked wild rice
2 cups water
1/2 tsp. salt
2 Tbs. vegetable oil
1 lb. ground buffalo chuck
1 medium-size onion, chopped fine
1/3 lb. fresh mushrooms, sliced
2 cups diced French bread
1 cup beef stock, heated
1/4 tsp. ground sage
salt
freshly ground pepper
4 buffalo T-bone steaks

Preheat oven to 350° F.

Wash wild rice and put into a saucepan with water and salt. Bring to a boil, cover, and let simmer for about 35 minutes, or until tender. Drain and set aside. Meanwhile heat oil in a skillet and brown ground chuck with onion and mushrooms, stirring frequently. Soak bread in stock briefly, then stir in cooked rice and ground meat, seasoning to taste with sage, salt, and pepper. Turn mixture into a greased casserole, cover, and bake for 1 hour. About 15 minutes before serving, barbecue steaks. Sprinkle with salt and serve on hot plates with wild rice dressing.

MAKES 4 SERVINGS.

MALLARD DUCKS FLAMED WITH BOURBON AND BRAISED WITH TURNIPS AND ONIONS

2 mallard ducks
1 tsp. dried rosemary
1 tsp. dried savory
1/2 tsp. dried thyme
salt
freshly ground pepper
6 Tbs. (3/4 stick) butter
10 small white turnips, cut into halves
20 small white onions
1 tsp. sugar
1/3 cup bourbon
1 1/2 cups duck or chicken stock

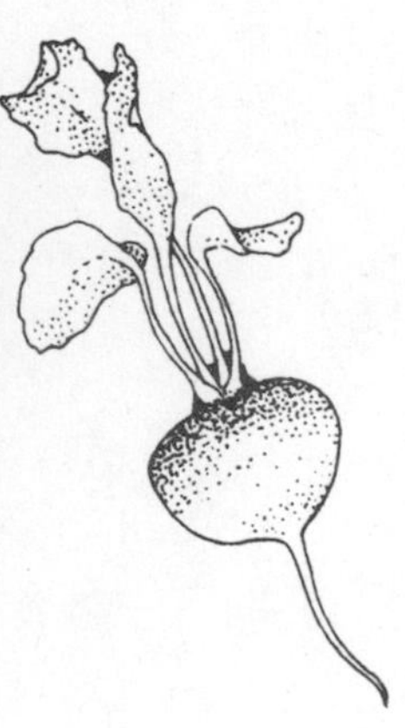

Preheat oven to 325° F.

Wipe out cavities of birds with a damp cloth. Crush herbs together and use half of this to sprinkle into cavities along with a generous amount of salt and pepper. Rub outsides of birds with salt and pepper too. In a flameproof casserole large enough to accommodate ducks with vegetables surrounding them, melt butter over medium heat and skim off foam. Brown ducks on all sides, then add turnips and onions to brown, sprinkling sugar over them and turning them until glazed. Warm bourbon, pour over birds, and set aflame, basting. Add stock and remaining herbs. Bring to a boil, then cover the casserole and bake for 1 hour. Uncover, baste, and raise heat to 375°

for a final 10 minutes. Split ducks in half. Skim off excess fat and boil down pan juices until almost syrupy. Pour this over duck halves, surround with vegetables, and serve with green peas and corn bread.

MAKES 4 SERVINGS.

WILD DUCK SOUP

The novelist Hervey Allen described a soup based on wild ducks so temptingly that a Chicago hostess, Peggy Harvey, was impelled to turn fiction into fact—with the following results.

2 wild ducks with giblets
1 medium-size onion, peeled
1 cup uncooked wild rice
1 quart hard cider, or half sweet cider, half dry white wine
1/4 tsp. ground sage
1/4 cup minced parsley
1 bay leaf
1/4 tsp. dried marjoram
6 cups water
1 scant tsp. arrowroot starch dissolved in 1 Tbs. water
salt
freshly ground pepper
1/4 tsp. freshly grated nutmeg
1 Tbs. dark rum

Put cleaned ducks, their giblets, onion, and wild rice into a pot. Cover with hard cider. Let simmer, covered, for about 2 hours, or until ducks are tender. Take out ducks, remove meat from bones, and cut into small pieces; remove onion and return meat to pot. Add sage, parsley, bay leaf, marjoram, and water. Let simmer for about 1 hour more—the longer it simmers, the smoother it gets. Just before serving, stir arrowroot-water mixture into soup, adding salt and pepper to taste; grate in nutmeg and add rum.

MAKES 6 TO 8 SERVINGS.

BAKED BREAST OF WILD DUCK

Canvasback ducks from Havre de Grace, Maryland, fed on wild celery before flying northward and were internationally acclaimed as one of America's great wild foods; Charles Ranhofer, famous as chef of Delmonico's, roasted them over coals and served them with squares of hominy samp dipped in egg and sautéed. An equally American accompaniment for ducks, wild or domestic, is wild rice.

3 mallard ducks
1 cup flour
salt
freshly ground pepper
4 Tbs. (1/2 stick) butter
grated rind of 1 orange
1 1/2 cups heavy cream
1/2 cup dry sherry

Preheat oven to 350°F.

Use a sharp knife to pry breasts from ducks. Season flour with salt and pepper and dust meat thoroughly. Melt butter in a heavy skillet and brown breasts evenly. Put them in a casserole, fitting snugly. Sprinkle with orange rind and pour over 1 cup cream and the sherry; sprinkle lightly with salt and pepper. Bake for about 1 1/2 hours; add remaining cream and continue baking for 30 minutes more.

MAKES 4 OR MORE SERVINGS.

SPIT-ROASTED WILD CANADIAN GOOSE WITH FRIED APPLES

1 Canada goose (4 to 5 lb.)
coarse salt
freshly ground pepper
5 tart apples
1 celery rib
2 pieces of fresh pork fat (approximately 3 by 5 in.)
4 Tbs. (1/2 stick) butter
2 to 3 Tbs. brown sugar
3 Tbs. dried currants soaked in applejack
1/4 cup applejack, warmed

Rinse cavity of goose, dry with paper towels, and rub in coarse salt and pepper. Stuff with 1 apple, quartered, and the celery rib; skewer or sew up vent. To roast, make sure the spit is under a good hot broiler or over very hot coals. Cover breast with pork fat, tying string around snugly. Place bird on spit and roast for 1 hour. About 20 minutes before serving, prepare fried apples by coring and peeling remaining apples, then slicing into fairly thick pieces. Fry in foaming butter, turning, and adding the brown sugar after 5 minutes. Continue to fry until golden, then add currants. Place apples around goose on a platter and just before serving, ignite applejack and pour, flaming, over all.

MAKES 4 SERVINGS.

WILD GOOSE CASSOULET

4 cups dried white navy beans
1/4 lb. Italian salami, cut into 1/4-in. cubes
3 cups dry white wine
4 tomatoes, peeled, seeded, and chopped
4 large onions, chopped
4 peppercorns
2 tsp. chopped parsley
1/4 tsp. dried rosemary
2 garlic cloves, minced
1 bay leaf
1 wild goose (8 lb.), cut into 8 to 10 pieces
salt
freshly ground pepper
1/2 cup olive oil
6 garlic sausages
1 cup fresh bread crumbs

Preheat oven to 200° F. *
Soak beans in water to cover for at least 10 hours. Drain, discarding any beans that float on the surface.* Put into a large lidded earthenware casserole. Add salami, 1 cup wine, the tomatoes, onions, peppercorns, parsley, rosemary, garlic, bay leaf, and enough water to cover. Cover the casserole tightly and bake for 6 hours, adding more water if needed.

Rub goose pieces with salt and pepper. Heat oil to sizzling, add goose, and brown lightly on all sides. Reduce heat, add remaining 2 cups wine, and let simmer, covered, for 30 minutes. Stir goose and sauce carefully into bean casserole. In another skillet sauté garlic sausages until well browned; remove, reserving fat. Stir sausages into casserole carefully; cover and bake in a 250° oven for 1 1/2 hours. Sauté bread crumbs in sausage fat and sprinkle over top of casserole. Bake, uncovered, for 10 minutes more to brown crumbs.

MAKES 8 TO 10 SERVINGS.

WILD GOOSE GUMBO

2 Tbs. butter
2 lb. fresh okra, trimmed and sliced
1 Tbs. flour
1/2 cup chopped celery
2 garlic cloves, minced
1 medium-size onion, chopped
1 green pepper, chopped
2 qt. water
2 bay leaves
2 Tbs. salt
1/3 cup tomato paste
1 wild goose, about 5 to 6 lb.

Heat butter in a large soup pot and sauté sliced okra. Stir in flour, adding celery, garlic, onion, and green pepper; continue to stir while cooking for about 5 minutes. Add water, bay leaves, salt, and tomato paste. Bring to a boil, then let simmer for about half an hour. Meanwhile cut goose into pieces and add to pot, cover and simmer for about 2 hours, or until meat is very tender; remove goose, extract all the meat from bones, dice, and add to gumbo. Let gumbo simmer for 15 minutes. Wild duck is used to make a similar gumbo, which is often served with a spoonful of cooked rice in each soup plate.

MAKES 6 TO 8 SERVINGS.

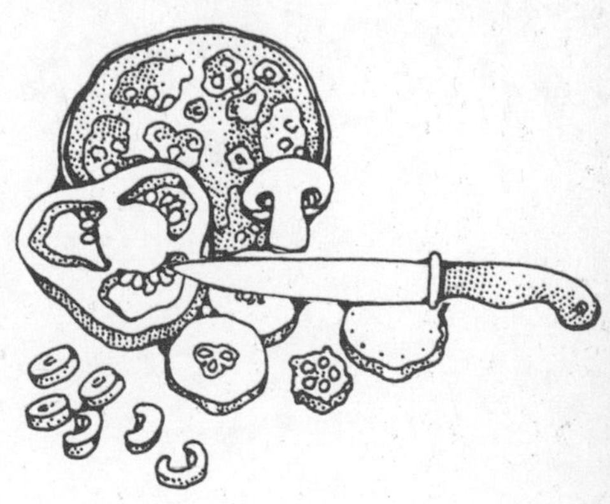

BREASTS OF GUINEA HEN WITH VIRGINIA HAM

2 guinea hen breasts, cut into halves
1 to 2 Tbs. butter
1 1/2 Tbs. minced shallot
8 medium-size fresh mushrooms, chopped
2 cups cream
1 1/2 Tbs. sherry
4 fresh mushroom caps
4 paper-thin slices of Virginia ham
4 slices of toast
4 whole fresh mushrooms, broiled

Remove skin from guinea breasts and sauté breasts in butter for about 10 minutes, turning to cook evenly. Remove from pan and keep warm. Add a little butter to the pan if necessary and sauté shallot and mushrooms for 1 or 2 minutes; cover pan, lower heat, and let simmer for 5 minutes. Add cream and sherry; when liquid is hot, add meat and let simmer for 10 minutes more. Meanwhile broil mushroom caps, heat up ham slices, and make toast. Place 1 slice of ham on each slice of toast, top with guinea hen breast, and pour mushroom-shallot sauce over all. Garnish each serving with 1 broiled whole mushroom.

MAKES 4 SERVINGS.

FRICASSEE OF HARE
(Virginia, c. 1780)

1 hare
1 cup flour
salt
freshly ground pepper
1/2 tsp. dried savory
6 Tbs. vegetable oil
1 small onion, chopped coarse
2 small turnips, cut into eighths
2 celery ribs, cut into 1/2-in. slices
1/4 cup chopped parsley
6 cups chicken stock
slice of lemon rind (about 1 1/2 in. square)
3 whole cloves
2 bay leaves
1/2 tsp. ground mace
1/2 cup fresh bread crumbs
2 Tbs. ground suet
2 tsp. finely minced parsley
1/2 tsp. dried thyme
1/2 tsp. dried marjoram
1 tsp. grated lemon rind
1/4 cup chopped ham
1 egg, well beaten

Cut hare into serving-size pieces. Mix flour, 1 Tbs. salt, several turns of the pepper grinder, and savory, then use to dredge pieces of hare. Brown hare pieces in oil in a skillet large enough to hold them in a single layer. Add onion, turnips, celery, and parsley and cover meat with stock. Bring to a boil, then let simmer over very low heat for about 2 1/4 hours, or until hare is very tender. Make ham balls by combining bread crumbs and suet with herbs, grated lemon rind, ham, and salt and pepper to taste; add egg and blend mixture thoroughly. Form into balls and roll in flour. Remove pieces of hare from stock and keep warm. Cook ham balls in stock for about 10 minutes; remove and keep warm along with meat. Make a paste of about 1/4 cup of flour and some of the hot stock, then mix into simmering stock and cook until sauce thickens. Return hare and ham balls to pan just long enough to get thoroughly hot, and serve from pan.

MAKES 6 TO 8 SERVINGS.

OPOSSUM AND SWEET POTATOES

1 opossum (about 2 1/2 lb.), skinned and cleaned
salt
freshly ground pepper
flour
1/2 cup water
4 medium-size sweet potatoes
2 Tbs. sugar

Preheat oven to 350° F.

Wipe opossum with a damp cloth and trim and discard excess fat. Mix salt with pepper and rub thoroughly into possum, inside and out. Sprinkle inside and out with flour. Put opossum on its back in a roasting pan with a tight-fitting lid. Pour in water, cover, and roast in oven for about 50 minutes. Cut sweet potatoes in half lengthwise and surround opossum with them. If water has evaporated, add enough to cover bottom of pan. Cover and return to oven for about 25 minutes more. Remove cover and sprinkle sweet potatoes with about 1/4 teaspoon salt and the sugar. Continue roasting until meat and potatoes become crisp on the surface.

MAKES 3 TO 4 SERVINGS.

CHUKKA PARTRIDGES, SPLIT, BAKED, AND BROILED

If you're a little short on the game you brought home, this is a good way to make one partridge do for two, particularly if you serve each half on a potato pancake with a good helping of red cabbage alongside. Of course, if you have plenty of partridges, be generous and offer both halves per serving.

2 chukka partridges
2 Tbs. butter, softened
salt
freshly ground pepper
1/2–3/4 cup Madeira
4 thin slices of fatback
1 doz., or more, garlic cloves, unpeeled
1/2 lb. fresh mushrooms, chopped coarse

Preheat oven to 400° F.

Use poultry shears or a sharp knife to cut through the breastbone and slice open each partridge from neck to tail. Flatten out and place in a baking pan just large enough to hold both birds. Rub them well on both sides with butter, salt, and pepper. Pour in enough Madeira so that the pan is filled by 1/4 inch. Put the birds in, skin side up, cover the breasts with fatback slices, and scatter unpeeled garlic cloves around. Bake for 30 minutes, basting every 5 minutes. Then add mushrooms, tossing them well in the basting juices, and bake for about 10 minutes more, or until the juices at the leg joints run clear when pricked. Then quickly brown under a very hot broiler, just long enough for the skin to get crackly and to darken slightly. If making potato pancakes, have them ready just before you slip the birds under the broiler. Cut birds in half if serving only half per person. Garlic lovers can squeeze the cloves over crusty bread and eat.

MAKES 4 SMALL SERVINGS.

FRESH PERCH WITH ALMONDS, PINE NUTS, AND OLIVES

Of freshwater game fish, as many yellow perch are caught by barefoot youngsters with a bent pin and a plump worm as any other way—and hundreds are brought home by adult anglers in most of the states. The recipe below has some Spanish-American influences developed in the Sierras.

1/2 lb. (2 sticks) butter
4 yellow perch, split
1/4 cup almonds, blanched
1/2 cup pine nuts
12 pimiento-stuffed green olives, sliced

Melt half the butter and brown perch, skin side down. Heat remaining butter in a separate pan and sauté nuts slightly. Spoon this mixture over perch to cook top side. When fish is tender enough to flake easily, transfer to a hot platter, pouring over it the nut-butter sauce, and garnishing with sliced olives.

MAKES 4 SERVINGS.

PHEASANT WITH CHORIZOS

Hunters in the Southwest enhance the game they bring home with recipes that reflect both Indian and Spanish influence. Highly flavored sausage, like chorizos, are as complementary to the wild taste of pheasants from sagebrush country as they are to venison (see recipe p. 381).

1/2 lb. sliced bacon, chopped
2 pheasants
2 medium-size onions, chopped
2 cups cooked prunes with juice
1 lb. chorizo sausages
2/3 cup port
freshly ground pepper
1/2 tsp. hot chili powder

Preheat oven to 375° F.

Fry bacon in a skillet, add pheasants, and brown on all sides. Drain all but about 2 tablespoons bacon fat and sauté onions for 2 to 3 minutes. Heat juice from prunes in a saucepan and in it cook chorizos for about 5 minutes. Remove sausages with a slotted spoon, then fry along with pheasants until browned on all sides. Put pheasants in a casserole, placing sausages on top, add prunes and prune juice, port, a liberal sprinkling of pepper, and the chili powder. Cover casserole and bake for about 1 ½ hours.

MAKES 4 SERVINGS.

PHEASANT WITH GJETOST SAUCE

Norwegian-American cooks in the Midwest often use the goat cheese of their ancestral kitchens in cooking, and in good hunting country they developed this unusual way of preparing pheasant.

2 pheasants
3 Tbs. butter
freshly ground pepper
½ cup, or more, cream
¼ lb. Gjetost cheese, shaved thin
8 to 10 juniper berries
2 to 3 Tbs. quince, red currant, or rowanberry jelly

Preheat oven to 375° F.

Brown pheasants in butter and turn them, with their juices, into as tightly fitting a casserole as possible. Sprinkle with pepper. Put casserole in oven for 30 minutes, then turn heat down to 225° and add about half the cream to pan juices; fit cover tightly and continue cooking for about 1 hour more, or until birds are well done. Remove and keep warm. Add Gjetost shavings and juniper berries to juice in casserole and stir over medium heat to melt cheese; stir in remaining cream, or more to taste; add jelly, and let it melt. Top pheasant with a little sauce when serving and serve remaining sauce in a sauceboat.

MAKES 4 SERVINGS.

POLISH-AMERICAN STUFFED PIKE

Old World ways with fish have been much adapted, and the northern pike of the Upper Midwest have been turned into delicious dishes like this one when brought home by Polish-American anglers. If the pike comes from a market, look it in the eye and be sure it is absolutely fresh.

2 pike (about 1 ¼ lb. each), split open
4 Tbs. (½ stick) butter
½ cup chopped onions
½ cup chopped celery
½ cup chopped apples
½ cup chopped fresh mushrooms
¾ cup fresh bread crumbs
1 egg, beaten
¼ tsp. dried thyme
salt
freshly ground pepper
3 Tbs. butter, softened
Warsaw Sour Cream Sauce (p. 446)

Preheat oven to 450° F.

Rinse fish and pat dry. Melt butter and sauté onions and celery over low heat for about 5 minutes. Add apples and mushrooms and sauté for 2 or 3 minutes more. Off the heat, stir in bread crumbs, blend in egg, and add thyme, salt to taste, and several turns of pepper grinder. Stuff this fruit-vegetable-crumb mixture into cavities of fish, skewering or sewing them up to hold in stuffing. Rub fish with softened butter, sprinkle with salt and pepper, and bake in a buttered baking dish under a foil cover for 30 minutes. Remove foil, brown in oven for 5 minutes, and serve with sour cream sauce.

MAKES 4 SERVINGS.

BRAISED QUAIL, SQUABS, OR ROCK CORNISH GAME HENS

4 small birds (about 1 1/4 lb. each)
salt
freshly ground pepper
1 cup flour
1/2 oz. dried mushrooms
1/2 cup water
6 Tbs. butter
2 Tbs. vegetable oil
1/3 cup finely chopped whole scallions
1/4 cup minced country ham
1/3 cup bourbon, warmed
3/4 cup chicken stock
pinch of dried thyme
1/4 tsp. dried tarragon
1/4 tsp. freshly grated nutmeg
1 bay leaf
4 tsps. chopped parsley

Sprinkle birds inside and out with salt and pepper, then dredge with flour. Soak mushrooms in 1/2 cup warm water for 30 minutes. Melt 3 tablespoons butter and oil in a large enameled pot and brown birds, 1 at a time, on all surfaces; remove, then wipe pot clean. Melt remaining butter and sauté scallions until white parts are translucent; then stir in country ham, mushrooms, and the water in which they soaked. Return birds to pot, add bourbon, set aflame, and baste birds. When alcohol has burned off, stir in stock and bring to a boil, adding thyme, tarragon, nutmeg, and bay leaf. Simmer for about 45 minutes, basting often. When tender, put birds on a heated platter in a warm place. Boil down juices in pot to about 1 cup, removing bay leaf. Pour sauce over birds. Sprinkle with parsley and serve.

MAKES 4 SERVINGS.

GRILLED OR BROILED QUAIL À LA GRECQUE

During hunting season in Florida, some Greek-American outdoorsmen develop an appetite for quail cooked as it is in Greece. Birds are frequently grilled over hot coals, rubbed first with a little oil, some garlic if desired, salt, and pepper—a technique that can be easily adapted to the backyard barbecue or to the oven broiler, provided you get your cooking medium good and hot.

3 quail
2 Tbs. olive oil
1/2 tsp. coarse salt
freshly ground pepper
1 or 2 garlic cloves, mashed
1/2 tsp. dried thyme (optional)

Mash oil, salt, pepper, garlic, and thyme, if used, together in a mortar. Then rub mixture over quail inside and out. Set birds on the grill or on the rack of preheated broiler, and grill or broil them for 5 minutes on each side.

MAKES 1 SERVING.

SQUIRRELS IN A CLAY POT

1 tsp. ground savory
1 tsp. dried marjoram
1 tsp. dried thyme
1 Tbs. coarse salt
freshly ground pepper
2 squirrels (about 1 lb. each), cut into 8 to 10 pieces each
2 large onions, chopped
3 oz. country ham with some fat, cut into strips
1 Tbs. sweet butter
1/3 cup red wine

Preheat oven to 450° F.

Crush herbs together along with coarse salt and add about 8 turns of pepper grinder then rub pieces of squirrel thoroughly with mixture. Place onion in the bottom of a presoaked 4-quart clay pot, put squirrel pieces on top, and then strew ham strips over. Dot with butter and cover with the clay top. Bake for 1 hour and 40 minutes. Remove and add wine, then bake, covered, for a final 20 minutes. Serve with spoon bread (p. 000).

MAKES 3 TO 4 SERVINGS.

LAKE TROUT SAUTÉED WITH FRESH SAGE

Anyone who has grown up in Minnesota knows what the taste of freshly caught trout can do to one, and there is some reason to think that the effect is greater on visitors. Before this recipe was tried, an acquaintance told a story about being the state's hostess for the duke and duchess of Windsor. When she served trout for the fish course, "the duke ate his first trout in two minutes flat and asked for a second." He might have liked the following presentation even better.

4 lake trout (1 lb. each)
butter
¼ cup chopped fresh sage
salt
freshly ground pepper

Wash trout in cold salted water and pat dry. Melt enough butter to cover bottom of a large skillet 1 inch deep. Add sage and let simmer for 1 minute. Slip in fish. Brown, then cover and cook slowly for 10 minutes on first side, turn, sprinkle with salt and pepper, then cook for 5 minutes on second side. Zucchini cooked with chopped black walnuts (p. 263) makes a delicious accompaniment.

MAKES 4 SERVINGS.

BLACK-WALNUT-BREADED PANFRIED TROUT

4 Rocky Mountain trout (about 1 lb. each), cleaned
coarse salt
freshly ground black pepper
⅔ cup ground black walnuts
½ cup fresh bread crumbs
¼ cup crumbs from Montpelier water biscuits or soda crackers
1 egg
3 Tbs. butter
3 to 4 Tbs. walnut oil
½ cup dry white wine or hard cider, or tea plus 5 to 6 drops of lemon juice
2 Tbs. mixed minced fresh herbs: parsley, chives, basil, or tarragon
1 lemon, quartered

Rinse trout under cold water, pat dry, and sprinkle inside and out with coarse salt and pepper. Mix walnuts, bread crumbs, and cracker crumbs, and spread out on wax paper. Break egg into a large saucer, beat lightly with a fork, then dip each trout into egg, coating each side. Next, dip fish into crumbs, coating thickly. Heat 2 tablespoons butter and 2 tablespoons oil in a large skillet; when almost smoking, put in trout and fry over medium heat for 8 to 10 minutes, depending on size, on one side and 4 to 5 minutes on other side. Add remaining butter and oil as needed. Remove fish to warm plate. Sizzle wine (or other liquid) into hot skillet; swirl around and let it reduce for about 1 minute. Add fresh herbs and pour over fish. Serve with lemon quarters.

MAKES 4 SERVINGS.

BRAISED WILD TURKEY

Knowledgeable hunters are apt to consider the wild turkey the most delicious of all game birds. They should be field-dressed immediately, especially when hunting on warm days that occur in spring and fall. When it comes to cooking, wild turkeys may be prepared according to any recipe used for domestic turkeys, with special effort taken to keep the meat moist.

1 wild turkey
salt
freshly ground pepper
1 lb. salt pork, sliced
1 qt. chicken stock
1 medium-size onion, sliced
1 medium-size carrot, sliced
2 or 3 parsley sprigs
1 large celery rib, chopped
1 bay leaf
1/2 tsp. dried thyme

Preheat oven to 400° F.
Wash turkey and dry with paper towels. Sprinkle cavity with salt and pepper, then stuff with half of sliced salt pork; lay remaining slices on turkey to cover, securing with toothpicks. Put turkey into oven to brown. Meanwhile combine stock, onion, carrot, parsley, celery, bay leaf, and thyme in a saucepan. When turkey has roasted for about 1 hour, remove salt pork from cavity and pour stock and vegetables over. Reduce heat to 300° and continue cooking for 2 to 3 hours more, or until meat is very tender. Baste at frequent intervals.

MAKES 6 TO 8 SERVINGS.

VENISON IN CABBAGE LEAVES

3 cups chopped or coarsely ground cooked venison (about 1 lb.)
2 cups cooked wild or brown rice
2 to 3 Tbs. butter
1 small head of cabbage
2 medium-size onions, chopped
salt
freshly ground black pepper
3 to 4 cups meat stock (venison, chicken, beef, etc.)
1 Tbs. cornstarch dissolved in 2 Tbs. water
1 to 2 tsp. guava jelly

Preheat oven to 350° F.
In a large mixing bowl stir together meat and rice; add butter in small bits and set mixture aside while preparing cabbage. Wash cabbage and remove outer leaves; reserve. Cook cabbage in boiling water for 10 to 12 minutes; drain and cool sufficiently to handle. Carefully peel off 8 perfect leaves without tearing. Chop reserved outer leaves, mix with onions, season well with salt and pepper, and spread on bottom of shallow casserole large enough to hold 8 stuffed leaves snugly; pour over this 1 cup stock. Put about 3 tablespoons meat-rice mixture on each of prepared cabbage leaves, roll up, and place, flap side up, on vegetable bed in casserole. Cut foil to cover, pushing foil down around edges of casserole. Cover and bake for 1 hour, checking liquid and replenishing as necessary. Blend cornstarch-water mixture into remaining stock to make a sauce; add guava jelly to taste; serve with stuffed rolls.

MAKES 8 SERVINGS.

VENISON LIVER PÂTÉ

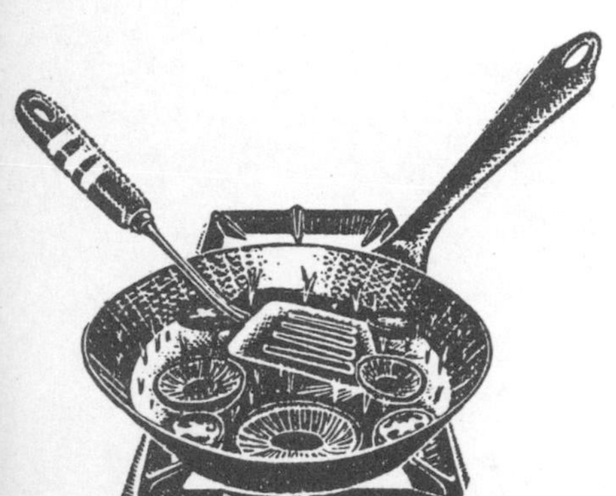

1 deer liver
2 Tbs. butter
1/2 cup diced salt pork
1 small onion, chopped fine
2 slices of white bread
milk
salt
freshly ground pepper
freshly grated nutmeg
rind of 1/2 lemon, grated
1/2 cup minced bacon
2 eggs, well beaten
2 bacon strips, blanched

Preheat oven to 350° F.

Use a sharp knife to cut liver into halves. Heat butter in a skillet and braise 1 half liver along with salt pork and onion. Cook for about 5 minutes and turn liver; meanwhile mince remaining raw liver half and soak bread in milk. Squeeze bread to remove excess milk, add to minced raw liver, and stir thoroughly, sprinkling in salt, pepper, light sprinkling of nutmeg, and lemon rind; blend in minced bacon. Finely chop cooked liver and add to mixture along with eggs, blending thoroughly. Grease a loaf pan and spread bacon strips on bottom. Pack in liver mixture. Bake for 1 1/2 hours. Serve hot on toast.

SERVES 8 AS AN APPETIZER.

ROAST LOIN OF VENISON

8-chop loin of venison (about 6 lb.)
2 1/2 cups California Cabernet Sauvignon or other good red wine
1 1/2 cups water
2 bay leaves
2 Tbs. minced fresh thyme, or 1/2 tsp. dried
8 juniper berries, crushed
2 onions, sliced
2 garlic cloves, minced
beef suet or fat to cover top of roast
4 or 5 strips bacon

*Preheat oven to 450° F.**

Have butcher partially separate chops, leaving enough uncut to hold roast in 1 piece when tied. Combine wine, water, bay leaves, thyme, juniper, onions, and garlic; pour over meat and marinate under refrigeration for about 36 hours, but baste meat often during this period.

Bring meat to room temperature.* Drain marinade and put venison into a roasting pan, spreading beef suet or fat and bacon strips on top of meat. Roast for about 18 minutes. Reduce heat to 350° and roast for about 15 minutes per pound, or until interior temperature reaches 140°. Remove from oven and let venison rest for about 10 minutes before carving. Serve with wild rice and baked tomatoes seasoned with fresh herbs.

MAKES 6 TO 8 SERVINGS.

CHICANO ROAST VENISON EYE OF THE ROUND

1 chorizo sausage (about 1/4 lb.), chopped
1/4 lb. cooked ham, chopped
1 garlic clove, minced
1/4 cup chopped red onion
1 small green pepper, chopped
4 lb. venison, eye of the round
salt
freshly ground pepper
paprika
3 Tbs. olive oil
hot water
1 bay leaf
4 whole cloves

Preheat oven to 350° F.

Mix sausage, ham, garlic, onion, and green pepper. Cut eye of round vertically and open butterfly-fashion. Spread stuffing mixture evenly, reshape meat, and secure with skewers or tie with string. Sprinkle all over with salt, pepper, and paprika. Brown all surfaces in oil, turning often. Remove and keep warm, deglaze pot with hot water; add bay leaf and cloves, and return meat to pot. Cover and roast in oven for about 2 1/2 hours, basting occasionally with pot juices.

MAKES 8 TO 10 SERVINGS.

ROAST MARINATED LOIN OF VENISON

4 to 5 lb. loin of venison
olive oil
juice of 1 lemon
3 medium-size onions, sliced
1 parsley root, scraped and sliced
1 celery root, peeled and sliced
freshly ground pepper
1/2 Tsp. dried thyme
8 juniper berries, slightly bruised
2 cups Cabernet Sauvignon or other red wine
salt
1/2 lb. salt pork
4 Tbs. (1/2 stick) butter, melted

*Preheat oven to 300° F.**

Rub all surfaces of loin with oil and sprinkle with lemon juice. Place on cheesecloth, covering meat with onions and root slices; sprinkle with pepper, thyme, and juniper berries, then wrap cloth securely around loin. Put it into a container just large enough to fit and pour wine over. Refrigerate for 48 hours, turning occasionally.

Bring meat to room temperature.* Unwrap and scrape away vegetables but do not rinse meat. Rub with salt and lard with salt pork. Roast in oven for 2 hours, basting with melted butter. Serve on a hot platter with pan juices as sauce.

MAKES 10 OR 12 SERVINGS.

BONED LEG OF VENISON

1 venison roast (5 lb.), rolled and tied
4 to 5 strips pork fat
2 1/2 cups red wine
1 cup cider vinegar
2 tsp. dried tarragon
1 tsp. salt
2 Tbs. prepared mustard
2 bay leaves
10 peppercorns
10 whole cloves
6 to 8 juniper berries
1 large onion, sliced thin
2 garlic cloves
1 Tbs. celery seeds

SAUCE:
2 to 3 Tbs. flour
2 to 3 Tbs. Madeira
1 Tbs. orange or lemon marmalade

*Preheat oven to 375° F.**

Cover meat with fat and tie. Mix remaining ingredients and pour over meat in a stainless steel or enameled receptacle. Cover loosely and let stand for at least 24 hours in a cool place; do not put in refrigerator. Turn meat frequently in marinade—every time you pass by is not too often. Drain meat but reserve marinade.* In a large skillet, brown roast thoroughly on all surfaces. Place it on a rack in a shallow roasting pan and roast for about 20 minutes, reduce heat to 350° and continue roasting until interior temperature is between 130° and 150°, depending on how well done you like it; reserve roasting pan. Remove to a hot platter and let rest before serving.

Make the sauce: Stir flour into fat in pan in which venison was roasted and cook, stirring constantly until it thickens. Stir in enough marinade to make a sauce, blending in Madeira and marmalade.

MAKES ABOUT 8 SERVINGS.

VENISON STEW PIE

1 1/2 lb. lean venison or leftover rare roast
1 Tbs. bacon or other fat
3 medium-size onions, chopped
2 garlic cloves, minced
2 cups seeded, peeled tomatoes
1/2 tsp. ground savory
2 cups stock
salt
freshly ground pepper
3 to 4 carrots, sliced
2 large celery ribs, sliced
2 cups peas (frozen may be used)

TOPPING:

1 cup flour
3/4 cup yellow cornmeal
2 tsp. sugar
1 Tbs. baking powder
1/2 tsp. salt
3/4 cup milk
3 Tbs. corn oil or melted shortening
1 egg, beaten

Preheat oven to 425° F.

Cut meat into bite-size pieces and sauté in fat in an enameled pot to seal in juices. Add onions and garlic and cook for 1 minute, stirring, until onion is translucent. Stir in tomatoes, savory, and stock, bring to a boili, and let simmer, covered, for 1 to 1 1/2 hours, or until meat is tender. Season with salt and pepper to taste, then add carrots and celery, adding peas the last 5 minutes; continue cooking for about 30 minutes more.

Make the topping: Combine dry ingredients, then stir in milk, oil, and egg and beat well. Transfer stew to a 1 1/2-quart baking dish and spoon cornmeal batter over meat and vegetables. Bake for about 25 minutes, or until topping has puffed uniformly and is lightly browned.

MAKES ABOUT 4 SERVINGS.

LEFTOVER VENISON LOAF

About 1 lb. cooked venison
1/4 cup (1/2 stick) butter, melted
1/3 cup fresh bread crumbs
2 Tbs. heavy cream
2 egg yolks
1 small bay leaf
1/4 tsp. dried thyme
1/4 tsp. ground allspice
salt
freshly ground pepper
1 Tbs. chopped parsley
4 lean bacon strips

Preheat oven to 300° F.

Remove fat from cooked venison, chop it, and measure 2 cups into a large bowl, stirring in melted butter that is no longer hot, crumbs, and cream. Beat in egg yolks one by one, then add bay leaf, thyme, allspice, salt to taste, and a few turns of pepper grinder. Grease an 8-inch loaf pan and lay 2 bacon strips lengthwise in the bottom. Pack in venison mixture, pressing it so that it is smooth and firm; top with remaining 2 bacon strips. Bake for 2 hours. Remove and let cool, then refrigerate overnight, and serve cold.

MAKES 8 TO 10 SERVINGS.

VENISON STROGANOFF

The secret of a good Stroganoff is to use tender meat, sear it quickly, and not let it stew in the sauce. So use only young deer meat and cut 1/4-inch slices from the leg, then slice into 1/4-inch strips. If the sour cream seems too rich for you, use part yogurt and serve the Stroganoff with rice, noodles, or spaetzle.

1 to 2 Tbs. vegetable oil
3/4 lb. tender, lean venison, cut into 1/4-in. strips
2 Tbs. butter
2 large onions, chopped
1/2 tsp. sweet paprika
1 garlic clove, minced
1/2 lb. fresh mushrooms, sliced
1 1/2 cups sour cream, at room temperature
1 tsp. tomato paste
salt
freshly ground pepper
dash of cayenne pepper

Pour enough oil into the bottom of a large skillet to make a film. Heat until almost smoking and toss in venison strips, then stir fry until they are just seared on all sides. Remove and keep warm. Add butter to skillet, then add onions, paprika, and garlic. Cook over moderate heat, stirring, for about 5 minutes, then add mushrooms and sauté for 5 minutes more. Stir in sour cream (if it's at room temperature, it won't curdle), tomato paste, salt, and pepper. Return venison to the pan and cook until heated through. Correct the seasoning and sprinkle top with cayenne before serving.

MAKES 4 SERVINGS.

VENISON STEAKS WITH MUSHROOMS AND GREEN PEPPERCORN BUTTER

The aromatic and pungent flavor of green peppercorns mashed into butter is just the right complement for quickly sautéed, tender venison steaks surrounded with browned mushrooms with a hint of garlic. Serve these with crisp panfried sliced potatoes and a green vegetable or just a sprig of watercress.

1/4 lb. (1 stick) butter
6 Tbs. pickled green peppercorns
2 Tbs. vegetable oil
2 garlic cloves, just crushed with the flat of a knife
1/2 lb. fresh mushrooms
8 tender venison steaks (2 to 3 oz. each and about 1/4 in. thick)
salt
freshly ground pepper
3 Tbs. red wine

Soften 6 tablespoons butter, then mash in green peppercorns. Melt remaining butter and the oil in a good-size skillet, and when sizzling, toss in garlic cloves. Cut mushrooms into quarters if they are large, halves if smallish; add to skillet. Sauté over moderate heat, seasoning with salt and pepper and tossing occasionally, for 5 minutes. Remove with a slotted spoon and keep warm. Now sauté steaks in the same skillet, 4 at a time if necessary so that the pan isn't crowded. Have the heat quite high and cook only a minute on each side. Salt and pepper well, remove to a warm platter, and when the last steak is done, toss in the wine, scrape up all the pan juices, and pour this little bit over the steaks. Top them with the green peppercorn butter and surround them with the mushrooms.

MAKES 4 SERVINGS.

PLANKED GREAT LAKES WHITEFISH

Once, on a cold, dreary day outside Anacortes, Washington, we had the warming reward of eating salmon that had been cooked outdoors on a hardwood plank. The method was that of the American Indians, and it was a common way to cook fowl, lobster, shad, and other fish from eastern rivers, and whitefish from the Great Lakes. The latter "has gained much favor," Fannie Farmer pointed out in 1896. "Our plank had been used long and often, gaining virtue with every planking," a man who grew up in nineteenth-century Michigan remembered. "It held two medium-sized whitefish cut down the back and pressed firmly on the board." For those who needed a recipe, one was provided in the 1857 edition of the *New Cookery Book* of Eliza Leslie, who cited the method as "superior to all others."

1 whitefish (3 1/2 to 4 lb.), cleaned and boned
coarse salt
freshly ground pepper
butter
3 bacon strips

Preheat oven to 375° F.

Season fish inside and out with salt and pepper. Heat a grooved oak plank in the oven, then oil it liberally and put fish in center. Cover exposed part of plank with coarse salt to keep from burning. Spread bacon strips on top of fish, then bake for 45 minutes.

MAKES 4 TO 6 SERVINGS.

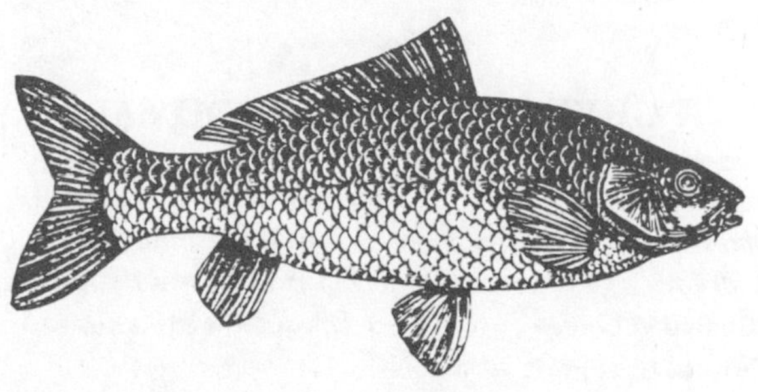

SALADS

ARTICHOKE AND GRATED CARROT SALAD

1 pkg. (9 oz.) frozen baby artichokes
1/3 cup water
1/2 tsp. salt
6 to 8 peppercorns, bruised
6 to 8 coriander seeds
juice of 1/2 lemon
1/4 cup olive oil
2 medium-size carrots, grated
3/4 Tbs. mixed minced parsley and fresh basil

Put artichokes into a saucepan with water, salt, peppercorns, and coriander, most of lemon juice, and most of oil; cover, bring to a boil, and let simmer for 5 minutes. Remove cover and boil until liquid is evaporated. Chill for several hours. Put chilled artichokes in center of salad bowl and arrange carrots around. Sprinkle with remaining lemon juice and remaining olive oil, then scatter herbs over all.

MAKES 4 SERVINGS.

BLUE CHEESE AND AVOCADO SALAD

1 large, very ripe avocado
1/4 cup sour cream
1 Tbs. grated onion
few dashes of Tabasco
1/2 cup crumbled blue cheese
3/4 cup California olive oil
1/4 cup wine vinegar
1/4 cup California Chablis
1 tsp. lemon juice

Mash avocado until smooth, blending in sour cream a little at a time. Stir in onion, Tabasco, and crumbled cheese. Add oil, vinegar, wine, and lemon juice gradually, tossing to mix lightly. Chill, and serve on lettuce leaves.

MAKES 4 SERVINGS.

BEET AND APPLE SALAD

1/2 cup heavy cream
1/4 cup sour cream
1/4 cup yogurt
4 medium-size beets, cooked
2 tart apples, peeled and cored
3/4 cup mayonnaise
1/2 tsp. prepared mustard
2 Tbs. chopped parsley or fresh dillweed
salt
freshly ground pepper

Mix the cream, sour cream, and yogurt together thoroughly and let stand at room temperature for several hours. Dice beets and apples into equal-size pieces. Mix mayonnaise and cream mixture; blend in mustard and parsley or dillweed. Toss with beets and apples. Taste, and season with a little salt and a few turns of pepper grinder as needed.

MAKES 4 SERVINGS.

BEET, CELERY, AND CUCUMBER SALAD

3 garlic cloves, minced
1/2 tsp. salt
1 cup fresh bread crumbs
1/2 cup pine nuts
1/2 cup olive oil
2 to 3 Tbs. vinegar
juice of 1/2 lemon
salt
freshly ground pepper
1 cup diced boiled beets, drained on paper towels
3/4 cup finely chopped celery
3/4 cup finely diced peeled cucumber

Combine in a mixing bowl garlic, salt, bread crumbs, and pine nuts. Mixing constantly, stir in small quantities of oil, vinegar, and lemon juice alternately, until total amounts are used up. Mixture should be moist but still granular, not soggy. Taste, and add salt only if needed and a few turns of pepper grinder. Toss this mixture with beets, celery, and cucumber. Arrange on lettuce leaves and serve cool but not chilled.

MAKES 6 SERVINGS.

BEAVER BAY CABBAGE, HAM, AND CHICKEN SALAD

12 red radishes
2 cups shredded white cabbage
2 cups shredded red cabbage
2 cups shredded leaf lettuce
1 cup strips of cooked chicken breast
1/2 cup strips of country ham
2 Tbs. chopped anchovies
6 Tbs. vegetable oil
2 Tbs. tarragon vinegar
1 to 2 Tbs. mayonnaise
freshly ground pepper
1 can Wisconsin whitefish caviar

Slice radishes very thin and put into a large salad bowl with cabbage and lettuce (or other salad greens). Toss, adding chicken, ham, anchovies, oil, vinegar, mayonnaise, and pepper to taste. (Salty flavor of ham, anchovies, and caviar should eliminate all need for salt.) Add caviar just before serving, or divide salad on plates and garnish with caviar.

MAKES 6 TO 8 SERVINGS.

PENNSYLVANIA PEPPER CABBAGE

2 cups thinly sliced cabbage
1 green or sweet red pepper, cut into match-size strips
1 1/2 tsp. salt
1 cup thick sour cream
1 Tbs. grated onion
2 Tbs. vinegar
1 Tbs. lemon juice
freshly ground black pepper or cayenne pepper
2 Tbs. mayonnaise

Toss cabbage and pepper strips with 1 teaspoon salt. Mix remaining 1/2 teaspoon salt with sour cream, onion, vinegar, lemon juice, and 6 or 7 turns of pepper grinder, or shake on cayenne to your own taste. Blend mayonnaise into this mixture and toss with vegetables.

MAKES 4 SERVINGS.

VARIATION: PEPPER CABBAGE WITH HOT DRESSING

2 tsp. sugar
1/2 tsp. dry mustard
freshly ground black pepper
1 Tbs. butter
1 tsp. flour
1/2 tsp. salt
1/2 cup vinegar
1 egg yolk
2 cups thinly sliced cabbage
1 green or sweet red pepper, cut into match-size strips

Put sugar, mustard, a few turns of pepper grinder, and vinegar into a saucepan and bring to a boil. Melt butter in another saucepan and stir in flour, salt, and egg yolk. Blend in vinegar and let simmer for 4 minutes. Pour over cabbage and pepper strips and toss.

CHEF'S SALAD

The origin of this salad is not, apparently, a matter of record, but it may have been made first in the kitchen of the Ritz-Carlton, where a recipe used by Louis Diat called for smoked ox tongue as one of the meats and watercress as the only green leaf.

DRESSING:

1/2 tsp. salt
2 Tbs. vinegar
6 Tbs. olive oil
freshly ground pepper

SALAD:

1/2 head of iceberg lettuce, shredded fine
1 scallion, minced fine (white part only)
1 cup strips of ham or tongue (1/4-in. wide by 2 in. long)
1 cup similar strips of chicken or turkey
1 cup similar strips of Swiss cheese
1 medium-size tomato, cut into 1/2-in. wedges
1 tsp. each of fresh parsley, basil, or tarragon, or a combination, minced

Mix dressing and pour about half of it over lettuce and scallion; toss thoroughly. Arrange lettuce in bottom of salad bowl and over it arrange other ingredients in decorative patterns. Pour remaining dressing over all and sprinkle with one or more of minced herbs.

MAKES 6 SERVINGS.

JUDITH'S CHICKEN AND GRAPE SALAD

1 chicken (3 to 4 lb.), steamed (see p. 317)
2 cups Homemade Mayonnaise (p. 400)
salt
freshly ground pepper
1 tsp. lemon juice
2 doz. seedless green grapes, peeled
lettuce leaves
1/3 cup almonds, toasted
1 tarragon sprig, minced (optional)
1 Tbs. mixed minced fresh chives and parsley (optional)

Cut good white and dark meat from chicken into fair-sized dice (save wings and drumsticks for a picnic). Toss with mayonnaise and season to taste with salt, pepper, and lemon juice. Fold in peeled grapes. Toast almonds in 400° F. oven for about 5 minutes. Serve over fresh lettuce leaves, topped with almonds and a sprinkling of herbs.

MAKES 6 SERVINGS.

PENNSYLVANIA DUTCH COLESLAW

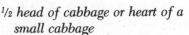

1/2 head of cabbage or heart of a small cabbage
1 carrot
1 small white onion, or 2 or 3 whole scallions
1 tender celery rib

DRESSING:

1 Tbs. sugar
2 Tbs. vinegar
1/2 cup heavy cream
1/4 tsp. salt
freshly ground pepper
minced parsley

Cut away hard core of cabbage and shred remainder very fine. Peel and grate carrot; mince onion or scallions and celery; mix all vegetables together. Combine ingredients for the dressing, dissolving sugar in vinegar before adding cream. Toss with vegetables, then let mature in refrigerator for 2 to 3 hours before serving.

MAKES 4 SERVINGS.

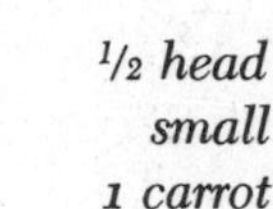

FLAKED CRAB SALAD

2 cups cooked crab meat
2 Tbs. grated onion
2 small carrots, cut into match-size strips
3 Tbs. finely chopped celery
6 Tbs. olive oil
2 Tbs. tarragon vinegar
2 Tbs. mayonnaise
cayenne pepper
salt

Flake crab, removing any bits of bone, then toss with vegetables. Continue tossing with oil, vinegar, and mayonnaise and season to taste with cayenne and a little salt. Serve on crisp lettuce or romaine on chilled salad plates.

MAKES 4 SERVINGS.

CRAB SALAD LOUIS

No one seems to know which of the many West Coast cooks named Louis may be memorialized in this recipe for enhancing the fresh delicacy of crab meat, but it has been recorded that Crab Louis was served as early as 1914 at Solari's, a San Francisco food establishment much revered by the local cognoscenti. There are almost infinite variations of ingredients, and the method here is based on James Beard's memory of "the finest Louis I have ever eaten," as prepared at the Bohemian Restaurant in Portland, Oregon, about the time that World War I began. This is sparer than the Solari version, which called for mustard pickle in the sauce, as well as Worcestershire sauce.

1/2 head of iceberg lettuce
1 lb. fresh crab meat, flaked
1 cup Homemade Mayonnaise (p. 400)
1/3 cup whipped cream
2 to 3 Tbs. chili sauce
2 to 3 Tbs. grated onion
2 to 3 Tbs. chopped parsley
cayenne pepper
3 to 4 eggs, hard-cooked and quartered
3 to 4 tomatoes, cut into wedges
6 to 8 small frozen artichokes, thawed

Shred lettuce and divide among 4 plates. Divide crab meat and arrange on top of lettuce. Mix mayonnaise with cream, chili sauce, onion, parsley, and cayenne to taste; spread over crab meat generously. Garnish each plate with hard-cooked eggs, tomatoes, and artichokes.

MAKES 4 SERVINGS.

CUCUMBER AND BEET SALAD

1 cup diced cucumbers, seeds removed
1/2 cup diced cooked beets
1 tsp. salt
2 Tbs. vinegar
2 Tbs. minced shallots or scallions (white part only)
3/4 cup sour cream
1 tsp., or more, minced fresh dillweed (optional)

Toss cucumbers and beets in salt and let stand for 1 hour. Drain well. Mix remaining ingredients and toss lightly with vegetables, sprinkling with dillweed if available.

MAKES 4 SERVINGS.

FISHERMAN'S SALAD

1 can (2 oz.) flat anchovy fillets, well drained
3 Tbs. red salmon or whitefish caviar
1 cup diced mozzarella or other bland cheese
1 cup marinated artichoke hearts, chopped coarse and drained
3 eggs, hard-cooked and minced
1 Tbs. minced fresh thyme
lettuce
romaine

Chop anchovies very fine and combine with caviar, cheese, artichokes, and eggs. Sprinkle with thyme. Tear up enough lettuce and romaine for 4 persons and toss with other ingredients.

MAKES 4 SERVINGS.

JELLIED FRESH FRUIT SALAD

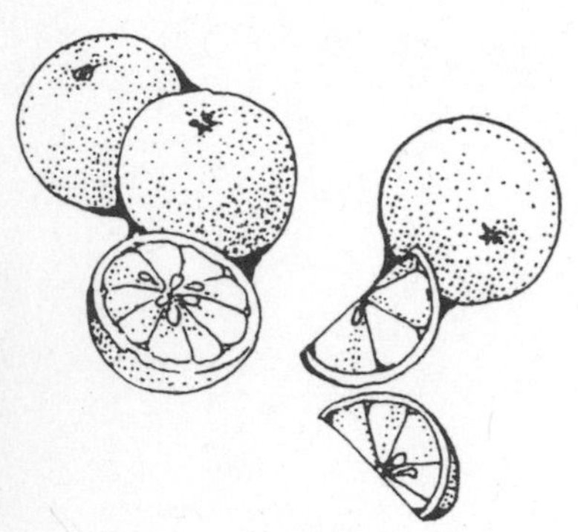

2 envelopes unflavored gelatin
1 cup cold water
3/4 cup sugar
1 1/4 cups freshly squeezed and strained orange juice or mixture of orange and grapefruit
1/4 cup mixed fresh lime and lemon juice
1/2 cup dry sherry
pinch of salt
vegetable oil
1 small avocado or 1/2 large, sliced
1 medium-size pear, peeled, cored, and sliced
1 large navel orange, peeled and sectioned
2 doz. grapes, peeled and seeded
cream cheese balls rolled in fresh herbs (minced parsley, chives, basil, or tarragon)
watercress for garnish

Dissolve gelatin in 1/2 cup cold water. Meanwhile heat sugar with remaining 1/2 cup water until thoroughly dissolved. Remove from heat and blend in gelatin. Add orange juice, lemon and lime juice, sherry, and salt. Oil a ring mold that will hold 2 quarts. Pour a little fruit juice aspic over the bottom and chill. Meanwhile prepare the fruits. When gelatin has set, arrange the fruits in attractive alternating patterns around the ring and fill the mold with the rest of the aspic mixture. Chill for several hours. Serve with cream cheese balls in the center and sprigs of watercress around.

MAKES 8 SERVINGS.

GARBANZO SALAD

1 cup cooked garbanzos (chick-peas)
1 1/2 Tbs. minced whole scallion
1 1/2 Tbs. minced green pepper
1 1/2 Tbs. red wine vinegar
3 Tbs. California olive oil
1/2 tsp. salt
freshly ground pepper
1/2 tsp. minced fresh green chilies
1/2 tsp. ground cuminseed

If cooking your own garbanzos, soak them overnight like any dried legume. Cook them for several hours in water or, better yet, in liquid left from boiling ham, tongue, or corned beef. Drain. Mix with remaining ingredients, arranging romaine leaves around before serving.

MAKES 4 SERVINGS.

GAZPACHO SALAD

Sometimes spelled "guzpacho," sometimes called Spanish salad, the layering of vegetables in an icy vinaigrette sauce was not an uncommon way of serving salad in antebellum Southern homes. Early versions of gazpacho, as a matter of fact, were known to Greeks and Romans. In America, a Virginian identified as "Col. Talbott" is the source of an ancestral recipe, while "Miss Evelyn's" formula, published in Mrs. S. R. Dull's *Southern Cooking*, is based on an Andalusian penchant for using mayonnaise instead of a blending of oil and vinegar. Gazpacho, however spelled or put together, may well have entered the American scene generally as a result of the first Spanish settlements in the Southeast. Here is an adaptation of Colonel Talbott's method.

2 medium-size cucumbers, sliced very thin
1 large red or other onion, sliced very thin
3 tomatoes, peeled and sliced
1 cup stale bread crumbs
oil and vinegar dressing
1/4 cup chipped ice

Fill a glass dish with layers of vegetables, each sprinkled with crumbs. Cover with salad dressing, garnish with lettuce or watercress, and chil thoroughly. Just before serving, sprinkle on chipped ice.

MAKES 4 SERVINGS.

FLORIDA GREEK SALAD

1/2 head of cabbage, shredded fine
1 tomato, seeded and chopped coarse
1/2 green pepper, cut into match-size strips
1/3 cucumber, peeled and diced
1 small carrot, cut into match-size strips
1 small onion, chopped coarse
1 jar (8 oz.) herring fillets in wine sauce
2 tsp. sugar
1/2 tsp. salt
freshly ground pepper
1 to 2 Tbs. olive oil
2 to 3 tsp. vinegar

Mix vegetables and stir in herring. Sprinkle with sugar and salt and several turns of pepper grinder. Add oil and vinegar and toss to coat vegetables. Taste and adjust seasoning for palatable sweet-sour flavor. Cover and refrigerate for at least 8 hours.

MAKES 4 SERVINGS.

HAM AND CHEESE SALAD

1 cup diced cooked country ham
1 1/2 cups diced mozzarella or other mild cheese
1/2 cup finely chopped celery
1/4 cup minced whole scallions
3 to 4 Tbs. chopped ripe olives
1/4 to 1/2 cup chopped fresh mushrooms
1/4 cup mayonnaise
1/4 tsp. dried basil
1/4 tsp. dried marjoram
1/4 tsp. dried oregano

Combine ham, cheese, celery, scallions, olives, and mushrooms with enough mayonnaise to bind, and sprinkle in herbs. No other seasoning is needed if well-flavored country ham is used. Arrange lettuce in a salad bowl and mound salad mixture in center.

MAKES 4 SERVINGS.

NEW ENGLAND HERRING SALAD

6 to 8 kippered herring
2 small beets, cooked, peeled, and sliced
2 tart Greening apples, peeled and sliced
2 or 3 scallions, minced (white part only)
salt
freshly ground pepper
6 Tbs. olive oil
2 Tbs. tarragon vinegar
1 tsp. dry mustard
2 to 3 Tbs. minced fresh dillweed, or 1/2 to 1 tsp. dried

Tear kippers into small strips, then blot with paper towels. Toss in salad bowl with beets, apples, scallions, and a little salt only if needed; grind in several turns of pepper mill. Add oil, vinegar, mustard, and dillweed, and toss again. Chill and serve on lettuce leaves.

MAKES 6 SERVINGS.

HEART OF PALM SALAD

2 celery ribs, diced
2 Tbs. carrot shavings
2 Tbs. green pepper, cut into slivers
1 scallion, minced (white part only)
1/4 tsp. dried marjoram
1/4 tsp. dried oregano
freshly ground pepper
1 tsp. salt
1 can hearts of palm, diced
juice of 1/2 lemon or lime
1 Tbs. mayonnaise
about 1 Tbs. vinegar

Mix vegetables with herbs, seasoning, and hearts of palm. Add citrus juice and mayonnaise, and toss. Add vinegar according to taste. Chill well before serving.

MAKES 6 SERVINGS.

VERMONT POTATO SALAD

New potatoes are waxier and, we think, just right for a summer picnic salad like this one. Don't be deterred if the vegetable bin has only baking potatoes, however. The texture of the potatoes will be mealier and they will absorb more mayonnaise, but the result is, in either case, perhaps *the* most American of all vegetable salads.

6 medium-size potatoes
1 Tbs. white wine vinegar
2 tsp. coarse salt
freshly ground pepper
1 cup Homemade Mayonnaise (p. 400)
cream or lemon juice
2, or more, scallions, minced (including some green)
2 Tbs. finely chopped green pepper
1/4 cup minced parsley mixed with minced fresh basil, tarragon, or dillweed
2 eggs, hard-cooked and sliced or quartered
2 tomatoes, cut into wedges
watercress for garnish

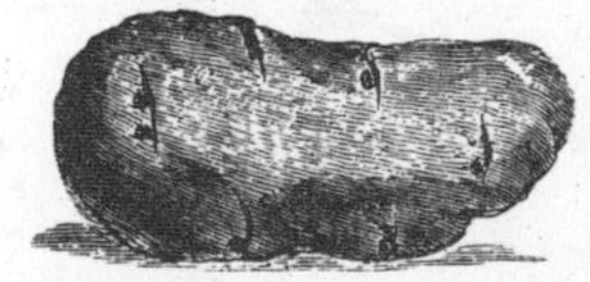

Scrub potatoes and boil in their jackets in salted water for 25 to 40 minutes. Pierce to test for doneness (new potatoes will take less time). Let cool a bit, peel, and dice. Toss with vinegar, salt, and pepper. Gently fold in mayonnaise thinned with a little cream or lemon juice. Season with salt and pepper, and add scallions, green pepper, and herbs. Chill before serving. Garnish with hard-cooked eggs, tomatoes, and watercress.

MAKES 4 TO 6 SERVINGS.

SMOKED SALMON AND AVOCADO MOUSSE

3 large avocados
1/3 cup heavy cream
1/3 cup béchamel sauce
2 tsp. lemon juice
2 Tbs. Homemade Mayonnaise (p. 400)
salt
freshly ground pepper
1/3 to 1/2 cup coarsely chopped smoked salmon
1 Tb. unflavored gelatin
2 Tbs. water

Blend avocado pulp with cream, béchamel sauce, lemon juice, and mayonnaise; add salt and pepper to taste. Stir in smoked salmon. Blend gelatin with water and dissolve over low heat, then work into salmon-avocado mixture. Oil a mold and pour in mixture. Chill for about 4 hours. Slice and serve on lettuce leaves with lemon quarters.

MAKES 4 TO 6 SERVINGS.

SAUSAGE, SARDINE, AND GREEN BEAN SALAD

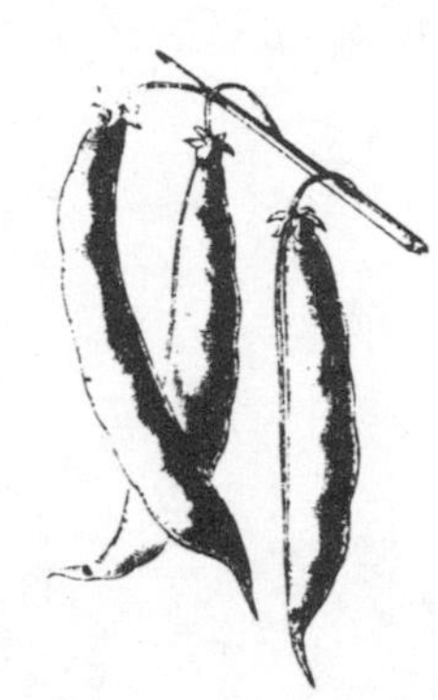

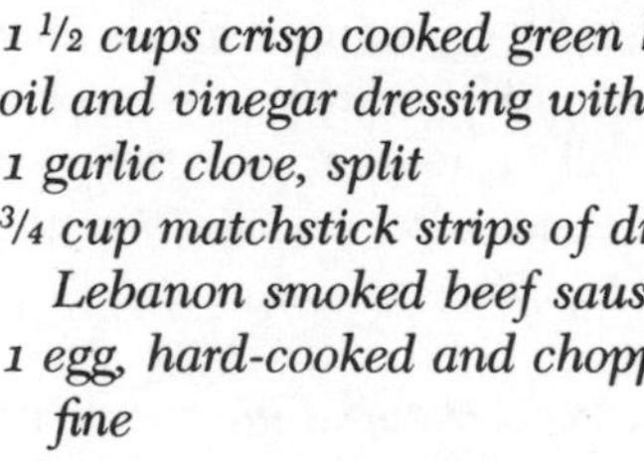

1 1/2 cups crisp cooked green beans
oil and vinegar dressing with garlic
1 garlic clove, split
3/4 cup matchstick strips of dry Lebanon smoked beef sausage
1 egg, hard-cooked and chopped fine
1 Tbs. minced chives
1 tsp. ground savory
salt
freshly ground pepper
4 large canned sardines

Put beans into a glass bowl. Make a garlicky French dressing and pour over beans, then set aside for 2 or 3 hours. Rub a wooden salad bowl with cut sides of garlic clove, then put in sausage, egg, chives, savory, salt to taste, and a few turns of pepper grinder; toss well. Add beans and dressing and toss again. Serve on lettuce cups and top each serving with a sardine.

MAKES 4 SERVINGS.

SHRIMP, BACON, TOMATO, AND EGG SALAD

6 bacon strips
1 1/2 cups cooked small shrimps
3 to 4 Tbs. mayonnaise
2 Tbs. lemon juice
2 or 3 sprigs of fresh dillweed, or 1/2 tsp. dried
1 tsp. minced fresh tarragon (optional)
1/2 tsp. salt
1 Tbs. vinegar
3 Tbs. olive oil
freshly ground pepper
1 small head of Boston lettuce
few sprigs of watercress
2 large tomatoes, cut into wedges
2 eggs, hard-cooked for 10 minutes only and quartered

Fry bacon until well cooked, then drain on paper towels. Wash cooked shrimps and pat dry; mix with mayonnaise, lemon juice, and herbs. In a salad bowl mix salt and vinegar, then add oil, stirring hard with a wooden spoon. Add several turns of the pepper grinder. Put lettuce leaves in a salad bowl, add watercress, tomatoes, eggs, and bacon bits; toss until well mixed. Pile shrimps in center and serve salad with toasted rye bread.

MAKES 6 SERVINGS.

SPINACH, BACON, AND MUSHROOM SALAD

1/4 lb. very fresh young spinach
8 bacon strips
4 medium-size fresh mushrooms
1 1/2 Tbs. lemon juice
1/4 cup olive oil
salt
freshly ground pepper

Wash spinach leaves thoroughly, remove tough stems, then shake or spin dry. Fry bacon until crisp, drain on paper towels, and crumble. Slice mushrooms thinly after removing only tough end of stems. Tear spinach leaves into 3 or 4 pieces each and toss with mushrooms and bacon. Sprinkle with lemon juice, oil, salt, and several turns of pepper grinder. Toss again, taste for seasoning, adding salt and pepper if necessary. Serve immediately.

MAKES 2 SERVINGS.

LOUISIANA SWEET POTATO SALAD

1 cup grated raw sweet potato
2 cups diced apples
1/2 cup broken pecans
3/4 cup raisins
1/2 cup chopped celery
6 Tbs. Homemade Mayonnaise (p. 400)

Put sweet potatoes into a salad bowl and add apples, pecans, raisins, and celery. Stir in a spoonful of mayonnaise at a time to make salad as moist as desired. Serve in lettuce cups.

MAKES 8 SERVINGS.

CHEESE-STUFFED TOMATO SALAD

4 large ripe tomatoes
1 egg
1 Tbs. flour
1 Tbs. sugar
1/2 cup milk
1 Tbs. wine vinegar
6 oz. cream cheese, at room temperature
6 oz. dry-curd cottage cheese, at room temperature
1 Tbs. minced fresh basil
1 Tbs. minced fresh tarragon
1 tsp. salt
freshly ground pepper
2 eggs, hard-cooked and chopped fine
2 to 3 Tbs. minced chives

Hollow out tomatoes to make cases with shells about 1/2 inch thick, removing all seeds; chill for several hours. In a saucepan, mix together egg, flour, and sugar, stir in milk, and cook over low heat for about 5 minutes, stirring constantly as mixture thickens. Off the heat, add vinegar, then stir mixture into cheeses, stirring until smooth. Mix in herbs, salt, and several turns of pepper grinder. Spoon cheese mixture into chilled tomatoes, sprinkle liberally with chopped eggs, then with chives. Return to refrigerator and chill for 1 hour or more.

MAKES 4 SERVINGS.

VEGETABLE SALAD

1 medium-size cucumber
1 cup cooked peas
1 cup diced cooked carrots
1/4 green pepper, chopped
2 medium-size tomatoes, diced
1/2 medium-size red onion, sliced thin
1/4 cup minced parsley
1 cup Homemade Mayonnaise (p. 400)
2 Tbs. chili sauce
salt
freshly ground pepper
1 Tbs. chopped fresh basil (optional)

Peel cucumber, slice into quarters lengthwise, scrape out seeds, and cut into bits about the size of peas and carrots. Mix all vegetables together and toss with mayonnaise and chili sauce. Season to taste with salt and pepper, and sprinkle with fresh basil if available. Serve in a bowl lined with salad greens.

MAKES 4 SERVINGS.

WALDORF SALAD

Oscar Tschirky, who became famous as Oscar of the Waldorf and was maître d'hôtel from that hotel's opening until his death, created this salad for a "society supper" to which 1,500 persons came from Boston, Baltimore, and Philadelphia; these social lights were invited to a preview of the Waldorf when it opened in March 1893. For Sheila Hibben, food editor of *The New Yorker*, his creation was a mixed blessing. She thought his combination of apples and mayonnaise headed American housewives in the wrong direction "and bred the sorry mixture of sweet salads" that remain very much on the gastronomical scene. Someone else seems to have added nuts to Oscar's salad, which, truth be told, can be a happy addition when homemade mayonnaise is used (particularly with some walnut oil added) rather than the more common sweet salad dressing.

1 cup diced crisp tart apples
1 cup diced crisp celery
1/3 cup coarsely chopped walnuts
3/4 cup Homemade Mayonnaise (p. 400, using walnut oil)

Toss apples and celery with nuts, then fold in mayonnaise. Chill and serve on lettuce leaves.

MAKES 6 SERVINGS.

MINNESOTA WILD RICE AND BEEF SALAD

2 cups julienne strips of rare roast beef
1 1/2 to 2 cups cooked wild rice or other rice
2 to 3 Tbs. pine nuts
1 small white onion, minced
2 to 3 Tbs. chopped green pepper
1 cup sour cream
1 1/2 to 2 Tbs. Dijon mustard
2 to 3 Tbs. wine vinegar
1/2 tsp. sugar
1/2 tsp., or more, dried chervil

Mix together beef, rice, pine nuts, and vegetables. Season sour cream to taste with mustard, vinegar, sugar, and chervil. Toss meat and rice mixture with dressing and refrigerate for an hour or so. Serve on lettuce leaves.

MAKES 6 SERVINGS.

GREEN GODDESS DRESSING

George Arliss, the British actor who was later a great Hollywood star, made such a hit in the early 1920s in a play called *The Green Goddess* that its run in San Francisco inspired the creation at the Palace Hotel of an anchovy-flavored, meadow-colored mayonnaise to dress salad greens and to be served as Western style dictates at the beginning of a meal.

8 to 10 anchovy fillets, chopped
1 or 2 scallions, minced (white part only)
3 to 4 Tbs. minced parsley
1 1/2 Tbs. minced tarragon leaves
3 cups Homemade Mayonnaise (p. 400)
3 Tbs. tarragon vinegar
3 Tbs. minced chives

Combine anchovies, scallions, parsley, and tarragon. Mix well with mayonnaise, adding enough vinegar to give the consistency of heavy cream; stir in chives. For a green salad, rub a wooden bowl with garlic before putting in washed and dried mixed greens. Add dressing and toss until well mixed.

MAKES ABOUT 3 1/2 CUPS.

POPPY SEED DRESSING

Poppy seeds were among the many things that American Shakers raised, packaged, and sold, as well as used in their own simple but imaginative cooking. Mennonite cooks dressed orange and grapefruit slices or red cabbage with oil and vinegar flavored with poppyseeds and onion juice; and Helen Corbitt, whose knowledge of United States gastronomy stretched from Pennsylvania to Texas and from sea to sea, perfected a poppy seed dressing to be made in a blender. The recipe that follows is good on all combinations of fruit and on avocado slices.

1/2 cup sugar
1 tsp. salt
1/2 tsp. dry mustard
1/3 cup vinegar
1 Tbs. grated onion
1 cup vegetable oil
1 tsp. poppy seeds

Mix sugar, salt, mustard, and vinegar. Stir in onion. Add oil very slowly, a little at a time, beating constantly until thick. Stir in poppy seeds.

MAKES ABOUT 1 1/2 CUPS.

HOMEMADE MAYONNAISE

3 egg yolks, at room temperature
1/2 tsp. salt
2 Tbs. vinegar or lemon juice, or 1 Tbs. of each
1/4 to 1/2 tsp. dry mustard (optional)
up to 2 cups good oil, or combination of olive, vegetable, or other oils

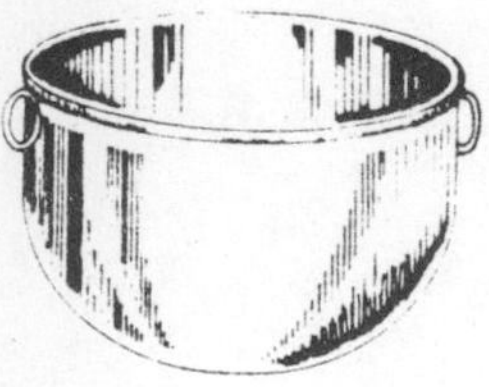

Beat egg yolks until thick and lemony. Add salt, just 1 tablespoon vinegar or lemon juice, and mustard if you use it, and beat again thoroughly. Now start adding oil very slowly, drop by drop, beating constantly and making sure each drop is absorbed before next is added. Proceed slowly until 1/2 cup oil has been assimilated, then start adding more quickly. When mayonnaise is very thick, add a little of remaining vinegar or lemon juice, and continue adding oil until you have desired consistency. Correct seasoning. If storing, keep refrigerated in tightly sealed jar.

Variations: For a more mustardy mayonnaise, halfway along add 1 tablespoon mustard seeds and as much more as you like when correcting seasoning at the end. For a subtle variation in flavor, try using half walnut oil, particularly delicious with Waldorf Salad (p. 398)

CASSEROLES, LUNCH AND SUPPER DISHES

STUFFED ARTICHOKES

4 large globe artichokes
1 lemon, cut in half
4 Tbs. (1/2 stick) butter
3 Tbs. olive oil
3 Tbs. finely minced shallots or scallions (white part only)
1 1/2 cups finely diced ham
1 garlic clove, minced fine
1 cup cooked wild rice
2 Tbs. chopped parsley
pinch of dried thyme
1 tsp. dried tarragon
salt
freshly ground pepper
2 Tbs. freshly grated Parmesan cheese
1/4 cup fresh bread crumbs

Preheat oven to 425° F.

Trim the tops and stems from artichokes, snip off thorny tips of leaves and remove small, tough outermost leaves. Rub cut surfaces with lemon. Steam artichokes on a trivet over boiling water in a heavy, tightly lidded pot for 45 to 50 minutes, or until a leaf pulls out easily. Melt half the butter in a skillet with 1 tablespoon of oil. Sauté shallots or scallions for a few minutes, then add ham, garlic, wild rice, herbs, and salt (if necessary) and pepper to taste. When artichokes are done, scrape out the center down to the heart, and spoon out all the choke. Fill centers with ham and rice mixture so that it heaps over the tops and spills down some between the leaves. Sprinkle cheese and bread crumbs over the top, dribble on remaining 2 tablespoons oil, and bake for 10 minutes.

MAKES 4 SERVINGS.

ASPARAGUS WITH HAM SAUCE

3 Tbs. butter
2 1/2 Tbs. flour
2 cups milk
1/4 cup canned puréed chervil, drained
2 cups finely minced ham
1 1/2 lb. fresh asparagus, or 2 pkg. (10 oz. each) frozen asparagus, cooked
4 eggs, hard-cooked

Melt butter in a saucepan, stir in flour, and cook for 3 or 4 minutes. Off the heat, stir in milk; return to heat when smooth and cook until sauce thickens. Stir in chervil and ham. Be sure asparagus is hot. Chop 3 hard-cooked eggs and stir into sauce. Slice remaining egg. Garnish each serving of asparagus with sauce and slices of hard-cooked egg.

MAKES 4 SERVINGS.

AVOCADO WITH CREAMED PHEASANT

1 ripe avocado
lemon juice
salt
freshly ground pepper
1 1/2 cups small chunks of cooked pheasant
3/4 cup leftover gravy from pheasant or stock made from pheasant carcass thickened with a little cornstarch
1/4 cup heavy cream

Preheat oven to 425° F.

Cut avocado into 1/4-inch slices. Place in the bottom of a buttered shallow baking dish. Sprinkle with lemon juice, salt, and pepper. Toss pheasant chunks on top. Mix gravy or thickened stock with heavy cream and pour over. Bake for 10 to 15 minutes.

MAKES 4 SERVINGS.

AVOCADO BAKED WITH CHICKEN AND HAM

1/4 lb. (1 stick) butter
2 Tbs. chopped onion
1/4 cup flour
3/4 tsp. salt
3/4 tsp. paprika
3/4 tsp. dried rosemary, ground
1 1/2 cups chicken stock
1 1/2 cups sour cream, at room temperature
2 cups diced cooked chicken
1 cup finely diced country ham
1 medium-size avocado, diced
1/2 cup fresh bread crumbs

Preheat oven to 350° F.

Melt 6 tablespoons butter and sauté onion until golden in color. Stir in flour, salt, paprika, and rosemary. Cook over low heat until mixture is smooth and bubbling. Off the heat, stir in stock, return to very low heat, and stir constantly until sauce comes to a boil. Remove from heat and stir in sour cream, a little at a time. Fold in a chicken and ham, then add avocado. Pour into a 1 ½-quart baking dish. Blend bread crumbs and remaining butter over medium heat, then spread over contents of baking dish. Bake for 30 minutes.

MAKES 6 SERVINGS.

BAKED TUNA-STUFFED AVOCADO

2 Tbs. butter
2 Tbs. flour
1 ½ cups heavy cream
milk
½ tsp. dried thyme
½ tsp. dried rosemary
1 tsp. salt
freshly ground pepper
½ lime
2 medium-size avocados
2 cans (7 oz. each) tuna, drained and flaked
sesame seeds

Preheat oven to 350° F.

Melt butter in a saucepan, stir in flour, and heat, stirring for about 2 minutes, or until smooth. Off the heat, stir in cream and continue to stir until smooth; return to heat and cook for about 5 minutes, or until sauce thickens. If it seems too thick, add a little milk, Stir in thyme, rosemary, salt, freshly ground pepper to taste, and a squeeze of lime juice. Cut avocados into halves and then into ¼-inch-thick slices. Cover bottom of a small baking dish with avocado slices. Stir tuna into sauce, letting it warm up, then pour sauce over avocado slices. Sprinkle with sesame seeds and bake for 12 to 15 minutes.

MAKES 4 SERVINGS.

AVOCADO-STUFFED PANCAKES

1 egg
pinch of salt
½ cup milk
⅓ cup flour
1 ½ Tbs. butter, melted
1 Tbs. sugar
1 Tbs. Cointreau

FILLING:

1 large avocado, mashed
1 tsp., more or less, sugar
1 lime
3 Tbs. finely chopped pecans
2 Tbs. Cointreau

Beat egg, salt, and milk together thoroughly. Stir in flour to make a smooth batter, adding half the melted butter as you stir; blend in sugar and Cointreau. Heat a small skillet with a cooking surface of about 5 1/2 to 6 inches, brush it with some of remaining butter, and let it sizzle but not brown. Pour in just enough pancake batter to cover bottom of hot pan as thinly as possible. Tilt pan from side to side to spread the batter evenly. Cook the pancake 1 to 1 1/2 minutes, or until it moves when pan is shaken. Turn and cook for about 30 seconds on other side; remove pancake. Return pan to heat, brush with more butter, and repeat process, stacking pancakes on a plate.

Make filling by mixing avocado with sugar to taste. Grate rind of lime and reserve. Cut lime in half and squeeze juice into avocado mixture. Add pecans and blend thoroughly. Spread out pancakes, light side up, and spoon filling across center of each cake, dividing equally; roll up, then place on serving plates. Sprinkle with grated lime and Cointreau.

MAKES 2 SERVINGS.

GRANDFATHER'S BAKED BEANS AND DUCK

More Americans descend from families who moved south from Canada than many people think. In the Maritime Provinces, where this recipe began its journey into the Upper Midwest, baked beans are as popular as they are in Boston, "home of the bean and the cod."

1 lb. dried pea beans
6 cups beer
2 cups beef stock
2 bay leaves
1 medium-size onion, chopped
1/2 cup chopped candied gingerroot
1 lemon, chopped
1/4 cup maple sugar
1/2 cup unsulphured blackstrap molasses
2 Tbs. Worcestershire sauce
1 Tbs. Dijon mustard
1/2 tsp. ground cuminseed
1 tsp. ground savory
freshly ground pepper
3/4 cup diced salt pork
1 duck (4 to 5 lb.)
1/2 cup water

Preheat oven to 350° F. *

Soak beans in 4 cups beer overnight. Mix remaining 2 cups beer with stock, combine with beans soaked in beer, and pour all into a 4-quart baking dish. Add bay leaves, onion, gingerroot, lemon, maple sugar, molasses, seasonings, and salt pork.* Cover and bring to a boil, then put baking dish in oven and bake for 3 hours, adding a little water every 30 minutes as necessary; there should be enough liquid to cover beans by 1 inch.

Cut duck into 4 or 6 pieces, pulling fat away from meat. Render fat in a skillet large enough to hold all of duck pieces flat. Brown the pieces for 8 to

10 minutes, turning often so that all surfaces are seared; when browned, transfer to baking dish and push down into beans and liquid. Pour off duck fat from skillet and stir in water, scraping up brown bits on bottom of pan and letting liquid sizzle for about 1 minute; pour over duck and beans in baking dish. Cover and continue baking for 3 to 4 hours, checking occasionally and adding water, if necessary, to keep beans covered. When done, they will have absorbed most of the liquid, including any fat that may still come from duck; the meat should be falling off the bones.

MAKES 4 TO 6 SERVINGS.

BLACK-EYED PEAS WITH HAM, SAUSAGE, AND DUCK

2 cups dried black-eyed peas
1 Tbs. salt
1 bacon strip, cut into squares
1/2 cup rendered duck fat
2 onions, chopped
1 celery rib, chopped
1 small green pepper, chopped
1 lb. pork sausages, cooked
1 cup diced country ham
leftover pieces of cooked duck
1 tsp. sweet red pepper, minced
2 Tbs. butter
1 cup crumbled stale baking powder biscuits or dry bread crumbs

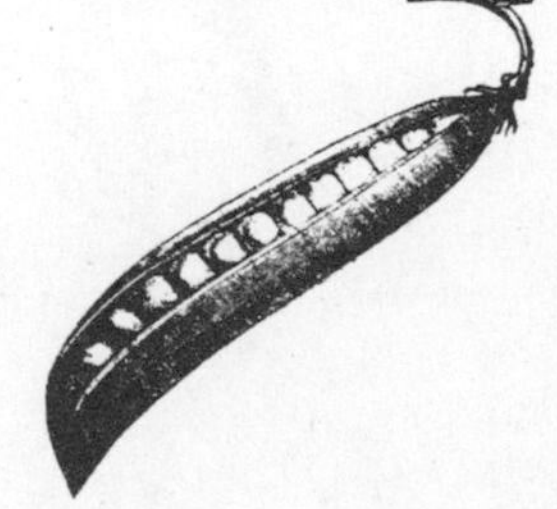

Preheat oven to 350° F.

Soak peas overnight. Drain; cover amply with fresh water. Add salt and bacon, bring water to a boil, and let simmer for 1 hour. Melt 2 tablespoons duck fat in a skillet and sauté onions, green pepper, and celery for 5 minutes. Cut sausages into sections and add, with ham, to vegetables; stir well, then add with duck and red pepper to peas. Stir in rest of duck fat and transfer to a 3-quart casserole with enough liquid in which peas cooked to barely cover. Melt butter and stir in crumbs; mix well and spread evenly over casserole. Bake for 1 hour.

MAKES 6 SERVINGS.

TEXAS BLACK-EYED PEAS AND SHRIMP

3/4 cup palm oil or peanut oil
1/2 cup finely chopped onion
2 garlic cloves, chopped
1 cup chunks of raw peeled shrimp
1 cup diced country ham
1/2 cup freshly made tomato sauce
2 Tbs. finely minced fresh hot red pepper
2 Tbs. dried shrimp or crayfish
2 cups cooked black-eyed peas (see above)

Heat oil in a large saucepan and slowly cook onion and garlic for about 4 minutes. Add shrimp and cook for 8 to 10 minutes. Stir in ham and tomato sauce and let simmer for 10 minutes. Add hot red pepper and dried fish, turn heat very low, and continue simmering 5 minutes until shrimp are tender. Combine with cooked peas and a little water if mixture seems too dry. Reheat.

MAKES ABOUT 6 SERVINGS.

MASHED LIMA BEANS IN SAUSAGE RING

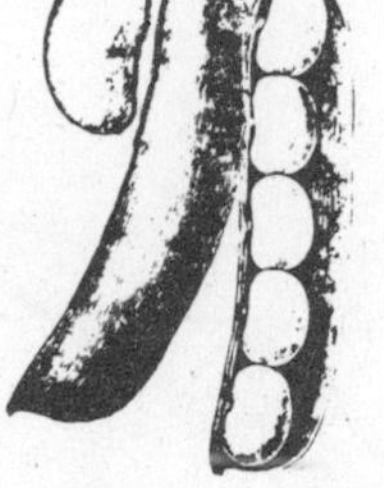

1 lb. highly seasoned bulk sausage
1 1/2 cups soft bread crumbs
1/4 cup grated onion
1 tsp. prepared mustard (optional)
1/4 cup chopped parsley
2 eggs, slightly beaten
6 Tbs. crushed cornflakes or stale corn bread
2 cups mashed cooked lima beans

Preheat oven to 350° F.

Grease an 8-inch ring mold thoroughly. Mix sausage with crumbs, onion, mustard if desired, parsley, and eggs. When thoroughly blended, press cornflakes or corn bread into greased surface of mold, coating evenly. Pack meat mixture into mold, then bake; after 15 minutes draw off fat that has collected and continue baking for 15 minutes more. Meanwhile carefully heat mashed lima beans just long enough for bubbles to appear. Turn baked sausage ring upside down on plate and fill center with mashed beans.

MAKES 4 SERVINGS.

PINTO BEANS AND SMOKED HAM HOCKS

1 lb. dried pinto beans (about 2 cups)
4 smoked ham hocks
1 onion, chopped
1/2 tsp. dried red pepper flakes
2 qt. water
1/2 tsp., more or less, salt

Wash beans in running water, removing any foreign bits (it should not be necessary to soak beans). Put hocks, onion, and red pepper in pot with water, bring to a boil, and let simmer, covered, for 1 hour. Add beans and continue simmering for about 2 hours, or until beans have doubled in size and are very tender; their skins should not crack or loosen, so do not let liquid boil. Add salt to taste. Drain and save liquid for soup.

MAKES 6 TO 8 SERVINGS.

DRIED OR CHIPPED BEEF WITH POACHED EGGS AND MUSHROOM SAUCE

about 1 cup dried beef
2 Tbs. butter
2 Tbs. chopped onion
2 Tbs. chopped green pepper
1/4 cup sliced fresh mushrooms
2 Tbs. flour
2 cups milk
2 to 3 Tbs. very dry sherry
1/4 tsp. dried marjoram
1 egg, hard-cooked and chopped
salt
freshly ground pepper
4 fresh eggs
4 baking powder biscuits or 4 baked or mashed potatoes
2 Tbs. chopped parsley

Separate leaves of dried beef under cold running water to freshen. Melt butter and gently sauté onion and green pepper, then add mushroom slices, stirring frequently for 3 to 4 minutes. When mushrooms begin to color, add beef and stir to coat with butter. Sprinkle in flour while continuing to stir. Off the heat, slowly whisk in milk, then return to heat and let milk warm up; stir until sauce is smooth and thick. Add sherry, marjoram, and chopped egg. Add salt only if beef is not overly salted to begin with; add pepper to taste. Poach eggs and place on split halves of baking powder biscuits; cover with beef-mushroom sauce. (Baked potatoes may be split open and substituted for biscuits; or beef may be served with mashed potatoes.) Sprinkle with parsley just before serving.

MAKES 4 SERVINGS.

DRIED BEEF AND SWEET POTATOES

4 medium-size sweet potatoes
1/4 lb. dried beef
1 small onion, grated
2 Tbs. butter
2 Tbs. flour
1 3/4 cups milk
salt
freshly ground white pepper
pinch of grated nutmeg
1/2 cup bread crumbs
1/4 cup grated cheese (Cheddar or Gruyère)

Preheat oven to 350° F.

Cover sweet potatoes with boiling water and cook for 10 to 15 minutes, or until skin slips off easily. Cut into 1-inch dice. Shred dried beef and mix with onion. Melt butter over low heat and stir in flour, slowly cooking for 2 or 3 minutes. Off the heat, stir in milk, return to heat, and whisk continuously until smooth and thickened. Add salt sparingly, then pepper and nutmeg. Mix together sauce, sweet potato dice, and beef, then turn into a 1 1/2-quart casserole. Sprinkle top with bread crumbs, then with cheese.

Bake for 30 to 40 minutes, or until mixture is bubbling and the top has turned golden.

MAKES 4 SERVINGS.

CALF'S BRAINS AND SPINACH BAKED IN PASTRY

1 recipe Basic Piecrust (p. 459)
1 calf's brain
1 Tbs. vinegar
salt
1 pkg. (10 oz.) frozen spinach
1 Tbs. butter
½ cup chopped ham
freshly ground pepper
¼ tsp. ground cloves
1 Tbs. minced parsley

SAUCE:
2 Tbs. butter
2 Tbs. flour
1 cup milk
salt
freshly ground pepper
2 Tbs. prepared horseradish

GLAZE:
1 egg mixed with 1 Tbs. water

Preheat oven to 450° F. *

Roll out pastry to a rectangle 6 by 12 inches and place on a greased cookie sheet; chill while preparing filling. Soak brains in cold water for 30 minutes; drain, then put into a saucepan, cover with fresh water, and add vinegar and 1 teaspoon salt. Bring to a boil and let simmer very gently for 15 minutes. Meanwhile cook spinach in salted water for 5 minutes, drain thoroughly, then return to pan to toss with butter until moisture has evaporated. Let cool, then chill. Now drain poached brains and rinse with cold water until cool enough to handle; remove membrane and cut into ¾-inch pieces. Toss with ham and add salt, pepper, cloves, and parsley (amount of salt depends on saltiness of ham).

Make the sauce: Melt butter, blend in flour, and cook gently for 1 minute, stirring continuously. Off the heat, whisk in ¾ cup milk and return to heat long enough to thicken. Season to taste with salt and a few turns of pepper grinder. Stir 1 cup of sauce into meat mixture. Thin remaining sauce with remaining milk, add horseradish, and set aside in a warm place. *

Spread spinach on pastry, leaving a 1-inch border. Spread brain-ham mixture on top. Draw long sides of dough toward each other and paint nearest side with egg glaze; overlap farther side by 1 inch, gently pressing into glaze to seal. Then flip roll over so that seam is on bottom; tuck in the two ends. Paint the roll, top and sides, with egg glaze. (Use leftover dough, if you wish, to make decorative shapes; place these on top and paint with glaze.) Bake for 10 minutes; reduce heat to 375° and continue baking for 20 to 25 minutes more, or until pastry is crisp and golden. To serve, cut into slices and serve horseradish-cream sauce separately.

MAKES 4 SERVINGS.

CALIFORNIA BAKED FLANK STEAK WITH EGGPLANT

1 flank steak (about 1 1/2 lb.)
salt
freshly ground pepper
flour
2 Tbs. chopped suet or vegetable oil
1/2 large green pepper, chopped coarse
1 large onion, chopped coarse
2 cups cooked tomatoes or tomato purée
1 tsp. minced dried basil
1 purple or white eggplant (about 1 lb.)
1 1/2 tsp. salt
1 egg, beaten
2 Tbs. butter, melted
freshly ground pepper
1/2 tsp. oregano
1/2 cup dry bread crumbs
1 large tomato, sliced
2 Tbs. grated Cheddar cheese
1/4 cup grated Monterey Jack cheese

Preheat oven to 350° F.

Use a sharp knife to score meat into 1-inch diamonds on both sides; sprinkle all over with salt and pepper and dredge thoroughly with flour. Heat suet or oil in a fireproof shallow casserole just large enough to hold meat flat and sear steak over high heat. When it is lightly browned, strew green pepper and all but 2 tablespoons onion over it and cover with tomatoes or purée. Sprinkle with basil, cover, and put in oven for 1 hour. Peel and slice eggplant; put slices into saucepan with salt and about 1 inch of boiling water. Cover tightly and cook for 10 minutes. Drain. Beat eggplant until puréed, then mix in egg, butter, a little pepper, reserved 2 tablespoons of onion, oregano, and bread crumbs. When meat has baked 1 hour, spread mixture over flank steak and sauce, then sprinkle with cheeses. Return to oven, turn heat up to 375°, and bake for 45 minutes more. Steak should be soft enough to cut with a spoon.

MAKES 6 TO 8 SERVINGS.

MEAT AND CHEESE LOAF

1 1/2 lb. ground chuck
1/2 lb. ground veal
2 cups grated Monterey Jack cheese
1/2 cup chopped shallots
10 juniper berries, crushed
1 1/2 tsp. salt
freshly ground pepper
2 eggs
2 to 3 Tbs. minced celery leaves
2 cups buttermilk
1 1/4 cups fresh bread crumbs
4 bacon strips

Preheat oven to 350° F.
Lightly mix all ingredients except bacon. Pack into a large greased loaf pan. Arrange bacon strips on top of meat loaf and bake for 1 1/2 hours.

MAKES 6 TO 8 SERVINGS.

EMPAÑADAS WITH BEEF FILLING

The Spanish-Indian influence on American food may be most recognizable along the Rocky Mountain spine of the country—from foothills towns like Jerome, Arizona, to Butte, Montana (where, one July day in 1902, two hot tamale vendors were fined five dollars apiece for shouting too loud in an effort to sell their snacks in the frontier mining settlement). Empañadas are often sweet, filled with jam, jelly, or Spanish flan, but like Cornish pastries they make a substantial "meal in the hand" when the interior puffs out with a highly seasoned meat filling.

DOUGH:

10 Tbs. (1 1/4 stick) butter, chilled
3 1/2 cups flour
1/2 tsp. salt
1/2 cup cold water

FILLING:

1/4 cup vegetable oil
1 dried hot red pepper
2 medium-size onions, chopped
1/2 tsp. paprika
3/4 lb. ground beef round or chuck
1 sweet red pepper, roasted, skinned, and chopped
1/4 cup raisins
2 tsp. capers, drained
1/2 tsp. oregano
salt
freshly ground pepper
2 eggs, hard-cooked and chopped
10 small pitted green olives

GLAZE:

1 egg, beaten with 1/2 tsp. sugar

Preheat oven to 450° F. *
Make the dough: Cut the butter into 1/2-inch pieces and place in the bowl of a food processor or electric mixer along with flour and salt. Process with the metal blade for about 15 seconds or mix with the mixing blade or dough hook until the butter is broken up, then add cold water and mix until dough forms a ball, adding a little more water if necessary. Dough should be moist but not sticky. Remove from the bowl and pat into a flat round. Cover with plastic wrap and let rest in refrigerator for at least 30 minutes. Then remove and knead the dough for about 2 minutes. Flour your working surface and roll dough out to a thickness of 1/8 inch. Using a saucer of about 5 1/2-inch diameter, cut circles out of dough. Stack them, separated by plastic or wax paper, and refrigerate while making filling. You should have about 10 circles, using scraps, rekneading them, and rolling them out.

Make the filling: Heat oil in a skillet and sauté dried red pepper until it turns black. Remove and sauté onions with paprika until soft. Add ground beef, stirring and breaking up meat until it loses its color. Add sweet red pepper, raisins, capers, and oregano; season liberally with salt and pepper to taste. Stir in egg and let mixture cool thoroughly.*

Assemble the empañadas: On each circle of dough now place about 1/4 cup filling off center with an olive on top. Wet the edge all around and then fold the dough circle over to make a half-moon, patting down the filling a bit to distribute evenly. Press the edges together, fold over the edge once to seal tightly, and crimp. Paint tops with egg glaze and place on greased cookie sheets, 1 inch apart. Bake for 20 minutes.

MAKES 6 TO 8 SERVINGS.

TACOS DE CARNE

1 lb. lean beef chuck
5 Tbs. vegetable oil
1 small onion, chopped
1 garlic clove, minced
1/4 tsp. cuminseed
1/2 tsp. ground coriander
1 Tbs. chili powder
1/2 cup water
8 tortillas
shredded lettuce
1 medium-size avocado
sour cream

Do not grind meat, but chop it with a sharp knife into 1/4-inch pieces. Heat 4 tablespoons oil; sauté onion and garlic for 1 or 2 minutes, then stir in meat and let it brown. Bruise cuminseeds and add along with coriander and chili; stir in water and let mixture absorb it. In a skillet heat remaining oil and heat tortillas until soft. Slice avocado. While tortillas are hot, fill each with shredded lettuce, 2 or 3 avocado slices, some sour cream, and some of seasoned meat mixture. The contrasts of hot and cold temperatures, spicy and bland flavors, is exquisite.

MAKES 4 SERVINGS.

CALIFORNIA CARNE CON CHILE

6 red ancho *chilies*
1 Tbs. flour
1 large onion
2 garlic cloves
1/4 cup fat
2 lb. beef chuck, diced
1/2 tsp. ground coriander
1/2 tsp. dried thyme
1/4 tsp. ground cuminseed
salt
freshly ground pepper
2 or 3 canned green chilies

Split open red chilies and soak in hot water for 1 hour. Drain and remove seeds and pith, then put through a meat grinder with onion and 1 garlic clove. Heat half the fat in a skillet and stir in flour, cooking slowly until flour takes on color. Stir in ground chili mixture and cook for 5 minutes. In another pan sauté beef in remaining fat until well seared on all sides. Mash remaining garlic clove and add to beef along with seasonings. Add ground chili mixture and cook for about 10 minutes, or until meat is tender. Mince green chilies and stir in. Serve with cooked pinto or pink beans.

MAKES 6 SERVINGS.

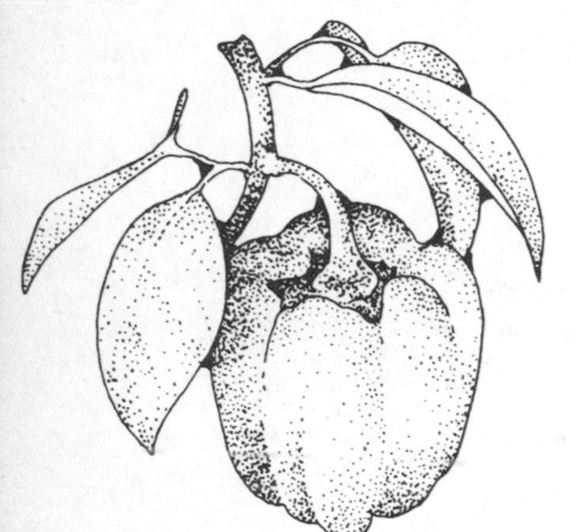

ARIZONA CHILI WITH RICE

½ lb. link pork sausage
2 onions, chopped
1 green pepper, chopped
2 garlic cloves, minced
1 ½ lb. beef round
2 Tbs. chili powder
4 medium-size tomatoes
2 tsp. wine vinegar
1 ½ tsp. brown sugar
1 tsp. salt
1 Tbs. dried oregano
1 tsp. cuminseed
1 bay leaf
1 cup ripe olives
2 cups cooked red kidney beans
2 cups uncooked rice

Cook sausages in an enameled cast-iron pot for about 10 minutes, turning to brown all surfaces; remove. In the sausage fat cook onions, green pepper, and garlic for 2 to 3 minutes, stirring occasionally. Cut beef into ½-inch cubes and stir into onion mixture to sear on all sides. Stir in chili powder. Peel and chop tomatoes, retaining juice and adding both to pot. Add vinegar, brown sugar, salt, and oregano; pound cuminseed in a mortar and add along with bay leaf. Cover pot and cook for 1 ½ to 2 hours, or until meat is tender. Remove bay leaf; cut sausage into short lengths and add along with olives and beans. Cook rice in a large pot of boiling salted water for about 17 minutes and drain. Serve rice and chili in separate heated serving bowls.

MAKES 8 SERVINGS.

BAKED BROCCOLI WITH HAM AND CHEESE

1 large bunch of broccoli
salt
3 Tbs. butter
3 Tbs. flour
3 cups milk
3 Tbs. puréed chervil, or 1 tsp. dried
freshly ground pepper
butter
1 cup postage-stamp-size flakes of country ham
¼ lb. mozzarella cheese, cut into ¼-in. slices
sweet paprika for garnish

Preheat oven to 350° F.

Cut buds away from broccoli stalks and put into a bowl of cold water with a little salt. Peel and cut up stalky pieces, making them about thickness of bud stems and about 1 by 1 ½ inches in length. After 30 minutes of soaking put stalk pieces into boiling water and cook for 5 minutes. Then add buds and continue cooking for 10 minutes. Meanwhile make the sauce: Melt butter in a saucepan and stir in flour, cooking gently 2 minutes. Off the heat, gradually stir in milk, blending until smooth. Return to heat and cook slowly, stirring occasionally as sauce thickens. Blend in chervil and several turns of pepper grinder. (A salty country ham eliminates need to add salt.) Stir in ham flakes. Drain broccoli thoroughly and pat dry with paper towels. Butter a 1 ½-qt. casserole and put in broccoli, then cover with ham and sauce. Cover contents of casserole with cheese. Sprinkle with paprika and bake for 25 minutes, or until cheese blisters and has taken on color.

MAKES 4 SERVINGS.

PENNSYLVANIA DUTCH STUFFED CABBAGE

2 cups chopped cooked fresh pork
1 cup chopped cooked ham
½ cup finely chopped fresh mushrooms
1 tsp. ground savory
½ tsp. salt
freshly ground black pepper
8 large cabbage leaves, blanched
1 qt. pork or chicken stock, boiling
2 Tbs. butter
2 Tbs. flour
1 Tbs. minced chives

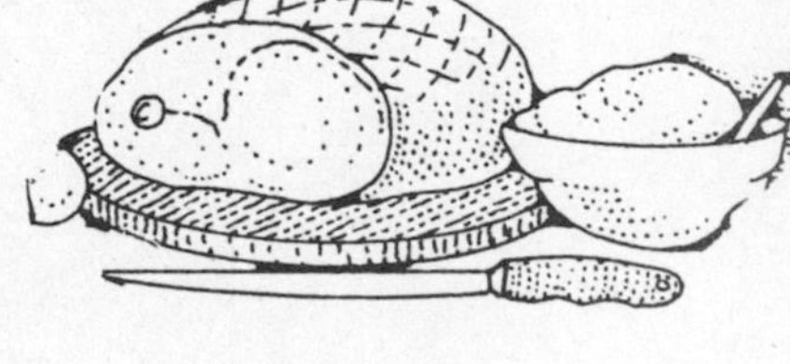

Mix together pork, ham, mushrooms, savory, and salt, and grind in pepper. Divide stuffing mixture among cabbage leaves, tuck in ends of each, and wrap like a package. Put these side by side in a single layer in a pan, cover with boiling stock, and let simmer for 30 minutes. Remove stuffed cabbages with a slotted spoon and keep hot. Mix butter, flour, and chives into a smooth paste, then add stock, a little at a time, to liquefy; stir into stock in pan. Let sauce thicken over medium heat before pouring over stuffed cabbage leaves on a serving dish.

MAKES 4 SERVINGS.

BAKED CABBAGE WITH CHOPPED MEAT

4 cups finely chopped cabbage
1 small onion, minced
½ cup slivered sweet red pepper
2 eggs, separated
½ cup heavy cream or evaporated milk
1 ½ tsp. salt
freshly ground black pepper
½ tsp. dried rosemary
1 ½ cups cooked veal heart and ham, chopped together

Preheat oven to 375° F.

Cook vegetables in boiling water for 7 to 8 minutes; drain and pat dry. Beat egg yolks with cream or evaporated milk, adding salt, a few turns of pepper grinder, and rosemary. Mix cooked vegetables with veal and ham (any leftover meat can be used), then stir into sauce. Beat egg whites until very stiff, then fold carefully into vegetable-meat mixture. Transfer to a buttered 1 1/2-quart casserole and bake for about 45 minutes.

MAKES 4 SERVINGS.

CAULIFLOWER WITH SHRIMPS

1 1/2 Tbs. butter
1 1/2 Tbs. flour
2 cups milk
salt
1/2 tsp. sugar
2 Tbs. sour cream
1 lb. freshly boiled shrimps, peeled
1 large cauliflower
2 Tbs. dry sherry

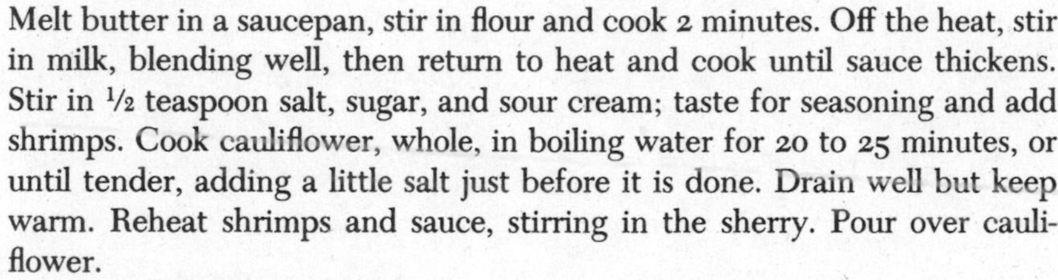

Melt butter in a saucepan, stir in flour and cook 2 minutes. Off the heat, stir in milk, blending well, then return to heat and cook until sauce thickens. Stir in 1/2 teaspoon salt, sugar, and sour cream; taste for seasoning and add shrimps. Cook cauliflower, whole, in boiling water for 20 to 25 minutes, or until tender, adding a little salt just before it is done. Drain well but keep warm. Reheat shrimps and sauce, stirring in the sherry. Pour over cauliflower.

MAKES 4 SERVINGS.

CHAYOTES STUFFED WITH SHRIMP AND HAM

Belonging to the squash family, chayotes are common in parts of Florida, Puerto Rico, Louisiana, Texas, New Mexico, Arizona, and California, as well as in specialty fruit and vegetable stores in other places; they are usually called mirlitons in New Orleans, where they are grown in many backyards, or they may be known in some regions as vegetable pears or christophines. Some chayotes have smooth, pale green skins, and all are roughly pear shaped, with delicate, pale green flesh.

2 chayotes (about 1 lb. each)
4 Tbs. (1/2 stick) butter
1/2 lb. ham, chopped fine
1/2 lb. shrimps, cooked, peeled, and chopped
1/4 cup chopped shallots or scallions (white part only)
2 garlic cloves, minced
1 tsp. dried thyme
1 large bay leaf
1 cup stale bread cubes
1 1/2 tsp. salt
freshly ground pepper
dash, or more, of Tabasco
1/4 cup fresh bread crumbs
1/4 cup chopped parsley

Preheat oven to 350° F.

Cover chayotes with boiling water and boil for about 1 hour, or until tender. When cool, cut into halves and scoop out pulp, leaving shells about 1/4 inch thick. Melt butter in a skillet and add chopped chayote pulp, ham, shrimps, shallots or scallions, garlic, thyme, and bay leaf. Cook gently for 20 minutes. Soak bread cubes in water and squeeze dry, then add to stuffing mixture along with salt, pepper, and Tabasco. Fill shells with mixture; mix crumbs and parsley and sprinkle over tops. Bake for about 15 minutes, or until browned.

MAKES 4 SERVINGS.

CHEDDAR PUDDING

2 Tbs. butter
2 whole eggs
2 egg yolks
1 cup milk
2 cups grated sharp Vermont Cheddar cheese
9 large Montpelier water biscuits or unsalted crackers
salt
freshly ground pepper
3 Tbs. chopped celery leaves or mixed chopped parsley and fresh chives
paprika for garnish

Preheat oven to 350° F.

Butter a 1-quart casserole liberally. Beat whole eggs with egg yolks and milk, and add cheese. Crumble biscuits with a rolling pin and sprinkle one-third of them over the bottom of the casserole; add salt and pepper and half of the egg-cheese mixture. Repeat, then strew chopped greens over and top with last layer of biscuits dusted with paprika and dotted with remaining butter. Bake for 35 to 40 minutes, or until puffed up and set. Serve with broiled fresh tomatoes.

MAKES 4 SERVINGS.

CABOT CHEDDAR AND ONION PIE

CRUST:

1 1/3 cups flour
2 Tbs. lard, chilled
5 Tbs. butter, chilled
1/2 tsp. salt
3 Tbs. ice water

FILLING:

10 bacon strips
2 eggs
1 cup milk
1 Tbs. granulated flour
1/2 tsp. salt
freshly ground pepper
pinch of cayenne pepper
2 Tbs. butter
2 good-size onions, chopped fine
3/4 lb. Vermont Cheddar cheese, grated

Preheat oven to 450° F.

Mix crust and chill for a few hours, or 1 hour in the freezer will do. Roll out, then fill a 9-inch pie pan, crimping the edges. Set a slightly smaller pie pan on top to hold down crust, or line with foil filled with dried beans. Bake for 8 minutes, then remove extra pan or filled foil, prick bottom all over, and bake for another 2 or 3 minutes. Meanwhile cook bacon slowly, squeezing out all fat. Beat eggs with milk, flour, salt, pepper, and cayenne. Drain bacon and wipe skillet free of grease; crumble bacon. Melt butter in same pan and sauté onions slowly until translucent. Now blend together bacon, egg mixture, sautéed onions, and cheese and pour into partially baked shell. Bake for 30 minutes. Let set for a few minutes before cutting.

MAKES 6 SERVINGS.

SOUFFLÉED CHEESE SANDWICHES

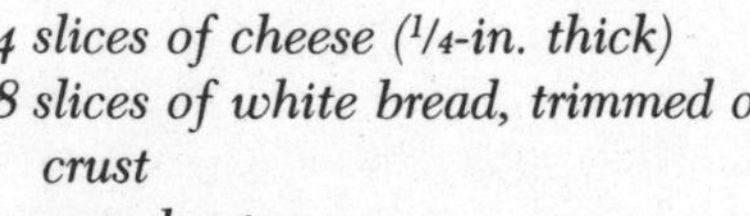

4 slices of cheese (1/4-in. thick)
8 slices of white bread, trimmed of crust
2 eggs, beaten
2 cups milk
butter or bacon fat
1/2 tsp. salt
freshly ground pepper

Preheat oven to 325° F.

Put each cheese slice between 2 slices of bread and press firmly together to make 4 sandwiches. Beat eggs and milk together until blended. Use a shallow rectangular pan or heatproof dish just large enough to hold 4 sandwiches; butter it well, or use bacon fat for added flavor. Cover bottom with sandwiches and pour egg-milk mixture evenly over all. Sprinkle with salt and a turn or two of pepper grinder. Let stand for 45 minutes. Put in oven and bake for 45 minutes, or until puffy and golden brown.

MAKES 4 SERVINGS.

MINCED CHICKEN SAM WARD

Lately Thomas, Sam Ward's distinguished biographer, points out that in the 1870s and 1880s Ward was recognized as America's premier authority on all matters pertaining to food and wine. "The evidence is ample of Sam's preeminence in the American hierarchy of the table, ranking second to none," Thomas wrote, adding that "his worthiness of association with the brightest luminaries of the French firmament" is beyond doubt. Here is Ward's recipe for chicken with mushrooms. Others are to be found on page 54.

1 large chicken
1 lb. fresh mushrooms
3 Tbs., or more, butter
2 cups white wine
1 large potato, cooked
heavy cream
4 bacon strips, cooked crisp

Clean chicken and boil until done. Remove all meat from bones and chop into fine dice; set aside. Chop mushrooms and sauté in about 3 tablespoons butter for 4 or 5 minutes, stirring occasionally. Add white wine, bring to a boil, and let it reduce to one-third. Meanwhile put potato through a grinder. Add chopped chicken to reduced wine-mushroom mixture and stir in potato to bind mixture. Add just enough cream to make a smooth, thickish blend. Serve piping hot, topped by crisp bacon in half slices.

MAKES 8 TO 10 SERVINGS.

OLD DOMINION CHICKEN AND OYSTERS OVER CORN BREAD

American cooks have been combining chicken and oysters since the earliest colonial days. In one method, called Chicken Smothered in Oysters, chicken pieces were baked in milk, then "smothered" in a mixture of cream and oysters with their liquor. Following is a seventeenth-century shortbread that demonstrates why cornmeal was so accepted when wheat flour was in short supply; it is delicious.

4 Tbs. (1/2 stick) butter
5 Tbs. flour
1 3/4 cups chicken stock
1/2 cup heavy cream
1/2 tsp. salt
4 or 5 drops of Tabasco
1 tsp. lemon juice
2 Tbs. minced parsley
1 1/2 pt. oysters, with their liquor, at room temperature
2 cups diced cooked chicken, at room temperature
1 recipe Everyday Corn Bread (p. 204), freshly made and still warm

In a saucepan melt butter and stir in flour until smooth. Off the heat, stir in stock until mixture is free of lumps, then return to heat and let simmer over lowest heat for about 5 minutes. Stir in cream, salt, Tabasco, and lemon juice. Poach oysters in oyster liquor for 5 minutes or less, until they have just become plump. Drain and fold into sauce, adding diced chicken. To serve, cut squares of warm corn bread, split, and put bottoms on a serving platter. Cover with half of chicken-oyster mixture, top with remaining corn squares, and pour sauce over. Sprinkle with parsley.

MAKES 6 SERVINGS.

CHICKEN LIVERS MADEIRA

1 lb. chicken livers
1/4 cup finely diced country ham
1 1/2 Tbs. butter
1 1/2 Tbs. vegetable oil
1 tsp. ground sage
salt
freshly ground pepper
4 slices of bread, cut diagonally to make 8 triangles
1/4 cup Madeira

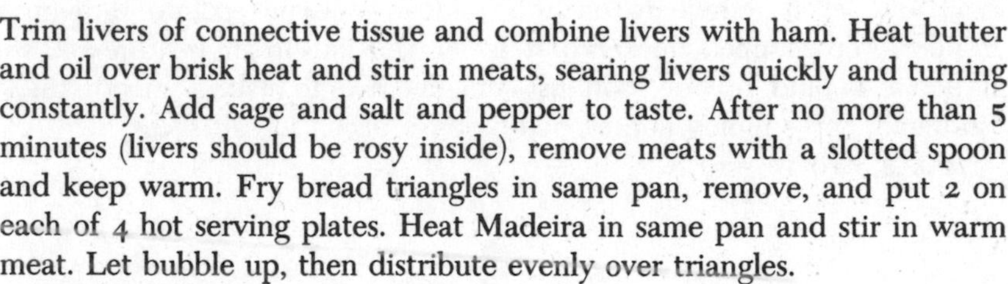

Trim livers of connective tissue and combine livers with ham. Heat butter and oil over brisk heat and stir in meats, searing livers quickly and turning constantly. Add sage and salt and pepper to taste. After no more than 5 minutes (livers should be rosy inside), remove meats with a slotted spoon and keep warm. Fry bread triangles in same pan, remove, and put 2 on each of 4 hot serving plates. Heat Madeira in same pan and stir in warm meat. Let bubble up, then distribute evenly over triangles.

MAKES 4 SERVINGS.

CHICKEN SOUFFLÉS WITH MUSHROOM SAUCE

1 cup finely chopped cooked chicken
1 tsp. dried tarragon or 1 Tbs. chopped fresh
1 Tbs. chopped parsley
2 shallots or scallions, chopped very fine (white part only)
salt
freshly ground pepper
4 Tbs. (1/2 stick) butter
3 Tbs. grated Parmesan cheese
3 Tbs. flour
1 cup rich chicken stock
3 egg yolks
4 egg whites

SAUCE:

3/4 lb. fresh mushrooms, chopped coarse
3 Tbs. butter
2 Tbs. flour
1 cup chicken stock
1/4 cup Madeira
salt
freshly ground pepper
up to 1/4 cup leftover cooked chicken, minced fine (optional)

Preheat oven to 400° F.

Mix finely chopped chicken with tarragon, parsley, shallots or scallions, and salt and pepper to taste. Set aside while making the soufflé base. Prepare 4 individual straight-sided baking dishes of at least 1 cup; or, if a single soufflé is preferred, use a 1 1/2-quart mold; grease with 1 tablespoon of the butter, then sprinkle the bottom and sides with half the cheese. Make collars of foil to extend the molds by 1 inch and butter inside of foil. Melt remaining butter over low heat, add flour, blend, and cook for 1 minute. Off the heat, add stock, beat until smooth, return to heat, and stir as sauce thickens. Let simmer for a minute, then remove and add egg yolks one by one, beating in thoroughly. Add the chopped chicken mixture, season with remaining cheese and more salt and pepper (the base should be highly seasoned). In a clean bowl beat egg whites, with a pinch of salt until they form soft peaks. Beat one-third of egg whites into soufflé base, then gently fold in remaining two-thirds. Turn into prepared molds and place in top third of oven. Reduce heat to 375°. Small soufflés will be done in 20 minutes; the larger in 30.

Meanwhile prepare the sauce: Sauté mushrooms in sizzling butter, tossing occasionally, for about 5 minutes. Sprinkle on flour, then add stock and stir until thickened. Add Madeira and let sauce simmer to reduce a bit. If there is an extra bit of chicken, mince it very finely and add it to the sauce for body. Serve sauce in a large sauceboat.

MAKES 4 SERVINGS.

BUTTERMILK CAKES STUFFED WITH CHICKEN, HAM, AND WALNUTS

This is one of those dishes of the Harvest Century that used the bounty of the farm, but it can be a treat today when made with cultured buttermilk and, if necessary, chopped dried beef instead of country ham.

STUFFING:

2 cups diced cooked chicken
1 cup chopped or diced cooked country ham
1/4 cup finely chopped black walnuts
1/2 tsp. dried rosemary
3 Tbs. butter
3 Tbs. flour
1 cup chicken stock
1/2 cup buttermilk
1/4 cup heavy cream
3 to 4 Tbs. bourbon
1 recipe Buttermilk Pancakes (p. 215)

Preheat oven to 400° F.

Make the stuffing: Mix chicken, ham, black walnuts, and rosemary. Melt butter and stir in flour; cook over low heat for about 4 minutes. Off the heat, stir in stock, blending until smooth; then stir in buttermilk, cream, and bourbon. Return to heat and cook until sauce thickens, stirring constantly. Reserve half the sauce and stir meat mixture into remainder; keep warm.

Make the buttermilk pancakes. Have a casserole large enough to hold 4 cakes flat on the bottom. Spread each cake with chicken-ham mixture, making 4 stacks 3 cakes high and divide mixture evenly among them. Pour reserved sauce over all and sprinkle with cheese. Bake for about 5 minutes, or until all is bubbling.

MAKES 4 SERVINGS.

CRAB MEAT AND MUSHROOM SCALLOP

4 Tbs. (1/2 stick) butter
1 shallot or scallion (white part only) minced
4 medium-size fresh mushrooms, (about 1/4 lb.), sliced thin
2 Tbs. dry white wine
2 Tbs. flour
1 cup milk
1 generous cup fresh lump crab meat
pinch of salt
freshly ground black pepper
1 tsp. dried tarragon
2 Tbs. dry sherry
1 egg yolk
1 Tbs. heavy cream
4 tsp. mixed dry bread crumbs and grated Cheddar cheese

Melt half the butter in a skillet and sauté shallot or scallion and mushrooms, coating everything well with butter; add wine and let simmer for 5 minutes. Remove from skillet and keep warm. Melt remaining butter and blend in flour. Off the heat, stir in milk, whisk well, return to heat, and let thicken, stirring constantly. Add mushrooms, shallots, crab meat, salt, 2 or 3 turns of pepper grinder, tarragon, and sherry. Beat egg yolk with a little cream, add a little hot sauce, and stir, then a little more sauce; combine with crab mixture and heat, stirring gently. Do not let boil. Fill 4 scallop shells or small, shallow baking dishes and sprinkle each top with a teaspoon of crumb-cheese mixture. Put under broiler and serve when bubbling and golden.

MAKES 4 SERVINGS.

CALIFORNIA CRAB TOSTADOS

Informal dining became a way of life in California long before its popularity spread to the rest of the country. Maybe it was inevitable that the West Coast's delectable Dungeness crab should have been recognized by cooks with Spanish forebears as a natural and surprising basis for filling tostadas.

2 cups frijoles refritos *(refried beans)*
4 tortillas
1 1/2 cups shredded Monterey Jack cheese
1 cup shredded iceberg lettuce
1 lb. cooked Dungeness crab meat
1 doz. cherry tomatoes, cut into halves
1/2 cup pimiento-stuffed green olives, sliced
1/4 cup guacamole
3 to 4 pickled chili peppers

Heat beans thoroughly and spread evenly on tortillas. Sprinkle with cheese, lettuce, and crab, evenly divided. Garnish with tomatoes, sliced olives, and top each tostado with your favorite guacamole mixture and a strip or 2 of chili pepper, to taste.

MAKES 4 SERVINGS.

SPAGHETTI WITH BLUE CRAB AND TOMATO SAUCE

Delicious! A labor of love that is worth the effort.

2 medium-size onions, chopped
1/4 cup olive oil
2 or 3 garlic cloves, minced
1/4 cup minced celery
1/2 cup minced parsley
1/4 cup fish stock, or 2 Tbs. clam juice and 2 Tbs. water
4 medium-size tomatoes, peeled and chopped, juice reserved
1 1/2 Tbs. salt
freshly ground black pepper
1/2 tsp. sugar
8 live hard-shell blue crabs (about 5 in. in diameter)
3/4 lb. uncooked spaghetti
3 Tbs. chopped fresh basil

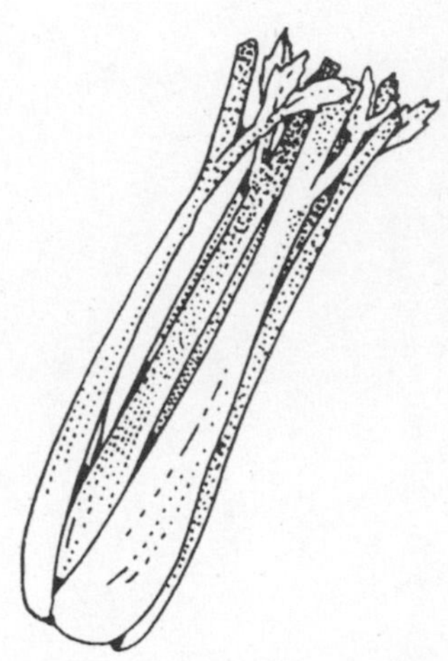

In a large, heavy pot sauté chopped onions in 3 tablespoons oil, adding garlic, celery, and parsley; cook over very low heat for about 10 minutes. Add liquid and tomatoes with their juice and bring to a boil. Add salt, pepper, and sugar. Pick up 4 of the crabs with tongs and very quickly drop them into the tomato mixture and cover. Reduce heat to medium and cook for 10 minutes, then remove crabs and set aside. Repeat with remaining crabs.

Heat a large pot of water to boiling. Keep tomato sauce simmering over low heat. Meanwhile crack shells of crabs and remove all of the meat and juices. This can be done over the pot so you don't lose any of the juices; scrape all meat away from shells, breaking claws, and using skewer to loosen bits of crab. When water is boiling, toss in spaghetti in big handfuls, pushing top ends down into water, and add remaining 1 tablespoon salt and remaining 1 tablespoon oil. Cover and boil for about 12 minutes. Drain well and serve on piping-hot plates with hot crab sauce and chopped basil divided equally.

MAKES 4 SERVINGS.

STUFFED CUCUMBERS WITH GROUND LAMB

4 cucumbers (7 in. long)
4 cups ground cooked lamb
1 Tbs. minced fresh oregano
1 Tbs. puréed chervil
salt
freshly ground pepper
1/2 cup pine nuts

Preheat oven to 325° F.

Soak cucumbers in cold water for 15 minutes. Cut into halves lengthwise and scoop out seeds, leaving a shell 1/4 to 1/3 inch thick. Boil them for 15 to 20 minutes. Mix lamb with oregano and chervil, add salt and pepper to taste, and stir in pine nuts. When cooked cucumbers are cool enough to handle, divide meat mixture evenly, spooning into cucumber hollows and mounding neatly on top. Bake on a rack in a shallow pan for about 10 minutes.

MAKES 4 SERVINGS.

EGGS BENEDICT

Few dishes are more American than this combination of poached fresh eggs, smoked meat, English muffins (a truly Yankee breakfast staple), and hollandaise sauce. The ornate sandwich came into being as a cure for too much "night before" when Lemuel Benedict, a Wall Street stockbroker—according to the research of George Lang—developed the habit of ordering "toast, a few slices of crisp bacon, two poached eggs and a gooseneck of hollandaise sauce. Later in life," Lang added, "Benedict felt that Oscar of the Waldorf, who admired and copied this concoction, became a Benedict Arnold by exchanging some of the elements, including the toast for the English muffins, the bacon for ham, then adding truffles and *glace de viande*." Nowadays grilled Canadian bacon is used as often as ham, and few American housewives have either truffles or meat glaze at the ready. A footnote of some interest is supplied by Edna's Cafe in Minneapolis. Edna's daily special consists of an English muffin covered with homemade hash browns that have been mixed with melted cheese and topped by two basted eggs.

2 recipes Hollandaise Sauce (p. 441), warm
4 English muffins
2 Tbs. butter, softened
8 slices of Canadian bacon or country ham
1 tsp. vinegar
8 eggs
salt
freshly ground pepper
paprika or cayenne pepper for garnish

Split English muffins, toast, butter, and keep them warm. Fry meat lightly. Fill a large skillet with water, add vinegar, and bring to a boil. Drop in eggs one by one; lower heat until water is barely simmering, and poach eggs slowly, spooning water over the yolks—they should cook for about 3 minutes. Meanwhile put 2 halves of buttered muffins on each plate, topping with meat slices. As eggs are done, remove with a slotted spoon and drain before nestling one egg on each muffin half. Spoon over warm hollandaise and sprinkle with a little paprika or cayenne. Serve immediately.

MAKES 4 SERVINGS.

CAMBRIAN BAKED EGGS

butter
8 eggs, at room temperature
salt
freshly ground pepper
2 cups Cheese and Pimiento Sandwich Spread (p. 188)
1 tsp. minced chives

Preheat oven to 375° F.

Thoroughly butter 4 individual heatproof serving dishes. Carefully break 2 eggs into each dish. Sprinkle with a little salt and several turns of pepper grinder. Crumble about 1/2 cup of cheese spread over each dish of eggs, then sprinkle with minced chives. Bake for 15 minutes; check to see if eggs are set. Finish by turning oven to 500° for 5 minutes.

MAKES 4 SERVINGS.

AN AMERICAN FRITTATA

This tempting "pie" may be perceived as a cross between a quiche and an omelet. Following is one of the formulas we tinker with, depending on mood and contents of the refrigerator. Imagination is what's called for here.

8 eggs
3 to 4 oz. boiled ham, cut into 1/2-in. squares
2 oz. cheese, crumbled
1/4 lb. chopped cooked zucchini or other leftover vegetable
2 tsp. chopped herbs (such as parsley, chives, basil, or oregano)
salt
freshly ground pepper
4 Tbs. (1/2 stick) butter
1 large onion, chopped
2 garlic cloves, crushed

Beat eggs and add ham, cheese, zucchini, herbs, and salt and pepper to taste. Sauté chopped onion and garlic in about half the butter until translucent, then scrape all into egg mixture. Melt remaining butter in a shallow 1-quart baking dish that will take direct heat (or an iron-handled frying pan works well). Turn dish to cover sides with butter and pour egg mixture into it. Cover and cook over low heat for about 10 minutes, or until egg has begun to draw away from sides. Then finish cooking about 6 inches below broiler so that top of *frittata* becomes golden and firm.

MAKES 4 TO 6 SERVINGS.

HANGTOWN FRY

Before it became known as a gold miner's headquarters, Placerville, California, was called Hangtown because of an incident of summary Western justice. How the omelet-like dish known as Hangtown Fry got its name may be obscured by the enthusiasm of the Forty-niners for tall stories. A likely version has it that this recipe was created when a miner who'd struck it rich sought to satisfy his hunger by ordering the most expensive items a restaurant cook had on hand. In the bonanza fresh country eggs were worth their weight in gold, so the hungry miner ordered them cooked with bacon, and topped with oysters—and a meal still served in tradition-saluting San Francisco eating places was born.

1/2 lb. lean bacon
2 Tbs. butter
6 medium-size oysters, or 12 small Olympia oysters
1/4 cup flour
1 egg, beaten
1/4 cup cracker crumbs
6 eggs
salt
freshly ground pepper

Fry bacon strips in a large skillet, remove, and drain on paper towels. Remove bacon fat and put butter in skillet to melt. Dip oysters into flour, then into beaten egg and cracker crumbs; fry in butter, turning so that they are crisp on all surfaces. Beat the 6 eggs, seasoning with salt and pepper, then pour over oysters. Cook until bottom is firm, then turn and cook like an omelet, adding bacon strips to top. Divide into 3 or 4 parts and serve on hot plates.

MAKES 3 TO 4 SERVINGS.

STUFFED EGGPLANT WITH COOKED MEAT

2 medium-size eggplants
salt
freshly ground pepper
1 medium to large onion, chopped
2 garlic cloves, minced
3 to 4 tablespoons vegetable oil
2 to 3 cups cooked beef, pork, or veal, chopped fine
3 Tbs. minced parsley
1 tsp. dried mint leaves
3 cups chopped tomatoes, fresh or canned
1/2 cup freshly grated mild cheese

Preheat oven to 350° F.

Remove stems from eggplants and slice into halves lengthwise. Use a melon ball scoop to remove eggplant pulp, leaving 3/8-inch shell; sprinkle with salt and pepper. Chop pulp, combine with onion and garlic, and sauté in oil, stirring frequently; season to taste. When vegetables are cooked, in about 15 minutes, stir in meat, parsley, mint leaves, and tomatoes. Arrange eggplant shells in baking dish just large to hold them snugly, then spoon in mixture of meat and vegetables in equal mounds. Sprinkle tops with grated cheese and bake for about 40 minutes.

MAKES 6 TO 8 SERVINGS.

EGGPLANT WITH BEEF AND CHEESE

1 medium-size eggplant
2 to 3 Tbs. bacon fat
1/2 cup chopped onion
1/4 to 1/2 cup chopped green pepper
3/4 lb. ground beef
tomato sauce
1 cup grated Cheddar cheese
1 1/2 tsp. salt
freshly ground pepper

Preheat oven to 350° F.

Peel and dice eggplant. Put into a saucepan, cover with boiling water, and cover pan. Let stand for 15 minutes, then drain. Melt bacon fat in a saucepan and sauté onion and green pepper for about 5 minutes; stir in ground beef, tomato sauce, cheese, eggplant, salt, and several turns of pepper grinder. Heat thoroughly, turn into a 2-quart casserole, and cover. Bake for about 30 minutes; remove cover and continue baking for 15 minutes more.

MAKES 4 SERVINGS.

LASAGNA BAKED WITH HAM AND SPINACH

This is uncompromisingly American—wide noodles so common in Italian neighborhoods, spinach in a style reminiscent of the *spanakopita* of citizens with Greek and Turkish backgrounds, and ham from a country smokehouse in the Ozarks, the Virginia Piedmont, or from a Vermont hillside village.

SPINACH SAUCE:

1/4 cup corn or other vegetable oil
1 large onion, chopped fine
2 lb. fresh spinach, chopped fine
1/4 cup minced fresh dillweed, or 1 1/2 Tbs. dried
1 tsp. dried lemon thyme
1/2 tsp. salt
freshly ground black pepper
1/4 cup heavy cream
1/2 lb. mozzarella cheese, diced fine
4 eggs, beaten
butter

PASTA:

1 lb. uncooked lasagna

HAM SAUCE:

6 Tbs. (3/4 stick) butter
1/2 cup flour
1 to 2 cups milk
3 cups finely chopped country ham
freshly ground pepper
1/2 cup grated Swiss cheese

Preheat oven to 300° F.

Heat oil in a large skillet and sauté onion over low heat for about 5 minutes, then add spinach, cover, and cook for 5 minutes more. Remove cover, add dillweed and other seasonings, and cook slowly for about 10 minutes. Scrape out into a bowl and let mixture cool. Add cream, cheese, and eggs. Butter a 2-quart baking dish.

Cook the pasta in boiling salted water and let it drain well. Melt butter in a saucepan and stir in flour until a thick, smooth paste is formed. Add milk a little at a time to make a thick sauce (it should be too thick to drop off spoon). Stir in ham and a few turns of pepper grinder (salt will not be needed if ham has a good country character).

Cover bottom of a buttered baking dish with a layer of lasagna. Spread half the spinach mixture over this and cover with another layer of lasagna. Spread this with half the ham mixture. Repeat layering until all of spinach is used and the dish is topped by ham mixture. Sprinkle top evenly with cheese to form a crust. Bake for 1 hour; then turn up oven to 500° for last 5 minutes to brown cheese slightly, or put dish under broiler.

MAKES 4 TO 6 SERVINGS.

HAM SOUFFLÉ WITH MUSHROOM SAUCE

7 Tbs. (not quite 1 stick) butter
2 Tbs. minced scallions (white part only) or shallots
3 Tbs. flour
1 cup milk
4 egg yolks
1 cup finely ground country ham, at room temperature
2 Tbs. grated cheese (Wisconsin asiago, Parmesan, or very dry sharp Cheddar)
5 egg whites
1 recipe freshly made Simple Mushroom and Madeira Sauce *(p. 444)*

Preheat oven to 375° F.

Melt 4 tablespoons butter and sauté scallions or shallots for about 5 minutes. Stir in remaining butter and flour and cook over low heat for 2 or 3 minutes. Remove from heat and stir in milk, eliminating all lumps; return to stove to thicken sauce. Off the heat, drop in egg yolks, 1 at a time, stirring briskly with a wire whip as each is added. Stir in ham and half the cheese; sprinkle bottom and sides of buttered soufflé dish with remaining cheese. Beat egg whites until stiff and fold 1 to 2 tablespoonfuls into cheese-ham mixture, then turn mixture into egg white bowl and fold gently until barely blended. Tie a buttered paper or foil collar around soufflé dish and pour mixture into it. Bake for 35 to 40 minutes. Top each serving of soufflé with mushroom sauce.

MAKES 4 SERVINGS.

PANCAKES WITH HAM-FRUIT SAUCE

1/4 cup raisins
1/3 cup lemon juice
3 to 4 Tbs. applejack
3 Tbs. red currant jelly
1/4 cup orange fruit preserves
1 Tbs. butter
2 cups finely diced cooked country ham
1/3 cup maple sugar
1/4 cup slivered almonds
1 recipe Thin Pancakes *(p. 215)**, warm*

Soak raisins in cold water for about 30 minutes, then drain. Put them in a saucepan, cover with cold water, and bring to a boil; continue boiling until raisins have absorbed all the water. Add lemon juice, applejack, currant jelly, and preserves (a combination of apricot and orange is good, or plain marmalade). Bring this mixture to a boil and remove from heat. Melt butter and brown ham in it. Sprinkle with maple sugar and stir for 1 minute or more, then stir in fruit mixture and almonds. Serve hot pancakes with plenty of butter and a sauceboat of this tangy sauce.

MAKES 4 SERVINGS.

FLAMING HOT DOGS

Scores of guests have consumed this dish with gusto and with little clue as to its ingredients. Hostesses not so surreptitious serve it from a chafing dish.

1 lb. skinless frankfurters
6 Tbs. (3/4 stick) butter
1/2 lb. fresh mushrooms
1 garlic clove, minced
1 tsp., more or less, salt
freshly ground pepper
1 Tbs. minced parsley
1/4 cup applejack, heated

Cut frankfurters into quarters lengthwise, then into 1/2-inch pieces. Heat butter and sauté frankfurters for 5 minutes. Wipe mushrooms with a damp cloth, trim stems, and cut caps into quarters. Add mushrooms along with garlic, salt, and several turns of pepper grinder, to frankfurters. Cover and cook for 5 minutes, stirring occasionally to coat mushrooms with butter. Sprinkle with parsley. Just before serving pour applejack over all and set aflame.

MAKES 4 SERVINGS.

LITTLE VIENNA SOUFFLÉED SANDWICH

3 eggs, separated
1/2 tsp. dry mustard
1/4 tsp. salt
1/2 tsp. paprika
1/4 tsp. cayenne pepper
1 lb. skinless frankfurters
8 slices of toast

Preheat oven to 350° F.

Beat egg yolks until lemon colored. Stir in mustard, salt, paprika, and cayenne. Beat egg whites stiff enough to form peaks; gently fold into beaten yolks. Split frankfurters and arrange on toast in a shallow pan large enough to hold all pieces side by side. Pour soufflé mixture over and bake for 25 to 30 minutes, or until slightly browned.

MAKES 4 SERVINGS.

JAMBALAYA SOUFFLÉ

2 cups, or less, leftover jambalaya (see p. 339), at room temperature
2 cups milk
2 cups water
1/2 cup flour
2 Tbs. butter
4 eggs, separated
1/2 tsp. salt
freshly ground black pepper
1 Tbs. grated cheese

Preheat oven to 350° F.

Chop jambalaya so that all ingredients are of uniform size. Heat milk in a 2-quart saucepan. Meanwhile carefully stir water into flour until mixture is smooth and runs easily. Melt butter in hot milk (do not let it boil), then gradually add flour mixture, stirring constantly for about 5 minutes, or until thickened. Stir in chopped jambalaya and set aside. Beat egg yolks, then beat a little at a time into hot jambalaya mixture. Add salt and a little pepper. Let cool. Beat whites to form peaks and fold into mixture. Butter a 2-quart soufflé dish, then sprinkle in cheese, turning and shaking dish to distribute cheese evenly. Bake for 40 minutes or more, or until soufflé is firm in center and the risen top is delicately browned.

MAKES 4 SERVINGS.

COOKED LAMB IN CHILI SAUCE

3 Tbs. vegetable oil
1 onion, minced
2 garlic cloves, minced
3 Tbs. flour
3 to 4 Tbs. chili powder
1/2 tsp. ground coriander
3 to 4 Tbs. red wine vinegar
salt
2 to 3 cups bite-size pieces of cooked lamb
1 to 1 1/2 cups lamb or chicken stock

Heat oil in a skillet and cook onion and garlic for 2 to 3 minutes, or until translucent. Stir in flour, eliminating lumps, and cook for about 3 minutes. Meanwhile mix chili powder, coriander, and vinegar. Stir into skillet mixture, and add stock, a little at a time, to make a smooth sauce. Add lamb, spoon sauce over meat pieces, and warm over lowest possible heat. Serve with boiled rice.

MAKES 4 TO 6 SERVINGS.

LAMB AND EGGPLANT CASSEROLE

1 large eggplant
1 medium-size onion, chopped
1 lb. lean uncooked lamb, cut into 1-in. cubes
5 to 6 Tbs. butter, melted
1/2 cup heavy cream
salt
freshly ground pepper
2 tomatoes, peeled, seeded, and cut into 1-in. pieces
3 Tbs. minced parsley

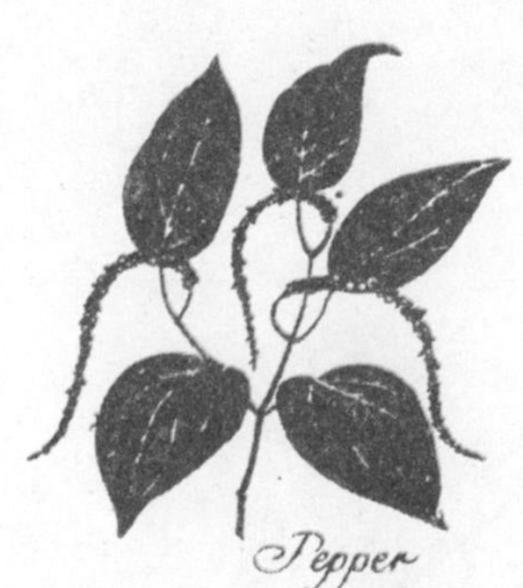

Preheat oven to 450° F.

Prick eggplant all over with a fork and bake for 45 minutes. Mix onion, lamb, and 2 tablespoons butter. Put into a 1 1/2-quart casserole and bake alongside of eggplant for 30 minutes. Remove eggplant when soft inside, peel it, and mash the pulp; stir in remaining 3 or 4 tablespoons butter and the cream, then season with salt and freshly ground pepper to taste. Blend the eggplant and tomatoes. into the casserole meat and return to oven, reducing heat to 350°. Bake casserole for 20 to 30 minutes. Sprinkle top with parsley just before serving.

MAKES 4 SERVINGS.

LENTILS WITH SPANISH SAUSAGES

German-Americans make fine lentil soups, and other United States cooks with Middle Eastern or Indian backgrounds use lentils in many imaginative ways. Spanish-speaking citizens of the Southwest sometimes combine them with hot sausages.

3/4 cup dried brown lentils
1 tsp. salt
1 qt. boiling water
1/2 lb. chorizo sausages
1 large onion, chopped
1 green pepper, chopped
2 garlic cloves, minced
1 cup drained plum tomatoes, chopped
salt
freshly ground pepper
2 bacon strips, cut into halves

Wash and drain lentils. Add salt to boiling water and dribble in lentils. Cook over medium heat until water has been absorbed and lentils are tender but not mushy—about 35 minutes. Meanwhile in a skillet let sausages simmer in 1/4 cup water, pricking them several times. When water has been absorbed and pan is covered with fat from sausages, add onion, green pepper, and garlic, and sauté until soft. Add tomatoes and mix well; add salt and pepper to taste. Cut sausages into bite-size pieces. Put a layer of lentils into a casserole, spread sausage and tomato mixture on top, then another layer of lentils. Arrange bacon strips in halves on top. Put casserole under broiler until bacon becomes crisp and lentils bubble.

MAKES 4 SERVINGS.

MUSHROOM-EGG-BARLEY CASSEROLE

1/4 cup uncooked barley
2 cups boiling water
3 Tbs. chopped green pepper
2 cups sliced fresh mushrooms
5 Tbs. butter
2 Tbs. flour
2 cups milk
1/4 cup grated Sardo or Parmesan cheese
4 eggs, hard-cooked
1 tsp. salt
freshly ground black pepper

Preheat oven to 350° F.

Pour barley slowly into water and cook for about 30 minutes, or until tender; drain and set aside. Sauté green pepper and mushrooms in 2 tablespoons butter for 5 or 6 minutes. Meanwhile in a 1 ½- to 2-quart flameproof casserole melt 2 tablespoons butter, stir in the flour, and cook over gentle heat, stirring constantly, for about 2 minutes. Off the heat, blend in milk, then return to heat and whisk until smooth and thickened. Stir cheese into sauce, then mix in eggs, barley, sautéed vegetables, and remaining butter. Season to taste with salt and pepper. Bake for 30 to 40 minutes, or until a crusty surface forms.

MAKES 4 SERVINGS.

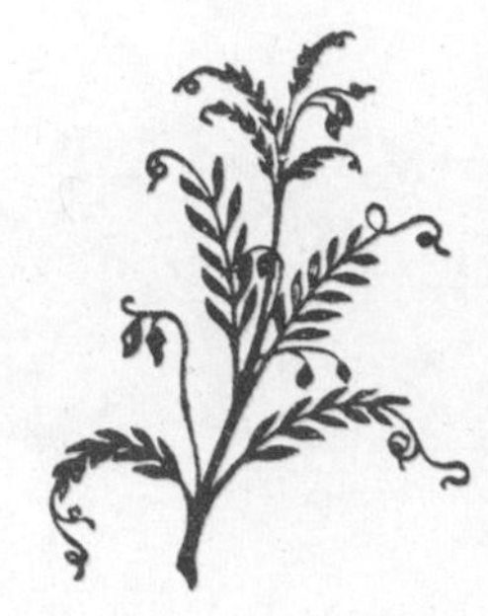

OYSTERS AND HAM JENNY LIND

Legends left behind in many United States cities after Jenny Lind's triumphal tour in 1851 refused to die, leaving among other things several dishes bearing her name. The singer wrote letters home that told of her longing for familiar foods, but she also cooked, while in this country, some of her favorites herself. Before a concert she often had a creamy soup to which she added sago or tapioca, and she is said to have prepared a tomato-oyster chafing dish supper for some St. Louis admirers. Oysters and ham Jenny Lind was first done this way, the story goes, by a St. Louis doctor at whose house she was entertained.

1 Tbs. butter
1 Tbs. bacon fat
2 Tbs. flour
1 cup oysters, liquor reserved
½ cup heavy cream
½ tsp. salt
⅛ tsp. hot red pepper sauce
½ tsp. celery salt
¼ tsp. paprika
½ cup chopped cooked ham
2 Tbs. sherry, cider, or white wine
2 patty shells

Melt butter and bacon fat in a chafing dish over hot water. Stir in flour to make a smooth paste. Off the heat, add oyster liquor and slowly stir in cream. Cook for about 4 minutes while mixture thickens. Add seasonings, oysters, and ham. Cook until oysters plump up and curl at edges. Stir in sherry, cider, or wine, and serve immediately in patty shells.

MAKES 2 SERVINGS.

OYSTER-SPINACH CASSEROLE

24 large oysters, drained
2 pkg. (10 oz. each) frozen chopped spinach, cooked and drained
4 Tbs. (1/2 stick) butter
2 medium-size onions, chopped
1/2 cup small whole fresh mushrooms
1 garlic clove, minced
1 tsp. salt
Tabasco
1/4 cup sour cream
2 eggs, beaten
lemon juice
1 cup loosely packed fresh bread crumbs

Preheat oven to 350° F.

Set aside 12 whole oysters; chop remainder and mix with spinach, which has had as much moisture as possible pressed out. Melt 2 tablespoons butter and sauté onions, mushrooms, and garlic for about 5 minutes, stirring often to cook mushrooms evenly. Stir in spinach and oysters, salt, a dash or two of Tabasco, and sour cream. When mixture is hot, remove from heat and stir in eggs and a liberal sprinkling of lemon juice. Butter a 2-quart casserole and put reserved 12 oysters on bottom, then pour in hot spinach mixture. Melt remaining 2 tablespoons butter and stir in bread crumbs; spread over spinach. Bake for 30 minutes, or until mixture bubbles and crumbs turn golden.

MAKES 4 SERVINGS.

WALLIS WINDSOR'S OYSTER AND HOMINY PIE

During World War II the Duchess of Windsor put together a small book of her native Maryland recipes and turned the proceeds over to charity. She said her husband had great appreciation for food that was typically American; few dishes are more so than this one.

1 1/2 cups canned cooked whole hominy
1 qt. oysters, drained, liquor reserved
3 Tbs. butter
1/2 cup milk
1/2 tsp. salt
freshly ground pepper
1/2 recipe Basic Piecrust (p. 459)

Preheat oven to 400° F.

Put alternate layers of hominy and oysters into a buttered 1-quart casserole. Combine oyster liquor, milk, remaining butter, salt, and a few turns of pepper grinder; pour over oysters. Make pastry dough according to instructions and roll out very thin; trim to fit over top of casserole, making slashes for steam to escape. Bake for 30 to 40 minutes, or until crust is well browned.

MAKES 6 SERVINGS.

MEAT-STUFFED PEPPERS

4 large green peppers
1 large onion, chopped fine
2 1/2 Tbs. vegetable oil
2/3 cups cooked kasha, cracked wheat, or bulgur
3 cups finely chopped cooked lamb or other meat
2/3 cup cooked rice
3 whole scallions, chopped fine
salt
freshly ground pepper
1 tsp. ground cinnamon
freshly grated nutmeg
5 to 6 Tbs. minced parsley
2 cups canned plum tomatoes with juice, chopped
1/2 cup lamb or chicken stock or water

Slice off top of peppers and remove seeds and white pith; cook in boiling water to cover for about 3 minutes. Sauté chopped onion in oil until soft but not browned, then mix with kasha, meat, rice, and scallions. Season with salt to taste, a few turns of pepper grinder, cinnamon, a few gratings of nutmeg, and parsley. Stir until well blended, then pack into prepared peppers, moistening with a little oil. Put chopped tomatoes into a deep saucepan, season with salt and pepper, adding stock or water. Cook slowly for 5 minutes. Put in stuffed peppers, open tops upward. Cover saucepan and cook for about 20 minutes. Serve with tomato sauce spooned over peppers.

MAKES 4 SERVINGS.

PORK-FILLED TAMALE PIE

Like the word *tomato*, *tamale* is an Indian term derived from the Nahuatl language, and the food itself was known in eastern America when Captain John Smith arrived. Hot tamales were sold by street vendors in the early days of Texas and throughout the West, much as they are available today in highway restaurants. Tamale pies, a sort of casserole version, have become common in kitchens from coast to coast and are recognized as being thoroughly American.

1 1/2 lb. lean pork, cut into 1-in. cubes
1 onion, chopped coarse
1/2 cup chopped celery
1/2 cup chopped green pepper
2 garlic cloves, minced
1 cup tomato purée
1 qt. hot water
1 Tbs., or more, chili powder
3 Tbs. flour
salt
1 cup hominy grits
1 qt. plus 3 Tbs. cold water
3 Tbs. butter, melted
3 eggs, beaten
2 pimientos, chopped
1/2 cup olives, pitted

Preheat oven to 375° F.

Trim fat from pork and cook it gently in a skillet. Remove cracklings and brown pork cubes on all surfaces. Stir in onion, celery, green pepper, garlic, and tomato purée, then cover with hot water; let simmer for 10 minutes. Mix chili powder and flour with about 3 tablespoons cold water and set aside. Measure grits and cover with 1 cup cold water. Bring remaining 3 cups of water to a boil in top part of a double boiler, stir in grits, bring back to a boil over direct heat, then cook over hot water, simmering gently for about 20 minutes. Stir chili powder-flour paste into pork and cook slowly as sauce thickens. Remove grits from stove and stir in butter and eggs. Grease a shallow baking dish lightly and put in enough cooked grits to make a 1/4-inch lining. Pour in pork mixture, and sprinkle with pimientos and olives. Carefully spread remaining grits over top to form a thin crust. Bake for about 25 minutes, or until pie filling begins to bubble up through topping.

MAKES 6 TO 8 SERVINGS.

RICE CROQUETTES

3/4 cup uncooked rice
3/4 cup boiling water
1 1/2 cups milk, scalded
1 1/2 Tbs. butter
3 egg yolks
1 egg yolk beaten with 1 Tbs. water
1 cup fine bread crumbs
lard for deep frying
1 cup raspberry and currant jelly

Wash rice in several changes of water. Combine it with the boiling water in a deep saucepan and cover tightly. Cook about 30 minutes until rice has absorbed all the water. Add milk. Fork rice over lightly. Cook in top part of a double boiler over hot water until soft; remove from heat. Stir in butter; let cool for 5 minutes. Stir in the 3 egg yolks. Spread mixture on a platter to cool. Make balls the size of a golf ball. With your thumb, press a good hollow into the top of each ball. Chill 2 hours.

Heat lard to 375° to 385° F. Roll croquettes in egg yolk beaten with water, then in crumbs, then in egg again. Fry croquettes 6 to 7 minutes until golden brown and drain on brown paper. Keep warm. At serving time put some jelly in the hollow of each croquette.

MAKES 4 SERVINGS.

DIXIE BAKED RICE AND SAUSAGE MEAT

2 cups cooked rice
1/2 cup minced parsley
1 lb. Southern-style smoked pork sausage meat
1/2 cup finely chopped green pepper
2 cups chopped peeled fresh tomatoes or canned
3 Tbs. butter, melted
1/2 cup fresh bread crumbs
1/4 cup grated mild cheese

Preheat oven to 350° F.

Mix rice and parsley together in a large bowl. Spread sausage on bottom of a cold skillet and cook very slowly until meat is lightly browned. Pour off all but 2 tablespoons fat and push cooked meat to one side; sauté green pepper in sausage fat for about 10 minutes, but do not burn. Stir together meat, green pepper, and tomatoes, mixing well. Stir sausage mixture into rice, blending thoroughly. Brush a 1 1/2 quart baking dish lightly with melted butter and pour in rice-sausage mixture. Mix remaining melted butter with bread crumbs and spread over top. Sprinkle with cheese and bake for 30 to 40 minutes.

MAKES 4 SERVINGS.

RICE WITH DUCK AND HAM

2 Tbs. bacon fat or butter
1 medium-size onion, chopped
1 celery rib, chopped
1 cup uncooked rice
2 1/2 cups freshly made rich duck or chicken stock, hot
1 cup canned tomatoes with juice, chopped coarse
1/4 tsp. dried oregano
1/4 tsp. dried basil
1/4 tsp. dried marjoram
1 1/2 to 2 cups diced cooked duck meat
1/2 to 1 cup diced country ham
salt
freshly ground pepper

*Preheat oven to 300° F.**

In an ovenproof skillet melt fat and sauté onion and celery for about 8 minutes, stirring frequently so that vegetables turn color slightly but do not brown. Stir in rice and sauté for 2 minutes, mixing with vegetables and coating each grain with fat. Pour in stock. Add tomatoes. Sprinkle in herbs, then stir in duck and ham. Add very little salt if ham is country-cured; grind in a few turns from pepper mill. Cover pan tightly and let simmer over very low heat for about 45 minutes.* Remove cover from rice mixture (there should be some liquid) and put in oven for 5 minutes; turn off heat and leave rice in oven for 5 minutes more before serving.

MAKES 6 SERVINGS.

RICE WITH TOMATOES, CHILIES, AND CHEESE

3 small canned green chilies, seeded and chopped
1 garlic cloves, minced
1/2 cup canned tomatoes, drained, juice reserved
2 Tbs. drippings or other fat
1 white onion, chopped
1/2 cup uncooked rice
butter
1/2 cup stuffed olives, halved
3/4 cup shredded Monterey Jack cheese

Preheat oven to 350° F.

Put chopped chilies, garlic, and tomatoes into a blender. Add enough water to reserved tomato juice to make about 1 1/2 cups; add this gradually while spinning vegetables to make a thin purée. Melt fat in a skillet, add onion and rice, and sauté until rice is golden, stirring almost constantly. Stir in puréed tomato mixture, bring to a boil, cover, and let simmer for about 40 minutes, or until rice absorbs all liquid and each grain remains separate. Butter a 1 1/2-quart casserole and spoon in half of rice mixture, then sprinkle in olives and grated cheese; top with remaining rice and cover casserole. Bake for 30 to 45 minutes.

MAKES 4 SERVINGS.

SMOKED SALMON QUICHE

pastry dough for a 9-in. quiche pan
2 egg yolks
1 whole egg
3/4 cup milk
1/2 cup heavy cream
1/8 tsp. ground mace
1 1/4 cups smoked salmon, chopped coarse
freshly ground pepper

Preheat oven to 425° F.

Line a 9-inch quiche pan with pastry dough and partially bake for 10 minutes.† Remove quiche shell and reduce heat to 375 degrees. Beat egg yolks and whole egg with milk and cream. Season with mace. Distribute

†If you have a baking stone, you won't have to partially prebake the crust. Instead (to borrow from Julia Child) use a quiche ring set on foil on a cookie sheet. Then after filling, simply slide the ring and foil directly onto hot tiles or baking stone to bake, thus producing a crisp bottom crust. Bake a total of 30 minutes at 425°.

salmon over the bottom of the pastry, then pour egg mixture on top. Sprinkle with several turns of pepper mill. Bake for about 35 minutes, or until pastry is lightly browned and custard is set. Remove from oven and let settle for about 5 minutes before serving.

MAKES 6 TO 8 SERVINGS.

SPINACH WITH BRAISED CHESTNUTS AND CHICKEN LIVERS

1/3 lb. chestnuts
4 Tbs. (1/2 stick) butter
1/2 cup chicken stock
1 Tbs. Madeira
1 lb. fresh spinach, trimmed of stems
salt
3/4 lb. chicken livers

SAUCE:
2 Tbs. butter
3 Tbs. flour
1 1/2 cups milk
salt
freshly ground pepper
freshly grated nutmeg
2 Tbs. dry white wine or vermouth
1/4 cup grated Parmesan cheese

Use a sharp knife to cut a cross in each chestnut, then drop into a saucepan of cold water; bring to a boil and boil chestnuts for just 1 minute. Use a slotted spoon to remove a couple at a time, then peel away both shell and inner skin; reserve pan. Braise chestnuts slowly in a small, tightly covered saucepan with 2 tablespoons butter, the chicken stock, and Madeira for about 25 minutes; shake pan occasionally and check to make sure liquid has not evaporated; if necessary add a little water or more stock. Meanwhile blanch spinach in 1 cup boiling water with a little salt for 3 to 4 minutes, or until spinach is barely tender. Drain; chop coarsely. Clean and trim chicken livers, cutting each into 2 or 3 pieces. Sauté them in remaining 2 tablespoons butter over fairly high heat for 1 or 2 minutes on each side; leave in pan and set aside.

Make the sauce: Melt butter, stir in flour, and cook for 1 or 2 minutes. Off the heat, add milk, mixing until smooth. Return to heat and whisk as mixture cooks and thickens, adding salt, pepper, and nutmeg to taste. Add wine.

In a shallow baking dish spread out half the spinach. Slice chestnuts and return them to pan in which they cooked; use a rubber spatula to scrape chestnut juice and sliced nuts into baking dish, spreading evenly over spinach. Scrape out chicken livers and juices and spread over chestnuts. Top with remaining spinach, then pour sauce over all. Sprinkle with cheese. Put under broiler until everything bubbles and cheese turns golden.

MAKES 4 SERVINGS.

BUTTERNUT SQUASH STUFFED WITH PORK, APPLES, AND CHESTNUTS

2 medium-size butternut squashes
6 Tbs. (3/4 stick) butter, softened
salt
freshly ground pepper
2 cups small dice of cooked pork
1 large tart apple, peeled and diced
8 roasted and peeled chestnuts, diced
3 whole scallions, chopped
1 tsp. crumbled dried sage leaves

Preheat oven to 350° F.

Split the squashes lengthwise and scoop out seeds. Rub with a little of the butter and fill centers with about 1 teaspoon of butter each. Salt and pepper them and bake for 40 minutes. Remove from the oven. To make the filling, pour the hot butter from the centers into a bowl, and mix it with apple, chestnuts and herbs. Now scoop out the partially cooked flesh from the shells, trying not to break the skin. Chop squash pulp coarsely and fold into the filling; correct seasoning. Pile filling mixture evenly into shells, dot with remaining butter, and cover loosely with foil. Bake for 30 to 35 minutes.

MAKES 4 SERVINGS.

STUFFED YELLOW SQUASH

2 summer squashes (about 1 lb. each)
3 Tbs. butter
3 to 4 Tbs. finely chopped shallots or onions
1 1/2 cups finely chopped fresh mushrooms
2 garlic cloves, minced
2 cups finely diced ham
1 tsp. dried thyme
1 bay leaf
1 cup stale bread crumbs
salt
freshly ground pepper
1/2 cup fresh bread crumbs
1/4 cup minced parsley

Preheat oven to 350° F.

Cut each squash into 2 equal pieces that will lie flat; scoop out centers to leave shell about 1/8 inch thick. Chop pulp and set aside. Melt butter in a skillet and sauté shallots or onions, mushrooms, and garlic. Add squash pulp to skillet along with ham; stir in thyme and bay leaf. Soak bread cubes 2 to 3 minutes in 1 cup of water. Season squash mixture lightly with salt and pepper. Stir in soaked bread cubes. Divide this mixture among the 4 squash shells, sprinkling tops with crumbs and parsley. Bake for about 25 minutes.

MAKES 4 SERVINGS.

SWEET POTATO SHEPHERD'S PIE

4 large sweet potatoes
3/4 cup cream or half milk, half cream
sprig of fresh mint, or 1 tsp. crumbled dried
6 Tbs. (3/4 stick) butter
1 large onion, diced
1 green pepper, cut into match-size strips
1/2 lb. fresh mushrooms, chopped coarse
2 cups finely diced cooked lamb
2 Tbs. flour
1 cup lamb stock†
1 tsp. ground savory
several gratings of fresh nutmeg
2 to 3 Tbs. chopped parsley
salt
freshly ground pepper
1/2 large rutabaga, cut into match-size strips
2 carrots, cut into match-size strips

Preheat oven to 350° F.

Boil sweet potatoes in salted water until tender—about 30 to 40 minutes. Meanwhile let mint simmer in cream for about 5 minutes, then strain; discard mint. Drain and peel sweet potatoes when cool enough, then mash them with the warm cream and 2 tablespoons butter. Sauté onion in remaining butter for a few minutes, then add green pepper and mushrooms and cook until just tender—about 5 minutes. Add lamb, toss, and brown slightly, then sprinkle in flour, stirring and cooking for a few minutes. Gradually add stock, stirring until thickened. Season with savory, nutmeg, parsley, salt, and pepper and let simmer very gently while you blanch rutabaga and carrots in salted water for 2 minutes. Drain and toss with lamb mixture. Correct the seasoning and spread on the bottom of a shallow casserole dish. Spread mashed sweet potatoes over the top and let bake for about 30 minutes, or until bubbling.

MAKES 6 TO 8 SERVINGS.

†Make stock from scraps and bone if you are using a leftover leg of lamb roast; otherwise use veal or chicken broth; any leftover gravy could be included, too.

TURKEY WITH BROCCOLI AND CHEESE

After it opened in August 1905, the White Turkey Inn near Danbury, Connecticut, gained many enthusiasts for its American bill of fare. It often served turkey slices with broccoli under a cheese sauce, and so, a half century later, did Albert Stockli at his airport restaurant called the Newarker. When chicken was substituted, a similar dish became known as chicken Divan.

1 lb. broccoli, cooked until just tender
2 Tbs. butter
8 slices of cooked turkey breast
1/2 cup milk
1/2 cup chicken stock
1 Tbs. arrowroot starch
1/2 cup heavy cream
1 cup hollandaise sauce
1/4 cup dry bread crumbs
1/2 cup grated Vermont cheese

Preheat oven to 375° F.

Break up broccoli into individual buds. Grease a shallow baking dish with 1 tablespoon butter, cover the bottom with turkey slices, and top with broccoli. Heat milk, stock, and remaining butter. Mix arrowroot with cream and stir this paste into hot milk mixture; cook slowly until sauce thickens, stirring constantly. Off the heat, stir hollandaise into the cream sauce, blend well, and pour over broccoli and turkey. Sprinkle with bread crumbs and cheese. Bake for about 15 minutes.

MAKES 4 SERVINGS.

ZUCCHINI AND RICE CASSEROLE

2 medium-size zucchini (about 1 lb. each)
2 cups cooked rice
1/4 cup minced whole scallions
2 Tbs. chopped fresh basil
3 Tbs. butter
2 Tbs. sour cream
2 Tbs. heavy cream
1/2 tsp. salt
freshly ground pepper
1/3 cup bread crumbs
2 Tbs. grated Parmesan cheese

Preheat oven to 375° F.

Grate zucchini and toss with rice, scallions, and basil. Butter a shallow baking dish and fill with zucchini-rice mixture. Mix together sour cream and heavy cream. Sprinkle with salt and pepper and spread top with cream mixture. Bake for 30 minutes. Add bread crumbs and sprinkle top with cheese; increase heat to 450° and bake for 10 minutes more.

MAKES ABOUT 4 TO 6 SERVINGS.

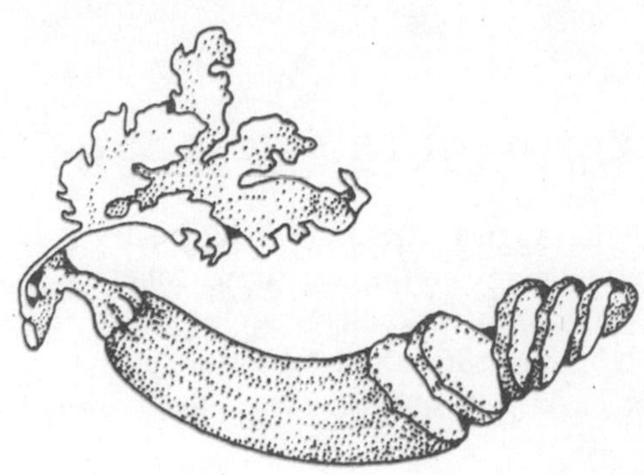

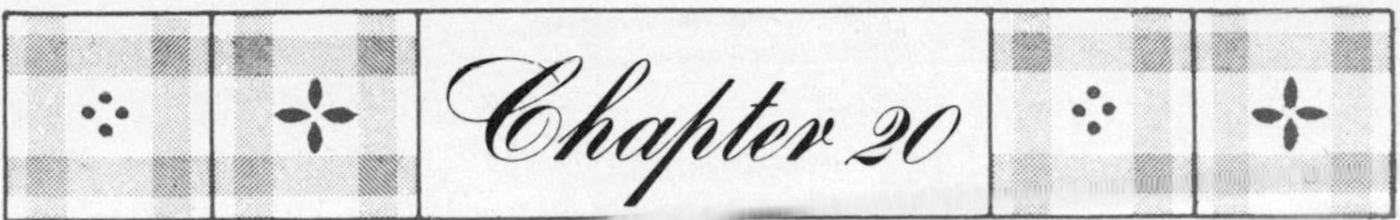

Chapter 20

SAUCES

RICHMOND BARBECUE SAUCE

This sauce complements all meats and is an especially poignant accent for pork. Spit-roast—either indoors or out—a pork shoulder with its skin still on for 5 to 6 hours, basting often so that meat almost falls off the bone when finished.

1 Tbs. dry mustard
2 to 3 Tbs. grated maple sugar or other sugar
1 tsp. celery seeds
1 tsp. salt
1/2 to 3/4 tsp. dried red pepper flakes
1 tsp. freshly ground black pepper
1 cup tarragon vinegar

Combine mustard, sugar, celery seeds, salt, red pepper flakes and black pepper. Stir into vinegar and boil for about 5 minutes.

MAKES ABOUT 1 CUP.

NEVER-FAIL BÉARNAISE OR HOLLANDAISE SAUCE

Sarah Tyson Rorer, whose *Philadelphia Cook Book* was published in 1886, urged Americans to serve béarnaise sauce with broiled steak, smelts, or "lobster chops." As for hollandaise, notwithstanding its Netherlander name, it is essentially French. When it first entered American cookbooks, fussy recipes called for washing the butter, but this step has no effect on the texture of the sauce. Some cooks are afraid of making hollandaise, but we've found this simple method to be almost foolproof. If it does overheat and curdle, try whisking in a little cream.

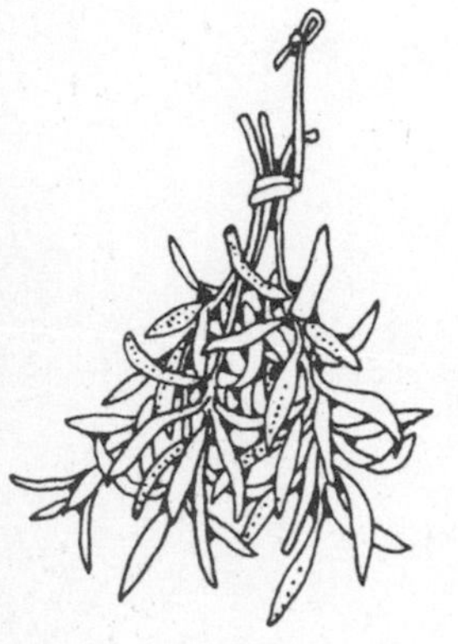

FOR BÉARNAISE:

1 teaspoon dried tarragon
2 teaspoons chopped shallots
1/4 cup wine vinegar
1/3 cup white wine or vermouth

FOR HOLLANDAISE:

2–3 teaspoons lemon juice
2 egg yolks
1/4 lb. (1 stick) sweet butter
salt
freshly ground pepper

For béarnaise, place tarragon, shallots, vinegar, and wine or vermouth into a small saucepan and bring to a boil, reducing to two-thirds of original volume. Strain tarragon mixture into the cool part of a double boiler. For hollandaise, simply place 2 teaspoons lemon juice in the top of the double boiler. Place over (but not touching) boiling water, which should be kept at a slow, steady boil. Pour the egg yolks over either the tarragon essence or the lemon juice and whisk vigorously about half a minute until they just begin to feel a little thick, then start adding cold butter, tablespoon by tablespoon, whisking steadily, allowing each to melt before adding the next. When all the butter is used and the sauce has become thick enough, put the top half of the double boiler into a pan of cold water for a few minutes to stop the cooking. Add salt and pepper to taste, and for the hollandaise, a little more lemon juice.

MAKES ABOUT 1 CUP.

PEPPERY BARBECUE SAUCE FOR BEEF

1 cup (2 sticks) butter, melted
2 1/2 cups water
1/4 cup red wine
1 1/4 tsp. dry mustard
1 Tbs. sugar
2 tsp. salt
2 tsp. chili powder
1/8 tsp. cayenne pepper
1 1/2 tsp. Worcestershire sauce
1 tsp. Tabasco
1/4 tsp. freshly ground black pepper
1 Tbs. paprika
1/2 cup finely minced onion
1 garlic clove, minced fine
1 tsp. dried marjoram
1 tsp. dried thyme
1 Tbs. lemon juice

Put all ingredients into an enamelware saucepan; stir to blend flavors. Boil over moderate heat for 20 minutes, stirring occasionally. Brush on meat while broiling or use as a marinade.

MAKES ABOUT 4 CUPS.

WHITE CLAM SAUCE

4 Tbs. (1/2 stick) butter
1/3 cup olive oil
1/2 to 3/4 cup chopped onion
1 tsp. dried basil
1 tsp. dried oregano
1 tsp. dried rosemary
3/4 cup minced parsley
2 cans (7 oz. each) minced clams
1/4 cup white wine
1/2 cup grated Parmesan cheese
1/4 cup grated Sardo cheese
salt
freshly ground pepper

Heat butter and oil in a skillet and sauté onion over very low heat for 25 minutes. Rub dried herbs between fingers and sprinkle over onion, cooking for 5 minutes. Stir in parsley, cover, and cook for 10 minutes. Add clams and wine and cook for 5 minutes, then stir in cheeses; add very little salt and pepper to taste. Toss with buttered pasta—rigatoni, shells, linguini, etc. Be sure serving plates are hot, and have plenty of extra Parmesan or asiago cheese to serve on the side.

MAKES ABOUT 4 CUPS.

GREEN HERB SAUCE

Excellent with cold fish and seafood or poultry; also delicious as a dip for crisp raw vegetables.

1 cup coarsely chopped watercress
1 cup coarsely chopped fresh spinach
2 Tbs. chopped green leaves of scallions
2 Tbs. chopped Italian parsley
2 Tbs. chopped fresh basil
2 Tbs. chopped fresh tarragon
2 Tbs. fresh dillweed
2 Tbs. fresh chervil
1 egg, hard-cooked
2 Tbs. cottage cheese
1 cup yogurt
1 Tbs. tarragon vinegar
4 canned sardines
1 dill pickle
salt
freshly ground pepper

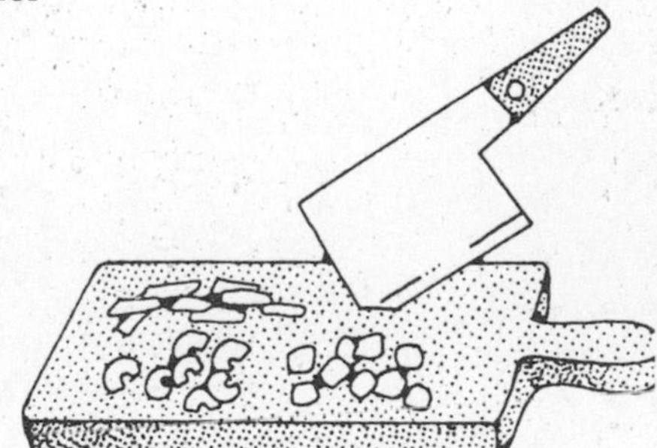

Put all but the last 2 ingredients into a blender and spin until smooth. Season with salt and pepper to taste.

MAKES ABOUT 4 CUPS.

FERRY FARM MAPLE-HONEY SAUCE

This syrup, an absolutely brilliant complement to buckwheat cakes for breakfast or lunch, is also uniquely American and a fine example of native cookery. Dating from colonial days, it is still served in Kentucky and Virginia and was a favorite sauce for waffles and pancakes that Washington's mother, some say, frequently made at her Ferry Farm. Similar combinations, with maple as the predominant flavor, were developed in other regions.

1/2 cup strained pure honey
3/4 cup maple syrup
2 tsp. ground cinnamon
1/2 tsp. caraway seeds

Combine honey and maple syrup in a small saucepan and heat slowly. Add cinnamon and caraway and bring to a hard boil. Serve hot.

KENNEBEC FRENCH-CANADIAN MAPLE BUTTER

1/2 cup grated maple sugar
4 Tbs. (1/2 stick) sweet butter, softened

Blend maple sugar into butter. Serve on waffles, pancakes, or hot toast.

OZARK MAPLE-BUTTER WHIP

1/4 cup maple syrup
1/2 cup (1 stick) butter, softened

Combine syrup and butter and whip until fluffy. Serve on waffles, pancakes, or hot corn bread.

SIMPLE MUSHROOM AND MADEIRA SAUCE

For hamburgers, leftover beef, game, croquettes, and many other uses.

1/4 lb. fresh mushrooms
2 Tbs. butter
2 Tbs. flour
3/4 to 1 cup beef stock or canned consommé
salt
freshly ground pepper
1 tsp. minced tarragon, or 1/2 tsp. dried
1 to 2 Tbs. Madeira

Wipe mushrooms clean with a damp cloth. Remove stems and chop fine; slice caps. Melt butter in a saucepan and sauté stems and caps for 3 to 4 minutes. Sprinkle in flour, cook, and stir gently for 1 more minute. Pour in stock, adding seasonings to taste along with Madeira; stir until thickened and smooth.

MAKES ABOUT 2 CUPS.

LEMONY MUSTARD SAUCE

A tangy accent for fish, or cauliflower, celery, asparagus, and for Jerusalem Artichoke and Celery Root Salad (p. 197).

4 Tbs. (1/2 stick) butter
2 Tbs. flour
1 1/2 cups boiling water
3 large egg yolks, beaten until light
juice of 1 lemon
1/2 tsp. French herb mustard
scant tsp. salt
liberal sprinkling of cayenne pepper

Melt butter in a saucepan and stir in flour to make a smooth paste. Add boiling water slowly, stirring constantly to eliminate all lumps. Off the heat, stir in egg yolks, mixing thoroughly. Blend in lemon juice, mustard, salt, and cayenne.

MAKES ABOUT 2 CUPS.

OYSTER SAUCE

1 pt. oysters with liquor
3 Tbs. butter
3 Tbs. flour
1/2 cup heavy cream
1/2 cup white wine
1/4 cup fish or chicken stock (optional)
1 Tbs. lemon juice
1 tsp. good brandy
salt
freshly ground white pepper
pinch of cayenne pepper
1 Tbs. minced parsley

Poach the oysters in their own liquor until the edges curl; drain and keep warm. In a separate pan melt butter, add flour, and stir over low heat for a minute or two. Off the heat, add drained oyster liquor, cream, and white wine plus another 1/4 cup oyster liquor reserved from Chicken Breasts with Oyster Stuffing (p. 310). (If making the sauce independently and there is no additional oyster liquor at hand, use an equivalent amount of fish or chicken stock diluted with a little water.) Return to the heat and stir until well blended and fairly thick. Let cook slowly for a minute or so, then add lemon juice, brandy, and seasonings to taste; taste carefully and correct. If too thick, add a little more liquid. Finally add drained oysters; if they are large, cut each into 2 or 3 pieces. Serve in a sauceboat, sprinkled with minced parsley.

MAKES 2 CUPS.

SALT PORK AND MILK GRAVY

As indicated on page 17, salt pork dinners were common enough in the New England past. Today in the village of West Winfield, in upstate New York, a restaurant popular among the affluent local farmers specializes in salt pork and milk gravy; the gravy also accompanies boiled chicken similar to that served by Daniel Webster's mother, and there are hot baking powder biscuits or johnnycakes on the side. There are also at this New York hostelry old-fashioned pumpkin muffins, usually served with creamed codfish—other typical examples of the basic cooking of colonial America.

1 lb. salt pork with streaks of lean meat
1 cup flour
1 1/4 cups milk

Cut salt pork into slices 1/2 inch thick. Soak slices in warm water for 2 to 3 hours, changing water several times. Dry slices on paper towels and dredge with flour. Fry slowly, about 10 minutes, in a greased skillet, turning occasionally, until slices are brittle, with crackly brown surfaces. Remove all but 3 tablespoons of fat. Stir in 3 tablespoons flour and blend well. Stir in 2 tablespoons milk, eliminating all lumps; stir in 2 more tablespoons milk and blend well. Gradually add remaining 1 cup milk and cook over low heat until gravy thickens. Serve hot over freshly baked biscuit or mashed potatoes.

MAKES 4 SERVINGS.

WARSAW SOUR CREAM SAUCE

Excellent with Polish-American Stuffed Pike (p. 375), other fish, or cooked vegetables.

4 egg yolks
1 1/2 cups sour cream
1 1/2 to 2 Tbs. lemon juice
1/2 tsp. salt
1 to 2 Tbs. rose paprika
3 Tbs. minced parsley

Beat egg yolks in top part of a double boiler; stir in sour cream and lemon juice over simmering water; beat continuously until sauce thickens. Add salt and enough paprika to turn the sauce to a subdued pink. Stir in parsley just before serving.

MAKES ABOUT 2 CUPS.

DESSERTS

MRS. JEWETT'S APPLE CAKE

1 cup shortening
1 cup sugar
1 cup diced apple
1 cup plus 1 tablespoon flour
½ tsp. salt
1 tsp. ground cinnamon
1 Tbs. chopped nuts (optional)
1 Tbs. raisins (optional)

Preheat oven to 325° F.

Put shortening into a mixing bowl and blend in sugar and finely diced apple. Sift flour with salt and cinnamon, and stir into apple mixture. Add nuts and raisins if desired and stir well. Pour into greased rectangular pan. Bake for 30 to 35 minutes, remove, and let cool on a wire rack. Serve warm with whipped cream.

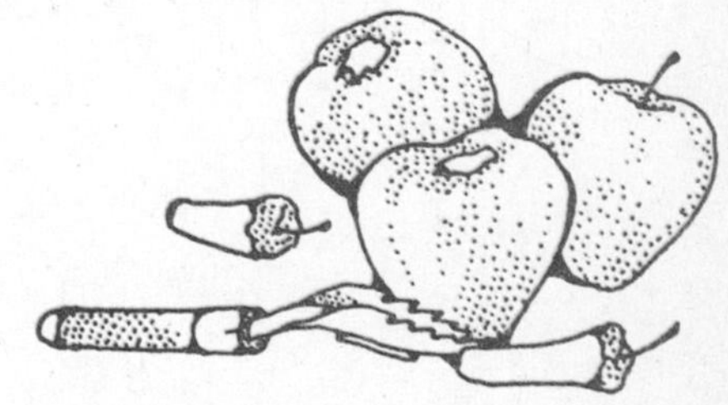

CARVERSVILLE BLACK WALNUT CAKE

A veteran retailer of nuts of all varieties once said he could be sure anyone who asked for black walnuts was either a Southerner or a Midwesterner. This recipe migrated to eastern Pennsylvania.

1/2 cup (1 stick) butter, softened
1 cup plus 2 Tbs. sugar
2 whole eggs
1 tsp. vanilla extract
1 tsp. orange juice
2 cups cake flour
2 1/2 tsp. baking powder
3/4 tsp. salt
3/4 cup milk
3/4 cup black walnut bits
1/4 cup confectioner's sugar

Preheat oven to 350° F.
Cream butter and sugar together; add eggs, vanilla, and orange juice, mixing thoroughly. Sift together flour, baking powder, and salt, then stir into first mixture along with milk and nuts. Spoon batter into a greased and floured loaf pan (9 by 5 by 3 inches). Bake for 1 hour and 10 minutes. Remove from oven and cover top with confectioner's sugar.

DURGIN-PARK BLUEBERRY CAKE

There are many regional variations of New England's tea cakes made with blueberries, and the recipe of Boston's well-known Durgin-Park restaurant is often adapted. Sometimes it is served as a dessert with a lemony sauce; to finish a festive meal, a Wisconsin cook serves hot blueberry cake direct from the oven, with a scoop of ice cream.

3 cups flour
4 tsp. baking powder
3/4 tsp. salt
2 eggs, beaten
3/4 cup sugar
2 Tbs. butter, melted
1 1/2 cups milk
1 1/4 cups blueberries
extra flour

Preheat oven to 400° F.
Sift flour, baking powder, and salt together. Blend eggs with sugar, then combine with butter and dry ingredients. Stir in milk to make thick batter. Dust berries with extra flour and add to the batter, mixing well. Spoon batter into a greased baking dish (9 by 14 by 3 inches). Bake for about 1/2 hour.

MAKES ABOUT 6 SERVINGS.

BLUE-RIBBON CARROT CAKE WITH ORANGE GLAZE

As mentioned on page 161, carrot cake was Americanized in many ways as a result of newfound popularity in the 1960s and thereafter. Viola Schlichting used this recipe to win a blue ribbon at a Texas county fair.

1 1/4 cups vegetable oil
2 cups sugar
2 cups sifted cake flour
2 tsp. baking powder
2 tsp. baking soda
1 tsp. salt
2 tsp. ground cinnamon
4 eggs
3 cups grated carrots
1 cup broken pecan meats

ORANGE GLAZE:

1 cup sugar
1/4 cup cornstarch
1 cup freshly squeezed orange juice
1 tsp. freshly squeezed lemon juice
2 Tbs. butter, softened
2 Tbs. grated orange rind
1/2 tsp. salt

Preheat oven to 325° F.

Combine oil and sugar, mixing thoroughly. Sift together dry ingredients, then sift half of the sifted seasoned flour into the sugar-oil mixture and blend well. Sift in remainder alternately with eggs, adding 1 egg at a time and blending well after each addition. Stir in carrots, add nutmeats, and blend thoroughly. Pour into a greased 10-inch tube pan and bake for about 1 hour and 10 minutes.

Meanwhile make the glaze: Put sugar and cornstarch into a saucepan and slowly stir in orange juice and lemon juice. When mixture is thoroughly blended, stir in butter, orange rind, and salt. Cook over low heat about 5 minutes until thick and satiny. Let cool before glazing cake. When cake is ready, remove from oven and set on a wire rack to cool. Remove cake from pan, split into 3 layers; spread orange glaze between layers and on top and sides of cake.

MAKES 6 TO 8 SERVINGS.

CHOCOLATE CUSTARD CAKE

3 oz. unsweetened chocolate
1/2 cup condensed milk
1 cup granulated brown sugar
1 egg yolk
2 cups cake flour
1 tsp. baking soda
1/2 tsp. salt
1/4 lb. (1 stick) butter, softened
1 cup white sugar
2 eggs
3/4 cup buttermilk
1 tsp. vanilla extract

FROSTING:

1 cup condensed milk
1 1/4 cups sugar
5 oz. unsweetened chocolate
1/4 lb. (1 stick) butter
1 tsp. vanilla extract

GARNISH AND DECORATION:

2 Tbs. mint jelly
12 pecan halves

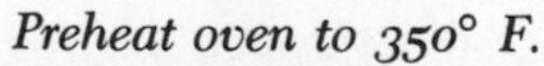
Preheat oven to 350° F.

Melt chocolate with condensed milk, brown sugar and egg yolk in top part of a double boiler over hot water, stirring until smooth and thickened.

Remove from heat and set aside. Sift together flour, baking soda, and salt. Cream butter and add white sugar gradually, beating consistently until fluffy. Separate eggs and add yolks to the butter mixture 1 at a time, beating after each addition. Now add flour mixture alternately with milk. When thoroughly blended, stir in chocolate custard and vanilla. Beat egg whites until they form soft peaks and fold them into cake batter. Butter well and flour lightly, knocking out excess flour, two 9-inch cake pans, and distribute batter evenly into them. Bake for 30 minutes, then let cool in the cake tins for about 10 minutes; turn out onto wire racks.

Make the frosting: Combine condensed milk and sugar in a heavy saucepan. Bring to a boil, stir once, then reduce heat and let simmer, without stirring, for 6 minutes. Remove from heat. Blend in the chocolate, then butter, then vanilla. Let cool, stirring occasionally. When sufficiently cool and thick, spread about one-third over 1 layer, place the next layer on top and coat the surface of that with mint jelly. Spread the rest of the frosting over the top surface and sides of the cake. Set pecans around the edge for decoration.

MAKES 1 DOUBLE-LAYER CAKE.

DATE AND NUT CAKES

3 eggs
1 cup chopped dates
3 Tbs. sugar
1 cup chopped walnuts
1 Tbs. bread crumbs

GARNISH:
1 cup heavy cream
1 tsp. sugar
1/2 tsp. vanilla extract

Preheat oven to 375° F.

Separate eggs; beat yolks until lemon colored. Toss dates with 3 tablespoons sugar so that they don't stick together, then mix with walnuts and bread crumbs and add to yolks. Beat whites until they form stiff peaks, then fold into date mixture. Butter muffin tins and fill three-quarters full. Bake for 12 minutes. Remove and let cool a little on wire racks. Beat cream, add 1 teaspoon sugar, and continue to beat until stiff; then blend in vanilla. Serve a dollop over each slightly warm cake.

MAKES 12.

DEVIL'S FOOD CAKE

Chocolate cakes are popular from coast to coast. There are numerous variations on devil's food, including a favorite of "coeds" in the Boston suburbs that was called Wellesley fudge—its chief difference being the use of twice as much chocolate. The Wellesley confection was first served in a small upstairs tearoom on Wellesley Square, later at the Blue Dragon, in days when any undergraduate caught smoking off campus was summarily expelled.

1 tsp. baking soda
1/2 cup sour milk
2 oz. unsweetened chocolate
1/4 lb. (1 stick) butter, softened
2 cups brown sugar
3 egg yolks
1 tsp. vanilla extract
1/2 cup coffee, hot
2 cups sifted flour

Preheat oven to 350° F.
Stir baking soda into sour milk. Shred chocolate; put into a 1/2-cup measure and fill with boiling water to make 1/2 cup of liquid chocolate. Cream together butter and half the brown sugar; beat remaining sugar into egg yolks, then blend with butter-sugar mixture, beating thoroughly. Stir in liquid chocolate, vanilla, and coffee, and continue thorough beating. Stir in flour alternately with sour milk, beating the mixture for 3 more minutes. Spoon into a greased loaf pan (9 by 5 by 3 inches) and bake for about 35 minutes.

MAKES ABOUT 8 SERVINGS.

FILBERT CAKE

Pioneer cooks found American hazelnuts abundant in the South and in Midwestern states such as Kansas, but nowhere were these nuts turned into tempting desserts more often than in Oregon. This excellent version is not unlike a very popular Salem dessert.

7 eggs
1 cup vanilla sugar, or 1 cup plain sugar with 2 tsp. vanilla extract
flour
1/8 tsp. salt
1/8 tsp. ground cinnamon
freshly grated nutmeg
1 tsp. rum
1/2 lb. filberts
1/4 tsp. cream of tartar
confectioner's sugar (optional)
1 cup heavy cream, whipped (optional)

Preheat oven to 325° F.
Separate eggs, putting whites into a very clean white metal or copper bowl. In another bowl, beat yolks until lemon colored, then add vanilla gradually, beating continuously until sugar is all absorbed. Sift in 2 tablespoons flour and salt, then add cinnamon and a few gratings of nutmeg along with rum. Pulverize filberts in a blender, half at a time. When very finely ground, stir small amounts into batter by lightly crumbling the nuts through your fingers to loosen their density; beat well into mixture. Beat egg whites with

cream of tartar until they form peaks. Mix one-fourth of beaten whites into batter to lighten, then turn batter into the bowl of remaining whites, carefully folding to keep lightness. Butter a 10-inch tube pan generously; sprinkle with flour and shake out excess; pour in batter and bake for 1 hour. Let cool in the pan, then turn out onto a wire rack. To serve, slip onto a cake plate and sprinkle well with confectioner's sugar or heap with whipped cream and sprinkle with extra nuts.

MAKES 10 SERVINGS.

GENERAL ROBERT E. LEE CAKE

In the 1950s women of the Olivet Episcopal Church in Franconia, Virginia, collected recipes, many of which dated back to the Old Dominion. Some had been jotted in a book used by the Lee and Washington families, and a separate contribution was Mrs. Robert E. Lee's own recipe for this citrus-flavored cake as preserved by Miss Edna Lee: "Twelve eggs, their full weight in sugar, a half weight in flour. Bake it in pans the thickness of jelly cakes. Take two pounds of nice 'A' sugar, squeeze into it the juice of five oranges and three lemons together with the pulp. Stir it in the sugar until perfectly smooth, then spread it over the cake as you would do jelly—putting one above another till the whole of the sugar is used up." Variations of the recipe and ingredients appear in a number of kitchen manuals published in the nineteenth century; in *Housekeeping in Old Virginia, from 250 of Virginia's Noted Housewives*, Mrs. Isabella Harrison pointed out in the recipe she gave that Mrs. Lee's confection must be made "exactly like a Sponge cake," but her instructions were just about as vague as the original. The method below may be more helpful.

CAKE:

5 large eggs
1 cup sugar
1 Tbs. grated orange rind
2 tsp. grated lemon rind
2 tsp. lemon juice
2 tsp. orange juice
cream of tartar
salt
1 cup sifted flour
1 cup grated fresh coconut

FILLING:

3 large egg yolks
1/3 cup sugar
3 Tbs. lemon juice
2 1/2 Tbs. sweet butter
1 tsp. cornstarch
1 Tbs. water

FROSTING:

1/4 lb. (1 stick) sweet butter, softened
2 1/2 cups sifted confectioner's sugar
1/3 cup lemon juice
1 large egg yolk
1 Tbs. grated orange rind
2 tsp. grated lemon rind
pinch of salt

Preheat oven to 350° F.

Butter three 8-inch cake pans. Separate eggs and use an electric mixer in a large bowl to beat egg yolks with 1/2 cup sugar until thick and pale yellow; stir in orange rind, lemon rind, lemon juice, and orange juice. In another bowl beat egg whites with cream of tartar and a pinch of salt until they form peaks. Gradually beat in remaining 1/2 cup sugar, then continue beating until mixture is stiff. Fold this meringue into egg yolk mixture, alternately adding 1 cup sifted flour sifted again with 1/4 teaspoon salt. Divide batter and fill buttered pans. Put them on middle rack of oven and bake for 25 minutes. When cakes are done, set aside to cool, then invert onto wire racks.

Meanwhile make the filling: Combine egg yolks, sugar, lemon juice, and butter in a saucepan. Cook over moderate heat for 5 minutes, whisking briskly, until mixture thickens. In a bowl mix cornstarch with water and stir this paste vigorously into lemon mixture until mixture is shiny. Set aside, covered with wax paper, and chill.

Make the frosting: Using an electric mixer, cream butter with sifted confectioner's sugar, adding about 1/4 cup sugar at a time, until light and fluffy. Stir in lemon juice, egg yolk, orange rind, lemon rind, and salt; mix well.

Put 1 cake layer on a plate and spread with half of filling. Top with second layer and spread on remaining filling. Place third layer on top and spread top and sides of cake with lemon frosting. Sprinkle coconut evenly over frosting.

MAKES 1 TRIPLE-LAYER CAKE.

KEN'S UPSIDE-DOWN CAKE

Most Americans grow up on upside-down cakes of one kind or another, usually made of pineapple rings with a cherry in the middle and a gooey brown bottom; sometimes apples are used, or bananas, or another fruit in season, and the fluffy white cake with one egg is usually puffy and rather bland. Ken Wollitz, a gifted musician from California with a fine palate, is addicted to upside-down confections. His contention is that the cake should have far more substance and texture for balance against the candied fruits it supports, and after much study he devised this recipe calling for a pumpkin bread base with nuts and an unusual combination of fruits. It may sound far out, but it is delicious.

approximately 20 dried apricots
1/2 recipe Pumpkin Bread (p. 207)
1/2 cup chopped walnuts
4 Tbs. (1/2 stick) butter
3/4 cup dark brown sugar
3/4 cup whole cranberries, cooked, or canned whole cranberry sauce is fine

GARNISH:
2 cups whipped cream

Preheat oven to 350° F.

Soak apricots in boiling water to cover while preparing cake. Follow instructions for mixing pumpkin bread batter, adding chopped walnuts at the last. Melt butter in a skillet and add brown sugar, heating until melted and blended. Pour into a well-buttered pan (7 by 11 inches or equivalent) and arrange apricots on the bottom in a decorative pattern; surround apricots with cranberries, filling in all the interstices. Pour batter over fruits and bake for 45 minutes to 1 hour, or until a straw inserted comes out clean. Turn out onto a platter and serve warm with whipped cream.

MAKES 12 SERVINGS.

LADY BALTIMORE CAKE

There are plenty of stories to go with this splendid cake, almost as many as there are recipe variations. It seems to be true that novelist Owen Wister, tarrying in Charleston, was so taken by the city and a cake he first ate there that he borrowed the name of the cake for the title of his 1906 romance, *Lady Baltimore*. It also may be true that the "original" recipe became the property of the Misses Florence and Nina Ottolengui, who managed Charleston's Lady Baltimore Tea Room for a quarter of a century and annually baked and shipped to Owen Wister one of the very American cakes his novel had helped to make famous. The following method is simpler than some but results in a cake that tempts one to eat it with a spoon.

1/2 lb. (2 sticks) sweet butter, softened
2 cups sugar
3 1/2 cups sifted cake flour
4 tsp. baking powder
1/2 tsp. salt
1 cup milk
1/4 tsp. almond extract
8 egg whites
pinch of cream of tartar

FILLING:
1 cup chopped mixed nuts
1/2 cup dried raisins, yellow and brown mixed
8 dried figs
1/4 cup sherry or rum (optional)

ICING:
3 egg whites
1 1/8 cups sugar
1/4 cup cold water, or substitute 1 Tbs. with rum or brandy
1/2 tsp. cream of tartar
pinch of salt
1 1/2 tsp. vanilla extract (less if liquor is used)

GARNISH:
pecan halves

Preheat oven to 375° F.

In a large bowl cream butter, add sugar slowly, and beat until fluffy. Sift flour again with baking powder and salt. Add flour alternately with the milk and finally almond extract to butter-sugar mixture and beat batter until smooth and light. Beat egg whites with cream of tartar (unless using a copper bowl) until stiff but not dry. Mix well one-quarter of the whites into the batter, then fold in the rest. Butter well three 9-inch cake pans, dust with flour, and shake out excess. Turn equal amounts of batter into the pans and bake for 25 minutes. Let cool on racks.

Make the filling: Chop nuts, raisins, and figs together; if you like, steep them in sherry or rum for a while, then drain. Spread equal amounts of filling over tops of 2 layers, then place one on top of the other.

Make the icing: Mix egg whites, sugar, water, cream of tartar, and salt in the top part of a double boiler over boiling water. Beat continuously for 7 minutes, maybe a little more, until the mixture will stand in peaks when beater is lifted and turned up. Remove from the heat. When cool, add vanilla. Spread generously over top and sides of cake. Decorate rim with pecan halves and a little wheel of pecans in the middle.

MAKES 1 TRIPLE-LAYER CAKE.

MAPLE-BOURBON CAKE

1/4 lb. (1 stick) butter, softened
1/2 cup sugar
2 eggs
2 1/2 tsp. baking powder
2 cups flour
1/2 tsp. salt
freshly grated nutmeg
1/2 cup maple syrup
1/2 cup bourbon whiskey
1 1/2 cups coarsely chopped pecans
confectioner's sugar

Preheat oven to 350° F.

Work butter into sugar until it is evenly distributed. Add eggs, 1 at a time, beating mixture thoroughly. Put baking powder, flour, salt, and a liberal grating of nutmeg into a bowl and blend well. Add maple syrup and bourbon alternately, then stir in pecans. Pour into a small greased loaf pan (9 by 5 by 3 inches). Bake for 45 to 50 minutes. Sprinkle with confectioner's sugar.

MAKES 6 TO 8 SERVINGS.

MAPLE LAYER CAKE

2 cups all-purpose flour
2 1/2 tsp. baking powder
1/4 lb. (1 stick) butter, softened
1 1/4 cups confectioner's sugar
1 tsp. vanilla extract
5 egg whites
pinch of salt
1/8 tsp. cream of tartar
1/2 cup milk

AUNT LUCY'S VERMONT MAPLE FROSTING:

1 1/2 cups pure Vermont maple syrup
2 egg whites
pinch of salt
1/4 cup walnuts

Preheat oven to 375° F.

Sift flour and baking powder together three times. Cream butter with sugar until light and lemon colored. Add vanilla. Beat egg whites with salt and cream of tartar until they form peaks. Add milk and flour alternately to butter-sugar mixture, blending well. Finally mix in about one-quarter of whites to lighten, then gently fold in remaining whites. Turn into 2 buttered and floured 9-inch cake pans and bake for 25 minutes. Let cool on wire racks.

Meanwhile make the frosting: Boil syrup until it spins a thread. Beat egg whites with salt until they are stiff but not too dry. Add syrup gradually and keep beating until cool and of spreadable consistency. Spread frosting over cake, stacking one layer on top of the other. Decorate with walnuts.

MAKES 1 DOUBLE-LAYER CAKE.

MARBLE CAKE

1/4 lb. (1 stick) butter, softened
2 cups sugar
2 eggs, beaten
3 cups cake flour
1 tsp. cream of tartar
1/2 tsp. baking soda
1/2 tsp. salt
1 cup milk
1 tsp. vanilla extract
3 Tbs. unsweetened powdered cocoa
boiling water
confectioner's sugar (optional)
1 recipe Mocha Frosting (opposite) (optional)

Preheat oven to 375° F.

Cream the butter and add sugar slowly, beating constantly until sugar is absorbed and mixture is fluffy. Add the eggs. Sift dry ingredients together, then start adding alternately with milk, beating with each addition. Then add vanilla. Moisten the cocoa with just enough boiling water to make a smooth paste. Remove about one-third of the cake batter to another bowl and beat in cocoa until smooth. Grease a 10-inch tube pan or a decorative round cake mold. Using 2 spoons, start adding the 2 batters, first the white, then a dollop of the chocolate here and there, swirling it slightly to form a marbled pattern. Knock tube pan on the counter to even the batter; don't smooth or mix the 2 batters. Bake in the top third of the oven for 1 hour. Remove and cool in the pan for about 10 minutes before turning out. Marble cake can be served simply sprinkled with confectioner's sugar, or it can be frosted with Mocha Frosting.

MAKES 8 SERVINGS.

MOCHA FROSTING

3 Tbs. freshly made strong coffee
3 Tbs. butter
1/4 cup heavy cream
1/8 tsp. salt
1 tsp. vanilla extract
2 cups confectioner's sugar

Pour coffee into a saucepan and stir in butter. Heat cream and add to coffee when warm. Stir in salt, then remove from heat. When mixture is cool, add vanilla and beat in sugar, a little at a time. When smooth and spreadable, frost any suitable cake.

MAKES ENOUGH FOR 1 DOUBLE-LAYER CAKE.

LESLIE JONES'S OATMEAL CAKE

1 1/4 cups boiling water
1 cup rolled oats
1/4 lb. (1 stick) butter, softened
1 cup white sugar
1 cup brown sugar
1 tsp. vanilla extract
2 eggs, beaten
1 1/2 cups flour
1 tsp. baking soda
1/2 tsp. salt
3/4 tsp. ground cinnamon
1/4 tsp. grated nutmeg

TOPPING:

4 Tbs. (1/2 stick) butter, melted
1/2 cup brown sugar
3 Tbs. half-and-half or evaporated milk
1/3 cup chopped nuts
3/4 cup shredded coconut

Preheat oven to 350° F.

Pour boiling water over oats, cover, and let stand for 20 minutes. Beat butter until creamy; gradually add both sugars and beat until fluffy. Blend in vanilla and eggs, then stir in oats. Sift together flour, baking soda, salt, cinnamon, and nutmeg; add to creamed mixture and mix thoroughly. Pour this batter into a well-greased and floured 9-inch square pan. Bake for 50 to 55 minutes. Remove from oven but leave in pan.

Make the topping: Combine all topping ingredients, blending until smooth. Spread over top of cake, then put it under the broiler just long enough to glaze. Good either hot or cold.

MAKES 9 SERVINGS.

MICHIGAN APPLESAUCE TORTE

2 1/8 cups fresh bread crumbs, made from homemade white bread
5 Tbs. butter
3 eggs, separated
2 cups applesauce
2 Tbs. vanilla sugar
pinch of salt
2 Tbs. plain sugar
1/3 cup mixed chopped walnuts and filberts
1 cup boiled custard, chilled, or whipped cream

Preheat oven to 350° F.

Sauté 2 cups bread crumbs in 4 tablespoons butter, tossing continuously over very low heat until they turn golden brown. Beat egg yolks thoroughly, then add applesauce and vanilla sugar. In a separate bowl beat egg whites with salt until almost stiff, then add plain sugar and beat until peaks form. Mix one-quarter of stiff whites into applesauce batter, then carefully fold in remainder. Fold in chopped nuts. With remaining 1 tablespoon butter generously grease a shallow cake pan (8 to 9 inches) and sprinkle with remaining 2 tablespoons bread crumbs. Pour in applesauce mixture and smooth out. Bake for 1 to 1 1/4 hours. Remove from pan. Chill overnight and serve with cold boiled custard or whipped cream.

MAKES 8 SERVINGS.

HELEN KNOPF'S MEDFORD, OREGON, PRIZE PEAR TORTE

Fruit growing is profuse in each of the Pacific states, but no orchard was more prolific than the Medford acres once presided over by the distinguished New Yorker who, in more youthful days, won a ribbon for this original recipe.

2 eggs
1 cup sugar
1/2 cup flour
2 1/2 tsp. baking powder
1/4 tsp. salt
1 1/2 cups stewed or canned Bartlett pears, drained and well mashed
1 cup English walnuts, broken

Preheat oven to 350° F.

Beat eggs until light; add sugar and continue beating. Sift flour, add baking powder and salt, and sift again. Fold flour mixture into egg and sugar alternately with the pears. Fold in walnut meats. Oil a shallow rectangular pan about 14 by 12 inches, then dust it lightly with flour; pour in batter. Bake for 30 to 40 minutes. Torte is done when toothpick or straw comes out clean. Serve warm.

MAKES 6 TO 8 SERVINGS.

BASIC PIECRUST

In older American cookbooks pie dough was made with pork leaf lard, a method still used by some people who prefer the traditional flavor and texture. (See following recipe.) Tastes, however, do change. We use mostly butter with a little lard, preferring animal fat to vegetable shortening. The latter of course can be substituted for lard by those who watch cholesterol counts, or for any other reason. This recipe will make a two-crust 9-inch pie or one 10-inch bottom crust; if a smaller crust is called for, leftover dough can be wrapped and frozen for future use.

2 cups unbleached flour
1/2 tsp. salt
1/4 lb. (1 stick) butter, chilled
3 Tbs. lard, chilled
about 5 Tbs. ice water

Mix flour and salt together. Cut in butter and lard; use pastry blender or fingers to mix until dough is the consistency of cornmeal. Dribble enough ice water into mixture so that is holds together. Scoop up this dough and put onto a floured surface. Smear dough out in about 2 or 3 strokes with the heel of the hand, then scrape it together into a ball. Flour ball lightly and refrigerate for 2 hours or more.

To make a double piecrust: divide dough into 2 slighly uneven portions. Roll out the larger half; if it cracks, just pinch it together, then line a 9-inch pie pan, pressing dough firmly into angles of sides. Refrigerate the lined pie pan and the remaining dough while making pie filling. After putting filling into pie shell, roll out the smaller portion of chilled dough and drape it over the filling; then press dough together along the rim, crimping with a fork and trimming away excess.

To bake empty pie shells, line a 10-, 9-, or 8-inch pie pan, according to need, with roughly half the dough; press in firmly, then cut around edge, leaving a 1/2-inch overhang. Fold this margin under and press all around with the tines of a fork, or crimp with fingers. Butter outside of another pie pan just one size smaller and press it on top of dough lining original pie pan. Bake for 8 minutes in a preheated 425° F. oven, then remove top pan, pricking bottom of pastry with a fork in several places. Reduce oven heat to 375° and return pastry shell to oven for 2 minutes more for partially baked, 10 to 15 minutes more, or until lightly golden, for fully baked. For a sweet pie or tart, take shell from oven after first 8 minutes, brush bottom with 1 tablespoon apricot jam or currant jelly, as indicated in specific recipes, then return to 375° oven.

To make small pastry shells, follow the method above, lining small tart molds or muffin tins with pastry. To bake blind, cut foil to fit individual mold and fill with dried beans or rice for first 8 minutes of baking, then remove and bake at lowered heat for another 3 to 4 minutes.

MAKES ONE DOUBLE CRUST FOR A 9-INCH PIE OR A SINGLE CRUST FOR A 10-INCH PIE.

LARD PIE CRUST

For a fruit pie nothing can beat the old-fashioned pie crust made with unadulterated leaf lard, put away when the pig was slaughtered. Today most commercial lard is so full of preservatives that the genuine pork fat flavor is lost. It is better to substitute a vegetable shortening like Crisco if you can't get the real thing. Incidentally, this dough can't be made successfully in a food processor.

2 cups flour
1/2 teaspoon salt
3/4 cup lard or vegetable shortening
6–7 tablespoons ice water

Mix the flour and the salt thoroughly. Cut the lard or shortening up into rough, smallish pieces and toss into the flour. Using either your fingertips or a pastry cutter cut the lard into the flour rapidly until the mixture resembles coarse meal. Dribble in the ice water, lightly gathering the ball of dough together as it become moistened. Wrap in plastic wrap and let rest, refrigerated, for 15–20 minutes. You'll have enough dough for a 9-inch pie with a bottom and top crust.

ALEXANDER PIE

The birth of the brandy Alexander cocktail may be obscured in alcoholic mists, but the first brandy Alexander pie seems to have been made sometime after the end of Prohibition. Not that brandy hadn't been almost essential to good mincemeat pies for generations; it's simply that some temperate cooks seem to think that evolving a pie filling from a cocktail recipe is a little like gilding the lily. In the freewheeling 1970s the gilding of pies of all flavors took the form of paintings; top crusts of some pies baked commercially by New York artists looking for added income were decorated with portraits, landscapes, patchwork, even pornography.

1 envelope unflavored gelatin
1/4 to 1/2 cup water
2/3 cup sugar
1/8 tsp. salt
3 eggs, separated
1/4 cup Cognac or applejack
1/4 cup crème de cacao
1 cup heavy cream, whipped
1 recipe graham cracker crust *(see p. 466)*

GARNISH:

1/2 cup grated chocolate or chocolate curls
1/2 to 1 cup whipped cream

Sprinkle gelatin into a saucepan containing water; add 1/3 cup sugar, salt, and egg yolks; stir thoroughly. Over low heat continue stirring until gelatin is entirely dissolved and mixture thickens. Do not boil. Off the heat, stir in Cognac and crème de cacao. Let cool, then chill 2 to 3 hours in refrigerator until mixture starts to thicken at edges. Beat egg whites until peaks form; gradually beat in remaining 1/3 cup of sugar, then fold all carefully into thickened gelatin mixture. Fold in about 1 cup whipped cream. Pour pie mixture into a 9-inch pie pan lined with graham cracker crust. Chill for several hours or overnight. Garnish with remaining whipped cream and chocolate gratings or curls.

MAKES 6 TO 8 SERVINGS.

NATURAL BANANA CREAM PIE

1 1/2 cups whole wheat pastry flour
1/4 tsp. salt
4 Tbs. (1/2 stick) butter
1/4 cup cold-pressed corn oil

FILLING AND TOPPING:

1 1/2 cups milk
3 eggs
1 tsp. vanilla extract
1 cup heavy cream
3/4 cup strained natural honey or Grade A maple syrup
2 bananas, sliced

Preheat oven to 400° F.

Use a pastry cutter to blend flour and salt with butter; then mix in oil with fingers. Carefully add just enough water to form dough into a ball. Without chilling, roll out dough on a pastry cloth, then press smoothly into 9-inch pie pan. Flute edges and prick with a fork. Bake for 8 minutes, then remove and let cool. Reduce oven to 350°.

Bring milk to a boil, meanwhile beating together eggs, vanilla, and honey or syrup and 1/2 of cream. Stir hot milk into beaten egg mixture. Fill pie shell with mixture and bake pie for about 45 minutes; let cool. Top with sliced bananas. Whip remaining 1/2 cup cream with 3 tablespoons honey or syrup and spoon evenly over banana layer. Chill for 1 hour or more.

MAKES 8 SERVINGS.

BOSTON CREAM PIE

Harvey D. Parker, who opened his Boston hotel in 1856, was host to distinguished people from all walks of life, including such members of the Saturday Club as Ralph Waldo Emerson, Henry Wadsworth Longfellow, Oliver Wendell Holmes, Nathaniel Hawthorne, and John Greenleaf Whitter, who came to the Parker House regularly to stimulate one another intellectually and praise the hostelry's American bill of fare. Boston cream pie had been on that menu since the day Parker House opened, yet the fact that it is really a cake disguised by this misnomer remains unexplained. When the layers of vanilla cream filling are transformed into stratifications of raspberry jam, this dessert is equally famous, and again for reasons unknown, as Washington pie.

CAKE:

6 Tbs. (3/4 stick) butter, softened
1 cup sugar
2 eggs
1 3/4 cups all-purpose flour
1/2 tsp. salt
2 tsp. baking powder
1/2 cup milk
1/2 tsp. vanilla extract

FILLING:

2/3 cup sugar
1/3 cup all-purpose flour
pinch of salt
2 cups milk, scalded
2 egg yolks
1/2 tsp. lemon extract

TOPPING:

confectioner's sugar

Preheat oven to 375° F.

Cream butter with all but 2 tablespoons sugar. Beat eggs until lemon colored; add remaining sugar and beat again. Blend egg-sugar mixture into creamed butter and beat until fluffy. Sift together dry ingredients, then add, alternately with the milk, to the batter and continue beating until all is absorbed. Add vanilla. Turn into 2 well-buttered 8-inch cake pans and bake for 25 minutes. When done, turn out onto wire racks to cook.

Make the filling: Mix sugar, flour, and salt together in top part of a double boiler. Blend in hot milk slowly and cook gently over simmering water, stirring occasionally, until thickened, about 15 minutes. Beat egg yolks, blend a little of the hot mixture into the eggs to warm them, then add to the rest of the mixture and continue cooking for another 3 or 4 minutes. Remove from the heat and season with lemon extract. When custard is cool, spread between cake layers. Using a shaker, sprinkle top liberally with confectioner's sugar. To serve, cut into pie-shaped wedges.

MAKES 6 TO 8 SERVINGS.

APRICOT CHIFFON PIE

In France the word *chiffon* has been used to describe fabric that is smooth and silky, and sometimes it has been used in the vernacular as a synonym for "gossip," or "conversation of airy nothingness." Nowhere but in America is it a description for smooth and silky confections from the kitchen that are among desserts characteristic of the twentieth century.

5 1/2 oz. dried apricots
3/4 cup apricot nectar or orange juice
3/4 to 1 cup sugar
1 envelope unflavored gelatin
1/4 cup cold water
2 egg whites
1 prebaked 8-in. pie shell (see p. 459) or graham cracker crust (see p. 466)

Place apricots in the top part of a double boiler, cover with water, and cook over boiling water, uncovered, for 20 minutes. Remove from heat; spin in a blender with apricot or orange juice to purée. Return to double boiler, with as much sugar as needed, depending on sweetness of juice. Meanwhile soften gelatin in cold water, then stir into sweetened purée and mix well; set aside to cool. Beat egg whites until stiff, then fold carefully into cooled purée. Turn into pie shell or crumb crust and chill for several hours before serving.

MAKES 6 SERVINGS.

BOURBON-PECAN PIE

Westering Southerners found pecans growing wild as they moved into Louisiana and Oklahoma, but it was a black gardener named Antoine who grafted sixteen trees on a plantation in Louisiana sugar country to produce the best pecans the South had known. Pecan pie is one of the reasons gastronomes come to the Lowell Inn in Stillwater, Minnesota, where it is made with white sugar. In Louisville, Marion Brown's recipe calls for maple syrup and maple meringue. Here the mystery flavor is a sip of Kentucky's own bourbon.

1/3 cup butter, softened
1/2 cup dark brown sugar
3 eggs
1/4 tsp. salt
1 cup dark corn syrup
1 Tbs. Kentucky bourbon
1 cup chopped pecans
1 Tbs. flour
1/2 recipe Basic Piecrust (p. 459)

GARNISH:
8 to 10 whole pecans, cut into halves
1/2 cup heavy cream (optional)
2 Tbs. sugar (optional)
2 to 3 Tbs. Kentucky bourbon (optional)

Preheat oven to 450° F.
Cream butter and add brown sugar slowly, beating constantly until all is absorbed and mixture is fluffy. Add eggs, one by one, beating continuously, then add salt, corn syrup, and bourbon. Toss pecans with flour, then fold them into filling. Make pie dough according to instructions and use it to line a 9-inch pie pan, holding down pastry by placing another pan on top,

or lining with foil filled with beans; bake for 10 minutes. Remove from oven, remove extra pan or foil, and prick bottom of crust with a fork. Pour in filling. Reduce heat to 350° and bake for 35 minutes, or until pie is firm. Decorate top by making border of pecan halves and bake for 5 minutes more. Serve tepid; pie may be garnished with whipped cream flavored with sugar and bourbon.

MAKES 8 SERVINGS.

HONEY CHEESECAKE PIE

1/2 recipe Basic Piecrust (p. 459)
8 oz. cream cheese, at room temperature
1/2 cup honey, warmed
3 eggs
1/4 tsp. salt
1 1/2 cups milk
ground cinnamon

Preheat oven to 450° F.
Make pastry dough according to instructions and set aside in refrigerator. Cream cheese until soft. Mix honey, eggs, salt, milk, and about 1/4 teaspoon cinnamon. Stir into cheese and blend thoroughly. Line an 8-inch pie pan with pastry and pour in filling. Sprinkle with cinnamon. Bake for 10 minutes; reduce heat to 325° and bake for 25 to 30 minutes more. Let cool, then chill in refrigerator for several hours.

MAKES 6 SERVINGS.

CONCORD GRAPE PIE

It seems generally accepted that Norsemen arrived on America's Atlantic coast and called it Vinland because of the abundance of grapes. One of the most famous of vineyard fruits growing in New England is the Concord grape, which was developed by Ephraim Bull from a vine he found "among our wildings" in Concord, Massachusetts. The wine produced by this hybrid may be as "incredibly mediocre" as Alexis Lichine has said, but Concord grapes themselves are fine to eat, and they make an admirable Yankee dessert.

2 lb. Concord grapes
3/4 cup sugar
1 1/2 Tbs. lemon juice
1 Tbs. grated orange rind
1 1/2 Tbs. flour
1/2 recipe Basic Lard Piecrust (p. 460)
2 Tbs. butter

Preheat oven to 450° F.
Peel grapes and put pulp into a saucepan and skins in a bowl. Cover saucepan and cook slowly for about 10 minutes, or until seeds have sepa-

rated. Put through strainer to remove seeds. Mix skins and strained pulp with sugar, lemon juice, orange rind, and flour, and set aside for 20 minutes. Meanwhile make pastry dough according to instructions and line a 9-inch pie pan with it. Pour filling into pie pan and top with butter. Cover with pastry lid, fluting edges, and pricking on top. Bake for 10 minutes, then reduce oven to 350° and bake for 30 minutes more.

MAKES 6 TO 8 SERVINGS.

GREEN TOMATO PIE

This has long been a favorite among New Englanders, who are apt to have lots of green tomatoes on hand when the frost comes early and the still-unripened tomatoes have to be gathered in a hurry. Crusts, of course, were almost always made with lard, but we've found that our standard more buttery, crumbly crust holds its own well with the long cooking required before the tomatoes soften and yield their lovely, surprising flavor.

6 medium-size green tomatoes
1/2 recipe Basic Piecrust (p. 459)
2 Tbs. butter
1 cup sugar
1/2 tsp. freshly ground allspice
1/2 tsp. ground cinnamon
1/2 cup cider vinegar
1 tsp. flour

Preheat oven to 425° F.

Slice tomatoes paper-thin. Prepare pie dough according to instructions and line bottom of a 9-inch pie pan with it. Dot a little of the butter on the pastry in the pan, then spread on layers of tomatoes, topping each layer with some sugar, spices, vinegar, butter, and a sprinkling of flour until all ingredients are used. Roll out remaining dough and cover pie, crimping edges and trimming. With remaining scraps of dough roll out a small piece, curl it around a finger, then make a small cross in the center of the top crust and insert it, forming a chimney to allow steam to escape; turn out edges for a more decorative rosette. Bake for 20 minutes, then reduce heat to 375° and continue baking for 35 to 40 minutes. Serve slightly warm with a wedge of Vermont cheese.

MAKES 6 SERVINGS.

LEMON MERINGUE PIE

A pie can always be turned out for dessert as long as there are lemons in the house, and American cooks have devised many recipes. President Calvin Coolidge is said to have favored a simple lemon custard pie. The even more common lemon meringue, ever present in public eating places, is one more dish served at Boston's Parker House that has become a classic in the American repertoire. And a special version gained fame swiftly when it went on the menu of the Lion House Social Center in Salt Lake City. The following version is based on a method worked out in the 1960s by the late Michael Field in collaboration with Dr. Paul Buck, a food scientist at Cornell University. The determined Mr. Field devoted days to making one lemon meringue pie after another until he eliminated the "weeping" common to meringues that sit around on counters; his trick was to use a little calcium phosphate powder, a food-grade phosphate product available in drugstores and suggested by Dr. Buck; the gingersnaps sprinkled on the crust help to keep it from getting soggy.

3/4 cup sugar
1/4 cup cornstarch
pinch of salt
1 3/4 cups cold water
6 egg yolks
2 Tbs. grated lemon rind
2 Tbs. butter
1/2 cup freshly squeezed lemon juice
2 Tbs. pulverized ginger snaps
1 prebaked 9-in. pie shell (see p. 459)
5 egg whites
1/2 cup vanilla sugar or 1/2 cup plain sugar mixed with 1 or 2 drops of vanilla extract
1/2 tsp. cream of tartar
1/2 tsp. calcium phosphate powder (optional)

Preheat oven to 325° F.

Prepare the filling by blending sugar, cornstarch, salt, and water together in a saucepan and cooking slowly, stirring constantly, for 2 minutes. Remove from heat. Drop egg yolks, 1 at a time, into the hot mixture, beating thoroughly after each addition. Return cornstarch-egg mixture to heat, add lemon rind, and let simmer for 6 or 7 minutes, or until smooth and very thick, beating constantly as it thickens. Off the heat, beat in butter, a little at a time, then lemon juice. Let custard cool to room temperature. Sprinkle pulverized gingersnaps on the bottom of pie shell, then pour filling in evenly. Now beat egg whites until foamy, then add mixture of vanilla sugar, cream of tartar, and calcium phosphate, a little at a time, until whites form stiff peaks. Spread the meringue over the lemon filling, making decorative swirls and peaks if you wish. Bake for 25 minutes, or until meringue is golden. The pie must cool at room temperature for at least 3 hours before serving, but don't refrigerate to hurry it.

MAKES 6 SERVINGS.

LIME PIE WITH GRAHAM CRACKER CRUST

This recipe for frozen lime pie comes from a cook who brought the high style of Virginia cooking to New York when she opened a tiny restaurant called Mr. & Mrs. Foster's Place. It is a reservations-only oasis where cosmopolitans sample American food untainted by institutionalized kitchens. Lime pie made in this fashion is common in parts of the South. It uses neither evaporated milk nor the gelatin common to most Florida lime pies; it is as fresh as any fruit ice cream. Two kinds of limes are grown in Florida; the Persian, sometimes called Tahiti, is about the size of a small lemon; the so-called Key lime is juicy, yellowish, small, and seedy; it grows from Miami to Fort Myers. Key limes are preferred by many Floridians who grow their own. A third type of lime, planted by Spanish explorers, grows along Georgia's Ogeechee River, but it is rarely found in the twentieth century except by blacks who know the Georgia back country.

CRUST:

1 1/4 cups graham cracker crumbs
1/4 cup superfine sugar
4 Tbs. (1/2 stick) butter, softened

FILLING:

5 eggs, separated
3/4 cup superfine sugar
2/3 cups freshly squeezed lime juice
2 tsp. grated lime rind
pinch of salt

TOPPING:

1 1/2 cups heavy cream, whipped
1 lime, sliced thin
or
fresh strawberries
sugar

Preheat oven to 350° F.

Make the crust: Mix all crust ingredients together thoroughly, then press evenly into a 9-inch pie pan. Bake for 10 minutes; let cool to room temperature.

Make the filling: Beat egg yolks in the top part of a double boiler over hot but not boiling water until very thick. Gradually beat in 1/2 cup sugar until mixture turns pale yellow and is thick enough to form a thread when dribbled off beater. Stir in lime juice and grated rind and heat again over simmering water until mixture will coat a spoon. Mixture should not boil. Turn out into a large bowl and let cool to room temperature. Beat egg whites with salt until soft peaks form. Gradually beat in remaining 1/4 cup sugar until mixture is stiff and shiny. Stir one-third of this into cooled yolk mixture, then fold in remainder and turn into cooled pie shell. Bake for 15 minutes, then set aside to cool; chill in refrigerator before freezing. Cover with plastic wrap when frozen.

Take pie from freezer about 10 minutes before servings. Cover with whipped cream and decorate with thin slices of lime or fresh strawberries dipped into sugar.

MAKES 6 SERVINGS.

MAPLE-WILD RICE PIE

Minnesota and Wisconsin housewives, with access every fall to the Chippewa harvest of wild rice (even at the source wild rice is expensive), seem to be increasingly inventive in developing recipes for every meal. A delightfully nourishing breakfast dish requires equal parts of cooked wild rice and cream of wheat or oatmeal; raisins and brown sugar are added to taste. In this formula for a dessert of surprising texture, two products much used by American Indian cooks are combined.

3 eggs, slightly beaten
1/2 cup brown sugar
2/3 cup maple syrup
1/3 tsp. salt
1 1/2 cups cooked wild rice
1/2 recipe Basic Piecrust (p. 459)
1 1/2 cups heavy cream, whipped (optional)

Preheat oven to 350° F.

Combine eggs, sugar, maple syrup, and salt. Blend in wild rice, mixing thoroughly. Prepare dough according to instructions and line a 9-inch pie pan with it. Pour in filling and bake for about 45 minutes, or until filling of pie puffs slighly in the middle. Whipped cream is the ideal garnish.

MAKES 6 TO 8 SERVINGS.

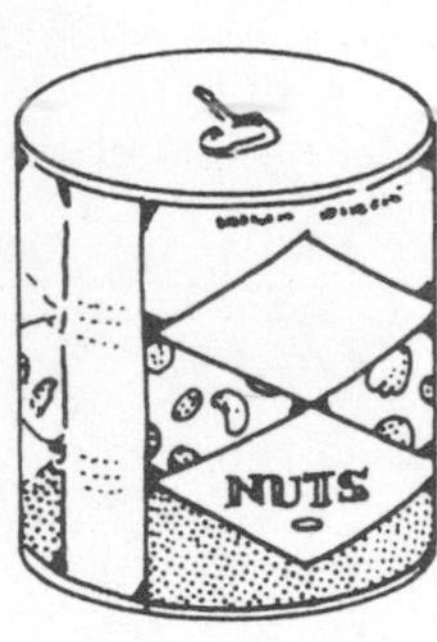

PEANUT PIE

2 eggs
1 cup dark corn syrup
1 cup sugar
1 tsp. maple syrup or vanilla
1 cup salted peanuts
1/2 recipe Basic Piecrust (p. 459)
2 Tbs. butter, softened

Preheat oven to 350° F.

Beat together eggs, corn syrup, sugar, and maple syrup and stir in peanuts. Prepare pie dough according to instructions and fit it into a 9-inch pie pan. Pour in filling. Dot surface with butter. Bake for about 45 minutes, or until filling sets firmly.

MAKES 6 TO 8 SERVINGS.

PUMPKIN PIE

Passing through western Wisconsin, where a good many Scandinavians live, some travelers like to stop at the Norse Nook in the village of Osseo. Over the years the proprietor, Helen Myhre, built a reputation for the best pies one could order in a midwestern restaurant. She also celebrated December 13 by cooking a traditional Norwegian meal replete with lutefisk, lefse, rutabagas, cranberries—and pie, either mince or pumpkin, whichever a customer might prefer. The recipe below was awarded a blue ribbon at a county fair held north of Milwaukee.

2 eggs, slightly beaten
2 cups mashed cooked pumpkin
3/4 cup sugar
1/2 tsp. salt
1 tsp. ground cinnamon
1/2 tsp. ground ginger
1/4 tsp. ground cloves
1 1/2 cups evaporated milk
1/2 recipe Basic Piecrust (p. 459)

Preheat oven to 425° F.

Blend together all ingredients except piecrust in order given. Prepare pie dough according to instructions and line a 9-inch pie pan with it. Pour filling into pie shell. Bake for 15 minutes, then reduce heat to 350°. Bake for 45 minutes more.

MAKES 8 SERVINGS.

ST. ANTHONY FALLS SALT PORK AND APPLE PIE

A New Englander who came to Minnesota as a girl in 1856 wrote down this recipe sixty years later: "You cut the pork so thin you can almost see through it. Cover the bottom of a pie tin with it, then cut the apples up on top of this. Put two thin crusts one on top the other over this, then when cooked, turn upside down in a dish and serve with hard sauce. This recipe," she added, "is over a hundred years old but nothing can beat it."

8 to 10 tart cooking apples
3/4 cup maple sugar or brown or white sugar
1/2 tsp. ground cinnamon
1/2 tsp. grated nutmeg
1 Tbs. flour
salt
8 to 10 postage-stamp-size slices of salt pork
1/2 recipe Basic Piecrust (p. 459)

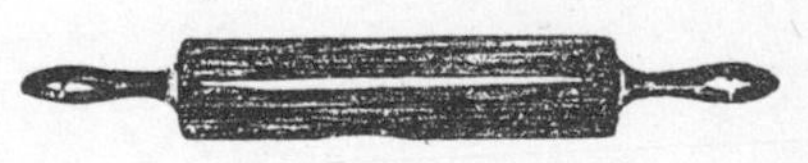

Preheat oven to 450° F.

Peel and core apples and slice very thin; spread slices in bottom of a deep pie dish. Sprinkle with sugar, cinnamon, nutmeg, flour, and very little salt. Arrange salt pork slices on top; if they are sufficiently thin, they will disappear, leaving nothing but an ineffable old-fashioned flavor. Prepare dough according to instructions and roll it out. Cover pork and apples with pastry dough and pinch down edges; make slits in dough to allow steam to escape. Bake for 10 minutes, then reduce heat to 350° and continue baking for 30 to 40 minutes more.

MAKES 8 SERVINGS.

CONNECTICUT MAPLE-TOPPED SQUASH PIE

1/2 recipe Basic Piecrust (p. 459)
3 eggs, well beaten
3/4 cup brown sugar
1 tsp. salt
1/2 tsp. ground cinnamon
1/2 tsp. freshly grated nutmeg
1/2 tsp. ground ginger
2 cups milk, hot
2 cups cooked winter squash, strained

GARNISH:
1 cup heavy cream
1/4 cup maple syrup

Preheat oven to 450° F.
Prepare pie dough according to instructions, and line a 9-inch pie pan with it, fluting the edges with your fingers. Mix together eggs, brown sugar, salt, cinnamon, nutmeg, and ginger, then gradually stir in milk and squash. Pour into uncooked pie shell and bake for 10 minutes; reduce heat to 325° and bake for 30 minutes more. Remove from oven and let cool. Whip heavy cream until peaks form, then carefully pour syrup in a fine stream over whipped cream, turning cream to fold in syrup. Spread lightly over pie in swirls.

MAKES 6 SERVINGS.

SWEET POTATO PIE

1 1/2 cup mashed cooked sweet potatoes
4 eggs
1/3 cup sugar
2/3 cup milk
1/3 cup orange juice
2 Tbs. honey
pinch of salt
2 Tbs. applejack or brandy
1/2 recipe Basic Piecrust (p. 459)
13 pecan halves

GARNISH:
1 cup heavy cream
1 to 2 tsp. sugar
1 Tbs. grated orange rind
1 Tbs. applejack

Preheat oven to 450° F.
Make sure sweet potatoes are free of lumps. Beat eggs until very light, then add sugar and sweet potatoes, stirring until well mixed. Stir in milk, orange juice, honey, and salt, then stir in applejack or brandy. Prepare pie dough according to instructions and line a 9-inch pie pan with pastry. Pour in mixture and bake for 10 minutes. Reduce heat to 350° and bake for 30 minutes more. While pie is hot, put 1 pecan half in center and arrange other nuts around edge.

Make the garnish: Beat cream over ice until it peaks, then beat in sugar, grated orange rind, and applejack. Use as garnish for each wedge of pie cut.

MAKES 6 SERVINGS.

TYLER PUDDING PIE

A recipe popular for many decades in Virginia and other parts of the South, Tyler pudding pie was named for President John Tyler and has been made by so many generations of Tyler women that each of several variations is said to be authentic. Whether made by Miss Mary Lee Tyler of Haymarket, Virginia, by a granddaughter in Richmond, a great-granddaughter in Louisville, Kentucky, or a relative in Washington, D.C., the Tyler dessert has been extolled as "a culinary masterpiece." If it isn't truly that, it is characteristic of Southern plantation food and a fitting end to a good meal. "Rich?" asked Harriet Ross Colquitt in presenting her Savannah version. "Of course, but was it not presidential fare?"

3/4 cup white sugar
3/4 cup granulated brown sugar
1/4 lb. (1 stick) butter
1/2 cup heavy cream
3 eggs
1 tsp. vanilla extract
1 partially baked 9-in. pie shell (see p. 459)
2 Tbs. grated coconut

Preheat oven to 450° F.

In the top part of a double boiler over simmering water, mix both sugars together; add butter in pieces, then cream, and heat until butter has melted. Beat well, then slowly pour the warm mixture into them, continuing to beat. Add vanilla and turn into partially baked shell. Bake for 35 minutes, the sprinkle coconut over the top and bake for another 5 minutes more or until coconut is lightly toasted.

MAKES 6 SERVINGS.

KEY WEST PAPAYA AND PINEAPPLE TART

1 papaya
2 slices of fresh pineapple (1/2 in. thick each)
1/2 cup sugar
1/2 cup water
2 limes
1/3 cup apricot jam
1 10-in. pie shell, baked with a coating of apricot jam (see p. 459)

Peel papaya, split into halves, scoop out seeds, and slice flesh into 1/4-inch strips. Cut pineapple slices into small wedges. Put sugar and water into a saucepan, bring slowly to a boil and cook for 1 minutes, then remove from heat. Add juice of 1 1/2 limes and steep papaya strips 10 minutes in this syrup. Cut remaining 1/2 lime into very thin slices and cut slices into halves. Add pineapple wedges to syrup and let stand for 15 to 20 minutes. Remove pineapple and papaya pieces from syrup and add lime slices to it; boil syrup for 3 or 4 minutes and remove lime slices with a slotted spoon. Combine apricot jam with half of remaining syrup and boil for about 5 minutes, or until reduced to a glaze and quite thick. Arrange papaya strips as spokes in bottom of prebaked pie shell. Fill spaces in between with pineapple wedges and slivers of lime. Spoon apricot glaze over all. Serve cool, but do not refrigerate.

MAKES 8 TO 10 SERVINGS.

PLUM-GUAVA LATTICEWORK TART

CRUST:

1 cup all-purpose flour
pinch salt
pinch sugar
6 Tbs. (3/4 stick) butter
2 Tbs. vegetable shortening or lard
3 Tbs. ice water

FILLING:

about 1/3 cup guava jelly
12 small fresh plums, cut into halves and pitted
1 tsp. sugar
1 tsp. flour
heavy cream (optional)

*Preheat oven to 425° F.**

Mix dough lightly and refrigerate for at least 2 hours before rolling out to a very thin sheet.* Line an 8-inch pie pan with a thin layer of dough. Spread about half of guava jelly evenly on bottom. Arrange halved pitted plums, skin side down, over the bottom, fitting them in snugly. Put a little jelly in center of each half plum, then sprinkle with mixture of sugar and flour. Roll out remnants of dough left from lining pie pan, and cut into strips. Make loose latticework across top of tart and pinch down ends to join with bottom pastry. Bake for 15 minutes, then reduce heat to 350° and bake for 20 minutes more. Serve warm with heavy cream if desired.

MAKES 6 SERVINGS.

RHUBARB AND STRAWBERRY TART

1/3 cup currant jelly
1 10-in. pie shell, baked with a coating of currant jelly (see p. 459)
2 lb. rhubarb
1 cup sugar
1 tsp. cornstarch
1 1/2 pt. fresh strawberries

GARNISH:

1 cup whipped cream flavored with 1 tsp. sugar and 1 to 2 Tbs. strawberry or other liqueur

Preheat oven to 375° F.

Melt currant jelly in a saucepan and brush bottom of baked pie crust with some melted jelly, reserving rest. Cut rhubarb into large chunks and place in a casserole; sprinkle sugar mixed with cornstarch over, and cover the casserole. Bake for 20 to 25 minutes, or until fruit is soft but not mushy. Remove rhubarb with a slotted spoon and place in cooled pie shell. Add rhubarb juice to remaining currant jelly and cook over medium-high heat until it forms a thick syrup. Remove stems of strawberries and cut them into halves, then arrange them, rounded side up, over rhubarb. Brush strawberries generously with syrup, letting it penetrate to rhubarb underneath. Let the tart cool, but do not refrigerate. Serve with flavored whipped cream spooned on in strips or piped through a pastry tube over the fruit.

MAKES 8 TO 10 SERVINGS.

BANANA COOKIES

In *The Notions of a Travelling Bachelor*, James Fenimore Cooper listed bananas among tropical fruits "as common as need be" in New York markets during the 1830s. But the great popularity of the fruit in the United States had to wait until the improvement of refrigeration and transportation facilities, a generation or so after Captain Lorenzo Baker of Wellfleet in 1870 brought the first ship loaded exclusively with bananas into Boston harbor. Breads, pies, and cakes made with bananas—and cookies, too—were soon thereafter being turned out by innovative American cooks. A delicious variation of traditional banana cookies results when a little finely minced candied gingerroot is scattered over the tops just before baking. The sharp ginger gives a pungent accent to the banana flavor.

2 large ripe bananas (about 1 cup)
2/3 cup (1 stick plus 2 2/3 Tbs.) butter, softened
1 cup sugar
1 tsp. vanilla extract
2 eggs
2 1/4 cups flour
2 tsp. baking powder
1/4 tsp. baking soda
3/4 tsp. salt

TOPPING:
mixed ground cinnamon and sugar
3 Tbs. finely chopped candied ginger

Preheat oven to 400° F.

Mash bananas. Cream butter and sugar together, beating until fluffy, then blend in vanilla. Stir in bananas, then eggs, 1 at a time, beating well after each addition. Sift dry ingredients together, then stir into batter. Scoop up batter with a teaspoon and drop onto ungreased cookie sheets. Sprinkle liberally with cinnamon and sugar or candied gingerroot. Bake for 12 minutes, then remove to racks to cool.

MAKES ABOUT 4 DOZEN.

CHARLESTON BENNE SEED WAFERS

Benne seeds, brought over from Africa during slave-trading days, are known by most Americans as sesame; imaginative black cooks used them in many ways.

1 cup flour
1/2 tsp. baking powder
1/4 tsp. salt
3/4 cup (1 1/2 sticks) butter, softened
2 cups brown sugar
2 eggs, beaten
1 tsp. vanilla extract
3/4 cup sesame seeds

Preheat oven to 325° F.
Sift flour, baking powder, and salt together. Cream butter and gradually add brown sugar, beating constantly until it is all absorbed and mixture is fluffy. Beat in eggs, then vanilla. In a large skillet toast sesame seeds, shaking and stirring constantly to distribute heat evenly, until they turn taffy color. Add them to batter. Oil a large cookie sheet. Drop batter by the teaspoonful, leaving at least 1 1/2 inches between the drops on the cookie sheet for batter to spread; bake in upper third of oven for 10 minutes, *only one sheet at a time.* Let wafers cool for about 1 minute, then scrape them up briskly but gently with a spatula and let cool on wire racks. Repeat until batter is all used.

MAKES ABOUT 6 DOZEN.

NINTH-FLOOR BROWNIES

Brownies have been made on the ninth floor of a certain apartment building in Manhattan for probably as many years as that vintage structure has stood. Nobody seems to know the origin of this American confection, but they vary from one region to another, sometimes characterized by an almost fudgelike consistency. In the mid-1970s a health restaurant long famous in Corona del Mar, California, added to its reputation by offering apricot brownies. The true brownie is very "New World" in its use of chocolate, which has been available to cooks since early colonial days.

1/4 lb. (1 stick) butter
2 oz. unsweetened chocolate
1 cup sugar
2 eggs, slightly beaten
1 tsp. vanilla extract
1/2 cup flour
pinch of salt
1/2 cup chopped walnuts

Preheat oven to 325° F.
Melt butter with chocolate in the top part of a double boiler and mix well over hot water. Sift sugar and stir in eggs, then fold into chocolate mixture

along with vanilla. Stir in flour, a little at a time, along with salt. Finally stir in walnuts. Pour this batter into a greased 9-inch square pan. Bake for about 30 minutes; don't bake too long, for brownies should be slightly moist and chewy and never dry.

MAKES 16 TO 24 SQUARES.

DATE ICEBOX COOKIES

1/4 lb. (1 stick) butter, softened
2 cups brown sugar
2 eggs, well beaten
1 cup finely chopped nutmeats
1 cup dates, chopped
3 1/2 cups flour
1 tsp. baking soda
1 tsp. salt
1 tsp. vanilla extract

Preheat oven to 375° F.

Cream butter and sugar, gradually adding a little of each and beating until smooth. Add eggs, nuts, and dates. Sift flour, baking soda, and salt together, then add to other ingredients. Add vanilla and stir well. Turn dough out onto a floured surface, divide into halves, and shape 2 long sausagelike rolls. Wrap each in floured wax paper and refrigerate for several hours. Remove from refrigerator and cut into slices about 1/8 inch thick. Place slices on a greased cookie sheet and bake for 10 minutes.

MAKES ABOUT 50.

LOUISE SHELDON'S FUDGE BARS

Just before the turn of the century the word *fudge*, which until then was used almost entirely to connote deceit of one kind or another, was given a new definition as the term for a candy mixture that in New England was often made with maple syrup. As the availability of chocolate increased throughout the country, that flavor became the most popular, resulting in many variations, such as fudge bars or the Wellesley fudge cake, long a campus favorite in Massachusetts.

1 cup flour
1 tsp. baking powder
1/8 tsp. salt
3 Tbs. butter
2 oz. unsweetened chocolate
1 cup sugar
1 egg, well beaten
1/2 cup chopped nutmeats
1 tsp. vanilla extract

Preheat oven to 375° F.

Sift together flour, baking powder, and salt. Melt butter with chocolate over very low heat. Beat sugar into egg; stir in melted chocolate and butter, then sifted flour. Stir in nuts and vanilla and mix well. Spread batter very thin on a greased 17-by-14-inch baking sheet, and bake for 20 minutes or less. When cool, cut into squares.

MAKES ABOUT 2 DOZEN.

OATCAKES

2 3/4 cups rolled oats
1/4 lb. (1 stick) butter, softened
1/3 cup condensed milk
1/2 tsp. salt
1/4 cup pure maple syrup

Preheat oven to 325° F.

Make oatmeal flour by spinning oats in a blender until they have the consistency of stone-ground flour. Transfer to a mixing bowl and add butter with a pastry blender or mix with your fingers. Mix in condensed milk, salt, and maple syrup. When well mixed, spread onto a generously buttered pan (about 6 by 10 inches). Bake for 15 to 20 minutes, or until oatcake shrinks from the sides and is slightly browned on top. Remove and immediately cut into 18 cakes, but let cool in the pan before trying to remove the pieces; they will be crumbly. Eat still slightly warm; if kept, spread with a little butter and reheat in a medium oven for 4 or 5 minutes. They can also be kept frozen. Delicious for tea.

MAKES 18 THIN CAKES.

PEANUT BUTTER COOKIES

The flavor improves when freshly roasted peanuts are shelled, peeled, and chopped, then combined with freshly ground peanut butter, as the original recipes dictate. But as long as the ingredients are the best available, this recipe results in cookies that are perhaps more exclusively American than any others.

1 cup peanut butter
1/4 lb. (1 stick) butter, softened
2 tsp. vanilla extract
1/2 cup light brown sugar
1 cup honey
2 eggs
2 1/2 cups flour
1 tsp. baking soda
1 cup unroasted peanuts, chopped fine

Preheat oven to 375° F.

Cream together peanut butter and butter; add vanilla. Beat in sugar and honey, then stir in eggs, 1 at a time; beat until batter is smooth and light. Sift flour and baking soda together and stir into batter, then finally fold in peanuts. Scoop up batter with a dessert spoon and drop onto lightly greased cookie sheets. Press down with the flat of a fork to smooth the top of each mound, making cookies about 1/3 inch in height. Bake for 12 minutes.

MAKES ABOUT 6 DOZEN.

WINTER SQUASH COOKIES

All the varieties of winter squashes, including pumpkin, turn up often in old recipes for cookies and sweets and always seem to add a good color and special texture.

3/4 cup (1 1/2 sticks) butter, softened
3/4 cup sugar
1 cup grated raw winter squash or carrot
1 large egg
grated rind of 1 orange
2 cups flour
2 tsp. baking powder
1/2 tsp. salt

Preheat oven to 375° F.

Cream butter, then add sugar gradually, creaming until smooth. Beat in grated vegetable and egg and continue beating until light. Sift dry ingredients into this batter, a little at a time, and mix well. Drop the batter from a teaspoon onto well-greased cookie sheets, pressing the mounds down lightly with your fingers. Bake for 12 to 15 minutes, or until golden brown at the edges. Remove while warm to wire racks to cool.

MAKES ALMOST 40 SMALL COOKIES.

BLUEBERRY BREAD PUDDING

This dessert may also be made with raspberries, huckleberries, or blackberries.

1 pt. blueberries
2 Tbs. water
1/3 cup, more or less, sugar
about 1/4 loaf homemade white bread, 1 or 2 days old
1 to 2 Tbs. butter
heavy cream

Place picked-over berries in a heavy saucepan with water and sugar and bring slowly to a boil. Let simmer for 5 to 10 minutes, depending upon ripeness of berries, until they are soft but still holding their shape. Meanwhile slice the bread very thin; if it is presliced, split slices into halves; remove crusts and butter one side lightly. Line a small bowl (less than 3 cups) with bread slices, buttered side down, cutting and shaping more slices to press in and fit snugly so that bottom and sides are lined and leave no gaps. Spoon berries into bread-lined bowl, reserving some of juice, and fold bread slices over, adding a slice to cover top completely. If juice does not saturate all of bread, spoon some of reserve over top. Set a saucer on top and press down. Refrigerate bowl for at least 6 hours. Serve with heavy cream.

MAKES 4 SERVINGS.

BROWN SUGAR PUDDING

3 slices of homemade white bread
2 Tbs. butter
1 1/2 cups brown sugar
2 1/2 cups milk
2 eggs
1 tsp. vanilla extract
pinch of salt
1/2 tsp. grated nutmeg
1/2 tsp. ground cinnamon
heavy cream

Preheat oven to 350° F.

Trim crusts from bread and butter well on both sides. Sprinkle brown sugar over the bottom of a buttered 1-quart casserole. Warm milk, beat in eggs, and add vanilla and salt. Tear bread into small pieces and distribute over sugar, then add warmed milk-egg mixture. Sprinkle spices on top and bake for 45 minutes. Serve warm or chilled with heavy cream.

MAKES 4 SERVINGS.

HOMINY PUDDING WITH APRICOTS

3/4 cup dried apricots, chopped
2 Tbs. butter
2 cups milk, hot
1 cup cooked hominy grits
1/4 cup sugar
1/4 tsp. salt
1/4 cup slivered almonds
2 eggs, well beaten
1/8 tsp. ground cinnamon

Preheat oven to 350° F.

Soak apricots in water to cover for 30 minutes, or until soft. Melt half the butter in hot milk; stir in cooked grits. Combine sugar, salt, almonds, and apricots with eggs. Add cinnamon, then stir slowly into milk mixture. Butter a 1-quart casserole with remaining butter, fill with mixture, then set casserole in a pan of hot water and bake for 45 to 50 minutes.

MAKES 4 SERVINGS.

LENNOX HILL CHARLOTTE RUSSE

Charlotte Russe may have been created by the great French confectioner Carême; it may have received its appellation because it resembled a French hat style called *charlotte*, which, as Parisians said, was "garnished with shuttlecocks." But Charlotte Russe became the American hostess's most festive dessert in the latter part of the nineteenth century. Six Southern ladies, contributing to *Housekeeping in Old Virginia*, published in 1879, each gave their own versions, each as different as plantation hostesses could be.

12 to 18 ladyfingers
1/2 cup Madeira
2 envelopes unflavored gelatin
2 to 3 Tbs. cold water
1 qt. heavy cream
3/4 cup confectioner's sugar
1 tsp. vanilla extract
1/4 cup slivered almonds, toasted (optional)
or
1/4 cup crumbled macaroons (optional)

Line a 2-qt. glass bowl with ladyfingers. Sprinkle with about half of the Madeira to help make them adhere. Soften gelatin in water and the rest of the Madeira. Whip cream in a metal bowl over ice; when thickened, whip in sugar and finally the softened gelatin. Add vanilla. Pile the cream mixture into the lined bowl. Chill for at least 8 hours. Unmold. If desired, sprinkle almonds or macaroons over the top before serving.

MAKES 6 TO 8 SERVINGS.

MAPLE CRÈME BRÛLÉE

Crème brûlée had its origins in the grilled cream that was a seventeenth-century favorite at King's College, Cambridge. It appeared in at least one early American cookbook as Burnt Cream and is said to have been prepared often by Thomas Jefferson's cook, Julien. In Saint Louis and on the West Coast toasted California almonds are added and sometimes the local brandy or sherry. A Montpelier, Vermont, cook devised this truly American recipe.

6 egg yolks
1/4 cup vanilla sugar
1 cup milk, scalded
3/4 cup heavy cream, scalded
1/4 to 1/3 cup maple sugar

Beat egg yolks and add vanilla sugar, continuing to beat for 2 or 3 minutes. Gradually add milk and cream in a steady stream, then put mixture into a heavy saucepan over very low heat, or in the top part of a double boiler over simmering water, and stir continuously as mixture slowly thickens; it must not boil and should not exceed 165° F. Remove from heat when custard coats the spoon. Let cool, beating several times, then turn into a buttered shallow heatproof 1-quart casserole and chill thoroughly, for at least 4 hours, or overnight. Remove from refrigerator. Just before serving, sprinkle maple sugar over top to make a layer 1/3 inch thick. Run under broiler until sugar bubbles. Chill again briefly and serve from baking dish.

MAKES 4 TO 6 SERVINGS.

MAPLE-FLAVORED INDIAN PUDDING

In early Ohio, when some of the eastern counties were known as the Western Reserve, a common frontier dish, adapted by pioneer cooks from the Indians, was a mixture of cornmeal and maple syrup cooked with wild fruits or berries. With eggs and milk added, maple-flavored Indian pudding can be delicious, either with or without fruits but with a dollop of rich cream on top. One of the best ways to achieve at least a semblance of old-fashioned, heavy, unpasteurized cream is to mix "heavy cream" from store or milkman with cultured sour cream, as indicated in the recipe. It must, however, be made ahead of time and left to mature in the refrigerator an hour or more.

GARNISH:

2/3 cup sour cream
1 1/3 cups heavy cream

5 Tbs. yellow cornmeal
1 qt. milk, scalded
2 Tbs. butter, melted
1 cup maple syrup
2 eggs, beaten
1 tsp. ground cinnamon
3/4 tsp. ground ginger
1 tsp. salt
1 cup cold milk

Preheat oven to 300° F.

Make the garnish ahead of time: Shake sour cream and heavy cream together in a bottle and set aside in a warm place for 2 hours, then put in refrigerator for 1 hour or more.

Add cornmeal to scalded milk in a saucepan, stirring constantly to make sure no lumps form; continue cooking and stirring over low heat until thickened. Off the heat, stir in butter, maple syrup, eggs, cinnamon, ginger, and salt. Pour into a buttered 2-quart baking dish and bake for about 45 minutes. Stir pudding and whisk in cold milk, then continue baking for about 1 hour more. Serve pudding warm and top each serving with heavy or slightly whipped cream.

MAKES 8 TO 10 SERVINGS.

LEMON PUDDING

2 Tbs. butter, softened
1 cup sugar
grated rind of 1 lemon
juice of 1 lemon
pinch of salt
3 Tbs. flour
1 cup milk
2 large eggs
3/4 cup heavy cream (optional)

Preheat oven to 350° F.

Cream butter and work in sugar until all is absorbed. Add lemon rind, lemon juice, and salt. Stir in the flour alternately with the milk, blending until smooth. Separate eggs; add yolks to mixture and blend thoroughly. Beat egg whites until they form soft peaks, then fold in. Turn pudding into a 1-quart baking dish, set dish in a pan of hot water, and bake for 40 minutes. Serve tepid, or chilled with thick cream.

MAKES 4 TO 6 SERVINGS.

BESS TRUMAN'S OZARK PUDDING

The food preferred by President Truman and his wife was as American as it could be. When Winston Churchill came to Fulton, in the Trumans' home state, to make his "Iron Curtain" speech, he was the guest of honor at a dinner for which the menu included the famous Missouri country ham and this plain but wonderful dessert.

1 egg, beaten
3/4 cup, sugar
1/3 cup flour
1 1/4 tsp. baking powder
pinch of salt
1 medium-size apple, peeled, cored, and chopped
1/2 cup chopped walnuts or mixed nuts
1 tsp. vanilla extract
1 cup heavy cream, whipped
3 to 4 Tbs. rum

Preheat oven to 325° F.

Put egg and sugar into a mixing bowl and beat until very light. In another bowl sift together flour, baking powder, and salt. Blend this well with egg mixture and fold in apple, walnuts, and vanilla. Pour into a greased shallow baking dish and bake for 30 minutes; let cool. Stir rum into whipped cream. Serve pudding garnished with whipped cream

MAKES 8 SERVINGS.

PHYLLIS'S ORANGE JELLY

2 envelopes unflavored gelatin
1/2 cup cold water
1 3/4 cups boiling water
3/4 cup sugar
1 1/2 cups freshly squeezed orange juice
juice of 1 lemon
1 bunch of green seedless grapes (1 lb. or less), peeled

GARNISH:

1 cup lightly whipped cream (optional)
Cointreau

Dissolve gelatin in cold water, then pour on boiling water and mix well. Add sugar and orange and lemon juices, blending thoroughly. Spread grapes around a 1-quart mold, then pour the liquid jelly on top. Let cool, then set in the refrigerator to chill thoroughly. Serve turned out if you wish and garnished with lightly whipped cream flavored with a little Cointreau.

MAKES 6 SERVINGS.

OHIO RIVER PERSIMMON-BUTTERMILK PUDDING

1 large, not-too-ripe persimmon
1 1/2 cups buttermilk
1 cup sugar
2 Tbs. butter, melted
2 eggs, well beaten until foamy
1 cup all-purpose flour
1 tsp. baking soda
1 tsp. baking powder
1/4 tsp. salt
1/2 tsp. ground cinnamon
1/2 tsp. freshly grated nutmeg
whipped cream (optional)

Preheat oven to 450° F.

Peel persimmon, cut into small pieces, and spin in a blender with buttermilk until fruit is puréed and smooth. Add sugar and butter and stir well; stir in eggs. Sift dry ingredients into a large bowl and beat in fruit mixture, a little at a time, until well blended. Pour into a high-sided 1 1/2-quart baking dish. Bake for 15 minutes, then reduce heat to 375° and bake for 30 minutes more. Pudding should be nicely puffed up and browned. Serve warm with whipped cream. Also good cold with custard sauce mixed with a little sherry.

MAKES 6 TO 8 SERVINGS.

PINEAPPLE-LIME BAVARIAN CREAM

3 eggs
grated rind of 1 lime
juice of 1 lime
2/3 cup syrup from canned pineapple
1 to 2 Tbs. wine jelly (optional)
1 envelope unflavored gelatin
1/3 cup cold water
2/3 cup pineapple chunks, or 3 slices canned pineapple, cut into chunks
1/2 cup heavy cream

GARNISH:
1/2 cup whipped cream (optional)
1 or 2 pineapple slices (optional)

Separate eggs and beat yolks. Add lime rind and juice to egg yolks. Boil pineapple syrup, adding wine jelly if you have some (wine jelly with ground ginger is particularly delicious). When syrup is reduced to 1/2 cup, remove from heat and pour, in a slow steady stream, into the yolk mixture, stirring constantly. Place in the top part of a double boiler over simmering water and heat, continuing to stir, until thickened. Remove from heat. Soften gelatin in cold water and stir into the hot custard, then add pineapple chunks; let cool. Chill custard while you beat first the cream until stiff and then, in a separate bowl, the egg whites with salt until they form soft peaks. Fold both into the pineapple custard. Pour into a 1-quart ring mold or 6 sherbet glasses and refrigerate for 6 to 8 hours if Bavarian cream is to be unmolded, for only 3 or 4 hours if served in individual glasses. The center of the mold can be filled with whipped cream and additional pineapple slices cut into whatever shape you want.

MAKES 6 SERVINGS.

SOUTHERN RICE-FRUIT PUDDING

2 cups cooked rice
1 egg, beaten
1/2 cup sugar
2 cups half-and-half or rich milk
1/2 cup chopped dried apricots
1/2 cup chopped dates
1/2 cup chopped pecans
2 or 3 pieces of candied gingerroot, chopped
1/4 tsp. freshly grated nutmeg
1/2 tsp. vanilla extract
2 Tbs. butter, melted
1 recipe Lemon and Wine Sauce *(p. 485)*

Preheat oven to 350° F.

Put rice into a large mixing bowl. Combine egg and sugar and stir into rice. Add half-and-half, apricots, dates, pecans, and candied gingerroot, then grate in about 1/4 teaspoon nutmeg. Add vanilla and butter and stir well.

Pour into a greased 1 1/2-quart baking dish and bake for about 1 hour, or until pudding is firm in the center. Meanwhile prepare lemon and wine sauce and serve with sauce.

MAKES 6 SERVINGS.

WELSH-AMERICAN SNOWDON PUDDING

Welsh Americans include the Virginia-born father of Thomas Jefferson, and numbers of them live in every part of the country. This recipe is a part of the heritage of family cooks in Minnesota and Wisconsin, and the accent of lemon marmalade that distinguishes it from other steamed puddings makes it worth the effort. If necessary, an orange marmalade can be substituted.

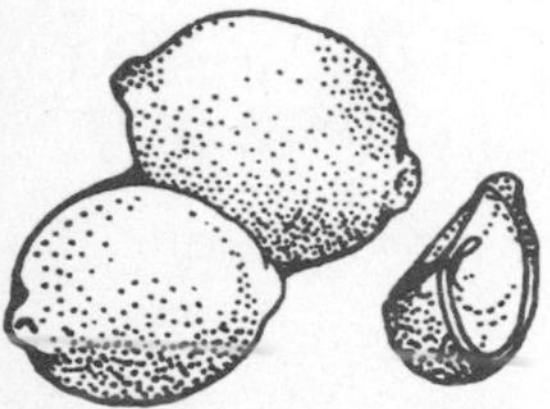

1/2 cup raisins
butter
1 cup bread crumbs
1 cup chopped suet
3 Tbs. flour
3/4 cup lemon marmalade
3/4 cup light brown sugar
6 eggs, well beaten
grated rind of 2 lemons
1 recipe Lemon and Wine Sauce (opposite)

Cut raisins into halves with a very sharp knife. Butter a 2-quart mold and press raisins, cut side down, into butter, making a decorative pattern. Stir together bread crumbs, suet, flour; then stir in marmalade, sugar, eggs, and lemon rind. Beat well, pour into mold, and cover with wax paper and a lightly floured cloth; secure with a length of string. Place filled mold on a wire rack in a kettle and pour in boiling water to reach three-quarters the way up mold. Cover and steam for 2 hours. Meanwhile prepare lemon and wine sauce and serve with sauce.

MAKES 8 TO 10 SERVINGS.

GEORGIA SWEET POTATO PUDDING

1/4 cup sugar
1/2 cup cane syrup
1/2 cup milk
2 cups grated raw sweet potatoes
1/4 tsp. ground cloves
1/2 tsp. ground allspice
2/3 tsp. ground cinnamon
4 Tbs. (1/2 stick) butter
2 small eggs, beaten
1 recipe Lemon and Wine Sauce (opposite)

Preheat oven to 375° F.

Mix all ingredients except butter and eggs. Put butter into a flameproof casserole and cook over low heat to melt. Beat eggs into sweet potato mixture. When butter is melted, pour mixture into casserole and stir until it is hot. Bake for 20 minutes, then stir crust developing on sides and bottom into pudding. Repeat twice more before removing casserole after pudding has baked a total of 40 to 45 minutes. Meanwhile prepare lemon and wine sauce and serve with sauce.

MAKES ABOUT 6 SERVINGS.

LEMON AND WINE SAUCE

1/2 cup sugar
2 Tbs. cornstarch
1 1/2 cups water
1 lemon
4 Tbs. (1/2 stick) butter
1/2 cup sherry

Put sugar, cornstarch, and water into the top part of a double boiler and cook over boiling water, stirring constantly for 10 minutes. Grate half of lemon rind, then squeeze all of juice. Remove thickened sugar mixture from heat and stir in lemon rind and juice along with butter and wine. Serve warm.

MAKES ABOUT 2 CUPS.

AVOCADO ICE CREAM

1 cup milk
1 cup light cream
1/2 cup sugar
3 egg yolks, well beaten
1 cup mashed ripe avocado
1/2 cup chopped pistachio nuts

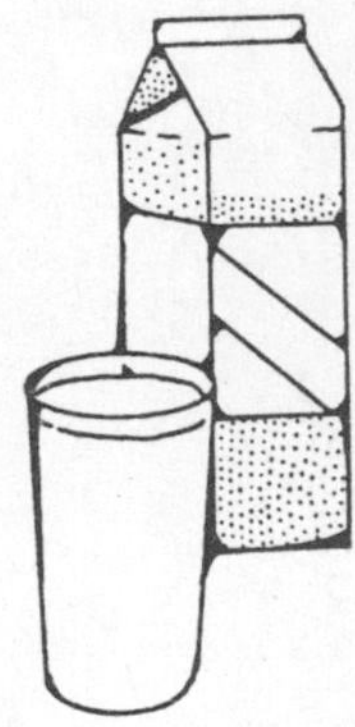

Combine milk, cream, and sugar and bring to a boil, stirring constantly. Pour over egg yolks and blend well. Add avocado and pistachios, stirring until smooth. Let cool, then turn into refrigerator trays; freeze. When firm, put into a chilled bowl and beat until smooth. Return to trays and refreeze. Repeat beating in chilled bowl. Freeze for 2 hours more and serve.

MAKES ABOUT 1 1/2 QUARTS.

OLD DOMINION GREENGAGE ICE CREAM

Some time after small, green, delicious plums were first cultivated in England, they acquired the surname of Sir William Gage, and colonial plum orchards were started in Virginia before the Revolution. Mrs. Raffold's cookbook provided Old Dominion ladies with a recipe for ice cream that required no mechanical freezer, and her cookbook also told them how to make greengage preserves. The two combined became a favorite dessert at the King's Arms in Williamsburg.

1 jar (11 1/2 oz.) greengage preserves
juice of 2 small lemons
1 cup sugar
1/4 tsp. salt
3 cups heavy cream
3 cups milk

Mix all ingredients and pour into a flat freezer container. Freeze for 2 hours. Remove from freezer and beat. Return to freezer and continue freezing. Remove and beat again. Freeze until firm.

MAKES 2 QUARTS.

PLUM PUDDING ICE CREAM

Frances Parkinson Keyes, a transplanted Virginian who lived in New England and later spent much time in Louisiana, was a novelist with a probing interest in American food; she wrote once of finding an old newspaper recipe for a Christmas dinner ice cream invented by Yankee cooks. This is the way plum pudding ice cream was made for a twentieth-century holiday:

1 cup raisins
1/2 cup chopped candied orange rind or dried currants
applejack or other brandy
1 cup sugar
4 oz. unsweetened chocolate
1 qt. buttermilk
3/4 tsp. ground cloves
3/4 tsp. ground cinnamon
1 tsp. vanilla extract
4 egg whites

A day ahead, put fruits into a bowl and barely cover with applejack; set aside to macerate at least overnight; most of liquid should be absorbed. Put sugar, chocolate, and about 3 tablespoons of buttermilk into a saucepan or the top part of a double boiler over hot water and heat just enough to melt chocolate and meld it with sugar; stir in cloves, cinnamon, and vanilla. Beat egg whites until peaks form. Combine sugar-chocolate mixture with remaining buttermilk, then fold in egg whites. Pour into freezer containers and freeze for about 3 hours, then stir well. Repeat at 3-hour intervals twice.

MAKES 12 OR MORE SERVINGS.

LEMON-ORANGE-BANANA SHERBET

1 1/2 cups sugar
2 1/4 cups water
juice of 2 1/2 lemons (about 1/3 cup)
juice of 2 1/2 oranges (about 1 cup)
2 bananas, sliced
1 1/2 tsp. mixed grated orange and lemon rind

Put sugar and water into a saucepan, mix well, and bring to a boil, then let simmer just long enough to dissolve sugar. Let cool. Put half of juices and half of bananas in a blender and spin until bananas are puréed; repeat. Pour into a large bowl and mix well with sugar syrup, adding grated rind. Beat thoroughly, then pour into a 2-quart freezer container. Cover and freeze for about 1 hour, or until mushy. Remove and beat well before returning to freezer for 30 minutes. When sherbet is again mushy, beat again and return to freezer until it is firm.

MAKES ABOUT 1 QUART.

PUMPKIN MERINGUE ICE CREAM PIE

1 1/2 cups heavy cream
3 egg yolks
3/4 cup brown sugar
1 scant Tbs. cornstarch
pinch of salt
1 1/4 cups mashed cooked pumpkin
3/4 tsp. ground ginger
3/4 tsp. ground cinnamon
3/4 tsp. grated nutmeg
3/4 tsp. grated lemon rind
2 Tbs. dark rum
1 1/2 cups heavy cream, whipped
3/4 cup finely chopped walnuts
1/3 cup finely minced preserved gingerroot
1 prebaked 10-in. pie shell *(see p. 459)*

MERINGUE:
2 egg whites
pinch of cream of tartar
scant 1/2 cup vanilla sugar

Scald cream. Beat yolks until lemon colored; stir in brown sugar and cornstarch, then add hot cream. Cook in top part of a double boiler over boiling water until custard begins to thicken (180° F), then stir in salt; remove from heat. Mix pumpkin with ginger, cinnamon, nutmeg, and lemon rind, then stir into custard. Beat mixture over ice while adding rum. When cool, fold in whipped cream, walnuts, and gingerroot. Freeze in ice cream freezer, or in a metal bowl in refrigerator freezing compartment. Beat twice during first 2 half-hour periods of freezing. Soften ice cream made in refrigerator by removing to lower shelf; when it reaches a stiff but spreadable consistency, fill pie shell and return to freezing compartment.

Just before serving, beat egg whites with cream of tartar until peaks form; add vanilla sugar gradually until mixture has firm meringue consistency. Spread meringue over ice cream, making sure edges are neatly sealed; put under broiler until lightly browned. Serve immediately.

MAKES 6 TO 8 SERVINGS.

VERMONT MAPLE PARFAIT

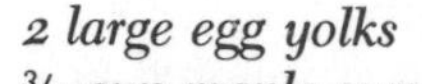

2 large egg yolks
3/4 cup maple syrup
2 cups heavy cream

GARNISH:
1/2 cup heavy cream, whipped
1/2 tsp. sugar
1 tsp. rum (optional)
1/3 cup chopped walnuts

Beat egg yolks in the top part of a double boiler until lemon colored. Heat maple syrup to boiling point, then pour it slowly into egg yolks, beating continuously. Cook over boiling water until eggs coat spoon (170° F). Cool mixture over ice, beating well; set aside. Over same ice beat 2 cups of heavy cream, preferably with a whisk, until stiff and doubled in volume. Fold in maple-egg mixture until well blended, then turn into parfait glasses, filling not quite full. Cover with plastic wrap and chill in freezer for at least 6 hours. Before serving, whip remaining 1/2 cup heavy cream and add sugar and rum. Spoon a little cream over each parfait glass and top with walnuts.

MAKES 8 SERVINGS.

ZABAGLIONE

An Englishman who went to Sicily intent upon devising his own recipe for sherry instead contrived to make the first Marsala. This led someone else to invent zabaglione; the word means eggnog in Italian, and the dish is so popular in the United States that the New York chef Albert Stockli took it one step further and served it ("especially to those who pass up rich cakes or tarts") as a foamy hot garnish for fruit, which he called Zabaglione Creole.

4 egg yolks
3 Tbs. sugar
1/2 cup Marsala
sliced berries, peaches, or apricots (optional)

In a large bowl that can be placed over hot water (a copper bowl is excellent), beat egg yolks and sugar together for 2 or 3 minutes until lemony colored and thick. Now place the bowl over a saucepan of barely simmering water and continue beating, preferably with a large whisk to allow for strokes that whip air into the egg mass; add Marsala and continue to beat steadily until mixture is warm and so frothy that it has tripled its original size. Spoon into high-stem glasses and serve immediately. Or arrange sliced berries, peaches, or apricots in glasses and pour zabaglione over.

MAKES 4 SERVINGS.

APPLE CRUNCH, OR DELIGHT–OR HEAVEN

Just about every American household had its favorite simple, crunchy apple dish in days when a complete meal wasn't complete without a homemade dessert. This was a favorite in our family, handed down by parents and cherished by our children. The dish went by any of the above names. It can be made with peaches, when in season, or with rhubarb (with additional sugar), but apples always rank first.

6 to 8 medium-size tart apples
sprinkling of grated nutmeg
1/2 tsp. ground cinnamon
1/2 cup, more or less, sugar

TOPPING:
2/3 cup flour
2/3 cup sugar
4 Tbs. (1/2 stick) butter

Preheat oven to 375° F.

Peel and core apples and cut into slices. Toss in a baking dish with nutmeg, cinnamon, and sugar; more or less may be added according to how sour or flavorful apples are.

Make the topping: Mix flour and sugar together. Cut butter into small pieces and blend lightly with fingertips into dry mixture. Sprinkle this crumblike mixture over apples. Bake for about 45 minutes, or until apples are bubbling over onto browned, crusty top.

MAKES 6 TO 8 SERVINGS.

APPLE DUMPLINGS

PASTRY:
1/4 lb. (1 stick) butter, chilled
1/4 cup lard, chilled
1 3/4 cups all-purpose flour
1 tsp. salt
6 Tbs. ice water
4 rather small, firm tart apples
4 tsp. brown sugar mixed with 4 tsp. butter, or
3 or 4 tsp. raisins, steeped in 2 Tbs. rum, plus 4 tsp. butter

SYRUP:
1 cup dark brown sugar
1 1/2 cups water
2 Tbs. butter
heavy or slightly whipped cream

*Preheat oven to 450° F.**

Prepare pastry by cutting butter and lard into flour; add salt and enough ice water to hold together. Chill for at least 30 minutes. Peel and core apples and spoon one of the two fillings into the centers, topping with butter to fill holes completely. Roll out pastry fairly thin. Place a stuffed apple on dough; roughly trim dough in a circle around apple so that there will be enough to cover apple when you draw it up. Pinch top together with a little water. If the folds seem too thick, trim them and seal seams with water. Repeat with the remaining apples and put them all in the refrigerator for about 20 minutes.* Mix syrup ingredients in a small saucepan and boil slowly for 5 or 6 minutes. Paint apples with syrup and quickly put in oven for 10 minutes; then reduce heat to 350° and bake for 35 minutes more. Continue to paint dough with syrup every 10 minutes while baking. Serve with thick or slightly whipped cream.

MAKES 4 SERVINGS.

JEANNETTE LOWENSTEIN'S BLINTZES

BATTER:

1 tsp. sugar
2 eggs
2 Tbs. vegetable oil
1 tsp. vanilla extract
1 cup milk
3/4 cup sifted flour
1/2 tsp. salt

FILLING:

1/2 lb. cottage cheese
1/4 lb. cream cheese
1 egg
2 Tbs. sugar
1/2 tsp. salt
1 tsp. vanilla extract
1/2 tsp. ground cinnamon
1/2 tsp. grated lemon rind
matzoh meal to thicken

1/4 lb. (1 stick) butter, melted
1 cup sour cream (optional)
ground cinnamon (optional)
confectioner's sugar (optional)

Beat all batter ingredients together until smooth, or spin in a blender for 1 minute or a little more. Refrigerate for at least 1 hour. Combine ingredients for filling, adding just enough matzoh meal to make mixture quite thick. Brush bottom of a 6- or 7-inch skillet with enough butter to cover lightly. Pour about 2 tablespoons batter into pan, tilting to spread batter evenly around bottom. Cook over medium heat for about 1 minute, or until lightly browned on one side only. Turn out, brown side up. Brush butter lightly into pan again and repeat, buttering and making blintzes until all the batter is used up. Pancakes may be stacked with layers of filling or, as each blintz is baked and turned out, place a spoonful of filling in center, fold up sides, and carefully roll. Before serving, brown rolls in butter. Add a dollop of sour cream to each hot blintz and dust with cinnamon; or, if you prefer, omit sour cream and dust with sugar and cinnamon.

MAKES 6 TO 8 SERVINGS.

WILD ISLAND BAKED BANANAS

4 bananas
2 Tbs. sweet butter
3 Tbs. brown sugar
1 lemon
sprinkling of shredded coconut (optional)
1/4 cup coconut liqueur or rum
heavy cream

Peel and split bananas and arrange them in 1 layer in a large ovenproof serving dish. Distribute dots of butter and the sugar on top, then squeeze the lemon over. If using coconut, sprinkle it over and add the liqueur or the rum. Place about 8 inches under a broiler; baste once or twice. Serve hot with thick cream.

MAKES 4 SERVINGS.

BANANAS BAKED WITH GUAVA JELLY

Some Key West cooks, and some in tropical Florida, have small home-grown, tart Cattley guavas from which they make excellent jelly. But the commercial jelly, available throughout America, makes an interesting dessert when served with cream cheese, and an even better one in this combination that is accented by coconut cream.

1 cup heavy cream
1/2 cup shredded unsweetened coconut
4 firm bananas
1/3 cup guava jelly
2 Tbs. butter
2 Tbs. rum, warmed (optional)

Preheat oven to 350° F.

Several hours ahead mix cream and coconut and set aside. Peel and slice bananas, and place them in a buttered baking dish. Distribute guava jelly over them and dot with butter. Bake for 20 minutes, turning once and spooning melted jelly over bananas. Serve warm with coconut cream, pouring flaming rum over the dish if desired.

MAKES 4 SERVINGS.

BANANAS FOSTER

For decades this characteristically New World concoction of fruit and ice cream has been a favorite dessert at Brennan's in New Orleans. It is common in many homes in the South, as well as in restaurants of some pretension in Miami and elsewhere. If you like chafing dish cookery, try this at the table.

4 Tbs. (1/2 stick) butter
1/3 cup brown sugar
1/2 tsp. ground cinnamon
4 ripe bananas, sliced lengthwise
1/2 cup banana liqueur
1/3 cup white rum
4 large scoops vanilla ice cream

In a skillet melt butter and stir in brown sugar and cinnamon. Add banana slices and sauté until they begin to turn brown; you may have to do this in 2 lots, depending on size of pan. Pour banana liqueur and rum over all and set aflame, tipping the pan so that flaming liquid is well distributed. Quickly divide bananas among 4 plates, top each with ice cream, and spoon sauce over.

MAKES 4 SERVINGS.

BANANA SOUFFLÉ

3 medium-size ripe bananas
juice of 1/2 lemon
2 Tbs. dark rum
3 Tbs. flour
3/4 cup milk
3 egg yolks
5 egg whites
pinch of salt
1/3 cup plus 1 to 2 Tbs. sugar
1 Tbs. butter, softened

Preheat oven to 375° F.

Mash bananas through a sieve or whisk in a food processor or blender along with lemon juice and rum. Blend milk slowly with flour in a small heavy saucepan, whisking and heating slowly until well blended and thick. Off the heat, beat in egg yolks, one by one. Then add mashed bananas. Beat egg whites with salt. As they begin to stiffen, add sugar gradually, beating until thick. Mix one-quarter of the egg whites into the milk-flour-banana base, then turn the lightened base into the egg white bowl and fold in remaining whites carefully. Butter the sides and bottom of a 6-cup soufflé mold, then sprinkle sugar over. Gently pour the soufflé mixture into the mold and bake for 30 minutes.

MAKES 6 TO 8 SERVINGS.

BAKED FRESH PEACHES

4 medium-size fresh ripe peaches
1/2 lime
2 Tbs. chopped hazelnuts
2 Tbs. butter
2 Tbs. brown sugar
1/3 cup sauterne or scuppernong wine
1/2 to 3/4 cup sour cream

Preheat oven to 400° F.

Peel peaches, cut into halves, and remove pits. Rub with cut side of lime and place in a baking dish just large enough to hold fruit. Mix chopped hazelnuts with butter and sugar, then spread in even amounts over peaches. Pour wine around fruit. Bake for 20 minutes, basting once. Serve warm with dollops of sour cream.

MAKES 4 SERVINGS.

FRESH PEACH COBBLER WITH PEACH OR APRICOT JAM

12 peaches
juice of 1/2 lemon
2 Tbs. flour
1/4 cup sugar
2 Tbs. peach or apricot jam
2 Tbs. butter

TOPPING:
1 1/2 cups sifted all-purpose flour
1/2 tsp. baking powder
1 Tbs. sugar
5 Tbs. butter
1 egg
1/2 cup soured cream or milk

GARNISH:
1/2 cup heavy cream
1 tsp. vanilla sugar, or 1 tsp. plain sugar with a drop of vanilla extract

Preheat oven to 425° F.

Butter a 9- or 10-inch cake pan or shallow round casserole. Slice peaches, sprinkle with lemon juice, and arrange loosely in cake pan or casserole; mix flour and sugar and sprinkle over fruit. Spread fruit with jam and dot with 2 tablespoons butter. Sift flour, baking powder, and sugar, cut in 5 tablespoons butter, and mix lightly. Beat egg with soured milk or cream, then stir into flour until mixture is smooth, but don't overmix. Divide dough into 8 portions and drop in small rounds on fruit. Bake for 30 minutes. Serve with cream whipped with vanilla sugar.

MAKES 8 SERVINGS.

PLUM DUFF WITH CHERRY LIQUEUR

1 lb. fresh plums cut into halves
1/2 cup sugar
1/3 cup kirsch
2 tsp. tapioca
1 large egg
3 Tbs. vanilla sugar, or 3 Tbs. plain sugar with 1/4 tsp. vanilla extract
pinch of salt
1/8 tsp. cream of tartar
3 Tbs. sifted flour
1/8 tsp. almond extract
heavy cream

Preheat oven to 325° F.

Use a flameproof dish that will hold plum halves snugly; distribute plums in a single layer. Mix sugar, kirsch, and tapioca and pour over fruit, then stew for about 10 minutes on top of the stove. Meanwhile separate egg and beat yolk in a small bowl. Slowly add vanilla sugar until smooth and lemon colored. In a separate bowl, beat egg white with salt and cream of tartar; when stiff, fold in beaten yolk, then stir in flour and almond extract. Spread this batter over plums and bake for 30 minutes. Keep warm and serve from baking dish with heavy cream.

MAKES ABOUT 4 SERVINGS.

RHUBARB STOCKLI

Swiss-born chef Albert Stockli, who was responsible for many creative dishes featured at New York's Four Seasons in the 1960s, was a great enthusiast for the natural bounty of the United States. A lover of rhubarb, he originated this splendid dessert in response to a request for a dish that would celebrate the tart, colorful fruit that is seldom used except in pies or stews served as desserts.

1 lb. rhubarb, peeled and diced
3/4 cup water
1/2 cup sugar
3/5 cup Madeira
1 lemon
1/2 cup dry vermouth
7 egg yolks
8 slices of zweiback, cubed

Combine rhubarb, water, sugar, and about 1/3 cup Madeira in a saucepan, and let simmer for 5 minutes. Squeeze lemon and add juice with vermouth; continue to simmer for about 5 minutes more, or until rhubarb is tender; drain and reserve liquid. In a glass or stainless steel bowl, beat egg yolks lightly and blend in rhubarb liquid; place bowl over boiling water and beat vigorously with a wire whip until mixture is light and frothy. Off the heat, stir in remaining Madeira and fold in cooked rhubarb. Divide zweiback cubes among dessert bowls and pour rhubarb on top.

MAKES 6 SERVINGS.

COLD RHUBARB SOUFFLÉ

4 cups chopped unpeeled fresh rhubarb
1 3/4 cups sugar
1 envelope unflavored gelatin
2 tsp. crème de cassis
1 cup heavy cream
4 egg whites
pinch of cream of tartar
1/2 cup vanilla sugar, or 1/2 cup plain sugar with 1 tsp. vanilla extract

GARNISH:

12 large fresh strawberries, cut into halves (optional)

whipped cream (optional)

Preheat oven to 350° F.

Toss rhubarb and sugar in a casserole and put in oven to stew for about 20 minutes, or until rhubarb is soft. Drain, reserving liquid; purée rhubarb in a blender or put through a food mill. Dissolve gelatin in crème de cassis. Boil reserved liquid until reduced to ½ cup; let cool, then stir into dissolved gelatin. Use a balloon whisk to whip cream in a metal bowl over ice cubes, letting in as much air as possible so that volume is almost doubled. Beat egg whites with a pinch of cream of tartar until almost stiff, then add vanilla sugar and continue beating until stiff peaks form. Fold whipped cream into rhubarb purée, then fold in egg whites. Make a collar of wax paper or foil about 2 inches high and fit it to a 2-quart soufflé dish, tying it a little below the rim; pour in rhubarb mixture. Chill overnight or for at least 6 hours. To serve, remove collar. Garnish with strawberries and whipped cream squeezed in swirls from pastry tube, if desired.

MAKES 6 TO 8 SERVINGS.

INDEXES

General Index

Recipe Index

°indicates that the recipe is to be found within the text in the first section of the book. Although integrated in the narrative, these recipes are sufficiently detailed so as to be used just as those in the Recipes section are.